Shakespearean Tragedy

Its Art and Its Christian Premises

Shakespearean Tragedy

Its Art and Its Christian Premises

ROY W. BATTENHOUSE, 1912-

Indiana University Press

Bloomington · London

SECOND PRINTING 1971
Copyright © 1969 by Indiana University Press
All rights reserved
No part of this book may be reproduced or
utilized in any form or by any means,
electronic or mechanical,
including photocopying and recording,
or by any information storage and retrieval system,
without permission in writing from the publisher.
The Association of American
University Presses' Resolution on Permissions
constitutes the only exception to this prohibition.
Library of Congress catalog card number: 69-15991
Published in Canada by
Fitzhenry & Whiteside Limited,
Don Mills, Ontario, Canada
Manufactured in the United States
of America
253-18090-2

To Marian and
Anna Marie

Contents

Preface

My purpose has been to reexplore basic issues in the interpretation of Shakespearean tragedy. Chiefly these turn about the implications of structure and metaphor, since the meaning of each story is latent in the form of its action and language. One important dimension is the tragedy's moral significance, which Shakespeare evidently understood more profoundly than his heroes do, and for which he provides us many clues. Yet if we are to read these adequately, we need to be able to recognize them and their range of import. Much can elude our vision or be misconstrued, if we bring to Shakespearean tragedy intellectual preconceptions of a romantic or Hegelian cast, as did A. C. Bradley, for instance. A better preparation, as some of our recent critics have been saying, is a sensibility alert to the historic concepts and world view of mainstream Christianity. For this was the heritage most likely to have furnished Shakespeare his fundamental premises, and clusters of paradigm for understanding tragic fall in human life, and a symbolism for signalling its meaning. When probing the many-sided implications of his art work I have therefore taken particular care to investigate the pertinence of Christian lore.

In illustration of what such an approach can reveal, Part I of my book is devoted to a close reading of a nowadays rather neglected tragedy, Shakespeare's early *Rape of Lucrece*. This narrative poem, if we but pay due attention to its details, and especially to those through which Shakespeare has reshaped the story as given by Ovid and Livy, can be shown to have a surprisingly complex meaning. That meaning depends, however, on a basically Augustinian perspective, the one used covertly by Chaucer in his *Legend of Good Women*. This fact, once we discover it and put it to the test, makes possible our seeing how important to Shakespeare's art of tragedy is a whole constellation of compositional devices—irony, parody, analogy, prefiguration, multilevel perspective and an enigmatic symbolism—all of these cohering with an implicitly medieval moral theology and sense of history.

With these initial insights as an incentive, I next turn to a broadranging search for an adequate theory of Shakespearean tragedy in general. The three chapters of Part II explore many matters in an interlarded fashion: the general history of comment on Shakespeare's tragedies, the relevance of major medieval ideas to the shaping of his work, the way in which biblical paradigms echo in a play's structure, the precise sense in which his tragedies may properly be called Christian, and an assessment of the continuing influence of Aristotle's principles, both moral and poetic. Various of these matters involve debatable issues. I can hope only to have advanced the present state of discussion in the direction of interpretations that are defensible and fruitful. In developing my argument, I draw from almost all of Shakespeare's tragedies, but from some only briefly in connection with specific problems. Several of the tragedies, however, receive a rather full analysis. In Chapter II, for instance, *Romeo and Juliet* is the culminating illustration of the perspective to which that chapter has been leading; and in Chapter III the progress of discussion brings up *Antony and Cleopatra* as an appropriate play for close examination; then in Chapter IV *Hamlet* becomes the obvious test case for the aspect of theory there being considered. My concern in these chapters is to open up frontier aspects of the poet's art, which other scholars may then find intriguing enough to explore further. Originally and until persuaded otherwise by my publishers, I intended to title my book simply "Toward Understanding Shakespearean Tragedy." That still represents the spirit of my inquiry.

Part III returns to a methodologically simpler procedure, that of offering comment on two of Shakespeare's late tragedies. On *King Lear*, I undertake to amplify and round out what other critics have said as to its essentially Christian structure. Then the chapter on *Coriolanus* returns to an approach like that used in Chapter I, a close reading based on source comparisons, in order to demonstrate Shakespeare's transcendence of Plutarch's outlook. I regard this play as being, among other things, a parable for the Plutarchans of Shakespeare's own time. That is, the drama has been shaped to reveal by implication Plutarch's flawed vision, as well as and alongside that of Coriolanus. The insight behind Shakespeare's reordering of story stems, here again, from Christian tradition.

The two Appendixes are of an auxiliary nature. The first presents a pair of incidental instances of Augustine's usefulness for Shakespeare. More substantial is Appendix II, which extends the study of the Lucrece legend in Chapter I by demonstrating how Chaucer's version of it paved the way for Shakespeare's, and how on the other hand Thomas Heywood's version slides into a jumble of neoclassical morality for the sake of producing a spectacular melodrama. Heywood's treatment, when compared with Chaucer's, offers interesting testimony to the existence of competitive perspectives within Renaissance times, as well as to the difference between hackwork and Christian art. My study of this was originally a part of Chapter I, but has been transferred to an appendix so as not to retard the momentum of the book's concentration on Shakespeare.

Since most of the chapters have developed out of papers written for sundry occasions in recent years, I am indebted to all who have prompted them. A brief version of the chapter on *Hamlet,* for instance, was first drafted in 1961 for the Catholic Renascence Society meeting in Detroit; my analysis of *Lucrece* was offered in germ at an *MLA* meeting in 1961 and more fully in 1964 at a convention of the Association of Canadian Teachers of English; a considerable part of my chapter on *Lear* has been read to several audiences and published in *Stratford Papers on Shakespeare* (Toronto, 1965), edited by B. W. Jackson. These three essays had the further benefit of faculty discussion in forums at the University of Western Ontario during my service there as a Visiting Professor in 1963–64. Two other chapters (II and III) depend a good deal on an essay I contributed to *The Tragic Vision and the Christian Faith* (New York, 1957), edited by Nathan Scott, and on another written for *The Centennial Review* (Winter, 1964). A fellowship given by the Guggenheim Foundation in 1958–59 aided me during an early stage of the study, and a sabbatical leave from Indiana University for the spring of 1967 has provided time for completing the book. To all these sources of encouragement I am grateful. I wish to express thanks also to my colleagues Merritt Lawlis, Alfred David, and Mary Elizabeth Campbell for helpful comments on one or other of the manuscript's chapters, and to James H. Jones of Northern Michigan University for a critical reading of the whole, and to innumerable seminar students over the years who by query or comment have sharpened my study. My colleagues Charles Forker, Mary Gaither, and the late William Riley Parker have given help also. Finally, I owe more than thanks to my wife, who both by encouragement and by offered assistance has lightened my task and shepherded its progress.

Indebtedness to the published ideas of fellow scholars I have tried to indicate, chiefly in notes, although these inevitably bypass some references either inadvertently or to conserve space. In the notes the reader will also find, frequently, important comments of a supplementary nature. And the index will help him locate, among other things, the various places in the book where each tragedy emerges or reemerges for attention. All citations from Shakespeare, unless otherwise indicated, are from G. B. Harrison's *Shakespeare: The Complete Works,* published by Harcourt, Brace and World, Inc., New York, the 1952 edition. It has seemed to me generally unnecessary when quoting Shakespeare to give act, scene, and line reference; but occasionally such identification has been tucked in for emphasis or when a phrase might be difficult to locate. In footnote references to books published through a university press I have usually named the publisher rather than the place of publication. In citing well-known journals my title abbreviations are those standard among bibliographers. To the staff of Indiana University Press I am grateful, lastly, for painstaking care in the book's editing and styling.

Bloomington, Indiana   ROY W. BATTENHOUSE
November, 1968

Shakespearean Tragedy

Its Art and Its Christian Premises

Let those who think I have said too little, or those who think I have said too much forgive me; and let those who think I have said just enough join me in giving thanks to God.

—AUGUSTINE, *City of God*

PART

I

An Exercise
in Reading

I

Shakespeare's
Re-Vision
of
Lucrece

At the age of thirty—after having written *Richard III* and before completing *Romeo and Juliet*—Shakespeare published his *Rape of Lucrece* (1594). This tragic story in narrative verse was immediately and for a generation afterwards very well received, going into six further editions. When in 1600 *England's Parnassus* appeared, there were included in this popular anthology thirty-nine quotations from *Lucrece*. And soon thereafter Gabriel Harvey named *Lucrece* along with *Hamlet,* as in his view the notable works of Shakespeare which "have it in them to please the wiser sort." What kind of artistry can have elicited such high esteem for *Lucrece*? The fact that Harvey's comment occurs on a margin of his copy of Chaucer may be significant.

Today's historians of literature see in the poem's tuneful rhetoric the tradition of Ovid. But only rarely does anyone sense, besides this, a sophisticated psychology of tragedy—perhaps as intricate as that of Chaucer's *Troilus,* whose rime-royal stanza Shakespeare is here using. Probably because *Lucrece,* unlike Chaucer's *Troilus,* depicts a love which is consummated in violence and then plunges the heroine into a nightmare of grief, almost all readers since Dr. Johnson's era have misliked this work of Shakespeare's. Johnson himself (a moralist with scant understanding of tragedy) found lapses of judgment in it, which condescendingly he attributed to Shakespeare's straining as a young poet to write in a self-consciously tragic manner.

Using Johnson's view as a springboard, the editor of the new
Arden text (1960) has outspokenly voiced his own more bitter
distaste. *Lucrece* is a young man's idea of tragedy, F. T. Prince believes, "and the imagination of the young man in question is a curious blend of health and morbidity, a bundle of self-contradictory
impulses." Lured by a "craving for sensation," says this critic, the
poet has misused his talents, and as a result it is "only too obvious
that the poem, as a whole, is a failure." Its whole conception of
tragedy, in Prince's view, is not only youthful but crude and vulgar.
Hence if *Lucrece* is a tragedy, he remarks, it is "not by the author of
Lear or *Othello*," but rather to be looked on as "Shakespeare's projection of his own immature spirit." It is tragedy (borrowing a
phrase of Miss Bradbrook's) in the newspaper sense of "something
that slaps you in the face" with its senseless horror. And its basic
weakness may be described (in a phrase Hazlitt used of *Measure
for Measure*) as that of "an original sin" in the subject matter.[1]

So extreme an indictment on the part of an editor seems to me
improper. And in this case it is wholly unwarranted. It exemplifies,
however, the loose thinking too often given rein by impressionist
criticism. For can it be valid to assume, as Prince does, that because
Tarquin and Lucrece are nightmarish in their imaginings, their
outlook must be taken as "a true equivalent" for "a phase in
Shakespeare's vision of reality"? Is Shakespeare seeing no more of
reality than his tragic characters see? Furthermore, has our critic,
when borrowing the phrase "original sin," bothered at all to probe
the concept's theological meaning? Would he think the author of
Genesis 3 an "immature" writer for having told a story with
"original sin" in it? And, as for the notion that *Lear* and *Othello*
contrast with *Lucrece* on the score of subject matter, what careful
reader of these later plays dare affirm that the mad and sensational
imaginings of Lear, or of Othello, are any freer of sin than the
violence we watch in Tarquin or the suicide we witness in Lucrece?
The writing of any tragedy, surely, requires the mimesis of actions
involving "excess" and implying sin—but not implying thereby a
sick poet with an aberrant vision of reality.

Toward a rehabilitation of the artistic greatness of *Lucrece,*
there has appeared a more recent essay by Harold R. Walley.[2] Here
the poem is defended as a work carefully structured and designed
to give a "systematic elucidation of tragedy." In Walley's view, it
"lays the foundation of Shakespeare's whole subsequent treatment

of tragedy" and fairly bristles with anticipations of his later dramatic work. The psychology of evil in Tarquin, for instance, closely correlates with that in Macbeth. Like Macbeth, Tarquin knows that his enterprise is impious; yet when driven by appetite he resorts to sophistic argument to confuse the issue and confute his own conscience. Both protagonists overwhelm moral inhibitions by descending to a merely pragmatic fear of consequences and then to brute force. When Tarquin, invoking Love and Fortune as his gods, completely abandons himself to "Desire" as his pilot and "Beauty" as his prize, the result is a gradual paralysis of reason, in which might supplants right. As Walley remarks, this theme of justice overthrown by self-interest can be found not only in *Macbeth* but, with equal pointedness, in *Troilus and Cressida*. And Lucrece's plight after rape, he suggests, is comparable to that of Hamlet or Lear, who likewise lament their victimization by an outrageous world. When benumbed by shock, Lucrece seeks to exclude herself from society and gives way to bitter reproaches against the very conditions of life. Further, she finds herself in a dilemma. For although she may be blameless in the rape, the facts of her case are not proof against suspicion. How then can she escape from the imputation of disloyalty to her husband, Collatine? In her agony, the only remedy seems to be, finally, that of suicide as a personal consummation, while asking of her friends a pledge to revenge the wrong that has befallen her. The poem's total story entails, as Walley reads it, "the very rationale which underlies the whole of Shakespearean tragedy." Hence *The Rape of Lucrece* is "a key document in Shakespeare's coming of age as an artist."

1 The problem of perspective

I consider Walley's main contention valid, and his supporting analysis correct, as far as it goes. Yet it falls short, in various ways, of a fully adequate focus on the causes of tragedy. Tarquin's motive has not been quite grasped in its deepest dimensions, and Lucrece's responsibility has been seen only as she herself envisions it. Omitted in this picture are her own self-deception and its causes, and her husband's significant folly, and in the background the tragedy of Roman civilization as a whole. Lucrece's tragedy, in its implications, needs to be seen as that of all Rome. It rests, as I shall be showing, on a tragic flaw that is distinctively Roman yet typically human. Precisely what this flaw is, Walley has not perceived, simply because like most other readers he has overlooked the story's persistent ironies. Yet these ironies are available to us through innumerable verbal clues. And when pondered they bring to the classical story a special perspective, the product of a heritage of Christian interpretation.

Modern-day lack of enthusiasm for *Lucrece* (Walley excepted) goes back, as I have indicated, to the limited perspective which emerged with English neoclassicism. Viewed from within such limits, the purpose of the poem's rhetoric seemed merely ornamental. By 1780 we find Edmund Malone apologizing for the "wearisome circumlocution" of *Lucrece* and asking readers of his *Shakespeare* to pardon this "great defect" in view of the fashions of an earlier age. Openly or tacitly expressed, this impatience with the poem has echoed down to our day.[3] Geoffrey Bullough, for instance, can see only that Shakespeare has transformed Ovid's "terse and clear-cut tale" into "rich if tedious eloquence." He salutes the poet's "full-scale exercise in lyrical and descriptive dilation" but considers it undramatic.[4] T. W. Baldwin, while granting a "dramatic instinct" in the poem, yet ends his two-chapter analysis on a wan note: "the drama is pretty well stifled under the swaddling clothes of Renaissance rhetorical ornamentation, so that the result is neither good narrative, nor good drama."[5]

Are these critics justified in thinking the rhetoric nonfunctional to plot and characterization? Shakespeare in his dedication of the earlier *Venus and Adonis* had promised Southampton a forthcoming "graver labour." Did he mean by this a labor of merely ornamental engraving, a show of his skill in grammar-book exercises? Surely something more, I believe: the retelling of an ancient tragedy in a seriously revelatory way—or, as Walley says, designing it "to bring home to men's business and bosoms the broad significance of certain historical events."

But where was the "broad significance" of those events to be found? Could it be truly found in the 132 lines on Lucrece in Ovid's *Fasti*? Or in Ovid's text when supplemented by the slightly more detailed account given in Livy's history (and translated into English prose by Painter in 1566)? These were Shakespeare's chief sources in the opinion of critics,[6] and all told they are scant ones. Their substance is adequately conveyed in the brief prose Argument with which Shakespeare prefaces his poem. Let me suggest, however, that this Argument sums up the legend as the Romans understood it,[7] whereas Shakespeare's own profounder understanding is embedded in the poem which follows. That is, theirs can be an outward "cover" for his version, now to be offered within such a husk.

The inner story, we immediately discover, not only expands into 1855 lines but, astonishingly, achieves this huge enlargement while completely omitting the first episode of the Roman legend. The noblemen's visit to Rome for a testing of their wives, and finding that only Lucrece vindicates her husband's commendation, is told in the Argument but is absent from the poem itself. We enter on the story as if *in medias res*. A lust-breathing Tarquin is on his way, alone, to Lucrece's house. Even more significantly, his lust has arisen without his ever having seen Lucrece. In this respect, the situation is somewhat like that in Shakespeare's *Cymbeline,* although the deliberate villainy of Iachimo in that later version of the wager story, derived from Boccaccio, is centrally intellectual and therefore satisfied, in the upshot, with a nonsexual triumph.

"It seems to be unlikely," remarks one modern editor of *The Rape of Lucrece,* "that Tarquin should desire Lucrece before he sees her"; this "mechanical" improvement "loses more than it gains."[8] But is Shakespeare's alteration merely a mechanical one? It does indeed lose something—namely, the basic assumption of the Ovid-Livy tale, that Tarquin's lust has as its cause his earlier sight of a chaste Lucrece, modestly engaged in spinning a war-cloak for her husband, and saying tearfully to her maids as she directs the work: "Whenever I picture him to myself in the midst of battle, I tremble, I feel ready to die, sudden cold strikes at my heart" (Ovid, as translated by Charlotte Porter). It loses this important assumption, that an idyllically pious wife, whose one concern is her husband's safety, has by her very sanctity aroused a sexual lust in her husband's friend, through his witnessing her at work and then beholding her beauty as she rises to embrace lovingly her returned husband. What Shakespeare's revised beginning gains, instead, is a quite different cause for the tragedy—an untested boast of a chaste Lucrece on the part of her husband. On this more problematic base Shakespeare has set his version. It permits, in turn, a significantly variant psychology and a deeper rationale for the whole story. I would suggest, indeed, that all of Shakespeare's subsequent rhetorical inventions—including such major ones as Tarquin's internal debate, Lucrece's sermon when under threat, her long aftermath of complaint, and even the Troy tapestry introduced for her contemplation—function as a development of this new rationale.

In other words, Shakespeare is dilating the classical legend not simply with rhetoric, but rather *through rhetoric* with a truth hidden from the Romans and their story-tellers. Unlike his tragic heroine Lucrece, who cannot read "the subtle-shining secrecies/ Writ in the glassy margents" of Tarquin's "parling lookes" (100--101), Shakespeare can read these secrecies and can trace them to their complex source. Furthermore, he can read certain subtle shinings on the glassy margins of Lucrece's own face, since (as he has her say significantly in line 1253) "Poor women's faces are their own faults' books." That is, there are facts in her face which covertly contribute to the tragedy, and which can be imaginatively indicated through the parleyings Shakespeare invents for her in the course of Tarquin's visit. As narrator of the encounter he can provide a kind of perspective glass—like that described by Bushy in *Richard II* II. ii. 18–20 (written around 1594). In a perspective glass, the griefs of human beings "show nothing but confusion" when gazed on directly, yet reveal significant "form" when "eyed awry."* Shapes of grief, says Bushy in that important passage, are "naught but shadows/ Of what is not." Only by eyeing these shadowy shapes *awry* will we discover that they are but the vision of "false sorrow's eye."

The metaphor of a perspective glass suggests a concept common in medieval art—the distinction between a work's surface of "beautiful lie" and a truth hidden under this fiction, the kernel beneath its husk, its fruit amid the chaff. All such metaphors involve the notion of a double perspective, through which a covert meaning is discoverable inside an overt one. In *Lucrece,* therefore, may not Shakespeare be giving us, on the surface of his poem, the grief of "false sorrow's eye," and at the same time inviting us to eye awry this surface that we may thereby discover what is being falsified? If we will but "attend each line" (as Shakespeare invites us to do in line 818), I think we will find easily enough this double perspective. The tragic tale requires, for its surface movement, a rhetoric

---

* A perspective painting of Edward VI, now in the National Portrait Gallery, was one of the curiosities of Shakespeare's day. It consists (Carroll Camden tells us, *MLN,* LXXII, 252) of a glass-fronted box displaying a painting "which appears grotesquely distorted when viewed through the glass, but is a life-like representation when viewed through a peep-hole at one end of the box."

of woe; yet built into that rhetoric are hidden "forms" for a wry reading of the tragedy. In this respect Shakespeare has restyled, and gone quite beyond, Ovid and Livy.

But where could Shakespeare have found sources for the marginal vision I have just defined and postulated? Might he have found a source in Chaucer's tale of Lucrece in *The Legend of Good Women*? Various critics have surmised that the *Legend* was possibly or probably known to Shakespeare, but most seem to feel, as Kittredge does, that Shakespeare's *Lucrece* "owes nothing to Chaucer."[9] Those scholars who have compared most closely Shakespeare's story details with Ovid's and Livy's have seen in Chaucer's version so little additional to the Roman version that they think him either an uncertain influence on Shakespeare, as Ewig does, or a "negligible one," as Baldwin does. What they have overlooked, however, is Chaucer's irony in the *Legend*. Such oversight is understandable, since most of our specialists in the study of Chaucer have likewise failed to see this irony. But I am certain of it, on the basis of a careful reading which I shall provide separately in an appendix (see Appendix II). Chaucer's irony in celebrating the "goodness" of Lucrece is exactly the point at which Shakespeare could have learned from him.

Yet Chaucer's way of telling the Lucrece story is not quite Shakespeare's. Chaucer, I think, was covertly making a farce of Ovid's martyrology, while on the surface keeping his own version studiously deferential to Ovid, almost as brief, and seemingly in accord with the order of episodes as given by Ovid. Shakespeare, on the other hand, was transubstantiating Ovid into the magnitude required for serious tragedy, while reformulating Ovid's episodes to support an intricately incremental tragedy on the theme of "ambitious foul infirmity" (see line 150). Nevertheless, what Chaucer and Shakespeare have in common is double perspective. Both bring to the Roman tale a wry underside of perception which evaluates the classical world view moving at the surface. The "source" for which we should inquire, in both these authors, is the source which makes possible their marginal perception. In Chaucer's case, we have our clue to such a source when he casually fumbles a reference to Augustine at the beginning, and then at the very end bungles a reference to the Bible. These two Christian sources are, surreptitiously, the basis for the true meaning of Chaucer's tale. Likewise they are so for Shakespeare's tale, even though Shakespeare does not openly name either one. A moral vision whose source is St. Augustine (especially his chapter on Lucrece in *City of God* I. 19), and behind him the Bible, ultimately accounts for the art with which Shakespeare has thoroughly reformulated classical story.[10]

2 Polar forms of covetousness

To show how this is so, let us now examine the rich texture of Shakespeare's *Lucrece*. I shall be developing my reading through close attention to detail, since the configurative significance for which I am contending requires a full demonstration. Its cumulative fascination will amply reward my patient reader, who will discover, to his delight, a poetic complexity too long overlooked.

First let us note how, at the poem's very outset, Shakespeare focuses on the unwise boasting of Lucrece's husband, Collatine. In Tarquin's presence, Collatine has praised Lucrece "at such high-proud rate," that kings might be "espoused to more fame" but never to so peerless a dame as his. In fact, Collatine thinks of Lucrece as his highest heaven—a view which Shakespeare as narrator criticizes indirectly, by commenting on the transitoriness of all happiness that is centered on the gifts a man possesses.* Moreover, the poet remarks that Collatine's boast, perchance, was what tainted Tarquin's heart with envy, thus stirring up in him the fires of lust. With a delicacy of touch the poem is intimating that what was referred to in the Argument as simply the "pleasant humor" of the Roman noblemen is tainted, actually, with passions which any reader of Genesis would recognize—pride followed by envy. These make of Tarquin "this devil." He has become a "false worshipper" of an "earthly saint," Lucrece. But note the word *earthly*. It hints at a mistaken worship, quite antecedent to Tarquin's false dealings. The worshipping of an earthly beauty implies idolatry, which is one kind of falsity; it can issue in another kind, treachery.

Next, the poem tells us of Lucrece's two conspicuous endow-

---

* I am not attempting to distinguish between the poet and the narrator, although this might be done. I assume the narrator is Shakespeare, speaking from a stance of storyteller which permits him to hide deftly the full import of what he is saying, so that only alert readers will readily discern it. Alternatively, one might suppose the narrator an invented persona, assigned an awareness somewhat less profound than the poet's but allowed to speak commonplaces which carry a meaning larger than he knows.

ments: virtue and beauty. But the white of the one and the red of the other are located, in Shakespeare's description, in her "face" simply. There they make show of themselves—not at peace but in a constant combat to outdo each other. Very prettily, Shakespeare describes how the two colors oscillate in vanquishing each other:

> When virtue bragged, beauty would blush for shame;
> When beauty boasted blushes, in despite
> Virtue would stain that o'er with silver white.

Behind the prettiness of this warfare, there are moral implications. Note that virtue's only activity here is to brag, or alternately to stain, while beauty's is to blush shamefacedly, or alternately to boast blushingly. What Shakespeare calls "this heraldry in Lucrece' face" hints at a nature dialectically ruled by two ambitious forces, each guided by no purpose other than (as he says) to "underprop" the "fame" of Lucrece. It is this fame which has attracted Tarquin, who in order to vindicate his own fame now feels he must vanquish Lucrece's fame, and who himself is inwardly at war between affection for beauty and his virtuous conscience. In him, as our story will reveal, a bloody lust vanquishes his pale virtue, and then in response Lucrece's pallid virtue dominates over her own red blood. (Meanwhile Shakespeare suggests indirectly, in lines 1511–1512, that blushing-red is a sign of guilt, and paleness of cheek a sign of "the fear that false hearts have.") Thus nature's strife between red and white becomes, as I read it, an emblem of a dialectic which encompasses the story's whole action, enslaving man and woman alike to a tragic love of fame, protean in its mutability.

Thirdly, let us observe that early in the poem, soon after Shakespeare has brought Tarquin and Lucrece under the same roof, he pauses for three stanzas (20–22) to moralize on covetousness and its effects. To covet honor, wealth, or ease, he says, is to engage in a "thwarting strife," in which we gain only bankruptcy and death. Stanza 22, in particular, sums up the metaphysics of this paradox:

> in venturing ill we leave to be
> The things we are for that which we expect.
> And this ambitious foul infirmity,
> In having much, torments us with defect
> Of that we have. So then we do neglect
> > The thing we have, and, all for want of wit,
> > Make something nothing by augmenting it.

This explanation of evil is the traditionally Christian one, and here it is being offered us as a vantage point from which to assess the more limited understanding possessed by the characters within the tragedy. If we apply the narrator's moralizing to a judging of Tarquin only—as we may be tempted to do by the fact that it is applied immediately to "doting Tarquin"—we will be falling into a moral myopia, like that of Lucrece and her Roman admirers. Although Shakespeare is permitting such a trap for unwary readers, if they yield to it they will be indulging superficial emotions which the poem as a whole, when rightly pondered, can purge. Actually the narrator's theme applies universally to the full range of events to come within the total story. Covetousness will figure later, for instance, in the poet's comment that Tarquin's "greedy eyeballs" treasonously mislead his heart (368–69). But also it will crop up in Lucrece's moralizing—through which unwittingly she describes herself—when she speaks of "The aged man that coffers up his gold . . . And useless barns the harvest of his wits" (855–59). Here the word "barns," incidentally, carries an allusion by Shakespeare to the parable of the covetous rich man in Luke 12.[11]

If I may now recall two of St. Augustine's most famous passages, it will become evident that covetousness can take either of two closely allied forms: one, an abandoning of personal honor in the blind pursuit of a fleshly good; or secondly, an abandoning of fleshly good in the blind pursuit of a personal honor. A paradigm of the first, I suggest, is Augustine's story in *The Confessions* (II. 9–18) of his youthful pear-stealing; and a paradigm of the second is his story in *The City of God* (I. 19) of the suicide of Lucrece. In polar ways, these may have a pertinence to the two major sections of Shakespeare's narrative. Let us therefore digress to take a look, first, at the pear-stealing episode in *The Confessions*.

Augustine there describes himself as running headlong into shamelessness. What compelled the theft, he says, was not a famished poverty, but rather a delight in the theft itself because it would be misliked. "Fair were the pears, but not them did my wretched soul desire; . . . I gathered only that I might steal." Once gained, the pears were scarcely tasted before he flung them away. Hence it can be inferred that what he chiefly loved was the audacity of his act, and the fact that it was foul. Yet, on more final analysis, Augustine concludes that he loved not the villainy itself, but rather a kind of "maimed liberty," which was but a darkened

shadow of Divine omnipotency. He sees a likeness between this boyish act of his and the adult tyrannies of Catiline—of whom it was
said that he was cruel lest through idleness his hand or heart should
grow inactive. All such savageries, in Augustine's view, are but a
mimicking of God's freedom; they have their root in a coveting
of sovereignty.

Does not the behavior of Shakespeare's Tarquin parallel Augustine's explanation? Note that although Tarquin professes Lucrece's
beauty as his prize, he nevertheless discards her after the rape, having barely tasted her body. Moreover, in advance of the rape he
acknowledges that his desire is mere dotage, against both law and
duty; "Yet strive I," he says (line 504) , "to embrace mine infamy."
Infamy has become for him a perverse form of fame-seeking. Basically what he loves is his own resoluteness, and the illusion of
power which his fearlessness of consequences gives him, and in
particular the satisfying sense of activity he gets from striking his
falchion against flint, or in setting his foot upon the light. It is
utterly futile, therefore, for Lucrece to emphasize in her pleas the
dishonor and ruin Tarquin is bringing on himself. He already
knows that, but is subconsciously enjoying his own capacity to
dare such a doom. From the outset of his enterprise, the very
blameworthiness of his design has excited his will. Actual physical
sight of Lucrece, in Shakespeare's reading, has not been the initial
cause. Later, in the bedroom scene, when at last Tarquin has full
opportunity to survey her beauty as she lies sleeping "like a virtuous monument," Shakespeare's five stanzas of anatomical description (lines 386–420) conclude with a sixth telling us that such
gazing actually "qualified" and "slacked" Tarquin's rage of lust,
until his eye began to tempt his veins. Plainly, what he chiefly
covets is a proof of his audacity.

And what triggers his final enacting of a conquest is Lucrece's
offering opposition by lecturing him on its forbiddenness. Her
negatives, as Tarquin himself comments, are a "let" (a word meaning "hindrance" but suggesting also "permission") , which turns
not the tide of his uncontrolled passion, but rather "swells [it] the
higher." This is true, also, of other negatives he encounters. The
fact that his conscience opposes his crime in a long internal debate
becomes to Tarquin a reason for overriding reason in order to
show his own bravery.[12] Likewise when he faces ominous external
warnings—the frightening cries of weasels, the smoke blown from

a torch onto his face, the needle in Lucrece's glove which pricks his finger—he "in the worst sense" construes their denial. They are but "lets," he says, which "attend the time." That is, they help make his adventure an exciting pastime.

Walley has claimed rightly, I believe, that the psychological pattern in Tarquin is basically that of Shakespearean characters such as Macbeth. In a character of this type there is an open acceptance of what is known to be a crime, a deliberate flouting of the moral sense. But what about another type of tragic hero—the type represented in Hamlet, Brutus, or Othello? Does not Shakespeare more often, and more typically, choose for his tragic hero some self-deluded champion of virtue, rather than a conscious villain? Should we not in the present instance, therefore, look to Lucrece rather than to Tarquin as our model for highest tragedy? Our present poem, as a matter of fact, is named after Lucrece. Perhaps hers is the tragedy in which Shakespeare has summed up his most subtle insights into evil.

But this second type of tragedy, as I have already suggested, has also its paradigm in the pages of St. Augustine. Whereas Augustine associates his pear-stealing with what he calls a Babylonian mire and with Catiline, Rome's worst, on the other hand he associates Lucrece with Rome's boasted best, yet with Rome's most characteristic fault, an inordinate love of glory. To Augustine, Lucrece's obsessive fear of scandal and her ultimate suicide illustrate the moral contradictions inherent in a misplaced idealism. He brings up her story as a capital instance of pagan heroism at its alleged noblest, then shows such nobleness to be self-deceptive and illogical, the product of a superficial and distorted notion of virtue. Later, in Book V of *The City of God,* he rates ambition for glory as "nearer to virtue" than crude avarice, but underscores for his readers the pitiableness of those Roman heroes who sacrificed wealth, and even life itself, simply that men might think well of them. Theirs is the sad story of "splendid vices." In coveting praise, Rome has gained only an empty and tragic eminence.

Augustine's "compassion" for Lucrece, we may recall incidentally, is the one point on which Chaucer cites him, leaving to the knowing reader to recall what else Augustine had to say. But later, without citing Augustine, Chaucer borrows from him when expanding Ovid's one-line explanation of Lucrece's fall (Succubuit famae victa puella metu) into a seven-line apology for "These

Romeyn wyves." They so loved "name," says Chaucer, that Lucrece
for fear of scandal lost both her wit and breath, becoming thus so
"ded" that she "feleth no thyng, neyther foul ne fayr." This could
mean, ironically, that she sensed no difference between good and
evil, so spiritually dead had she become. Love of name can have
tragic consequences.[13]

Shakespeare's treatment of Lucrece, like Chaucer's, accounts for
her fate in terms of a Roman love of fame, and there are occasional
hints of kinship to Eve's vanity in Genesis. By a close reading we
can sense these factors from the very beginning of Lucrece's encounter with Tarquin. Why does she blush in giving "reverent welcome" to her visitor when he stares at her with "still gazing eyes"?
Why is she unsuspicious of his "wanton sight"? The narrator says
she "little suspecteth" and is impressed by his shows of honor, his
"plaits of majesty." When he avoids speaking of the purpose of his
coming and makes excuses, why is she still unalarmed? The poem's
clue is in the fact that he "decks with praises Collatine's high name"
and "stories to her ears her husband's fame." He praises Collatine's
"*bruised* arms and *wreaths* of victory"—an equivocal kind of chivalry, we might say. Lucrece responds "with heaved-up hand" to
express her joy, and "wordless so greets heaven." But is she saluting
heaven—or, rather, Tarquin for his story-telling? (Some five hundred lines later, we find her heaving up *both* her hands to Tarquin,
a gesture that could represent ambiguously either plea or surren-
der.) She stayed "after supper long," we are told, in conversation
devoted to his questionings.

On retiring to bed Tarquin has memories of how, holding his
hand, she "gazed for tidings in my eager eyes," while in her face
her color rose to deep red, then blanched to white; and how, with
her hand "locked" in his, she both trembled and smiled. Tarquin
innocently attributes these actions to her "loyal fear," but Shakespeare may be suggesting that the fear thus displayed is less loyal to
Collatine than this parleying couple realizes. In any case, we have
here a broad spectrum of compromising detail—all of it by way of
marginal addition to Ovid and Livy. Ovid has only four lines, in
which he tells us simply that the good woman, thinking no evil of
her visiting kinsman, gave him welcome and a supper at her table,
after which "came the hour for slumber," presumably right after
supper. Chaucer impishly, I think, omits the prefatory supper. He
has Tarquin enter the house late at night, as a thief, through a win-

dow—thus implying, for the surface reader, Lucrece's utter lack of any opportunity to suspect evil, but giving the alert reader a hint as to her knack for leaving windows open, through a negligence due perhaps to subconscious motive. A subconscious preparation in Shakespeare's Lucrece seems indicated by a detail given of her bedroom sleeping. When the intruding Tarquin draws the curtains of her bed, he sees a "pearly sweat" on the hand that is lying outside the coverlet.

In all versions Lucrece awakens to find Tarquin in her bedroom. But in Shakespeare's version Tarquin's threat, that if she denies him he will not merely slay her but devise scandalous circumstances to blacken her reputation, moves Lucrece to plead—after a lengthy silence, and then with sighs prefacing her eloquence—not for life but for reputation. She preaches a long sermon on lust's dishonor, by which actually she increases its fascination. Why does Shakespeare have her react in this way? Is he not contriving to show, in anticipation of the second half of his poem, that a concern for self-justification on her part is leading her even now, not to avoid ruin but to tempt it? "If thou deny," Tarquin warns her, "then force must work my way." So, deny she does—as if subconsciously she wished force to work his way, but only after she has had time to excuse herself from responsibility. "Tears *harden* lust," says Shakespeare—and then shows us Lucrece aiding such hardening in Tarquin by her own tearful looks. (Like Shakespeare's later heroes, Richard II and Hamlet, she seems covertly to desire some "plight" that will facilitate a self-pitying and self-vindicating role.)

Surely if Lucrece really wished rescue, she has plenty of time to cry out for it; for Shakespeare, in contrast to Ovid, makes much of Tarquin's long dallying. And surely there are servants in the house to answer calls for help; for Tarquin's own threat mentions a household "slave,"[14] and the Argument has mentioned housemaids. (One of them comes "fleet-winged" at Lucrece's call the next morning; and a hint that this maid was awake to goings-on the night before is given in her statement that she was "stirring ere the break of day.") Shakespeare is but giving his reader time to realize that actually Lucrece's resort to complaints is her way of escaping from calling for help, and that her spinning out a lecture to Tarquin is a way of pulling her own wool over her sheepish eyes. Indeed, her pleas have an underside of intimated invitation to sexual play, as for instance in the lines:

> Thou look'st not like deceit; do not deceive me.
> My sighs, like whirlwinds, labor hence to heave thee.
>> If ever man were moved with woman's moans,
>> Be moved with my tears, my sighs, my groans.

This is whip-saw moralizing: no and yes in the same breath. It gives special irony to her rhetorical question: "And wilt *thou* be the school where Lust shall learn?"; and then to her rhetorical answer, "Thou back'st *reproach* against long-living *laud*." This epitomizes what, blindly, she is herself doing.

In her steadfast determination to upbraid *his* sin, Lucrece is being completely successful in failing to see how her preachings apply to herself:

> Men's faults do seldom to themselves appear.
> Their own transgressions partially they smother.
> This guilt would seem death-worthy in thy brother.
>> Oh, how are they wrapped in with infamies
>> That from their own misdeeds askance their eyes!

Here her surface woe is fabricating a denunciation of man, which Shakespeare's context is universalizing to include woman. Any reader less self-deluded than Lucrece cannot fail to be reminded of the biblical sermon: "Why beholdest thou not the mote that is in thine own eye? . . . Can the blind lead the blind? Shall they not both fall into the ditch?" Into the ditch, inevitably, they both do fall.

A contrasting story, well known to most Elizabethans and certainly to Shakespeare, was that of the biblical Susanna. The virtuous Susanna, we may recall, was sexually propositioned and threatened both with a blackened name and a rigged public trial if she refused. Yet after brief reflection she chose to cry out for help; whereupon the household servants came to her aid, and then at the trial an unexpected Daniel rescued her reputation. If measured by this paradigm, Lucrece's shortcomings would be obvious.

3 Ironies in Lucrece's lament

After the rape we see Lucrece obsessed by feelings of shame and disgrace. She thinks now only of the burden of "offense" put upon her. In Shakespeare's words, she "bids her eyes hereafter still be blind," while she beats her breast and "prays she never may behold the day." Here the poet is hinting at the real measure of Lucrece's fault—her desire to shut her eyes against daylight examination of her action and, instead, treasure her own fancies of truth. No wonder she is unable to recognize (as Augustine so carefully does) that a rifling of the body involves no true dishonor unless the will consents to such an act. It would be fatal to her fancy of herself if she were to search into the meaning of "consent."

Fearing for loss of social status, Lucrece now luxuriates in grief, virtually wrapping herself in a cocoon of it. She breaks out in self-pitying expostulations against Night, Opportunity, and Time— as if these were gods determining her destiny, rather than means which she has misused and could better use in another way. She inconsistently both blames them and invokes their aid. And we hear her call on smoky Night to let not Day behold the face of Lucrece, which "Immodestly lies martyred with disgrace." In this phrase she unwittingly confesses her own "immodesty" and hints at the "lie" her martyrdom presents in being devoted to disgrace, not grace. Such are Shakespeare's subtle ironies of diction. A stanza later he lets her complain that

> The light will show, charactered in my brow,
> The story of sweet chastity's decay

—a statement true certainly of Lucrece's chastity, although she is wriggling for some way to disprove it. Essentially her chastity is even now decadent, and thus makes her sour-faced rather than sweet.

Four stanzas later she introduces a beautiful simile. She complains that she is like a drone bee, her honey lost, stolen from her by a "wandering wasp" that has crept into her "weak hive" and sucked the honey which as a chaste bee she kept. Figuratively this is truer than its speaker realizes. Her chastity has indeed been weakly guarded—by buzzing complaints as impotent as any drone's, both now and from the moment she first used them against Tarquin. Moreover, the wandering wasp which has sucked her honey may figure, not solely Tarquin (as she supposes), but her own waspish dawdling, which has emptied her chastity of all its substance, and is even now distracting her from the final end of bee-ing (metaphorically the proper end of every human "being"), the producing of honey.

A similar irony attends her complaints against Opportunity. Bitterly she accuses Opportunity of failing to be "the humble suppliant's friend," of never showing her presence to the lame and the blind. Hence,

> The patient dies while the physician sleeps;
> The orphan pines while the oppressor feeds;
> Justice is feasting while the widow weeps;
> Advice is sporting while infection breeds.
> Thou grant'st no time for charitable deeds.

But surely the "thou" who here grants no time for charitable deeds is actually Lucrece herself, who instead of seeking to be a physician is sporting herself in advice-giving, while infection breeds within *her*. It is she who is neglecting the "patient" in herself and feeding on oppression, while weeping lamely like a widow—although she has in fact a husband. The multiple ironies of human self-delusion (intensified by a feminine proclivity to self-pity and evasive argument) are here Shakespeare's tragic theme. "Why work'st thou mischief in thy pilgrimage?" Lucrece asks of Time, but never thinks to ask of herself. In her view, Time is the enemy, injurious and irresponsible Time. If only Time would grant her now the return of one past hour, she sighs, she herself could prevent this night's dread storm and its wrack! But with her next breath she is using the *present* moment to stir up and fan in herself a tempest of hate toward Tarquin, for whom she begs Time to devise "extremes beyond extremity."

> Stone him with hardened hearts, harder than stones,
> And let mild women to him lose their mildness,
> Wilder to him than tigers in their wildness.

Here she is making herself into the very tiger she invokes.

Marvellously the sweet melody of Shakespeare's verses is aiding the irony. For all the while the tiger passion is mounting in Lucrece, it is coming through to us in rime royal. The poetic form, smooth as silk, is in contrast to its subject matter, the hectic moral state of Lucrece. In drama such a distancing of the psychological action would scarcely be possible; human emotion as emergent in public dialogue would there need to be imitated.[15] But here what is being narrated is the development of Lucrece's indignant imagination, and that can be done in a style that surges smoothly like the waves of a sea, even though the subject matter be moral madness. Listen, for example, to the stanza in which Lucrece continues her prayer to Time to lay its curse on Tarquin:

> Let him have time to tear his curlèd hair,
> Let him have time against himself to rave,
> Let him have time of Time's help to despair,
> Let him have time to live a loathèd slave,
> Let him have time a beggar's orts to crave,
>> And time to see one that by alms doth live
>> Disdain to him disdainèd scraps to give.

The final lines here, I think, reflect the biblical parable of Dives and Lazarus—that is, in Shakespeare's mind, not Lucrece's. She is simply imagining how fit a punishment for Tarquin it would be for him to end up as a beggar craving "orts," but denied even such scraps by some fortunate beggar who "by alms doth live." But who is this more fortunate beggar who by alms doth live, and yet disdains giving scraps to the neighbor? Ironically, its immediate representative is none other than Lucrece herself, now in the act of disdaining any scrap of mercy toward Tarquin, ignoring the fact that mercy is the alms by which she (and all of us) can live. Morally, therefore, it is Lucrece who is even now in hell—tearing her hair, helping to despair—by her very act of begging this fate for Tarquin. A timeless truth thus peeps out at us, both through and under Shakespeare's time-borne lines and time-worn imagery.

Lucrece's expostulations to Night, Opportunity, and Time have alternated between blaming and begging. Weaving her feelings through a maze of contradictions—which Shakespeare is letting us see as the vanity of reasonings motivated by vanity—Lucrece regards these cosmic powers as irresponsible yet somehow responsible for her infamy. They are in her view detestable traitors, to whom she nevertheless calls for divine aid in establishing justice. Time, for example, she rails at as being a murderer (line 929), yet ends by asking that Time teach her how to curse the thief (Tarquin? or herself?) with a madness of self-murder (line 996). Such a madness is precisely what *we* can see she has been taking time to teach herself.

Having touched on suicide, she breaks off her harangue. Deploring what she calls "this helpless smoke of words," she resolves on a "remedy indeed to do me good." Since in Shakespeare's art the "smoke of words" has been the very means by which she has been making herself helpless, what kind of "good" may we expect? Appropriately, that of a forged martyrdom. But there is the further irony that Lucrece's proposal now to "let forth my foul defiled blood" is actually a remedy analogous to Tarquin's: he, merely in a different way, had let forth his foul blood (the lust of his defiled nobility). Shakespeare has already told us that Tarquin's act "defaced" his "soul's fair temple," leaving as legacy a "spotted princess." Now this spotted princess can be seen in Lucrece, intent on razing her own soul's temple, her body of flesh and blood.

"My honor I'll bequeath unto the knife," she vows, recalling thus the knife Tarquin had cowed her with, and through which now illogically she hopes for remedy. "So of shame's ashes shall my fame be bred." (A latter-day reader can hardly avoid thinking here of the similar heroism of Shakespeare's later Romans—Brutus, Antony, and Cleopatra.) But before Lucrece can pitch herself to such an action, she must first justify herself—not quite as Tarquin did, by deliberately overriding conscience, but (like Brutus in *Julius Caesar*) by a shifting and self-contradictory conscience. Her mad reasonings weave, in Shakespeare's telling, a tapestry of beautiful ironies. There is her argument, for instance, that since what she sought to live for is gone, she can now "clear this spot" by death, which will cover "slander's livery" with a "badge of fame." The illogic here is in proposing death as a remedy for what is already dead, and fame as a remedy for slander. "I am the mistress of my fate," she boasts in another stanza,

> And with my trespass never will dispense,
> Till life to death acquit my forced offence.

But if indeed "mistress" of her fate, how did she become the victim of any "forced" offence? Or why cannot the trespass be now dispensed by forgiveness? "Mistress of my fate" is a claim that here makes no sense unless, ironically, it means mistress of her trespass, which she is forcing herself to find indispensable to her life. That is, she would rather die than give it up.

The height of Lucrece's nonsense, perhaps, comes with her boast that "in my death I murder shameful scorn." Actually, will not her death merely illustrate a shameful scorn, Lucrece's own scorn of life? Scorn (as readers of Matthew 5:22 know) is not murder's victim but murder's motive. Lucrece's logic is topsy-turvy. Yet Shakespeare, by the doleful tone of his verses, keeps the irony subdued. He is writing tragedy, not satire, and hence must avoid overt mockery, must keep pathos uppermost.

Shakespeare maintains this delicate balance by spinning out

Lucrece's anguish long enough that it can become for us an object of contemplation. And to further distance it, he shows Lucrece catching at mirrors of herself in classical story. One such digression is her turning to the nightingale, Philomel, to join in a singing of ravishment and languishment. (Philomela, we may recall, was another of Chaucer's "good" women.) "Make thy sad grove in my disheveled hair," begs Lucrece, so that "While thou on Tereus descant'st, / I'll hum on Tarquin." But note that Shakespeare has placed this request against an early morning setting, in which birds of day are singing mirthful melody. Against these Lucrece wilfully shuts her ears, to hearken instead to this one bird of night. She calls day's birds "mocking birds" and bids them be mute. "A woeful hostess brooks not merry guests," she says. But Shakespeare-as-narrator has tucked in the comment: "Great grief grieves most at that would do it good." Self-pity, he goes on to imply, is a prelude to lawless behavior: "Grief dallied with nor law nor limit knows." Can any reader of this scene doubt the poet's maturity as moralist and psychologist?

Observe, further, how skilfully he has integrated the Philomela motif into his larger story. He shows Lucrece fascinated with the "thorn" at Philomela's breast. He shows her resolving to keep Philomela's "woes waking" by fixing "a sharp knife" to her own heart, that she may imitate "well" the wretched nightingale. Significantly, Lucrece does not altogether lack an awareness of the wrongness of such action:

> "To kill myself," quoth she, "alack, what were it,
> But with my body my poor soul's pollution?"

Moreover, it would be "a merciless conclusion," she admits, for any mother to slay her second baby because the first had died. But these glimmerings of truth are evaded by immediately burying them under a maze of contrary reasoning—that by making "some hole" in her "blemished fort" she can provide escape for her troubled soul; that by spending her blood she can ensure revenge on Tarquin; that by bequeathing her honor to the knife "fame" shall be bred; and that by leaving to Collatine this example of her "resolution" she can "boast" herself his true friend.

As we listen to such argument, are we not reminded, perhaps, of similar make-believe persuasions on the part of Shakespeare's suicides in his later *Julius Caesar* or *Antony and Cleopatra*? There is some resemblance, also, to the logic by which Hector, in *Troilus and Cressida* (II. ii) , is shown arriving at his "resolution" to disregard the moral laws of nature: affection for the "fame" which in time to come may "canonize" him overwhelms all else. But this desire for worldly canonization proved to be Hector's ruin, and Troy's with him. It may be significant, therefore, that in the present poem Troy's dismal story is the theme of a tapestry on which Lucrece next fixes her attention. It furnishes her a major mirror for self-study, and chiefly fills up the hours while she is awaiting the delivery of her letter to her husband.

Surely Shakespeare has not introduced this long digression, as some critics seem to think, merely to exercise his rhetoric on a set piece. More likely he is seizing an opportunity to project Lucrece's Roman plight against the larger canvas of Greek story—and also, in accordance with his general understanding of tragedy, to show her (like Hamlet) seizing on this opportunity to work herself up emotionally for a later "let go" release into self-dramatization. Even though the digression takes 217 lines, one-ninth of the poem, we need not suppose with Sir Sidney Lee that this "delays the progress of the story beyond all artistic law."[16] Rather, it belongs to Shakespeare's artistic purpose to affiliate new Troy's developing tragedy to old Troy's, and to show how the imagined past helps precipitate Lucrece's latent revenge motive. Lucrece herself may be blind to various of the figurative Troy-Rome parallels, or distort the ones she does seize on. Yet the poem's reader may grasp them, if he will, and thereby gain perspective on Lucrece. We are to be shown how Lucrece reads Troy's prototypal tragedy for clues to her personal tragedy. And while she reads we can ask: With how much self-understanding is she capable of reading? Her shallowness as an explicator of great art can then become for us both amusingly pathetic and a caveat for explicators like ourselves.

Lucrece identifies herself, we observe, first (at line 1447) with the despairing Hecuba, in whose face "all distress is stelled," and then finally (at line 1546) with credulous Priam, who was beguiled by the "outward honesty" of subtle Sinon. How appropriate for Lucrece is either one of these self-identifications? Putting her own feelings into Hecuba's mouth, she rails on Pyrrhus. Comparing herself with Priam, she declares Tarquin to be the Sinon through whom "my Troy" perished, and again vents her revenge feelings. But all the while she is raging against the violence and guile of the

Greeks, she seems wholly unaware that their motive for such actions was basically the same as the motive she herself now cherishes, namely, glory for oneself by avenging a rape. Is not she herself about to incite her own husband to become a Pyrrhus-like destroyer of Rome's royal family? And will she not go about her revenge with quite as much "saintlike" show as Sinon used in beguiling Priam? There is Shakespearean irony, therefore, in her lament that Sinon's "borrowed tears" were but a hellish means for burning Troy with water:

> Priam, why art thou old and yet not wise?
> For every tear he falls a Trojan bleeds.
> His eye drops fire, no water thence proceeds.
> > Those round clear pearls of his that move thy pity
> > Are balls of quenchless fire to burn thy city.

Lucrece's own pearl-like tears presently will hide a fire that will burn new Troy's institution of kingship; and many a Roman will bleed for every tear she sheds, betrayed to this ruin by pity for her.

Lucrece, of course, is blind to this deeper analogy between Troy's tragedy and her own Roman situation. Self-pity prevents her from seeing that her own tears are more like Sinon's than like Hecuba's; and, further, that if she is seeking in the Troy legend for some woman with whom to identify herself, a truer parallel would be the beautiful young Helen rather than motherly old Hecuba. Lucrece's outcry against Helen thus carries a special irony:

> Show me the strumpet that began this stir,
> That with my nails her beauty I may tear.

The strumpet whose beauty Lucrece here clamors to tear can be found, equivalently, in the present situation, in Lucrece's own hidden self. Shakespeare so hints by placing the "me" of the first line in a position of latent iambic stress. What the speaker pleads to be "shown," she is shown to be.[17]

4 The import of her suicide

We turn next to the climactic scene of Lucrece's self-immolation. She has been preparing for this moment of public show while awaiting the gathering of an audience. When writing her summoning letter, we are told, she was but *hoarding* her passion (note this motif of covetousness in line 1318), in order to spend it when her husband would be at hand to hear her sighs and groans. These, she hopes,

> may *grace the fashion*
> *Of her disgrace,* the better so to clear her
> From that suspicion which the world might bear her.
>
> (Italics mine)

Here, by way of contrast to Lucrece, we may wish to recall what Augustine had written (*City of God* I. 19) of the Christian women who had been raped by the Goths during the sack of Rome (in 410 A.D.) : "They declined to avenge upon themselves the guilt of others, and so add crimes of their own to those crimes in which they had no share." Unlike Lucrece, he says, they did not let their shame drive them to homicide. They were content to be esteemed pure "in the witness of their own conscience" and "in the sight of God"; for they did not burn with shame, as did Lucrece, at the thought that endurance of another's foul affront might be construed as complicity in it. They declined to "evade the distress of human suspicion, lest they thereby deviate from the divine law" (tr. Marcus Dods).

Shakespeare, I think, understands Lucrece's staged suicide as paganism's dark substitute for the Christian Passion story. That is, her "My blood shall wash the slander of mine ill" (line 1207) parodies the Christian hope of being washed in the blood of the Lamb. Lucrece as lamb will enact a "martyrdom" formally similar to, but morally the opposite of, a true atonement. To convey this implication, he lets her ritualize her "show" with details suggestive of a priestess in some Roman cult. When her congregation arrives, they find her "clad in mourning black" and with blue circles streaming "like rainbows" round about her eyes. These details suggest a martyr of romantic-bizarre visage. They are a deft revision of Ovid's portrait. Ovid had pictured the grieving Lucrece as like a "mother" at the funeral of her son. In his version, her friends immediately offer comfort and ask the cause of her grief; whereupon she veils her "modest" face and breaks into tears which flow like a running stream. But Shakespeare is suggesting a more equivocal kind of modesty. Lucrece's "tear-distained" eyes, he says, looked "red and raw," and their blue circles "Foretell new *storms*." Moreover, her look reflects such "deadly cares" that Collatine can only

stare "as in a trance" for a long while. Then, as he is able at last to
make loving inquiry, his phrases (through Shakespeare's diction)
carry an ambiguous import:

> Sweet love, what *spite* hath thy fair color spent?
> Why art thou thus attired in *discontent?*
> *Unmask,* dear dear, this moody heaviness . . .
> (Italics mine)

Lucrece's response at this point is to "sigh" three times to give
her sorrows "fire"—probably Shakespeare's parody of a preacher
invoking the Trinity before beginning his sermon. Then she addresses herself to speaking, and beginning with a promise of "Few
words," launches into seven uninterrupted stanzas of "sad dirge"
on the theme of "foul enforcement." Superficially her manner may
be construed as simple embarrassment; but the artistry of it suggests a deliberateness, if only subconscious on her part, yet given
significant form by Shakespeare. The prefatory three sighs, followed by a sevenfold organization of message, hint analogy to
Christian ritual, but on a theme the utter opposite of Christian
"good news." Following a five-line preface, the story of the rape is
set forth in 42 lines (a number symbolic of evil) [18] and organized
with great neatness—first a one-stanza statement of theme, then a
three-stanza account of the rape, concluded by two stanzas of meditation on its tragedy.

Ovid's simpler account has been much altered. He had written
of Lucrece's response:

> Ter conata loqui: ter destitit: ausaque quarto:
> Non oculos ideo sustulit illa suos.

> (Thrice she essayed to speak, and thrice gave o'er, and
> when the fourth time she summoned up courage she did
> not for that lift up her eyes.—J. G. Frazer, tr., Ovid's *Fasti,*
> London, 1929.)

Here the phrase "essayed to speak" implies a struggle for courage,
whereas the "sighs" of Shakespeare's Lucrece are a fan to "fire" up
the speaker's grief. And Shakespeare has omitted all mention of
downcast eyes. Furthermore, when Ovid's Lucrece does speak, she
can only gasp out two questions:

> Hoc quoque Tarquinio debebimus: eloquar, inquit,
> Eloquar infelix dedecus ipsa meum.

("Must I owe this too to Tarquin? Must I utter," quoth
she, "must I utter, woe's me, with my own lips my own
disgrace?"—tr. Frazer)

Beyond this, Ovid says, she could tell but a part of her story before
collapsing again into tears and matronly blushings (*matronales
erubere genae*). Shakespeare, in revising, has carefully avoided
Ovid's suggestion of matronly feelings and of speech becoming
tongue-tied through shame. Rather, his Lucrece is a sinuous orator
and quasi-(actually pseudo-) saint.

Having rounded out her dirge, Shakespeare's Lucrece pauses to
take note of the "speechless woe" into which it has plunged Collatine. Then, in order to awaken Collatine's "frenzy," she devotes
three stanzas to deftly pleading with him and his lords to "plight"
their "faith" to her by revenge on the foe. When the whole congregation consents, but longs to be told the foe's name, Lucrece delays
this revelation for three more stanzas while she raises and debates
with them a third topic, namely, how she may be acquitted of foul
offense. In these stanzas she elicits, only to reject, their offer of dis-
pensation. Then in a final stanza (the seventh in this second half
of her discourse, which has been devoted to revenge) she reveals
Tarquin's name amid a paroxysm of sighs which culminate in the
self-stabbing.

This climactic stanza, by reason of its crucial position in the
story, warrants our keenest attention:

> Here with a sigh, as if her heart would break,
> She throws forth Tarquin's name: "He, he," she says,
> But more than "he" her poor tongue could not speak
> Till after many accents and delays,
> Untimely breathing, sick and short assays,
>   She utters this: "He, he, fair lords, 'tis he,
>   That guides this hand to give this wound to me."

There are unmistakable hints of orgy in these lines. Not only the
"sighs" and "delays," but especially the untimely breathing, "sick
and short assays," suggest an analogy to sexual climax. Besides,
there is an obvious undertone of glee in the reiterated "he, he."[19] I
have been quoting the modernized punctuation of Harrison's edition, but Shakespeare's punning on the syllables *he-he* is perhaps
clearer in the original (Rollins Variorum text): "She throwes
forth TARQVINS name: he he, she saies"; and then, "She vtters this,

he he faire Lords, tis he." May we not imagine Lucrece, as she reaches the end of this penultimate line, pausing momentarily in a suspended "tizzy" of elation? Then, with stress on *That,* she guides the knife downward into her bosom. Emblematically, we have been shown martyrdom in an obscene mode, a religious "dying" which Shakespeare hints, figuratively, is a kind of masturbatory self-rape.

Lucrece's withholding of Tarquin's name until the moment of her suicide is unique to Shakespeare's version. In Ovid's version, as we have noted, Tarquin was named in Lucrece's very first sentence of reply to Collatine. Moreover, Ovid does not thereafter at any time show Lucrece requesting revenge. Instead, he tells us that after the suicide, when Brutus volunteered a vow of revenge over her dying body, she moved her sightless eyes by way of approval. Such modest demeanor accords with Ovid's whole portrait. He reports (as Shakespeare does not) that Lucrece took care, even in dying, to sink down decently. Livy, however, had pictured Lucrece verbally asking for revenge, midway in the course of her speech, and announcing Tarquin's name at that point. Her whole speech of confession, in response to her husband's question whether all is well with her, has in Livy's version a more straightforward and un- hesitating tone than in Ovid's. It reads in Painter's translation:

> No, deare husband, for what can be wel or safe unto a woman, when she hath lost her chastitie? Alas, Collatine, the steppes of an other man be now fixed in thy bed. But it is my bodye only that is violated, my minde God know- eth is guiltles, whereof my death shall be witnesse. But if you be men, give me your handes and trouth, that the adulterer may not escape unrevenged. It is Sextus Tarquin- ius whoe being an enemie, in steede of a frende, the other night came unto mee, armed with his sword in hand, and by violence caried away from me (the Goddes know) a wo- ful joy.

Her refusal of pardon for her forced offense, which Ovid tells in a mere two lines, is elaborated by Livy in some detail. Lucrece's friends affirm that "her bodye was polluted, and not her minde, and where consent was not, there the crime was absente." And she replies:

> I praye you consider with your selves, what punishmente is due for the malefactor. As for my part, though I cleare my-

self of the offence, my body shall feele the punishment; for
no unchast or ill woman shall hereafter impute no dishon-
est act to Lucrece. (Painter's translation)

Thus determined to punish her body, she draws out a hidden knife
and stabs herself. Whatever details beyond these we find in Shakespeare's version of the scene are his own invention. He has followed
Livy in making Lucrece easily articulate, but has developed for her
a more elaborate eloquence, deviously beguiling. He has patterned
for her a fascinating swan song, which rapturously enacts a ritual
of dark passion.

What Shakespeare's reconstructed scene further implies is that
Lucrece, through her mode of publishing Tarquin's guilt, has re-
embodied in her own actions Tarquin's spirit. In a polar but analogous way, she has figuratively repeated his devilish triumph. Indeed, her method of vindication parallels, although in telescoped
form, the stages by which in the earlier bedroom scene her visitor
had seduced her. Tarquin, let us recall, had begun his suit by pleading in excuse his own helplessness, "ensnared" by the beauty in her
face (specifically its color of blushing-red and pale-white anger).
So, likewise, Lucrece pleads to her husband in self-excuse (but now
with tear-red eyes and pallid trembling) the helplessness of her
own "poor weak self," entrapped by fear of Tarquin's visage (specifically his "scarlet lust" and ghastly threats). In both cases there
is the heraldry of red in league with white. In both cases the pleading becomes a disowning of responsibility, with the speaker self-
pictured as mere victim of fatal forces. And in each case the effect
on the hearer is to encourage a further fatalism. Thus, in the bedroom scene Lucrece's response was first some broken sighs, then a
tide of moralizing complaint undercut by signs of acquiescence. In
the public scene Collatine's response to Lucrece is figuratively
parallel: first a voice "damn'd up with woe" that drinks up its own
breath; then a "violent roaring tide" of sighs and sorrows, which
(although in this case not verbalized) are described as making "a
saw" (equivalent to Lucrece's earlier resort to moral saws) that
both pushes back and draws on grief. In the bedroom scene the
dallying was ended when Tarquin, sensing Lucrece's sympathetic
passion, cried: "Yield to my love" or else suffer the consequences of
being slain and afterwards disgraced by scandal. In the later public
scene it is ended when Lucrece, sensing her husband's "frenzy,"
cries in effect: Yield to my revenge or else suffer the consequences

of drowning in woe and being reputed no knightly champion. It is this threat that hypnotizes.

In this second instance, of course, the wiles of feminine insinuation cloak the naked threat. Lucrece's demand, "Be suddenly revenged," is beguilingly preceded by the clause "for my sake, when I might charm thee so." But the implication that a stigma of dishonor will result if compliance should be refused is made clear—first by associating "honorable faiths" with the merit of "revengeful arms," and then by adding that "Knights, by their oaths, should right poor ladies harms." Thus Lucrece seduces her audience. The absurdity of righting harms by revenge is overlooked. "Each present lord," we are told, promises aid, "As bound in Knighthood to her imposition." So subtly have they been *imposed* on, they remain unaware of how *benighted* is the *bondage* they are accepting. The wiping away of what Lucrece calls her "forced stain" seems to them a noble obligation. The ironic truth, however, is that Lucrece's stain at Tarquin's hands was actually no more "forced" than is now the general public's unwitting stain on its own honor in yielding to Lucrece's lust for revenge. In reversible ways, both the "victimized" Lucrece and now (through her) the victimized public have been drawn into complicity with evil because of a shallow notion of honor, a dread of loss of fame. Lucrece's rape has ramified into a "rapturing" of all Rome.

In retrospect, a careful reader may wonder whether Shakespeare was not foreshadowing this aspect of Lucrece's accomplishment earlier, when among the figures in the Troy tapestry he included "grave Nestor"[20] (1401 ff.). Let me recall the passage, italicizing parts of it:

> There pleading might you see grave Nestor stand,
> As 'twere encouraging the Greeks to fight,
> Making such sober action with his hand
> That it *beguiled* attention, charmed the sight.
> In speech, it seemed, his beard all silver white
>   *Wagged up and down,* and from his lips did fly
>   *Thin winding breath* which purled up to the sky.
>
> About him were a press of *gaping faces*
> *Which seemed to swallow up his sound* advice.
> All jointly listening, but with several graces,
> *As if some mermaid did their ears entice* ...

This reads like a parallel to Lucrece's mermaid-like beguiling of the Romans—with advice that charms by its sound while morally unsound. The diction of the passage has focused the tragic moment in a covertly comic light. Dr. Johnson was perhaps half-right about Shakespeare, when he wrote in his *Preface* of 1765: "In tragedy he is always struggling after some occasion to be comick . . . ." Shakespeare, however, is not struggling; the comic occasion lies in the very struggles of tragic mankind when looked at with figural perspective.

If we will return our attention to the actual content of the public pleading of swanlike Lucrece, nesting in her grief, we can see how carefully Shakespeare has focused for us the thin and winding character of her argument. He has given it an up-and-down contradictoriness (already implicit in Ovid's and Livy's story but not appreciated by them), and slyly has embellished this waggishness. Thus he has Lucrece begin her speech by saying that "no excuse can give the fault amending"—but then has her turn, immediately, to five stanzas which plead extenuating circumstances. Next he has her declare her mind pure—but in a context of excuse-seeking:

> Oh, teach me how to make mine own excuse,
> Or, at the least, this refuge let me find:
> Though my gross blood be stained with this abuse,
> Immaculate and spotless is my mind.

By Shakespeare's irony, this excuse is locating the stain not in her body (as in Livy's version) but in her *blood*—and in what she will call two lines later her mind's "poison'd closet" (which readers of Matthew 6:6 would identify with the "closet" of one's heart, the inner will). Lucrece is reasoning desperately and confusedly: she is begging her audience to allow her the "refuge" of claiming a spotless mind, by disowning responsibility for that mind's "closet." In effect she is hypnotizing herself and auditors by winding excuse on excuse. Then comes her request for revenge. Associated with her power to "charm," it is urged with a statement which is quite illogical as an argument for revenge: "The help that thou shalt lend me/ Comes all too late." How very true, ironically.

The question Lucrece then puts, "May my pure mind with the foul act dispense?" is pure rhetoric of an equivocal kind. It asks for self-dispensation, a request in itself foul. But by it Lucrece successfully prompts her auditors to declare that her "mind untainted" clears her "body's stain." Still, she covets something more finally convincing—may we not call it a *fool-proof* remedy—through letting her heart direct her hand to the slaying of her body. The poem's early reference (in line 154) to making "something nothing" is being climactically fulfilled.

> "No, no," quoth she, "no dame hereafter living
> By my excuse shall claim excuse's giving."

Here we see negative affirmation and moral double-talk epitomized. And the wordplay on "excuse" is Shakespeare's special contribution. By it he is able to characterize Lucrece (in line with what he had hinted in the bedroom scene) as a woman who can so talk as both to *deny* excuse and to *proffer* it at the same time. The logic of her argument has become a snake-like coil: a refusing of "excuse" is turned into an excuse for refusing other dames any excuse for ever yielding to the lust of "He he"—the shame of which must now excuse (and glorify) her suicide. It is farcical morality, but in its blindness pathetic tragedy.

5 Brutus and Collatine

The aftermath of the suicide is the poem's final section. Here attention shifts to the reaction generated by Lucrece's ritual blood-bath. The chief actors now are Collatine, who all along has been too hypnotized to interrupt his wife's paroxysm, and Brutus, a bystander who emerges from the shadows to assume command. As we watch these two, Shakespeare may intend us to be reminded, once again, of equivalent figures in the Troy tapestry. He had depicted in that tapestry, among its background personages, an Ajax of "blunt rage and rigor" and a "sly Ulysses" whose mild glance "showed deep regard and smiling government" (1394 ff.). These two Greeks prefigure, I suggest, Collatine and Brutus in the Roman story. For Collatine now reacts with dumb rage, while Brutus smoothly turns the debacle into a bid for political leadership. As Collatine remains momentarily dream-bound, Brutus steps forward to pluck the knife from the side of Lucrece. The situation is thus analogous to Ulysses' outwitting of Ajax in obtaining the armor of the slain hero Achilles.

Shakespeare next shows us how Brutus shrewdly uses for his own policy the honored knife, while Collatine fumbles about madly in "deep vexation." Collatine, we are told, desperately bathes "the pale fear in his face" in "key-cold Lucrece' bleeding stream." (Key-cold sounds like a pun on cuckold—perhaps to support the irony of his baptizing himself in what line 1745 has called "black blood," putrified.) When he tries to speak, he can only babble incoherently, sometimes through his teeth tearing the name "Tarquin" in a tempest of woe and desire to be revenged. But meanwhile Brutus, who had been thought by the Romans to be a silly jeering idiot, now begins to "clothe his wit in state and pride." He makes use of the "deep policy" of which he is capable. "Advisedly" he chides Collatine, asking him if it be revenge or mere "childish humour" to strike at oneself for the "foul act" which caused Lucrece to bleed. (Such phrasing does not specify what caused the foul act—was it perhaps, ironically, both revenge and childish humour?) Then turning to the assembled Romans, Brutus calls on them to join him in kneeling,

> To rouse our Roman gods with invocations
> That they will suffer these abominations,

with which Rome is disgraced. (The syntax, again, is ambiguous: Is he protesting abominations; or is he, rather, asking the gods to permit new ones?) Priest-like, he swears "by the Capitol that we adore" and "by chaste Lucrece' soul" to revenge her death. Then he seals this oath, appropriately, with a kissing of the fatal knife.

The Roman auditors, overcome with wonder, approve the words and act of Brutus. They kneel and repeat his vow. Is this not figuratively a kind of Black Mass? It ends with the worshippers going forth "with speedy diligence" to parade Lucrece's body through the streets. Thus, says Shakespeare,

> The Romans plausibly did give consent
> To Tarquin's everlasting banishment.

"Plausibly" this concludes what the poem's Argument had promised, the story of how Rome's government passed "from kings to consuls." But is Shakespeare seeing moral gain—or sad tragedy—in this event? Has he not shown us yet one more seduction?

Shakespeare has carefully ritualized the religiosity of this final scene, probably in order to highlight for Christian readers its parody of true religion. He has depicted Brutus as the master artist of a piety guided by "policy." Such a portrait owes something perhaps to Dante's estimate of Ulysses—a prototype for all counsellors of fraud. In any case, Shakespeare's scene has so reshaped and embroidered on details from Ovid and Livy as to transform the total import. Ovid had reported simply that Brutus tore the blade from the corpse, and waving it aloft, swore by the "chaste blood" of Lucrece and by her Manes, or ghost, "that shall be divine to me," to proscribe forever Tarquin and his race. (The motif here of a vowed revenge against an adulterous tyrant, in the name of a Ghost hailed as divine, anticipates Hamlet.) But Shakespeare has deftly suggested moral ambiguity, both in the Lucrece whose ghost is here being exalted, and in the motives of Brutus, who in canonizing her is using religion to serve political ends. (For Brutus it is "the Capitol that we adore"—just as, similarly, in the Bible those who adored the Temple were seduced to make a hero of Barabbas, not Christ.) Can any reader really suppose that Shakespeare is personally approving the kind of religion around which Brutus is rallying Roman devotion?

Shakespeare could have known, simply by reading Augustine's City of God, Book IX, that Rome's worship of Manes or tutelary spirits was deadly in its effects and a central cause of Rome's ultimate downfall. In other books of the City of God, Shakespeare could have found a full catalogue of the "abominations" which the Roman gods "suffer," and which their worshippers suffer by suffering such gods. These abominations, in Augustine's view, included such practices as the banishing of princes, civil war, and orgies of adultery and suicide—all the result of human self-delusions due to an idolatrous will-worship, and to a ridiculously pathetic coveting of honor and fame. Such is the total truth about Rome, I think, which Shakespeare has beautifully caught and illustrated in the welter of ironic contradictions which his poem narrates.

As poet, he has also brought his story full circle. The Collatine who at the beginning joyed in nothing so much as a boasting of his wife is now at the end to reap no other joy than the boasting of her suicide. Henceforth he can worship her valor by expending his own in brute service under Brutus, Rome's substitute for Tarquin. It is to this sterile destiny, rather than to any fireside comforts of a home with children in it, that Collatine's "loyal" wife Lucrece has led him. May we not say, then, that Lucrece's beauty is to Rome what

Helen's was to Troy? And this sense of the relation of Troy's tragedy to Rome's, let us note, is also implied at the beginning of the
City of God, when Augustine ascribes the whole fall of Rome to a
worship of those discredited gods which Aeneas foolishly carried
on his back, all the way from burning Troy to Tiber's watery banks.

Some critics possibly will object that we have gone beyond the
poem in our commentary and engaged in mere speculation. What
right have we to ferret out an art work's implications, or to attempt
through inference to consolidate its obscure import? Shakespeare
himself, I think, helps us to reply through a stanza in which he
describes the artistry of the worker of the Troy tapestry (1422–28):

> For much imaginary work was there.
> Conceit deceitful, so compact, so kind,
> That for Achilles' image stood his spear
> Grip'd in an armèd hand; himself behind
> Was left unseen, save to the eye of mind.
> A hand, a foot, a face, a leg, a head,
> Stood for the whole to be imaginèd.

This stanza seems clearly to say that no great work of art can be
appreciated properly unless the reader brings to it "the eye of the
mind" and an ability to go behind signs to the realities they signify.

6 The poem's three levels

Shakespeare's poem is profoundly moral, but by now it should be
evident that its moral is no simple one. We are invited to grasp it,
in fact, at no less than three levels of meaning. The poet announces
these, very craftily, in a stanza near the mid-point of his work, immediately after Lucrece's six stanzas of expostulation to Night. As
she turns next to imagining the dreadful fate which "telltale Day"
may have in store for her, she cries out:

> *The nurse,* to still her child, will tell my story,
> And fright her crying babe with Tarquin's name;
> *The orator,* to deck his oratory,
> Will couple my reproach to Tarquin's shame;
> *Feast-finding minstrels,* tuning my defame,
> Will tie the hearers to *attend each line,*
> How Tarquin wronged me, I Collatine.
> (813–819; italics mine)

Indirectly Shakespeare is here telling us, I would say, that the Lucrece legend in the future may take any one, or more, of three possible versions. The simplest of these will focus on Tarquin and his frightful villainy, thereby making the story's emotional impact, and its moral, turn about the ruin caused by a big bad wolf. Or secondly, the story can take on an added "deck," the result of a binocular vision. The focus then will be that of an orator, weighing judicially Lucrece as well as Tarquin, and finding blame in both parties. Thirdly, the story can be *sung* within a three-dimensional perspective, in which the background figure of Collatine is considered, and the tragedy is then so tuned as to reveal the wrong committed against family welfare, the defaming of the husband-wife relationship.

The nursemaid's version, the orator's version, and the feast-finding minstrel's version are thus three successive levels of understanding, related to each other like a nest of spheres or the layers of an onion. The nursemaid's version, Shakespeare implies, is superficial, good enough only for frightening infants. The orator's version, however, is for adult minds, for a public interested in the complex apologetics of a case, and prepared jury-like to size up its moral aspects. The minstrel's version, finally, is for royal listeners at a feast —for seasoned minds eager to be entertained with comprehensive insight, and alert therefore to watch for it in every well-tuned line. In distinguishing these three levels, did Shakespeare perhaps have in mind, respectively, Ovid's version, Augustine's version, and his own version? Certainly Ovid's brief poem, while smooth and picturesque, is ethically superficial. Augustine's oratorical treatment by comparison is ethically profound, yet yields dialectic rather than poetry. Shakespeare as minstrel seems to have absorbed and reorchestrated these predecessors.

The story as told by Ovid had been one of pathos simply. It relied for its impact on the contrast between a vicious Tarquin and a modest Lucrece. *Agna lupo* is its theme, the innocent lamb caught by a ravening wolf. Tarquin's lust is traced, therefore, not as in Shakespeare to a husband's boast, but to Tarquin's own sight of Lucrece's winsome form and incorruptibility (quod corrumpere non est) , evident as she rises (from amid humble needlework and from confiding to her maids her concern for her husband's safety) to greet this homecoming husband with an embrace about the neck and tears of joy. Shakespeare's version, as we have noted, omits these details of domestic virtue. But in Ovid it is precisely Lucrece's chastity which, by the memory of it which lingers in Tarquin's mind, arouses in him a burning lust, a dastardly plot, and the daring deed. At no time does he then pause for self-debate. Welcomed at Lucrece's house because he is her kinsman, he is given a friendly supper and then retires; but once the house is dark, he arises, draws his sword, invades the bedroom of the virtuous wife (nupta pudica), grasps her waist, and threatens to ruin her fame if she resists. Trembling like a lamb, Lucrece can say nothing; she is overcome by her "fear of fame." Even the next day she utters no expostulations. Instead she grieves like a mother over the death of a son, and sends at once for her old father and for her husband. On their arrival she veils her modest face and can scarcely speak. But solaced by them, she makes known Tarquin's outrage. Her shame is so great that although exonerated by them she refuses pardon and stabs herself, taking care to fall with modesty. Then as father and husband throw themselves moaning on her body, Brutus arrives on scene and proves his hidden courage. Seizing the bloody knife, he vows revenge and rouses the populace to banish the reigning Tarquin. This simplistic tale is the Roman one.

Orators such as St. Augustine, however, approach the story differently. When Shakespeare's Lucrece says that orators will "couple my reproach with Tarquin's shame," what she fears is reproach for contamination by the rape. Subconsciously she has also fugitive fears of public suspicion of her complicity in it. But specifically this second level of reproach for possible complicity and a more important further level, reproach for her suicide, are the added deck of meaning which the Christian Augustine developed. In that orator's comments Shakespeare could have read:

> She herself alone knows her reason; but what if she was betrayed by the pleasure of the act, and gave some consent to Sextus . . . and then was so affected with remorse that she thought death alone could expiate her sin? Even though this were the case, she ought still to have held her hand from suicide, if she could with her false gods have accomplished a fruitful repentance. However . . . if the truth were that both were involved in it, one by open assault, the other by secret consent, then she did not kill an innocent woman (*City of God* I. 19, tr. Marcus Dods).

Her whole case, Augustine goes on to explain, is in such a dilemma that "if you extenuate the homicide, you confirm the adultery; if you acquit her of adultery, you make the charge of homicide the heavier; and there is no way out of this dilemma, when one asks, if she is an adulteress, why praise her? If chaste, why slay her?" Of these two options, if the Romans are in agreement on exonerating Lucrece of adultery, Augustine is ready lawyer-like to argue from this hypothesis. For thereby he can show her self-slaying as having no moral justification at all, and hence Roman praise of her as utterly nonsensical. Yet by repeated and subtle implication he leaves open the other option too, even when consenting to waive it as a criminal charge. If she was not adulterous by consent to Tarquin, at least her suicide was "prompted not by the love of purity, but by the overwhelming burden of her shame." Her love was tainted by "the Roman love of glory in her veins." That was the basic impurity which caused her "proud dread" of losing fame.

Around Augustine's interpretation Shakespeare could develop his own more expanded reading. For with love-of-glory clearly posited as the root cause of Lucrece's act of suicide, the tragedy could be truly unified, since this same motive could be posited for Tarquin's act of rape as a more basic motive for it than mere sexual desire. The two crimes then interrelate by a fascinating polarity. Behind Tarquin's adultery can be shown his self-murdering of his reason, while behind Lucrece's self-murder can be shown her prior sin of adulterating human love. But to give this story its proper social frame, the role of Collatine too must be developed, a role left unexamined by Augustine, although by implication Collatine was included by Augustine with those Romans who unreasonably extol Lucrece out of their love of human glory. The full tragic cause comprises the ethos of a whole civilization.

Unlike Augustine, however, Shakespeare is a poet rather than an orator. That means that for him the art of mimesis must circumscribe and use the art of rhetoric. As a narrator of tragic psychology, Shakespeare has the task, not of resolving the ethical dilemma which Augustine had so ironically set forth, but of showing dramatically how the Romans could reason themselves into it, and how hero and heroine alike could sink themselves in its mazes. Having learned the causes of tragedy from Augustine, and the rudiments of story-telling from Ovid, Shakespeare was trying for the more complex role of Feast-finding minstrel.

Minstrels will say, says Lucrece, that I wronged Collatine. She means: wronged him by the scandal of her rape. But Shakespeare means, additionally: wronged him by serving, not his welfare, but his reputation; by speaking up, not for his sake, but for her own fame; and finally by sacrificing herself, not to bring him happiness, but to bind him and all Rome in a covenant of revenge and death. Moreover, Shakespeare can show how Collatine, too, through his own love of glory, has neglected to protect his wife, and even has stood idly by while she slays herself. There is irony, therefore, when Lucrece tells Collatine of Tarquin's threat that unless she took all "patiently" her shame would rest "on record" as "the adulterate death of Lucrece and her *groom*" (line 1645). Who is this groom? In one sense, he is the base houseboy whom Tarquin had in mind to place murdered in her bed. But in a deeper sense does not this lackey figuratively denote Collatine? When Collatine was away at war, did not Lucrece value him as lackeying to her own love of glory? And after the rape, did she not impatiently override his efforts to console, exploiting these for her own ends? Thus she has treated her husband like a base groom; and ironically he himself has accepted this role. In this respect, both have prostituted the husband-wife relationship. In them, family life has become tragically disordered by a mutual addiction to fame. But the community life of Rome as a whole reflects this same disorder.

Within such a Roman background Shakespeare can place the balancing tragedies of his two principals, Tarquin and Lucrece, reciprocal versions of tragic shame and waste. For if rape shames by its wastefulness, revenge wastes by its shamefulness. The two major sections of the poem may thus be said to display, in summary, two successive but interdependent phases of evil. Tarquin's quest shows us how things rank and gross in nature can grow in an unweeded garden. Lucrece's reaction, balancing this, shows us in what sense "lilies that fester" can smell far worse than weeds. An "expense of spirit in a waste of shame" is common to both, although in polar ways. Their polarity can be further understood if we will recall, from Shakespeare's later *Measure for Measure* (I. i. 32), the two sides of Duke Vincentio's warning: against, on the one hand, wasting one's self on one's virtues; on the other hand, wasting one's virtues on one's self. On these twin counts, the protagonists of *The Rape of Lucrece* prove wasteful. Hence, morally there are no "fine issues" to their story. But esthetically the art form of simple tragedy thus achieves its distinctive beauty. It mirrors faithfully the defective actions of noble persons and the sad consequences which coherently ensue.

7 *Lucrece* in relation to *King Lear*

How can we place this simple tragedy in relation to the more terrifying and abysmal tragedy of *King Lear*? The later work, written
twelve years after *Lucrece,* depicts moral defects of greater range
and variety. Yet it does not conclude with either suicide or the exiling of kings. It tells the story, rather, of a temporarily self-exiled
king, and of an attempted suicide by an adulterous Gloucester,
but also of an eventual rescue of both these persons by their children—one of whom, Cordelia, undergoes a genuine martyrdom, the
reverse of the suicide attributed to her in most of the source versions Shakespeare inherited. In other words, the poet is here showing that even in a pagan society the evil consequences of initial
human infirmity and defect can in time provide the emergent occasions for a discovery of regenerative self-knowledge. Tragic life
can reach a bottom, when (in the "far country" of the Prodigal) man
comes to himself and begins to turn homeward. Since this theme
corresponds to Christianity's reading of the canvas of human history in its broadest dimensions, it is not surprising that *King Lear*
was performed as a Christmas play in the year 1606. Its story is that
of a completed nighttime of tragedy, within which are discovered
the spiritual clues, at least, for an upward turn toward the day-
spring of comedy.

Tragic experience begins, let us say, always in some latent idolatry of the self or of some property of the self. As Augustine would
say, gifts are mistaken for gods, and to these mortal gods sacrifices
are then offered. But Shakespeare seems to have had Augustine's
insight to recognize that such false religion and false sacrifice are a
testimony to man's need of, and neglected capacity for, true religion and true sacrifice. If and when the world of what St. Paul
called the "old man" dies, the world of what he termed the "new
man" can begin to appear. History tells us, in fact, that when the
old world of Graeco-Roman civilization reached its bankruptcy (a
fate figured incipiently in *The Rape of Lucrece*) , a new world of
Christian values was destined ultimately to succeed it. In *King
Lear* Shakespeare prefigures this larger story, taking his protagonists into human bankruptcy and largely through it, to the point
where they glimpse at least some enigmatic sign of a life beyond
tragedy.

The fully completed cycle we can find, historically, in the career of Augustine himself. Recapitulating in his own experience Troy's penalty of burning for having coveted earthly beauty, and Rome's penalty of drowning in suicidal strife for having coveted worldly glory, Augustine discovered in the depths of his remorseful misery the beauty of a love he had neglected and the glory of a mercy he had banished. After this baptism, he could put his tragic past in new perspective. His writings, together with the Bible's, were probably Shakespeare's chief guides, both in understanding the nature of evil and in imaging its historical logic for the catharsis and enlightenment of a latter-day Christendom.

PART

II

The Premises
of Shakespearean
Tragedy

II

In Search
of an Adequate
Perspective

Any interpretation of Shakespeare depends in part on one's orientation. For each reader brings, when responding to a play or poem, a vision conditioned by his general store of knowledge and beliefs. His literary sensibility rests on premises—as to the nature of poetry and its genres, and at a deeper level as to the nature of man and of human destiny. Since these can vary from one critic to another, the history of interpretation abounds in differing judgments, at times clashing ones. Yet we do not on that account dismiss criticism as useless. We discover that each reading is relative to its perspective, and that some perspectives scant certain aspects of a work which another point of view helps bring to light. We therefore reject ultimate relativism, and suppose that each play has an objective structure whose significance can be progressively grasped as readers achieve a capacity for perceiving it.

This capacity must arise, as Robert Heilman has well said, from "a large enough philosophic base" from which to contemplate the literary object in depth and in breadth.[1] Such a base we can assume to have been available within the cultural tradition of Shakespeare's time. Even the nonacademic man could have had his sensibility nourished indirectly by it. In those social circles where it was being eroded, however, or in later times when shifts of taste had obscured it, something less than an adequate understanding of Shakespeare would not be surprising. Prerequisite to any proper evaluation of his work is a general sense of the world view implicit in his whole poetic. To the degree that we, in our day, can recapture the premises immanent in the form given his dramas, we can hope to discern with accuracy and coherence each play's resonance of meaning.

The present chapter is directed toward searching for an adequate perspective in the sense just described. Our procedure will be to begin with a brief historical review. For we can use, as an incentive to fresh study, an acquaintance with what some of the more notable critics of the past have had to say on Shakespearean tragedy. Their observations can raise for us major problems of interpretation, if we study in each critic the nature of the philosophic base underlying his judgments. How, we may ask, is his orientation conditioning his pronouncements? And what aspects of Shakespeare's art are some perspectives neglecting or warping, which from another perspective might be more rightly appreciated and assessed? If our historical sketch proceeds in this evaluative way, beginning conveniently with Dr. Johnson, continuing through Coleridge and Bradley, and sampling a few of the more recent trends, we will discover various flaws in the criticism of the past and discern, through a winnowing, some of the more promising present-day understandings of Shakespeare's tragedies.

The remainder of the chapter will then be devoted to resolving a few of the controversial issues which lurk on the frontiers of study today. The reader will here find evidence for the thesis that a knowledge of Shakespeare's background in medieval Christian lore—which includes theology, symbolism, and the principle of analogy—can be of particular help toward a better understanding of his tragedies. As illustration, a brief reading of *Othello* and a fuller one of *Romeo and Juliet* will be offered from this perspective in the last two sections of the chapter. The considerations which prompt my efforts can be understood only by giving attention first to some landmarks in the history of comment on Shakespeare's tragedies in general.

1 Johnson, Coleridge, Santayana, and Shaw

Insofar as "common sense" is a sufficient guide, Dr. Samuel Johnson is often an excellent critic.[2] Among his editorial remarks on *Romeo and Juliet,* for instance, we read: "Juliet plays most of her pranks under the appearance of religion: perhaps Shakespeare meant to punish her hypocrisy." This suggestion, although too moralistic in its focus, may be nearer the truth than today's romantic interpretations. Johnson's comment on *Timon of Athens* is equally noteworthy: "The catastrophe," he says pointedly, "affords a very powerful warning against that ostentatious liberality, which scatters bounty, but confers no benefits, and buys flattery, but not friendship." What is sensible here is Johnson's recognition that the heroes of tragedy are not to be taken at their own self-estimate. He is quick to penetrate, likewise, obvious sophistries, such as the one in Lady Macbeth's appeal to her husband's "manhood": Shakespeare is here letting us see the glittering lure of a false fortitude. The reason for Macbeth's later reference to Duncan's "silver skin laced with his golden blood" is also rightly grasped by Johnson: these "unnatural metaphors" are a signal to us of the "artifice and dissimulation" in Macbeth's pretended grief. Elsewhere, when Johnson is paraphrasing knotty passages, his explication is often as exact as one could wish—as, for instance, of Hamlet's "To be or not to be" soliloquy.

On the other hand, Johnson's common sense involves prejudices. We see them misleading him, for instance, into guessing that the "golden story" of Lady Capulet's reference (in I. iii) may be to the *Golden Legend,* "a book in the darker ages of popery much read." A more significant instance is his whole attitude toward the witches which lure Macbeth. For here we see Johnson's inability to believe that evil can ever tempt in supernatural guises. Any poet, he remarks, who would nowadays make the whole action of his tragedy depend upon enchantment, and its chief events on the assistance of supernatural agents, would be "banished from the Theatre to the nursery, and condemned to write fairy tales instead of tragedies"; yet Shakespeare is not to be censured, since in his time such credulity was universally admitted and he turned it to advantage in a play warning against "vain and elusive predictions." Johnson seems unable to appreciate that Shakespeare is telling not really of elusive predictions but of the equivocation of fiends, who might in any age tempt human hopes. He seems unaware that witches were associated by the Elizabethans with the desert demons of Isaiah and the furies of classical literature,[3] and could therefore represent just as much reality as these. His rationalist perspective is reflected also when he comments on scenes in other tragedies in which evil takes on what we would term demonic perversions. The extrusion of Gloucester's eyes, or Othello's language of piety when murdering Desdemona, or Hamlet's contriving of damnation over the praying Claudius—all these Johnson wishes had been excluded, for he finds them too horrible to be endured in a drama.

We can be grateful that Dr. Johnson had the good sense to reject as false assumption the neoclassical unities of time and place, and also to oppose any rigorous exclusion of comic elements from a tragedy. Yet Johnson's apologia for a "mingled kind" of genre is based solely on the argument that "the course of the world" mingles joy and sorrow and that a comparable variety on stage furnishes the spectator emotional relief. This is a pertinent consideration, no doubt. It omits, however, what today we recognize as a further reason for the comic scenes, namely, their indirect commentary on some theme in the tragedy, their figurative play about one or another of its motifs—as, for instance, in the play on "equivocation" by the drunken Porter in *Macbeth*. Johnson dislikes all quibbles and conceits. He dislikes also what he considers vulgarity —for instance, the "low jest" of Antony on the "horned" herd of Basan, and some of Cleopatra's feminine arts. In an important sense, as we shall see, the basic design in Shakespeare's plays eludes him. It does so partly because, with his common sense approach, he neglects the possibility of multiple meanings in Shakespeare's language, and partly because he assumes an audience of homogeneously reasonable beings, overlooking the fact that some auditors might prefer a more mysterious kind of truth.

This is notoriously the case in Johnson's avowed preference for Tate's version of *King Lear*, which altered Shakespeare's ending in order to reward Cordelia in political terms. On this he comments:

> A play in which the wicked prosper, and the virtuous miscarry, may doubtless be good, because it is a just representation of the common events of human life: but since all reasonable beings naturally love justice, I cannot easily be persuaded, that the observation of justice makes a play worse; or, that if other excellencies are equal, the audience will not always rise better pleased from the final triumph of persecuted virtue.[4]

In Shakespeare's version he complains of finding only an "incidentally enforced" moral, that "villainy is never at a stop, that crimes lead to crimes, and at last terminate in ruin."

But has Johnson here grasped the meaning of *King Lear*? Does not Shakespeare show villainy actually coming to a stop, when Edmund before dying discovers his better self? And have not Edmund's very crimes led, indirectly, to Edgar's maturing into a national deliverer, and to Albany's elicited perception of a heavenly justice in human affairs? There are some other moral facts, too, overlooked in Johnson's reading—for instance, the fact that Lear's final cry,

> Do you see this? Look on her, look, her lips,
> Look there, look there!

may be the play's answer to Kent's early prayer, "See better, Lear!" And what of Lear's experience of forgiveness in Act IV? Is there no significant reward in his having found, amid misery, this moment of blessedness? Or no triumph of virtue in his having come —after "the great rage . . . is killed in him"—to "live / And pray, and sing" with Cordelia? Johnson's moral vision seems to have lost something of the large philosophic base of his Christian heritage. In asking that a tragedy exhibit the poetic justice which "all reasonable beings naturally love" he is reducing justice to the measure of man's "natural" reason.

How is it that Johnson can say, as he does in his *Preface,* that Shakespeare "seems to write without any moral purpose"? The explanation, basically, is that Johnson cannot understand the distinctive logic of Shakespeare's tragedies. He thinks their plots "loosely formed"; asserts that the catastrophe in them is "improbably produced"; and conjectures that Shakespeare did not always fully comprehend his own design. In short, his own notion of probability is at odds with Shakespeare's. Hence we find him explaining, in an essay prefaced to the *Shakespear Illustrated* of Mrs. Lennox, that the poet lived in an age when men's minds "were not accustomed to balance Probabilities, or to examine nicely the Proportion between Causes and Effects." Shakespeare's reputation for excellence, we are told, depends not on the "naked Plot or Story" of his plays, "not on the Fiction of a Tale." It depends, rather, on Shakespeare's great attention to "the Scenes" of nature, and to incidents which mirror faithfully human habits, manners, sentiments, and passions. Shakespeare's art in connecting these scenes, and in ordering the course of their incidents, Johnson supposes to have been rather haphazard. In Shakespeare's day, he explains patronizingly, plays were written which "by changing the catastrophe, were tragedies to-day and comedies tomorrow." A history was then regarded as a series of actions "with no other than chrono-logical succession, independent on each other, and without any tendency to introduce or regulate the conclusion." And tragedy was much like this history. Hence in his tragedies Shakespeare catches at "opportunities of amplification," instead of "inquiring what the occasion demanded." He has scenes of undoubted excel-lence, but "perhaps *not one play* which, if it were now exhibited as the work of a contemporary writer, would be heard to the con-clusion" (italics mine). Always there is "something wanting" in Shakespeare's tragedies. The dramatist exercised his skill of inven-tion, not in perfecting his plots, but in affecting "a disproportion-ate pomp of diction and a wearisome train of circumlocution," at times sinking into trivial sentiments, or obscurity, or quibble.

F. R. Leavis, in writing of Johnson as a critic of Shakespeare,[5] has singled out two faults in Johnson's perspective. One is that it cripples an appreciation of metaphor and of what Leavis calls the "exploratory-creative use of words upon experience." The other is a "moralistic fallacy and confusion," which prevents Johnson from understanding that works of art (in Leavis' phrase) "enact their moral valuations," rather than starting with an abstractly formu-lated moral which the dramatist then proceeds to demonstrate. But these two blindspots, I think, are not quite the whole of John-son's trouble. And Leavis too much reduces them to an ignorance of artistic process. Johnson's imperceptiveness was perhaps not so much in the area of metaphor (where we noted his appreciation of one of Macbeth's) as in the area of wit and tragic irony. And his second major limitation is not exactly, as Leavis would say, that "for Johnson a moral judgment that isn't *stated* isn't there" and that he demands of the dramatist a play "conceived and composed as statement." The trouble, more profoundly, is that Johnson is unhappy over the implicit moral which he does find *enacted,* when Cordelia can "perish in a just cause," or when "the harmless and pious Ophelia" suffers an untimely death. These catastrophes offend his sense of "poetical justice" and "poetical probability"—norms which reflect his philosophic presuppositions, no less than his artistic predilections. Johnson should have asked himself: What is probability in drama? Is it not (as a recent scholar has defined it) whatever is "believable within the assumptions of the life-frame imagined by the dramatist"?[6] Johnson's basic difficulty is that

Shakespeare's life-frame often seems to him unsuitable for belief, not quite rationally conceived.

In short, Johnson's incapacities are rooted in his Augustan world view and his distaste for history, together with his loose sense of literary genre. He has a neoclassical ideal of moral order, and on not finding this exemplified in Shakespeare's tragedies he assumes the poet was careless of moral issues because of "the barbarity of his age." Would that the poet had risen to a concern for justice independent of time and place, for it is always a writer's duty "to make the world better"! But to this contention one might reply: Is Nahum Tate's ending of *King Lear* in any way really conducive to making the world better? One reason, surely, for its not surviving as theatre after the period of 1680–1830, is that audiences have not found it illuminative of the human condition; it simply does not do justice to our sense of historical experience. We feel Tate's sense of justice is too rationalistically convenient. It is he, rather than Shakespeare, who "sacrifices virtue to convenience." Viewing with a perspective different from Tate's and Johnson's, a twentieth-century critic can hail Shakespeare's *King Lear* as "a miracle play," revealing our world as a "miraculous world."[7] The revealing of life's potentiality for miracle is more satisfying, to most men's moral sense, than an exemplification of neoclassicism's concept of justice.

Let us turn next to Coleridge's criticism. Here we encounter idealism in another guise than Johnson's. Drawing elements from Plato, Spinoza, Kant, and Schelling, Coleridge fashioned his own distinctive philosophy. Its orientation has been well described as an amalgam of the "organic vitalism" of romanticism with the "rationalism and idealism" of classicism.[8] Like Johnson, Coleridge sees Shakespeare as a poetic imitator of nature's universals. But whereas Johnson thought of these universals as "those general passions and principles by which all minds are agitated," a "general nature" discoverable through external observation and study, Coleridge viewed them as the creative stirrings of nature, the *natura naturans* which works from within by a process of evolution.

Coleridge therefore sees Shakespeare as working in the spirit of nature, imitating by imagination its evolving germ and active being. He likens him to a Proteus, who "darts himself forth and passes into all the forms of human character and passion," becoming all things yet remaining ever himself.[9] By meditation, Shakespeare changes himself into the Nurse of *Romeo and Juliet* or into the Constable of *Much Ado*. That is, he assumes their characters by imitating certain parts of his own character or exaggerating such as exist in possibility in his own nature. His dramatic characters thus develop as symbolic embodiments of "fragments of the divine mind" that is drawing them. "Shakespeare is the Spinozistic deity—an omnipresent creativeness." He has a "holiness of genius" like the divine effluence which created all the beauty of nature. True genius in a poet acts creatively "under laws of its own origination." Moved by an instinct for self-perfection, every true poet, by using some part of his own hopes, yearnings, and imperfections, makes of these a shadow embodiment in art, "a sort of prophetic image" of what he is not but may be. In Shakespeare's characters, therefore, what we behold are "ideal realities" which the poet has naturalized to his own mind's conception, and which he projects as particular dream modes of human nature, wherein we may see, however dimly, "that state of being in which there is neither past nor future but all is permanent in the very energy of nature." In the plays of Shakespeare every man "sees himself, without knowing that he does so"—like a traveller beholding his own figure in mountain mist—a figure "dressed in all the prismatic colours of the imagination" and magnified to proportions of grandeur.

In Coleridge's view, if we may summarize, the dramatist is regarded as a kind of pantheistic creator, who by imaging forth a gallery of particularized modes of his own universal human nature gives us prophetic enlargements of our potential selves and thus a similitude of the panorama of life. What are the consequences of such a theory? One consequence is a tone in criticism which differs markedly from Johnson's. Coleridge communicates the thrill he feels of contact with Shakespeare's imagination. He finds both esthetic pleasure and a participative self-expression in the activity of thinking himself into the feelings of beings in circumstances different from his own. He annotates, more or less, his experience of trying to share in the moods and thoughts of characters in the process of their development. Imagery is important to Coleridge, because in it he sees something of the poet's own spirit coloring the passion or character then foremost in the poet's mind. All earlier English critics, he feels, have been blind to this key he has to Shakespeare's greatness. A dramatic character's prodigality in beautiful words, which sometimes annoyed Johnson, Coleridge values as embodying a psychic movement colored by the author's exuberance of wit and fancy and symbolic of some moral truth.

With this perspective Coleridge can sometimes catch aspects of character psychology which Johnson overlooked. Hamlet's horrible words over the praying Claudius, for instance, he explains as an excuse Hamlet makes for not acting; they reflect Hamlet's disposition to indecision in doing the justice he had resolved on. There is considerable insight in this interpretation, I think, although it remains incomplete unless we can explain why Hamlet makes excuses. Elsewhere I find interesting Coleridge's explanation of Hamlet's capering with the cellarage ghost. Ludicrous jesting, he comments, is a mode for relaxing a tense mind, and Hamlet is using it to emancipate his mind from terror. Further:

> Add too, Hamlet's wildness is but *half-false*. O that subtle
> trick to pretend the acting *only* when we are very near *be-*
> *ing* what we act. (Italics mine)

Here Coleridge has perceived that Hamlet's subconscious mind is engaging in trickery, pretending to act mad when, in fact, his real state of mind is "nigh akin to" mania. But if so, could we not push this observation even further? If Hamlet is tricking himself into a half-false interpretation of his mania, is he not acting—but acting a self-deception? Coleridge does not realize where his own point could lead, nor can he quite integrate his partial insights with his total understanding of the play.

Let us recall Coleridge's overall view of *Hamlet*. He begins by telling us that Shakespeare's mode of conceiving characters "out of his own intellectual and moral faculties" was that of conceiving some one faculty "in morbid excess" and then placing himself, thus "mutilated," under given circumstances. The faculty which is in excess in Hamlet is his power of meditation on inward thoughts, to the neglect of outward action. Thus in Hamlet's first soliloquy we see in him, says Coleridge, a "craving after the indefinite" such as easily besets a man of genius, but along with it a disproportionate aversion to real action; and in later speeches Hamlet substitutes "the seeing of his chains" for the breaking of them, and by delay becomes the victim of circumstances. Here is a hero whose genius, Coleridge thinks, leads him to "a perfect knowledge of his own character" as being strong in motive, but yet too weak to carry into act "his own most obvious duty." Hamlet has an overbalance of imagination. Hence although called upon to act "by every motive human and divine," this great object of his life is defeated by his doing nothing but making resolutions to act. Shakespeare is thus enforcing a great moral truth: man needs a "healthy balance" in his faculties. And Polonius is another instance of this truth. His advice to Laertes, says Coleridge, is full of wisdom, but its speaker is unable to apply his wisdom to appropriate action in his situation.

On what grounds may we criticize Coleridge's interpretation? Certainly we may question, for one thing, his notion of action. For in fact the play has been one long story of Hamlet's acts—in thought, word, and deed—all as aspects of a revenge action which culminates with the killing of the king. But also we may ask whether indeed this action, either as a whole or in any of its phases, was an "obvious duty" in the eyes of anyone except Hamlet or his father. When this father demands revenge, is he invoking a divine motive—or an all too human one? May not Hamlet be both deceived and engaging in self-deception, when later he taunts Ophelia, or stabs Polonius, or consigns Rosencrantz and Guildenstern to their death? Is Hamlet's flaw really an excessive use of his faculty of meditation? Could it be, rather, a misuse of this faculty, through neglecting to meditate on "intents . . . charitable"? Does his initial desire to be freed of his flesh give evidence, simply, of an excessive craving for "the indefinite" while evading action? Does it not display, rather, an action of resentment against the Everlasting's canon, and a wish to evade divine law? How can Hamlet be said to have a "perfect knowledge of his own character," when he knows not the meaning of his longing for self-slaughter, and when he puzzles so often over his own motivation? Likewise, how "full of wisdom" can we consider the maxims of Polonius, when we see all of them centering on a selfish pragmatism? The basic imperfection in the moral character of Polonius or of Hamlet, we may reply to Coleridge, consists not in their failure to carry their sense of duty into action, but instead in their defective notion of duty. That is, their tragedy arises not because one of their psychic faculties, that of thought, overbalances some other faculty; it arises because they misdirect thought, tying it to self-glorifying ideals. Whereas Coleridge would view the play as Shakespeare's bodying forth of the consequences which develop from modes of mental life mutilated by imbalance, we can bring the play's facts into far better focus if we regard Shakespeare as dramatizing an action of revenge, in which the disordered wills of the main participants mutilate their own human natures by choosing rites of duty that are "maimed" rites. I shall amplify this point in a later chapter.

Perhaps because Coleridge had been fascinated by Spinoza's philosophy, he scants the concept of human free will. He analyzes a dramatic personage usually in terms of a ruling passion, and tends to assume that free will means the free development of a predisposition determined by this person's mode of nature. Thus Richard II, in Coleridge's view, is predisposed to a womanish weakness; he "possesses feelings which, amiable in a female, are misplaced in a man and altogether unfit for a king." The play, then, shows us how this quality of character displays itself, from first to last, in variableness and a yielding to circumstance. Othello, to cite another example, has a predisposition to unsuspiciousness. This characteristic of his nature, Coleridge remarks, "almost sanctifies" him in our eyes. Othello is never jealous, in Coleridge's view; rather, his passion is that of a "moral indignation" that virtue should so fall as he believes it to have done in Desdemona. "He could not have acted otherwise than he did by the lights that he had"; but the lights he had—those of his unsuspicious nature—permitted Iago to force on him a mistaken view of Desdemona. As a third example, we may take Coleridge's comment on Cassius in *Julius Caesar*. Here he names envy as the basic disposition, but goes on to suggest that this passion is something "constitutional" in Cassius by derivation from his parents. Shakespeare is showing that it is something Cassius "cannot avoid, and not something he has acquired." Blame is thus thrown from the will of man, says Coleridge, to some inevitable circumstances. This kind of explanation crops up also in his comment on Edmund in *King Lear*. Edmund's circumstance of birth as a bastard is to blame for his villainy. In Lear, likewise, circumstances of old age and of habits fostered by rank are responsible for this hero's "by no means unnatural" mixture of selfishness with a "loving and kindly" nature. "Old Age, like infancy, is itself a character" in Lear, says Coleridge; its natural imperfections make Lear "the ample play-room of nature's passions." Never does Coleridge analyze the acts of will by which these passions are given play. Nor does he, like more recent critics, see a later educating of Lear through experience. Coleridge has often been praised as a psychologist of character; but the streak of determinism in his psychology has been insufficiently recognized. In my judgment, it largely prevents his understanding the human will's contribution to tragedy.

And along with Coleridge's necessitarianism, I would note also his impressionistic evaluations of romantic love, which are often highly subjective. In *Troilus and Cressida,* for instance, he thinks Shakespeare intended to contrast Cressida's "wanton" passion with "the profound affection represented in Troilus, and alone worthy the name of love." Here Coleridge is accepting Troilus' own self-estimate, while on the other hand taking his estimate of Cressida from her most severe critic, Ulysses. Is such a procedure justifiable? It overlooks, for one thing, the fact that Cressida turned to Diomede only after Troilus took no steps to keep her, did nothing to forestall her being handed over to the Greeks.

Elsewhere, we find Coleridge propounding another questionable contrast—between the passion of Cleopatra, which he reads as simply "the habitual craving of a licentious nature," and the innocent and pure love he sees in Romeo and Juliet, a love which blossoms out of heartfelt "spontaneous emotion." In Romeo and Juliet, he goes on to rhapsodize, passion has the spirit of youth and of spring, mixing virtues and precipitancies. The lovers have a yearning to complete their natures in a perfect union. This union, even in its rashness, is contrived by Providence, Coleridge believes, as a step in the exaltation of human nature to "a higher and nobler state." It draws up the body to the mind, which is "the immortal part" of our nature. It consists, Coleridge explains, in a reverence for the beautiful, by which we rise, as Plato has said, "from affection to love, and from love to the pure intellectual delight, by which we become worthy to conceive that *infinite in ourselves,* without which it is impossible for man to believe in a God" (italics mine). Coleridge even likens this exaltation to "our marriage with the Redeemer of mankind." Is he not here blindly confusing romanticism's religion of love with Christian belief?

How does he evaluate the suicide of the lovers? He evades direct comment, although amid his rhapsodizing we can pick up his passing reference to Romeo's "rash death," the effect of "youth," and to Juliet's ending her life in "a long deep sigh, like the breeze of the evening." When commenting on the tomb scene, he speaks only of Romeo's gentleness softened by love and sorrow, and when commenting on Juliet's taking of the potion in a fit of fright, he remarks: "How Shakespeare provides for the finest decencies!"

What Coleridge is overlooking is the equivocal decency of escape into drug taking, and the "madman" Romeo becomes in his gentleness. Earlier, however, he has explained that "the whole catastrophe of the tragedy" is brought about by the death of Mercutio, a man whose perfect gentlemanliness and amiability make him so endearing that we feel the necessity of Romeo's interfering in the feuding to avenge his death. This scene, says Coleridge, serves to show how Romeo's aversion to activity is "overcome and aroused to the most resolute conduct." Coleridge's admiration for Romeo's resolute conduct, let me suggest, stems from the same perspective by which he judged Hamlet's lack of resoluteness as that hero's only flaw. Coleridge's moral sense, W. K. Wimsatt has remarked, rests ultimately on feelings belonging to "obscure ideas" and a subjective experience of an indefinite sublime.[10] Was this the case with Shakespeare? I shall contend, later in this chapter, that Shakespeare distinguished kinds of love from a quite different perspective.

The emphasis on Shakespeare's characters, for which Coleridge is chiefly remembered in all histories of criticism, carries as its corollary a disinterest in the plots of Shakespeare's plays. Coleridge never bothers to study the shape of the plot in any one drama. He believes that for Shakespeare plot was "a mere canvas and no more." It was of no dramatic interest except on account of the characters. Shakespeare "never took the trouble of inventing stories," says Coleridge, but instead contented himself with borrowing suitable ones, while directing his whole imagination to bringing before us a gallery of richly individualized persons, giving us the pleasure in each case of beholding "just the man himself." That this pronouncement overlooks not only a few plays of Shakespeare for which we have almost no story source, but also the important changes of plot which Shakespeare made in his borrowed stories in reformulating their logic, I think we need not here pause to argue. Let us note, however, the consequences of Coleridge's view. It entails a loss of concern for genre. Nowhere does he distinguish tragedy as a particular form of the human story, one in which the kind of action being imitated by a dramatist is intended to arouse our pity and fear, and which therefore usually takes human downfall as its subject. Instead, he talks broadly of "dramatic interest," which the poet achieves by exhibiting to us forms of experience illustrative of man's moral being.

As regards drama in general, Coleridge redefines unity of action to mean "totality of interest," produced through a homogeneity and proportionateness in all the parts which make up the artist's landscape of character. Action, as thus viewed, seems to exist for the sake of well-painted character portrayal; it seems to have little to do with a unity achieved through the dramatist's charting a beginning, middle, and end for some significant mode of human purpose. Not man's choices and deeds as related to his destiny, but man's powers of heart and mind as exhibited in symbolic form, Coleridge takes to be the focus of drama. He hails Shakespeare as "the pioneer of true philosophy" for having presented the spectator "the great component powers and impulses of human nature" individualized in their "different combinations and subordinations." We may comment that this suggests, rather, the art of the kaleidoscope.

In keeping with his theory of poetry as organic form, Coleridge can declare that Shakespeare "never wrote at random" and that every word or thought in his dramas is a clue to the "consistent whole" of his mind. By saying this he is perhaps intending to rebuff Dr. Johnson's contention that Shakespeare sometimes wrote carelessly. Yet, as a matter of fact, the consistent whole of Shakespeare's mind sometimes proved to be to Coleridge quite as puzzling or distasteful as to Johnson. He is even more indignant than Johnson, for instance, over the plot of *Measure for Measure*. This play's "comic parts" are disgusting, he remarks, and its pardon of Angelo is both unjust and degrading to the character of Mariana, since Angelo's "lust and damnable baseness" should be unforgivable. Here is an instance, we may infer, where Coleridge's customary respect for Shakespeare's "holiness of genius" has been dashed by the specifically Christian holiness which Shakespeare has introduced as the cause of his play's happy ending. And Coleridge has difficulty with aspects of other plays as well. He finds "low" and "disgusting" the whole of the Porter scene in *Macbeth*; and so (since Shakespeare did not write at random) he conjectures that an interpolator wrote this scene. We can be grateful that elsewhere Coleridge defends Shakespeare's use of wordplay and conceits; yet he ends by admitting that sometimes these may be excused only by the taste for "quaintness" in Shakespeare's time. And the only way he can explain Romeo's oxymorons "O brawling love! O loving hate!" is to conjecture that Shakespeare has here neglected for the moment his dramatizing of Romeo's character and is letting us see, instead, his own imagination in the process of "hovering between images." In *Julius Caesar,* Coleridge confesses himself unable to understand what character Shakespeare intended Brutus to have. Does it not lower the intellect of this noble republican, he asks, to have him say he knows "no cause" to spurn Caesar? Here Coleridge's blindness to Shakespeare's grasp of the psychology of self-dividedness in a tragic hero can serve us as a clue to Coleridge's limitations as a philosopher-critic.

The defect in Coleridge's Shakespeare criticism, basically, is that it depends on a medley of romantic theory which simply does not fit adequately the more traditional principles implicit in Shakespeare's art. Though Coleridge may be quite correct in hailing Shakespeare as a "profound philosopher," his own philosophy tends to distort and misconstrue that profundity. Yet he is sometimes judged to be the greatest of Shakespearean critics, largely because he does talk about what we all hope to find in Shakespeare, clues to our own human nature and its moral responses. And perhaps also because, for readers with sensibilities vaguely religious but unanchored to traditional theology, it is comforting to be told that Shakespeare "entered into no analysis of the passions or faiths of men, but assured himself that such passions and faiths were grounded in our human nature." Faiths, that is, are grounded in human psychology, just as are our passions; and no further scrutiny of either is needed. This is Coleridge's belief, traceable in large part, I think, to Spinoza's genial natural religion, in which the intuitive philosopher takes over the role of sage. If Spinoza is believed, that God is simply the total creativity in nature, evolving variegated modes of Himself as His partial manifestations, then why should not a philosophical poet, working in the spirit of nature, imagine out of his own subconsciousness a world of characters each of whose mode of feeling is a partial shadow symbol of the infinite in their author's mind? It is by some such perspective as this that Coleridge can declare Shakespeare to be of no "religion, or party, or profession," but simply a genius of "oceanic" mind. The adequacy of this fluid assumption we shall have occasion to test further as our study proceeds.

The question of Shakespeare's religion lurks persistently in the background of criticism. When now and then it emerges into prominence in twentieth-century commentary, often the occasion is some critic's berating of Shakespeare for his lack of religion. G. B. Shaw and George Santayana, for instance, take this tack. It may be granted that these two critics are of little weight as Shakespeare scholars, yet I should like to devote a few paragraphs to their views because they highlight so obviously the point to which I have been speaking, the importance of a critic's own perspective in his evaluating of Shakespeare's.

Santayana comes to Shakespeare with a belief that poetry and religion are in essence identical. The function of both, he holds, is to provide fables which image a moral ideal to which reality ought to conform.[11] It is from this perspective that he admires Christianity: its system contains "as in a hieroglyph" a deep knowledge of the world; its Scriptures are "fictions" which allegorize man's moral life and its anticipated perfection. Did Shakespeare appreciate this truth? Santayana laments that he did not; that although given the chance to choose the Christian system he chose no system at all. He chose "to leave his heroes in the presence of life and of death with no other philosophy than the profane world can suggest"—a half-heathen sort of positivism, devoid of "victorious imagination." Santayana's essay on "The Absence of Religion in Shakespeare" decries the poet's indifference to the "lesson" of life, life's "relation to its own ideal."

But from what evidence is Santayana reasoning? Only from selected speeches presumed to be representative of Shakespeare's philosophy. Hamlet's speech on the "undiscovered country," for instance, is taken as indicative of an underlying positivism in Shakespeare's thinking. And Macbeth's speech on life as a petty pace to dusty death, signifying nothing, is selected as expressing Shakespeare's outlook in general. What causes Santayana to read drama in this illegitimate way? Why has he overlooked, for instance, Malcolm's rescue of Scotland by the "grace of Grace," or Ophelia's prayer for sick Denmark, that "God be at your table"? We can infer that Santayana's version of Christianity is preventing him from noticing signs of actual and orthodox Christianity, while at the same time his notion that a dramatist should fable his own religion in the "sentiments he attributes to his heroes" is precluding a proper understanding of the art of tragedy.

Shaw is like Santayana in expecting poetry to teach religion. He tells us that the theatre is "really the week-day church," for which artists should provide an "iconography for a live religion." For Shaw, however, the one "live" religion is the constantly evolving religion of Creative Evolution.[12] This he laments not finding in Shakespeare; and on not finding it concludes that Shakespeare had "no conscious religion" and must be regarded therefore as inferior to Bunyan. For whereas Bunyan, says Shaw, was aware of being moved by a power tending toward a goal beyond pessimism, and indeed identified himself with this "purpose of the world," Shakespeare never challenges us to triumph with new concepts. Shakespeare leaves us with the stultifying pessimism of Ecclesiastes; he gives us as the moral of his plays merely Macbeth's despairing cry, "Out, out, brief candle," or the cry in *Lear* that we are to the gods as flies to wanton boys. Only in Hamlet did he come close to the truth of Creative Evolution. For Hamlet is a man, Shaw surmises, who feels uncomfortable in Shakespeare's mere reach-me-down morality; a man who struggles against the misfit of duties dictated by conventional revenge and shows signs of evolving out of a Mosaic morality into a Christian perception of the futility of punishment. But because Shakespeare had not "plumbed his play to the bottom," Hamlet's perception slips away when he sends Rosencrantz and Guildenstern to their death. All told, Shakespeare failed to advance beyond "moral bewilderment" and a vulgar contentment with potboilers. His characters weakly collapse into false ideas or dreary platitudes.

The tone of Shaw's judgments is of course dictated by his flair for polemic and his desire to shock by iconoclastic pronouncements. Yet basically he is a romantic religionist like Santayana. We will have noted how he misunderstands tragedy by expecting its tragic heroes to develop an "enlightened" moral ideal as a message to the audience. His own philosophy, however, is more attuned to positivism than is Santayana's. The mission of the artist, he tells us in a postscript to *Back to Methuselah,* is to take life "a step forward on its way to positive science from its present metaphysical stage." The "new" morality of Ibsen, and of course of Shaw himself, seems to him self-evidently true. It is from this stance that he passes judgment on Shakespeare. We may note, however, that many of his comments seem to echo eighteenth-century prejudices. *Othello,* he declares, has "a pure farce plot," supported (as Rymer had complained) on the artificially manufactured trick of a handkerchief. Its characters are "monsters," and Othello's transports are an orgy of "magnificent but senseless music." *Romeo and Juliet* has nothing to recommend it but its music of metrical declamation; and it is "interlarded by the miserable rhetoric and silly logical conceits which were the foibles of the Elizabethans." Throughout Shaw's criticism, only the music of Shakespeare's language, and the "magic" of its stage-effects remain objects of admiration. He can not take seriously Shakespeare's plots in drama, and he views the characters as mere vehicles for "thought," thought of a kind he finds largely unpalatable.

Few readers nowadays are likely to accept Shaw's or Santayana's way of reading Shakespearean tragedy—although we must admit that there still persists, even in some academic circles, the practice of plucking out the cry of despairing Gloucester as if it were Shakespeare's own, the very eye by which to read the play's message or motto.[13] Such misreading is a carryover, in part, of the Victorian theory of Edward Dowden that Shakespeare personally was "in the depths" of a philosophical despair during a tragic period in life; and in part it reflects the perspective of Swinburne, who from his standpoint in pagan humanism could find only "darkness" in *King Lear*. But A. C. Bradley is notable for having answered Swinburne by focusing on the total action which develops in *Lear* and finding there a drama of "purgation." Although Bradley held that in the years 1601 to 1608 Shakespeare was "burdened in spirit" by the dark and terrible look of the world, he saw this as turning Shakespeare to a form of drama through which he could study in history the process by which conflict leads to a final reconciliation. Bradley is usually regarded as having brought to a climax the long romantic tradition of character analysis, yet his renowned *Shakespearean Tragedy* of 1904 is almost equally important for its attempt to appreciate plot. What impresses Bradley in *Lear* is the "law and beauty" in the play's whole action. And in the other tragedies he examines he shows a concern not alone for character, but also for Shakespeare's implied theory of tragedy. Let us now examine that theory in some detail.

2 Bradley

From what philosophical perspective does Bradley interpret the tragedies? He claims, in his initial and very important chapter on "The Substance of Shakespearean Tragedy," that he is reasoning solely by induction from "the facts" in the dramas and gathering their underlying idea merely by his "native strength and justice of perception." But is this truly the case? Not if we take seriously his own earlier essay of 1901 on "Hegel's Theory of Tragedy." For there, after reviewing Hegel's theory and offering only minor amendments of his own, he calls his amendments "trifling" in comparison with "the theory which they attempt to strengthen and to which they owe their existence."[14] And in fact his own steeping in Hegel was of long duration. While a Fellow at Baliol, a close friend of his had been Professor T. H. Green, a notable moralist of Kantian and Hegelian stamp, who at his untimely death in 1882 left Bradley the editing of his *Prolegomena to Ethics* (1883), which Bradley tidied up and prefaced with a twenty-four page "digest" of his own. Nor did Bradley's addiction to Hegelianism ever wane. Anyone who reads his Gifford Lectures of 1907 on *Ideals of Religion* (not published until 1940) will find in them a creed, the center of which is man's "human ideal" in place of traditional dogmas. One of its chapters, for instance, is entitled "Man as Finite Infinite"; and elsewhere man is described as "neither limited being nor unlimited, but the passage of limited being into unlimited" in search of his own perfection. Accordingly, evil is defined simply as the imperfection of finitude, from which man is freed when he "refuses to acknowledge as himself anything but the self which is united to the infinite, and is *a function of its will*" (italics mine). Religion, thus understood, is "escape from evil" through man's becoming united by worship to "the principle of the whole" within himself, the developing human-divine which is God. Bradley is very much a religious thinker. His Hegelianism, however, is but a latter-day form of the German idealism which had influenced Coleridge. We need to bear this in mind as the perspective by which, in fact, Bradley is approaching Shakespeare and reading the plays.

What is the substance of Shakespearean tragedy as Bradley sees it? Tragedy, he tells us, is a "convulsive reaction" within the supreme power that governs the tragic world. It is a story of calamity brought about by spiritual conflict involving waste—yet sometimes intimating to us at the end that the "heavenly spirits" whom we see perishing are vanishing "not into nothingness but into freedom." The conflict is that of "forces" colliding within persons and generating strife between persons. These forces consist of "whatever can animate, shake, possess, and drive a man's soul"—doubts, scruples, ideas—whether good or evil. Bradley's "forces," we may note, are remarkably like Coleridge's "powers" of the psychic life. And Bradley sees them as parts of "a moral order and its necessity," which seems to him to determine, far more than do the individuals caught up in it, "their native disposition and circumstances and, through these, their action." This moral order "poisons itself" in producing evil. But it also reacts, from the necessity of its nature, against attacks made on it by the persons whom evil inhabits. Those persons are both within the moral order and produced by it. It "produces Iago as well as Desdemona, Iago's cruelty as well as Iago's courage." Hamlet, or Antony, or Macbeth are the "parts, expressions, products" of this order; "in their defect or evil *it* is untrue to its soul of goodness and falls into conflict and collision with itself." In "making them suffer and waste" themselves, this moral order suffers and wastes itself. But when, in order to "save its life and regain peace from this intestinal struggle," the moral order casts them out, it loses "a part of its own substance." Bradley rounds off his chapter with the following epitome of his theory:

> The whole or order against which the individual part shows itself powerless seems to be animated by a passion for perfection: we cannot otherwise explain its behaviour towards evil. Yet it appears to engender this evil within itself, and in its effort to overcome and expel it it is agonised with pain, and driven to mutilate its own substance and to lose not only evil but priceless good. That this idea, though very different from the idea of a blank fate, is no solution of the riddle of life is obvious; but why should we expect it to be such a solution? Shakespeare was not attempting to justify the ways of God to men, or to show the universe as a Divine Comedy. He was writing tragedy, and tragedy would not be tragedy if it were not a painful mystery. Nor can he be said even to point distinctly, like some writers of tragedy, in any direction where a solution might lie.[15]

To this we might reply, for one thing, that Bradley seems to misunderstand the *Divine Comedy*. What Dante there attempted was a review of the representative "ways" of the human will and the reward of each within a Christian eschatology. Moreover, there is painful mystery aplenty for each of the souls dwelling in *Inferno* —precisely because the true moral order has provided this as a punishment for those who have disregarded Divine light, thus crippling their own intellect. If Bradley had but looked for this truth, he might have found indications of it in the careers of Hamlet or Othello or Macbeth. But instead Bradley has been betrayed by his Hegelianism into supposing that the agony of Shakespeare's tragic heroes manifests an agony in the moral order of the universe. If this animated order, he reasons, can move toward self-perfection only by first engendering evil in itself to provide an intestinal conflict; and if it can regain its own peace only by expelling something of its own "substance" of priceless good; and if Shakespeare's heroes are but "parts" of this universal history, driven by the same "necessity" which drives the whole—then it follows that those heroes are developing toward self-perfection through their very self-conflicts, since these are but preface to a final mutilating sacrifice by which the moral order (and in some paradoxical way, many an expelled hero too) is "saved," self-translated by a wasting purgation.

This vision of Bradley's, we may comment, is no mere philosophy of tragedy; it is a tragic philosophy. What does he mean by saying that Shakespeare cannot be said to point "in any direction where a solution might lie"? Actually, Bradley himself is doing some pointing! But while pointing he is wrapping his wand with an aura of mystery, and blurring its edges, perhaps fearing to see too distinctly, or to let his readers quite perceive, the implications of his own theory. It is significant, I think, that Bradley never wrote on Shakespeare's comedies. He seems to have considered them frivolous, no serious reading of the mystery of life. He remarks, in wayside comment, that *The Winter's Tale* can end happily because its characters "fail to reach tragic dimensions"; and he finds a "scandalous" ending in *Measure for Measure* when the Duke proposes marriage.[16] His idea of tragedy, however, suffers from its dependence on Hegel's philosophy of history, which we may recall Jacques Maritain has criticized as "but the gnosticism of history" and "spurious" as philosophy.[17] Hegel confuses, Maritain explains, "necessary laws" with "necessitating laws" and disregards or ignores in practice the free will of man. Or, as George Thomas has recently commented, Hegel's monistic idealism "deprives men of real freedom by treating their passions and actions as necessary effects of the divine will," subordinating thus the interests and happiness of men to the ruthless purposes of Absolute Spirit.[18] Such is the philosophy which, all too often, Bradley has read into Shakespeare's tragedies.

Although Bradley believes that Shakespeare is showing man "as in some degree, however slight, the cause of his own undoing," and therefore a responsible agent, his whole perspective scants the nature of the human will and of choice. His language repeatedly implies that persons are the product of forces generated in them, rather than souls or selves forming their own purposes in response to opportunities. Aristotle, let us recall, had said (*Poetics* VI. 13) that persons in drama "do not act so as to represent character; but through their actions they take on character." But this seems not to be Bradley's view. He describes action as "deeds expressive of character," and says that action issues *from* character. What then, *is* character, and how is it formed? Bradley regards it as a given bundle of "forces"—thoughts, desires, passions, habits of mind, or genius. These are said to issue in outward deeds. Overlooked here is the fact that, in traditional psychology, thoughts and desires are themselves actions, which take their character from being moved or restrained by the human will. When Bradley says that "action is the translation of thought into reality," he is omitting to say that action is first of all the preferring of a certain kind of thought. In a tragedy, in fact, is it not by acts of preferring evil thoughts, or by an ignoring of good ones, that a hero reaches the decisions which result in his outward deeds—deeds which while existentially real may be essentially hollow? This perspective seems to elude Bradley.

In his initial chapter, Bradley generalizes that tragic heroes are marked by "a predisposition in some particular direction" and by "a total incapacity, in certain circumstances, of resisting the force which draws in this direction." The "tragic trait," he goes on to explain, consists of "a fatal tendency to identify the whole being with one interest, object, passion, or habit of mind." If I understand these statements, they are saying that man is tragic when any particular aspect of his life enslaves his whole being. The explanation sounds rather like Coleridge's notion of an unbalancing of the self through the predominance of some one faculty. Bradley calls this tendency that of "infatuated men." But in the same breath he mystifies the reader by calling it a "gift" which carries "greatness" with it, and which when joined to "genius" or "immense force," makes us realize with *admiration* "the full power and reach of the soul." And three pages later, he adds that the "greatness of soul" exhibited by the tragic hero is "the highest existence in our view" and seems to call for "our worship." Thus by a strange (and certainly strained) logic, Bradley has here made an infatuated one-sidedness of disposition the very basis for the soul's achieving *full* reach and *highest* existence—a greatness warranting both admiration and worship!

Miss Lily B. Campbell is justified, I think, in accusing Bradley of loose terminology and bewildering concepts. His moral universe, she complains, is "without morals and without moral responsibility and without moral arbiter"; and as for his famed "psychology" of character, it is "untrue to psychological thinking in any period."[19] She might more accurately have said that it is a psychology which is not much more than a variation of Coleridge's, and hence true to a romanticism which has cast its shadow over Shakespeare for a century and a half—a fact which largely accounts for the many misunderstandings of Shakespearean tragedy which even today haunt us, a few of them still prevailing, I think, in Miss Campbell's own interpretations. It should be conceded, however, that Bradley's sketching of traits in various Shakespearean characters is often helpful when he is not tied strictly to his theory, as for example in his reading of Banquo, or Emilia, or Gloucester. And he traces rather well, although impressionistically, Lear's emerging insight.

But there can be no doubt that Bradley is judging out of an essentially romantic perspective when he asserts, for instance, that Antony "touches the infinite" in the passion that exalts and ruins him. Or, again, when he declares that at the end of *Coriolanus* we feel "exultation in the power of goodness," because the hero has "saved his soul," to which loss of life is as nothing. Or when he finds, even in heart-withered Macbeth, something "sublime" in his defiance of hell and heaven. Or when he writes of Othello, that at the end our "pity itself vanishes, and love and admiration alone remain," leaving us for the moment exulting in the power of "love and man's unconquerable mind."[20] This can scarcely be what Aristotle meant by a catharsis of pity and fear. For does catharsis arise from admiration dispelling pity, or from love replacing fear? And if we may pursue a bit further Bradley's view of Othello: Can we hold that "there is not a syllable to be said against" this hero before the middle of the play, when suddenly in his outburst of jealousy we realize that Iago's "poison" has been at work? Just how "good" is Othello's love *before* Iago starts working on it with his deceptiveness? Bradley has failed to notice Othello's initial self-righteousness and jealousy for reputation, which makes this hero liable to being tempted by Iago; and he overlooks also the self-justification which motivates Othello's suicide at the end.

Bradley's reading of *Hamlet* warrants our attention as a kind of paradigm of his sense of tragedy. He begins with inferences as to what Hamlet was like "just before his father's death": a nature not one-sidedly intellectual but "healthily active." But then came "the ghastly disclosure of his mother's true nature," a moral shock which poisoned Hamlet's mind. It "forced" him into melancholy, a pathological condition. Yet even in this morbid state, and in conflict with it, there persisted what Bradley considers "healthy" feelings—Hamlet's "love of his father, loathing of his uncle, desire of revenge." Bradley regards the Ghost as a representative of "that hidden ultimate power" of the universe, a majestic messenger of divine justice, who gives Hamlet a commandment which, beyond doubt, he *ought* to have obeyed.[21] Hamlet's later fear that the Ghost might be a devil is interpreted as an "unconscious fiction" on Hamlet's part, an excuse for delay. Why does Hamlet delay what Bradley terms his "sacred duty"? Because Hamlet's "healthy motives" are retarded by his melancholy. But at last Fate descends, forcing on Hamlet the killing of Claudius—and bringing with it his own mortal wound. And then, as Hamlet lies dying, "all the nobility and sweetness of his nature" are revealed in a wonderful beauty. His world-wearied flesh reaches its haven, as flights of angels sing him to his rest; and we bow our heads murmuring, "This was the noblest spirit of them all." For now, the "very divinity" of Hamlet's thought, which has rendered him powerless in the world's "petty sphere of action," suggests to us a "sense of the soul's infinity" along with our sense of the doom which is its offspring. Though this cannot be called religious drama in a specific sense, says Bradley, it is a reminder that the apparent failure of Hamlet's life is not the ultimate truth concerning him.

Let us note that this interpretation has foreclosed, on merely arbitrary and impressionistic grounds, the whole question of whether Hamlet's love of his father and desire for revenge were, in fact, healthy feelings. Do we not need to question that assumption, considering the antic madness into which the revenge-motive propels Hamlet? Is it really healthy to idolize one's father as Hamlet does, or to hate Claudius in the way he does? But, further, we will have noted the religious tone in Bradley's total reading. And is this not in contradiction to his own contention, elsewhere, that Shakespeare "practically confined his view to the world of non-theological observation and thought," and that he painted this secular world "without the wish to enforce an opinion of his own, and, in essentials, without regard to anyone's hopes, fears, or beliefs"?[22] Granted that Shakespeare did not *enforce* any belief of his own, may we nevertheless ask: Did he really *intimate* the belief Bradley finds?

It is one of the curious facts of latter-day Shakespeare scholarship that critics who have quoted Bradley's above statement, in order to argue (as Roland Frye, for instance, does) that Shakespeare's works "make no encompassing appeal to theological categories,"[23] seem unaware of the crypto-theologizing which underlies Bradley's view, a theologizing of gentlemanly but insinuating kind. This theologizing is masked, of course, behind a fashionable reserve. Disarmingly, Bradley assures his readers that Shakespeare's personal creed, whatever it was, was of "no material influence" on his presentation of life. Yet from the plays Bradley repeatedly hazards inferences as to Shakespeare's faith, quite specifically so in his later essay on "Shakespeare the Man." There he tells us that Shakespeare's religious position in middle life seems to be "much like Hamlet's." And he goes on to characterize Shakespeare as having a lively sense of "conscience" connected with "the power that rules the world and is not escapable by man." Shakespeare never doubted, says Bradley, that "to be good is to be at peace with that unescapable power"; and to this "natural piety" Shakespeare may have added, as he grew older, some approximation to conventional Christian ideas.[24] It is plain, I think, that Bradley has attributed to the dramatist just such belief as Bradley's own permitted him to educe. *That* belief, we are to infer, *did* influence Shakespeare's painting of life.

It was Bradley's good fortune to write at a time when his intellectual public was attuned to Hegelianism—so much so that many Christian theologians were favoring it. But this vogue, so central to the liberal humanism of a naturalistic idealism, has now waned. And with its waning we are perhaps free, at last, to see whether some other ground of vision than the various religio-philosophic ones ascribed to Shakespeare by romantic critics may not provide us a better perspective on his dramas.

We need to be cautious, however, of a complaint often nowadays heard, that Bradley's fault was to mistake characters in drama for persons in real life. That particular charge is unfair or misleading.

For even when Bradley speculated about events before the opening of the action in *Hamlet,* or about possible conversations between the Macbeths antecedent to the play, his concern was to account for lines in the text, so as to provide a consistent understanding of the dramatic personages. From earlier criticism he inherited the biographical question of whether Macbeth already had children, but himself wisely remarked that it "does not concern the play." When reading Lady Macbeth's reference to having "given suck," he perhaps unwisely pursued the inference that she may have had a child, now either alive or dead. But in this instance his real fault was that of neglecting the symbolic import of the speech. Elsewhere, too, Bradley is not sufficiently aware of the symbolism with which Shakespeare has enriched his imitations of life. But surely those critics who would wholly disassociate art from the human life it imitates are going too far in a contrary direction.[25] I mean that we should expect great drama to present not simply man's gestural behavior but, inside that, his modes of psychic action, selectively embodied. The dramatized "self" which is taking on qualities of character needs to be believable. At the same time, the import of this person's action can be highlighted by a symbolic language, carrying what our New Critics call themes. The basic flaw in Bradley's analysis of character, it seems to me, was not that he confused fictional persons with live ones, but rather that he somewhat obscured the full order of values in relation to which the persons in Shakespearean drama act. And, further, that his metaphysic, by hypostasizing "forces," tended to depersonalize persons: so that we find him writing of Macbeth, for instance, not that this man showed great energy in doing evil, but that "Evil . . . shows in *Macbeth* a prodigious energy."

In treating action, Bradley blurred both its rootage in human choice and its thematic aspects. He skimmed impressionistically over the imagery of drama—as, for instance, when he reviews it in *Macbeth* and then concludes: "It is as if the poet saw the whole story through an ensanguined mist, and as if it stained the very blackness of the night." But was the poet, in fact, seeing his story as if through a bloody mist? Do we not, rather, get Shakespeare's perspective on the "blood" in this story through a wayside comment by Ross (in II. iv) : "Thou seest the heavens, as troubled with man's act, / Threaten his bloody stage"? Quite specifically, in this speaker's verdict, the blood is of man's making and is offensive to heaven. What the now-darkened face of earth needs is "living light" to kiss it. Bradley ignored Ross's speech. In stressing the play's atmosphere of doom, he missed seeing how the play's imagery was functioning to reveal a judgment, like that of the biblical doomsday, on the "sacrilegious" act of Macbeth. Clearly, Shakespeare sees this act as importing an unnatural order, shaming to the fair face of nature which heaven should sanctify. To analogize Macbeth's contending against "obedience," Shakespeare tells us of Duncan's horses, which have broken from their stalls. (A literary source for this portent, let me suggest, may be Augustine's *City of God* III. 23, which reports an occasion when Rome's horses broke from their stalls, thus portending "a sea of Roman blood.")

Bradley was aware of "the fascination of the supernatural" in *Macbeth,* but he associated this with merely fatal forces—with an "unearthly" light playing about the head of "the doomed man." Consequently, he slurred over the roles of Malcolm and of pious Edward, whom the play shows to be acting in the name of a nature sanctified by the light of grace. It is characteristic of Bradley's discussion that nowhere in his two chapters on *Macbeth* does he use the word "unnatural" in reference to Macbeth or his Lady (despite Shakespeare's emphasis on this in III. iv. 10 and V. i. 79) , but manages instead, frequently, to call these two persons "sublime." And, to our astonishment, he speaks of Macbeth as nearer to the "heart" of the moral order, and more valuable to it, than Malcolm.[26]

From the New Critics has come help in remedying this defect. L. C. Knights's essay of 1933, entitled provocatively "How Many Children Had Lady Macbeth?," is an attack chiefly on Bradley's philosophy of nature, which obscures, Knights argues, "those passages in the play in which the positive good is presented by means of religious symbols," by various images of grace and of the holy supernatural. Has not Shakespeare suggested, through the opening report on Macbeth's valor, a violence that is unnatural in quality? And, for contrast, has he not used imagery of husbandry in Duncan's speech, and images of love and procreation to surround Duncan's castle? Further, do not Malcolm's speeches of pretended self-accusation (in IV. i) serve to summarize the hellishness of Macbeth in contrast to the virtues of "justice, verity, temperance, stableness," which are Malcolm's true norm and the play's as well? Shakespeare's point, says Knights, is that Macbeth's tragedy lies in his defiance of natural values which have supernatural sanctions.[27]

Accepting this insight, later critics have enlarged on the further meaning it opens up in the play. Shakespeare, they explain, is showing how Macbeth by his action inverts fundamental values of fertility, fealty, and grace; how he plunges into a world of surmise where nothing is but what is not; dwarfs his own manliness and thwarts his deepest needs; binds himself to a concept of time as mere duration; exhausts his energies in "successes" he cannot conclude; hardens his heart progressively against repentance; and finally brings on himself a Judgment Day, like the one by trumpet-tongued angels which he had earlier imagined but had overleaped through recourse to an "if" world of hypothetical reality.[28] Very likely, there is analogy to the biblical Herod in Macbeth's fear of the heavenly cherubin, and in his later slaughter of various innocents; and his eventual defeat by Malcolm, who returns with tree branches, suggests by its imagery the biblical theme of a "righteous branch" as deliverer, a theme which in Old Testament prophecy figured the promised end of exile. In many respects *Macbeth* is a Christmas play. Francis Fergusson recently has brilliantly charted its overall action in terms of two major movements: Macbeth's *downward* outrunning of "the pauser, reason," through his leaps of equivocation, and Malcolm's counteractive *upward* outrunning of hesitant reason, through his faith in heavenly powers.[29] The drama, as thus read, depends on traditional Christian principles of understanding and on medieval principles of analogical structure.

3 The historical critics and their successors

Can a sensibility attuned to traditional Christian modes be of help, equally, in rectifying misjudgments of Shakespeare on the part of the so-called historical critics? It has been typical of these rivals of Bradley to turn to Elizabethan frames of reference—to the theatre conventions and character types of the age, or to its popular books on psychology and morals—in search of an approach to Shakespeare more scientific than Bradleyan impressionism. But the results have been less than satisfying. Usually we are aware of a gap of some kind between the frame adduced and the Shakespearean drama it is supposed to fit. The offered background has not illuminated the work of art as much as was promised.

Frequently, in fact, one historical scholar's appraisal has clashed with another's. *Othello,* for example, has been explained by E. E. Stoll in terms of conventional theatre devices and a magic of poetry covering over the "specious and unreal psychology" of its characters; but Lily B. Campbell sees in this same play a tragedy of jealousy in accord with an Elizabethan theory of the passions and of the ruin which punishes enslavement to passion; and Bernard Spivack proposes yet a third historical reading: that Shakespeare's dramaturgic need for a "pattern of opposites" gave him opportunity to exalt in Othello and Desdemona the richest possibilities of Renaissance *l'amour courtois* (Shakespeare's "own highest sentiment") as over against the Renaissance atheism of Iago.[30] Does any of these readings quite satisfy? Miss Campbell's may be near the truth, but is questionable when she claims a perfect love in the early Othello before his victimization by Iago. Her approach would attribute to Shakespeare a Tudor moralism; Spivack would attribute a faith in courtly love; and Stoll (as he says elsewhere[31]) can find "no theology or theodicy, no philosophy" at all in any of Shakespeare's dramas. Do such judgments arise from an adequate philosophical base?

Stoll can be charged with judging by a naive norm of psychology of his own, largely of Ibsen's kind. And, further, if we turn to his essay on *Romeo and Juliet,* we can detect his own crypto-religion in his raptures over romantic love and its "triumphal hymn" of *amor vincit omnia.* This play is a "romantic tragedy of fate" in his view, and it implies no fault in the lovers, although there is some occasional "bad" writing by Shakespeare, as for instance in Juliet's outburst over Tybalt's death.[32] But one result of such intuitive and subjective historicizing is Stoll's contention that, since passion is "an affair of the imagination, not of the intellect," Shakespeare's plays in this respect are "scarcely dramas" but rather lyric and poetical dreams.[33] Drama's structure, which reflects the poet's intellectual base, is thereby virtually eliminated from consideration. As a critic, Stoll is a romanticist in sentiment, yet in the rationalist tradition of Shaw when accounting for Shakespeare's appeal solely in terms of stagecraft and musical effects. *Othello,* in his view, is absurd as an image of life, yet successful in enthralling a theatre audience through reviving the convention of the "calumniator credited." To this explanation, Heilman has well replied: ". . . the critic's responsibility is to try to find out with what trans-conventional life the poet has inspired the actions."[34]

Heilman's book on *Othello* is a capstone to various New Critical studies—notably by Leavis, Kirschbaum, and Bethell—in which a psychology of self-deception in the hero is found to be basic to the play's action and meaning. Taking for granted that the play is "emphatically Christian," Heilman devotes his attention to versions of love which give thematic form to the action—versions which range from Iago's *invidia* (hate as love) and Othello's "possessive love" to the contrast provided by Desdemona's *"agape* in a world distraught by *eros."* The Christian myth, Heilman acknowledges, is not explicitly dramatized but present in the background as generic and archetypal, an "auxiliary mode of conception forced upon us by the vast range" of the individual dramatic person. Thus, for instance, Iago with his "shadowy miming of conscience," and his improvising of spurious justifications in an effort to "look normal," is a mode of Everyman's envy, and in that sense one of us in some measure; while at a symbolic or metaphysical level he has something of the character of Satan. Othello, likewise, is first of all an individual person, but at a symbolic level is affiliated with Judas. This approach, it seems to me, effectively removes the confusions in the views of both Stoll and Spivack.

Spivack's book, devoted mainly to a study of Iago, starts from Stoll's premise that the Elizabethan soliloquy is "the truth itself," and from L. L. Schucking's premise that "substantially correct and sufficient" reasons for a character's behavior are intended by the dramatist when stated in soliloquy. We ought therefore, he argues, to be able to read Iago's behavior in terms of the motives of sexual jealousy and desire for office which he gives us through soliloquy. But why is it then that Iago's actual behavior in the play does not seem to us that of a jealous husband or of a man ambitious for office? Is it not, Spivack asks, that Iago's behavior is still largely being dictated by an archaic allegorical motive lacking in psychological explanation, the Vice's delight in showmanship? Drama was undergoing, Spivack reasons, an evolutionary transition from one convention to another, and the inevitable result was a hybrid drama that did not cohere, a mixture of conventions in which naturalistic motives were blurred by a non-naturalistic motive taken over from allegory. But because for the Elizabethan audience the popularity of an archaic "formula" counted for more than the "human validity" of which it deprived drama, Shakespeare and his fellows utilized bravura elements of old spectacle, at a time when the theatre was in pilgrimage from metaphorical to literal, from *Everyman* to Ibsen. Note that Spivack's explanation is in terms of the theatre's pilgrimage, not man's. His conclusion is that Iago is a conflation of two theatre types, the medieval Vice and the Renaissance atheist, a "double image" to which Shakespeare assigns the propagandistic voice of *homo emancipatus a Deo*.

But does not this way of combining the background elements leave us with an Iago whose personage is mere visage and voice? It supposes no inner coherence in Iago's psychology, attributing his character instead to theatrical make-up. There is a half-truth here, I think: the character of jealous husband and aggrieved subordinate is indeed made-up, as is also the character of show-off manipulator and cynical philosopher. But these character-images are being made up by Iago himself, by that human self in him which underlies conventional character and takes on character to suit its sense of need —in this case a felt need for conventions of motive to cover up an irrational envy. Envy is the basic and real motive, and we see it peeping through in his wayside confession that the "daily beauty" in Cassio's life makes his own ugly by comparison. The other motives Iago voices are but the would-be motives he is trying to convince himself of. At bottom, he is a deceiver self-deceived; and he is not really "emancipated man," but only *homo fugens,* a soul seeking escape from truth and from his own humanity. When thus viewed, Iago is Shakespeare's coherent dramatization of the inconsistencies in which envy involves a man. One could say that the story of Iago, at its literal level, is simply that of a clever revenger. But once one begins probing what revenge means, one discovers additional dimensions implicit within the literal: a likeness to the vice Envy (Iago's tropological dimension), a likeness to boastful Satan (an allegorical dimension), and a likeness to Reprobate flight (the anagogical dimension). Thus Iago is a life-like person, multivalently symbolic.

If we next examine Miss Campbell's historical approach, taking for example not her chapter on *Othello* but the one on *Hamlet,* we can detect shortcomings of another kind. Here either the Tudor psychology and philosophy which are invoked, or the application of this lore to the play, leave us with several unanswered questions. Why should we suppose, for instance, that Hamlet's theory of tragedy is Shakespeare's own basic theory? Granted that Hamlet thinks of tragedy as an "o'ergrowth of some complexion" breaking down "the pales and forts of reason," can we infer from this that Shakespeare designed his play to demonstrate Hamlet's theory? Is he showing simply how this hero's complexion of melancholy, an excess of grief, "sins in failing to follow reason"? Miss Campbell's phrase here is itself puzzling. Can Hamlet's grief "sin," unless by some fault in Hamlet's own reasoning which is causing the grief to be excessive in the first place? Is reason a mere "fort"? Is it not, rather, a governing power which can itself sin by acting defectively? And if this latter be Hamlet's actual situation, then must we not say that it is Hamlet himself who sins by *misdirecting* his grief? But Miss Campbell does not see the matter in this way. When discussing, later, Hamlet's delay in revenging, she remarks that through grief Hamlet "has failed to kill the King." To this we might reply: Has not a wilful reasoning decreed the wrong thing? Can a man whose grief is "excessive" arrive at a truly reasonable judgment as to his duty toward the King? Miss Campbell herself seems half-aware of a problem; for although in this chapter she describes Hamlet's duty as one of a "public vengeance" delegated by God, her later essays (in Appendices A and B) waver on this point in a confusing manner. Perhaps one handicap stems from the kind of moral psychology she is bringing to the play. It sounds merely Stoic or Platonic, if we read carefully her formulation of it:

> Shakespearean tragedy made concrete Elizabethan moral teaching, and that teaching was centered about the conflict of passion and reason in man's soul. When passion rather than reason controls the will, man errs or sins.[35]

Did Shakespeare understand sin in quite these terms?

As my questions have been indicating, there is a more complex tradition of moral psychology which can do fuller justice to Hamlet's experience than his own theory, or than the theory Miss Campbell has put together out of Plutarch, the Renaissance Stoics, and occasional Tudor treatises. It can be found in Augustine, Aquinas, and medieval Christian philosophy in general. According to Augustine, human passions are not sinful except as "ill-directed" by a wrong will; their moral goodness depends on their being "rightly placed." The will "could not become evil, were it unwilling to become so"; and its defections are not to things in themselves evil, but to an inordinate fondness for mutable goods. Moreover, "the reason must be subject to God if it is to govern as it ought the passions."[36]

And Aquinas further clarifies this matter by explaining that the reason is a power which can sin, that is, act defectively, either by neglecting to know what it is able and ought to know or by failing to direct the other powers of the soul. Reason is the counsellor of the will and the principle of its act. All sins involve a departure from "right reason"; but since man's reason is right insofar as it is ruled by the Divine will, the departure itself is "an act of reason" —not a simple "deprivation of reason," as Cicero and the Stoics held.[37]

This explanation of the role of the human reason in an act of sin continues to be stressed in at least some of the treatises of Shakespeare's own day. Consider, for instance, *The Sinners Guyde* (1598), a work whose interesting lineage is described on its title page as follows: "Compiled in the Spanish / Tongue, by the Learned / and reverend Divine, F. Lewes of / Granada. / Since translated into Latine, Italian, and French. / And nowe perused, and digested into English, by / Francis Meres, Maister of Artes, and student in Divinitie." In Granada's treatise, as digested by Meres, let us focus on the following passage:

> . . . the first root of all sinnes is the errour of the under-standing, which is the counsailor of the will. For . . . our understanding beeing corrupted, the will also is corrupted which is governed and guided of it; therefore they [the tempters] endeavour to colour evill with good, and to sell vice under the show and semblance of vertue, and so to hide the temptation, that it seemeth not temptation, but reason. For if they assault any man by ambition, by covet-ousnesse, by wrath, or desire of revenge, they perswade him, that it is altogether agreeable unto reason to desire this, that this or that affection desireth; and that it is against reason not to lust after that, that it lusteth after. After this manner they pretend reason, that they may so much the more easily deceive them, who are ruled by reason. Where-fore, it is very necessary that we should have sharpe-sighted eyes, that we may see the hooke lurking within the baite, least wee be deceaved with the shadowe and likelihood of goodnes. (pp. 374–375)

As this passage makes clear, man's understanding is corrupted and errs if it countenances the deceptive reasoning with which some tempting object, such as revenge, is presented as "good." This psychology of moral evil is pertinent surely to Hamlet, as well as to other revenge heroes such as Othello or Brutus. And as a psychology of ambition it fits also Macbeth, whose fall into temptation has been shown by W. C. Curry to be patterned in accord with the analysis of sin which Aquinas had formulated.[38]

I have quoted from Meres in order to make the point, also, that a medieval strain of thought characterizes Shakespeare's earliest of literary critics. Francis Meres was an Anglican clergyman whose chief enthusiasms seem to have been Chaucer, Shakespeare, Granada, and the Church Fathers. *The Sinners Guyde* contains much quoting from Augustine, Gregory the Great, and Bernard. Frequently it includes allegorical interpretations—for instance, the following on Lazarus:

> . . . how great a miracle it is that God should raise one four
> dayes dead and stincking: that is, to convert one buried
> in the custome of sinning. The first of these four dayes, as
> saith Augustine, is the delight of the pleasure in the heart:
> the second is the consent: the third is the deed: the fourth
> custome: and he that is come to this fourth day, as Laza-
> rus, is not raysed up, unless it be with the loud voyce and
> teares of our Saviour. (p. 273)

Furthermore, if we turn to Meres' *Palladis Tamia* (1598—the same year as his *Sinners Guyde*), we find that this compendium of jewelled similes and literary comparisons draws its citations almost as often from the Church Fathers as from the popular Plutarch, Seneca, and Pliny. Fathers such as Chrysostom, Basil, Nazianzen, Ambrose, and others furnish not only the bulk of citations under the various theological topics of the volume but also many under topics such as "Parents," "Children," "Princes," and so forth. Meres never cites—so far as I can find in a rather careful reading—from any Protestant theologian.

This is worth noting, I think, in view of Roland Frye's recent claim that patristic and scholastic writers were "less than immediately relevant" to the culture of Shakespeare's day, and that "medieval responses" to Shakespeare's plays "would scarcely have occurred to Elizabethans."[39] Frye has overlooked evidence from Meres. Patristic writers, plainly, were very immediately relevant for this Elizabethan, whose whole *Palladis Tamia* is organized by a medieval interest in analogies and in literary *figura*. Moreover, patristic and scholastic works were of indispensable importance to another notable contemporary of Shakespeare, Thomas Lodge, several of whose popular works we know to have been largely cribbed from these sources.[40] And the indebtedness of John Donne to patristic writers is everywhere evident. I reported some years ago my tabulations of the authorities Donne cites in his collected sermons: Augustine about 340 times; Chrysostom, Jerome, and the medieval Bernard over a hundred times each; Ambrose and Basil almost as often; but Calvin and Luther less than twenty times each.[41] These sermons had a large public following. Frye is of course right in saying that Luther and Calvin stand out as influencing sixteenth-century opinion; but he seems to ignore the fact that in England there was a strong holdover of the older theology. We may therefore need to qualify considerably his thesis that Luther, Calvin, and Hooker "epitomize the major religious attitudes of Shakespeare's culture."[42] While Luther and Calvin no doubt influenced one notable stratum or stream within Elizabethan culture, there were concurrently other strands of attitude, and Hooker in fact represents a position closer to Aquinas than to Calvin.

As to where Shakespeare stood intellectually amid these various currents, we can only judge inferentially through a close study of his plays—not by *a priori* generalizations regarding the climate of the age. Frye's decision to use Calvin and Luther, chiefly, in glossing Shakespeare's theological references is questionable. For we must take into account, first of all, that these references are being made, not by Shakespeare directly, but by dramatic personages of many kinds—some of them pagans, others backsliding or sham Christians, and some bona fide Christians. To evaluate their utterances we therefore need, along with attention to dramatic context, a broad general knowledge of Western forms of religion and philosophy and an ability to recognize both well-balanced and ill-balanced or decadent versions of piety. Admittedly, Luther and Calvin can here often be helpful, since their knowledge in such matters is considerable. Yet since their interpretations or emphases are not always quite those of the Fathers or Schoolmen, there remains the question which of these traditions more closely accords with the total understanding implicit in Shakespeare's placing of his characters' views and their consequences. We need constantly to keep in mind in literary criticism that any concept of "the Elizabethan mind" is an insecure generalization. There were many Elizabethan minds, and Shakespeare's was no average one.

The Elizabethan background includes, in fact, so broad a spectrum of philosophies that, simply by focusing on one strand or other, various critics have produced quite diverse readings of Shakespeare. In the 1920s and 30s, attention was often given to Machiavelli, or Montaigne, or Seneca, in a historical search for the dramatist's source of vision. Particularly widespread then was the belief that Shakespeare's own faith rested in the Stoic ideal. L. L. Schücking, for instance, held this view, on the ground that the tragic heroes whom Shakespeare shows as the victims of passion often voice admiration for a life governed by reason. In Schücking's view, Shakespeare was experimenting with Neo-Stoic stage conventions from a stance in Stoic faith. He was a "baroque artist," who in a Senecan manner played up to his audience's interest in grotesque forms of passion—hence Hamlet's "exaggerated" revenge-lust over the praying King, or Lear's "eccentric" outburst against the chastity of women.[43]

But about this time T. S. Eliot countered with the view that Shakespeare had apparently no philosophy at all, or merely the "rag-bag philosophy" of his times, which by his poetic art he transmuted into something rich and strange, something with a "submarine music" as its underlying design.[44] Shakespeare's world at the end of the sixteenth century, Eliot explained, was one of "mixed and muddled scepticism," a world filled with "broken fragments of systems"—and this was the material enforced on the poet "to use as the vehicle of his feeling in writing himself and his times." For it is a poet's business, Eliot averred, not to think, but simply to "express the greatest emotional equivalent of thought." Hence, qua poet, Shakespeare's business was to "express the greatest emotional intensity of his time, based on whatever his time happened to think." But since at that time the thinking most widely diffused was a strain of Senecanism, this is the philosophy we find given emotional quality in Othello's final speech and in Hamlet's similar flair for self-dramatization. It is an attitude the reverse of Christian humility, but it was Shakespeare's ill luck to work with a philosophy inferior to Dante's, and we can hardly say whether or not Shakespeare believed the philosophy he was using and expressing. Shakespeare became "the representative of the end of the sixteenth century," just as Dante had been the voice of the thirteenth century, by starting from "his own emotions" and fabricating out of his agonies something impersonal. In writing *Hamlet,* however, the initial emotion, that of torture over a mother's guilt, was (so Eliot surmised) baffling to Shakespeare and defeated his effort to find for it a proper artistic formula. In this play, and similarly in *Measure for Measure,* Shakespeare got bogged down in "intractable" material.

Eliot's view here that the ideas and emotions of an age are for the poet materials he works with, working them up into art whether or not he believes in them, can be a salutary emphasis on the poet as craftsman. But even if we grant that Shakespeare qua poet was a fabricator, need we conclude that a fabricator's sole business is to empower ideas with their emotional equivalent? Dante did something besides giving an emotional quality to ideas when presenting, for example, Farinata and Cavalcante, two of his contemporaries; he associated their believed-in ideas with a tragic heroism and with a kind of nobility appropriate to the circle of the heretics. It would be imprecise to say simply that the poet is here using their ideas to make poetry. Rather, he is making a poem about a pilgrimage which has as one of its episodes an encounter with the felt thought these persons voice. And both through the placing given such thought and through the details selected for exhibiting its moral quality, Dante is introducing us to an understanding of life which depends on principles of insight traditionally Christian. His total activity qua poet includes certainly the activity of understanding and ordering the materials he is using.

Eliot's misjudgment of *Hamlet* and of *Measure for Measure* stems from a failure to study closely the total action in these plays and also the significance of Shakespeare's having placed the action in the one case in the genre of tragedy and in the other that of comedy. In reading *Othello* Eliot does better. But why does he not ask whether his own perception that Othello's final attitude is the reverse of Christian humility may not have been Shakespeare's in writing the scene? If it seems to Eliot that Othello is here "endeavoring to escape reality," how could Eliot have got this impression unless the very form of Shakespeare's art implies it—or else Eliot should claim only that he is judging Othello by bringing in from the outside his own ethical judgment. But does not the play itself implicitly judge Othello by showing us the "reality" he is fleeing? Had Eliot but pondered more closely the total play he could have found the reality of a spirit of forgiveness in Desdemona which Othello is neglecting, and also the fact that Shakespeare has set

Othello's absorption in self against a background of visiting Venetians whose attitudes contrast with Othello's.

Eliot's shortcoming is that although he can perceive, by reason of his own Christian sensibility, the self-dramatizing pride of Othello, yet he is not understanding it in relation to the play's structure because he presupposes a Shakespeare who did no thinking of his own but merely expressed through heroes the thought of his age. "The thought behind Shakespeare," says Eliot, "is the thought of men inferior to himself," and he could not, out of his own thinking, supply "the difference in quality between a St. Thomas and a Montaigne or a Machiavelli or a Seneca." By stating the situation thus, Eliot overlooks the fact that the tradition of St. Thomas or of his Christian allies was still alive within the Elizabethan age, and secondly that in a play the particular quality of any voiced idea is serving to characterize some mode of action which the playwright is placing in relation to its consequences. Eliot as moralist is insufficiently concerned with art's task of imitating action.

Because Eliot has so often insisted on the value of tradition, J. C. Ransom has called him "The Historical Critic." Yet Eliot's sense of history is in one basic respect surprisingly limited. It reflects, as René Wellek has rightly noted, an almost Hegelian view in treating each age as a cohering temper of thought for which its poets serve as mouthpiece. Furthermore, Eliot's characterization of Shakespeare's age as one of scepticism and rationalism is an over-simple one. It is partly responsible, I suspect, for Eliot's uncritical acceptance of the premises of J. M. Robertson (a modern positivist) when reading *Hamlet*. If Eliot's historical sense had been keener, he might have conceived the possibility, at least, of Shakespeare's belonging to the same intellectual tradition as Dante. For why might not Shakespeare be dramatizing, by a light of understanding inherited from Christianity, various and sundry currents within his Elizabethan age—not as systems of thought, indeed, but as the emergent "felt thought" of characters engaged in modes of action representative of human life, and hence pertinent by analogy to latencies in the Elizabethan scene? That is a way by which a poet can write for his age while yet not being wholly of it. He can have a special vantage point for seeing into the "muddles" of his own times; and as artist he can then imitate through story the moral action of the human psyche through which such muddles develop and bring on a probable fate. To understand this as Shakespeare's role as artist would be to credit him with a mature historical sense.

Modern historical approaches to Shakespeare, if I may now venture a general assessment, have not been really historical enough. Too often they have merely taken for granted the validity of their own historiography. Approaching Shakespeare with views limited by some Renaissance or more modern interpretation of history, they have neglected giving proper attention to a medieval-Christian sense of history which continued, however unofficially, into Elizabethan times. Hence although much useful information about aspects of that age's culture has been provided by our students of background, they have judged the logic of Shakespearean drama by formulas which more or less distort and even at best fall short of full justice to the import of his art. But this consequence is a result, secondly, of having slighted the dramatic mode and in particular the requirements of tragedy. Insufficient care has been taken to distinguish between ideas expressed by personages in a tragedy and other ideas guiding the dramatist in his plotting of what happens to those persons. Can the reasonings of a tragic hero, and of other persons whose advice-giving forwards the tragic action, be exempted from contributing somehow to the disaster which ensues? Is not Shakespeare indicating the inadequacies of certain voiced ideas by showing the plights into which they entrap their spokesmen? Here is where plot, as revealing by its logic an imitation of the logic of history, has such principal importance. The developing fate which a plot discloses overarches the thought of characters, putting it under judgment.

In partial reaction against historical approaches, the New Critics have focused on the integrity of each play as a whole. They have stressed starting from one's direct experience of a play, attending carefully to its language, and probing from within for its order of values. What matters to them is what the dramatist has made of his materials, not the mines from which he quarried them. And they see criticism as simply a coherence of response by a sensitive intelligence to significances within the poetic work. Yet by what lamp has their intelligence been aided? Are no extra-literary principles needed for the refining of a critic's sensibility? On this point a few of the New Critics, such as Leavis or Empson, have been evasive and even disdainful of examining the norms from philosophy or theology implicit in their critical practice. This may explain why

Leavis, in his otherwise excellent essay on *Othello,* can see in that play's ending only "a superb coup de théâtre" and a "radically un-tragic" speech by the hero; or why, elsewhere, when Leavis touches on the question of the final meaning of tragic experience, he soon arrests his discussion by saying it does not suit him to "threaten" the reader with theory.[45] Leavis fears "metaphysical ambitions" and would rely solely, in the liberal tradition of Matthew Arnold, on his general sense of "positive cultural" values. But other New Crit-ics are not so limited. L. C. Knights, for instance, has admitted a concern for creative insights by "religious teachers and philoso-phers," and in some recent essays on Shakespeare's politics he re-peatedly brings up the critic's need to understand the "medieval insistence" on the moral basis of politics. Shakespeare's politics, he asserts, "cannot be defined simply in terms of the Tudor view of history and the commonplace of order and degree"; rather, Shake-speare's political wisdom indicates some correspondence with medieval forms of thinking, which we ought to explore in Dante, St. Thomas, John of Salisbury, and the author of *Piers Plowman.*[46] Likewise Heilman, as we have noted earlier, occasionally draws on Christian categories, as does Fergusson similarly from his back-ground in the study of Dante. Thus the New Criticism is becoming increasingly interested in Shakespeare's philosophy of history.

Amid interpretations of many kinds one can observe an accumu-lating awareness, during the last thirty years, that Christian back-grounds may have a special relevance to our understanding the quality of Shakespeare's art. I have already mentioned contribu-tions in this direction by recent essayists on *Hamlet, Othello,* and *Macbeth;* and on *Lear* there are nowadays many readers who hold that this play is a Christian tragedy although its setting is pagan.[47] Further, it has been argued by L. A. Cormican that a medieval idiom and a medieval ethic characterize Shakespeare's art in gen-eral, and by Miss Parker that an Augustinian or Thomistic meta-physic is evident in Shakespeare's whole conception of justice.[48] In the area of comedy, Nevill Coghill has probed Shakespeare's un-derlying theory and traced it to medieval Christian concepts, in contrast to the neoclassical concepts adhered to by Ben Jonson and other contemporaries.[49] Of particular comedies, the one to which critics have given the most attention for its Christian imagery, struc-ture, and theme is *Measure for Measure.*[50] But also they have found Christian imagery, and even biblical allegory, in *The Winter's*

Tale.[51] And recently these two comedies, along with *Much Ado,
All's Well, Cymbeline,* and *The Tempest,* have been studied as being in their structure Shakespearean developments of the medieval
miracle play.[52] *The Tempest,* with its motif of "Providence divine,"
has long been recognized as in some way Christian; but the New
Arden editor now ventures to speak of it as modeled on Fall and
Redemption in Scripture, and I have proposed the Joseph story as
its most striking prototype.[53] Interestingly, the New Arden editor
of *Pericles* traces this play's structure to a basis in miracle play, comparing it in particular with the Digby *Mary Magdalene.*[54] And in
recent essays on *The Merchant of Venice* and *Twelfth Night* the
formerly unfashionable term "allegory" is being openly used and
applied.[55] In fact, it has been applied to various other plays as well,
in a stimulating book by J. A. Bryant.[56] Bryant is quick to point
out, however, that the kind of allegory he senses in Shakespeare is
not that of some abstract and external truth illustrated through the
poetry, but rather a dimension of analogy and typology incorporated in the literal fable for the deepening of its dramatic import.

The catalog I have recited could be easily extended. Even Shakespeare's *The Phoenix and the Turtle,* for instance, has been shown
to owe its terminology to medieval Scholastic theology.[57] But what
is perhaps more to the point is the increasing number of respectable
scholars who are announcing Shakespeare as "intellectually" a
Christian throughout his poetic works, claiming this as a helpful
key to their full meaning, and sensing in Shakespeare's fugitive biblical echoes important clues.[58] Sometimes the convictions of these
critics are thinly supported, or accompanied by a questionable explication of text; but that is a frailty to which all critics are liable.
Discrimination from a new perspective cannot mature in a trice.
Besides, since this perspective is often allied to more general interests in myth and ritual, it is sometimes confused with foreign an-
thropological lore. But there seems good reason for believing that
a scholar such as S. L. Bethell was pointing in the right direction
when he asserted (in 1944) that "Shakespeare's world is the world
of folk legend more profoundly understood—a development, in
fact, of medieval Christianity."[59] In any case, this is a more likely
thesis than the contrary one of Curtis B. Watson, that "Shakespeare
reflects the Christian values of his age to a lesser degree than pagan
humanist morality."[60]

One reason for thinking so is our awareness of recent scholarship in the area of medieval literature. The study of Chaucer has of late been both disturbed and revivified by new investigations in medieval symbolism, which are likely to influence in the future our perspective on Shakespeare. Chaucer's so-called "secular" tales are no longer seen as independent of his religious heritage. Not only is his *Troilus* interpreted nowadays as influenced in large measure by the predominantly Christian insight of the Middle Ages, but even his *Miller's Tale* and *Merchant's Tale,* for example, have been read as artistically shaped by motifs in Christian morality and doctrine.[61] It has been discovered that the medieval concept of allegory can apply not merely to dimensions in the text of Scripture but also to the symbolic art of secular tales, and that when these latter are approached with this perspective many of them reveal a richer and more complex meaning than had heretofore been supposed. Hence multilevel interpretation is returning to something of the favor it enjoyed prior to the Age of Enlightenment. A major key to Chaucer's symbolism, it is being argued, is to be found in patristic and medieval works of Scriptural exegesis; and accordingly such scholars as D. W. Robertson and R. E. Kaske have been diligently mining these sources for the meanings they attach to such things as plants, animals, birds, gardens, and numbers, as well as for understanding a general theory of art as involving the double values of "kernel" and "husk," a *sententia* within the *sensus* of a story. Supporting this interest are such other recent publications as Henri de Lubac's two-volume *Exégèse médiévale,* English translations of Jean Danielou's studies in this area, and a serious concern with Christian typology in books by Austin Farrer and Erich Auerbach. Auerbach's stress on "figural realism" as the distinctive genius of Christian art has made clear that literary "style" itself carries metaphysical and theological presuppositions. Hence stylistic analysis remains incomplete unless attention be given to the ontological reference and mythic quality of language. In Anglo-Saxon studies, meanwhile, the significance of Christian symbolism in the structuring of *Beowulf,* for instance, is today widely acknowledged.

But how can such lore be further appropriated for an attuning of our sensibility to the patterns in Shakespeare's plays? As a sample although minor illustration, I would suggest that if Chaucer is invoking for satire a reference to the Song of Songs in the *Miller's Tale,* and also in the *Merchant's Tale* when old January sings that "The turtles voys is herd, my dowve sweet," as R. E. Kaske holds,[62] then equally it is likely that Shakespeare is using this same biblical allusion, nonsatirically, for his pastoral scene in *The Winter's Tale,* when Florizel betroths himself to Perdita with the words, "So turtles pair / That never mean to part" (IV. iv. 153); or again in the final scene in which Paulina calls herself an "old turtle" as she plights troth with Camillo. The whole complex of pastoral imagery in this play may be an instance of romance conventions heightened and brightened by biblical associations. Even so small a detail as the Old Shepherd's looking for "two of my best sheep" (III. iii. 65) may glance analogously at Leontes and Polixenes, the "twinned lambs that did frisk i' the sun" in Act I before they wandered into jealousy and had to be returned to their fold by the story's shepherding and gracious persons. If so, this allusion (among others) signalizes a Scriptural core within the play's whole plot.

Or let me illustrate, from another play, how biblical allusion can be used to implant irony. If Chaucer's characterizing of his Summoner as a lover of "leeks" is important, as Kaske has explained,[63] because it symbolizes the backsliding "cupidity" of the leek-loving Israelites of Numbers 11:5, then it may also be significant that Shakespeare has Henry V wear a "leek" (IV. vii. 109) during a campaign which rests for its moral justification on warping the meaning of Numbers 27:8. That is, Shakespeare has got Henry's number: this Christian "star of England" of the play's surface *sensus* is being interpreted through its *sententia* as a cupidinous Egypt-lover. And that this is scarcely happenstance is confirmed by a parallel text to Numbers 11:5 in a New Testament Epistle (2 Peter 2:22), the one about the dog returning to its vomit and the sow to its mire. For Shakespeare twice sounds this text from Peter, once allusively in *2 Henry IV* (I. iii. 97–99) and then verbatim in *Henry V* (III. vii. 68). Thus the hidden moral meaning of Henry's whole career is glanced at through the symbolism of the paired Old Testament and New Testament texts I have cited. The play has these clues to its meaning alongside and within an otherwise chauvinistic surface appeal.[64] Shakespeare's Fluellen, who believes "there is figures in all things" (IV. vii. 35), speaks more truly than he knows when he figures King Henry as like Alexander "the Pig."

My task in this book, however, is to elucidate Shakespeare's tragedies rather than his comedies or his history plays. How can a Christian symbolism be operative in the structuring of a tragedy? And can it give us perspective for a theory of tragedy? In tentative ways I shall explore these matters in the remainder of the present chapter, and then more extensively in the chapters which follow.

4   Tragedy and biblical analogue

In interpreting Shakespeare's tragedies there is a pitfall, it seems to me, if we speak of a tragic hero as a Christ figure. G. Wilson Knight, for instance, has yielded to this in his reading of *Timon of Athens.* Timon, he says, is "Christ-like" in his suffering, and when Timon's servants wander abroad separated "they are as disciples of the Christ meeting after the crucifixion."[65] These comments have been vigorously objected to by Roland Frye,[66] who does not pause, however, to tell us what is wrong with Knight's analogy. What is it that makes the analogy a tempting one? Plainly, it is the fact that Timon is shown as a man who bountifully gives of his goods to his neighbors, only to find himself eventually scorned and rejected. The ungrateful Athenians, in Knight's view, slaughter the love of a blamelessly generous Timon by preferring "the gold of coins to the gold of love." But this interpretation fails to ask whether the "love" Timon gave was actually true charity or merely a vain love of his own virtue, a kind of fool's gold. It notably overlooks the warning of I Corinthians 13, and instead condones Timon's cursing of ungrateful man as evidencing a heavenly indignation on his part. I would not deny all analogy between Timon's love of *timia* and Christ's service of *agape,* but would suggest rather an analogy of contrast. That is, there is in Timon's story some shadow similarity to the outward form of the Christ story, but by way of blind analogy. Knight's mistake lies in his blurring the difference between a dark analogy and a true likeness, thus assimilating Timon to Christ. The mistake has come about, probably, through a Nietzschean influence to which Knight pays tribute in a footnote appended to his chapter on *Timon.*

Replying to Frye, Knight has recently denied that his many studies of Shakespeare are pervasively Christian.[67] Rather, he explains, he has "always in morality's despite viewed Shakespearian tragedy as in some indefinable, Nietzschean, way an advance" over Christian belief; and he has "not wasted valuable time in trying to guess what some long forgotten Elizabethan sociologist or theologian" might have thought on any point. This is no doubt largely true. In fact, Knight's disdain for historical theology may account, in part at least, for the impressionistic mysticism which in much of his writing irks many of today's readers. Yet in his essays on various of Shakespeare's comedies, and notably in *"Measure for Measure and the Gospels"* in his *The Wheel of Fire,* Knight has invoked not Nietzschean but New Testament passages mainly, and in a way which has proved of great help to other students.

On balance, the range of Knight's thought can only be called eclectic—at times a use of Christian lore in a kind of cut-flower way (typical of a modernism which neglects the roots from which its sensibility still draws residual nourishment), and at other times a toying with some super-truth of Nietzsche's as a guiding mythology. One unfortunate result is that philosophical distinctions, and Shakespeare's text as well, frequently get blurred under the musical patterns of Knight's mystic intuition. Nevertheless, his theoretical concept of drama as an "expanded metaphor" has been very valuable. It has stimulated many studies of Shakespeare's imagery in recent years, which happily have progressed beyond the techniques of cataloguing to a pondering of the symbolic import of particular plays. And for approaching the tragedies, Knight has raised what is certainly a challenging concept by asserting that "each of Shakespeare's tragic heroes is a miniature Christ." Elaborating on this, he has said that since the Christian Mass is "at once a consummation and transcending of pagan ritual," the unique act of the Christ sacrifice "can, if we like, be seen as central" to the world of Shakespearean tragedy.[68]

Can such a concept be in any way useful? I find Northrop Frye, the Toronto critic, apparently thinking along similar lines when he includes Christ in his list of tragic heroes, and then later suggests that for a theory of tragedy one looks naturally to "the psychology of the will to power, as expounded in Adler and Nietzsche."[69] The difficulty I sense in both the Knight and Frye approaches is that neither seems quite to allow for a genuine transcendence of pagan ritual by the Christian. For if, as Frye asserts, the "great majority" of tragic heroes possess a hubris or proud soaring of mind which brings about their catastrophe, how can we suppose Christ to be one of these, unless we part company with the traditional view of Christ? Or, again, if the "typical" tragic hero is, as Frye thinks, a person "somewhere between the divine and the all too human," can the Christ of traditional theology fit this type?[70]

The theologian E. J. Tinsley has recently made the point that

Christ, the "new" man, put aside his status "in a way which is the *reverse* of the tragic hero's manner." St. Luke's Passion narrative, he notes, shows Christ as interceding for others and dying the death of a righteous man. In short, as Tinsley sums up: "The New Testament shows Jesus passing through the tragic without presenting him tragically." But this New Testament perspective, Tinsley observes, has been warped by certain nineteenth-century romanticists. For example, Albert Schweitzer portrayed Christ as a figure of tragedy in a way quite foreign to the New Testament. "Schweitzer's Christ, a tragic hero who storms Jerusalem to force the hand of God, is nearer to classical tragedy or Wagnerian romanticism than the New Testament, where the evidence suggests that to try to force God's hand, Zealot-fashion, was the continuing temptation of the mission of Jesus, not its basis."[71]

Is there then, possibly, a confusion somewhat like Schweitzer's underlying Northrop Frye's naming of Christ among tragic heroes? Or does he perhaps think Christ a tragic hero in some unspecified but nontypical way? Even if the latter be the case, how can we refer to Christ in formulating a theory of tragic heroism?

Since Frye's position seems to me less than clear, let me return to Knight's. Every Shakespearean tragic hero, he would say, is "a miniature Christ," whether the hero be good, bad, or indifferent. In only one possible sense, I think, can this be true—a sense quite different from what I judge Knight to intend. There is a theological sense (more recognized by Aquinas than by Calvin) in which every human being has a potentially Christlike nature. An indestructible trace of God's likeness is residual even in sinners, who nevertheless are thwarting and perverting this potentiality. In this limited sense we might say that Shakespeare's Richard II, for instance, is not utterly wrong in likening himself to Christ, even though he has been secretly Cain-like toward his uncle Gloucester, and is Adam-like in neglecting the care of his garden-kingdom. But in styling himself a martyr, Richard is blindly overlooking the difference between the charitable Christ and his own selfish version of Christian behavior. He is a defective Christ figure, and unwittingly parodies Christ. Indeed, when he comes down from Flint castle in III. iii. in order to give up his crown with a spectacular show of would-be piety, just after having boasted of angels' support, may not this whole action be Shakespeare's emblematizing of an analogy to the "Cast thyself down" advocated by Satan in Luke 4:9?

Of other Shakespearean tragic heroes, even of the pagan ones, I think we may say the same: that simply as human beings they have a potential Christliness, but that in them this natural potentiality is crippled and distorted by an overlay of sin. In the typical tragic hero, therefore, we recognize a significant moral gap between the character of this hero's suffering and Christ's suffering. In action this difference amounts to an upside-down orientation of the human will as compared to Christ's. Figuratively, it is the difference between the Old Adam's blind purposing and the New Adam's redemptive purposing.

If, then, we are looking for an ultimate archetype for the tragic hero, why not speak of him as a figurative Adam? Adam is related to Christ by analogy, in the way in which the Old Adam in everyman is related to the potential New Adam in him: the first is but the mistaken shadow-version of the second. From this point of view, the agony and "sacrifice" we see in a typical tragic hero is not at all identical with Christ's but rather its rival analogue. Thus we can grant the insight of the Cambridge anthropologists that tragedy is related to ritual sacrifice, yet we are pointing out at the same time that the rituals of tragedy are historically those of goat-song, and that a scapegoat-sacrifice is not the equivalent of that of the Lamb of God. The Christian Mass is a wholly transformed version of scapegoat ritual. Christ's Passion fulfils the tragic hero's "passion" in a transfigured sense—by analogy, but across a moral gulf which gives irony to the tragic hero's career by comparison. We may properly call the passion and death of Judas tragic, but not that of Christ in any strict sense. Christ as hero offers a rectification of tragic heroisms of all kinds.

The concept of tragic heroism as a parody of the Christ story has been half-rightly grasped in a recent essay on *Timon* by Jarold Ramsey.[72] At Timon's first banquet, as Ramsey notes, we hear a comment by Apemantus on the men who "eat" Timon by dipping their meat in his blood while he "cheers them up to it," and a prediction that the fellow who "now parts bread" with Timon will be the first to kill him. Does not such spectacle, Ramsey asks, imply a monstrous parody of the Last Supper? It is followed, in Act II, by Timon's betrayal by three followers, a kind of parallel to Christ's being denied three times by Peter. In Act III, there is again imagery suggesting ritual sacrifice. When Timon is beset by stewards demanding that he pay their masters, he responds by inviting them to

"Cut my heart in sums" and "Tell out my blood." Then he prepares another banquet—this time a sort of mockery of baptismal
ritual—in which he splatters their faces with water, while invoking
as their blessing a curse. After this he withdraws from the world to a
"cave," where he broods on his misanthropy. Finally, he descends to
enact a suicide, by which he goes to his "everlasting mansion"—
not in an Eternal Father's house, however, but in the "salt flood" of
nature's sea.

It seems to me Ramsey is justified in calling this total story-
pattern a caricature of Christ's. Yet he is mistaken, surely, when he
speaks of Timon as initially blameless, and then interprets his ruin
as due simply to his practicing, in an extreme form and excessive
way, "Christian moral directives." Shakespeare, in Ramsey's opinion, is showing that the idealism of Christian ethics is "potentially
cruel, destructive, and perhaps impossible to live by"; the dramatist is challenging the validity of New Testament teachings. I would
say, rather, that Timon's ethic is never Christian at all, but only a
man-centered Greekish analogue which unwittingly apes Christian
charity.

We can find a comparable dark-shadowing of Christian pattern,
I may add, in the Roman story of *Julius Caesar*. That is, the drama
is here structured in terms of a beginning in triumphal entry on a
holiday, then a climax with the slaying of its hero at "the ninth
hour," and finally a return of his ghost from the dead to inspire a
martyr-like death by his godson Brutus. By Christian philosophers,
suicide has aptly been called "the last sacrament of the Stoic religion." Brutus celebrates it with a sense of victory. A dagger (so
Cassius has preached in Act I) is the power "every bondman in his
own hand bears" to cancel his captivity; it makes "the weak most
strong." It is the gift of the gods, says Cassius, for defeating "tyrants." What an irony there is in such a religion! Dramatically its
pattern of a purging sacrifice for the "renewal" of Rome—a renewal
memorialized by a bathing of murderers' hands and later of citizens' napkins in Caesar's blood—would seem to any Christian audience a parody of Redemption. The holiday of Lupercal, at which
Caesar makes his bid for kingship by playing weak and humble,
parodies the Christian Passover at which Christ was humble in a
different way. And when Antony, after Caesar's death, enlists disciples by displaying the "wounds" of the dead Caesar, do we not
have a counterfeit parallel to the resurrected Christ's offering his

wounds for the view of Thomas the doubter? Brutus and his party of "Roman actors" resemble the Pharisees of biblical story: they meet by night, seal their compact at three o'clock in the morning of Rome's spring festival, and look for a sun that will arise from the south and find its "high east" over the Capitol. Their victim, however, is no Christ but a hero constant as the "northern" star in refusing a petition for mercy toward a "banished brother." These and other symbolic details in Shakespeare's structuring suggest that it is by shadow-analogy to biblical paradigm that a Roman chronicle covering three years of time has been compacted dramatically within what seems a few days and a night.[73]

Let me mention, incidentally, a somewhat more complex way of understanding the relationship between Christ's bid for kingship and Caesar's. Christ's is related by typology to Abel's death at the hands of Cain, whereas Caesar's can be related by typology to the death of Remus, slain by Romulus. Augustine (in *City of God* XV. 5) points out that there is a similarity, but also a difference, between the Abel-Cain story and the Remus-Romulus story. The first he calls an "archetype" of the hatred that subsists between Two Cities, the Heavenly and the Earthly, which the brothers Abel and Cain respectively represent. The second he calls an "archetype" of the strife within the Earthly City, between two brothers of that city. Romulus and Remus figure the desire for the glory of ruling which divides the Earthly City against itself. Together their antagonism corresponds to Cain's, which in Scripture is viewed as the heritage of Adam's disobedience; but Abel's love of God prefigures the promise of a New Adam in Christ. Bible paradigm is thus the superior analogue to Roman paradigm.

Because Christ is the recapitulated "fulfilment" of Adam, we are more likely to find in Shakespeare's comedies than in his tragedies true analogies to Christlike behavior, or to Old Testament foreshadowings of it in such figures as Noah, or Joseph, or Daniel. Thus, for instance, we can rightly discern a genuine Christliness in gracious Hermione, something Daniel-like in Portia, something Joseph-like in Prospero, and something Noah-like in Rosalind's bringing to the "ark" of marriage eight persons (see *As You Like It* V. iv. 36) . For in the genre of comedy, moral fulfilment and rectification crown the end. In the genre of tragedy, on the other hand, the misdirections of human love, which in comedy lurk as a passing threat, dominate the central action and carry the story's tragic heroes to misery and usually to death. Tragedy and comedy are, in drama as in life, two differing modes of action: that of comedy transcending by a reverse movement what was fatal in the tragic mode. Hence, in tragedy, if any analogy to Christ is suggested by the hero's behavior it must take the form of an ironic or dark analogy—as, for instance, the inverted likeness to Christ in Lear's crowning himself with weeds, or in Macbeth's ritual supper with his thanes. On the other hand, an occasional "innocent" death in a tragedy, by someone other than the titular hero, can truly suggest Christ's—as, for instance, Cordelia's death by hanging, or Duncan's being killed between two grooms.

Parenthetically, let me concede that the reader is not strictly required to recognize the analogies I have just mentioned. Some of them are not signalized by any verbal allusion to Bible story; and Shakespeare's story of course fascinates even when appreciated solely in its literal terms. Yet there is a gain in emblematic quality if echoes of typology are recognized. For whenever a drama—whether by its diction, or plot, or both—uses imagery resonant of biblical associations, any reader who carries biblical archetypes on the horizons of his consciousness may be prompted to discern their relevance to the play's secular story (as he was expected to do, for example, in the "secular" portion of the *Second Shepherds' Play*), and thereby he can place the poet's episodes within a more ultimate overplot of meaning. And a reader of Shakespeare has ground for doing so, in that the figurative shape of such episodes as I have mentioned is in each case the dramatist's invention, not provided by his literary source.

Let us note further how in a tragedy such as *Macbeth,* for instance, the hero's action has a tendency to adumbrate features of Old Adam behavior or experience. One critic has seen in this play "the Adam and Eve story over again, with the Witches in the role of the Serpent."[74] Yet even more than this is suggested; for in various phases of the action other critics have seen additional biblical analogies—to Ahab and Jezebel in the way the crime is urged and planned by the wife; to Judas in Macbeth's false welcoming of Duncan to supper; to Saul in Macbeth's apostasy and commerce with witches; to Herod in Macbeth's slaughtering of Macduff's "babes" and his threatening to hang on a "tree" a truth-telling messenger.[75] These analogies, any or all of them, involve aspects of what may be called the experience of Adamkind. They arise, now and then, to a reader's mind because of the play's imagery or shape of episode, and they punctuate the literal story with a typological import. This is not allegory in a literal form, however, such as one finds in morality plays, or in a more polished guise in Spenser's *Faerie Queene*. The drama is not being used to illustrate antecedently conceived ideas. Rather, the secular history it presents is carrying overtones of symbolism through flickering analogy to biblical history.

5 Othello as a Judas

This point can be pursued by turning to another of the tragedies, *Othello*. What analogies are suggested in its imagery or by its action, and how can these enlarge our understanding of the total drama? Othello in Cyprus has been likened to Adam in a paradise by Paul Siegel,[76] who notes also the satanic malice with which Iago sets about untuning the harmony of the newlyweds. This analogy probably occurs to many readers, although in several respects it is an imperfect one. Desdemona is scarcely Eve, or at most distantly so; she chides Iago for his "profane" talk. And Othello, if somewhat like an Adam, nevertheless does not fall by hearkening to his wife in the way Adam did. Obliquely, however, there is an element of analogy. For when Othello says that no contentment of soul could be more "absolute" than his welcome by Desdemona, and then adds that "I dote / In mine own comforts," he is evidencing a uxoriousness which makes possible the later jealousy into which Iago tempts him.[77] Othello's very concept of bliss has Adam's fault at its basis; then, on top of this, a betrayal of Desdemona develops as a second fault representative of Adamkind's history in some later phase. Since Othello from the start lacks Adam's original innocence, his tragedy has a more complex paradigm than the Genesis one.

The analogy closest to the completed circuit of Othello's career is the one touched on by Siegel when he remarks that this hero's act of self-murder follows the example of Judas. In Scripture the deadliest extent of Adamkind's tragedy is instanced in Judas. And in Othello's own last speeches (although he may be unconscious of this) there are signals of an analogy in his likening himself to "the base Judean" who threw away a pearl "Richer than all his tribe," and in his final comment:

> I kissed thee ere I killed thee. No way but this,
> Killing myself, to die upon a kiss.

Even if we follow those editors who prefer to read "Indian" (Quarto, 1622) instead of "Iudean" (Folio, 1623) , the twin images of priceless pearl and deadly kiss are sufficient to evoke biblical echoes. The Judas who betrayed with a kiss, and whose bargaining away of Christ-the-pearl inverted tragically the parable of the merchant of Matthew 13:45, resembles Othello all too obviously. Othello has become "egregiously an ass," as Iago predicted (II. i. 318) , and in this respect is the Jud-as of Elizabethan proverb (see *Love's Labor's Lost* V. ii. 631) . Furthermore, the fact that Judas was Christ's only disciple from his own tribe of Judah, and thus was a traitor to family in betraying Christ, must have made him in Shakespeare's eyes a particularly apt archetype for the domestic tragedy of Othello.

In what more specific ways could the story of Judas be parallel to the tragedy of Othello? Let us recall some aspects of the biblical account. In Matthew 26 (see also John 12), Judas is concerned for the worldly value of a certain "alabaster" cruse, and not for the mystery which this vessel is devoted to celebrating. When the ointment from the alabaster is poured out on the feet of Jesus by Mary of Bethany (in Western tradition usually identified with Mary Magdalene), it signifies her understanding of his mission of sacrifice in the work of atonement. Judas does not understand the mystery of atoning sacrifice. He upbraids Mary's act, by the norm of his own narrower kind of righteousness. He thinks her alabaster vessel should have been committed solely to his treasury, so that he could use it for conventional works of patronizing generosity. Need I expound the analogy of this attitude to that of Othello in his worldly valuing of the "monumental alabaster" (V. ii. 5) of Desdemona's body? Throughout the drama he has supposed that her body should be devoted solely to himself and his own ideals of nobility—and not at all to that "reconciliation" in the name of "grace" for which Desdemona pleads (in III. iii. 47) because she wishes to "atone" (IV. i. 244) Othello and Cassio. Judas so resented Mary's act that he decided, then and there, to turn to Christ's enviers to make a covenant for Christ's betrayal. Othello similarly, in his self-righteousness, turns from Desdemona because he is resentful of her Christlike hope for atonement, and makes a covenant with her envious adversary, Iago. At a Last Supper during which Christ speaks of his body as a memorial unto the "forgiveness of sins," Judas arises from the table to go out into the night to keep his bargain of betrayal with a kiss. Likewise Othello, in a final scene of bedroom communion with Desdemona, has no mind for forgiveness but instead, in loyalty to his own blind sense of justice, mocks the reality of communion by celebrating it perversely with a deadly kiss. Judas discovered afterwards, to his shame, that he had betrayed "innocent blood"; and because he was then unable to undo the earthly consequences of his act he hanged himself. Even in his remorse he had not come to understand the meaning of forgiveness. The same is true of Othello, even though he too has seen forgiveness exampled before his very eyes in the spirit of the righteous one he has victimized. Thus Othello's tragedy involves not merely the "mistake" of having conspired against and slain an innocent person but the deeper sin of rejecting grace—by neglecting the "mercy" to which Desdemona was dedicating her alabaster body while also preserving this "vessel" (IV. ii. 83) for Othello.

We need not infer that Shakespeare was equating Desdemona with Christ. In terms of the analogy she is Christlike merely as a faithful follower, like Mary Magdalene. She quite sufficiently identifies herself by her oath "As I am a Christian" (IV. ii. 82) , and in the bedroom scene by her cry "Heaven have mercy on me!" (V. ii. 33) . This does not mean that her life has been without fault. Indeed, earlier in the play, out of her pity for human suffering, she has committed a number of indiscretions.[78] One of them is glanced at, I think, by the clown in Act III, scene iv, when he jests: "I will catechize the world for him; that is, make questions and by them answer." The clown is here wittily suggesting that Desdemona is better at catechizing than at understanding her pupil—which is certainly the case in her manner of approaching Othello on Cassio's behalf. In this sense, there is some truth in her ultimate testimony, after Othello has strangled her, that "Nobody, I myself" is responsible for her death—although it is also true that she dies "guiltless" of Othello's specific charge, and yet is forgiving this fault in her "kind lord." These three utterances, spoken almost surrealistically as if from a world beyond death, carry the paradox of a humble confession of fault on the part of a Christian who fulfils charity in her death. Shakespeare is maintaining the real-life complexity of Desdemona's virtue. Yet at the core of the play's meaning is a Christlike martyrdom by Desdemona, fumbling though it be.

This mystery a Judas-like Othello has profaned by backsliding into the noble "barbarian" he was before his baptism. His tragedy can be traced to a majestic loyalty to blind ideals. No intentional malice but rather a self-centered mode of virtue has caused him to fall victim to Iago's tempting insinuations, and later, when the facts are set right, to pursue a vain glory one more step into a brutally honorific suicide. Othello thus returns to the action by which in Aleppo once he established his sense of righteousness—when he took by the throat a Turkish traducer of the Venetian state and smote this "uncircumcized dog." (Shakespeare may be here depicting, by analogy, the temper of those called Judaizers in the New Testament, who took pride in a circumcision of the flesh while neglecting circumcision of the heart.) Othello is displaying at this moment a noble indignation but devoid of all patience and mercy. To vindicate his retaliatory justice he is punishing a culprit, now his own flesh, and prejudging how the state might rule on the matter. This is the story of an aristocratically self-sufficient man—such as we might potentially be, and such as Judas seems to have been. It arouses not our contempt but our pity and fear.

Once we ponder Othello's overall likeness to Judas, it makes fully coherent his underlying psychology. I do not mean that we see him as deliberately cuing his attitude by reference to Judas; indeed, the final allusion in his mouth is probably more of Shakespeare's making than comprehended by its speaker. To us, however, it becomes a clue for understanding this hero as a man whose love of name has made him blind to charity; and thus his jealousy can be seen as something more than a sexual jealousy. We can be aware, in retrospect, of a jealousy for personal honor which both preceded and continues after the episode of disbelief in Desdemona's chastity. And this explains why, in the midst of his sexual jealousy, Othello could exclaim:

> I had been happy if the general camp,
> Pioners and all, had tasted her sweet body,
> So I had nothing known. Oh, now forever
> Farewell the tranquil mind! Farewell content!

His peace of mind is dearer to him than Desdemona. Hence, ironically, he would rather have her defiled and himself ignorant of it, if thereby he might retain an undisturbed confidence in himself. But does not such a narcissistic love of self-image accord with his attitude at the beginning of the play? "My parts, my title, and my perfect soul / Shall manifest me rightly" has been his boast. He has felt no compassion for Brabantio, or later for Cassio. Having developed none for Desdemona either, he is consistent in denying compassion ultimately to himself, his own flesh and blood.

Othello's stance in his first scene, when Brabantio with officers comes to seize him, is emblematic and constitutes in fact something of a parody of Christ's attitude when arrested at Gethsemane. Othello says chidingly to his accusers: "Keep up your bright swords, for the dew will rust them." Christ had said to Peter: "Put up your sword into the sheath; the cup which the Father hath given me, shall I not drink it?" The situations have a strange affinity. But Christ's gentle rebuke was to an over-eager defender, not to his arresters; and it was said out of a willingness to suffer humiliation, not with Othello's intention to "out-tongue" complaints against him. In the drama, it is an instance of inverted analogy. And it is possible, perhaps, to see another such upside-down analogy to Christ at a midpoint in the play, when Othello is offered a handkerchief by Desdemona to soothe his anguished head but impatiently brushes aside this napkin. Any playgoer familiar with the Veronica legend (one of the Stations of the Cross in churches) might see here a parody of Christ's suffering brow and a contrast to Christ's acceptance of Veronica's napkin. Whether Shakespeare had in mind these analogies some readers may doubt. But one can say that in the two episodes I have mentioned, both of them at important points in the drama, their artistic shape takes on added meaning if referred to the paradigms I have cited, and we know Shakespeare to have invented both scenes without any hint from Cinthio.

He has invented also a later scene in which Othello, after rejecting Desdemona's testimony that "Heaven" knows her honesty, retreats into the self-pity of an ironic Job. Here, in the verbal references to "affliction," "sores," and "patience," all scholars have recognized allusions to Job. But by implication Shakespeare is portraying a grotesque aping of holy Job. Job when tested called on Heaven to resolve his perplexities. Othello is taking his whole vision of life from a Satan-like Iago. And after saluting patience only conditionally, Othello soon calls on the "cherubin" Patience to "look grim as Hell!" Thus he would make the cherubin's office, traditionally that of charity, sanction his own demand for revenge. Ever since his vow by "yond marble heaven" (III. iii. 460), his justice has reflected a heart turned to stone. As a would-be priest of this heaven, Othello can weep only over Desdemona's supposed apostasy from his own ideal, and over his own supposed obligation to offer her up in sacrifice to it. He begins Act V, scene ii, by communing self-centeredly with his own soul and its sense of "cause"; and then, as if aping a celebrant at a service of Tenebrae, he ritualizes his task to "Put out the light, and then put out the light." He is thus like the Judas who gave himself to the "night" of a Pharisaic self-righteousness. The accumulative analogies I have touched on are all coherent with the Judas one, which resonates finally in Othello's speech of suicide.

Many of us are familiar with Northrop Frye's useful distinction between two kinds of response to a work of literature.[79] One kind is a participating sense in time, our absorption in the narrative as it moves in its spontaneous continuity—a precritical response largely. The second kind is a detached response, a consciousness of theme— that is, of what the story is all about when contemplated in its unifying structure. Although these responses somewhat overlap in experience they are distinguishable. The second is our sense of the story's total design, the response by which we see in the words and actions of a character something beyond what they mean to their speaker in the play. We then see the ironies with which the playwright has highlighted the tragic hero's career and we become aware of the analogies by which they are signalized. We discover thus what may be called the "overplot" (Harry Levin's term) and what medieval theorists would have considered the allegorical dimension of the literal fable.

Shakespeare's art in this respect is more subtle than that of, say, Marlowe's *Dr. Faustus,* in which morality play conventions openly interpret each step. Faustus freely confesses his ambition to be a mighty god by outflying Scripture. Quite aware that the god he serves is his own appetite, he deliberately engages in necromancy in order to sell his soul to the devil. Tragedy in this vein is largely exemplum, the illustration of an antisaint's career.[80] As in *psychomachia* drama, the theological aspects are explicitly labelled: "Hell strives with grace for conquest" in the breast of Faustus; good angels and bad angels stalk the stage; the face of a Greekish Helen outweighs the attraction of a vial of "precious grace"; and at the end, the hero's last-minute vision of Christ's saving blood in the firmament is outweighed by a guilty terror of God's wrath. Visible devils carry off this damned man and a chorus moralizes on his "hellish fall." No Shakespearean drama is didactic in this overt and immediate fashion. That is because Shakespeare's focus is on historical verisimilitude—on tragedy as it emerges cumulatively in the arena of temporal events. We may recall, however, that such a focus is also characteristic of the Bible's story of Judas, or Achitophel, or Saul, or Herod. They are not shown debating their eternal destiny or, in the end, carried off to hell. If we infer their fate in eternity we do so on the basis of the moral quality of their behavior before and at death.

Of *Othello,* some readers have sentimentally supposed that the hero ends his life "saved" by punishing himself, or at least that the evidence for his damnation is inconclusive.[81] But is not Shakespeare implying otherwise? The Judas analogy invites us to judge Othello, ultimately, by the light of Christian commentary on Judas. Historically, such commentary begins with Peter's lament, in Acts 1, that Judas has "turned aside" from fellowship in the ministry of Christ to go "to his own place"—a place interpreted (by Peter's allusion to Psalm 69) as one of darkened eyes and "punishment upon punishment" from God's anger. Commentary of a more explicit kind was familiar to all readers of Augustine, or Dante, or Calvin. Judas "passed from this life," Augustine said (*City of God* I. 17), "chargeable not only with the death of Christ, but with his own: for though he killed himself on account of his crime, his killing himself was another crime." This act "rather aggravated than expiated" his guilt, since by despairing of God's mercy "he left to himself no place for healing penitence." His so-called "repentance," Calvin explained (*Institutes* III. iii. 4), was no "gospel" repentance, since it apprehended only misery and terror for sin, and not Christ's medicine for sin. Such a "repentance" was unlike Hezekiah's or David's, in Calvin's view, but like Cain's or Saul's. Indeed, it was "nothing but a sort of entryway of hell . . . already entered in this life." Dante, understandably, saw Judas as destined for the lowest circle of hell.

With this general tradition of moral analysis Shakespeare was no doubt familiar, either through reading or indirectly through the sensibility of the Christian community in which he lived. He reflects the tradition in his portrait of Othello, who is not shown as achieving a Christian penitence. When made aware of his crime against Desdemona, Othello partly shuffles off responsibility for it onto fate, the stars, and his merely "unlucky" deeds. Instead of being contrite for his vengefulness, he blames only his folly and ignorance. He blames his ignorance of Desdemona's innocence—but not his own ignoring of Christian duty in having sworn a "sacred vow" to serve revenge, nor his now continuing to ignore Christian duty by turning to self-slaughter. On Othello's last speech, Gratiano comments: "All that's spoke is marred." And Gratiano is a commentator who has earlier told us what a "desperate" turn involves: it involves a "fall to reprobation" (V. ii. 209). Othello is clearly among the reprobate by Shakespeare's implication.

Othello's own sense of damnation must be shown, however, as somewhat limited and confused. That is, it would be inappropriate to portray him as measuring his own damnation in relation to his neglect of charity. Hence when he speaks of hell, he views it simply as the place of punishment for betrayers of justice. "I were damned beneath all depth in Hell / But that I did proceed on just grounds," he says, just before the evidence is supplied him that he has indeed proceeded on unjust grounds. Then, as a deserved retribution for his crime, he calls on devils to whip him and roast him in sulphur. But in thus damning himself he is presumptuously playing God, while overlooking the divine Spirit to which Desdemona's action has testified. Blindly he imagines that when "we meet at compt," her look will "hurl my soul from Heaven"; whereas, in fact, only his own pride is doing that. Confusedly he wishes to prove himself "honorable" by killing himself.

Is it true, then, that Othello has loved "not wisely but too well"? Surely not in the sense that he has loved Desdemona too well. Rather, he has loved her not enough, through unwisely loving too well his own honor. A quasi-religion of honor guides his final "sacrifice" of himself.[82] We may say of his suicide that it is related to Christian sacrifice by disjunctive analogy—just as Dante's bleeding wood-of-the-suicides is inversely analogous to the holy wood of Calvary. It is we, however, and not Othello, who can understand it thus. His vision must be from within a narrower frame than that which is implied in the play's total design.

6 The imagery's import in *Romeo and Juliet*

From a traditional Christian point of view suicide is always sinful, except when the consequence of a special command from God (as in Samson's case), or when the mind is deranged, as is plainly the case in Ophelia's death. Does a play such as *Romeo and Juliet* imply this same general judgment? Does its structure suggest that its author was understanding the tragedy from a Christian point of view? This is a lively issue in Shakespeare criticism, and one which can properly challenge our careful analysis. If we are to deal with it, however, we must consider the suicide of the lovers in its full dramatic context, in which it arises as the culmination of the whole action of the story and not as an isolated episode. Further, we need not suppose that Shakespeare's intent is to moralize—in any case, not on the literal suicide, which may be (as for Cleopatra) merely the consequence of a prior and more basic sin. As a playwright of tragedy, Shakespeare is seeking, we may assume, to exercise and purge our pity and fear by what he reveals. His aim is not to blame but, as artist, to imitate action while including the action's moral quality in the imitation. What must concern us, then, is the poetic diction and symbolism through which that moral quality is revealed. As in our analysis of *Othello,* we can likewise in the present play use the imagery of tragedy to question the romantic perspective on tragedy.

The romantic reading of *Romeo and Juliet,* which prevails even in recent commentary, holds that the lovers are flawless victims of circumstances, or mischance, or a malign fate. G. I. Duthie, for instance, takes this view in his edition of the play.[83] After debating whether the lovers are in any way responsible for their doom, he concludes that it is "not part of the basic design" that we should regard their fate "as directly caused, even partly, by their own character flaws." There is nothing we can hold against Romeo, he believes, unless we insist on "the (admitted) validity of moral conceptions that have no meaning for Shakespeare in this play." How can we blame Romeo, he asks, for killing himself on believing Juliet dead, "since he has, from his first vision of her, regarded her as his whole life"?

This critic's own final clause, however, can be our clue to Shakespeare's answer. That is, Romeo's regard for Juliet as his "whole life" is at the root of the tragedy, because of the idolatry and self-deception involved in such an attitude.[84] The lovers idolize each other, and in doing so make a religion of their passion. The first clear signal of this fact comes at a point structurally important in every Shakespearean tragedy, the end of Act I. Here, in a love duet antiphona. y sung, Romeo casts himself in the role of a pilgrim visiting his "saint" Juliet and seeking as the "fine" of his devotion —that is, both as its "end" and as its penitential "satisfaction"—a kiss at her "holy shrine." Juliet is in a mood sympathetic to this imaginary saint worship. She asks for service in the form of prayers to herself, since "Saints do not move, though grant for prayers' sake." Already in imagination she is here eternizing herself as an immovable deity, foreshadowing dramatically her role in the tomb in Act V. In kissing her, Romeo sees his kiss as a prayer, and her lips as a purging absolution: "Then move not while my prayer's effect I take. / Thus from my lips by thine my sin is purged." But at this point, half breaking the spell, comes the wit commentary of a more realistic logic:

> JUL.   Then have my lips the sin that they have took.
> ROM. Sin from my lips? Oh, trespass sweetly urged!
>   Give me my sin again.
> JUL.   You kiss by the book.

By what "book" have they kissed? The context of a worship involving secret "sin" suggests the Book of Courtly Love. Is this perhaps Verona's code-book for courtesy and "mannerly" love?[85]

The comments of critics on this scene have been various and inconclusive. Let me cite a few:

> It is hard to see what better first encounter could have been devised. . . . There is something sacramental in this ceremony, something shy and grave and sweet; it is a marriage made already. And she is such a child; touched to earnestness by his trembling earnestness, but breaking into fun at last . . ."—Granville-Barker.[86]

> . . . instead of the long and tedious process of getting acquainted and making love, there is a wooing which is lifted above the level of life by rime and brought within the compass of a sonnet. This way of courting and mating is appropriate in Shakespeare's romantic Verona . . . —E. E. Stoll.[87]

> This is a strange conversation for a boy and a girl. Certainly, it is not Shakespeare's aim to mirror nature here. Do romance and poetry explain it fully? I hardly think so. The religious imagery is too insistent, too sustained. It suggests allegory.—John Vyvyan.[88]

By "allegory," Vyvyan here means the theme that love is a pilgrimage, which he judges to be the play's meaning. Though he thinks its elaboration unnatural as conversation between wooers, he supposes that Shakespeare is thereby announcing a religious love like Dante's, which for Romeo will replace the "fume of sighs" of his earlier vain fantasy over Rosaline. Stoll would justify it, rather, as a convention of romantic courtship, appropriate to Verona, and acceptable to a theatre audience because of the "high poetical ways of talking generally" which Shakespeare is stage-managing to charm us emotionally. Granville-Barker, on the other hand, seems to regard it as in character for expressing the shy but "sacramental" feelings of marriage-minded young lovers. Juliet's final line, "You kiss by the book," he interprets as a bit of fun for hiding her childlike embarrassment. But none of these three critics is paying attention to the delight in worship and "trespass" with which the lovers are bookishly conducting their courtship.

Would Dante have seen here an anticipation of sacramental marriage—or merely its mock image? Has Romeo cast off his former "artificial night"—or is he but re-creating it now with Juliet's co-operation? (The wit and the spirit of this wooing is far different from the public jesting of the ladies and lords in *Love's Labor's Lost*. There romantic love was treated as a fanciful "humour" to be mocked in the process of attaining self-knowledge.) Romeo is taking his religious conceits seriously. He continues them in his sighs to "dear saint" and "fair saint" in the orchard scene, when he has "night's cloak" to hide him and Juliet has "the mask of night" to screen her blushes. Benvolio, who has followed Romeo as far as the orchard wall, has commented: "Blind is his love, and best befits the dark." Although Benvolio at this point does not know of Romeo's new mistress, his comment seems applicable beyond his immediate ken. Romeo has entered this orchard, as he entered the earlier party, as an interloper self-invited. Yet we see him translating his action in terms of sacred vocation, even though he is half-aware of its mundane aspect as a venturing for "merchandise." His quest has had its start, perhaps emblematically, in his being able to read "the letters and the language" (I. ii. 63) of a guest list. May Shakespeare be suggesting, figuratively, that Romeo is a superficial reader of love's *letters*—one who impetuously turns their meaning into the "trespass sweetly urged" of his fashionable sonneteering?

Metaphors of book and reading in connection with love are recurrent in the play. Romeo's love, the Friar remarks (II, iii. 88), "did read by rote and could not spell." The Friar here has in mind Romeo's rumored love for Rosaline; yet his comment may be, for Shakespeare, equally pertinent to the love Romeo has begun to devote to Juliet. And meanwhile we have witnessed an earlier scene which turns about the theme of Juliet's "reading." We have overheard Lady Capulet (in I. iii.) instructing Juliet in the ritual of love quest: she is to "read o'er" the volume of a "face" at a nighttime feast, to find out what her "liking" is. In this "precious book of love," Lady Capulet goes on to say, Juliet will discover an "unbound" lover, who lacks only a "cover" to beautify him. Obviously this metaphor involves wordplay: by Lady Capulet at a social level ("unbound" meaning "bachelor"); but by Shakespeare, no doubt, at two further levels—the sexual ("unbound" meaning "naked"), and the moral ("unbound" in the sense of "irresponsible," a lover who needs the cover of some disguise or "mask" for his self-abandonment).

The book of love, evidently, has lurking ambiguities. For who is this prospective lover? Lady Capulet has in mind the "valiant Paris," kinsman to Verona's prince. But she is unaware of another lover of more bookish face, the legendary Paris who may be hidden in Verona's Romeo. Will not Juliet, by her liking for this secret lover, become the "face" that launches Romeo's ship on dangerous seas? We will hear later of the dashing rocks which Romeo as voyager welcomes and dares (V. iii. 118), because he thinks to find "immortal blessing" (II. iii. 37) in Juliet's kiss—as did the ancient Paris (or Marlowe's Faustus) in Helen's.[89] Juliet is idolized as Romeo's sole "Heaven"—once he has ignored his own mind's premonitory warning of the dire consequences that may lurk in the "night's revels" at Capulet's house. Rashly he entrusts the "steerage of my course" to a nameless "He" (I. iv. 112), who is later identified by allusion as the blind god, Cupid (II. ii. 80–81).[90] This is courtly love's hidden story, which Lady Capulet does not realize may lie in the "book" Juliet will read. She promises:

> That book in many's eyes doth share the glory
> That in gold clasps locks in the golden story.
> So shall you share all that he doth possess,
> By having him, making yourself no less.

But, actually, what glory will he—the lover whose golden story Juliet will find to her liking as she reads love's book—come to possess and share with her? Juliet will later glimpse the undercover truth: a "serpent heart" beneath the "flowering face" (III. ii. 73).

> Was ever book containing such vile matter
> So fairly bound?

Courtly love's book is indeed fairly bound—bound, one may say, as blind Cupid is in much medieval iconography, "hoodwinked with a scarf" (I. iv. 4).

The book by which Romeo loves, and Juliet too, teaches "faith" and pilgrimage. We have noted this language in the sonnet of I. v. 95, and its significance is later highlighted when Mercutio calls Romeo a "Young Abraham Cupid" (II. i. 13). Abraham is the Bible's paradigm for a pilgrim of faith. But there is a Shakespearean irony in associating his name with Cupid. For in what sense are Cupid's devotees like Abraham? Are they not blind versions of Abraham? Cupidinous lovers, as the play will indicate, are led by a faith—in glories of the "eye," the "I," and the "aye" (that shadow-trinity on which Shakespeare puns in III. ii. 45–50); and by a hope —of the promised land of a dark orchard and its bitter-sweet fruit; and by a love—of passion itself as "death-devouring." Are not these the shadow-virtues of a false religion? (Compare Olivia's comment in *Twelfth Night* I. v. 246, when told of the first "chapter" in Orsino's book of love: "Oh, I have read it. It is heresy.")

In obedience to *eros* and *liebestod*, Romeo can overleap walls, alike mural and moral. Significantly, he is ready from the start to put off his Christian name at Juliet's suggestion.

> I take thee at thy word.
> Call me but love, and I'll be new baptised.
> Henceforth I never will be Romeo.

Elizabethan auditors, if witty enough to recall their theology's association of rebaptism with Anabaptist heresy, may well have been startled by Romeo's vow here. Juliet herself is startled a bit: "What *man* art thou that, thus *bescreened in night,* / So *stumblest* on my counsel." I have italicized the *sententia* I think Shakespeare is conveying. Juliet, of course, understands only the literal sense of her words. She is intuitive enough, however, to sense an impropriety when Romeo goes on to offer to swear by the moon. She edits out the inconstant moon, asking Romeo to swear rather by "thy gracious self, / Which is the god of my idolatry" (II. ii. 13–14). But is this revised oath any less auspicious of tragedy?

A moment later, Juliet's native intuition warns her that her contract has been "too unadvised," too much like lightning, and without joy. But then, reaching for some cover for her love, she rushes into her plan for a secret marriage. In Act III, similarly, she can recognize but suppress her glimpse of Romeo as "beautiful tyrant," and thus can turn to naming him, without shame, her "true knight." Rather than be untrue to this knight of her night, Juliet will later declare herself ready to leap

> From off the battlements of yonder tower;
> Or walk in thievish ways; or bid me lurk
> Where serpents are; . . . (IV. i. 78–80)

In these lines Shakespeare has hidden an allusion to the Temptation of the Tower (in Luke 4:9 the temptation to vainglory), and an allusion to its parallel (in Gen. 3:5), the temptation to be "as gods" by accepting a serpent's thievish dare. All readers of Milton should immediately recognize such allusions. It is a curious fact that most readers of Shakespeare have not.

In Juliet's epithalamium, sung in solitude and not as a community hymeneal, we find numerous half-submerged images of Blind Cupid. Here at the center of the play (III. ii), Shakespeare by his motifs is enlightening his audience as to the "dark" nature of the lovers' love:

> Spread thy close curtain, love-performing night,
> That runaways' eyes may wink, and Romeo
> Leap to these arms, untalked of and unseen.
> Lovers can see to do their amorous rites
> By their own beauties; or, if love be blind,
> It best agrees with night.

Curtaining night, runaways' eyes, an "unseen" lover welcomed with a winking leap—these are the images by which Juliet invokes a blind love,[91] that she may learn "how to lose a winning match." The winning "match" that is lost in being won is more than sexual in its range of connotation. It suggests, morally, the Pyrrhic victory in which the play will end, and also carries wordplay on "match" —in the triple sense of "paired" lovers, love as a "game," and a putting of "fire" to the powder which (so Friar Laurence has remarked, III. i. 10) will "consume with a kiss" and in its triumph die, like a flash in the night. The game is but keener, the sport of it more aristocratic, if the hawk be "hooded," as Juliet wishes herself to be as she continues her epithalamium. More truly than she knows, Juliet is "sold" to a bit of white snow on a raven's back. She is "in love with night" and would banish the sun. In her "heaven," let Romeo substitute for the sun—when he is dead and "cut up in little stars" to give heaven a proper "face"! This is a love which worships face. It also harbors a death wish, in its longings for a cosmic immortality. But the immortality of stellification, obviously, is paganism's substitute for Christian transcendence. What it transcends is not sin and sorrow, which it secretly loves, but instead human community and life itself. True, Juliet's and Romeo's love is no crude sensualism;[92] it is an idealistic eroticism. Yet it truncates both Platonic and Christian mysticism by lacking the final goal of Plato's *eros,* union with an invisible beauty; and it is notably devoid of the gift of Christian *agape,* which finds fulfilment in actions of caretaking and husbandry.

It is significant, I think, that when the lovers part in the morning after their night of love, neither one of them so much as suggests that, instead of parting, they go together to Mantua. Juliet had pled to go with Romeo in Arthur Brooke's version of the story; but to Shakespeare any such concern for the daytime needs of the fellow lover seemed improbable for the kind of love his drama is presenting. He therefore beautifies the lovers' parting, instead, with a daysong which scholarship can trace to models in the cult literature of courtly love, and on which Francis Fergusson has commented:

> There is something sinister about Courtly Love and its Daysongs. In that tradition love is always amoral, all-powerful, and so wonderful that it can be fulfilled only in or through death. The common, daylight world is always love's enemy, the secret night its only friend. It is appropriate that the Daysong should be the form of the scene which marks the turning point in the story [of Romeo and Juliet].[93]

On the whole psychology and myth of courtly love, recent perspective has been aided by Denis de Rougemont's study. He noted as typical features of this love the following: a twin narcissism in the lovers; their half-conscious wish for suffering and death; their secret need for some "obstruction" to the course of their love in order to stimulate *askesis*; the motif of love as religion and as war; and the story-motif of a love-potion as an alibi for passion. Finding these features in Tristan and Iseult, he pointed to Romeo and Juliet as exhibiting a similar pattern.[94] Miss Mahood, in following up this lead, has traced in Shakespeare's play the *leitmotiv* of Death as bridegroom, and has noted also the ambiguity in the Prologue's reference to the "death-marked love" of Romeo and Juliet. This phrase can mean either a love "marked out for death," foredoomed; or it can mean a love which takes death as "its objective," its sea-mark in sailing. The first meaning suggests helpless lovers; the second suggests lovers who elect to die.[95] Romantic readers of the play, by taking the upper side of the phrase, have supposed the Prologue to refer to some thwarting by malignant stars. But why not the undermeaning, that the lovers have their stars crossed—that is, they sail by a mistaken light?

The whole texture of the play, it seems to me, carries a tension between these two perspectives. The first represents the surface sense by which the lovers interpret their doom. The second reveals a deeper truth which they fugitively glimpse and ignore, but which a sophisticated audience can see full well by attending to their actions and to Shakespeare's diction. Many auditors may miss seeing it, of course, while the play is in motion. Yet they can have second thoughts when remembering the play's accumulative design—the figural content which haunts the literal. No work of art is complete in the immediate impression it gives. It calls for rumination—like that redigestion which biblical commentators saw as praiseworthy in animals that "chew the cud."

It was standard Christian teaching, both in medieval and in Elizabethan times, that the stars cannot cause any act of human choice, unless a man willingly gives over his mind to their influence. Their power was described as solely that of inclining the mind through influencing the body and its humors—not a sufficient cause of choice in any wise or temperate man. "For all that results therefrom," Aquinas explained, "are certain passions, more or less violent; and passions, however violent, are not a sufficient cause of choosing, since the same passions lead the incontinent to follow them by choice, and fail to induce the continent man."[96] Intemperance is due to a defect of will; for man has the power of taking counsel in all matters relative to his actions, as to whether to give his passions a loose or a tight rein, and as to what kind of good he uses them to pursue.

Shakespeare's play gives us, at the beginning of Act V, an instance of how Romeo neglects his mind's power of taking counsel. Romeo is shown thinking on a dream he has had, that Juliet came and found him dead but miraculously revived him by her kisses; he is imagining a restorative love. But a moment later, when Balthazar arrives with a report of Juliet's funeral, Romeo rejects Balthazar's plea for patience and gives way to his own despair. Thus he puts aside his former hopeful thought, which he might have found potentially true, had he but taken the trouble to seek out the Friar for information. His cry, "Then I defy you, stars!" is paradoxical. For while it testifies verbally to Romeo's belief in freedom of choice, he in fact is choosing not to use his reason to investigate, but instead is giving way to the "mischief" that is "swift to enter the thoughts of desperate men" (line 36). In the name of free will, he is giving rein to "pale and wild" looks and to a suicidal purpose. Intemperately, he is taking his passion as his star.

Many interpreters of Act I have supposed a radical change in Romeo when he first meets Juliet. In his mooning over Rosaline they recognize all the symptoms of a post-Petrarchan love-sickness, but imagine that all this is cured when he finds "real" love. Actually, however, what he discovered was but another object of worship, a Juliet-"sun" instead of coldly Diana-like Rosaline. Whereas Rosaline would not "ope her lap to saint-seducing gold," Juliet reciprocates Romeo's love. Through this experience he becomes more sociable. Yet the change merely accords with Benvolio's recipe:

> Tut, man, one fire burns out another's burning.
> One pain is lessened by another's anguish.
> Turn giddy, and be holp by backward turning,
> One desperate grief cures with another's languish.
> Take thou some new infection to thy eye,
> And the rank poison of the old will die. (I. ii. 46–51)

With Juliet, Romeo has a new "infection." It represents, in fact, a turning "backward"—to a clandestine love, which socially is "giddy." But is it not the same "religion of mine eye" as was affirmed in I. ii. 93?

"Minds swayed by eyes are full of turpitude"—so Shakespeare tells us in his *Troilus* (V. ii. 112). Romeo is Troy-like in his loves. Or, if we may refer to another paradigm, he is like the "courtly" young man of ancient Carthage, whom St. Augustine describes as follows in his *Confessions:*

> I sought what I might love, in love with loving, and safety I hated . . . For within me was a famine of that inward food, Thyself, O God; yet through that famine I was not hungered; but was without all longing for incorruptible sustenance. . . . To love then, and to be beloved, was sweet to me; but more when I obtained to enjoy the person I loved. . . . I would fain, through exceeding vanity, be fine and courtly. I fell headlong then into the love wherein I longed to be ensnared. (III. i. Pusey's translation)

Does such a portrait differ from what we are told of Romeo by the Chorus as Prologue to Act II of the play? The facts (if we omit their theological interpretation) are the same: "young affection" gapes to be heir to "old desire." So (the italics are mine) :

> Now Romeo is beloved and loves again,
>   *Alike bewitched* with the charm of looks,
> But to his foe supposed he must complain
>   And she *steal* love's *sweet bait* from fearful hooks.

That Juliet is his "supposed" foe[97] adds challenge to the adventure.

Fortunately, Juliet is "as much in love" as Romeo. Mercutio, who does not know this, is nevertheless not wrong, symbolically speaking, when he associates Romeo's beloved with Dido, Cleopatra, Helen, and Thisbe. All are types of tragic amour-passion. Of Dido's secret love with Aeneas, Virgil had written: "she calls it marriage and with that name veils her sin" (*Aeneid* VI. 172). Juliet veils hers with the outward form of a marriage rite by Friar Laurence,[98] but in a context having little or none of the inward purpose a church marriage should signify. Essentially, hers is a Carthaginian type of love, only more youthful than Dido's. The youthfulness of Romeo and Juliet allies them, of course, to Pyramus and Thisbe, whose legend in Ovid is the generally acknowledged "source" of the Romeo and Juliet legend. But what Shakespeare thought of Pyramus and Thisbe we can easily infer, if we but glance at his comic treatment of their tragedy in a play being written during this same year, 1594, *A Midsummer Night's Dream.* Here appear, delightfully exaggerated, the basic motifs of amour-passion: the "lanthorn" by which Pyramus and Thisbe love is the moon; they commit suicide by "old Ninny's tomb";[99] the lion that threatens them is actually harmless; and they expend their passion, first, in thanking the "wicked" but yet "sweet and lovely wall" for providing them a chink to "blink through," and later in equally rhetorical invocations of "Furies fell," fate, tears, and death. It takes only a change of artistic tone to transfer this farce into the vein of high tragedy, as Shakespeare does in *Romeo and Juliet*. Morally, the substance is the same.

Why, incidentally, has Shakespeare invented Mercutio, out of little but a name in Brooke's account? Does Mercutio function in the play, as some commentators feel, as the scoffing sensualist who sets off by contrast the idealistic love of Romeo? Or is he the pure poet of the Queen Mab speech, which other readers adore for its soaring imagination? Perhaps he is something of both; but how exactly? Critics such as Schücking and Shaw have been puzzled by a disturbing inconsistency in Mercutio's exhibiting, on the one hand, a lighthearted poetic and, on the other hand, an indecent wit; and Granville-Barker has remarked in disappointment that we learn little about Mercutio "unless it be that a man may like smut and fairy-tales too."[100]

Basically, I would suggest, Shakespeare is using Mercutio as a kind of internal chorus, by whom Romeo's love is being assessed with a two-sided realism. One side is the ethical realism of the speech on Queen Mab (I. iv). Note that under all the delicate fancy with which this Queen is described, she is also called a "hag." She is the midwife of earthly dreams—making lawyers dream on fees, ladies on kisses, and a soldier on the cutting of throats. And she elicits these dreams, we are told, by a touch of moonshine, spider web, and film. Surely this speech is more than decorative. Shakespeare through Mercutio is here defining Verona's courtly world, by telling us the nature of the "fairy" who captivates human beings to the service of cupidity in its many forms. At the same time it lends irony to Mercutio's character, in that he does nothing to use his wisdom toward curbing his own "vain fantasy" for quarreling. He merely accepts this human foible lightheartedly, while taunting even the cautious Benvolio with it. "Why, thou wilt quarrel with a man," he jests (III. i), for tying his new shoes with old ribbon, "And yet thou wilt tutor *me* from quarreling!"

Mercutio is as fatalistic about his own "humour" as about the humour of the madman-lover which he recognizes in Romeo. His fatalism, in fact, is analogous to Romeo's; and so is his fashion-mongering sword play. He is, so to speak, a bolder and more worldly version of Romeo. Just as he knows that lovers (including Romeo) are victims of a hag-fairy, so also he knows, and wittily says just before his Queen Mab speech, that Romeo's love is a sexual game. And since Mercutio's scenes of jesting are by Shakespeare sandwiched before and after Romeo's scenes of lovemaking to Juliet, hints are thereby offered to the audience that Romeo's "idealistic" love is, after all, grounded in bewitching dream on the one hand and idle sport, wild-goose chase, on the other. With a wit that is both bawdy and metaphysical, Mercutio likens Romeo to "a great natural that runs lolling up and down to hide his bauble in a hole." Romeo is a fool—that is, just as every "natural" man is when pursuing an antic love.

But Mercutio is also important, thematically, in pointing up the analogy between love song and dueling. Tybalt, he says, "fights as you sing prick song." By thus linking love duet with duelling, Mercutio prepares the audience for Romeo's shift from the one to the other. Implicit here is the idea that these are but the two sides of one coin: fashionable quarreling and courtly romancing are polar activities. Both have been foreshadowed earlier in Romeo's own salute to "brawling love" and "loving hate"—the twin emotions belonging to the "Misshapen chaos of well-seeming forms" which Romeo reproves yet desires. As polar forms of "Serious vanity," they are rooted in a dialectic I have already noted; namely, that a religion of the "eye" is paradoxically also a religion of the "I"—that is, of self-esteem. Hence when Romeo feels his reputation at stake, after his naive efforts at peacemaking between Tybalt and Mercutio have miscarried and disgraced him, he can rush to meet Tybalt with a "fire-eyed fury" that actually outdoes Tybalt's. Shakespeare, in order to bring out this point of Romeo's concern for self-esteem, has had to change Brooke's version, in which Romeo fought solely for physical self-defense.

In Act V, for the same reason, Shakespeare again departs from Brooke by adding Romeo's slaying of Paris. This later episode clinches the thematic paradox of "brawling love," along with the moral paradox of "sin" committed out of devotion to a "face" supposed heavenly. No wonder there is so much oxymoron in the rheotoric of this drama; it highlights the pointedly foolish behavior of the lovers. Incidentally, let me recall that Augustine's description of his Carthaginian period was loaded with oxymorons—such as "barren seed plots," "beclouded brightness," and so forth (*Confessions* II. ii). Such is the similar state of Verona in a hot July.

The action of Romeo's visit to the tomb is shaped by Shakespeare as a kind of upside-down analogy to the Easter story. To the sepulchre of his beloved, Romeo hastens with mattock and crowbar to force open the "jaws" of death, that he may there set up his "everlasting rest" with worms! He comes, by torchlight, to engage in what Paris rightly calls "unhallowed toil." He slays Paris for attempting to stop him, then prepares himself for a "dateless bargain to engrossing death."[101] Hailing Juliet's beauty as a feast of light, he raises and drinks his cup of poison—a kind of blind *figura* of the Christian Mass. Since in the time scheme of the play it is now Thursday night, we recognize here a celebration which travesties the Thursday Last Supper of Christ. Romeo's rite climaxes a religion of love which has transcended reason—but by plunging into desperate dream. His devotion to *eros* has become a shadow-aping of *agape*. It is significant, also, that this takes place just before Lammastide—that season in the church year when the first fruits of the earth are offered up to God. For in Romeo's offering of his youthful manhood to the "lean abhorred monster" Death, and in Juliet's similar offering of her newly ripe womanhood, we have a tragic parody of Lammastide festival. An oath of old Capulet's, uttered earlier in the play, may have a thematic pertinence: "God's bread! It makes me mad." He and all Verona make mad use of God's bread.

In connection with the symbolism of the play's time scheme, I should like to hazard a further observation. Shakespeare has clearly located the action within five days, between around nine o'clock on a Sunday morning (I. i. 167) and very early on a Friday morning (V. iii. 203). Now if we recall that Christ's Passion began with his trial on the midmorning of a Friday and culminated in his resurrection at dawn on a Sunday, we can say that *his* Passion occupied exactly that portion of the week *not* occupied by Verona's drama of amour-passion. Is this fact a mere happenstance? May not Shakespeare be deliberately assigning to the "misadventured piteous overthrows" (Prologue I) of Cupid's saints a placing in the non-salvific portion of the week? Both Dante and Chaucer in some of their works used specific time-settings for symbolic purposes.[102] Why not Shakespeare? We can think of other reasons, of course, for his limiting the action of *Romeo and Juliet* to a few days, rather than spreading it over the nine months of Brooke's account: speed is necessary to the "mood" of the impetuous love being dramatized; it serves also to prevent the surface reader from scenting too easily an illicitness in the love affair;[103] and further, a compression of the events tightens dramatic unity. But these dramaturgic reasons cannot account for the particular span of days Shakespeare chose.

In Brooke's version, we may recall, the first meeting of Romeo and Juliet was placed during "the Christmas games," and the slaying of Tybalt on the Monday after Easter. Was Brooke aware, we may wonder, of the irony of having the lovers begin their "unhonest desire" (as he calls it) under the aegis of Christmas; or of placing the feud's new "mischief" on the day after Easter? Perhaps he was simply following Bandello's chronology, which is the same. Yet when Brooke in his September graveyard scene has Romeus say, "Helpe Peter, . . . helpe to remove the stone," is he not deliberately echoing Easter language, probably for the sake of irony? Sensing Brooke's fumbling attempts at Christian irony, Shakespeare seems to have decided on a better way for focusing this implication.

Shakespeare's irony begins with the opening of his play—in the fact that at nine,[104] on a day we later discover was a Sunday, no one in Verona seems to think of attending church. This small detail Elizabethans might have retrospectively noticed, since their own government levied fines for nonattendance at church. Consider, moreover, the meaning of Sunday: theoretically it owes its origin to Easter, and represents an extending of Easter by memorializing its mystery as the foundation for the community's each new week. We of a post-Christian temper may have forgotten this fact, yet it is embedded in our society's calendar. In Verona, similarly, the hot sun of July is having much more influence than Easter's supernatural Sun. Servants such as Sampson and Gregory are itching for a fray, talking cockily of their preference for "choler" over a "collar" and for "flesh" over "fish." Their markedly unregenerate mood contrasts ironically with the historic connotations of their own Christian names (i.e., with the ideal Samson, who bowed himself to serve God, or the ideal Gregory, who as Pope embraced the shepherding concept of "servant of the servants of God").

Quite evidently, Verona is a city of backsliding Christians, and that fact is important to Shakespeare's setting for his story. Within this setting there then develops the blindly heroic love of Romeo and Juliet, which culminates in suicide at about the very hour on a Friday morning when Peter wrongly drew his sword at Gethsemane. And Friar Laurence, a moment later, betrays his calling by fleeing out of fear, as the weak Peter had done. Could Shakespeare have had in mind the biblical paradigms of Holy Week? Let us say merely that the shape of his drama permits our sensing, on reflection, analogies which lend a penumbra of implicit irony to the literal action in the play. Verona's passion drama closes appropriately on a gloomy dawn, with the sun clouded or not yet risen (V. iii. 305) and its Prince Escalus fumbling to clear up the night's ambiguities by a trial hearing. Is this situation unlike Pilate's of ages ago—when he asked "What is truth?" and would not stay for an answer?

The drama ends also with Capulet and Montague burying their feud with a handshake. This gesture is noble; yet its motive may be little more than their instinctual desire for a self-rehabilitation in the public eye. Their Prince has just moralized the calamity as a punishment by Heaven on their hate. Understandably, they respond with shows of love to cover their disgrace. But we note that no tears are shed (even though Romeo's mother has been shedding them, and in fact has died of grief during the night). And there is an unmistakable undertone of rivalry, with a tinge even of commercialism, as the fathers contend in promising statues of gold in honor of their dead children. May Shakespeare be suggesting here a ceremony by which Verona is canonizing new household gods, to minister henceforth to the city's religion of the eye?

Some of the play's auditors may remember at this point that gold was called "saint seducing" in Act I. Or they may recall Romeo's wayside comment on gold in Act V: "worse poison to man's souls," he calls it, than the murdering drugs the destitute apothecary sells. Or other readers may recall the delusiveness of gold in Shakespeare's *Merchant of Venice*. "Gilded tombs do worms infold. . . . Your suit is cold" was the message given the Moroccan prince when he unlocked the golden casket he had chosen. Of if we turn to *Troilus and Cressida,* the body of an unnamed man in "goodly armor," so "fair without" but "putrified" at the core, seems to be Shakespeare's emblem for the fate of a pagan chivalry of love and war. Although Verona achieves a temporary peace through the "Poor sacrifices" it makes, we may doubt that these will suffice for a long-lasting peace. (Bandello in his account remarks that the peace did not last any great while afterwards.) There has been attained, as the play's Prologue promised, a burying of strife—but not of the human proclivity to one-up-manship. It is the Earthly City's peace, useful for its moment of civil agreement, yet far short of a heavenly peace, which St. Augustine had described as a "most harmonious fellowship in the enjoyment of God and of one another in God."[105]

The "golden story" of I. iii. 92 has thus come to its close, with little real self-discovery by Verona's participants in the drama. We may note that Prince Escalus, while politely including himself in the dictum "All are punished," does so in a glancing way which deflects the major blame on others—"And I, for winking at *your* discords . . . ." The phrase almost praises, indirectly, his own good nature. But did he, in fact, wink at discords? That is scarcely the impression he has given in the play's opening scene. There he thundered at them and threatened death to future brawlers. What he has chiefly winked at, we may say, is his true duty as a ruler, his duty to work out a reconciliation by group conference. He has substituted, like a policeman, a few separate summonses for laying down the law:

> You, Capulet, shall go along with me,
> And, Montague, come you this afternoon.

Thus the antagonists are never brought together in his chamber, but instead Escalus has paraded his own authority in the public eye —as he does again at the end of the play. This has been substituted, moreover, for any genuine policing of the streets—with the result that Romeo, and later Paris, get themselves into trouble through benevolently but unwisely undertaking to do the Prince's work for him, when undeputized they try to arrest a brawler.

In Act III, the Prince's only other appearance, he has blinked at Benvolio's testimony and swept under the rug the question of justice. Here his primary concerns were to placate Lady Capulet's demand for revenge and at the same time to display himself as merciful through reducing his edict of death to mere banishment— which of course simply shoved the genuine problem out of sight, and prevented discovery of the secret marriage which, had it been revealed, could immediately have ended the civic problem by reconciling the houses. At the close of Brooke's version of the story, we may recall, the nurse is upbraided by the Prince because the marriage

> . . . might have wrought much good, had it in time been knowne,
> Where now by her concealing it, a mischief great has growne.

Yet this speaker (and Brooke too) lacks an awareness of how the Prince himself has contributed to concealment. By failing to examine Romeo, has he not failed to nurse justice? Shakespeare, unlike Brooke, knows the Prince to be morally no better than the socially inferior nurse on whom Brooke, moralistically, has his "sage" Escalus decree a severe punishment. Shakespeare's view is given us indirectly through the Friar's comment that the Prince has "rushed aside the law" (III. iii. 26). We may miss seeing and seizing the import of this remark because (by the dramatist's irony) the Prince's act is being accounted praiseworthy by the Friar, who foolishly is telling Romeo: "This is dear mercy and thou see'st it not." Actually, it is dear in the sense of *costly* to the state and to that general welfare which both a Prince and a Friar should be guarding. Yet no one in Verona perceives the falseness of the "mercy" here practiced. Even we of the audience, if we are to catch the point, need the help of Shakespeare's latent wordplay on *dear* and on *see'st, seiz'st* and *ceased*. The play through its diction is challenging us to see into the tragedy's enigma, so that *we* may cease to be blind.

Shakespeare's Escalus all along has been practicing a patchwork politics in place of true statesmanship. We need to recognize that in this respect he is a blind and tragic ruler,[106] just as Friar Laurence, Verona's other official guardian of community welfare, is equally so and for the same reason, namely, a lasping into pretentious devices out of a kind of vanity for feeling important,[107] while neglecting thereby the heart of his responsibility. Moreover, these two heads of church and state have never conferred on community problems. Each has preferred doing things on his own. And this isolation of role (a strangely absolute separation of church and state) is reflected in analogous forms of individualism all the way down the social scale. Self-glory, by inducing mischances, is a basic cause of tragedy in Verona; and it is not eradicated even at the end.

Does Friar Laurence achieve humility, finally, when under arrest? Note the evasiveness of his plea: "And *if* aught in this / Miscarried by my fault, let my old life / Be sacrificed . . . ." Even in this very speech there are the twin faults of self-pity and of a winking at his own cowardice in having fled. Moreover, his recital of events distorts by suppressing telltale details. When he reports that "a noise did scare me from the tomb," he omits to say that this noise came from the watch, whom he knew to be approaching. Thus he evades seeing and admitting that what scared him, really, was not the "noise" but the prospect of loss of reputation if arrested. Similarly, when he reports that Juliet "would not go with me," he is omitting to confess that he had first proposed to "dispose" of her in a sisterhood, and then had disposed of his own responsibilities of "brotherhood" by forsaking her. It is all very analogous to Romeo's behavior: he too had fled, not taking Juliet with him when he left Verona, and never thinking to stay by her side and confess to the authorities his guilty secret. "Discovery" on the part of the chief persons in a Shakespearean tragedy seems to be limited, usually, to the discovery of being trapped by some mischance or fate, with little or no accompanying perception of how one's own moral fault has led him into the trap. The human proclivity for evasion is the drama's covert truth. Friar Laurence can mention in his report (line 233) "their stol'n marriage day," yet fail to infer from this his own complicity in thievishness.

Shakespeare's Friar differs significantly from the Friar of Brooke's poem. He lives a life more remote from his parish, is less active in professional services, and less learned. When old Capulet and Escalus speak well of him, their words imply acquaintance from a distance, no firsthand knowledge. Shakespeare has omitted the following details from Brooke's account: the Friar's "Doctor of Divinity" degree; his popularity for wisdom, which caused both the old and the young in Verona to run to him for his offices of "shrift"; his having served as a spiritual guide to Romeus from earliest childhood; his advising against a clandestine marriage, forcing Romeus to postpone it, and agreeing to it finally out of a concern, mainly, to avoid the couple's living in sin; his providing Romeus and Juliet with premarital instruction and submitting them to shrift before the ceremony; his conscientious self-examination when confessing to Prince Escalus, declaring himself innocent of murder but admitting that his soul is somewhat spotted with the "small and easy crime" of having put in use his "ancient artes" of potion making; his confessing that he hid himself from "the watchmen" out of fear; his declaration that he considers himself, in God's eyes, "the sinfullest wretch of all"; and his retiring to a hermitage for lifelong penance after his acquittal from criminal charge. Brooke, in short, makes the Friar's fault that of a momentary compromising of conscience, which is later recognized as such. Shakespeare evidently thinks inappropriate to tragedy this kind and degree of self-discovery.

Brooke had prefaced his poem by telling the reader to behold in it the doings of "superstitious friars." In the poem itself the chief manifestation of superstition occurs when Friar Laurence, to rescue Juliet from a second marriage, backslides into resorting to a potion while rationalizing as follows:

> Deere daughter, quoth the fryer, of good cheere see thou be,
> For loe, saint Francis of his grace hath shewed a way to me,
> By which I may both thee, and Romeus together,
> Out of the bondage which you feare assuredly deliver.

Shakespeare no doubt felt this speech violated probability. That a learned Franciscan should thus misuse the authority of St. Francis, deliberately and with St. Francis in mind, was highly unlikely. It implied too much premeditation in wrong choice, rather than a simple-minded stumbling. Brooke's version here rests on a propagandistic Protestant conception of friarly duplicity; just as elsewhere his version takes a dig at the venality of friars by mentioning a secret room where, in the Friar's youth, he used to hide his feminine friends. Such aspersions Shakespeare avoids. Shakespeare, I think, was concerned to show "superstition" in a different and more subtle form, the form in which it can tempt everyman— the superstition of secularizing one's approach to human crises by turning to worldly nostrums rather than gospel mystery for a solution, and doing this impulsively out of an intention supposedly benevolent. Superstition in this sense is characteristic of all Verona. The irreligion of such action is never perceived by Shakespeare's Friar, any more than others in Verona ever perceive their own analogous idolatries.

To carry out this conception of the tragedy, the dramatist needs a morally naive friar, comparable to the naive lovers. Friar Laurence is therefore a bumbling romantic, seemingly more "innocent" than earlier authors had portrayed him.[108] Shakespeare knew, no doubt, that Franciscanism originally was nonacademic in temper. Its distinctive themes were two: fellowship with Christ's suffering, and companionship with nature in giving praise to God. In Laurence we see a friar in whom the first of these has disappeared. The second he retains—in the form of a love of nature so seemingly winsome that we may not notice how, in fact, it hollows out the Franciscan concept. Shakespeare has Laurence enter the play carrying a willow basket for collecting flowers and weeds—at a sunrise hour when, probably, most friars instead would be saying their prayers. This friar's plucked flowers are analogous, figuratively, to the proverbs and theological truisms we hear him speak. He is stocked with a nice handful of them, but in practice will be applying them apart from the contextual charity in which their meaning should root.[109] His baleful weeds, on the other hand, are analogous to the spurious comforts he will minister when lovesick youths come to him in their distress.

In Act III, when Romeo arrives tearful and remorseful over having slain Tybalt, why does not the Friar advise shrift and give him formal confessional counsel—or, more tactfully, an informal equivalent of shrift through some well-directed questions? What we overhear, instead, are worldly consolations which unwittingly travesty Franciscan teaching:

> What, rouse thee man! Thy Juliet is alive,
> For whose dear sake thou wast but lately dead.
> There art thou happy. Tybalt would kill thee,
> But thou slew'st Tybalt. There art thou happy too.
> The law, that threatened death, becomes thy friend
> And turns it to exile. There art thou happy.
> A pack of blessings lights upon thy back,
> Happiness courts thee in her best array;
> But, like a misbehaved and sullen wench,
> Thou pout'st upon thy fortune and thy love.

A homicide is here being numbered among "blessings," and Romeo is being urged to recognize, not his sins, but his triply happy good luck. He is misbehaving, he is told, by scowling at fortune. Let him rouse himself to a "manly" response and hasten to Juliet's bed! Through the Nurse's ecstatic approval* we get Shakespeare's ironic comment:

* The Nurse, of course, is a character type deriving from the bawd of Roman comedy. When we see her, on the way to the Friar's cell, calling on Peter to bring "my fan," perhaps Shakespeare is foreshadowing in this comic Peter, as in an emblem, the role Friar Laurence will figuratively play. This servant is called Peter, I suspect, to suggest an absurd likeness to his biblical namesake—as do, elsewhere, the servants Abraham and Sampson.

> Oh Lord, I could have stayed here all the night
> To hear good counsel. Oh, what learning is!

The "learning" is all being directed, we may note, toward reviving
a love which Romeo has referred to, only a moment earlier, as
"doting" (III. iii. 67). The Friar's proverb, that "madmen have
no ears" (line 61), is thus true ironically of himself, since instead
of seizing on this word "doting" as an occasion for offering correction by charity's norms, he is turning to "philosophy" and disputa-
tion ("Let me dispute with thee of thy estate").

Suicide is unreasonable, this friar argues, because it would be an
act of disloyalty to the self—to the self Romeo owes to Juliet, no
mention being made of the self's duty to God. For the alert spectator, there is beautiful irony in Laurence's saying:

> Thy wit, that ornament to shape and love,
> Misshapen in the conduct of them both,
> Like powder in a skill-less soldier's flask,
> Is set afire by thine own ignorance,
> And thou dismembered with thine own defense.

The Friar's own ignorance is here so misshaping his own "defense"
(a metaphor which carries wordplay reference to school disputa-
tions) that he is actually dismembering his role as cleric by setting
fire to his own wit—and in the process putting a match to the powder of romantic passion in the lovers, whom he has been warning
against the violent ends of violent delights.

Why does he not apply to himself, we ask, his earlier aphorism:
"Too swift arrives as tardy as too slow"? Or the maxim with
which, in Act II, he had concluded his impetuous decision in favor
of a clandestine marriage: "Wisely and slow. They stumble that
run fast"? By his ironic blindness to his own proverbs, the Friar
finds himself in Act V stumbling at "graves" in the night. For the
theatre audience, here is a visual emblem of an upside-down Franciscanism: a friar accoutred with "crow" and spade, spurring himself on with the pathetic cry, "Saint Francis be my speed!" When
his whole enterprise eventually collapses—predictably in muddle
rather than miracle—some of the play's thoughtful auditors might
respond to the Friar's evasive confession by murmuring:

> Be plain, good son, and homely in thy drift.
> Riddling confession makes but riddling shrift.

The interpretation I have been giving of the Friar differs both from the usual romantic one and also from the "Elizabethan" one proposed by Franklin Dickey. Dickey would see in Friar Laurence a "consistent voice of moderation and wisdom" opposing the gusts of passion in Romeo, and would argue that Romeo's "disregard of the Friar's reasonable counsels" dooms the lovers. He calls Laurence, therefore, "a true chorus whose words give the necessary moral base from which to judge the tragedy."[110] I accept the view that the Friar is a kind of chorus, but am concerned to point out how inconsistent and tragic his choral "wisdom" is. It miscounsels Romeo, and later Juliet, by ignoring the Christian standard incumbent upon all clergymen and especially Franciscans. When, for instance, the Friar upbraids Romeo for "hollow perjury" to "Thy dear love sworn," he is thinking only of Juliet and quite overlooking the "dear love" to which every Christian swears allegiance at baptism, and which every Franciscan binds himself to practice. The Friar's very perspective here is a perjury to his Ordination vow. Or, again, when at the mock funeral for Juliet the Friar moralizes to the parents,

> Oh, in this love, you love your child so ill
> That you run mad . . .

is there not dramatic irony in that he himself, by his ill love for their child, is now running mad with pretenses for his own face-saving? "Confusions cure lies not in these confusions," he says; and this statement, by Shakespeare's irony, is truer than its speaker knows. To this irony we may ascribe also Laurence's use, ten times in his funeral sermon, of the pronoun "you" or "your"—but only once of the pronoun "us," and then in a usage which lacks all compassion:

> For though fond nature bids us all lament,
> Yet nature's tears are reason's merriment.

Reason is this Friar's norm, not love; and in its name he is proposing to override "nature." Indeed, the "merriment" he is invoking is analogous to the "merry dump" which Peter, a moment later, officiously asks of the musicians. But there is a hidden comic meaning, I think, in the "silver sound" for which Peter begs to relieve his "doleful dumps." It depends on the signification which "silver" has in the *Merchant of Venice*—there a symbol of self-love in the name of "deservings," and its actual reward a fool's head. Shakespeare's usual practice is to make language please us in two ways simultaneously: by its surface truth and by its deeper truth. Here is a nice instance. What the Friar and his surrogate Peter call "merriment" is associated by Capulet with "sullen dirges" (line 88).

The Friar's advice-giving in general, throughout the play, is further and finally analogized by Shakespeare, I think, to the "musty seeds" and "skins / Of ill shaped fishes" which "make up a show" on the shelves of the Mantuan apothecary. These metaphors are marvellously apt, when one considers how basic to Christian teaching are the symbols of "seed" and "fish"—they virtually define the Christian vocation, which in Friar Laurence has become "musty" and mere "skin" of ill shape. The whole eleven-line passage describing the apothecary's shop (V. i. 38–48) is much more than picturesque local color. It serves as a dramatically distanced mirror of the other druggist in the play, Friar Laurence—as if the telltale relics of his Verona world were here collected in a Mantuan archeological museum. Laurence, like his Mantuan counterpart, is stocked with "simples" which witness to a beggarly destitution—in his case, however, a destitution not financial but moral. (And this figurative truth applies also, by analogy, to other personages in Verona's world. A twentieth-century writer might aptly title the whole play *Packthread and Caked Roses* by borrowing those metaphors from line 47.)

The poverty of Shakespeare's Friar is a poverty in respect to the mysteries of gospel. Like the sentimentalists at Calvary, who offered as a medicine for anguish a sponge of vinegar and gall, Friar Laurence has given Juliet an escape drug. He has thus neglected Holy Communion—that is, the pastoral wisdom this sacrament implies, the "cure" whose mystery should constitute his priestly vocation. By a substituting of magic flask for holy cup, he has induced a mock sacrifice by Juliet, a disingenuous "two days buried" (V. iii. 176). Indeed, its forty-two hours of artificial sleep is but a false and shadow-parallel to Christ's salvific forty hours* in the region of the

---

* Augustine, *On the Trinity* IV. 6, explains the mystical reasons for this number. Painter's story speaks of Juliet's sleep as "40 houres at the least." Why Shakespeare adjusted this to forty-two hours we can only guess—possibly to suggest that Juliet's "death" is defectively like Christ's (since in number symbolism "two" has connotations of imperfection); or perhaps simply because, at the level of a naturalistic time scheme, somewhat more than forty hours must elapse. As critics have discovered, however, a literal forty-two hours is difficult to make fit with the play's episodes; for even if Juliet drank the potion as late as three o'clock on Wednesday morning she would then awake as early as nine

dead. The Friar's preaching, moreover, has substituted the theme of moderation for that of rectification—as if a less excessive doting were the chief need of the lovers. What they more basically need, however, is an "ordinate" love, freed of idolatry, a love which would give each created thing only its proper due in the total hierarchy of goods and values. This the Friar does not see, partly because he is misled by his ambition for the fame of peacemaker. By his immediately approving of a clandestine marriage, he abets inordinate love. There is dramatic irony in his proposing to "make short work" of incorporating "two in one"; for by thus abbreviating the meaning of marriage to a two-in-one relationship he is overlooking the Three-in-one dimension which sanctifies Christian marriage. The Friar's arithmetic is reductive. We have already learned that the lovers are poor readers (Romeo reads "by rote and could not spell"), but now we know also that the Friar is a poor figurer. All his attempts to figure out "solutions" end in disaster.

In the Friar's final recital of events, chance is made to seem solely the cause of the disaster. But suppose we examine closely the "chance" event of Friar John's failure to deliver a letter to Romeo. Is this mischance unrelated to a character flaw in Friar Laurence? Chance and choice may in fact be interdependent rather than mutually exclusive factors in a tragedy. Why, let us ask, has Laurence not chosen to communicate with Romeo through Balthazar, as he

---

o'clock on Thursday night, whereas the time references in V.iii suggest a later hour, conceivably between midnight and four o'clock in the morning, the hour stated by Da Porto, whose account spoke of a forty-eight hour sleep. Had literal accuracy been Shakespeare's concern, he could have written "eight and forty" without harm to the scansion of his verse; or else "two and fifty," which would let us presuppose Tuesday near midnight as the time of the potion-taking. Shakespeare may have wished instead, however, to use a number carrying figuratively evil connotations—such as forty-two does in Rev. 11:2 and in other biblical passages. For any reader who may be interested in number symbolism, let me mention also the fact that for artists in the medieval tradition the number eleven connoted something defective—which might account, possibly, for Shakespeare's picturing the Apothecary's shop in exactly eleven lines (and for his organizing of the tragedy of *Richard III* to cover eleven days of dramatic time—as calculated by P. A. Daniel). Since I realize how far-fetched such a consideration must seem to the modern mind, I suggest it with trepidation. Yet there is support from Augustine, *City of God* XI. 30: "we must not despise the science of numbers, which, in many passages of holy Scripture, is found to be of eminent service to the careful interpreter."

had promised to do (III. iii. 169)? Why does he send a friar, instead, and communicate only by letter (IV. i. 123)? If he had but, even then, told Friar John his urgent "news" by word of mouth, disaster might have been averted. How? Friar John, in that case, might in conscience have raised questions with Laurence about the whole business; or he might have decided independently to inform the Prince or arouse the watch; or, in any case, he would surely have seen to it that a message reached Romeo. (If any quarantine blocked his own path, he would have spoken over it to some other messenger.) For Laurence, however, any opening of his purpose to a brother Franciscan is not to be considered. Why? Subconsciously he is aware, we may infer, of the guiltiness of his project, and hence must hide it within an envelope. But at the same time, in order to reassure himself psychologically that he is behaving like a responsible pastor, he needs to surround his dispatch with an aura of churchliness, which also will give his letter a reassuring "face" of authority in Romeo's eyes by having an ecclesiastic, and not lowly Balthazar, deliver it. Precisely because the spirit behind this letter is not to be looked into, the letter itself must be "covered" with as fair a show as possible.

Once we state the matter thus, however, we have epitomized a motif basic to the play: the substitution of *letter* for *spirit,* and of cover for kernel. Through a minor episode Shakespeare is analogizing his theme. The Friar's forgetfulness of Balthazar, which to some critics has seemed evidence of Shakespeare's carelessness with details, is intended actually to nudge us into grasping the playwright's understanding of the subtle psychology of tragedy and its meaning.

The full meaning of *Romeo and Juliet,* I have been contending, is to be found only through weighing its symbolism and total logic. The perspective of the Prologues, for instance, represents only the limited vision of Verona's citizenry as voiced by this chorus. The focus of the initial Prologue is on the play's official moral, whose latent ambiguities are left unexplored. Its purpose is to engage our sympathy and prompt our pity and fear. But then, while our spellbound emotions are being exercised within this frame, the dramatist weaves into the action archetypal echoes, through wordplay and emblematic scenes, which offer for our intellect a deeper significance whenever (either during or after our moment in the theatre) we are ready to decipher it. This deeper meaning, in one sense, is simply Brooke's "moral" reimagined in a more sophisticated, unpropagandistic way.[111] In another sense, however, it is purely intellectual: a recognition of the wonderful mock analogy to Christian story which is provided us in the storybook of Cupid's saints. How marvellously their religion of love unintentionally mimics a Christian love of religion! From this recognition, there can then arise for us a moral which is not didactic but confessional: "There but for the grace of God go I."

We can say this because our emotional response has undergone a progress in the course of the play, a movement toward catharsis. The catharsis is achieved, it seems to me, by the drama's eliciting of our emotion at two levels. Most immediate is the appeal to our instinctual sympathy for the lovers, especially through a rhetoric of romance which lures us to identify ourselves with their feelings and outlook. To some extent every auditor is caught up in fearing the external obstacles which the lovers fear, and in pitying their suffering from what seem traps of circumstance. This naive response (typical of teenagers, but felt also by older auditors, for whom it indulges a nostalgic reliving of youthful dreams) takes on an intensification through the accumulating mishaps which entangle the story's beautiful and gifted protagonists, until finally the disaster of their death brings to rest our pity and fear in a resigned acceptance of the hard fact of human mortality. But all this while the dramatist has also been challenging a deeper level of our emotions—our half-conscious fear for the rashness in such a love and our pity for the desperation in its courage. It is this second level of emotion which is (or can be on later reflection) enlightened by the ironies built into the drama. Through these our penchant for a self-identification with the lovers is progressively brought under judgment by insight. And our insight feeds in us a pity which becomes compassion, and a fear which begins to dread death less than what now can be recognized as its moral cause, namely, a blind love. A pity and fear of this kind, if heretofore neglected or atrophied in us, is given opportunity to revive and mature. Thus our emotions acquire a better health. For while at a surface level the acted out tragedy has been permitting us to expend vicariously our unexamined sentimentality, at another level it has been awakening in us more enlightened forms of emotion—experienced by each auditor, however, only insofar as his attention is well tuned and using a good antenna. The dialectic between the two levels I take to be the purgative process of the play. In a concluding section of Chapter III I shall be examining more fully this concept of catharsis.

Our search for perspective in the present chapter has brought us, in a roundabout way, to an outlook quite different from that of Coleridge, or Shaw, or Stoll. We began our review by noting their views of *Romeo and Juliet* and other of Shakespeare's tragedies, in order to show how the implications of his art can be warped by a critic's inappropriate philosophical orientation. The *Weltanschauung* of many a critic has been, during eras of neoclassicism and romanticism, ill adjusted to perceiving the inner grain of Shakespeare's text. Unfortunately a background of medieval perspective, which in this chapter I have invoked for refurbishing our discernment, was largely neglected soon after Shakespeare's day and only nowadays is helping to correct misapprehensions. Moreover, we need to realize how very recent, only within less than a century, has been the establishment of professorships in English Literature, which today make possible a concentration on explicating the classics in our language. Background aids for approaching these works have been gradually assembled. Now the nuances and intricacies of text, which invite a more than casual intelligence, can be given the attention they challenge and deserve.

But is there not some danger, a sceptic may ask, of "reading into" Shakespeare things not there? One can only reply that the danger is perennial but not to be surmounted by retreating into superficiality. Any drifting into an anti-intellectual stance risks reading into Shakespeare an unlikely crudity. Occasionally such a reaction crops up even among academics—as, for instance, in this statement:

> Although everybody knows that the first impact of a play, and perhaps the most lasting, is visceral, the critics are fascinated by its intellectual dimension, even though it is unlikely that all, or even many, of their acute perceptions and wide-ranging insights could possibly be discerned amidst the excitement of a performance.[112]

The comment here may seem sensible—except that it implies on the playwright's part little concern for insight by his auditors during or beyond their moment of theatre. Should we presuppose that for Shakespeare "the excitement of a performance" had more lastingness than some possible review by the mind's eye? Why assume that visceral impact is the essence of import? Shakespeare's own colleagues, we happen to know, encouraged a rather different estimate. Heminges and Condell, in their preface "To the great Variety of Readers" of the First Folio, wrote:

> . . . we hope, to your divers capacities, you will find enough, both to draw, and to hold you: for his wit can no more lie hid, then it could be lost. Reade him, therefore, and againe, and againe: And if then you doe not like him, surely you are in some manifest danger, not to understand him.

Reading and rereading, these men of the theatre believed, was basic to appreciation—especially for revealing Shakespeare's wit, his remedy against our misunderstanding. And Ben Jonson was of a similar opinion. The art of Shakespeare, Jonson declared in his poem of tribute, is "alive still, while thy Booke doth live, / And we have wits to read."

Of all art forms in English, Shakespearean tragedy is our richest. For understanding it our liveliest questions turn, it seems to me, about the theoretical premises underlying tragedy and about the symbolic language through which drama amplifies its import. The chapters to follow will treat of further aspects of these matters.

III

Toward Clarifying
the Term
"Christian Tragedy"

Until rather recently it has been unfashionable to describe Shakespeare's art as Christian. The prevailing assumption, in the wake of Shaw and Stoll, has been that the dramatist had little or no interest in theology, and that his world view was somehow independent of Christian influences. Few readers, perhaps, have gone as far as J. M. Robertson ("the great disintegrator"), who viewed Shakespeare as groping his way out of "the aftershine of medieval day-dream" toward the "sanity" of Auguste Comte. But Churton Collins, at the turn of the century, could describe Shakespeare as a "theistical agnostic"; and A. C. Bradley was assuring the public that religious ideas did not "materially influence" Shakespeare's representation of life. By 1924, John Masefield's *Shakespeare and the Spiritual Life* was voicing a high-sounding liberalism: Shakespeare "held to no religion save that of humanity and his own great nature." "Orthodox religion," Masefield went on to say, "whether as ritual or as dogma, seems to have meant almost nothing to him."[1]

Similar sentiments are still frequently proclaimed. D. G. James, for instance, is confident in his *Dream of Learning* (1951) that the Elizabethan dramatists, including Shakespeare, "did not think as Christians." By and large their imaginations were "free of any religious prepossessions" and attuned to the secular humanism of Francis Bacon. Hence Shakespeare

> . . . did not write as a man of faith. He may have died a
> Papist; he did not write as a Christian. This seems certain.
> He writes without a philosophy; and we cannot say that
> his writings are Christian writings. And yet he conducted

> a poetic and dramatic exploration of human experience
> which is without parallel for both depth and range in the
> world's history. (p. 26; cf. p. 91)

But is there indeed no "parallel"? Has James taken into consideration the depth and range of human experience recorded in the Bible? Curiously he seems to assume that even if Shakespeare was a
Christian this fact would not have influenced the "depth" with
which his poetry explores life.

The grounds for questioning this assumption we have touched
on in our previous chapter. They depend, for one thing, on taking
seriously a premise which O. C. Quick, for instance, has emphasized:
that "the work of art expresses the soul of the artist." In explaining
how this is so, Quick commented on the difference between Shakespeare's practice and that of some modern playwrights:

> Shakespeare at first sight seems not to be expressing him-
> self at all, and his own personality remains an enigma. The
> moderns, on the other hand, seem to be doing little else
> than express themselves, and we are left in no doubt as to
> what they think and feel. But the truth is that Shake-
> speare's greatness manifests itself in the self-repression
> which allows his characters and situations, as it were, to
> speak for themselves uninterrupted by his own personal
> comments. His creative mind is immanent in them all, and
> we can only reach its essential thought and feeling by a
> deeper appreciation of the meaning and value of the drama
> as a whole.[2]

To hold that Shakespeare's thought is "immanent" in the total
structure of his work is not quite to say, as John Arthos more recently has suggested, that a "frame for understanding" was "imposed upon" Shakespeare by the Christian centuries.[3] The issue is
better put by Irving Ribner, who contends that "the moral and
metaphysical assumptions behind Shakespeare's plays were Christian because he was a Christian" and chose these assumptions rather
than alien ones for the shaping of his plays.[4] This premise seems to
me a defensible one, if pursued carefully—with more care perhaps
than Ribner himself quite achieves in his *Patterns in Shakespearian
Tragedy* (1960). Meanwhile, H. S. Wilson's *On the Design of Shakespearian Tragedy* (1957) has likewise posited a basic relation between Shakespeare's art and his religion:

No one, presumably, will dispute that there is a religious
faith reflected in the plays and that this faith is Christian.
To hesitate to call it Shakespeare's, as some would, is surely
a misplaced scrupulosity; it seems only common sense to
call it Shakespeare's, if it is there. The important critical
question concerns the precise quality of that Christian
faith and the way it becomes significant in the plays. (p.
217)

Wilson is here presuming, however, what many critics are as yet un-
ready to grant. Moreover, his discussion leaves largely unclarified
both aspects of the "important critical question" he mentions. What
is the "precise quality" of Shakespeare's Christianity? And in what
"way" does it become significant in a particular play? These are
matters nowadays much in debate.

Inevitably, such questions generate occasional misconceptions
and even partisan fears. Roland Frye, for instance, in his *Shakespeare and Christian Doctrine* (1963) sees today's Shakespeare scholarship as threatened by what he takes to be a school of "theologizers"
bent on turning the plays into works of propagandistic intent. He
is able to spot, it is true, some instances of loose reasoning in the
writings of Knight, Siegel, and Ribner. But in his eagerness to rebut
all analogical method he neglects to winnow its good use from its
sometimes ill application.[5] At the same time, his own view that "in
Shakespeare's dramas there is rarely any appeal to sanctions beyond
those available to the pagan citizens of Rome" (p. 96) seems questionable, if tested for example against *Macbeth* or *Measure for Measure*. And when we are told, further, that the "total dramatic structure" of Shakespeare's plays could be supported as well "by the
ethics of the virtuous heathen as by those of the Christian church"
(p. 94), we wonder why, in that case, Frye has not used these heathen
equally with Christian theologians for glossing religious references.
We cannot but wonder, too, whether "total dramatic structure," in
Frye's view, rests simply on sanctions taken over from source materials, or whether there is not some personal shaping by the playwright to reflect his own belief. One reviewer, László Kéry, has
inferred from Frye's study that, since Christian tradition took no
central position in "the conception" of any of Shakespeare's works,
the proper way to approach Shakespeare must be from the "much
broader notions of the Renaissance."[6] This would imply a Shakespeare whose ultimate values were sub-Christian. I doubt Frye

means this, but the imprecision of his argument tempts misunderstandings.

On a question which has thus in our times become controversial, clarification is much needed. What meaning can there be in the term "Christian tragedy," in particular as applied to Shakespeare? There would be no controversy, I assume, if this term were generally reserved for tragedies which have Bible story as their subject matter, such as Peele's *David and Bethsabe* or Milton's *Samson;* for then it could be taken for granted that "Christian" carried a denotation like that of the adjective "science" in our term "science fiction." But most users of the term "Christian tragedy" have in mind not story classification, but a Christian quality in the *Weltanschauung* of the author. A few, now and then, have used the term for all tragedies set within countries nominally Christian, or written by authors nominally Christian. But so broad a usage can be next to meaningless. For the temporal setting of a play has nothing to do with the insight by which an author penetrates its events; and, on the other hand, mere membership in a Christian church does not automatically bestow Christian insight. Ben Jonson, although a Christian and for a time a Roman Catholic one, wrote his tragedies by the light of premises predominantly neoclassical. Various eighteenth-century dramatists did likewise. Although admittedly the term "Christian tragedy" can be used in diverse senses, the most meaningful usage would seem to be in connection with some distinctively Christian understanding of man implicit in the art work, as evidenced by a mimesis of human experience in accord with principles of discrimination traditionally Christian.[7]

It is in this sense that I consider the word "Christian" a valid way of characterizing Shakespearean tragedy. It runs the risk, however, of being associated with the loose and half-informed notions of Christianity which many moderns have. That is, it can be misused as an umbrella under which to attribute to Shakespeare sentimental meanings, or impressionistically didactic ones, which his plays do not really imply but which the critic develops and denominates as Christian. This failing, to which any of us may be liable unless protected by firm historical knowledge in matters theological, seems to me occasionally evident, for instance, in the books by Wilson and Ribner noted above. Basically, both these critics have absorbed a great deal of Bradley's Hegelian romanticism; hence when they encounter talk of "love" or "providence" in a tragedy, they tend to evaluate these ideas romantically, while nevertheless characterizing their interpretations as Christian. This is possible because, since we have discovered through literary history that Christianity was important to most Elizabethans, we feel justified in using its vocabulary, but at the same time unwittingly confuse its meaning with modern sentiment. Even rather learned Roman Catholics can fall into this trap. Monsignor I. J. Semper's *Hamlet Without Tears* (1946) is a notable instance. In this study Prince Hamlet is interpreted as a champion of Christian orthodoxy and even a Thomistic philosopher, simply because Hamlet's sentiments include a vocabulary which sounds enough like that of St. Thomas that if we compare texts loosely, and feel toward Hamlet an uncritical admiration, the two thinkers can hopefully be identified in their ethics. Relying on Bradley's prestige, the unsuspecting Monsignor sees Hamlet as fulfilling God's will in "perfect conscience" and departing for heaven as the play ends. Hamlet is therefore a hero over whom we need shed no tears. But if such be the case, what happens to the traditional concept that tragedy should arouse pity? Semper does not ask this important question.

Too often modern readings of Shakespearean tragedy, it seems to me, harbor twin sources of confusion: on the one hand, a failure to take seriously the concept of tragic genre and its requirements; and on the other hand, a lack of theological precision in judging the ethics of tragic heroes. The crucial questions in practical criticism, as H. S. Wilson rightly said, involve assessing "how" Shakespeare's faith is present in his art of tragedy and the "precise quality" of that faith. But both these matters, in a modern climate, are more slippery than Wilson was aware. They require of the critic an adequate theory of tragedy and also an historical grasp of moral theology— alongside a scrupulous reading of Shakespeare's text. The hero's utterances must not be confused with the playwright's feelings. And further, we ought not to suppose that if the tragedy as a work of art is to be called Christian its hero must have or develop a Christian ethic. Rather, what may be said to qualify a tragedy as Christian is the author's unstated Christian world view, by the light of which he understands and orders what happens to, and within, a hero whose attitude and choices are morally defective. As George Peele long ago said of Marlowe, a tragedian's task is to write "passions for the souls below"—for "wretched souls." This implies a wisdom in the author above the protagonist's, yet devoted through empathy to delineat-

ing this hero's dark voyage of misunderstanding, amid circumstances which will make it credible, and with a logic making it
emblematic of the potentially tragic in everyman.

The pitfalls in criticism to which I have been referring beset not
only the nowadays semifashionable "Christian" approaches to
Shakespeare but also, in a different way, their opponents and detractors. In this rival camp are critics who read Shakespeare as concerned for a "faith in man"; or else as challenging any and all faith,
because bewildered by an unfriendly universe. In this sense, they
see the dramatist as an exponent of a "tragic sense of life," a tragic
"world picture." Often they suppose, or indeed assert, that the art
form of tragedy is irreconcilable with Christian faith. There is here
a basic misunderstanding, which I believe needs our close consideration. In what respect do these interpreters misread Shakespeare, and
by what interrogation can we perhaps bring them to revise their
assumptions?

In the present chapter, I shall proceed by offering, first, a running
critique of some arguments by critics who would deny a Christian
vision in Shakespeare, and then of some contrary readings by spokesmen who claim as Christian various interpretations which seem to
me sometimes valid but other times dubious. My purpose here will
be to illustrate from both groups some of the typical confusions
which in day-to-day practice hamper our understanding of Shakespeare, and to suggest clues for a more defensible perspective. My
own theory of tragedy will emerge through remarks on the various
tragedies which come up for review. Then, by way of elaborating
my view of tragic *anagnorisis,* and also in order to illustrate how a
Christian art can reshape pagan story, I shall offer some fairly
lengthy comment on *Antony and Cleopatra.* Finally, as a further
contribution to theoretical issues, the last section of the chapter will
be devoted to the troublesome question of *catharsis,* with an attempt
at applying this concept to several of Shakespeare's tragedies.

1 A critique of obstructing arguments

Is the writing of tragedy incompatible with a holding of the Christian faith? By critics who suppose that it is, a medley of arguments
has been put forward. Let us consider, for instance, those of Clifford
Leech, first developed in 1950 and often subsequently antholo-

gized.[8] In his view, "we cannot expect to find true tragedy anywhere in the Middle Ages, except here and there in early times when literature was not thoroughly Christianized." This statement overlooks Chaucer's narrative tragedy of *Troilus and Criseyde*, to which Chaucer himself gave a Christian meaning. The Christian basis of Chaucer's concept of tragedy has been made clear by D. W. Robertson.[9] Leech, perhaps because writing prior to Robertson's studies, associates all tragedies with what he calls "the tragic view of things," based on "a faith in man, and in the impersonality of divine justice." He would trace the flourishing of tragic drama in Elizabethan times to "a weakening of medieval faith and some return to stoicism." We need not be surprised, therefore, that he reads tragedy in largely stoic terms. The "tragic picture," he explains, is one of an indifferent universe and of gods remote if not actively hostile, amid which certain characters enlist our admiration by their power to endure torments with a clear-eyed fortitude. How, then, does he interpret *catharsis,* tragedy's final effect on us? He hesitates over formulating an interpretation, but suggests finally that "we are aroused to withstand destiny, to strive to meet it with fortitude and the clear eyes of the tragic figure." The tragic hero, he thinks, arouses not merely our admiration but also pride in the "fine flower" which this hero's humanity achieves in the face of an unjust universe. Thus we experience an "equilibrium" of Terror balanced by Pride—pride in seeing man justify his existence.

Would Aristotle accept this interpretation of catharsis? I think not. It substitutes admiration for pity, and an equilibrium of our emotions in place of their purgation. Moreover, it may be questioned whether heroes such as Othello or Hamlet actually achieve a humanity of "fine flower" and clear-eyed understanding. Perhaps they seem to, if we presuppose a stoic estimate of man's humanity. But did Shakespeare?

We cannot see tragedy aright, Leech believes, "unless we recognize that the divine justice it mirrors is an indifferent justice, a justice which cares no whit for the individual and is not concerned with a nice balance of deserts and rewards." This contention is the heart of his case for an irreconcilability between tragedy and the Christian picture of life. The following Shakespearean instances are adduced as evidence:

> Desdemona and Ophelia are guilty of nothing more than
> weakness, yet they are destroyed; Lear is hot-tempered and

foolish, yet no one will claim that he deserved to endure madness and the storm on the heath; Cordelia refuses to play her father's game, and is hanged for it; Gloucester begets Edmund and his eyes are plucked out. . . . Moreover, the plays frequently include a number of minor characters whose sudden and cruel deaths do not arise out of any fault of their own: Lady Macduff and her son, Polonius, Rosencrantz and Guildenstern, the brave servant in *King Lear* who tries to save Gloucester from blindness . . .

In short, the evil to which these characters are subject is either disproportionate to their minor faults or in no way related to any fault.

What can be said in reply? For one thing, it seems to me that each of these cases, in its Shakespearean context, is much more complex than Leech's surface review would indicate. In several, there are faults he has not named or faults at a level deeper than he has named, which contribute at least indirectly to the disasters which ensue. An initial self-righteousness in Cordelia, a mad wilfulness in Lear, a superstitiousness in Gloucester, and a weather-vane deviousness in Polonius might be mentioned, for instance. But more important is the fact that Leech is presupposing that a Christian world order must involve a divine justice like that of eighteenth-century "poetic justice"; and hence that if a dramatist presents us a less "reasonable" and more mysterious kind of order, his vision is un-Christian. This is a premise on which William Elton, in a very recent study of *King Lear,* likewise grounds his rejection of Christian readings of this play.[10]

But "poetic justice" in Thomas Rymer's sense is in fact not a Christian idea at all, only quasi-so and reductionist. A "nice balance of deserts and rewards," as regards temporal evils, is not taught in the Bible. On the contrary, we find there a long list of innocent martyrs, from Abel to John the Baptist and various of Christ's disciples. Moreover, if we consult Aquinas, we find him explaining that not all evils with which man is punished are penal, or simply so. Some are in whole or in part medicinal, or in some cases, satisfactory for the sins of others:

> We must observe that sometimes a thing seems penal, and yet is not so simply. . . . Evil is a privation of good. And since man's good is manifold, viz. good of the soul, good of the body, and external goods, it happens sometimes that man suffers the loss of a lesser good, that he may profit in a

greater good, as when he suffers loss of money for the sake of bodily health, or loss of both of these, for the sake of his soul's health and the glory of God. In such cases the loss is an evil to man, not simply but relatively. . . . And since such like are not punishments properly speaking, they are not referred to sin as their cause, except in a restricted sense: because the very fact that human nature needs a treatment of penal medicines is due to the corruption of nature which is itself the punishment of original sin. For there was no need, in the state of innocence, for penal exercises in order to make progress in virtue; so that whatever is penal in the exercise of virtue is reduced to original sin as its cause. (*S. T.* I–II. 87.7.)

Sometimes, moreover, a person bears the debt of another man's punishment by a union of love, and this has the quality of "satisfactory" suffering, if it is taken on voluntarily. In other cases, punishment for another's sin may be inflicted, for instance, on children for their parents, or on servants for their masters; and if this is borne patiently it is medicinal, since intended for the good of man's soul (I–II. 87.8). In the light of such teaching, need any Christian auditor of Shakespeare's tragedies feel an incompatibility between his faith and the instances he sees of medicinal and satisfactory suffering?

Leech's generalizations about tragedy are too impressionistic and reductive to fit the full facts of Shakespearean tragedy. Suppose, for example, we test his idea that in *King Lear* "justice operates like an avalanche," and that the tragic writer "believes in . . . the powerlessness of the human will to interrupt a chain of disasters." How true is this if we consider Edgar's role in the play? Do we not see this disinherited son, in Act IV, devising a way to turn his father's will from suicide into a discovery of "miracle"? A moment later, we see Edgar preventing Oswald's attempt to seize Gloucester, and still later we see him halting Edmund's attempt to hide guilt and outface Albany. Thus at least some potential disasters can be turned aside, if a man of good will intervenes. Indeed, Edgar not only saves England from falling under Edmund's rule; he contributes something to Edmund's deathbed conversion. And earlier, at the play's midpoint, we have seen him interrupting the spiritual disaster of Lear's self-righteous isolation by offering fellowship. We have also seen Cordelia counteracting this same disaster in Lear by her acts of charity. If, at earlier times in this play, the human wills even of these two children are powerless except for making matters worse, that is traceable to an initial defensiveness on their part. Their own wills need medicining through adversity. But when medicined they become increasingly powerful, if not so far as to interrupt all disasters, yet to the preventing of some potential ones and a transforming of the meaning of others. We may recall, further, the tragedies of *Richard III* and *Macbeth* in which, amid adversity, the human wills of various persons are stimulated to an action which ultimately rescues the state from tyranny. Events of this sort suggest that Shakespeare, instead of believing in a powerlessness of the human will, was able to differentiate modes of the will's ability. By distinguishing between sin and punishment, the latter being understood as less essentially evil than the former, he could portray a world in which suffering serves either as a judgment on man's sin or, for some men, as a medicining of the will for prompting acts of benevolence.[11]

It is well to recognize also that the term "world picture" can be ambiguous. Does it refer only to the world of outward events, or may it refer to realms of spiritual value which surround human choices? In *Hamlet* Shakespeare shows us Laertes saying:

> Conscience and grace, to the profoundest pit!
> I dare damnation. To this point I stand,
> That both worlds I give to negligence.

What specifically is here tragic? The "both worlds" to which Laertes is referring are not tragic. They are the worlds of man's temporal and eternal happiness, which depend on conscience and grace for their maintenance. They are the acknowledged worlds which man and society in Denmark might cultivate. What is tragic is Laertes' resolution to disregard them in favor of the limited satisfaction of personal revenge. Principally, then, what Shakespeare is presenting is a mimesis of Laertes in the process of a tragic action, rather than a tragic world picture. And in the consequences which ensue, partly from this action and partly from analogous ones by other persons in the story, Shakespeare is furthering his complex account of how social life in Denmark comes to disaster, through a neglect of sanctions within the world picture which, if respected, could have turned events toward a happier outcome.

Critics who associate tragedy with a "tragic view of life" tend to turn drama into a vehicle for self-expression on the author's part.

According to Richard Sewall, for instance, the artist acts through his tragic fictions to fight against his destiny and state his case before God and his fellows. This is what Shakespeare was doing in *King Lear,* Sewall thinks.[12] He was testing and protesting his intuitions of the "blight" man was born for. Lear has "no comforter on his dark voyage," and whatever ambiguous victory he wins at the end is "not through Divine Grace" but "through his own unaided efforts." These comments seem to overlook the aid Cordelia gives Lear. Yet elsewhere Sewall remarks that Christian images and a Christian spirit "pervade" the tent scene. But since at the end the play "says nothing about salvation," we can not call its rationale Christian, he argues. I find this whole interpretation confusing and contradictory. How can there be a Christian spirit *anywhere,* unless Divine Grace is aiding it? And must a tragedy announce an entry into heaven by its hero in order to qualify as having a Christian rationale?

It may be instructive to note that Sewall's position comes to rest in an essentially Manichean world view. His final comment is that *King Lear* embodies the "tragic truth" that good and evil are both "eternally present" in *all* human actions. He is of course mistaken; for surely there is no evil present in the action of Cordelia when forgiving and reclothing her father, or in Lear's final act of yearning for signs of a "life" that would "redeem all sorrows," or even in Edmund's final action of repenting. There is evil in the world, but not in these acts. Sewall's mistake warrants mention, because occasionally other critics have maintained, likewise, that tragedy springs (to cite Miss Ellis-Fermor's phrase) from a "Manichaeistic balance" in the playwright's vision. The "tragic mood" of a tragedy, Miss Ellis-Fermor explains, depends upon a kind of equilibrium "between the religious and the non-religious interpretations of catastrophe . . . , to neither of which the dramatist can wholly commit himself."[13] This is similar to I. A. Richards' pronouncement: "Tragedy is only possible to a mind which is for the moment agnostic or Manichean. The least touch of any theology which has a compensating Heaven to offer the tragic hero is fatal."[14] Such statements seem to me near the truth in one sense, but very misleading in another sense.

These critics intend to say, I infer, that the dramatist himself must be of a Manichean mind when writing tragedy. This I would deny of Shakespeare, while yet granting that the mood of his tragic heroes is often Manichean. For example, when Lear cries out, "But

to the girdle the gods inherit, / Beneath is all the fiend's," this reading of human nature is basically a Manichean one. So also is Hamlet's reasoning in his apology of self-excuse offered to Laertes. In
both these instances human nature is seen as the victim of rival
powers. But in each case this interpretation stems from the speaker's
failing to consider the actual role of the human will in deeds of
fiendishness or madness. Moreover, this vision contradicts what the
speaker's own best religious sense has at other times intimated to
him. In Lear's case, Cordelia's ministrations as rescuer have given
evidence of an undivided human nature. Her acts of charity have
testified to a responsible and wholesome vision, offering cure for
the hero's misvision. Lear has foolishly committed himself, not exactly to a "non-religious interpretation," but rather to a "no good
divinity" which has betrayed him into disaster. And Shakespeare,
as author of this drama, cannot be said to be hesitating agnostically
between religion and nonreligion, nor committing himself to a
Manicheistic mood. As artist, he is delineating an action in which
the sinful hero falls into Manicheistic explanations yet is haunted
by inklings of a better vision.

A loosely Manichean reading of Shakespearean tragedy can be
found in A. P. Rossiter's *Angel with Horns* (1961), as its title metaphorically suggests. The word "Manichean" appears only late in
the book, however, at a point where Rossiter is speculating on one
of Bradley's statements. Bradley had said that the Shakespearean
tragic hero is a far more valuable "part" of the moral order's substance, and "nearer to its heart," than the part which remains in a
Fortinbras or a Malcolm. Rossiter comments that he finds this difficult to understand,

> unless I conclude that the 'moral order' has a *double* heart:
> i.e. that the universe is quasi-Manichean, and that human
> greatness (which is one God's 'good') is the evil of the *other*
> God (i.e. the God of order and degree). I cannot think
> Bradley meant this. Yet such a view can result from seeing
> Renaissance *virtu* superimposed on Christian order; *Virtu
> contra Ordinem.* (p. 266)

It seems to me Rossiter is perceiving—but without realizing that it
is one of the consequences of Hegelianism—that Bradley's theory is
so next door to Manichaeism as to be at times tantamount to it. For
if, as Bradley holds, the hero is to be valued and cherished for his

admirable "greatness," yet finds this greatness subject to a fatality which "wastes" it, what can be causing this wastefulness, unless some God opposing another God within the universe?

Rossiter more or less adopts and follows up this implication. Shakespeare's tragic heroes, in his view, are noble in Renaissance *virtu* and admirable for their "passional distinction." Their tragedy therefore lies in a wasting of this natural excellence by some order alien to it (hypothetically, a Christian order), which Rossiter supposes Shakespeare is challenging as something grotesquely moral. Shakespeare is presenting this order as an evil one. Hamlet is to be seen as "the good mind in an evil world." He is the victim of its traps of circumstance. He is a man of intelligence, generosity, and fineness, who is destroyed by mean and clumsy forces around him. Even when at war with himself, Hamlet is at war with "a self or selves produced by uncontrollable circumstances." That is why the play is a tragedy: it symbolizes the conflict between two antinomies, "circumstance" and "inner value," whose contradictions and opposition are man's tragedy. "Shakespeare's tragedies have rejected the 'Tudor-Christian' concept of a moral and just world." The only way to evade this conclusion, says Rossiter, is by a theory of "tragic flaw," extracted from Aristotle, which has the effect of shifting all blame from the universe; but to press this approach is to "destroy tragedy."[15]

Whereas Rossiter is proud of Shakespeare's supposed espousal of Renaissance humanism, a critic such as D. D. Raphael in his *The Paradox of Tragedy* (1960) writes from an opposite desire to defend Christianity from the "humanistic creed" which he supposes all tragic writers adopt. The result is very much the same. For Raphael sees tragic art (including Shakespeare's) as committed to an admiration for the hero's defiance, and an attributing to the universe a "waste of good." And this he criticizes as incompatible with a biblical view. The pleasure we find in tragedy, he thinks, "is the result of regarding the hero as more sublime than the power he opposes"; hence it is "quite implausible to suggest that Shakespeare's tragedies rest on Christian theology."

But does not such interpretation wrongly presuppose that the hero's "defiance" is being celebrated by the playwright, rather than simply imitated as a tragic fact? Raphael is being misled, it seems to me, by a confusing of the fact of human tragedy with the dramatist's art of tragedy, and further by uncritically accepting Bradley's notion that the universe is forced to "waste" good for the sake of tragic process. Since Bradley thought Cordelia an instance of this, so does Raphael: "unless her fate is shown," he says, "not to be a waste of goodness, Shakespeare's treatment of it is not Christian."[16] Raphael seems unaware that actually the play contains evidence of something other than waste in the suffering Cordelia undergoes. When Edmund imprisons her, this fate is interpreted by Lear as a "sacrifice" on her part, on which the gods themselves "throw incense." Does a sacrifice waste goodness? When later Cordelia's hanged body is brought to Lear, does it not spur his mind ultimately to a quest for new seeing—comparable, perhaps, to the conversion to which Saul of Tarsus was induced by having beheld the death of St. Stephen? In a profound sense St. Stephen's death did not waste his goodness, since through it he offered a haunting and lasting witness to the life of charity he embodied. What was wasted was the persecutor's evil will. Providential order permits sinful men to waste their energies. It permits also, on the part of innocent persons, miseries which can be endured as sacrifices, through which higher goods are testified to and become efficacious.

Let us recall St. Augustine's discussion of divine providence in *City of God,* Book I. Temporal afflictions, he reminds his readers, are visited both on good men and bad. Christians were not spared sufferings during the sacking of Rome, since calamities are given to all men to test and try the human spirit. For anyone like Job, adversity will serve to manifest one's fortitude and teach an unmercenary love of God. For others, it serves to correct faults of vanity, or of selfish love of safety or good name. Tribulations winnow the wheat from the chaff. They prove, purge, and clarify the good man, but at the same time ruin or exterminate the wicked. Or, as Augustine elsewhere remarks *(Reply to Faustus* XXII): "The great husbandman of the vine uses the pruning hook differently in the fruitful and unfruitful branches; yet he spares neither good nor bad, pruning one and cutting off another. There is no man so just as not to require to be tried by affliction in order to advance, or establish, or to prove his virtue." Such teaching, surely, is in no way incompatible with what the play *King Lear* implies.

On other Shakespearean tragedies, the arguments of critics who reject the concept of Christian tragedy can go astray in other ways. Laurence Michel's view of *Hamlet* may be mentioned as a particularly interesting instance.[17] For Michel emphasizes, as rather few

readers do, the sub-Christian behavior of prince Hamlet. Yet he
infers from this, mistakenly, that the play's art cannot be called
Christian. He is right, surely, in his comments on Hamlet's penchant for mono-dialogue, solipsism, and nihilism; and he offers excellent argument for judging as un-Christian the tone of Hamlet's
attitude toward providence in Act V. But can we logically infer
from this that the play is depicting "the destruction of anthropocentric humanism"? Do we not need to state the matter somewhat
more precisely? I would say that the play tells the story of the destruction, not of an "ism," but of Hamlet and of the whole house
of Denmark, through their yieldings to an anthropocentric humanism. The play, in other words, does not simply "assert destruction."
Rather, it imitates the tragic action of men. And may we not relate
their action's disastrous end to a neglect, both by Claudius and by
Hamlet, of those angels and ministers of grace which, early in the
play, each had had enough conscience to invoke? Michel would insist that "the Tragic Vision and Christianity are incompatible."
But of whose tragic vision is he speaking? Why equate the hero's
vision with the playwright's own?

Some critics oppose a viewing of Shakespeare's tragedies as Christian by taking quite another line of argument. It turns about a professed concern to protect drama from overinterpretation. This is an
understandable reaction against the diversity of judgment which
has cropped up among readers who have attempted theological
approaches. The reaction takes refuge, however, in a general scepticism. On finding critics disagreeing, for instance, on the question of
whether the final moral state of Hamlet or of Othello is that of a
"saved" soul, the sceptic can retire into denying the validity of the
whole question. If it were important to the drama, wouldn't Shakespeare have made the answer explicitly clear? Such is the rejoinder
of Sylvan Barnet in a well-known essay[18] which warrants our careful consideration. Yet it may be recalled that it was Bradley who
first touched on the question of "salvation" in Shakespeare's tragic
heroes; and many other non-Christian approaches have ended by
talking about it. If they have found it a relevant question, may it
not indeed be so, even though readers, both Christian and non-
Christian, may sometimes misjudge in pronouncing on it?

It is "harmful," Barnet thinks, to analyze Shakespeare's plays in
terms of Christian theology, because "the business of tragedy, unlike that of a religious system, is not to explain the world, but to

portray an aspect of it." Tragedy, he goes on to say, "does not claim to offer the whole truth, nor does it require an act of faith to be believed. It sets forth a kind of experience which everyman knows, presenting suffering and death as the hard facts which most men feel them to be." Shakespeare's plays show "the material fall" of heroes. This fall is "generally accompanied by an increased awareness of the nature of life, but such profit is gained at the expense of life." The ethics in the plays "partake of Christian ethics, but they are not based, as Christian ethics in fact are, upon the eschatology of the Christian system." The tragic heroes have little in common with the heroes of Christianity. What is the final "moral" of *Othello*? Does Shakespeare "even wish us to draw one?" It is perhaps better, Barnet concludes, to accept "the immediate impressions yielded by the plays, and to see in these dramas not explicit eternal theological verities, portrayed on a canvas stretching from hell-mouth to heaven, but a picture of man's achievements and failures, hopes and fears, life and death."

Does not this argument oversimplify the alternatives? It seems to me to misconstrue the intent of most scholars nowadays using theological analysis. They are not contending that tragedies are morality plays. They recognize, though perhaps not always sufficiently, that tragedy is a particular kind of drama. Its business is to portray tragic action, and not "explicit theological verities" on a canvas. Barnet is right in thinking that tragedy's focus is the secular world, in which is set forth "a kind of experience which everyman knows." But may we not ask: What *range* of experience? Do we witness merely the "material fall" of heroes, or the moral causes as well? Does tragic drama invite us to nothing besides a vicarious reexperience of the "hard facts" of suffering? Does it not expect us to weigh the hero's disposition and mistaken action—his hamartia as related to his hopes and fears? Barnet has not explained how Shakespeare's plays "partake of Christian ethics." If the hero's ethic is not Christian but indicates instead "little in common" with that of Christian heroes, then *where,* or how else, *do* the dramas "partake" of a Christian ethic?

They *reflect* it, I would say, in two possible ways: through actions essentially Christian on the part of some other character in a tragedy, as for instance in Desdemona's behavior at death; or through wayside references to the Christian ethic by a speaker who is failing to live up to its standards, as in the words of Claudius at prayer. In both these ways, a Christian ethic is the play's implicit norm—in those plays, at least, which are set in Christian times. But does this not imply also a Christian eschatology? Barnet himself admits that eschatology is the "base" or ground of ethics in the Christian world view. Does he suppose Shakespeare unaware of this integral inter-relationship? When references to heaven, hell, and damned appear in the talk of Romeo, Hamlet, Othello, and others, how are we to read these? Do they not challenge us to distinguish between the hero's blind use of eschatological terms and their proper meaning in a Christian understanding? They refer to a dimension of experi-ence which cannot, reasonably, be excluded from consideration. Why should a critic refuse to ask whether the hero's action is damn-able? Is the question in itself "harmful"? More harmful could be the supposition that literary criticism is somehow independent of other disciplines, for this impoverishes criticism.

Let us take, for instance, the case of *Romeo and Juliet*. In Barnet's view, although "Shakespeare employs, of course, Christian imagery and terminology," the play is "not a Christian drama." The reason he gives is that "the supernatural seems to be not God but Fate." Furthermore, although the lovers commit suicide, yet "we cannot believe that Shakespeare sends them in a sixth unwritten but clearly imagined act to the seventh circle of Dante's Inferno." Note, for one thing, that Barnet is here smuggling in some theology of his own, of an impressionistic kind: he has named the supernatural as not God but Fate. Are God and Fate mutually exclusive? In the play, Prince Escalus traces the parents' fate to a punishment by "Heaven." Could not this same Heaven, although Escalus does not think out his premise, have been using the lovers' passion as their own scourge, punishing both themselves and others? Pity and fear should be our primary experience in witnessing tragedy. Yet plainly it is not unrelated to an awareness, while we watch the action or contemplate it afterwards, of moral causes and theological implica-tions in the seen disaster. In Escalus this awareness is incomplete; we can see more from our vision of the whole. We do not expect the author to step into his play to explain fully. For if all great art is, in Denis de Rougemont's phrase, a "calculated trap for medita-tion,"[19] our task as readers does not end with picking up surface im-pressions but includes a pondering of what the art object as a whole signifies.

Regarding Barnet's other remark, as to what we cannot believe

Shakespeare imagined, let us reply simply that no Christian critic supposes Shakespeare is "sending" any of his characters to hell. The dramatist presents, however, their acts of final choice—which cannot but have eschatological implications. W. H. Auden has well said that in an art work the moral data have a finality clearer than in real life.[20] Of *Romeo and Juliet* he writes:

> In real life, when a sane person commits suicide, it is always possible for a Christian to hope that, in the last split second, he or she made an act of contrition, but a character in a play is transparent; there is no more to him than the dramatist tells us. If a dramatist makes a suicide utter words of repentance before death, then he repents; if the dramatist does not, then he dies unrepentant and goes to Hell.

What Auden means is that such a "person" is headed for hell by his own bent—a judgment we can make of his character when we contemplate it with a Christian sensibility. If, however, a reader's sensibility lacks Christian categories, or if he stops short of using them, he grasps somewhat less than the potential meaning of Shakespeare's data. Auden is speaking of "the full tragic import" of the play.

Actually, few critics nowadays deny themselves eschatological inferences when interpreting "what happens" to Macbeth or Richard III. They openly speak of these characters as damned, or as experiencing already during their secular life the meaning of hell. *Macbeth,* in particular, is often described as a study in damnation.[21] When Auden, by applying moral analysis to *Romeo and Juliet,* infers that the lovers, by dying in a state of mortal sin, are hell bound; or when critics such as S. L. Bethell and Paul Siegel see this to be the case with Othello,[22] they are letting their criticism include, alongside other dimensions of understanding, a theological dimension which seems to be valid. They are not censuring, but simply discerning and placing an event's significance. If other critics do not believe in the relevance of the eschatological dimension, they can settle for less. After all, there is nothing to prevent critics, if they wish, from being even more thoroughly sceptical than Barnet, as are Shaw or Stoll, for whom the whole of *Romeo and Juliet* or *Othello* is incredible as an image of life, hence not to be believed in at any serious level. Nothing to prevent, that is, unless perhaps a haunting feeling that their spectacles have allowed to filter through something less than what the tragedy as a whole presents. Criticism must thrive as best it can amid such occupational hazards.

We have been reviewing, in this section of the chapter, various versions of the thesis that Shakespearean tragedy cannot be Christian drama. We have found this contention dependent, often if not always, on a tendency to identify the author's vision with the tragic hero's. Either additionally or alternatively, an "atmosphere" argument is sometimes advanced—that various characters voice despair, or that the evils inflicted on innocents suggest an unjust universe, or that chance lurking in ambush precludes a Christian world. In support of this impressionism, it is assumed that drama is a kind of canvas, on which the author paints his "tragic sense of life"; or else an exploratory voyage, during which he writes out his frustrations and testifies to his agnostic or Manichean conjectures. There is also, by some critics, a different and third line of argument, which we have mentioned already in Chapter II—that Shakespeare was no philosopher at all, but simply a technician who managed scenes for their theatrical magic. If so, his art would of course have no relation to Christianity, except as using its materials occasionally for color effects. One variant of this argument is that Shakespeare was basically a businessman, constructing weekday entertainments for box office gain, and hence far removed from any Sunday concerns. This view would presuppose either that drama is not to be taken seriously (despite Aristotle's requirement of a "serious" action in tragedy), or else that Christian insight is irrelevant to the serious issues of secular story. Common to all such arguments is a neglect of the significance of genre, and a shying away from the concept of tragic hamartia, in either its Aristotelian or Christian meaning, and a strained interpretation of catharsis or none at all.

2 Some theological misjudgments

But let us now turn to the other side of the present state of criticism. It cannot be denied that among critics who propose a Christian reading of Shakespeare there is often a failure to use Christian norms consistently. This may be illustrated by the interpretations of *Romeo and Juliet* offered by Siegel, Ribner, and Wilson, for instance.[23] Siegel would have it that in this play Shakespeare wishes his audience to free itself from "conventional religious attitudes" with regard to suicide and to view the lovers' noble romanticism as "part of the larger plan of divine providence" for bringing an end to the feud which has endangered the state. Ribner, while admitting that their suicide is difficult to reconcile with the play's "Christian framework," supposes it to be "a necessary sacrifice to the regeneration of the social whole." The play, in his view, has to do with "education" and "rebirth"—in particular, with Romeo's learning "to overcome evil by a process of growth which culminates in his recognition of the harmonious order of God." Ribner thinks it "absurd" to speak of a tragic flaw in either of the lovers. Wilson, aware of a quandary, writes more evasively. He finds, however, a "purity of motive" in the lovers and declares: "It is not their love that is blighted, after all, but their lives." Their self-destruction is "hardly more than their assent to compelling circumstance." The play's "Christian moral," then, is that providence uses their sacrifices to turn their parents' hatred into love.

In each of these readings, the meaning of the play seems to me distorted. I can find no evidence of any regeneration in Verona, or of Romeo's coming to recognize an "order of God," or of circumstances "compelling" the lovers, or of an unblighted ending in their love. These are all mistaken interpretations. It is no wonder that Ribner falls into speaking of the play as "imperfectly integrated," or that Wilson thinks it "deficient by the severest standard" of tragic art. Auden's reading is certainly preferable: "To kill oneself for love is, perhaps, the noblest act of vanity, but vanity it is, death for the sake of making *una bella figura*." The flaw of the lovers, and of Verona as a whole, is in Auden's view that of too much self-esteem, and the suicides reveal "in the profoundest sense, a failure to love, a proof of selfishness."[24] If read in this light, the play is a remarkable artistic success. Its art consists, we may say, in encouraging our identification with the lovers so that we may pity and fear their plight. But at the same time it challenges us to discern, either during the play or on later reflection, the moral causes of their fate —and on this ground to pity them more wisely, and to fear in ourselves any love as blind as theirs.

Readers not fully alert to the various forms of possible moral defect in human actions may misconstrue the deeper meaning of Shakespearean tragedy. When a hero such as Othello, for instance, commits suicide to punish himself, this does not imply that such an expiation is salvific. Occasionally, interpreters have thought that

Othello dies redeemed,[25] largely because they confuse this hero's remorse with Christian contrition. But had they pondered, by way of comparison, the inadequacy of Macbeth's remorse, or the teaching of Aquinas that a natural inclination to remorse remains even in "lost" souls (*S. T.* I–II. 85. 2), they could have avoided unwarranted inferences. Othello's remorse for having thrown away his "pearl," they could have perceived, is not rectifying but compounding his earlier urge to smite mercilessly.

A persistent temptation for unwary critics is to mistake tragic *liebestod* for a Christian martyrdom. Strangely, Siegel has slipped into this trap when reading *Romeo and Juliet,* despite his awareness that the traditional view of suicide was voiced by Friar Laurence when warning Romeo (in III. iii.) against "doing damned hate upon thyself." While granting that this would seem to imply the damnableness of Romeo's ultimate deed, Siegel prefers to believe that Romeo, "like the Christian saints," ends by renouncing the world to gain an everlasting life. Here the religious tone of Romeo's rhetoric has lulled Siegel into confusing Christian renunciation with a false substitute; and thereby he fails to be consistent with his own judgment in Othello's case, that suicide entails the hero's damnation. We shall be noting, when we study *Antony and Cleopatra* later in this chapter, how easy it is for numerous critics, even those attempting a Christian interpretation, to read romanticism's blind love as a salvific love. But let us turn attention, now, to a related area of misunderstanding—the nature of a tragic hero's obedience to Divine Providence. Do we not need to distinguish between a dutiful obedience and one that is, instead, unwittingly reprobate? Consider, for instance, *Hamlet.*

In readings of *Hamlet* there has been widespread confusion, since in this play the theological issues are unusually complex. With concepts of revenge, grace, conscience, repentance, and providence all challenging our assessment in the dramatic context, the task has often seemed bewildering. Even Virgil Whitaker, a critic uncommonly knowledgeable in matters of theology, has concluded despairingly that Shakespeare "found no profound meaning" in the action of *Hamlet.* "The system of Christian thought which plays so large a part in the language of the play," he complains, "is simply not reconciled with the action as a whole." And on the moot question of Hamlet's "salvation" at the end, he remarks that Horatio's hope "is not necessarily unfounded, but it is not founded on the action of the play," since no "genuine contrition" is evident in Hamlet. Without contrition, can he be a saved soul?[26]

Whitaker's pupil, Eleanor Prosser, bypasses this question in her *Hamlet and Revenge* (1967), where after making a strong case for the devilishness of the Ghost, she nevertheless slides into believing that Hamlet eventually fights his way out of hell to heaven. Miss Prosser relies, as at least a dozen other recent commentators have done,[27] on Hamlet's tone of serenity in resigning himself to "a divinity that shapes our ends," and on his confession of "a special providence" in the fall of a sparrow. These words, she supposes, clearly place Hamlet's "new orientation in the context of Christian faith."[28] But do they really? And is H. S. Wilson justified in saying that, since there is "no providence in the theodicy of the ancients," Hamlet's submitting to providence is proof of his purified motives?[29] Actually, Wilson is mistaken about the ancients. Plutarch's belief in providence, in the sense of an overarching divine justice, is attested in a well-known treatise; and such doctrine is conspicuous in the writings of Plotinus and other Platonists.[30] Seneca's *De Providentia* was well-known in the Renaissance. Might therefore Hamlet's doctrine, in fact, be more sub-Christian than Christian? Too often critics have not thought to ask. Roland Frye, among others, is confident that Hamlet is professing here "the grounds of a Christian hope" and a "readiness" which is "essentially and explicitly Christian."[31]

Since this question is of major importance, not only to the meaning of *Hamlet*, but to the whole theory of tragedy we are searching for in Shakespeare's general practice, let us explore it carefully. In doing so, we may wish to recall some of the judgments of critics who have seen, not salvation, but a pagan fatalism in Hamlet's final attitude. H. B. Charlton has written:

> The end is despair. . . . Worst of all, the recognition of the will's impotence is accepted as spiritual resignation; and the resignation is not seen as the moral abnegation, the *gran rifuto,* which it certainly is; on the contrary, it is phrased as if it were the calm attainment of a higher benignity, whereas it is nothing more than a fatalist's surrender of his personal responsibility.[32]

Moody Prior is of similar opinion. He comments that although there is an impression of quiet resignation in Hamlet's talk, "there is no suggestion of exaltation in a joyful possession of truth. . . . Moreover, it ends in an acceptance of uncertainty: 'Since no man knows aught of what he leaves, what is't to leave betimes?' " Prior likens this mood to the *ataraxia* of the Pyrrhonists and thinks it in no sense a Christian resolution.[33] E. M. Tillyard sees a mood of quietism, unaccompanied by any regeneration. Although the play in his view has a Christian framework, its hero attains something less than a religious enlightenment.[34]

Tillyard's testimony seems to me particularly significant, because he had hoped to find "regeneration," as (in his view) a requirement for "highest tragedy"; but on failing to find it in Hamlet, he decided the play should be called a "problem play" rather than a tragedy. I think Tillyard's proposed classification ill-advised, even though it has been taken up by a few subsequent critics, and tried out on other plays by Ernest Schanzer in *The Problem Plays of Shakespeare* (1963). It rests on a misconception of tragic art. Why should a play cease to be tragedy simply because the audience has the problem of assessing the validity of the hero's vision as compared to his neighbors' vision, or as compared to background norms which the hero is failing to meet? This, I should think, is intrinsic to tragedy, that the hero disappoint us by his defective understanding. But Tillyard, influenced by modern studies in ancient myth and ritual, is overeager to identify tragedy with a saving discovery by the hero. While I consider correct Tillyard's reading of Hamlet's final mood, he seems to me to extend unduly the requirements for tragedy. He acknowledges that Hamlet, without undergoing religious regeneration, "does change in some sort." Very well, but if so, why cannot a nonregenerative change suffice for tragedy? Aristotle was content with a reversal and recognition near the end of a tragedy. If we require additionally that the recognition involve a "rebirth" of a saving sort, are we not moving tragedy into the genre of comedy?

I am not suggesting that the genre of tragedy is violated if there be included, in some tragedies, a countermovement toward comedy on the part of subordinate characters (such as Malcolm in *Macbeth,* or Richmond in *Richard III,* or Edgar in *King Lear*), or that in a special case (such as *Lear*) this countermovement may not progressively provide the tragic hero himself glimpses of religious enlightenment. The Christian view of history, as scholars have recognized,[35] postulates something besides nature's cycles, a wayside opportunity for spiritual progress, even when enemies of the good act perversely, since the very destructiveness of their activities can spur what Jacques Maritain has called "indirect creative repercussions." Probably in all of Shakespeare's tragedies there is at least the ambiguous gain of a new equilibrium of civic peace when the play's conflict has come to its dead end. But a tragedy does not normally entail the salvation of the hero. It concludes, usually, with his death amid despair. According to Aristotle the best ending for a tragedy is an unhappy one. And if in Christian tragedy the final unhappiness implies also, usually, a soul lost in damnable error, this should not surprise us.

Is Hamlet so lost? Let us look closely at his confession of "a special providence in the fall of a sparrow." Is his faith here parallel to Christ's in Matthew 10:29? The whole context of that biblical verse carries as its theme God's watchful care. Man is in God's eyes "of more value than many sparrows" (verse 31). He should therefore put his trust in a heavenly Father, who can guard him as a sheep among wolves, so that he need not fear those serpent-like men who "scourge you in their synagogues" (verse 17). They can kill only the body, not the soul. If we measure by this Gospel teaching, is not Hamlet's faith tragically perverse? He is a self-proclaimed "scourge." His conscience is much like that of the blind synagogue. He has just gloried in killing Rosencrantz and Guildenstern, with the hope their souls may perish unshriven. He has praised his own "rashness" as the work of a divinity. And now, instead of facing the future with Christian cheer, he resigns himself to a weary readiness to let come what will come, shoving aside a "gaingiving" in his heart. Shakespeare tells us in *Richard III,* through Third Citizen:

> By a divine instinct men's minds mistrust
> Ensuing dangers . . . (II. iii. 42).

May not the warning in Hamlet's heart be the genuine "divine" he should be obeying? Instead, he indifferently awaits that moment of rashness in which we will hear him shout: "Then, venom, to thy work!" Is this the cry of a sheep, or of a serpent-like scourge?

Calvin, an authority whom Roland Frye should certainly respect, has some wise remarks on Christian providence in his *Institutes* I. xvii. 3–5. He warns against "profane men" who think it "vain for anyone to busy himself in taking precautions." "These fools," he says, "do not consider what is under their very eyes, that the Lord has inspired in men the arts of taking counsel and caution, by which to comply with his providence in the preservation of life itself." They plunge headlong into dangers, rejecting the Spirit's guidance, while covering up their own evil deeds with the name "God." They argue that they "could not resist God, who had so appointed from eternity." Then, "whatever does happen now, they so impute to God's providence that they close their eyes to the man who clearly has done it," and call crimes virtues. Calvin's theme is that God's providence does not relieve us of responsibility, does not excuse us from due prudence, does not exculpate our wickedness.[36]

In the light of such commentary, it seems likely that many in Shakespeare's audience would have seen in Hamlet a profane fool and ignorant scourge—and might thereupon have confessed, "There, but for the grace of God, go I." That is, they would have understood the tragedy's deeper meaning. They would have been familiar with the type of scourge represented, for instance, in Attila or Tamburlaine—a person of ungodly ambition who nevertheless served providence by punishing sins in others. Further, they could have remembered that proud Assyria in Isaiah 10 is called the rod of God's anger, His instrument but with an evil motive; and that in Joshua 23 the Israelites were warned that if they turned from God He would use the Canaanites as "a trap for you, a scourge on your side, and thorns in your eyes." Is not Hamlet just such an instrument of God, yet no child of His when acting as mousetrapper, scourge, and public irritant? Hamlet's willy-nilly yielding to providence is a blind obedience such as the Bible ascribes to the unrighteous.

Such a hero's distorting of the meaning of "special providence" does not, however, make the play un-Christian. On the contrary, *Hamlet* carries much evidence that its author's framework is Christian. Lurking in the drama's wayside passages is the Christian lore of a Marcellus, and of Claudius at prayer, and of Ophelia in her revenant role in Act IV, and of the Gravedigger singing at his work —and even of Hamlet himself in his oaths "By the rood" and "God-a-mercy." Hamlet might have been saved by his own oaths, had he but sworn them truly instead of vainly. Tragedy challenges us to see the difference between substance and shadow. It at the same time reveals the reality of providence to be such that even when Hamlet's knowledge of it has dwindled to a shadow, he can yet taste it in its withered appleseed. "Thou wouldst not think how ill all's here about my heart—but it is no matter." Does Shakespeare think it of no matter? Or do we? If we put this illness of heart alongside Hamlet's affirmation of "a divinity that shapes our ends," we discover dramatic irony. For heartsickness is an end to which Hamlet has brought himself by his own roughhewing—that is, by his neglecting the mysteries of Gospel providence and falling into a pagan and reductive view of providence.

3 The nature of tragic discovery

Although Hamlet would heroically cover over his illness of heart, it is one aspect of the drama's *anagnorisis*. We may compare it with the sense of guilt Oedipus felt on discovering who he was. More obscurely than Oedipus, because in Hamlet's case through inner testimony rather than by legal inquiry, Hamlet is discovering who he is and a despair is being voiced, although not in a bang but a whimper. There are implications in his having come to see, a moment earlier, that Laertes has a cause much like his own. This perception makes Hamlet sorry for having offended Laertes and leads him to resolve as reparation to court Laertes' favor. But note a deeper and unvoiced implication in the logic of this situation. If Hamlet expects Laertes to pardon the man who has killed his father, should not Hamlet himself be willing to pardon the man who has killed *his* father—and if so, what cause for revenge would remain? Is not Hamlet caught in an impasse of self-contradiction? He can meet this dilemma, we soon see, only by impaling himself on both its horns—that is, by acknowledging Laertes as a brother and offering apology, yet at the same time continuing a desire to beat him in a duel, under the mask of which there hopefully may arise opportunity for a wayside revenge. With an intention thus divided between pardon and revenge, Hamlet is no less a man to double business bound than his surface brothers but deadly rivals Laertes and Claudius. Only by not looking into this moral fact can Hamlet maintain his sense of "perfect conscience."

Inklings of the bewildered logic of his situation may be contributing, nevertheless, to Hamlet's sickness of heart. For marginally he has, even by his own standards of conscience, some sense of moral fault. In Act III he had confessed, although evasively, that his killing of Polonius was something to repent of; and now in

Act V he confesses to having forgot himself in attacking Laertes. He sees the illogic, we may infer, of his getting angry at Laertes for loving a sister in a way which parallels Hamlet's own love of father. Is he aware also, we may wonder, that by his calling the brother's love false and then summing up his own as in quantity thousands of times as great, he was by implication boasting merely a multiplied falseness in his love of Ophelia? In any case, he is now aware of having hurt the brother by some wildly shot arrows, and to ease his troubled sense of wounded name he laments over his mistake but pleads that it was unintended. The situation in this respect parallels that of Oedipus. Indeed, Shakespeare is very possibly analogizing in Hamlet the twin sins of Oedipus—namely, the Greek hero's unintended slaying of a father and his involving himself blindly in an antinatural version of love for woman.

Hamlet during his meditations in the graveyard has discovered, moreover, a more general and philosophic reason for despair. His earlier savage remark to Claudius about Polonius, that "we fat ourselves for maggots," is now more serenely voiced as he accepts as his own prospective fate the dusty destiny of an Alexander and other men of ambition. And that discovery has the effect of undercutting the value of his chosen role as a "mightly opposite" to Claudius, since it makes apparent a "fall" to which heroes come, as if no more than sparrows in their ultimate greatness. No wonder then that Hamlet now feels that the deep plots of men "pall"; the very devising of them is here recognized as evanescent labor, empty of real reward.

On the nature of Hamlet's self-discovery, Maynard Mack has commented: "The point is that he has now learned, and accepted, the boundaries in which human action, human judgment, are enclosed."[37] It might be somewhat more correct, I think, to say that Hamlet has learned the boundaries of *his* human judgment. That judgment has come to accept its own futility. It has learned what may be called the limits of the human condition, provided we add that Hamlet's graveside view of the human condition has a rather worm's eye perspective as compared to the First Gravedigger's cheerful view of death as a voyage with a biblical meaning for man.[38] Hamlet has become resigned to a fatalism. He would view his own human condition as that of a person not responsible for his madness, although to Horatio we have heard him praise rashness only a moment before. Hamlet's reasoning harbors contradictions which he is too confused to fathom. Hence he can find consolation only in the view that "A man's life is no more than to say 'One'." This is self-recognition in a tragic mode. It notably falls short, however, of the discovery made by Ophelia in Act IV: "Lord, we know what we are but know not what we may be." Ophelia's statement implied that we *may* come to be, through grace, Christian souls with God at our table. Hamlet's only hope is to be a hero in "story" after he dies.

Several reversals of situation, or what Aristotle called peripeteia, have brought Hamlet to his tragic anagnorisis. After rewriting the King's letters during the aborted voyage to England, he then wrote one to Claudius promising to look into the "kingly eyes" and reveal something. Quite evidently his intention was to face down Claudius and expose his treachery. But we see Hamlet arriving instead at a graveside and gazing into sockets of an eyeless skull; and by the end of this scene he has exposed himself to the public eye as guilty of a mad behavior. This makes him, unexpectedly, the object of the Queen's solicitude—"For the love of God, forbear him"—and of the King's "I pray thee, Horatio, wait upon him." Thus (like a shamed Oedipus) he is in no position for placing charges against other people. In a larger way, too, his fortunes are reversed. He had thought of himself at the end of Act I as a man born to set the world right by resetting the very "joints" of time. But now time is showing him to be its subject, one indeed for whom a doomsday has been set by the use to which he has joined time. Only an "interim" can he now call his, since soon messengers from England will be arriving, as Horatio reminds him, with reports of an act of his that can scarcely stand public assessment. In this situation Hamlet resigns himself to the role of instrument rather than agent, letting the King take the initiative.

A despairing self-abandonment is characteristic likewise of Macbeth's end, and of Othello's, and Romeo's. Typically it is climaxed by a final splurge of violence in an attempted vindication of dignity —just as, in a similar way, *Oedipus Tyrannus* concludes with the heroism of self-mutilation. Or we may recall the ending of *Richard II*. There the hero winds up his tragedy in a manner very like Hamlet's: he grabs a weapon from one of his attackers and with it slays two men, crying out as he does so, "Go thou, and fill another room in Hell." But earlier in this same scene, Richard's search had been for a resignation to the prospect of death:

> Nor I nor any man that but man is
> With nothing shall be pleased till he be eased
> With being nothing.

Richard finds "a kind of ease" in flattering himself with the thought that he is "not the first of fortune's slaves"; others before him have endured the like. This mood is similar to Hamlet's. Like Hamlet in his interim between graveyard and final battle, Richard follows thoughts which cycle between ambitious yearnings and a contentment with despair.

In Richard's case, it is significant that Shakespeare shows his fallen hero comparing the two sides of his mood to an entrapment of the mind somewhere between, but short of, two words of Scripture. "Come, little ones" (Christ's invitation to humility as the way to find rest for the soul) is as puzzling to Richard as "It is as hard to come as for a camel / To thread the postern of a small needle's eye" (Christ's warning of humility's impossibility for the worldly-minded man). These biblical counsels tantalize with their elusive meanings. Unable to reconcile them, Richard wavers between shadow-versions of them, between self-negation and self-justification. Sweet music is sour to him, since he recognizes in his own life "time broke in a disordered string" and thoughts which jar. "This music mads me, let it sound no more," he cries. He epitomizes his tragic discovery with the comment, "I wasted time, and now doth time waste me" (Compare Augustine, *Confessions* IX. [iv.] 10: "wasting away time, and wasted by time"). A few moments later, Richard turns to beating his prison keeper, while shouting:

> The Devil take Henry of Lancaster and thee!
> Patience is stale, and I am weary of it.

Like Hamlet, and also like Coriolanus, he dies under the blows of murderous adversaries.

But since Richard's dream has been that of a triumph as Heaven's "anointed," rather than as Heaven's "scourge," it is appropriate dramatically that he should die with a final cry for transcendence in otherworldly terms:

> Mount, mount, my soul! Thy seat is up on high
> Whilst my gross flesh sinks downward, here to die.

One critic, John Vyvyan, supposes that Richard in this last moment is achieving salvation by struggling toward a "kingship of his own soul."[39] But such a reading misunderstands salvation, which has its proper paradigm not in any storming of heaven but in Christ's words: "Father, into thy hand I commend my spirit" (Luke 23:46). The truth is that Richard dies self-deceived, and his dying attempt to scale heaven is pathetic. His hope for an immortality of the soul through a fleeing of the body is a gnostic hope. It is here tragically substituted for a Christian belief in the resurrection of the flesh. It magnificently characterizes, however, a histrionic Richard, who throughout his kingship has pretended to infinite rights with no finite responsibilities, and who has supposed kingship means *not* having to "live with bread like you, feel want, / Taste grief, need friends." This is "sacred" kingship in a false mode. But note that the hero's tragic ending has been shown by Shakespeare to be the consequence of an inability to understand the paradox contained in two "words" of Scripture. The only "discovery" therefore possible for Richard is the tragic one of an "untuned" lyricism, related by defect to a "music" he has failed to achieve.

In other of Shakespeare's tragedies, likewise, what the hero ultimately discovers is self-contradictions which he cannot resolve except by a violent death. Romeo for instance discovers, after his "savage-wild" duel in the churchyard, that he has killed a gentleman who is not only the kinsman of his friend Mercutio but also, like himself, a lover of Juliet, hence a man with whom he ought to be shaking hands. With feelings then swirling between remorse and self-pity, Romeo turns to burying both Paris and himself in a "triumphant grave." With equal illogic, he seeks forgiveness from Tybalt's spirit by offering him as a "favor" his own suicide. The case is much the same in *Julius Caesar*. Brutus discovers that Caesar's spirit, the spirit he had hoped to kill, now walks abroad to turn "our swords/ In our own proper entrails." This is anagnorisis in an Aristotelian form—the hero's encounter with some person through whom he becomes aware of a past mistake, and hence, of who he himself fatefully is. But Brutus would suppress full awareness, as Shakespeare shows by focusing on the confused reasoning of Brutus. When faced by a contradiction between his philosophy's judgment that suicide is a cowardly act and his resolve nevertheless not to be disgraced by the Rome he sought to free, Brutus abandons logic in order to accept fatalistically whatever the day's business may bring. To evade further self-knowledge, he rushes into battle. Then, when brought to confess himself beaten by Caesar's ghost and by "the world," he dramatizes his suicide as a "glory" by which he will outdo his enemies. In this act, as in Romeo's, we see a desperate effort to mask and transcend admitted defeat. The ending of *Richard III* is comparable, except that before death Richard discovers (through ghosts, the means to anagnorisis in this drama) a conscience which condemns him explicitly as guilty of villainy and self-hate. Yet this conscience prevails only for a moment, as if a fearful dream of the night. With the return of day, Richard dismisses conscience as "a word that cowards use" and devotes his action to a "pell-mell" bravery—"If not to Heaven, then hand in hand to Hell."

In none of these plays does anagnorisis lead to a regeneration of the hero. We note Romeo's desperate daring of "another sin upon my head," once he has discovered Paris, the means of his final anagnorisis. Confusedly he then turns to imagining himself "merry," like a lightning (not much enlightening) before death. Similarly, we sense a make-believe in the "joy" asserted by the dying Brutus. The earlier words of Lucius ring in our ears: "The strings, my lord, are false." We may recall also the early reasoning of Brutus himself: "Since the quarrel / Will bear no colour for the thing he is / Fashion it thus . . . ." And if we recall, alongside this, his injunction to his fellow conspirators in II. i.—to "look fresh and merrily" for the hiding of purpose, "as our Roman actors do"—we realize how theatrically Brutus is now putting on joy to disguise a sick heart. He is fashioning for himself a look of glory in order to avoid seeing his suicide for what it really is, a "vile conquest."

4 Anagnorisis and irony in
Antony and Cleopatra

Does not *Antony and Cleopatra* conclude with a similar display of make-believe by its heroes? On this question there has been a wide divergence among critics. On the one hand, romanticists such as G. Wilson Knight see in this play a metaphysic of "transcendental Humanism," in which life conquers death by a Phoenix-like love that is infinite and divine. At the end of the play, Knight believes, we are left "with a sense of peace and happiness, an apprehension of pure immortality."[40] Dover Wilson in part echoes this view by reading the play as Shakespeare's "Hymn to Man."[41] On the other hand, however, M. R. Ridley has characterized the passion of the lovers as "an *égoisme à deux*"; and to William Rosen the play's final events "approach the point of being ludicrous."[42] In Rosen's view, Cleopatra's suicide is her "consummate escape from the world and her most accomplished self-dramatization."

The romantic estimate, I would say, is little other than a latter-day amplification of the view the lovers assume. It is not ultimately Shakespeare's. As poet he is an adroit master of double perspective, as our earlier analysis of his *Lucrece* has shown. He knows well how to depict the psychology of self-fashioned dream, but his true view is the covert one which Ridley and Rosen have rightly sensed. The "transcendence" the lovers achieve is surrounded and punctuated therefore with Shakespeare's dramatic irony. The triumph in death which they imagine turns out to be both glamorous and hollow— evidence of a nobility in phosphorescent decay. Step by step the lovers delude themselves, fascinated from the start with their own dissembling and playacting. With soaring language they trick them- selves into a world of heroic lie, which becomes for them a compen- sating eternity for the earthly disasters into which they betray love. Appropriately to tragic art, Shakespeare does not moralize this truth but indirectly reveals it as the reality beneath the grandly pitiful and fearful events of his story. Let us turn to an examination of the play to show how this is so, and to discover with what larger implica- tions it is enriched.

Suppose we put aside for the moment the drama's first half and turn to its anagnorisis, a matter on which we have been focusing in other of Shakespeare's tragedies. Do we not find Antony and Cleo- patra arriving at a "discovery" which brings self-knowledge in a desperate sense only?[43] A remorse is evident, although more self- critical on his part than on hers, after their flight from Actium has disgraced them and reversed their fortunes. The immediate means of anagnorisis is here the flight itself, by which Antony recognizes in himself a person tied to Egypt's rudder. He then feels an over- whelming shame for having "offended reputation"; and Cleopatra cries out, "Forgive my fearful sails!" Yet this is not a self-knowledge which brings repentance. Antony does nothing toward giving up the rash doting for which he reproves himself, nor does Cleopatra give up her coquettish angling. His lament that "Now I must . . . dodge / And palter in the shifts of lowness" strikes us as an epitome of what both he and Cleopatra have been doing in this scene and will continue to do. With shifts and dodges, they will palter not only with Caesar but with each other. Their actions thus enter on a maze of self-contradiction. Cleopatra has such "full supremacy" over his spirit, says Antony, that she might command him "from the bidding of the gods"; yet two scenes later he is railing at her, himself now playing the role of a jealous god. Raging, he upbraids *her* for intemperance. What Antony's anagnorisis expands into, in these scenes, may be summed up in several phrases: "I / Have lost my way forever"; "Let's mock the midnight bell"; "I'll make death love me."

Discovery takes on a second phase when, in a later contest at sea, all of Cleopatra's ships desert, this time to join Caesar's. With fortunes now utterly hopeless, Antony cries out:

> O this false soul of Egypt! This grave charm,
> Whose eye becked forth my wars and called them home,
> Whose bosom was my crownet, my chief end,
> Like a right gypsy hath at fast and loose
> Beguiled me to the very heart of loss.

Here he recognizes that his "chief end" has been the bosom of a "Triple-turned whore," and that her eye is indeed a "grave" charm, since it has brought him to a shirt of Nessus, like that which destroyed Hercules. The "witch" shall die for it, he resolves. Yet the revenge to which he now turns for his chief end is essentially a reverse kind of jealous dotage. And when, a moment later, a report comes that Cleopatra has beaten him to the crownet of a love-death, by having already slain herself, Antony quickly tacks about in order to sail after and emulate her supposed courage.[44] His dream, at this point, of emulating Aeneas is Shakespearean irony, for it was by sailing away from Dido that the historical Aeneas showed *his* courage.

Cycles of mood are typical of tragic heroes. That Antony's mood has cycled around to a new version of his Actium behavior is a signal of the climax in his undoing. What is being fulfilled, perhaps, is a prediction we overheard in II. i—that a witchcraft-beauty could "keep his brain fuming. . . ./Even till a Lethed dullness." For here (in IV. xiv.) Antony is likening himself to a cloud of shifting shape, ready to dislimn. And he is interpreting courage in terms of "Unarm . . . . we must sleep . . . . Lie down . . . . couch on flowers." Such intellectual absurdity is the seal of a final despair. The "torch is out" indeed—not that of Cleopatra, really, but the light of his own reason. What remains is the darkly tragic knowledge that "force entangles/Itself with strength." And note how Shakespeare puns on the irony of this situation, by having the Mars-like Antony confess: "Now all labor/Mars what it does."

Even Antony's last labor, his attempt to ennoble death as a lover's bed, is undercut by comic aspects. He bungles his suicide, and lives to learn that Cleopatra has merely faked hers. His dignity is then reduced to being carried, marred of body, to a Cleopatra who is more concerned for her own safety than for his. Unceremoniously he must be hoisted up to her, with what Cleopatra in mock-irony calls "sport indeed." And when at last in her arms, he finds his own efforts to speak interrupted by hers. (This is characteristic: she had interrupted him six times in Act I, scene iii.) The whole scene has a different import from Plutarch's: Shakespeare's Cleopatra wipes away no blood on Antony's face, does not here greet him as husband, or forget her own misery for his.[45] Instead, she upstages him in self-dramatization. The very hyperboles in which she sings his greatness call our attention chiefly to herself.[46] And ironically, the self-discovery she proclaims after his death is that she has "no friend" except her own resolution. The Antony of her imagination, we infer, cannot be thought her friend.

Cleopatra's experience of tragic recognition, until this scene, has been minimal. She has known, earlier, moments of disfavor which always have seemed reparable by shifts of one kind or another. But now Antony's suicide confronts her not only with the loss of an idol of her affections but (more importantly) with imminent danger of public obloquy, since how can she henceforth avoid rebukes from Octavia, or be safe from display as a showpiece by Caesar? It is this fear, only marginally admitted, that makes of Antony's dying such a doomsday event for her. "O sun, / Burn the great sphere thou movest in!" she cries. Let there be a general conflagration of the world. For, otherwise, only by the operation of knife, drugs, and serpents can she keep "safe" her honor!

The size of Cleopatra's sorrow is proportioned to this half-repressed worry. Fear prompts, we can suspect, much of the fervor of her wish that she could quicken Antony with kissing. "Noblest of men, woo't die? / Hast thou no care of *me*?" Here the note of self-concern (which Shakespeare correlates with a linguistic lapse into the vulgar "woo't"—as in Hamlet's mouthing in the graveyard) hints the real nature of her plight. The absence of Antony makes the world seem for her no better than a sty—not simply because Antony can be imagined as the "crown o' the earth" and the world's "jewel," but because now she finds melting in her hands, and slipping from them, a crown and gem on which her own glory as Queen-mistress depends. The "garland" that is withering was *her* prize, the trophy to *her* greatness. This fact, not openly confessed, is our clue to why she rails at "the false housewife Fortune"—as if thereby to hide from her own offense of false housewifery. It can explain, likewise, her impulse to "throw my scepter at the injurious gods,"[47] for now her own status as an earthly goddess is at stake. Her threat brings to focus her resentment of the gods, whom paradoxically she would rival by her own self-deification. Shakespeare allows her the ironic self-recognition of desperation:

> impatience does
> Become a dog that's mad. Then is it sin
> To rush into the secret house of death
> Ere death dare come to us?

Implicit here is a haunting sense of sin, from which she can be free only by making herself first mad. For then (as a dog in a sty) she will be able to rush "becomingly" to the house of death which hides her secret fear of loss of status.

In this circumstance we see her turning instinctively, as Brutus had done just before his suicide, to a make-believe joy:

> What, what! Good cheer! Why, how now, Charmian!
> My noble girls! Ah, women, women, look,
> Our lamp is spent, it's out!

The lamp that is "spent," ironically, is here (while overtly that of Antony's life) covertly that of daylight reason and troublesome conscience. And the imagery further suggests the queen of a house of ill fame cheering up her girls. This underside of the truth, the quean or wench within the female monarch, is the secret of Cleopatra's gay self-abandon.

> Let's do it after the high Roman fashion,
> And make death proud to take us.

Yet such transcendence, of course, is the reverse of John Donne's "Death, be not proud." It accords, rather, with that of the cult which Plutarch mentions as flourishing in Alexandria during the days after Actium—the order called *Synapothanumenon,* of those who agreed to die together and made great feasts to their fraternity, while Cleopatra studied poisons for ease of self-destruction.

But just as there were shifts and delays between Antony's first declaring a love of death and his final suicide, so likewise in Cleopatra's case. Despite her famed "celerity in dying," she must so to speak hop a forty paces first, in order to make defect seem perfection, and thus delusively wind up our breathlessness into blessing what's riggish. Compare, in *Romeo and Juliet,* the penchant of the lovers for making *una bella figura,* as Auden has said.

Even when locked in her monument, Cleopatra squirms and wriggles—to probe the possibility of gaining a new earthly status from Caesar. In asking instruction of him

> That she preparedly may frame herself
> To the way she's forced to

is she not ambiguously inviting him to "force" her to be his mistress? But Caesar can be equally ambiguous. His reply is that he "cannot live / To be ungentle." That tells her nothing of what he means by "gentle." She desires to learn an "hourly" obedience, she replies, but first would gladly look him in the face. A moment later, when Proculeius breaks in, she stresses her determination never to submit to Octavia's chastising eye or to Rome's varletry. Then, through hymning to Dolabella her dream of Antony's "bounty," she seduces Dolabella to tell her Caesar's secret intentions.[48]

Thus forewarned, Cleopatra tries her most brilliant tactic for melting Caesar's purpose. She turns a defect into perfection, as regards her false account of money matters, by explaining that she has but kept some token for friendly use—for instance to induce Livia and Octavia to mediate on her behalf. Is she not implying that as Caesar's mistress she would know how to mollify his wife and sister? At the same time, through blushes and a tongue-lashing of Seleucus, she is advertizing her femininity and her need for a lordly understanding on Caesar's part, a "mercy" toward her frailties. But Caesar will not be seduced, even though she twice calls him "My master and my lord!" "Not so. Adieu," he replies; a "friend" only will he be. This is not what she wants. It leaves her with the choice of either living to see her arts disgraced in public parody or being "noble to myself" through suicide. A middle road, that of accepting personal humiliation in order to keep her kingdom for her sons, she never considers. Instead, she now issues orders to put into effect her contingent plan for the aspic trick.

Shakespeare has made the death scene itself a gorgeous spectacle of tragic irony. Every detail has an emblematic quality. The figs and the worm have obvious sexual connotations as well as symbolizing, more generally, an earthy lushness and the poisonous serpent this harbors. When the First Guard remarks afterwards, "And these fig leaves / Have slime upon them," we are reminded of the fig leaves of the Genesis story, there used as a cover for shame, or we think of the slime of the Nile, which Cleopatra herself had associated with decay and gnats. "Look you," says the clown, "the worm is not to be trusted but in the keeping of wise people, for indeed there is no goodness in the worm." Yet we see Cleopatra welcoming this "pretty worm of Nilus" (a Shakespearean pun on *nil us*);[49] for now nihilism is being imagined as liberty.

We perhaps here recall her earlier curse, "Melt Egypt into Nile. And kindly creatures / Turn all to serpents!" (II. 5. 78). She had invoked that curse when venting anger on a supposed "rogue" and "villain" who had brought her unwelcome news. But now she is fulfilling it in herself. Her words are truer than she knows when she resolves:

> I have nothing
> Of woman in me. Now from head to foot
> I am marble-constant . . . .

From head to foot she is in fact making herself marble-hearted—thus negating true womanhood for the stony immortality of an Egyptian mummy. Genuine motherhood (i.e., any care for her living sons) is being neglected, while constantly she dreams of the serpent she can nurse as her "baby." This magnificent parody of love is Shakespeare's invention, not mentioned by Plutarch.[50]

Added also by Shakespeare is the telltale fact (which Daniel had introduced in his account) that the crown Cleopatra calls for is set on her head "awry," giving her queenship a comic aspect. Further, her very kiss becomes one of death, when Iras falls dead after kissing her. "Have I the aspic in my lips?" she asks—and then speaks of her eagerness to have Antony spend his kiss on her lips. That would be her Heaven.[51] We recall at this point her earlier vow that if ever she were cold-hearted toward Antony, let Heaven dissolve her life by dropping a poisoned hailstone in her neck. Is this

not being figuratively fulfilled within a neck, poisoned with jealousy, which now we see Cleopatra dying to offer Antony? Jealous
love essentially is a paradoxical fire of cold-heartedness which dis-
solves life by slaying with its embraces. (Compare the kiss with
which Othello killed Desdemona, in the name of a "marble
Heaven.") In Cleopatra's case we note, as the final spur to her
suicide, a jealousy lest her so-called "husband" spend his kiss on
Iras. The moral irony of this Shakespearean detail is equalled only
by what follows, Cleopatra's placing of the asp as a kind of brooch
to her royal robe. Triumph can then be made satisfying by scorn-
fully calling Caesar an "ass"—after which comes the music of a
swan song, concluded by Charmian's comment:

> Death, in thy possession lies
> A lass unparalleled. Downy windows, close . . .

In a double sense, here, Cleopatra's eyes are "downy": feathered
with a swansdown loveliness, while shuttered down against the
light of truth. A lover of death, *alas,* can become *possessed* with
unparalleled *lies.*

Thus while on the surface of Shakespeare's dramatic scene there
has been resounding an entrancing lyricism, his symbolism and his
canny choice of diction have revealed an underside of parody,
reflecting his own metaphysical wit. He has furnished us, moreover, a counterpointing folk wisdom on the part of Egypt's rural
clown. This serves much the same purpose as do the remarks of the
Gravedigger-clown in Act V of *Hamlet.* Cleopatra's joy, in this
witty servant's estimate, is "joy of the worm." Those who die of
it, he adds, "do seldom or never recover." A woman "something
given to lie" may make "good report" of the worm; yet anyone who
will believe all that such reporters claim "shall never be saved by
half that they do." After this jest, and another on how the devil can
"mar" five out of every ten women (a parabolic jest which Shakespeare may be adapting from his recollection of the biblical virgins
who failed to keep oil in their lamps), surely at least a few of the
play's auditors, perhaps five out of ten, should be able to recognize
Cleopatra's love-death for what it is, a martyrdom *marred* by
vainglory.

Let us pursue further the wit of the play, even at the risk of discovering a Shakespeare cunning past man's thought. As we have
noted, scenes of low comedy in a tragedy provide the author a

medium through which he can toy with some major motifs in his main theme. With this in mind, let us recall from II. vii. Antony's mock-description of the Egyptian crocodile. This strange serpent, Antony tells Lepidus, moves with its own "organs," and "the elements once out of it, it transmigrates." The figurative relevance of this to Cleopatra, Antony's well-organed "serpent of Old Nile," can scarcely escape audience notice. Further, part of this lore's amusement depends on its outlandish superstitiousness—which for Elizabethan auditors could evoke their contrasting knowledge of Christian doctrine. That is, they could recognize in Egypt's notion of immortality a fake "mystery," the comic reverse of Christian mystery lore.[52] In this same scene, a remark by Lepidus may have a similar overtone for the audience. "I have heard the Ptolemies' pyramises," he says, "are very goodly things." Since Lepidus apparently means to say "pyramids," his slip of the tongue is comic as suggesting a drunken lisp. But besides this, I think, "pyramises" can be taken as a Shakespearean pun on the fiery "misses" of Egypt; or it can be heard as an allusion to Pyramus of Babylon, the Asian world's archetypal hero of love-death legend. And since Babylon and Egypt are synonymous in Christian typology, any indirect mention of Pyramus could remind an Elizabethan auditor of the whole catalog of paganism's "saints"—which in Chaucer's listing was headed by Cleopatra, and next to her, Thisbe. The immediate dramatic irony is that Antony might have recognized in the malapropism of Lepidus a prophecy of his own fate as a "Pyramus." (Just as Pyramus slew himself on mistakenly supposing his beloved dead, so likewise will Antony do.) Yet how many of *us* would be alert enough to catch "oracle" in the babblings of a winebibber?

Chaucer was certainly being ironic in his *Legend of Good Women*. There was "nevere unto hire love a trewer quene" than Cleopatra, he tells us, but at the same time pictures her as choosing, for the climax of her love, a pit full of serpents. His point, both sly and compassionate, is that she was a martyr to blind Cupid, even to the nth power of Cupid's godhead, a pitiably idiotic worship to which good women are prone—especially in Egypt, which Christians know to be a land of "fleshpots" and spiritual darkness, to which Babylon is a next door neighbor, both of them parodies of life's "promised land." Chaucer's reserve in not making this implication explicit is the mark of his ontological, rather than didactic, focus. In this respect he anticipates the genius of Shakespeare's art.

Both poets no doubt shared the estimate of Cleopatra which prevails in Western tradition. This estimate we can find stated explicitly in the final lines of Samuel Daniel's play, where the Chorus speaks of a greatness which "greatnesse marres, / And wrackes it selfe, selfe driven / On Rockes of her owne might." This nautical metaphor Shakespeare had used in *Romeo and Juliet,* where his play was analogizing the legend of Pyramus and Thisbe. In *Antony and Cleopatra* the metaphor of sailing is equally thematic, and present even in Cleopatra's semifinal "yare good Iras," and in her resolve to sail again for Cydnus—the river on which she had emblematized Voluptas, and to which she is now circularly returning. Circular love voyage implies whirlpool wrack. Such is the typified destiny of Cupid's saints. And this helps us understand why in various Elizabethan versions of Cleopatra's story she was so often associated with Helen of Troy, Circe, the Sirens, and a mermaid wantonness.[53] Like Narcissus, so Howell's *Fable of Ovid* (1560) tells us, she "drowned with desyre" of self-love.[54]

Whereas Roman authors emphasized usually Cleopatra's lustfulness and Antony's intemperance, Christian authors tended to focus on her hellish guile and on Antony's idolatry.[55] This latter stress on the falsely religious attitude of the lovers was a more ultimate dimension in characterizing them. That is, they were understood as parodies of Christian sainthood. Critics in our own day have not quite caught this perspective. Willard Farnham, for instance, has attempted to assess Cleopatra by balancing a case "for" and a case "against" her canonization in Cupid's catalogue of saints.[56] Although this approach would be congenial to Plutarch, who is always concerned to balance faults and virtues neatly, it misses the point that all of Cupid's saints are inevitably defective if looked at from a Christian perspective. Both Chaucer and Shakespeare, I would say, understood Cleopatra as belonging entirely and topmost among Cupid's saints, yet as tragic because that kind of sainthood is blind and self-defeating.

Precisely because pagan flight mimics Christian pilgrimage, and because an exclusive dependence on *eros* can counterfeit the higher version of love which Christians call *agape,* there is analogy between these two which renders the substitute version ironic. The evident analogy, however, has misled various modern critics. Too often they have stumbled into equating the two kinds of love. Irving Ribner, for instance, speaks of a "regeneration," a "redeeming" change, in the Cleopatra of Act V; and H. C. Goddard sees her as a "new self," listening "only to divine commands."[57] Similarly in S. L. Bethell's interpretation, both Antony and Cleopatra achieve an "eternal triumph" after being cleansed of all taint of selfishness by a "purgatory" of adversity; and to J. A. Bryant their final "selfless expenditure of themselves" embodies "the distinctly Christian ideal of humanity." These critics are confusing Christian ideals with pagan ones. They misread Caesar's comment on Cleopatra's "strong toil of grace," supposing it to imply a grace of Christian quality.[58]

No doubt there is analogy between natural grace and supernatural grace. Yet Bryant is mistaken in attributing to Antony a Samson-like final triumph and to Cleopatra a final "meekness." What these lovers embody, actually, is a simulacrum of such virtues, their ersatz version. When Cleopatra "looks like" she could catch another Antony in her strong toil of grace, Shakespeare is testifying to her magic for alluring, even in death, the hearts of some Antonys in the play's audience. If under the spell of the moment we allow ourselves to be caught, our second reflections should awake us to the realization of what salt fish we are. Perhaps the art of tragedy consists in this very temptation to confusion—for the sake of our subsequent recognition of our folly. That is, a tragedy's beguiling heroisms serve to prompt mistaken judgments, sc that then we can confess and evaluate our proneness to illusion.

How is it that a critic such as H. S. Wilson can conclude that the love between Antony and Cleopatra "reflects a distinctively Christian mode of thought and feeling"?[59] He does so because he sees, rightly enough, an analogy between their love and that of the Christian faith; yet he fails to see that these two kinds of love are morally contrary rather than compatible. He would read the play as a triumphant "vindication of the love of a man and woman," and would assert that their earthly love "does not raise any religious issue." Can an alert reader suppose this so? In retrospect, do we not find it untenable? We recall, for instance, the play's report of Cleopatra's dressing herself as a "new Isis" in a ceremony at Alexandria (an episode Shakespeare took over from Plutarch's story). We remember also, from earlier in the drama, Cleopatra's swearing "by Isis" (when threatening to give Charmian bloody teeth), and Charmian's prayer to Isis to bless cuckoldry (as Alexas aptly remarks, so that women may "make themselves whores"). Love, in Egypt, has *this* religious aspect. An impressive number of parallels between Cleopatra and the legendary Isis, especially as regards "the divine humanity which is common to Isis and Cleopatra," has been pointed out by Michael Lloyd.[60] Emblematically, Shakespeare is portraying her as an Isis-Venus-Juno, just as in Antony, similarly, he is showing the nature of a Bacchus-Mars-Jove. Thus a pagan polytheistic Trinity characterizes each of them.[61]

It will be worth our time to explore further the play's symbolism, since by doing so we can increasingly appreciate how a Christian dramatist uses typology to reformulate the facts of pagan love tragedy. Plutarch had said, of the lovers' meeting at Cydnus, that "there went a rumor in the peoples mouthes, that the goddess Venus was come to play with the god Bacchus, for the generall good of all Asia."[62] In Cinthio's *Cleopatra* (1583), however, an attendant comments to the lovers regarding this episode: "That day / The miserable ruin was declared / Of you yourself and also of your realm."[63] A Nuntius in Daniel's version offers a similar view, but more cryptically: Cleopatra did there show "what earth could shew" and what amazed all Asia with wonder (lines 1461–62). Shakespeare, avoiding even this much intrusive didacticism, hints his estimate, through the comment of an admiring but cynical Enobarbus, that the "holy priests" (i.e. of Asia) bless her riggishness. The kind of "prosperity" in store for Asia is also indicated by Shakespeare— through Enobarbus' comment that Cleopatra's playing left a vacancy in the marketplace, because all the citizens deserted it to gaze on her. This suggests a spellbinding that will make the city's prosperity short-lived.

Antony and Cleopatra do indeed transcend the world of Caesar by their ecstasies of flight into role-playing, at the expense of the business of life. "Let Rome in Tiber melt," and "Melt Egypt into Nile," well expresses the goal of their imaginative passion devoted to a Narcissus-like honor more entrancing than earthly duty. In one sense, their lives are richer than Caesar's, as every reader of the play feels. They have vibrancy, spontaneity, and infinite variety. They are playful, flexible, and adventuresome. The scope of their emotional outreach, although not identical with insight, is awesome. These lovers are spirited enough to demand of life a religious dimension, a new heaven and a new earth, whereas Caesar's world of values is restricted to the pragmatic order and a commonsense morality. His worldly prudence and calculated temperance is merely rational. They, on the other hand, celebrate the mysteries of nature's fertility. Yet their rites of love paradoxically unman Antony and make Cleopatra boyish, a fate further symbolized by Egypt's eunuch slaves and bastard princelings. A "gaudy night" celebrates Cleopatra's birthday, whereas "a prosperous day" of universal peace, when the three-nooked world shall bear the "olive," is Caesar's hope and achievement.

Shakespeare's own respect for Caesar's achievement is evident in *Cymbeline,* where there is implied the Christian view that Caesar Augustus provided an order of earthly peace within which a heavenly "Prince of Peace" could be born.[64] But Antony and Cleopatra, by contrast, have been portrayed as seeking their kind of peace in a divinizing of themselves. They have "Immortal longings," but in a form which parodies the Christian pattern of dying to the flesh in order to resurrect it. Moreover, Antony's turning to the "East" for his glory, and his mention of feasting "Three Kings" from the East, are Shakespearean touches for highlighting a parody of the Christ story—as are also Cleopatra's wish to outshine and supplant Herod and her being hailed finally as "Eastern Star." When we hear her so hailed by a Charmian who in Act I had wished for a "child . . . to whom Herod of Jewry may do homage," may we not suppose this to have been, secretly, Cleopatra's wish too?

Through other details also, Shakespeare seems to be suggesting a dark analogy to Christian legend in the story of Antony and Cleopatra. Antony's farewell supper in Act IV, for instance, has a tantalizing similarity to Christ's Last Supper.[65] There is a traitor at the table in the person of Enobarbus, who will later kill himself in remorse. Antony is trying to comfort his followers. He does so with phrases such as "Scant not my cups," "Haply you shall not see me more," "Tend me tonight two hours," and "I hope well of tomorrow, and will lead you / Where rather I'll expect victorious life . . . ." These words have a ring oddly like Christ's. But there is an underlying contrast to the Christian paradigm. Antony is inviting his men to "drown consideration" in drink; his purpose for the morrow is to "fight maliciously." On that next day, indeed, his most loyal follower, Scarrus—who for Shakespeare, let me suggest, may be a kind of parody of Christ's "beloved" disciple, John—is so inspired to the "sport" of war that he now fights

> As if a god in hate of mankind had
> Destroyed in such a shape. (IV. viii. 25)

For this, Scarrus is rewarded by being given Cleopatra's hand to kiss (compare Calvary's "Woman, behold thy son!" and "Son, behold thy mother," of John 19:27), while Antony cries out: "Behold this man" (a parody of the Ecce Homo of John 19:6). Perhaps even the detail of Scarrus' scar has an emblematic significance. It formerly, we are told, had the shape of a "T" (which suggests true sacrifice, prefiguratively that of the cross), whereas now it has the shape of an "H" (which suggests, besides the pun on "ache," an upended and overdone "T," perhaps a "Hades" wound).[66]

Shortly after this, Antony himself becomes an ironic Christ. His side pierced, he is lifted up limp on a stone monument, to commit there his spirit to Cleopatra's arms. Then we see Cleopatra, in turn, dead set against the kind of suffering which Christians associate with Calvary, and which Shakespeare's diction evokes. It would disgrace her if

> Mechanic slaves
> With greasy aprons, rules and hammers, shall
> Uplift us to the view.

Rather than any such submitting to Rome's rule, she resolves to "make / My country's high pyramides my gibbet"! Within Egypt's pyramid she then stages a self-immolation which unwittingly parodies a crucifixion.

Some readers may feel that I have been probing excessively the implications of Shakespeare's language. There may be a nettle danger here, I grant; yet if we run from it we risk not grasping the full import of the play. Shakespeare's details of story, it seems to me, serve two purposes simultaneously: the enriching of surface splendor with touches of realistic verisimilitude, while yet so selecting these as to point an underside of irony. And the full dimension of this irony includes some dark analogy to Christian lore by the echoing of a contrast.

Recent support for this way of reading the play comes from a note by Peter Seng on the "Egyptian Bacchanals" which conclude the galley scene of Act II. Seng has discovered that the song, "Come thou monarch of the vine," which a boy is brought forward to sing while Antony leads the Triumvirs in holding hands, has a stanza form, rhyme scheme, and metrics which duplicate those of the

Christian pentecostal hymn *Veni sancte spiritus*. He reasons that Shakespeare is here capping the ironic tensions of the Triumvirs' peace covenant with a parody of Christian pentecostal experience.[67] Marvelous parody it indeed is, especially if we consider its context in the drama—the patched-up nature of the peace these "brothers" are making. For the better sealing of their union, Caesar has approved a marriage of convenience, which Antony accepts; but we overhear the prediction of Enobarbus that "the band that seems to tie their friendship together will be the very strangler of their amity." This will prove true—not only because the friendship bond of a "holy" Octavia will be neglected by Antony, but because the motive for his doing so will be his preference for the spirit of Egyptian bacchanal, which will become a dissolvent, not a bond, of his political friendship with Caesar. And further, there is the irony that this will cause Enobarbus himself to turn traitor to Antony, since Enobarbus' own loyalty, as resting principally on conventional self-advantage, cannot hold up when Egyptian bacchanal takes over Antony.

Contextually we are aware also that the covenant between the Triumvirs is being made aboard a pirate's galley, a fit emblem of Rome's ship of state at this moment. ("Without justice, what are kingdoms but great piracies?" is a question St. Augustine asks in his *City of God*.) It is noteworthy, however, that Caesar, the one man on this ship who remains sober by scanting the wine of the festival, soon afterwards finds occasion to rid himself of the pirate Pompey, and then in a final contest at sea rids himself of Antony. Since Antony's break with Caesar is in the name of Pompey's honor, with which he closely associates his own (see III. iv), Antony is by implication a second Pompey, a greater pirate. And if we recall how in *Measure for Measure* Shakespeare had associated the name Pompey with bawdry, absurd pomp, and piracy, we realize that the moral aura there comically dramatized is serving here in *Antony and Cleopatra* as the subsurface of tragic story.

Another motif in Shakespeare's symbolism is embodied in the character Eros. The name and role of Eros had been briefly mentioned by Plutarch but is much expanded by Shakespeare, who sounds the name a total of twenty-one times. The first mention is when Enobarbus calls out, "How now, friend Eros!" at the beginning of Act III, scene v. The immediately preceding scene, let us note, began with Antony's words, "Nay, nay, Octavia . . . ." Through juxtaposing these scenes, Shakespeare may be suggesting that once Octavia is shuffled off by Antony he will turn to Eros for a substitute friendship. When we next see Eros, in III. xi, he is urging Cleopatra to comfort Antony; and by IV. iv. he has become Antony's armorer. But now Cleopatra is virtually identified with him when, arising from bed to give Eros assistance, she is called by Antony "The armorer of my heart." "False, false," Antony then mutters—with apparent reference to some misbuckling by Eros and Cleopatra, yet allowing the play's auditors to apply these words also in a moral sense. A few lines later, we hear Antony say: "Thou fumblest, Eros, and my Queen's a squire / More tight at this than thou." More tight at what? At buckling Antony into what will become, before long, his shirt of Nessus? This implication seems to overarch the literal dialogue. For when Antony in Act IV, scene xii, becomes aware of his Nessus-shirt, his outcry is against a bosom partner who has "at fast and loose / Beguiled me to the very heart of loss." And at this point, as Leeds Barroll has noted,[68] the ambiguity of Eros as Queen becomes the subject of an entrance confusion. Antony calls out, "What, Eros, Eros!"—but instead of Eros, Cleopatra enters. Antony thereupon shouts: "Ah, thou spell! Avaunt!"

The whole situation figuratively seems to epitomize Antony's plight: he would call in Eros to solace him, yet Cleopatra herself stands for *eros*. He adds the cry: "Vanish, or I shall give thee thy deserving." Ironically, both Eros and Cleopatra will later give themselves their deserving by vanishing into suicide. But, further, Antony's own suicide will be punctuated by the cry: "Eros!—I come, my Queen. Eros!—Stay for me." In this line, the identity of three-in-one (Antony, Eros, and Cleopatra) is complete. Antony dies the "scholar" of the other two. Recall, now, our previous comment that, metaphysically considered, eros is paganism's dark analogue of agape, its passion parody of Saving Passion.

Finally, some attention must be given to the play's echoes of the New Testament book of Revelation. Miss Ethel Seaton, who discovered many of these, has likened them to "sunken bells" sounding through the surge and swell of the poetry.[69] But what is their import? Do they serve, as she supposes, to convince us that the lovers must be viewed "as if children of light"? Not so, I think, unless we emphasize the *as if*. It is a scriptural commonplace that the devil and his disciples can seem to be angels of light. But the book of

Revelation pictures a doomsday on false and worldly lights, preparatory to the advent of a city which needs no light of the sun, since God is its light. Revelation promises "a new heaven and a new earth," to which there will come a New Jerusalem, "prepared as a bride trimmed for her husband" (Rev. 21: 1–2). Shakespeare's play begins with Antony's styling his dotage a "new heaven," and ends with Cleopatra's cry, "Husband, I come." But can we suppose Shakespeare thought Cleopatra a New Jerusalem bride? Or that he considered Antony's dream other than paganism's substitute for Christian apocalypse? When Cleopatra claims (in I. iii) that "Eternity was in our lips" and "none our parts so poor / But was a race of heaven," plainly it is not of a Christian "eternity" or *its* "heavenly race" that she is speaking. As her very first words in the play, Shakespeare has given her the line: "*If* it be love indeed, tell me how much." From then on, the play is devoted to indicating what this "if" version of love involves.[70] Its power to vex the course of world history is exhibited; and in this connection Shakespeare seems to have taken from the book of Revelation several motifs for "figuring" the meaning of his drama. Let us consider the possibly important ones:

1. *The great harlot.* In Rev. 17 she is an apocalyptic figure, symbolizing an evil genius in world history with whom the kings of the earth have committed fornication. Elizabethans who had seen or read Dekker's *The Whore of Babylon* (published in 1607, the year of Shakespeare's *Antony and Cleopatra*), would be especially familiar with her figure. In IV. iv. of Dekker's play she comes on stage as an Empresse attended by three worshipping kings. At her urging they report some of the "damned blasphemies" they have heard spoken of her: that she is "the superstitious Harlot"; that her robes are purple from being dyed in murder's blood; that the wine in her cup, while of sweet taste, is "rancke poyson"; that her beautiful brow has on it, in letters mystical, the name Babylon, meaning The Citie of Confusion; and that she makes kings think her fair by throwing mists before their eyes. Dekker is using this scene as emblematic of papistry's empire, and hence his kings are shown enbondaged to a Cardinal's view of this Empresse as the queen of heaven, who makes earth "all one with heaven."[71] Shakespeare's play has nothing to do with antipapal propaganda. But a Cleopatra who has been mistress to three kings—Julius Caesar, Pompey, and Antony—could certainly have reminded Shakespeare's audience of

the Apocalyptic harlot, especially when Antony refers to her as "Triple-turned whore." Moreover, in using Plutarch's description of her barge on the Cydnus, Shakespeare has added the statement that it "Burned on the water," like a burnished throne. This burning throne implies a demonic queenship. Compare, for instance, the Duke's cry in *Measure for Measure* V. i. 294: "And let the Devil / Be sometimes honored for his burning throne!"

2. *The beast with ten horns.* This is the creature (not mentioned in Miss Seaton's list of echoes) on which the harlot sits when enthroned upon the waters, according to Rev. 17:6. It symbolizes Antichrist. It is said to be full of "blasphemous names" (likewise in Rev. 13:1), because it takes to itself divine titles—as ten Roman emperors had done during the Apocalyptist's own lifetime.[72] This image is not limited, however, to any one historical application. It derives from Daniel 7:8, where the beast's ten horns signified (so modern scholars agree) the ten rulers of Syria's dynasty, the tenth being Antiochus Epiphanes, the desecrator of the Jewish temple, who forcibly tried to substitute Hellenic rites of worship. The Nebuchadnezzar regime was Daniel's "figuring" of this beast.

There is some evidence that Shakespeare may be applying this symbolism to Antony. We hear Caesar say (in III. vi.) that Antony, after being brought under Cleopatra's sway, "hath given his empire / Up to a whore, who now are levying / The Kings o' the earth for war"—whereupon exactly nine kings besides Antony are named. Plutarch had given a similar list of kings, but Shakespeare has slightly revised the number, possibly to make it symbolic of the biblical beast's horns. Earlier in the same scene, Caesar has told us of the Isis worship with which Antony and Cleopatra have enthroned themselves in Alexandria, when contemning Rome but using Julius Caesar's bastard Caesarion as a sanction for their monarchy. Such ritual implies an Asian Hellenism aimed at reviving Alexander's empire in a Ptolemaic version. The cultish aura of divine kingship which accompanies the proclaiming of "Kings of Kings" (compare Daniel's reference, 2:37, to Nebuchadnezzar as a "king of kings") makes the situation like the one which occasioned the book of Daniel.

Daniel's dream of a fifth monarchy to replace the world's four previous monarchies (see Daniel 2:24 ff.) had in Roman times, as Leeds Barroll has pointed out,[73] a parallel version among Asian nationalists. Very possibly, therefore, Shakespeare understands the monarchy attempted by Antony and Cleopatra as the Asian false substitute for the true theocracy symbolized by the "stone" in Daniel, which would introduce a fifth kingdom to last forever. In other words, the Antony and Cleopatra monarchy, if apocalyptically viewed, is new and divine only in an ironic sense, being actually the idol of Nebuchadnezzar's dream *redivivus,* of feet part iron and part clay. Figuratively speaking, it is a would-be messianic kingdom, but spurious. Cleopatra is merely Egypt's version of "Eastern Star." And Antony, whom she dominates, is a beast of the kind well indicated in his cry, "Oh, that I were / Upon the hill of Basan, to outroar / The hornèd herd!" (III. xiii. 126). The bull of Basan, in Psalm 22, was an antimessiah figure, a persecutor of the righteous. Antony's whipping of the innocent Thyreus (a parallel to Cleopatra's whipping of the messenger of peace in II. v.) accords with this implication. Here is typically a Herod-like behavior. Elsewhere, of course, Antony is accorded by Cleopatra a glamorous image: his delights are called "dolphinlike." Yet a dolphin is literally a whale, and as such might suggest to an Elizabethan reader the Leviathan of Old Testament typology.[74]

3. *A fallen star.* In Rev. 8:2–11:19 a series of calamities, in imagery which allies them to the plagues on Egypt in Exodus, is presented apocalyptically as a doomsday judgment on false world orders in history. Trumpets blown by angels announce various downfalls, including that of a "great star," which falls from heaven into the water, making the waters bitter and death-dealing (Rev. 8:10). Immediately next is a plague of darkness, in which a third of the sun and moon are eclipsed, so that a third of the day is kept from shining, and a voice cries out "Woe, woe, woe, to the inhabitants of the earth." Then, at the blowing of another trumpet, another star falls from heaven (Rev. 9:1). This star is given the key to a bottomless pit, from which come locusts with a power like that of scorpions (an image based on the fact that locusts have a serpent-like body); and we are told that "in those days shall men seek death, and shall not find it, and shall desire to die, and death shall fly from them." Then, in Rev. 10:6, an angel swears that "time should be no more."

Much of this imagery, as Miss Seaton has noted, echoes in Shakespeare's play at the moment of Antony's attempted suicide (IV. xiv. 106–109). A Guard cries out: "The star is fallen." Another adds: "And time is at his period." All cry: "Alas, and woe!" Antony then begs them to "strike me dead," but each refuses and Antony is left desiring death and unable to find it. Further, the association of Antony's fall with a darkening of a third of the day seems appropriate, when we consider that he is one of the Triumvirs who earlier has been hailed by Cleopatra as "Lord of lords!" His star has fallen, bringing an eclipse on Cleopatra's part of the earth. What else does his falling signify? The Apocalyptist's naming of the star of Rev. 8 as "Wormwood" accords figuratively with the inward decay and bitterness we see in Antony. These aspects of Antony's fate are prefigured, in fact, at the moment of his earlier breakdown into bitter anger in III. xiii, when he laments that the "good stars" which formerly guided him have left their orbs to shoot their fires into the "abysm of Hell." The "abyss," in Rev. 9:2, was the place which was opened up by the companion star to "Wormwood"—perhaps, in the symbolism of Shakespeare's play, by Cleopatra's star when it fell. In any case, the Apocalyptist's imagery of fallen star seems to be guiding Shakespeare's portrayal of the doom of Antony and Cleopatra. And since the Apocalyptist had correlated falling stars with his imagery (in 12:3) of the fall of a great dragon with ten horns, Shakespeare has included echoes of both these motifs.

4. *Forty-two months.* In Rev. 11:2 and 13:5 (which echo Dan. 7:25 and 12:7), this is the time span for the reign of evil forces. It is a conventional period, based on the fact that Antiochus Epiphanes forced a worship to the Olympian Zeus during three and a half years (168–165 B.C.).[75] Historically, three and a half years happens to be also the approximate time span of the usurped monarchy of Antony and Cleopatra, beginning with the Alexandrian rites of 34 B.C. and ending with Antony's death, August 1st, 30 B.C. Shakespeare did not know this modern chronology, and nowhere in his play is calendar time important. However, the number forty-two may have been in his mind as he wrote; for if we count up the number of scenes in the play we find there are forty-two. Interestingly, the Folio text lacks act and scene divisions, but editors have assigned them on the basis of the text's forty-two clearings of the stage. We need not suppose that auditors in a theatre would be numbering these as they unroll. While the play is in motion, the impression given would be simply that of an unusually awesome panorama of events. But since in any great work of art what interests the contemplative student afterwards is the articulated design of

its parts, I think it conceivable that Shakespeare may have thought to give the total tragedy of Antony and Cleopatra a structure in accord with the number symbolism associated with a period of evil glory. Since Cleopatra's planet is the "fleeting moon," her dominion lasts, figuratively, through forty-two moons. Let us note, incidentally, the balanced architecture of the forty-two scenes: twenty-one of them leading up to, and twenty-one following after, the turning point of Actium. Such care in organization is evidence against A. C. Bradley's complaint that this play is "the most faultily constructed" of Shakespeare's tragedies.[76]

Our concern in probing the language and structure of *Antony and Cleopatra* has been to demonstrate, through accumulative evidence, how a drama can carry clues to interpretation which are beyond the ken of its protagonists. A Christian author when dramatizing pagan times can punctuate his story with a figurative overplot, and its diction with an underside of meaning. Thereby he challenges us to grasp the final significance of the action by the light of a Christian *Weltanschauung*. A recent editor's remark that in Shakespeare's day "Western Europe knew very little of Egypt, either ancient or contemporary,"[77] is only half true. It overlooks the typological knowledge of Egypt which all readers of Scripture had, not merely from the book of Exodus but as a continuing symbolism throughout the Old and New Testaments and especially in the book of Revelation. Egypt, typologically, was a land of fleshpots, sorcerers, and bondage, whose rulers could vacillate between generosity and hardness of heart, and whose unholy civilization God punished by plagues. Would Shakespeare's auditors not have recalled these associations when viewing a play which echoes them in its imagery, and in which the name Egypt is sounded (see Bartlett's *Concordance*) in forty-two separate speeches? Additionally, the word "Egyptian" occurs eleven times. Only a scholar would wonder at these ill-omening numbers. Many an ordinary spectator, however, would sense in Antony's question, "O, whither hast thou led me, Egypt?" and in his twice-repeated final cry, "I am dying, Egypt, dying," a figurative and thematic summation of his tragedy.

These facts of symbolism can prompt us to modify somewhat the view of critics who would hold, as W. K. Wimsatt does, that *Antony and Cleopatra* is "a great poem, yet immoral." The play "celebrates" or "pleads for" certain evil choices, says Wimsatt, by presenting them "in all their mature interest and capacity to arouse human sympathy."[78] This is partly the case, no doubt. We do see evil choices being celebrated by the play's tragic personages. Yet what about the irony, invisible to these actors but built into the play? When, for instance, Eros hails Antony as "that noble countenance / Wherein the worship of the whole world lies" (IV. xiv. 85), is the play merely pleading for us to admire Antony? If we but give the line a double take, do we not recognize that *the world* indeed *lies* in worshipping face? This covert *sententia*, I suggest, is a moral which can mature our estimate of the morals of the tragic actors.

The classic concept of imitation, which ultimately Wimsatt mentions, seems to me our best approach. The play imitates, he suggests, "the reasons for sin, a mature and richly human state of sin." To this I would only add (what Wimsatt omits saying), that sin is richly human in the sense of "all too human"—with a richness which Shakespeare shows as maturing to the ruin of man's essential humanity. The play's artistic imitation of immorality implies an ontology. It shows us the awesomely pitiful glory of actions truly ab-hominable. If it arouses our sympathy for sin, it does so in order that by our witnessing sin's devastations we may be brought to pity the grandeur we have initially admired. A two-level mode in the dramatization forwards for us this recognition and ultimate self-confession.

The hallmark of any Christian tragedy, let us then say, is a certain quality of insight into downfall. A Christian playwright, in imitating a tragic action, will shape its development by what he knows of human history in general. The cultural setting of his play need not be limited to Christian times. The downfall of Antony and Cleopatra, or of Caesar or Brutus, can be made into Christian tragedy simply by perceiving, more profoundly than Plutarch does, the dimensional range of tragedy's causes and results. Beneath all other causes is man's mislocating of his chief end, in the process of his passionate quest for bliss.

There is no need to suppose, as H. S. Wilson does,[79] that some Shakespearean tragedies belong to "the order of nature" and others to "the order of faith." In all stories of human life, nature's health is influenced by the kind of faith one practices. The tragic hero (and others in his times) make their choices within an order of nature, yet by the light of attitudes taken in an order of faith—attitudes which are tragic by disregarding the "best" order of faith (e.g. Octavia's, or the Clown's) within the hero's own community. The dramatist, in imitating the vision of his tragic heroes, traces the progress of a self-induced blindness of vision, in which an idolatry of some kind (contrary ultimately to Christian faith, but more immediately to a native folk wisdom) is conditioning each hero's self-centered career and its destructive outcome. A delusive faith alienates the self from reality. Through a preference for appearance over reality, the tragic hero increasingly becomes a parody of himself, of reason, and of religious duty, while at the same time his rhetoric is being heightened by all the make-believe faith of the self's decay.

5 Toward understanding catharsis

Before concluding this chapter, let us return briefly to the question of the relation of Aristotle's *Poetics* to Shakespearean tragedy. We have already given passing attention to Aristotle's concept of anagnorisis and to Shakespeare's apparent use of it in an expanded sense. We have also explained how, for Shakespeare as for Aristotle, the art of drama rests basically on the mimesis of an action. In our next chapter we shall be attempting to describe how Aristotle's concept of hamartia relates to Shakespeare's more ultimate sense of its meaning. But first, in preparation for such discussion, it is pertinent to consider, through inference and tentative speculation, the possible meaning in Shakespeare's practice of one other of Aristotle's key items, catharsis.

Whether Shakespeare had ever read the *Poetics* we do not know. His Elizabethan contemporaries, however, had at least enough indirect knowledge of it to invoke frequently its doctrine of imitation; and a tragedy such as Bishop Watson's Latin *Absalom* (c. 1540) marks an early attempt to use Aristotelian principles.[80] In our day, interpreters of Shakespearean tragedy have tended to put aside Aristotle as being of little or no relevance.[81] Yet Virgil Whitaker, for instance, is among a few who continue to insist that Shakespeare had not only "a theology and ethics that derived in important respects from Aristotle," but also some help toward "an Aristotelian kind of tragedy" from the theory and practice current among Elizabethan men of letters. At least in Shakespeare's later tragedies, Whitaker believes, there is "a philosophic view of tragedy which allies him to Aristotle and to such thoughtful contemporaries as Sidney or Chapman."[82]

The whole question is complicated, however, by the likelihood that any Christian civilization inevitably will have introduced some qualification of meaning into concepts originally Greek. It is further complicated, moreover, by the fact that Sidney and Chapman (and other Elizabethans as well) seem to hold a more didactic view of tragedy, more moralistic in its focus, than Shakespeare's practice implies. Is he really, then, allied to their views, as Whitaker suggests, or does his practice, rather, rebalance their focus—perhaps in a direction that is both more germinally Aristotelian and more ultimately Christian? Chapman, we may recall, described the "soul, limbs, and limits" of a tragedy as consisting of "material instruction, elegant and sententious excitation to virtue, and deflection from her contrary" (Epistle to *The Revenge of Bussy D'Ambois*). And Sidney's *Apologie for Poetrie,* although perhaps, as Whitaker thinks, less bald than some other Elizabethan treatises in advocating a "poetic justice," nevertheless is obviously more moralistic than the impression we get, say, from Shakespeare's *King Lear.* Take for instance Sidney's generalization that "if evill men come to the stage, they ever go out (as the Tragedie Writer answered to one that misliked the shew of such persons) so manacled as they little animate folkes to follow them." Although such a statement seems approximately true, if we test it on *King Lear* or on other of Shakespeare's tragedies, does it not scant something in tragedy's perspective? For one thing, Sidney's reference to "evill" men seems not quite in tune with Aristotle's idea that a tragic hero of the best kind is a man more good than bad, who falls by some great mistake— alongside which I would mention the Christian orthodox idea that every man who does evil is, basically, a good man gone wrong. Granted that Sidney, when referring to evil men, may be intending merely our conventional shorthand expression for men who do evil things. Yet perspective makes a difference, and Sidney's is more moralistic than metaphysical or ontological.

A metaphysical perspective can also be moral, but with a difference of emphasis and tone. Consider, for instance, St. Augustine's discussion of evil:

> Worldly honor hath also its grace, and the power of overcoming, and of mastery; whence springs also the thirst of revenge. . . . The life also which here we live hath its own enchantment, through a certain proportion of its own, and a correspondence with all things beautiful here below. Human friendship also is endeared with a sweet tie, by reason

> of the unity formed of many souls. Upon occasion of all
> these, and the like, is sin committed, while through an
> immoderate inclination toward these goods of a lower
> order, the better and higher are forsaken. . . . For these
> lower things have their delights, but not like my God, who
> made all things. (*Confessions* II. v. 10, tr. Pusey)

The delight, the enchantment, the beauty of evil "goods"—in their
lower and mistaken order of good—is here included in Augustine's
theme. And does not this recognition of good in things evil accord
with Shakespeare's own confession, in his Sonnets, of the "graces"
in the fair youth who beguiled his love? "How many gazers mightst
thou lead away / If thou wouldst use the strength of all thy state!"
(sonnet 96). So lovely is this youth's beauty, even in its errors, that
one "Cannot dispraise but in a kind of praise" (sonnet 95). And of
the Dark Lady, later, this same speaker confesses (in sonnet 150)
that, even in the "very refuse" of her deeds, "There is such strength
and warrantize of skill / That, in my mind, thy worst all best exceeds"; and he cries out

> Oh, though I love what others do abhor,
> With others thou shouldst not abhor my state.

Shakespeare is here speaking in the *persona* of a man inside the
experience of evil, not outside it. Augustine's confession is similar,
in that he can put his sympathy, imaginatively, inside the delights
of evil love (note his pronoun "we"), although as a philosopher he
now transcends that mistaken experience and can view with detachment, yet compassion, its defects.

The art of tragedy for Shakespeare, as I see the matter, requires
a capacity for double vision—the capacity to see erring love's existential appeal from within, while yet understanding it from above
or outside. The presence of the "outside" understanding is infera-
ble, even for those whose perspective differs from the dramatist's,
through deft clues within the drama. In our previous discussion we
have noted how these emerge: through the tragic hero's flickering
awareness of standards he is betraying; further, through comments
on the hero made by other persons in the drama, whose own perspective, however, we must assess; and all this while, through a
heightening of the action with a symbolism both verbal and emblematic, which signals for us the deadliness of the "morals" being
practiced by the tragic personages. Yet the morals of these pro-

tagonists are presented from the inside, in order to engage and exercise our emotions, emotions at least half sympathetic to theirs. The other factors I have mentioned tantalize our intellect to question, and thus ultimately to confess, perhaps, the impurities in our own impulsive sympathies.

The Elizabethan apologists for tragedy, in those samples of their literary criticism which have come down to us, to some degree lack a sense of the full dimensions of tragedy's art. They incline to see in tragedy a moral exemplum. This emphasis stems in part from the influence of Horace and Seneca on Renaissance interpretations of Aristotle; and in part it is sometimes reinforced by a strain of puritanism among Elizabethan critics. Too often, therefore, poetry is defended chiefly for its moral utilitarianism. Thus, for Sidney, tragedy is "high and excellent" because it makes kings fear to be tyrants; and Puttenham praises it for showing "the just punishment of God in revenge of a vicious and evill life." In Nashe's view, tragedies are "sower pills of reprehension, wrapt up in sweete words"; for they never encourage any man to rebellion without also showing the wretched end of usurpers and "how just God is evermore in punishing of murther." Thomas Newton's apology for translating Seneca's tragedies was that the whole issue of every one of them beats down sin. And Thomas Heywood explained in his *Apology for Actors*: "If we present a Tragedy, we include the fatall and abortive ends of such as commit notorious murders, which is aggravated and acted with all the Art that may be, to terrifie men from the like abhorred practises."[83] By all these critics, tragedy is more or less reduced to the lesson that crime does not pay. In their eagerness to answer Plato's objection to poetry, that it stirs up unhealthy emotions, they commonly argue that it serves, rather, to warn against vice by exhibiting its depravity and punishment, so as to terrify the spectator into avoiding crimes. In drama we can see the effect of this emphasis, for instance, in the *Tragedy of Cleopatra* by Samuel Daniel, as noted in the previous section of our chapter. Daniel openly moralizes on Cleopatra's fall, and does much less justice than Shakespeare to the natural grace and fascination of her arts. The spectator is allowed too Olympian a stance; he is not lured into a quasi-identification with Cleopatra's emotional life.

For many Elizabethans the tragedies of Seneca, built about a contrast between passionate villains and men of reason, were influential as literary models. According to Stoic philosophy, all virtue is comprehended in rational self-control, while all vice is attributed to passion devoid of reason. A man of upright character will negate evil by becoming impervious to passion; but when character is deteriorated by passion it becomes rampantly mad. In Seneca's dramas, therefore, moral character is either black or white, and there is no mixed state of the human soul. His tragic heroes, typically, are murderous criminals crazed with blood and power.[84] The punishment they suffer is chiefly psychological, a loss of contentment of mind, which the onset of rage automatically entails. In much of Elizabethan drama these Senecan features are more or less reflected.

But does this pattern for tragedy resemble Shakespeare's? If we look at Shakespearean villains such as Iago or Richard III, we discover not hysterical revengers but singularly cold and adroit schemers. These men take pride in their reason's control of passion. Iago and Richard are fascinating to us because of their wit and their skill in playacting. In going about murder, they do not act for blood lust, but in proof of their cleverness and self-importance. When ultimately they suffer a downfall, this takes the form of an external loss of power through some final inadequacy in their vision or tactics, while internally their punishment is mainly that of a self-imprisonment within their own loveless existence.

In what sense does a spectator feel pity and fear while watching the drama of Richard III? Perhaps in this case we may feel pity chiefly for his victims, and a fear because we imagine ourselves in their predicament. If so, what purgation of our emotions takes place as we watch? Could it be that the quality of our emotion changes—that if we begin with pity for their plight, we find this pity qualified by an awareness of mistakes of theirs which are abetting it, so that ultimately our pity is for the ruin to which their blindness is making them liable? Our pity is in that way educated, refined from its initial sentimentality.

But is it only by these victims that our pity and fear are exercised? Do we feel toward Richard, the protagonist, merely a disapprobation and then a moral satisfaction when finally he is destroyed? I doubt this is the case. For surely Richard's despair in Act V draws our pity. Here we see him tormented by a conscience he had previously ignored. It is an aspect of the self he has not considered in his doctrine that "Richard loves Richard: that is, I am I." His self-love is revealed as self-hate. "There is no creature loves me," he cries, "And if I die, no soul shall pity me." Here his statement is only half-correct, for we of the audience who have been given this insight into his misery of soul pity him even now. He has committed his crimes in ignorance, we realize, of who he really is. Moreover, Shakespeare allows us a further ground for our pity. Richard in his despair is still ignoring a potential aspect of his conscience—the one voiced in the cry with which he began his soliloquy—"Have mercy, Jesu!" He neglects to give further consideration to mercy as a cure for guilt. This leaves us pitying the incompleteness of his penitence. For now when he tries to be courageous, he can do so only by banishing conscience and wasting what remains of his life in an empty show of outward bravado. There is a dramatic irony in his swearing "By the Apostle Paul" that he has been terrified by "shadows," since we know that in the Apostle's case a conversion came by probing the shadows of conscience—coming to terms with them rather than dismissing them. Some readers may not catch this irony. But for those who do, it furnishes an additional reason for pitying Richard and for fearing his disaster as one we might suffer.

All told, Shakespeare's drama is inviting a more enlightened pity and fear than Aristotle had envisaged, yet the goal of purifying these emotions through exercising them in viewing a tragedy is the same. Aristotle, it is true, in describing the best kind of plot for a tragedy, advised against one in which the downfall of an utter villain is exhibited. Yet, as Butcher has remarked, we need not infer a banning of the villain from all tragedies, since Aristotle elsewhere refers twice to the Menelaus of Euripides' *Orestes* as a character "gratuitously bad";[85] this Menelaus was perhaps tolerable in a tragedy of lesser kind emphasizing spectacle. Aristotle's objection was that a downright villain inspires neither pity nor fear. For "pity is aroused by unmerited misfortune, fear by the misfortune of a man like ourselves." This statement must be understood, however, in the context of Aristotle's whole philosophy. By "unmerited" misfortunes, he means miseries disproportionate to a man's faults; and he considers this the case whenever a man of typically healthy nature has acted from ignorance, not intending to do evil. Since the evil comes about accidentally to such a man's purpose, and not through deliberate choice, the misfortune is unmerited. (Christian thought is more complex on this point: earthly misfortunes may be visited on a man of good intentions to try him, rather than simply to reward the merit of his intentions;

and also they may punish secret faults of which he is unaware.) On the other hand, Aristotle thinks of a villain as one whose purposes are no longer properly human but rather those of a bestial depravity. Such a man is not "like us" and therefore cannot arouse our fear. In Shakespeare's outlook we can discern a modification of these premises. Richard's crimes are shown to be motivated not by animalistic depravity, but by a desire for revenge against nature for giving him a crooked back. They are intended by Richard as a means to the good of self-esteem. He pursues this good in ignorance of his true self, not realizing that his warped body ought not to be identified with his basic nature, since he has in fact a hidden or repressed soul capable of conscience. Thus Richard acts without intending the misfortune of self-hate and despair, yet faultily adopts a means to his intended good which lands him in this misfortune.

We may say that insofar as Richard has acted from ignorance, there is an element of involuntariness in his crimes. And is he not "like us"? Not like, perhaps, the run of the mill fellows among us whom we consider healthy; nevertheless, he is an instance of a spiritual blindness potential in everyman. This implication, more penetrating than Aristotle's view of villainy, depends on Shakespeare's inheritance of Christian philosophical principles. These enlarge the contextual circumstances of action and our reasons for pity and fear. They deepen, without abandoning, Aristotle's argument.[86]

St. Augustine, in his *Confessions* II. v. 11, takes up the matter of the so-called "gratuitously evil" man. That is what Sallust had called Catiline. But Augustine remarks that not even Catiline loved his own villainies; he loved rather something else, for whose sake he did them. "Would any commit murder upon no cause, delighted simply in murdering? Who would believe it?" Augustine asks. A criminal acts always for the sake of some beguiling good. A villain's monstrousness is merely an extraordinary case within the range of potential error to which human beings are liable. Shakespeare, with this background of understanding, could use a villain-hero in tragedy simply by treating Richard as not merely a villain. Though we hear Richard announce himself as a villain at the play's very beginning, that is not the whole truth about him. We are made aware that "villain" is the role Richard would make-believe as his nature, superimposing it on the human nature he would mock; and later we see the consequences of his having equated himself with his melodramatic self—with that shadow-self on which he preens himself at the end of II. i, asking for a mirror in which to admire it. These Shakespearean insights into the psychology of villainy give *Richard III* a subtlety lacking in a play such as Jonson's *Catiline*.

In the light of our discussion, we can amend somewhat a comment by Butcher. Rightly, he defends *Richard III* as a tragedy rather than a melodrama, but on grounds that are rather romantic:

> Wickedness on a grand scale, resolute and intellectual, may raise the criminal above the commonplace and invest him with a sort of dignity. There is something terrible and sublime in mere will-power working its evil way, dominating its surroundings with a superhuman energy. The wreck of such power excites in us a certain tragic sympathy; not indeed the genuine pity which is inspired by unmerited suffering, but a sense of loss and regret over the waste or misuse of gifts so splendid. (*Aristotle's Theory*, p. 313)

I can agree that we feel at the end a regret over Richard's misuse of his energies. But do we then still regard those energies as having been "superhuman" and sublime? When Richard declares before his last battle,

> Conscience is but a word that cowards use,
> Devised at first to keep the strong in awe.
> Our strong arms be our conscience, swords our law

he is being as resolute as ever in his kind of dignity; yet surely we perceive by now the intellectual bankruptcy of such a dignity. Only in Richard's own foolish estimate is he superhuman. His oration to his army cannot make appeal, as Richmond's does, to "God and our good cause"; it must resort instead to a picturing of his adversary as a "milksop" attended by vagabonds and rats. Richard's oration is obviously tawdry. And then when he exits invoking the spleen of dragons, but reappears crying "My kingdom for a horse!" any sense we might have had of something terrible and sublime is quite undone by our sense of the pitiableness of such absurdity. We remember perhaps, and apply to Richard, the play's earlier image of "a drunken sailor on a mast" (III. iv, 101). Rather then than Butcher's sympathy for "the wreck of such power," I think we feel a pity for Richard's misestimate of his capacities, and for his having (like Hastings) built "his hopes in air."

Also we come away fearing that such a disaster might have been ours too, had we been placed in Richard's circumstances. If we were deformed of body amid a society deformed by license, perjury, and opportunism—a society in which the King is living scandalously with Mistress Shore and the Archbishop is a trimmer easily cajoled into betraying "blessed sanctuary"—might not we, like Richard, take a morbid delight in outdoing this society on its own terms, by using Machiavellian arts to achieve a wooer's mastery over widow Anne and in all situations a mockery of traditional holiness? Is there not something almost sublime in the pleasure of becoming lyric about "my own deformity," studying "my shadow in the sun," and then demonstrating the power of one's actor-self to astound, plague, and dominate the less skilful hypocrisy of one's neighbors? Yet Shakespeare's drama, while tempting us by this dream of dignity, has in the course of its action shown us the dream's ultimate blindspot. Richard cannot beguile Queen Elizabeth in Act IV with the techniques he used on Anne in Act I. "Relenting fool, and shallow, changing woman!" he has boasted after she has given him in fact only an equivocal answer; and thus it is he who is fooled, and his wit proved shallow. His realism, which depends on supposing that immediate vantage and an illusion of security can be counted on to sway anyone but himself, is but a realism manqué, and he is self-deceived by a mistaken premise. Moreover, we have seen his intellect lapse into a misjudgment of Buckingham and a giving of confused commands when he finds his power evaded and then challenged by unanticipated events. And on the eve of the showdown at Bosworth field we have heard him confess:

> I have not the alacrity of spirit,
> Nor cheer of mind, that I was wont to have.

An attrition of his energies has overtaken him, comparable to that of Macbeth's in Shakespeare's later play, and its sequel is self-doubt, remorse, and despair, and then death in the service of a futile and vain activism.

How, then, does such a story purge our pity and fear? By arousing at the outset, I would say, our interest in the *seemingly* superhuman intelligence of Richard. We are encouraged, that is, to take a romantic view of evil. Out of a pity for Richard's deformity or because we find awesome his bold resourcefulness, we can become half-enchanted by this criminal. We then can perhaps let ourselves make-believe, as he does, that an unscrupulous wit is justifiable in a corrupt society, and that its skilful use may provide a sublime adventure. If we respond in this way we are releasing, for its exercise, the impure state of our own pity—i.e., of a pity in us which has become corroded more or less by our penchant for self-pity, pitiless toward society. The pleasure we take, with Richard, in making sport of the weaknesses of neighbors is, essentially, a deformed form of pity—the dried up version of it which the play magnifies in a Richard who pities only his bodily ugliness and fears nothing but the ignominy of losing out in the competition for worldly eminence. Such a person is fearless of outcries such as Anne's

> Either Heaven with lightning strike the murderer dead,
> Or earth, gape open wide and eat him quick.

For in this hero the emotion of fear has been deformed too, by a corrosive cynicism which has evaporated all credence in the reality of the supernatural. Hence Richard can make mock of "old odd ends" stolen out of Scripture (not realizing that his own end will turn out to be the "old odd" one Scripture tells of). But who of us can say we never have similar predilections? If and insofar as our own emotions of pity and fear have in them impurities like Richard's, we can be enlisted in a quasi-identification with him. Then the subsequent events of the drama work on our emotions, much as does a furnace fire when applied to a meltingpot containing rusty metal or crude ore. As the play proceeds, the accumulating crises stimulate in us insights which break down our initial form of pity and fear, eliminating the dross and allowing these emotions to recollocate. A purgation of this kind, it seems to me, is effected whenever a played tragedy is properly structured and its auditors are properly responsive.

There have been many interpretations of Aristotle's reference to catharsis in the *Poetics* VI. 3. So many, in fact, that today's drama critics often avoid the concept as too puzzling for deciphering. I would accept, however, Butcher's explanation that Aristotle means a clarification of the passions through the throwing off of some morbid element in them. And although I have modified somewhat Butcher's sense of how this is brought about, his comment that the effect is indirectly moral, not making men better morally but removing certain hindrances to virtue, seems to me right. There is a process of washing, a lustration, for which I have used the parallel analogy of a refining furnace which cooks out impediments to our more properly substantial emotional life. Thus a tragedy offers us opportunity for a learning to pity and fear what we ought to pity and to fear. Its function is the education of our emotions.

Feeling is a prerequisite to seeing, as we are reminded by Shakespeare in *King Lear*. Man "will not see / Because he doth not feel" (IV. i. 71). As a remedy for hardness of heart, the disguised Edgar (in mad Tom) proposes: "Expose thyself to feel what wretches feel" (III. iv. 34). And later he tells us that, "by the art of known and feeling sorrows," he has been made "pregnant to good pity" (IV. vi. 227). The hardest heart of all, we might say, is Edmund's; yet Edmund by exposing himself to what Goneril and Regan feel, and then to his own misery of defeat by a pilgrimaging Edgar, can repent. Of Hamlet, as Claudius can report: "He's loved of the distracted multitude, / Who like not in their judgment but their eyes" (IV. iii. 4–5). Yet by the time we have witnessed the full course and consequences of Hamlet's own distraction, our eye-liking for him can change into a more judicious love, compassionate rather than superficial, and thus more sound in its pity and fear than our earlier modes of these emotions.

Some of the alternative interpretations of catharsis we may briefly mention. The so-called Mithridatic interpretation was expounded in the Renaissance by Castelvetro, for instance. He regards pity and fear as harmful passions against which man needs to be insulated by exercising these passions on imagined scenes of misery and violence. An innoculation with distressful experiences through viewing a tragedy, he argues, inures the spectator's mind to their effects and thus enables the mind to bear them with equanimity.[87] This interpretation seems to rest on the Stoic ideal of gaining a mental superiority to passion's threat. Among other Renaissance moralists, a Christian interpretation of a didactic kind was popular. What is purged, in this view, are the soul's vices, through the spectator's exercising of his good emotions of pity and fear on scenes of pride, ambition, and lust. This comes close to the interpretation I have suggested. But it omits the important point that the spectator's pity and fear themselves need cleansing, and principally so, of elements dangerously sentimental in these emotions. Do we not experience most immediately, through a half-identification with the hero's emotions, the course of his form of pity and fear all the way to its final desperation and dead end? I say half-identification because as observers we are partly engaged and partly detached. While we are sympathizing with the hero, the feelings and views voiced by other characters make us aware marginally of aspects of his stance which he is overlooking and which carry dramatic irony. These at some point awaken our intellect to question, and progressively to crush, the element of blindness in our initial mode of pity and fear. A hint of this interpretation seems to me present in a brief comment on catharsis by the Englishman Robert Peterson in 1576, as cited by Marvin Herrick.[88] The cause for which tragedies were first devised, Peterson says, was that they "might draw forth tears out of their eyes that had need to spend them. And so they were by their weeping healed of their infirmity."

Among modern theorists, some have followed up and exaggerated an interpretation of catharsis developed by Jacob Bernays in 1857. They think of purgation as an expelling of the emotions of pity and fear. The final effect of tragedy, for them, is the spectator's relief when the accumulation of pity and fear, aroused by the play's events, is at last eliminated. But this way of applying a medical analogy has been objected to by Butcher, and more recently by D. M. Hill, who terms it the theory of the "bowel enthusiasts."[89] It is inconsistent, Butcher and Hill note, with the ethical philosophy of Aristotle, who regards all man's passions as good if tempered. Some sort of qualification of a man's pity and fear, rather than the removal of these emotions, was probably Aristotle's sense of tragedy's function.

A rather different reading of Aristotle, however, has been recently proposed by Gerald Else.[90] He would contend that what Aristotle meant was a purification, through the structure of the play's events, of the act of the hero, so that we come to regard him finally as "free of pollution" in his wrong-doing. The hero's assurance of his purity releases our tears. Else thinks there is no hint by Aristotle that the purpose of tragedy is to cure or alleviate pathological states in us; rather, its end is to gain our approval of the hero. A major weakness of this interpretation, it seems to me, is that Else can force only two of the extant Greek plays to fit his formula. He therefore argues that almost all Greek tragedy comported "things that were not dreamt of in Aristotle's philosophy," things damaging to Aristotle's credit as a critic.

Much more convincing is a theory offered on the basis of Freudian psychology by Roy Morrell.[91] Morrell sees tragedy as a "vicarious ordeal," in which we release our fantasy life through empathy with the hero and then see it thwarted by the hero's death, which serves as a death of "the old incomplete self" in us. By being brought to face the hero's developing sense of terror, we experience in our fantasy "something which has been evaded in the past." The dramatic effect, Morrell explains, depends on the fact that

> when the audience know the limits of the hero's strength, the nearness of his end, and the hero too knows it, but is desperately hiding the knowledge from himself—at such moments our critical faculty is stirring to waken, and our empathy is, as it were, being worked loose.

A disastrous end for the hero is essential for this catharsis, he argues, for only by the hero's failure can there be a break between us and our fantasy life in the play, thus setting free our own energies for a new readjustment to reality.

Morrell would identify this break, however, simply with the death of our illusions, whereby we are brought to the threshold of a new instinctive courage for facing reality. He thinks that in *Macbeth*, for instance, the dramatist must not encourage us to identify ourselves and our interests with Malcolm, lest the play become melodrama. This seems to me only half-true. The drama's attention to Malcolm in Act IV, I would say, is an important marginal means by which our break with Macbeth's fantasy is effected, and it also points our self-interests toward a proper order of courage, promised here in nature's subordination to divine grace. This adjustment to reality by Malcolm distinguishes *Macbeth* from Greek drama (except insofar as such a hope is foreshadowed in the *Oresteia*, for instance); and it marks a Shakespearean enlargement of Aristotle's sense of the cathartic benefit in rehearsing a story of error. In various other of Shakespeare's tragedies, however, this final hope is not present. They end, much like Aristotle's "ideal" type, with little more than the mortification of man's tragic illusions. Our signals for new direction in such a case are given only through the play's irony, yet an irony so framed as to carry a somewhat larger scope of reference than in Greek tragedy.

Let us briefly examine *Macbeth* as an instance of how Aristotle's principles are contextually reframed. Here, as in *Richard III*, the plot involves a hero who behaves villainously, although not with such boastful villainy as we saw in Richard. Macbeth's intent in his evildoing is to demonstrate valor—a good with which we can more easily sympathize than with Richard's "good," that of revenging his withered arm. Nevertheless, Shakespeare has the artistic problem of enlisting our sympathy for a hero who commits crimes while knowing that they involve a flouting of moral obligation. We can pity the "dead butcher" which Macbeth ultimately becomes, only if initially our pity is engaged by an awareness of the natural gifts his ambition is misusing. We are therefore shown Macbeth's bravery as a soldier, his struggles with conscience when tempted, and his nostalgic respect for things holy. We see him vacillate, because aware of murder's aura of damnation, before committing his first crime, and we see his remorse afterwards. Even when, in Act IV, his fears impel him to seek aid from midnight hags, though it be at the cost of blowing down churches and tumbling the very germens of nature into general disorder, Macbeth is to us not quite wholly a monster but a deeply despairing human being. "We can understand such a person and hence feel fear and pity of a kind for him," Ronald Crane has commented, "because he is only doing upon a grander scale and with deeper guilt and more terrifying consequences for himself and others what we can, without too much difficulty, imagine ourselves doing, however less extremely, in circumstances generally similar."[92]

In what way can Macbeth's story effect a catharsis of our emotions? Crane sees it as our sharing in a self-knowledge which the hero acquires through disaster. The catharsis is effected, he remarks, "not merely by the man's deserved overthrow but by his own inner suffering and by his discovery, before it is too late, of what he had not known before he began to act." The catharsis becomes complete when we feel "both that Macbeth is being killed in a just cause and that his state of mind and the circumstances of his death are such as befit a man who, for all his crimes, has not altogether lost our pity and goodwill." The hero's form of action, Crane believes, has a likeness to Aristotelian tragedy, in that a "basically good but incontinent man" comes to discover the difference between what an advantageous crime appears to be in advance and what it is discovered to be in its consequences. Yet *Macbeth* is not strictly Aristotelian, Crane feels, since its hero acted in "full knowledge" of the moral character of his actions.[93]

Suppose we ask, however: In what sense did Macbeth act with

full moral knowledge? Wayne Booth has commented that this hero both knows and does not know what he is doing.[94] Although aware of the immorality of his killing Duncan, says Booth, he has no conception of what will be the effects of this act on himself. He does not really know himself. Moreover, he lacks an understanding of two factors, outside his ambition, which are working on him: the equivocal promise of the witches, and the ideal of valor which Lady Macbeth is urging as necessary to his reputation as a man. Handicapped by a confused understanding on these matters, Macbeth's judgment is divided.

What Booth has described are aspects of ignorance more subtle than those Aristotle envisaged. And we can think of one more aspect of Macbeth's ignorance which Shakespeare reckons with in a way Aristotle could not have: Macbeth does not know what it means to "jump the life to come." He does not know how sterile can be a "success" which considers only the bank and shoal of time. True, he does have, as Helen Gardner has emphasized, a premonition that Duncan's virtues will plead, like angels, against the damnable act of the assassination, and that pity, horsed upon "the sightless couriers of the air," will blow the horrid deed in every eye, till tears drown the wind.[95] Yet it is unlikely that he is including *his own* eye when speaking of "every eye," or that he envisages what decisions may be made inside other human selves when pity has moved them to tears. He seems to be thinking, as his next speech indicates, solely of the loss he will suffer of "Golden opinions from all sorts of people." And if that is all, may not these be rewon in time, when the storm of indignation has blown over? Or, as Lady Macbeth suggests, may he not so contrive the murder as to transfer the public indignation to others than himself? By thus reasoning, he fails to appreciate fully what it may mean to lose heaven's blessing on one's everyday existence. Is the "life to come" merely one in eternity after our days in time are over? Might it not be, more importantly, a potential dimension of our present existence, which if disregarded, leaves time empty of basic satisfactions which the human heart needs?

Our pity and fear for Macbeth become in the course of the play progressively enlightened as to these several considerations. At the beginning, our pity may be limited simply to feeling sorry for a brave man who is being tempted into an act of crime, pity for this incontinent man whose passion is distracting his reason. Our fear, likewise, may be simply a fear that his project will fail, will tumble him in the attempt. Our pity for Duncan, at the same time, may be merely for a man whose unsuspicious nature is bringing him to earthly calamity; and our fear may be only that we, in such circumstances, could meet with a similar misfortune. Pity and fear, in these versions, are drossy emotions. They take their cue from Macbeth himself, who pities and fears in a foggy way. But these early feelings deepen as the tragedy deepens, through events which reveal the complex consequences of the hero's act. His mistake, we discover, is costing more than was envisaged. The criminal is suffering a distress, not in political terms only—and not a madness in the Senecan sense of raging passion—but chiefly a torment of bad dreams, anxieties, sleeplessness, and the desperation which accompanies a general attrition of his personal life.

We see in Macbeth something like what Sidney suggested as the moral meaning of tragedy, that the tyrant goes out "manacled" at the end of the play. Yet it is in a figurative sense only that Macbeth is manacled—in the sense that he comes to feel himself to be like a bear tied to a stake. What ties him is his own despair, and he is never literally enchained by his adversaries, who do little more than shake what is ripe for shaking. The reality revealed is that of the dreariness of a misspent life. An incremental tragic "recognition" of this emerges for Macbeth as various layers of his original ignorance are unpeeled, concluding with the recognition that the self is a victim both of the equivocation of the fiends and of a reduction of life to role-playing. Our pity and fear are thus pointed toward what we ought to pity and fear, any such impoverishment in *us*.

It is likely, of course, that some auditors will experience only partially, or not at all, the catharsis I have attempted to describe. I have been speaking of the potential effect in an ideal auditor, one alert to the whole of what the form of the tragic action invites. In any audience not all will be such, since people come to a play with their varying levels of intelligence and sensibility. Literary critics, too, if they read superficially or with an orientation out of tune with Shakespeare's, can respond defectively. A recent instance is the comment on *Macbeth* by Jan Kott, for whom this tragedy "produces no catharsis."[96] Kott sees only a tragi-grotesque "pure theatre," concerned to reveal "the absurdity of the human situation." He remarks:

> Suicide is either a protest, or an admission of guilt. Mac-
> beth does not feel guilty, and there is nothing for him to
> protest about. All he can do before he dies is to drag with
> him into nothingness as many lives as possible. This is the
> last consequence of the world's absurdity. Macbeth is still
> unable to blow the world up. But he can go on murdering
> to the end.

This reading distorts a half-truth. True, absurdity is being shown
—but located by Shakespeare in the world of Macbeth's soul, not
in the whole world of the play. Moreover, once Macbeth is con-
vinced of his absurd situation, he no longer desires to go on murdering. "But get thee back," he says to Macduff, "my soul is too
much charged/ With blood of thine already." If Macbeth's feeling
of guilt is here not wholly explicit, yet its existential equivalent, a
feeling of the choking burden of bloodshed, is very evident. "I'll
not fight with thee" is his first response. Yet he cannot bring himself
to yield to capture and thus to a public humiliation. Against this
he *does* protest, for to him any voluntary self-humiliation would be
damnable. "And damned be him that first cries 'Hold, enough!' "
he cries—here indicating that, for him, damnation is being thought
of in terms of worldly disgrace, not in terms of Heaven's disfavor.
By Aristotle's standards, we might possibly say that Macbeth is
showing courage in thus fighting, without compulsion, for honor's
sake (see *N. Ethics* III. 8). Yet, paradoxically, is not Macbeth's desperation compelling him? We pity, most of all, his defective version
of honor.

Outside Macbeth is a world of gracious nature, which he resists to
the bitter end, preferring a role-playing of valor as his final self-
justification and neglectful of the potential self he might have re-
covered by repentance. The spectator, however, by sharing Macbeth's experience of the "way to dusty death" becomes the more
ready to welcome a world of promise which transcends the shame
of death and circumscribes it. The spectator has been engaging in
two worlds. At the same time that he has been pitying Macbeth's
fate of being "aweary of the sun," and thus has discovered the wisdom of Ecclesiastes of the vanity of all life "under the sun," he has
seen emerging in Malcolm the higher wisdom of a redemptive
way of life under "powers above." This larger dimension of the
story is Christian, and in this respect modifies Aristotle's concept of tragedy. The range of tragedy's results and countervail-

ing opportunities has been more fully indicated than in Greek drama.

Hamlet accords more closely with Aristotle's sense of tragedy, and its hero is no villain. How is a catharsis of pity and fear effected in this instance? Surely, through the qualification of these emotions in us as they are progressively exercised and enlightened by events in the tragedy. We begin by pitying chiefly what Hamlet pities, his misfortune of living in an unweeded garden and the plight in which the ghost's revelation puts him. But soon our pity is distributed to include others in the play, who are suffering from the effects of Hamlet's isolation and antic behavior. His acts are not setting the world right, we feel, but making it worse. There is some resemblance here to the plight of an Orestes or an Oedipus. But unlike those Greek heroes, Hamlet is suffering a vacillation of purpose, perhaps because his ignorance regarding man's life after death leaves him uncertain as to what form of purpose is "nobler in the mind." When then he attempts a "virtuous" reform of his mother, he distractedly kills Polonius and entangles himself in crime. By the time he returns from England, he is acting only on impulse. And as he studies skulls in a graveyard, he becomes reconciled to death by his sense of the futility of human achievements. Our pity has become pity for a bewildered man, for whom the saving of name is the only value remaining. At this point he resembles somewhat a Greek tragic hero. But as we hear marginally the gravedigger's talk singing in our ears, we may be brought to pity, further, another dimension of Hamlet's misfortune, unperceived by him, his loss of the Christian world view. Not all auditors will grasp this level of his tragedy. Their pity and fear can be simply for Hamlet's disillusioned resignation to an inscrutable providence. Even so, they are experiencing a more educated pity and fear than that with which they began the play. But for others, who have sensed in Hamlet from the start a sub-Christian idealism, and later have been dismayed by his wildness of action, there will be pity for this hollow last stage of the hero's mistaken piety. Their fear will be for the double dimension of catastrophe in a man "like us." For they will now experience what Boethius recommended (*Consolation* IV. pr. 4)—pity for the man *spiritually* sick, even more than we pity the physically sick man. They will fear in themselves the hero's thwarting of his potentially true grandeur.

In many modern theatre productions of *Hamlet,* unfortunately, the larger catharsis I have just described is difficult to experience, because of cuts made in Shakespeare's text and an unequivocal romanticizing of the prince. Ever since the Restoration version by Thomas Betterton, directors have inclined to transform the play into "heroic tragedy." They have excised passages which would cast doubt on the validity of Hamlet's revenge, have omitted his "How all occasions do inform against me" in Act IV, have abbreviated the gravedigger's scene by omitting much of his talk, and very often have ended the play some forty lines short of its actual conclusion. Just recently, in 1967, a touring company of the Bristol Old Vic has been presenting a *Hamlet* which ends with a Horatio supporting Hamlet's head on his lap, on a throne platform otherwise denuded, while round about in a semicircle courtiers kneel with bowed heads as Horatio invokes flights of angels. This is the Hamlet of Bradley's interpretation. Admiration, not fear, is the emotion it aims to induce. The audience never hears Horatio's later comment to the English ambassadors, that their execution of Rosencrantz and Guildenstern was a bloody matter without warrant, and that "purposes mistook" have fallen on their inventors' heads. Nor does the audience witness the dead march, with peal of cannon, which marks the exit of Hamlet's body from the stage.

If we were allowed to hear the hedged tribute of "rites of war," offered by a victorious Fortinbras to a Hamlet who "was likely, had he been put on, / To have proved most royally," we might ask: Why has he *not* so proved? Has his failure been unrelated to his desire to sweep to revenge—"with wings as swift / As . . . thoughts of love"? What *kind* of love has now brought Hamlet to a downfall by its wings, alas, of wax? In contemplating this point, we could feel more pity and a genuine fear. For the form of the play would then be functioning with the potential it should have for evoking catharsis.

The tragedy's auditors, in that case, might respond with some kind of confession—if perhaps only a secular one, such as is voiced in Eliot's modern *Ash Wednesday*:

> Let these words answer
> For what is done, not to be done again
> May the judgment not be too heavy on us

The speaker in that poem, we may recall, has experienced an erosion of his liking for the "infirm glory of the positive hour" and a

turning from his desire for "this man's gift and that man's scope."
By wearying of a glory that has proved empty he is witnessing, although he may not know it, the truth of the Prayerbook's cry:
"Turn us, O Lord, and we shall be turned." That is, he is *being
turned* through experiencing the ashes of a misadventured hope.
And by this turn he is being returned to a mystery he may next
discover, that of divine grace—to which tragedy's catharsis is a
providential preface and propaedeutic. Catharsis, let us say, has a
continuum of modes, a potential spectrum of levels at which our
pity and fear may come to rest. One level is a simple accepting of
disaster. But the innermost level—to which some auditors may attain—could be expressed in the sigh, "Prevent us, O Lord, in all
our doings . . ." (the familiar Prayerbook cry), or in words like those
of the Prayerbook's litany: "From all blindness of heart; from pride,
vainglory, and hypocrisy; from envy, hatred and malice, and all
uncharitableness, Good Lord deliver us."[97] And if that confession
arises over and beyond the threshold of tragedy's catharsis, there is a
benefit to which the staged drama has served as an indirect means.

Tragedy, for the Greeks, ended with a recognition of the Dikê
which man cannot evade. For Christians, it ends with a recognition
of the Divine Providence to which all sons of Adam are subject.
The second of these two is but a larger horizon of the first. For if
Adam's original sin is the deeper truth behind the hamartia of
Oedipus, all tragedies in germ are analogues of Adam's. But Adam's
tragedy, by Christian hindsight, was "necessary" to bring us to
the new Adam, Christ. It was a "fortunate fall," a *felix culpa,* since
in the divine economy it prepared the way negatively for the repair
of life which divine grace, if sought, could bring. It is over the
knife-edge of disaster reviewed and pondered that tragedy hovers.
It offers a secular means for the recognition of our flawed inclina-
tions, by letting us experience them vicariously in the distanced
mode which art provides. Whether we then turn to a seeking of a
more reasonable good (the Greek implication) or of divine grace
(the Christian one) depends on how well we have understood the
disaster's causes, and on our readiness to relinquish the dead ends
we have witnessed.

There are two forms our pity can take in the course of a tragedy
—not unlike, I think, two of the moments recorded in Dante's
Divine Comedy. The pilgrim in that poem experiences one of
these early, in *Inferno* V, when he listens to Francesca's story with

such pity that he swoons. He has here imaginatively been caught up in her feelings, and by sharing her thoughts has reexperienced "the first root of our love." The other moment comes, in *Purgatorio* XII, when he has begun to climb the mountain of penitence under the guidance of reason in the person of Virgil. On a vertical rock, to the right of his path, he is allowed to study, incised in marble, various examples of humility from pagan and Christian story. But now Virgil directs his attention downward to examples of tragic story in the tombs under his feet, because the prick of remembering these, says Virgil, can give a spur to a man of pity. With sorrowing eyes and dignity of lament, Dante thereupon gives rein to his pity, a pity tempered now by a knowledge of the essential nature of evil as seen in its sculptured design. May we not say that, comparably in drama, our experience is moved in the direction of this contemplative view of tragedy, after earlier moments of having shared emotionally its existential pulse? The playwright's art, at one level, consists of an imitating of tragedy's immediate life and movement, while its other level is an emblematic figuring of tragedy's meaning *sub specie aeternitatis.*

IV

Hamartia in Aristotle, Christian Doctrine, and *Hamlet*

Within the broad movement of a tragic story from prosperity to misery, various motifs can be used to figure the action. Insofar as one's focus is on man in relation to nature and time, the metaphor of Fortune's wheel serves well enough as an interpretive image. Its implications, as in Chaucer's *Monk's Tale,* are that the world is mutable and its joys transitory, bringing for even the greatest of creatures a pitiful and fearful loss of estate. This is tragedy at the level of simple chronicle. But if one focuses on man's psychological story, a second kind of metaphor comes to prominence, that of the actor or masked self in a world of mirror and illusion. Here an alienation of the self bordering on madness is a persistent theme, and the story turns typically about the pitfalls that beset man's quest for identity. The tragedy becomes that of an inner breakdown —into self-deception, self-contradiction, and despondency, the signs of a lost humanity. And its misery includes the dreadful dreams and pitiable posturings which attend a mere role-playing existence. Or, thirdly, tragedy can include man's relation to the supernatural, his affair with the gods. Involved in this dimension is the hero's pretension to some priestly or prophetic task, in support of which there appear metaphors of ritual sacrifice. The theme turns then about man's effort to cleanse the state or the family, but as a missioner who comes to discover in himself a victim of evil fate. The fall we watch here is paradoxically that of flight—into a social isolation which culminates in some kind of scapegoat death. This is tragedy in its religious and communal aspect.

Of the three metaphors thus potential in a tragic hero—fortune's fool, distracted actor, and scapegoat minister—no one of them need be exclusive of the others. A missing of the mark of human happiness is involved in them all. The hero's suffered loss, whether of public position simply or also of psychic health and of friends, invites some explanation grounded in the mysteries of cosmic order and human purposing. Hence a serious dramatist will try to understand and suggest metaphysical and moral causes for the tragedy he tells. His imitation of it will include attention to the occasions and reasonings by which men become the victims of misfortune, or of sterile roles, or of self-destroying rituals. In sum, he will seek to illumine, as best he can, the characteristic logic and significant defect of human hamartia.

In the *Poetics,* Aristotle's single reference to hamartia is distressingly brief. But this treatise plainly was not intended to furnish a dramatist all the knowledge he could pertinently use in writing plays. Its distinctive focus precludes attention to the metaphysics or ethics of action; yet these sciences (so important elsewhere to Aristotle) are no doubt presupposed as furnishing a poet a background knowledge for understanding those forms of life which as artist he imitates.[1] When in the *Poetics* Aristotle uses terms such as "action," "hamartia," or "catharsis," he is assuming his own understanding of these, while focusing in his present treatise simply on describing their function in a drama of tragic kind. He is here concerned with what works well, rather than with explaining fully how it works. Some hamartia in the tragic protagonist is the factor necessary to the play's final function, its eliciting a purgation of pity and fear in the spectator. The particular psychology behind hamartia is a matter left to the individual playwright to supply. Each dramatist, presumably, will supply it by the light of whatever auxiliary knowledge he possesses. At the same time, Aristotle's own understanding of the meaning of hamartia may be gathered from his treatises on ethics. We may infer that he regarded his ethics as in general accord with the understanding of life presupposed in the bulk of Greek drama.

A critical problem nevertheless arises for us of a latter-day era: How far can Aristotle's principles, both artistic and moral, be considered still applicable to examples of tragedy written in Christian times? The complexities inherent in such a question go far toward excusing those critics who in despair have shelved it. We know, however, that in the sixteenth century Thomas Wilkinson had Englished *The Ethiques of Aristotle* (1547), and that in Latin the *Moralia* with commentary was in general use in England's universities. Latin translations of the *Poetics* could be had by import from Italy.[2] These facts do not tell us how well Shakespeare knew Aristotle (whose name he mentions only in *The Taming of the Shrew* and in *Troilus and Cressida*), but they testify to Aristotle's continuing importance.

We know, moreover, that at least some Elizabethan theologians were well-versed not only in Aristotle but in the remodeled Aristotelianism of St. Thomas and other schoolmen. John Harmar, Regius Professor of Greek at Oxford (1585–90), is described by Anthony Wood as a subtle Aristotelian well read in scholastic theology. Richard Hooker's thought, too, has its rootage in this tradition, as many historians have noted.[3] And John Donne, for instance, frequently cites from Aquinas favorably, even in public sermons.[4] Continental editions of the *Summa Theologica*—of which there were many within Shakespeare's lifetime—must have had some circulation in England even though marginal to the interests of most Elizabethans. Besides abridged editions, the following unabridged ones can today be consulted in the University of Illinois library: Lyon, 1575–77; Lyon, 1588; and Bergamo, 1590. Elsewhere I have seen listed a Lyon folio edition of 1562. One of these might have come to Shakespeare's attention through his associations with Catholics[5] or with learned Anglicans. More important, however, than any guesses as to whether or how well Shakespeare was versed in Aquinas is the provable fact that he knew the Bible very well indeed, and in addition the lore and moral vision of traditional Christianity. Hence his understanding of a term such as hamartia need not have rested strictly on Aristotle. More likely, it would have been informed by the accumulated moral theology Shakespeare had absorbed from the Bible, the Book of Common Prayer, and some of St. Augustine's more popular works, as well as from other Church fathers whose writings were quoted extensively both by Anglicans and Elizabethan Catholics in their numerous compendiums and tomes of controversy; although, besides this, some reading in Aquinas cannot be ruled out as a possibility.

Europe's two inheritances, surely, the classical tradition and the Christian, are not discontinuous. Medieval thought had allied them. And if by subordinating and reinterpreting the classical thought forms Aquinas could thus baptize Aristotle's ethics into the Christian scheme,[6] might not a Christian dramatist baptize Aristotle's *Poetics* in effect—not by rewriting Aristotle's treatise, but by employing his theory in the sense which a Christian vision makes possible? Drawing on a general heritage of Christian thought, whether acquired through books or otherwise, Shakespeare could have used Aristotle's traditional categories but with a Christian understanding imported into them. This is at least a possibility worth considering, trying out, and testing. For although it is no doubt true that most Renaissance theorists subjugated Aristotle's principles to those of Horace and to Senecan models, Shakespeare's own art in tragedy differs from this popular neoclassicism. He seems to have found his way, consciously or subconsciously, to a mode of tragedy more fundamentally Aristotelian,[7] and at the same time closer to Chaucer's psychological realism than to Ben Jonson's didacticism. Presumably it was by the light of medieval Christian premises that he enlarged on Aristotle's poetic.

In the previous chapter we have mentioned some of the subtle alterations which a baptized *Poetics* involves, and now it may be helpful to explore what could be involved as regards the most crucial factor in a theory of tragedy, the concept of hamartia. To understand what this could have meant to Shakespeare we can inquire briefly, first, what Aristotle meant by it, not merely as a formal principle in the *Poetics* but as given a moral content in his ethics. And then, through reference to traditional Christian ethics, we can suggest the revised and enlarged scope of meaning which hamartia takes on—what we may call its full potential of meaning, available for use by any Christian writer of tragedies capable of appreciating it and implying it in his own work. In short, Aristotle's concept when ontologized and Christianized can offer us, perhaps, a significant clue for the reading of Shakespearean drama. In support and illustration of this suggestion, I shall offer a reading of *Hamlet* in accord with it. Let me begin, however, with an attempt at tracing briefly the concept of hamartia in its historical evolution.

1 Aristotle and Sophocles

In describing "tragedy at its best" (in *Poetics* XIII), Aristotle associates hamartia with the measure of responsibility which the hero has in his own downfall, a measure which must be suitable for arousing our pity and fear. These emotions will not be aroused, says Aristotle, if the man who is shown passing from prosperity to misery is faultless or, on the contrary, if he is an utterly wicked man. There remains, then, the case of a man who is a mean between these extremes: a man who is "not eminently good or just," yet whose misfortune is not brought about by vice or depravity but by some failing, which Aristotle a moment later calls a "great failing" (*hamartia megale*). He explains that if the hero were wholly innocent, his misfortunes would offend our sense of justice; on the other hand, if he were wholly wicked, they would be merely what he deserves. Rather, his misfortunes must seem greater than he deserves, so as to arouse our pity; and he must be midway between good and bad, in order to be accepted as someone "like ourselves," thus enlisting our fear as his sad fate is revealed. When such a man comes from an illustrious family and yet falls into an unmitigated misfortune, we have the best kind of tragedy. Only a second best kind, says Aristotle, will show the hero as rewarded or reconciled with his enemies.

May we perhaps summarize as follows: in the best tragedy a greatly gifted but morally imperfect man makes a major error by which his life is blighted to the very end. But what kind of dreadful error can a deficiently good man make? Ingram Bywater has translated hamartia as an "error of judgment," derived from "ignorance of some material fact or circumstance."[8] This interpretation may be valid as far as it goes. But S. H. Butcher has contended for a wider area of meaning: the term connotes in Aristotle's ethics, Butcher believes, "an error due to inadequate knowledge of particular circumstances . . . such as might have been known." The error therefore "in some degree is morally culpable, as it might have been avoided."[9] It arises from a hasty or careless view of a special situation. W. K. Wimsatt reads Aristotle similarly. Hamartia connotes, he argues, an erroneous act amid an area of senses centering about "rash and culpable negligence" and shading out toward "a periphery of vice and passion."[10]

The truth of this broader reading, it seems to me, bears up well if we test it against *Oedipus Tyrannus,* the play which was apparently Aristotle's ideal. Does not Oedipus act negligently, rashly, and with proud self-assertion? Even within that segment of his life which the play covers, he is shown as irreverent toward the seer Tieresias, and unjustly angry at Creon, and impatiently violent toward the old Shepherd. His initial interest in solving the murder is founded on a self-protective motive—on the fear, as R. Y. Hathorn has remarked, that whoever murdered Laius may "do so to *me,*" rather than on a readiness to acknowledge that "what he did I might have done." The play, in Hathorn's view, is exhibiting in its hero a hamartia that is both moral and intellectual.[11] Even at the play's end, as R. B. Heilman has emphasized, Oedipus retains a motive of self-protectiveness. For although he then acknowledges his sin of parricide and incest, and punishes his eyes as a retribution, he yet attributes his shameful crimes to accident, rather than to his own faulty attitude. He does not, even now, rebuke himself for his acts of resisting the truth, or acknowledge that he has had self-righteous desires that have hampered his knowing what he had a capacity for knowing.[12] Does Heilman's point involve perhaps a more penetrating analysis of moral responsibility for ignorance than Aristotle would have given? Butcher, in the specific case of Oedipus, judges less rigorously and wavers in pinning down the nature of the guilt. While noting in Oedipus something of "proud self-assertion," Butcher comments that, broadly speaking, "circumstances" seem to be the determining factor in this hero's ruin. The slaying of Laius was "probably in some degree morally culpable," he says, yet on the other hand this original error seems to spring from "the necessary blindness and infirmity of human nature."[13] Such a balancing of the case may be close to Aristotle's view. Yet it verges on a contradiction by suggesting that a "culpable" act can spring from a "necessary" blindness. Just how necessary is the infirmity of human ignorance?

In the *Nicomachean Ethics* III. 5 (tr. W. D. Ross), Aristotle does not seem to regard ignorance as a necessary weakness in man. "We punish those who are ignorant of anything in the laws that they ought to know and that is not difficult," he remarks, because "we assume that it is in their power not to be ignorant, since they have the power of taking care." Each man, he goes on to say, is "somehow responsible for his state of mind" and of character. The man who is careless makes himself responsible for a self-indulgent state of character, like one who makes himself ill by disobeying his doctors. Aristotle is pessimistic, however, about the possibility of a man's recovering health of character once he has thrown away his chances. Such a man will not become well simply by wishing to be. Also, for Aristotle, there is a kind of fatalism regarding unjust acts due to "anger or to other passions necessary or natural to man" (*N. E.* V. 8). Acts of this sort he traces to man's failure to deliberate, and he extenuates this fault by saying that "it is not the man who acts in anger, but he who enraged him, that starts the mischief" by offering an "apparent injustice" which occasions the rage. Here are circumstances under which Aristotle is more ready to excuse man's guilt than are Christian authors, as we shall presently see. But before we pursue this point, let us turn to another matter.

In *Poetics* XIV, when speaking of situations which can best arouse pity and fear, Aristotle refers to Oedipus as an instance of a dreadful deed done in ignorance, and to the Medea of Euripides as an instance of a dreadful deed done wittingly. Both kinds, presumably, involve hamartia. They accompany Aristotle's advice to playwrights to choose a story in which "some such crime as murder" is done by friend against friend. Here, if we but recall the high value friendship has in Aristotle's ethics, we can infer that its betrayal must have seemed to him particularly heinous. Yet the dreadfulness of the crime, whether done ignorantly or consciously, need not mean that its basic motive is one of villainy. The injurious act can have arisen from some great failing in a person "like ourselves" not eminently good or just. When we use the modern term "tragic flaw," I think we usually have in mind both these aspects: a human moral imperfectness and, as a consequence, an act of misjudgment which is criminal and destructive.[14]

What can we say, then, of a heroine such as Antigone, whose culpability many critics would deny despite the fact that she hangs herself? Is not a modern romanticism coloring the spectacles of these judges? Even Butcher thinks Antigone an exception to Aristotle's formula, a sinless sufferer; Bernard Knox says she "was right" in her self-willed act of suicide; and Jacques Maritain, to my surprise, has remarked that she sacrifices her life to "the infinite transcendent good, that is, God.''[15] On the other hand, however, critics such as Gilbert Norwood, A. C. Schlesinger, Lane Cooper, and Wimsatt agree that Antigone's action is morally culpable; and we know this to have been the view, in Elizabethan times, of the poet-scholar Thomas Watson, whose Latin translation of *Antigone* (1581) includes an added pageant which moralizes on the faults of Antigone, Creon, and Haemon, while attributing to Ismene right reason and piety.[16] Interpretations along this second line, it seems to me, accord both with the play's implications and with an Aristotelian theory of tragedy. For if, as Schlesinger emphasizes, the intended ultimate effect of Greek tragedy is audience *insight,* through the drama's symbolic truth-telling, then (as he says) our sympathy for the characters "must not go so far as to preclude insight and judgment." Although the faults of a hero must not alienate our sympathy, yet Athenian philosophy and its poets do not contemplate an "unalloyed display of virtue" in tragedy's agents.

The *Antigone,* if read carefully, indicates clearly enough its heroine's penchant for twisting the laws of the gods to serve her own glory—just as Creon, in a polar way, twists human law. Neither of these opponents has patience for listening to the other or for profiting from choral counsel. Nor does Antigone have any of Ismene's concern for a balancing of duties. The reckless daring of Oedipus, as the Chorus comments, is renewed in this elder daughter. Defying all human restriction, she courts the rocky fate of a Niobe, even when aware that the Chorus is mocking her pretensions to divinity, and criticizing her dereliction from duty to the city, and terming her the victim of her own self-will. We note, further, the illogic of her reasoning. She would not defy her fellow citizens, she says, for the sake of any dead husband or child of hers, but only for her dead brother, who is irreplaceable. Can we miss seeing a Sophoclean irony in such a statement? In the name of love of brother, Antigone is conspicuously neglecting at this moment all brotherly concern for Haemon, her promised husband, besides continuing to scorn both uncle and sister. What a deadly and excessively literal sense of "brotherhood" she has! Its contradictoriness is equalled only by the illogic of her earlier invoking of "unwritten laws" against Creon while making her own will (as the Chorus remarks) "a law unto itself"; or by her final invoking, in her curtain speech, the gods of city and family to sanction suicide, an act which is essentially anticommunal. Such are the ironies of Antigone's self-deification. Both Plato and Aristotle (in *N. E.* III. 7) had disapproved of suicide. Sophocles has the Chorus comment by likening Antigone to Lycurgus, who was punished in stone for profaning the revels of the gods. On the other hand, when Creon relents, he is told that "proud men in old age learn to be wise." Prior to his grudging repentance, his stubbornness had been as excessive as Antigone's. Sophocles has been letting us see genuine tragedy—which includes but is larger than the melodrama of Antigone's outlook.

Aristotle, very reasonably, could have regarded both her and Creon as good but morally imperfect persons who have been brought to misfortune through a great error of judgment. This human failing he would have regarded as the consequence, centrally, of immoderation, since in his ethics moderation and prudence are essential for man's attaining of his proper end, which is happiness. Individuals are not laws unto themselves in Aristotle's view. They act faultily (see *N. E.* VII. 4) when they pursue excessively honor or victory or devotion to some member of the family. Granted that Aristotle considered honor the chief exterior good of the active life; yet he insisted that it not be loved over-ambitiously (see *N. E.* IV. 4). He emphasized *intelligent* conduct—conduct which flows logically from a correct estimate of life's natural goods. Like other Greek writers, he would not have approved the stubbornness of Achilles in the *Iliad* when an Ate of blind infatuation possessed this hero. In fact, he names Achilles in *Poetics* XV as a hero whose "defects" of character provide a proper type for tragedy; such a type, he says, can be ennobled by the dramatist's making it true to life and yet more beautiful, especially by taking care to make the man's inconsistencies "consistently inconsistent." According to Aristotle's ethics, honor is to be offered ultimately to the gods. But does Antigone do this? Bernard Knox concedes: "After her frank admission that she would not have done what she has done for husband or a child, she has little claim on the gods below, and those above do not claim her for their own."[17] Like her father in his act of self-blinding, Antigone persists in going a solitary way—independent of all considerations except, as Creon says, her worship of "Death, the god she loves." This fault, of course, is ironically Creon's too, unwittingly, until omens of the blight upon his doing bring him to relent, but too late to avoid the miseries of earthly disaster.

For understanding more precisely Aristotle's view, we need to consider closely what he means by a "misfortune not brought about by vice or depravity." Can there be any kind of moral disorder not involving vice or depravity? Perhaps Book VII of the *Nicomachean Ethics* can help us at this point. It carefully distinguishes vice and brutishness from what Aristotle calls incontinence. "Incontinence," he explains, "is *not vice,* though perhaps it is so in a qualified sense" (VII. 8). Incontinence and vice both lead to criminal acts. Yet they differ, in that vice is in accordance with choice, whereas incontinence is "contrary to choice." The vicious man has a criminal intention; he is self-indulgent "by choice" and hence unlikely to repent. But a man who is incontinent with regard to things in themselves desirable is self-indulgent unintentionally, un-deliberately. He simply follows his imagination without awaiting argument. He neglects the right rule. He neglects it, not because he thinks he ought to follow his pleasures without reserve, but because temporarily he delights in them too much. Thus he acts unjustly, but without guile or malice. This "incontinent" man (whom Aristotle thinks of as not vicious in a strict sense) may be our clue for understanding Aristotle's saying that a tragic hero falls "not by vice" but by some hamartia.

By distinguishing between a malicious or guileful act and a negligently self-indulgent one, Aristotle can say that the incontinent man is not wicked, but only "half-wicked" (VII. 10). He is like a man asleep, or drunk, or mad. He both knows and does not know what he is doing. He is, further, one of two types: either an excitable person who does not deliberate at all before acting, or else a person who, under pressure from appetite, does not abide by the conclusions of his own deliberation. Or, to restate the same distinction: either he acts impetuously on some general premise without attending to particular facts, or else he lets some particular proposition for which passion argues shove aside a general proposition which opposes. Thus he acts either from ignorance, or in ignorance, rather than by deliberate choice. In that sense his action is involuntary, even though in another sense he acts willingly. Socrates was wrong, Aristotle believes, in supposing that right action follows necessarily from a correct knowledge of the end to be pursued. Socrates failed to reckon with incontinence, which Aristotle understands as a flouting, when urged by desire, of the general knowledge of good and evil which a man has or could have by taking care.

But only the man who harms another "from choice," so Aristotle would insist (V. 8), is an unjust man or a vicious man. Aristotle's concept of choice, we may remark parenthetically, is not quite the same as we find later in Aquinas, since Aristotle's view of the human will turns about an intellectual preference, as applied to means in man's power, rather than about the response of a rational appetite when attracted to some end in the order of final causality.[18] In Aristotle's use of the term, "choice" is a self-controlled desiring based on deliberation. If deliberation is hampered, there is something less than a voluntary choice. Acts of injustice may then be done without intending vice. And when such is the case, their doer is not an "unjust man" in Aristotle's view, since his acts were without malice aforethought. They are simply "mistaken acts." Insofar as they have in them an element of involuntariness, they are both regretable and excusable. This is especially so when the act has resulted from anger, for anger is a passion more natural, more "common to all men" than other appetites, and less disgraceful, because "the man who is incontinent in respect of anger is in a sense conquered by argument" (VII. 6). Pardonable because not from choice, likewise, are actions done in ignorance of particular circumstances —such as ignorance of who one is, or of what he is doing, or of whom he is striking, or with what missile, or with what effect (V. 8). Harms done under such circumstances are excusable if the agent afterwards feels regret (III. 1).

Here Oedipus of Thebes is the example we think of. His moment of regret for his crimes, however, should not be equated with Christian repentance, since what it turns about is the recognition simply of a shameful mistake. A comparable example from Shakespeare might be Hamlet's remorse after stabbing Polonius. Of this, we shall say more later. But for now, let us note two instances of tragic mistake mentioned by Aristotle. In the *Nicomachean Ethics* VII. 4, when describing the undeliberate moral weakness of a person who is carried away by an excessive passion for "worthy" goods such as wealth, honor, or victory, Aristotle names in illustration Niobe's daring to rival the gods (by boasting), and the unreasonable devotion which Satyrus showed to his father (presumably in deifying him). Readers of Sophocles' *Antigone* may here recall that Antigone, on departing for her cave, compared herself to Niobe. For readers of Shakespeare, the example of Satyrus might be compared to Hamlet's excessive devotion to his father out of a "worthy" passion for honor. Aristotle, in terming such actions pardonable, is not approving them. Rather, he is including them among the pitiable instances of human error. And in other passages he acknowledges, as Wimsatt has noted, that chance itself belongs within the sphere of moral action; or, as we would say, accident-prone persons have something morally wrong in them.

2 The Bible, Augustine, and Aquinas

Now this notion of hamartia, while not identical with the Christian view, has a kind of congruence with it. The biblical view, we may say, understands the human frailty more precisely and more profoundly. Not merely a neglect to use reason in governing outward actions causes human mistakes, but, inside that, the fact of a human reason that is willing to neglect God's law. And this background kind of willingness is wilful in an "original" sense; it is a tragic inclination stemming from what later theologians have termed "original sin." Original sin, as described by St. Augustine (in *City of God*, XIV. 13), is a spontaneous pride of will, a paradoxical "undue exaltation" which takes place when the soul "abandons Him to whom it ought to cleave as its end, and becomes a kind of end to itself."

By this act (scarcely one of deliberate choice, rather one of voluntary neglect) man becomes benighted, frigid, and in his being more contracted. Thomas Aquinas enumerates the "wounds" it has brought on man: weakness, ignorance, malice and concupiscence.[19] The resulting flaw here described, let us note, includes even a kind of malice—the kind, says Aquinas, which we find mentioned in Genesis 8:21, man's proneness to evil imagination from his youth. (Aristotle had not taken this into account; he means something more deliberate when he refers to "malice.") Aquinas understands all four of original sin's "wounds" as the after-effects of a spontaneous wilfulness which, as such, is distinguishable from the will's subsequent mischoices under its influence. He explains that by original sin man's rational nature is not destroyed, or even in its root diminished; rather it has these obstacles now placed against its attaining its proper term.

Thus we may say that what Aristotle had described as the "incontinence" of yielding to natural passion is now seen, in Christian analysis, as resting on the prior fact of Adam's "sin of nature," caused by his yielding to self-love. This "sin of nature" is every-

man's tragic inheritance. Hence, except as men use their unde-
stroyed reason (in its root still undiminished) for a seeking of
grace to overcome this proneness (as Abel did), their ability to perform sinless acts is handicapped. In the state of original justice,
Aquinas explains, "the reason had perfect hold over the lower parts
of the soul, while reason itself was perfected by God and was subject to him"; but under original sin the soul's powers are left, as it
were, "destitute of their proper order." In this condition, the committing of further sinful acts readily follows. Augustine had explained that all sinful acts involve some kind of turning from the
immutable good. The soul takes this turn whenever it turns either
to itself, or to outward goods, or to downward ones: "It turns
towards its own when it wills to be its own master; towards outward good, when out of curiosity it strives to know things which
are the property of others, or which do not pertain to itself; to the
lower good, when it loves the pleasures of the body."[20] The three
forms of sin here distinguished were schematized in medieval moral
analysis as those of vainglory, avarice, and gluttony—the three
temptations to which Adam and Eve yielded and which Christ overcame, those named in I John 2:16 as the pride of life, the lust of the
eyes, and the lust of the flesh.

Anders Nygren, a modern Lutheran theologian, in comparing
the Christian view of sin with the Greek view, has contended that
for the Greeks

> ... man's innermost, spiritual self is good and perfect; that
> evil lies in its connection with the corporeal world of
> sense, which degrades and sullies it. The genuinely Chris-
> tian idea is the absolute opposite; sin is connected with the
> innermost being, the will, the spiritual self of man. The
> corporeal sensible world is God's good creation, which is,
> however, corrupted when used as an instrument for the
> will at variance with God, the spirit hostile to him.[21]

But Nygren's contrast is too blunt. It ignores certain more moderate forms of Greek and Christian statement. The will at variance
with God, if we consult Augustine, is regarded as only indirectly
hostile to God, through a neglect and a flight. Yet Nygren has cor-
rectly suggested that the Christian view locates sin principally in
man's will, not his body.

Evil arises, so Augustine insists (in *City of God* XIV. 2–6), not
from man's flesh, which in its own kind and degree is good, but from

man's willing to "live after the flesh"—that is, to yield to vices of the soul, which include not merely "carnalities" such as adultery and lasciviousness, but more importantly such "animosities" as idolatry, emulation, strife and envying (Galatians 5:19–20). Hence it is quite possible for a man "to abstain from fleshly pleasures for the sake of idolatry or some heretical error," yet in this way to be practicing damnable "works of the flesh" in the Pauline sense. These are comments we will do well to remember when, later, we analyze the character of Hamlet. For as we pick up Hamlet's tone of disdain for "solid flesh," we may wish to recall Augustine's further remark, a Christian paradox:

> He who extols the nature of the soul as the chief good, and condemns the nature of the flesh as if it were evil, assuredly is fleshly both in his love of the soul and in his hatred of the flesh; for these his feelings arise from human fancy, not from divine truth. (XIV. 5)

Augustine calls the attitude just described a Manichean one. The Platonic view, he goes on to say, tends somewhat in that direction, but is less censurable. It does not condemn the flesh; yet mistakenly it traces the origin of vice to the soul's being tied to a body which distracts the soul with corrupting desires. The Christian view, on the other hand, says Augustine, is that whatever corrupting desires man's body now harbors are not due to the body, which in itself is good, but to a punishment the body suffers as a consequence of the soul's original sin; "for it was not the corruptible flesh that made the soul sinful, but the sinful soul that made the flesh corruptible" (XIV. 3).

If Augustine had known Aristotle's view, he would no doubt have rated it even less censurable than the Platonist one. For Aristotle regards man's body as the locus of desires that are good if ruled by an uncorrupted reason. He deplores as "weak" the "incontinent" man who fails to use his reason or abide by it when his natural desires solicit. This weakness gives to such a man's action an involuntary quality. What Aristotle does not adequately explain, however, is how this weakness of the reason has become "common" in human beings. In the biblical view this state of character is due to the will's prior action of giving way to self-love. Aristotle comes close to this explanation when he regards the incontinent man's character as a natural frailty to which he is subject when his passions lead him to neglect his reason. But in the biblical view such weakness is not a frailty simply (although it is also that); more profoundly, it is a punishment for man's having ignored the divine rule as an aid to his human reason. St. Augustine sums up this situation in a sentence: "Disobedience punishes disobedience" (*City of God* XIV. 15). That is, man's passions disobey him because his own reason is not obeying God's law.

Aristotle's account of the incontinent man's frailty, nevertheless, has a kind of parallel to the Bible's account of mankind's shortcomings. For St. Paul declares in Romans, chapters 1–3, that the bulk of the human race has acted contrary to its own better judgment. The Gentiles, he says, although able to know the Creator through His creatures, have neglected such knowledge in favor of vain imaginings. And on the other hand, the Jews, although in possession of God's specific ordinances as their rule, have failed to practice what they preach. Here Aristotle's two kinds of incontinence (negligence in ascertaining fact, and a yielding to passion in the face of a higher rule) seem to be reflected, but translated within a larger context. When thus translated, the two kinds of "falling short" are by St. Paul plainly called "without excuse," because the Apostle has a stricter sense than Aristotle's of the will's accountability. Yet, somewhat like Aristotle, Paul sees a mixture of willing and nonwilling in man's hamartia: "that which I would not that I do."

Scholars have observed how the Greek term hamartia takes on a large scope of reference in the Septuagint. Hebrew words with such varying connotations as godlessness, presumption, idolatry, injustice, and disease are all sometimes translated in the Septuagint as hamartia.[22] It is noteworthy, in these instances, that the translators preferred hamartia over such other Greek words as *adikia* or *kakia*, probably because hamartia was less tied to a merely ethical sense; it could carry a general sense of wrong action.[23]

The Bible introduces a deeper meaning for hamartia but one not discontinuous with Aristotle's. The story of the Fall in Genesis, we may say, clarifies in an ultimate way that "error in judgment" by which tragedy entered the world. As a higher parallel to Aristotle's two kinds of incontinence, we have Eve's credulous ignorance, and Adam's willingness to set aside his knowledge; she is transgressing because she was "deceived," and he knowing better, but yet (as Augustine adds) deceived perhaps in thinking the sin venial and his apology for it admissible.[24] Thus there is an intellectual failure by both Adam and Eve, and at its center a moral weakness—a craving for undue exaltation, by which ironically the human will lapses from what could truly exalt it. Man's love becomes self-pleasing. Here, says Augustine (*City of God* XXII. 22), is that "root of error and misplaced love" from which crimes spring; here is the origin of "the profound and dreadful ignorance which produces all the errors that enfold the children of Adam."

Yes, criminal errors are due to ignorance, a "profound and dreadful ignorance." Yet such ignorance does not excuse man from responsibility. Augustine discusses this point at length in his treatise *On Free Will*. Through ignorance, he explains (III. 49–58), man "has not the freedom of will to do what he ought"; or "he cannot see what he ought to do or fulfill it when he will." Wrong things are thus done "by necessity." But this necessity is itself a penal state, the just consequence of Adam's sin, through which man has chosen the avarice which enslaves him. "All that a man does wrongfully in ignorance, and all that he cannot do rightly though he wishes, are called sins because they have their origin in the first sin of the will when it was free." Hence, men born into this ignorance should not murmur against God's justice. They should not seek to evade thus their *present* responsibility. For the same God who justly exacts punishment will mercifully remit it, *if men will only do what they still can,* namely, *confess* humbly their weakness *and seek* aid from Him.

> There is One present everywhere who, in many ways, by means of the creation that serves him as its Lord, calls back him who has gone astray, teaches him who believes, comforts him who has hope, exhorts the diligent, helps him who is trying and answers prayer. You are not held guilty because you are ignorant in spite of yourself, but because you neglect to seek the knowledge you do not possess. You are not held guilty because you do not use your wounded members, but because you despise him who is willing to heal them. These are your own personal sins.[25]

Man retains, Augustine insists, "the natural power to discern that wisdom is to be preferred to error and tranquility to toil, and to know that these good things are to be reached, not simply by being born, but by earnestly seeking them." Hence a man can be liberated from his ignorance, if he is willing to be.[26] But if he loves his own will, he will continue benighted and thereby self-betrayed into what Augustine calls "disgraceful error" and "painful effort."

Disgraceful error and painful effort: Are not these the hallmark of every tragic hero? What Augustine helps us see is that their root is not ignorance alone but an ignorance resulting from a misplaced love. Love of some temporal good in preference to God—a love that is pleasing to man's reason when that reason is centered on self —this is for Augustine the root of error. And Aquinas echoes Augustine. He names "inordinate love of self" as the source of every sin, and "aversion from God" as the formal cause of every sin.[27] Here then, precisely stated, is Christianity's unique insight into the nature of evil, and more particularly into what we may call the mystery of ignorance. And if, as I would suggest, the mystery of ignorance is centrally what tragedy turns about, then it can be said that whereas the Greeks penetrated this mystery but dimly, their Christian successors were able (by a higher light) to probe it more deeply so as to discern its large intelligibility.

Aristotle had approved a love of self. Not, it is true, in the sense of love of the irrational self, but in the sense of love of the rational element in man, by which man can do noble actions—those actions which bring him happiness in this life. The good man, he held (*N. E.* IX. 8), "loves most this part in him," his rational self. Aquinas accepts this argument, but with the important qualification that the rational self, as being in potentiality toward God as its object, cannot find its final happiness in any created good, but only in union with God, the Uncreated Good.[28] Man's reason is but the "proximate" rule of morality. It can show man good things, and guide his will, only insofar as it derives its light from the Eternal Reason. In its judgment of any particular good, the human reason can err, by neglecting to consider the Divine Law, or by holding that Law in contempt.[29] Aquinas therefore sums up the basic cause of sin in a way that both absorbs and goes beyond Aristotle. "The will," he says, "lacking the direction of the rule of reason and of the Divine Law, and intent on some mutable good, causes the act of sin directly, and the inordinateness of the act indirectly and beside the intention" (*S. T.* I–II. 75. 1). In this definition, it seems to me, we have an outline for all tragic action in its moral aspect. Tragic action is action intent on a mutable good, and neglectful of reason and the Divine Law, with the result that acts become rash without a man's having so intended. The rashness is accidental to a misdirected will.

On the nature of ignorance, Aquinas refines rather than rejects Aristotle. When, for instance, he cites Aristotle's statement that in human acts what is done through ignorance is involuntary, we find him qualifying this maxim with new distinctions and applications (*S. T.* I–II. 6.8). Simple involuntariness, he explains, applies only when man is "ignorant of some circumstance of his act which he was not bound to know." For instance, if a man *after taking proper precaution* does not know that someone is coming along a road, so that he shoots an arrow and slays a passerby, the slaying is involuntary. But when ignorance arises from some passion or habit, or when one does not take the trouble to acquire the knowledge he can and ought to have, his ignorance is voluntary as regards general principles of law, and as such is an "ignorance of evil choice," indirectly voluntary. Thirdly, sometimes ignorance is an "affected ignorance," as when a man wishes not to know in order that he may have an excuse for sin or not be withheld from sin, and this kind is directly voluntary.

Elsewhere Aquinas distinguishes ignorance from nescience, which denotes mere absence of knowledge. Ignorance, he explains (*S. T.* I–II. 76. 2), denotes a "lack of knowledge of those things which one has a natural aptitude to know." And some of these things we are under obligation to know, namely, all those without which we are unable to accomplish a due act rightly. Included here are matters which go quite beyond Aristotle's boundaries of vision. All men, says Aquinas, "are bound in common to know the articles of faith and the universal principles of right," and each individual is bound to know matters regarding "his duty or state." Neglecting to know any of these is a "sin of omission." Only "invincible" ignorance, that is, ignorance which can not be overcome by study, is without sin. Further, although "privation of grace is not a sin in itself, yet by reason of negligence in preparing oneself for grace, it may have the character of sin." It seems evident that Aquinas, following the Bible and St. Augustine, has here extended, beyond Aristotle's range, the frontiers of man's moral responsibility.

To what extent, Aquinas asks in *S. T.* I–II. 76. 3–4, does ignorance excuse sin in a subsequent act caused by the ignorance? Only insofar, he answers, as knowledge would have prevented the act as being contrary to the will, had knowledge been at hand. Only insofar as the act committed is not known to be a sin. Ignorance of some circumstance does not altogether and always excuse. For example, although one may not know that the man he is striking is his father, this ignorance does not altogether remove the sinfulness of the action if one knows that he is striking a man (which suffices for it to be sinful). Here Aquinas is restricting a loophole in *N. E.* V. 8, where Aristotle had called "involuntary" the striking of a father whose identity is unknown. Or, suppose that the striker is unaware that this man will defend himself and strike back, and that if he had known this he would not have struck him. Such ignorance, says Aquinas, does not affect at all the sinfulness of his striking the man. We can easily infer from this what Aquinas would have thought of Oedipus. Or, for that matter, what he would have thought of Hamlet's verbal striking at Claudius with veiled threats. Both cases would involve sinfulness. Aquinas emphasizes, however, that in all instances where the ignorance is not directly voluntary, a sinful act thus caused has a diminished gravity, since the will cannot be said to have consented directly but only accidentally. A slaying, for example, is less sinful when committed by a man when he is drunk. Yet such a man deserves punishment for both of two lesser sins, the drunkenness and the homicide.

Moral analysis of this kind, I suggest, could have offered Shakespeare a way of understanding and placing the nature of Hamlet's hamartia. Hamlet's various acts of violence, from this point of view, can be portrayed as being malicious only indirectly, inasmuch as Hamlet when doing them is virtually drunk—not literally with wine, but with vainglorious imaginations. ("As drunkennesse obscureth reason, so vaine glory corrupteth discretion" is a maxim quoted from St. Chrysostom by Meres in *Palladis Tamia*.) It is shortly after Hamlet's cry, "Now could I drink hot blood," that we see him ranting at his mother with verbal daggers, and then stabbing through the arras with a steel dagger. And is there not a similar intoxication as early as Act I, just after Hamlet has avidly drunk up the words of the Ghost? We see him, when excited by those words, recklessly banishing from his brain all customary norms of reason, and then capering about to swear oaths to an "old mole." Such actions done in an antic mood would have been regarded by Aquinas, we may suppose, as less sinful than if directly willed. Despite their "accidental" nature, however, he would see in them a voluntariness and hence a "vice," although in a diminished sense. In this respect, there is something like the "half-wicked" actions which Aristotle had ascribed to the "incontinent man."

Aquinas follows Aristotle when speaking of the ignorance which arises when a man is distracted by passion. In fact, in *S. T.* I–II. 77. 2–3, he uses Aristotle's metaphors of drunkenness and epilepsy to describe such a condition. But whereas Aristotle had named this condition "incontinence" (and thus not strictly "vicious"), Aquinas specifies it more exactly as a "sin of weakness," a vice of the soul. It is in the will's power, Aquinas explains, to give consent to an ignorant judgment, made by a reason which is impeded by an intensity of the sensitive appetite and a "vehement and inordinate apprehension of the imagination." In this way, a man fails to apply to the particular case at hand the habitual knowledge which in general he has. If his passion precedes an act of the will, it diminishes the sin of that act, yet does not altogether excuse it, says Aquinas, unless the cause of the passion be a natural sickness in nowise voluntary.

Is Hamlet's passion, we might ask, due to a natural sickness nowise voluntary? Is his will not in any way responsible for the melancholy grief in which we see him as the play opens, or for those later fits of hysteria which eventually he apologizes for as his "sore distraction"? This is a pertinent question, I think, despite the claims of critics such as E. E. Stoll, who would argue that Hamlet is not explainable in terms of any psychology at all but only in terms of theatrical makeup. Other critics have been not so sure. Dover Wilson, for example, admits Hamlet's "keen delight" in uncontrollable excitement, and hedges as to its voluntariness: it "appears nevertheless to have very little to do with his volition," Wilson says. Then, lamely, he falls back on Stoll's theory of magical makeup, yet in an appendix tries another tack by suggesting that "the defiled imagination of which Shakespeare writes so often . . . must be his own" (i.e., autobiographical).[30] Can such scattershot explanation really satisfy? On the other hand, can we be entirely content with J. H. Brock's psychoanalytic explanation, that a "manic depressive psychosis" in Hamlet made him "at times not responsible" during his emotional storms?[31] Or with Bradley's explanation that a morbid melancholy was "forced" on Hamlet by the moral shock of his mother's remarriage? T. S. Eliot, we may recall, arrived at a very different judgment: that the mother's remarriage does not warrant the intense disgust we find in Hamlet. In permitting Hamlet an emotion so disproportionate to its "objective correlative," so Eliot argued, Shakespeare botched his play. Here Eliot's initially right observation, I think, has led him to a wrong conclusion. Typically in any tragedy, I would say, the hero's reaction to external facts is inordinate if measured by *right* moral standards; it accords rather with the *defective* morality of the hero's will, an implicit fact in the play which furnishes a part of the total "correlative" to the emotion exhibited. Thus Hamlet's responses ought to be explained, not by supposing the play a failure, or by claiming that external events force a melancholy on the hero, or by hypothesizing a psychosis which eliminates responsibility, but rather by discerning the vice of soul which underlies Hamlet's encounter with his world.

In Hamlet's first soliloquy, for instance, do we not discern behind his grief what Aquinas would call an "inordinate apprehension of the imagination"? To picture Claudius as a "satyr" and Gertrude as bestial is an unwarranted exaggeration. It involves slander—if we may measure by strictly Christian norms.[32] And, concurrently, Hamlet is consenting to longings for suicide—despite his general knowledge that suicide is forbidden by Eternal law. He resents, longs to evade, this norm of reason. Then, in a later scene, when he breaks from his friends to follow the Ghost's beckoning, what we see is an emotional excitement and an imagining that his "fate cries out," a rash judgment which leads him to threaten to slay his friends—despite his general knowledge that murder is a sin. Still later, when he capers with the cellarage Ghost, despite his before-mentioned knowledge that a ghost could be bringing "blasts from Hell," may we not say that this action again evidences his will's neglect to use reason? Hamlet is here willing to swear to the Ghost's command *wherever* it comes from—whether from heaven, earth, or hell.

Such action may seem to some readers evidence of Hamlet's strength of resolve; but if read in the light of the moral psychology of Aquinas it is evidence, rather, of a "sin of weakness." And St. Thomas would trace all weakness of soul to a sinful concupiscence in man (in the form either of lust of the flesh, lust of the eyes, or pride of life), stemming from man's "original sin" of self-love, of which indeed such concupiscence is a punishment.[33] Thus Hamlet may be said to be half-right in his own explanation that his "sore

distraction" is a punishment, yet incorrect in thinking himself in
no way responsible for bringing it on, or for acting under its influence. His own self-love is its hidden cause. The perspective of St.
Thomas on this point represents an enlargement beyond Aristotle's,
a completing of Aristotle's categories by the light of biblical and
patristic texts.

Elsewhere (*S. T.* I–II. 19. 5–6), Aquinas specifically asks two
other questions, both very important to our consideration of the
moral roots of tragedy. The first is: Does an erring conscience bind?
The second is: Does an erring conscience excuse? The first concerns
those cases in which an erring reason proposes something as good
which is in fact evil, or proposes something as evil which is in fact
good. In such situations, is the will evil if it acts contrary to this
false judgment of the reason? Aquinas answers yes, the will is then
evil. For man's will is evil whenever it disobeys what he *thinks* to
be right, although we must call his evil in that case accidental only.
This point seems pertinent to the question of Hamlet's blameworthiness in delaying to take revenge on Claudius. Hamlet's excited reasoning tells him that revenge is a desirable good. It tells
him he "should have" fatted all the region's kites with the offal of
Claudius, and that he is a cowardly rogue to have been delinquent
in this duty. But this judgment may in fact be erroneous, because
dependent on a Pyrrhus model of justice—which conspicuously ignores an alternate model, the " 'Swounds" (Christ's wounds) by
which Hamlet is swearing. Is there moral evil, then, in Hamlet's not
being dutiful to his Pyrrhus-like conscience? If I read Aquinas
aright, he would say that so long as Hamlet remains ignorant of
his judgment's erroneousness and thinks revenge good, Hamlet's
will is evil in delaying the revenge, yet accidentally so.

But consider now the second question Aquinas raises: Is a man's
will good, on the other hand, when it abides by an erring conscience? To use Aquinas' own illustration, what about those men
who, in slaying the Apostles, thought they were doing God a service?
Aquinas answers that their will was evil, insofar as the error of
their conscience was itself voluntary, either directly, or through
negligence of what they ought to have known. Ignorance of the
Divine Law is inexcusable. "The will that abides by human reason
is not always right, nor is it always in accord with the eternal law."
For suppose a man who seeks vainglory: "he will sin whether he
does his duty for vainglory or whether he omit to do it." What a

dilemma man seems to be caught in! It looks irresolvable. But Aquinas insists that the man who seeks vainglory is in no genuine trap, but one of his own making. To escape, "he can put aside his evil intention." He can "lay aside his error, since his ignorance is vincible and voluntary."

Have we not here a key to the tensions within many a tragic hero? May not a dramatist let us see, in each of the tragedies he exhibits, that the seeming dilemmas of the hero are in reality self-made ones? Only by persisting in a self-pleasing love does man's ignorance become fatal. An implicit positing of this explanation of human disaster, it seems to me, is what can distinguish Christian tragedy. The writer of any tragedy needs, among other things, an adequately credible chain of moral causation for such action as he presents in his story. He needs to plot antecedents and consequences in character development according to some probable pattern. In his delineating of the quality of purpose in any action, and of stages in its developing psychology, a Christian playwright will shape his version of the story by the light of what he implicitly knows from traditional moral analysis and biblical paradigm. Such knowledge, even though it be present only half-consciously as he works, guides his selection of the detail by which he constructs his artistic imitation of life. A tragic action, as tending toward catastrophe, will require for its characters various modes of defective attitude—discernible by the artist at a level deeper than these characters can explain to themselves. He as their fashioner must understand these "persons" and their world better than they do, while providing for us of the audience signposts to such vision. In this respect Shakespeare excels. Hence the perennial fascination of his dramas.

To posit a self-pleasing love as central to every tragic hero does not, however, take us very far unless we go on to study, in a particular play, the specific cultural circumstances amid which the hero manifests this flaw and makes his great mistake. Yet this clue furnishes us a beginning. In part it explains various features which critics from time to time have noted in tragic heroes—features such as intense subjectivism, self-dramatization, flight from reality, and specious argument. Of Shakespeare's tragic heroes, A. H. Fairchild noted some years ago that all of them display an egoism and self-pity, an aversion to fact and truth, and a homicidal or suicidal mania.[34] More recently, John Vyvyan has declared that all of them are in some special way yoked with Judas, who "did betray the Best."[35]

In tragic heroes we must expect to see human failure writ large. That means, in terms of our discussion so far, some spectacular instance of inordinate love of glory for the self, such as human honor, or one of the other "worthy" goods which Aristotle said could be loved excessively. The imagined good must be such as might tempt us (and perhaps daily is tempting us) to a neglect of reason and Divine Law for its sake. Then, as the hero is shown defeating himself by his "purposes mistook," we can ponder the ironies of his self-delusion and, vicariously with him, experience at least what is well stated in T. S. Eliot's *Gerontion*:

> Neither fear nor courage saves us. Unnatural vices
> Are fathered by our heroism. Virtues
> Are forced upon us by our impudent crimes.
> These tears are shaken from the wrath-bearing tree.

Or perhaps, pondering further, we may discover the meaning of what Friar Lawrence teaches, yet fails himself to apply to the judging of his own actions, in *Romeo and Juliet*:

> Virtue turns vice, being misapplied,
> And vice sometime's by action dignified.

3 Sin's circularity in *Hamlet*

But let us now turn attention, more focally, on *Hamlet*. This play as a whole, as various critics of late have been saying, is the tragedy of all Denmark.[36] To understand this fact aright, however, we need a coherent view of the protagonist. And by what perspective can we find this? Does it make sense to say of Prince Hamlet, as Dover Wilson does, that he is "both mad and the sanest of geniuses," both "a miserable failure and the most adorable of heroes"? Such a reading, in its attempt to combine the "sweet prince" of romantic interpretation with the stage-puppet of Stoll's account, seems to offer us, not a "mysterious" character, as Dover Wilson claims, but instead an irresolvable contradiction. A fresh start from some other ground is needed. Yet it can not be one which reinstates a reading as simple as Peter Alexander's: "Hamlet is the most normal of Shakespeare's heroes, the man of unimpaired vision with an equally true discernment whatever side of our nature is in question."[37] For, somehow, we need to come to terms with W. F. Trench's insistence (as long ago as 1913) that "Hamlet himself finds it impossible to understand himself"; with H. B. Charlton's comments on Hamlet's distortions of reality; with Robert Speaight's stress on Hamlet's subjectivism and "divorce from reality"; and perhaps even with Ernest Jones's theory of an Oedipus complex.[38]

Some brief quotation from two recent books may suggest for us a valid focus. L. C. Knights, commenting on Hamlet's famous "To be or not to be" soliloquy, writes:

> It does not matter that in Hamlet's mind the thought of suicide merges with the thought of killing the king; what matters is the quite unambiguous sense of health giving way to disease, of a loss of purpose and a lapsing from positive direction. . . . Hamlet . . . is a man who has given himself over to a false direction of consciousness; and at each of the crucial points of the action Shakespeare leaves us in no doubt as to the inadequacy—and worse—of Hamlet's basic attitudes.[39]

And John Vyvyan, commenting on the relation of tragic horror to an "original flaw" in the hero's soul, writes:

> Hamlet is a study in degeneration from first to last, and that is the tragedy. . . . "Self-slaughter" is the initial theme of his first soliloquy. This, coming at the outset, is prophetic. . . . It was an inclination before he was tempted [by the Ghost]; and from the moment he yielded to the first temptation, self-slaughter is what he is doing throughout the play.[40]

With these statements I can in general agree.[41] What I would go on to note are two related points: 1) that a lapsing from health into an action of self-undoing is central to the Bible's story of man's fall; and 2) that any man's loss of positive direction is well symbolized by an arrow that miscarries. In both respects (at the level of participative myth and of metaphoric fact) the whole movement of Shakespeare's play dramatizes an action fraught with hamartia.

As Claudius remarks in a well-known passage (IV. vii. 21), a directionless arrow can turn back on the bow that sent it. Do we not find throughout the play *Hamlet* many such a peripety? Indeed, we can observe that the drama's whole action concludes, in one fundamental sense, very near where it began. That is, it ends with a fatal

duel by which a kingdom has been gambled away. When Fortune's
wheel has turned full circle, Denmark's entire royal family lies in
Act V where the elder Fortinbras lay after an earlier duel of honor
—dead, and the state's hegemony forfeit. Thus a second-generation
Norwegian, the once disinherited young Fortinbras, inherits the
Danish throne by Denmark's own default. Nor is this catastrophe
chargeable solely to Claudius. Both he and Hamlet (and others in
the action) have been reciprocally gaming in various ways, playacting, and engaging in sportive hunt. We may note that Hamlet's
final duel with Laertes, like that of the elder Hamlet thirty years
earlier, is fought for no public cause, but for a "wager." It is fought
as an exhibit of swordsmanship for the sake of personal glory. And
if we but recall at this point the traditional duties of kingship,[42] or
the traditional concept of the prince as a pilot to the ship of state,
must we not acknowledge a defection from princely duty on the part
of both Hamlets, father and son, no less than by the elder Fortinbras
and by Claudius? There may be a figurative meaning, along with
the literal, when Hamlet tells us in Act V that he has been in "con-
tinual practice" with the rapier, ever since the events of Act I.

In regard to Hamlet senior, the play gives us broad hints, in at
least two specific passages, that the duel of honor involved a love of
vainglory as its motive. The first such passage is in Act I in Horatio's
account of how

> Our last King,
> Whose image even but now appeared to us,
> Was, as you know, by Fortinbras of Norway,
> Thereto *pricked on by a most emulate pride,*
> Dared to the combat, in which our valiant Hamlet—
> For so this side of our known world esteemed him—
> Did slay this Fortinbras. Who by a sealed compact,
> Well ratified by law and heraldry,
> Did forfeit, with his life, all those his lands
> Which he stood seized of to the conqueror.
> *Against the which, a moiety competent*
> *Was gaged by our King,* which had returned
> To the inheritance of Fortinbras
> Had he been vanquisher . . . (italics mine)

Most readers, perhaps, overlook the phrase "pricked on by a most
emulate pride," because Shakespeare has deftly placed it syntacti-
cally where it *seems* to modify Fortinbras (for that is how Horatio
sees it); yet in fact it is a floating modifier which can equally well

pertain to "Our last King," as in moral logic it must, since the very effort to match Fortinbras involves matching his emulate pride. For the sake of this pride, Denmark's King has risked in wager its lands, an act of irresponsibility toward those lands and their citizens. And the King who did this is identical with the Ghost whose mission, we shall soon discover, turns about the defense of his personal glory. A second telltale passage, likewise carrying marginal implications easy to overlook, crops up in Act V, when the First Gravedigger is recalling the day on which King Hamlet overcame Fortinbras. "It was," says this clown, "that very day that young Hamlet was born." Readers have used this passage to "date" the double event. Its more important significance, however, is in what it tells us of the King's lack of consideration for the welfare of his newborn child and also of his wife—a clue for us, perhaps, as to why Gertrude could be tempted to find something attractive in Claudius, the brother whose solicitousness for her safety is evident throughout Shakespeare's play. Why this particular day for the duel? Gertrude's delivery of a child, evidently, was of less importance in her husband's mind than his own glory. Had there been newspapers in Denmark on that eventful day, whose achievement would have taken the headlines?

Further, if we pause to reflect on the elder Hamlet's triumph, we begin to realize that it was a Pyrrhic one. (This point partly explains the image of Pyrrhus introduced by Shakespeare in Act II.) King Hamlet's victory, although chivalricly glorious, was morally grandiose and foolish. Its long-term legacy to the people of Denmark is indicated in Act I: a "prosperity" in which, after many years of imperial *gloire,* the state's armament factories must yet now be kept humming night and day, even on Sundays. Such is the "out of joint" condition of the state which the young Hamlet quite overlooks in his narrower focus on the weeds that have sprung up in Denmark's royal "bed." Obsessed with attacking these weeds, Hamlet's policies will deracinate rather than mend. For in seeking to rehabilitate his father's ideals and predilections, he but runs a second and subsequent phase of the father's religion of honor, completing the cycle of its disastrous effects.[43] A remark of St. Augustine's may be used, perhaps, as appropriate to this sad story: "The wicked walk in a circle," says Augustine, ". . . because the path in which their false doctrine runs is circuitous."[44]

In its spiritual aspects, the world of *Hamlet* is not unlike a circular desert, even though in outward matters the play's action moves, as the genre of tragedy requires, from a state of temporal prosperity to an ending in misery. What the play's ending reveals is the graveyard fate to which a legacy of human vainglory leads. And in various lesser aspects of the action a *circular* turning can be seen: in the hero's whirling words and self-contradictory deeds; in his coming to see in his adversary Laertes a mirror of his own "cause"; in the desperate plot of Claudius which boomerangs on itself, with both cup and rapier returning against their owners; in the windy circumlocutions of Polonius, who more truly than he knows has bound his friends to him in "hoops of steel." Moreover, there is the incest theme, a matter of far larger import than its literal application to Denmark's royal bed. Incest, basically, is a love which circles about the self. As a metaphor it denotes the predicament of all Denmark, including the spiritual flaw of Prince Hamlet.

Let me illustrate some of the ways in which Hamlet's love is incestuous or, to use a variant term, narcissistic. In what sense does he love Ophelia? Is he ever concerned to understand her needs as a person? Does he cherish her welfare, or rather (like Troilus toward Cressida) her adulation, her "constancy" to *him*? Significantly, he fights (like Romeo) over his beloved's grave, rather than for her rescue while alive. Indeed, if we ask ourselves what Hamlet's fight in the graveyard is really for, must we not answer that it is for preserving his own self-esteem, his image of himself as a peerless lover? When he rants to Laertes that forty thousand brothers cannot equal his love, is it not because he cannot tolerate having his self-image overshadowed or rivalled? Earlier, he had sworn his love to Ophelia "by all the holy vows of heaven"—only to tell her later, "I loved you not." The whole pattern suggests an instance of love in love with itself, rather than love of neighbor. Madariaga, I think, attributes too crass an egotism to Hamlet in likening him to a Cesare Borgia,[45] yet undoubtedly a self-centeredness is the unwitting quality of Hamlet's idealism—as it is, similarly, for Romeo or Troilus. Typically, such idealism involves an idolatrous love. Hence we have Hamlet's verses referring to Ophelia as "my soul's idol." Also it expects idolatry in return. This we can infer from the picture Hamlet gives us, in his first soliloquy, of an ideal love relationship:

> Why, she would hang on him
> As if increase of appetite had grown
> By what it fed on.

These lines describe how Hamlet remembers Gertrude behaving when she was, in Hamlet's eyes, a very model of love. But also they are a clue to the kind of love (essentially doting) which Hamlet expects of Ophelia.

Another and related aspect of this pattern can be seen in the quality of the love Hamlet has for his father. For almost thirty years he has known his father; yet now what he remembers about him is not any good deeds done for family or community welfare but, rather, an Olympian splendor of personage. Cherished in Hamlet's "mind's eye" is simply the glory of his father's natural gifts. "He was a man, take him for all in all, / I shall not look upon his like again." And this imaged ideal remains unmodified, even after the father's Ghost has spoken of being doomed for "foul crimes done in my days of nature." It is as if those crimes were no part of Hamlet's concern. He gives them no thought, when fascinated by the more graphic story of a crime done against the father, and when empathizing with the father's lament over Gertrude's lapse from giving him sole honor. Never does Hamlet see his father as a sinful soul in need of divine grace, a man whom Hamlet might now succor by offering Christian prayers. Instead, he views him as the father views himself: as a godlike nature whose dignity has been sinned against. A vindication of this dignity becomes Hamlet's central concern.

In Hamlet's view, this dignity has an absolute value as the sole proper object of Gertrude's love; only some hellish mutiny in her can have caused her to remarry. Thus in the bedroom scene we find him holding up for Gertrude a "picture" of his father's godlike personage:

> See what a grace was seated on this brow—
> Hyperion's curls, the front of Jove himself,
> An eye like Mars, to threaten and command,
> A station like the herald Mercury
> New-lighted on a heaven-kissing hill,
> A combination and a form indeed
> Where every god did seem to set his seal
> To give the world assurance of a man.

The "combination" and "form" of human nature which is here being idolized accords with what we know of Hamlet's own earlier excellence as "The glass of fashion and the mold of form." It reflects an ideal of man as glorious through exhibits of formal excellence: through what the Greeks called *arete*.[46] Despite Hamlet's oath "by the rood" as he lectures Gertrude in this scene, he is not directing her love toward any Christian ideal of manhood; his ideal, instead, is a recrudescently pagan one. He is asking Gertrude to love, not God or neighbor, but a godlike figure who corresponds to that "piece of work" which we have heard Hamlet praise earlier in his apostrophe to man—a creature who is "the paragon of animals" and, as such, "the beauty of the world." From the point of view of any Christian moral theology, however, love of such an ideal would be recognized as a projection of self-love. It provides man no purpose of life other than the glorification of his own natural gifts.

Even though Shakespeare cannot have known Freud, there may be some measure of truth in the contention, now widespread among psychoanalyst interpreters, that Hamlet exhibits both an Oedipus complex and homosexual tendencies. The Freudian approach is modern and may not be the best. It is handicapped, I think, by its reductive naturalism.[47] Yet, in part, the Freudian vocabulary is congruent with that of Christian theology. On the question of homosexual tendencies, Shakespeare could have had some notion of this phenomenon, simply by reading St. Paul. Certain Greeks, according to Paul's explanation in Romans 1:24 and 27, have fallen into homosexual acts because of idolatrous imaginations. Instead of learning about God through His creatures, these men have given worship to images of man. When we hear Hamlet offering an apostrophe to man and idolizing his father, while in the name of this ideal he shows cruelty to both Ophelia and Gertrude, can we deny a factor of homosexuality—if not quite in the Freudian sense, yet in St. Paul's more profound theological sense of the concept? St. Paul's idea that literal homosexuality is a manifestation of man-centeredness is reflected, incidentally, in the common Elizabethan pun on the "malcontent" as a male-content. Psychologically, that is the drift of Hamlet's spirit.

On the related question of an Oedipus complex, the Freudian explanation is that Hamlet has a subconscious wish (allegedly everyman's infantile wish) to replace his father in his mother's affections; and that he is jealous of Claudius for having done this. Perhaps so. One argument the Freudians can use for this interpretation is Hamlet's reference to Lucianus as "nephew to the King." For if Hamlet is here hinting his own identification with Lucianus, is he not wishing, like this player, to murder a king (Gonzago being a symbol, ambiguously, for either Claudius or Hamlet Sr.) in order to get the love of this king's wife? But looking at the evidence in a more commonsense way, I would prefer to say simply that Hamlet has adopted, along with an idolizing of his father, the father's self-centered concern for his own dignity and glory. In this sense, Hamlet is jealous of Claudius: he wishes for himself, in the name of his father's dignity, sole proprietorship over Gertrude's love. He takes the view, in the bedroom scene, that it is against him (and *his* heaven) that Gertrude has committed a shameful act, namely, an adulteration of Hamlet's ideal.[48] Then, significantly, the only practical counsel he can offer his mother is the negative one to "avoid" Claudius, a counsel which tragically introduces a "void" in Gertrude's sense of responsibility—just enough so to cause her, in the duel scene, to avoid the loving request Claudius addresses to her, and to act on impulse to honor Hamlet instead. By thus neglecting a wifely obedience, Gertrude drinks her own death. In this event, she has not by any deliberate intention chosen Hamlet over Claudius, yet it seems clear that Hamlet has succeeded in his desire to make Gertrude his pupil. He has in effect substituted himself for Claudius in Gertrude's concern ("The Queen *carouses* to *thy* fortune, Hamlet") and thus has drawn her into his own fate of accidental death by poisoning. Even earlier he has done so to the extent of inducing her to lie for him—in her report to Claudius that Hamlet "weeps for what is done"; for, in fact, Hamlet has not wept. He nowhere in the play weeps; he is too self-centered to do so.

John Vyvyan has argued, not quite accurately, that the central thesis in *Hamlet* is that "The law we live by is within ourselves, and not outside." Vyvyan would suppose that Shakespeare's own ethic is summed up in the adage of old Polonius: "To thine own self be true."[49] This interpretation overlooks, however, the shortcomings in Polonius' vision. "To thine own self be true" can be a useful ethical principle, I grant, if set within the context of a proper knowledge of the self; but it is tragically false in a context which sees the self as the center of all relationships, as Polonius notably does in his advice speech taken as a whole. The concluding lines, moreover, seem to me to carry a Shakespearean irony: "And it must follow, as the *night* the day/ Thou canst not then be false to any man." Shakespeare's underside of meaning could be: When self-love is central, duty is followed naturally by a *spiritual dark-*

ness—in which one cannot then be false to any "man," since in this darkness the neighbor's *humanity* is no longer seen.

The precepts of Polonius go back to Isocrates.[50] Their total import, as critics have sometimes commented, is as worldly-wise as Lord Chesterfield's advice to his son. Such an outlook is unlikely to have been Shakespeare's own. He may have recalled, rather, Dante's placing in the vestibule of hell persons who were "true to self and self only." These self-lovers were pictured by Dante as "futile" souls treading a circular path in pursuit of a whirling banner, because through negligence of higher realities they have made "the great refusal" of man's proper intellectual good. Shakespeare perhaps knew also St. Augustine's generalization, that "when man lives according to himself . . . he lives according to a lie"; for man was "made upright, that he might not live according to himself, but according to Him that made him."[51] Texts such as these, I believe, are closer to Shakespeare's understanding of the self than is Aldous Huxley's Perennial Philosophy, on which Vyvyan relies. Even Vyvyan's concept of a "higher self" to which man must be true is a defective notion, unless we complete it by positing a divine Good beyond the self, in allegiance to which the self can become truly higher. "He alone has a proper love for himself," says St. Augustine, "who aims diligently at the attainment of the chief and true good; and that is nothing else but God."[52] This would be Christian orthodoxy's perspective on the schoolboy half-truth of Polonius' maxim. And as for the other adages in Polonius' lecture —for instance, those decrying borrowing and lending—not only does Shakespeare give ironic sidelight on them, by making evident Polonius' own dealings in borrowed proverbs and advice-lending, but also their half-truth needs a corrective of the kind Shakespeare's own *Merchant of Venice* offers, or of the kind various biblical texts offer (e.g. *Ecclus.* 29:2 and 10).

The vainglorious way in which Polonius is true to himself we can see from his various actions. In the name of protecting Ophelia's honor, he instructs her to distrust Hamlet's honor. In the name of finding out hidden truth about Laertes, he instructs Reynaldo to fish for it with falsehoods. Having commanded Ophelia to avoid Hamlet because he will only make a fool of her, he later avoids confessing this when reporting to the King and substitutes the self-flattering explanation that Ophelia was so commanded because Hamlet is a prince "out of [her] star," too noble for her.

Then, to advance his own status with the King, he offers his daughter as a decoy for finding out Hamlet's intentions. In short, the self to which Polonius is true is a whirling weathervane self, in love with its own conceit, neglectful of other goods. His or Laertes' injunctions to Ophelia to seek "safety" through "fear" seem to me to resemble, and to be almost as foolishly wise as, the advice-giving of Pistol in *Henry V* (II. iii. 52–55):

> Trust none.
> For oaths are straws, men's faiths are wafer cakes,
> And holdfast is the only dog, my duck.   ·
> Therefore, Caveto be thy counsellor.

Polonius functions in *Hamlet* as a comic and pathetic instance of worldly prudence and its code-fashioned judgments. We note that he thinks it idle to inquire what "Duty" is, so busy is he with its shallow shows. However, unlike Pistol's listener (the "Boy" who rejects Pistol's doctrine as "unwholesome food"), both Ophelia and Claudius accept the advice of Polonius, and with it a poison of unneighborliness. (This is one of many instances in the play of poison being poured into the ear; and in this sense the structure of the play is an expanded metaphor.) The tragic consequences of such counselling are many: an unexpected death by Polonius himself, Ophelia's descent into insanity, and the episode of Laertes' consent to treachery in the name of vindicating family honor, when in turn the poison of half-truth is poured into *his* ear by Claudius.

This pattern of events in the Polonius family is obviously analogous to a similar pattern at a superior level in the Hamlet family. To Denmark's royal prince we see offered, in an adjacent scene, the counsellings of a father's Ghost which tempt his son into mad actions precipitating, in turn, new treachery by Claudius and a pitiful death for Gertrude. Here the community of the kingdom, no less than the smaller community of immediate family, is being betrayed by a father's "advice." Thus through subplot and main plot, which as foils are polar versions of a common tragedy, the play is showing us how human welfare is defeated. The "good intentioned" sins of two fathers are visited on the children. An excessive love for these fathers and for the code of honor they inculcate dooms the interlocking families. All perish by yielding to norms and forms of glory all too human.

Yet such excessive love is paradoxically a defective love, a neglect of Divine Law. It is in this sense that we can apply, as Polonius cannot, a maxim of scholastic philosophy which Shakespeare allows Polonius to parrot: "This effect defective comes by cause." The cause of human defect (if only Polonius could trace it, as he boasts, to the center wherein it is hid) is in everyman's self-pleasing love —or, as a later clown tells us, in a wilful seeking of one's own salvation. From this cause (so the clown hints) arise those actions of self-defense which become pitiful cases of "se offendendo". Adam, the first gentleman ever to bear arms and become a gravemaker, could "dig" this truth for himself. Understandest thou the Scripture? Or art thou a heathen?

4 The Ghost's moral quality

The Ghost of Hamlet's father has been called the "linchpin" of the tragedy. Structurally this is so, because it is by his revisiting of Denmark that the play's revenge action is launched. And morally, the question of the validity of this Ghost's command is crucial to any interpretation of the play. Are his intents wicked, or are they charitable? Does he bring with him airs from heaven, or blasts from hell? These are questions Hamlet asks but never answers. They are indeed the right questions, but Hamlet in his excitement will not stay for an answer. The answer could be found, no doubt, among those "fond records" in his brain's book which Hamlet, in his distraction, would wipe from memory.[53] Having done this, he finds it sufficient to affirm to Horatio that "It is an honest ghost, that let me tell you"—a judgment which quite bypasses the question of charity, since "honest" connotes simply a frankness in *self*-communication.[54] Let us recall that in Dante's *Inferno* the damned can be honest in confessing such facts as they know, honest in conveying their own vision. Indeed, we have in *Macbeth* the authority of Banquo (I. iii. 123) to warn us that the "spirits of darkness" oftentimes "tell us truths"—but only to win us with "honest trifles" which in deepest consequence betray us to our harm. Souls in hell, according to Aquinas, retain their "natural knowledge." They retain even some "natural love" of God, but only insofar as God is "the principle of natural perfection"—*not* so far as He is "the principle of virtue or of grace and the other goods through which intellectual nature is brought to perfection by Him.[55] Hamlet never asks whether the command to revenge which the Ghost has given reflects a love for God as the source of virtue and grace.

Later, when Hamlet cannot understand why he has delayed in carrying out revenge, he does question whether the spirit he has seen "May be the Devil." He proposes then to test whether it is a "damned" Ghost. Yet here his method for testing invokes no Christian canons whatever by which to discriminate between a hellish and a heavenly motive in the Ghost. It aims instead to test Claudius. But suppose Claudius were to unkennel his guilt on seeing his secret crime mirrored in both the dumbshow and the playlet. How could his betrayal of a guiltiness prove anything other than the Ghost's "natural knowledge"? It could do nothing to prove the Ghost's demand for revenge a charitable commandment.

The whole play scene fails, as a matter of fact, to provide any public proof of Claudius' guilt. Although Dover Wilson would suppose that the King "rushes shrieking from the room," having been "caught—squealing" in Hamlet's trap, this interpretation (adopted for its staginess by some of today's producers) has been amply refuted by W. W. Lawrence, Robert Speaight, and other critics.[56] Speaight says: "Claudius rises, still in command of himself, and quietly asks for lights," thus bringing the entertainment to a close with "the minimum of fuss." This reading of the situation seems to me correct. Claudius did indeed see the dumbshow, but was too thoroughly in command of himself to betray alarm. He waited, rather, punctuating his attention with discreet questions, until he could assess the import of Hamlet's innuendo and then with dignity stop a play which was deteriorating into a hodge-podge. Afterwards, no one except Hamlet (and he only by presuming the evidence) infers that the King was showing guilt when he called a halt to the show. Even Horatio, who has been asked to watch closely and who has promised a sharp "detecting," is non-committal when questioned. The other spectators regard Hamlet as a madman dangerous to the state. Ironically, it is the "malefactions" of this guilty person, Hamlet, that have been proclaimed—by his general effrontery and his jumping into the show. Would that assessment not be our unqualified one too, if Shakespeare had not contrived to let us overhear Claudius confessing guilt in a private prayer (and in his earlier "aside" regarding the harlot-like hypocrisy of his "painted word")?

Further, may we not suspect that Hamlet's stated motive for putting on the play hides a deeper motive at the subconscious level? Has he not turned play producer, for one reason at least, as a desperate expedient for working himself up (through rehearsing his prior convictions imaginatively) into an orgy of revenge feeling, which may then enable him to act without thinking? He had experienced such a sense of release once before, under the excitement of a story poured into his ear by the Ghost; and now, by repouring that story in a playlet form, he can renew a former state of excitement with its attendant sense of uninhibited power. In short, he can recapture a daredevil antic mood, in which he can "let himself go."[57] In a profound sense, the staging of the playlet is a conjuring act on Hamlet's part—a revelling in occult arts in order to call up from the dead past a "croaking raven" that "doth bellow for revenge." The raven, in medieval lore, was a symbol of the devil.

Some scholars have argued that the Ghost comes from a Christian purgatory and that he speaks therefore with the moral authority of a saved soul. But such a view cannot hold up under close examination. Numerous critics have come to reject it.[58] The grounds on which it is quite impossible, theologically, for this Ghost's abode to be anywhere other than hell, or perhaps the Hades of the ancients (which is hell from any Christian view), I have set forth in a lengthy article (in 1951) and need not here repeat except briefly. Suffice it to say that souls in a Christian purgatory are holy souls, genuinely repentant of their sins, and inspired with charity. They are engaged in a crushing of the will's obstinate holding to its own judgment. They "desire the Sovereign Good with the most intense longing," says Aquinas, and they grieve over their delay in attaining to the divine vision. According to Cardinal Allen, they suffer in love of God's judgment toward themselves, in perpetual experience of mercy and grace, and in worship and confession of God's holy name. Nothing of these requisites can be discerned in the Ghost of the elder Hamlet. He is indignant over injuries done *him,* is full of self-esteem as regards his own "natural gifts," is contemptuous of Claudius as (by innuendo) mere garbage, and bases his revenge command not on any sanction from God but on an appeal to Hamlet's "nature" and love of father. In Act III he revisits, with eyes *glaring,* to reinforce this version of duty.

Proponents of the theory that this Ghost comes from purgatory have been unable to cite from any orthodox Catholic author any text to support the view that a spirit from purgatory ever returns to command revenge.[59] But they weakly claim that the qualification uttered by Hamlet's father, "Taint not thy mind," shows a spirit concerned for his son's welfare, and that the instruction regarding Gertrude, "Leave her to Heaven," seems to show a Christian forbearance. "Taint not thy mind," however, is surely not equivalent to St. Paul's "Let all be done in charity." It parallels, rather, Plato's counsel at the end of *The Republic* to keep one's mind unspotted —a counsel of mere self-perfection.[60] The "taint" the Ghost forbids is no doubt that of frenzy—the fault for which he seems to rebuke Hamlet in the bedroom scene. On that occasion, the Ghost's two concerns—to whet his son's revenge against Claudius, and to persuade Hamlet to forgo dagger-words against Gertrude—closely accord with the two injunctions of Act I. Mad violence against a mother was contrary to pagan ethics as being an act of impiety toward one's parent—the crime for which Nero was universally abhorred. But pagan conscience on this point, let us recognize, nevertheless falls short of being Christian. The Christian ethic forbids not simply the breakdown of reason into frenzy, but all spirit of contempt or vainglory. With this more inconspicuous imperfection the Ghost's mind is antecedently tainted, thus lending dramatic irony to his pleas against "taint." (This contradiction is comparable to that of his commanding revenge despite his own comment that murder is "most foul" even "in the best" of causes. Shakespeare has a subtle sense for the lurking logical fallacy, and existential absurdity, which accompanies moral evil. The sinner is always in some way divided against himself.) If this Ghost had health and charity he would counsel, even as regards Gertrude, not "Leave her to Heaven," but rather: "Have mercy, and pray for her soul and mine."

Charity's spirit can be found voiced in the play, but paradoxically under the mystifying babblings of the deranged Ophelia of Act IV. When she visits the court like some revenant from another world, she has suffered quite as much injustice as the elder Hamlet ever did. But her message is utterly different: "And of all Christian souls, I pray God. God be wi' you." And at her earlier entrance (since Shakespeare has given this revenant, like the Ghost, *two* speaking visits), her message was: "God be at your table." Note how the "table" image, as here used, reverses that of the "tables" on which Hamlet wrote revenge. It is a contrast between the "spirit" and the "letter" meanings of table. Through a mode of speech that is surrealistic (and thus wholly different from the surface realism of the Ghost's tale), Ophelia is giving us an instance of what we may call reason in madness, a motif developed comparably in *King Lear*. As in Lear, it arises to counteract a madness of reason, both in some earlier mode of the self and in an environing world of false stewards. Ophelia seems to include both herself and others like her in warning of the "baker's daughter" who was turned into an owl. And her reference to the "true love" of the pilgrim in "sandal shoon" implies a self-criticism for having neglected to look for a pilgrimaging kind of love. For her failure, in the ways these images suggest, she is repenting from within the depths of her consciousness, citing in admonition words which echo (as Miss Parker has noted) I John 3:2.

At her second entrance, she comes singing and bestowing flowers as aids to self-knowledge. To herself she offers "rue," the herb of grace, and then goes out to enact a penitence by crowning herself with nettles and weeds—as Lear had done in subconscious contrition. Identifying her forlorn self with the willow tree—an old folk symbol of unrequited love weeping over its image in the stream[61] —she mocks that willow with her coronet of weeds. May we not call this act the remorse of a "nymph" in whose orisons all *her* sins are now remembered? The "great command" by which Ophelia is afterwards allowed her "virgin crants" and "maiden strewments" seems, providentially, proper. For here the law's judgment reflects (if we follow a theological overtone in the Clown's talk) the "crowner's" quest law. Furthermore, in a figurative sense, Ophelia has ended her life as a kind of Jephthah's daughter, bewailing with pilgrimaging rites her sacrificed potential motherhood. She is the pitiable victim, like her prototype in Judges, of having welcomed home a father, in this case a father who parodies Jephthah. Her suitor, too, has acted like a false Jephthah in consigning her to an ironic "nunnery." In grief over her bewildering fate, she has retired to the mountains of her subconscious mind, and from that otherworld sanctuary brings back to the court world her prophet-like insights. When, finally, she sinks to her death while chanting snatches of old tunes ("laudes" in Q^2—i.e., the first of the day-hours of the Church), can we doubt that she warrants sanctified ground as her resting place? From her "fair and unpolluted flesh," may violets spring!

Perhaps a further comment should be added regarding Ophelia's character earlier in the play. Was she then, as some recent critics have been inferring, a sexually promiscuous girl and mistress to Hamlet? Or was she rather, as the older interpreters assumed, an innocent rose of May, whose only frailty was her pliability to parental schemes? A third view seems to me possible if we read her mad talk surrealistically, as its form would seem to demand. The reference in her Valentine song to the maid who came to her lover's bed can be metaphorical confession, rather than literal. That is, Ophelia has in the past invited a love relationship based on mutual idolization and coquettish impulse, and in this psycho-moral sense has prostituted love. No misdemeanor in any legal sense, but rather a spiritual failing of ontological kind is what her subconscious mind comes to recognize when her conscious mind is broken by disasters. If my suggestion is valid, then her mad scenes should be played on stage in a mood of "distanced" reflectiveness, with bursts of tripping fancy half-oracular in tone, rather than as they so often are played today, with a spectacularly emotional abandon as if to give verisimilitude to the ravings of an hysterical girl.

But let us return our attention to the Ghost and to the play's signs of his moral quality. His speeches alone are by no means our only clues for judging him. There is the background fact, already noted, of his "emulate pride" during his days as king. Then when he appears as Ghost and is solemnly charged to speak "By Heaven," he stalks off in silence—perhaps because Horatio's invocation of Heaven has forestalled him. On his reentry, the crowing of the cock (a bird associated with "wholesome" singing and "Our Savior's birth") prevents his speaking. He vanishes "like a guilty thing," so Horatio observes, and like an "extravagant and erring spirit" which cannot abide the light of day. The Ghost's next visit, to solicit Hamlet, is at midnight and he is clad in armor, making the "night hideous." Through this and other imagery Shakespeare seems to be suggesting a dark (i.e., perverse) version of a Christian Easter. Why have the father's bones "burst their cerements"? Why has the sepulchre opened its jaws "To cast thee up again"? Hamlet's friends sense a dangerous temptation. "Do not go with it," warns Marcellus. But Hamlet, like an impetuous disciple, rushes head-long to follow it, threatening to slay his friends if they withhold him. Such discipleship, if we consider its attendant circumstances, can be recognized as an upside-down parallel to Christian story. For this Ghost comes, as he confesses a moment later, from a "prison house," whose secrets are such as to make a man's hair stand on end. Such imagery suggests a life in hell. And we may note incidentally that later, in the bedroom scene, the Ghost's reappearance actually does make Hamlet's hair stand on end (III. iv. 122).

The Ghost's speech to Hamlet in Act I contains, nevertheless, various tag ends of Christian vocabulary. Dramatically this fact is important. It is evidence of a heritage whose meaning the Ghost is neglecting. He now refers to the last Sacraments, not as goods he desires for his family, but instead (superstitiously) as if they were a fire insurance he got caught without.[62] And he can conclude his speech to Hamlet with "Adieu, adieu, adieu," although this benediction is in nowise intended to commend Hamlet to God. In short, he retains the shell of a Christian faith, with none of its substance. He is thus a remarkably apt example of a Renaissance "gentleman": nominally Christian, while in his ethics recrudescently pagan.

Many an Elizabethan, as Fredson Bowers and others have shown,[63] held "religiously" to a morality justifying personal revenge for family honor, despite ecclesiastical and civil laws against it, and despite traditional moral teaching. A revived classical ethics, or a decadent chivalric code, or simply natural human instinct, was all too often preferred as a guide where the gentleman's sense of "dignity" was at stake. Shakespeare could therefore count on a good deal of empathy for the Ghost on the part of Elizabethan auditors: they would have felt him to be "like us," as Aristotle said a tragic figure should be. Dramatic impact is thereby achieved. But this cannot mean, as Robert H. West would argue,[64] that Shakespeare, out of a concern for dramatic impact only, has confused and deliberately mixed up the spiritual evidence regarding the Ghost, so that even in the last analysis we "cannot formally decide" what the Ghost is. It does not mean that if "we feel" the Ghost is from a Christian purgatory, then indeed he is so for us, and we need examine no further than our instinctive (and untutored) impressions. Rather, it means that Shakespeare was mirroring a contemporary temptation to confusion, and was challenging us to see what it means and how it becomes that way. We are invited, I think, as in all tragedy, to discover the difference between appearance and reality—perhaps, indeed, through an initial vicarious sharing in the hero's blind love of appearances, so that subsequently we may progressively discover the deeper reality we have initially overlooked. Yet, from the beginning, the playwright has been planting clues for our apprehending the real quality of the Ghost's spirituality, if or when we are ready to ponder them.

5 Hamlet's evasions

The moral flaw evident in the Ghost, his lapsing from Christian norms which are residual in his language but neglected in his judgments, is the same flaw we are shown more at large in Prince Hamlet. Repeatedly, Shakespeare allows Hamlet some Christian phrase which is in ironic contradiction to Hamlet's un-Christian attitude accompanying it. Thus there is indicated the fact that Hamlet might have avoided his downfall, had he but paused to think on the gospel truths vestigially present in his own vocabulary. Dramatically, Hamlet's bits of Christian language are important as evidence of canons he is bypassing in his yielding to self-pleasing imagination. Since he is not utterly without knowledge of the Christian rule, but impetuously overlooks it, his persistence in revenge is a fault of his own making. His ignorance is voluntary—and all the more ironic because Shakespeare lets Hamlet cry: "Let me not burst in ignorance." Deftly, Shakespeare is presenting an ignorance due to what Aquinas would call "sins of omission."

This point can be illustrated with numerous examples. In Hamlet's first scene on stage, we hear him say of his mother's remarriage:

> Would I had met my dearest foe in Heaven
> Or ever I had seen that day, Horatio.

Here the phrase about meeting one's foe in heaven reminds us of a wish which Christians ought to have (the salvation of self and enemy alike); but Hamlet is using the idea to express something abhorrent. A moment later we hear his oath, "For God's love"—thus heightening the irony. What he wishes, in the name of God's love, is a knowledge not of saving mysteries but of his father's Ghost, and (as we presently see) of the "foul play" which he suspects this day-avoiding visitor can reveal. A scene later, when he resolves to remember this Ghost's revenge commandment all alone in his brain, he does so (by Shakespearean irony) with the vow

"Yes, by Heaven." Here he is taking Heaven's name in vain, vio-
lating the third of the Decalogue's commandments, having earlier
violated its first and second ones. Then, after making an antic
compact with the Ghost, he demands an oath of secrecy from his
friends. This time he invokes as sanction: "So grace and mercy at
your most need help you." What relation can grace and mercy
have, actually, to the purpose Hamlet is treasuring in his heart?
Ironically they signalize for us the values Hamlet is bypassing. And
the same is true of Hamlet's later random oaths—for instance, his
" 'Sblood" and "by 'r Lady" when he is indignant that his father is
no longer idolized; and his oath " 'Swounds" as he grabs Laertes by
the throat. These oaths point to paradigms of Christian love which
Hamlet might have appreciated, had he but taken the trouble.
Auditors of the play may overlook this fact while the drama is
being staged; yet it is embedded in the fabric of the action for our
potential apprehension. Shakespeare, while engaging our imagination and emotions in a sympathy for Hamlet, is also at the same
time defining the tragedy of an ignorance due to neglect.

Shakespeare's story differs notably from its versions in Saxo and
Belleforest. These earlier chroniclers had set their tale in pre-
Christian times, and thus had been able to define the hero's motives simply in terms of a pagan vengeance efficiently carried out
—in Belleforest, in order to comfort the "shade" of an indignant
Horwendil in Hades.[65] On this level they were writing a success
story. Amleth, through using a madness wholly feigned, outwits the
publicly known slayer of his father and succeeds in destroying this
usurper and his court in a planned holocaust, after which he is
elected king by a grateful populace. This version avoids the deeper
question Shakespeare raises, that of an unintended ignorance in
the hero's moral purposing. Shakespeare turns into genuine tragedy a tale which in Saxo and Belleforest had been largely epic in
character and tone.

Occasionally I have been asked by students what other course of
action Hamlet might have taken. What other ethical option was
possible? I answer that if one poses this question as an ethical one
purely, and without regard to the kind of action Shakespeare needs
for his tragedy, then at least three other choices are conceivable for
a man in Hamlet's shoes. He might, if he could but acquire the
charity to desire a wholesome remedy for Denmark's ills, offer
himself for training in a Christian friars' Order. For obviously Den-

mark's lethargic church needs at least one holy man of God to re-awaken it; and the creative value of such a vocation for a prince is made plain by Shakespeare in *Measure for Measure*. Or, alterna-tively, Hamlet might have chosen a political role, such as Malcolm chooses in *Macbeth*, by fleeing suspected tyranny and then in exile awaiting such evidence of misgovernment as might justify a mili-tary invasion to take away the tyrant's power. Or, thirdly, he might have charged Claudius publicly with treachery and challenged him to a trial by combat—the procedure of Edgar in *King Lear*. In the Christian Middle Ages, this was the approved way of appealing for justice in doubtful cases. The vocation either of knight or of friar could have become a salvific one. But thus to turn the community's plight into a happy ending would be wholly unsuitable to what Shakespeare needs for tragedy, namely, a *tragic hero*. Hence, from the outset, Shakespeare so characterizes the disposition of Hamlet as to make improbable any of these ethical "might have done's." It is improbable that a Hamlet who has been accustomed to being the cynosure of all eyes would, on a sudden, humble himself to a role of patient rescue. (It is hard for a "rich" man, says Scripture, to enter "the kingdom of heaven.") So Shakespeare shows Hamlet choosing, instead, a private and "antic" form of priesthood, in melancholy suits of solemn black, and a mischievous version of statesmanship, in which the sword is used only for profitless duel-ing. Thus Hamlet's blind choices parody unintentionally the the-oretical "might have done's" of an enlightened ethic. For tragedy requires exactly such irony.

The Hamlet of Shakespeare, therefore, is a hero who comes to grief through his mistakes. And each of his mistakes stems from what Aquinas would have called a double carelessness: at the high-est level, neglect of Divine Law (through Hamlet's idolatry of his father's dignity and "commandment");[66] at a secondary level, neglect of the "proximate" rule of human reason (through his yielding to inordinate imaginations and unruly passions). Both levels of mistake are dramatized in Hamlet's reaction after hearing the Ghost's message. For here, in an episode which climaxes Act I and defines the basic quality of Hamlet's madness, we see him abandoning himself to conjuring, and lapsing into what Hamlet's friends call "wild and whirling words." A precedent in Elizabethan drama for this conjuring scene has been pointed out by Nevill Coghill.[67] In *Jack Juggler* (1570), Jack vows in proof of his name to play at juggling: "I will coniure the mole and God before" (line 110). This reference makes clear that the "mole" was a traditional devil figure, and that to conjure with him was conventional for a Vice character. However, Hamlet's consent to such an act of vice is less directly deliberate than Jack's, since it is in Hamlet's case the indirect consequence of his neglect of reason and Divine Law in consenting to the Ghost.

Antic behavior is not in accord with Hamlet's own ideal in saner moments—with his ideal of "blood and judgment . . . well commingled"; of using all gently and not ranting; of being immune to fortune and to passion's slavery. But it accords with a fault Aquinas had described: "A man who is in a state of passion fails to consider in particular what he knows in general . . . [for] the reason is somehow fettered so as not to exercise its act freely, even as in sleep or drunkenness" (*S. T.* I–II. 77. 2). The fact that Hamlet is, on this occasion, drunk with rapture would diminish the vice of his capering, in the view of Aquinas, by making it accidental rather than directly intended. But that does not, when we consider its prior causes, excuse it of voluntariness. It but makes it the more pitiful, and tragically human. We may wish to recall in this connection Chaucer's brief aside on tragedy in *The Knight's Tale* (I quote a modern translation for its pithiness of statement):

> We little know the things for which we pray.
> Our ways are drunken ways—drunk as a mouse;
> A drunkard knows quite well he has a house
> But what he doesn't know is the way thither,
> And for a drunk the way is slip and slither.[68]

It is through slip and slither, in moments of drunken excitement, that Hamlet commits his acts of violence. Dramatically, the irony of this fact is that no other than Hamlet had lectured Horatio a scene earlier on the tragedy of drink!

If closely looked into, all Hamlet's particular mistakes in the play give evidence of a culpable carelessness. His accepting of Osric's invitation to a duel is but a final instance. Here the circumstantial facts suggesting the likelihood of a trap are numerous: the King's known aptitude for underhanded murder; his obvious need to silence Hamlet; a desperate Laertes whom Hamlet has given cause for revenge, and then further has offended by mad attack at Ophelia's grave; and Osric's conspicuous willingness to let Hamlet make a fool of him, if thereby Osric can humor Hamlet into consenting to the duel.* If only Hamlet had used his reason to weigh these circumstances, surely he could have surmised what was in store for him. He has, moreover, a kind of misgiving in his own heart, which Horatio suggests he listen to. But this also Hamlet shoves aside, through a fatalistic urge to "Let be." His subconscious will, evidently, is courting an opportunity to let himself go —to let rashness be praised. Basically this same explanation, I think, can be made as to why, earlier, Hamlet makes the mistake of putting on a playlet which gives away, unintentionally, his own secret; why he then misjudges the King's departure from it as the frighted flight of a "pajock," although circumstances could have told him that Claudius was here making an exit much to his credit in the public eye; why Hamlet makes no effort, in the bedroom scene, to find out what is behind the arras before stabbing through it; and why, afterwards, he makes no effort to avoid being sent to England, although he has forewarning of the plan. He prefers to tempt fate by neglecting reasonable considerations. A negligence is evident, indeed, even in his most famous soliloquy. He there refers to the afterlife as "the country from whose bourn no traveller returns," despite the fact that he himself has talked with a returned traveller in the person of his father's Ghost.

Robert Heilman has analyzed acutely the "quest for ignorance" in several of Shakespeare's tragic heroes.[69] He has commented on Lear's "stubborn clinging to blinders," and on Macbeth's "rejection of perceiving" by a narcoticizing of what he knows—through slipping into violence as both "a surrogate for knowing" and a barrier against it. Hamlet's case, I have been showing, corroborates this pattern for tragedy. Hamlet's subconscious quest is to evade his own knowledge of heaven's canon against self-slaughter. He does this by counting his life "at a pin's fee"—and other people's

---

* Because Hamlet rates Osric as a "waterfly," many producers of the play have thought him wholly effeminate and have played him as merely laughable. But I find convincing Nevill Coghill's contention that Osric beneath his waterfly disposition is actually quite sophisticated, "a man who knows that his task is to bring Hamlet at all costs to fight the proposed duel. Therefore Osric puts up his smokescreen of affected language. Every time Hamlet starts aside from the wager into some digression, Osric brings him back to it with a short turn. In the end the fish is landed, and even the watchful Horatio has been deceived by the angling Osric." See *Talking of Shakespeare* (London, 1954), ed. John Garrett, pp. 46–47.

lives too. True, he can feel enough compunction to "repent" for having slain Polonius, yet even here he evades genuine repentance by excusing his act as something Heaven has "pleased" to do through him, who is Heaven's scourge and minister. Here Heilman has noted Hamlet's impulse "to hedge repentance around with implicit self-justification," and has noted further that Hamlet's plea to Gertrude, "Forgive me this my virtue," is spoken to justify a claim to being "kind," rather than in self-criticism. In neither apology, we may add, is Hamlet repenting of his spirit of contempt. Nor does he resolve to be more humane in the future toward human fools like Polonius. On the contrary, he turns almost immediately to new imaginations of ecstatic slaughter: his "two schoolfellows" are but "adders fanged," whom it will be most sweet "sport" to blow to the moon! "They must sweep my way / And marshall me to knavery. Let it work."

Hamlet's notion of himself as Heaven's scourge should recall for us the biblical concept elaborated most clearly in Isaiah 10.[70] There the Assyrian is called the "rod" of God's anger, used providentially for punishing the sins of backsliding Israel. But Assyria's intentions are not truly righteous, only speciously so. Assyria has no desire to honor God, but rather its own glory. Hence Isaiah declares that when the day comes that Assyria begins to vaunt itself before God, attributing its victories to its own arm, God will cast this scourge into the fire and destroy his glory. In the case of Hamlet, have we not perhaps reached this point of boasting, either at the end of the play scene when Hamlet boasts to Horatio the success of his mousetrap, or more finally at the end of the bedroom scene when he flaunts in imagination the glory of his "craft"? If so, perhaps we may add that at these moments Hamlet is being cast, without realizing it, into the fire that will destroy him—the fire of the aroused anger of Claudius.

By the time Hamlet calls himself Heaven's "scourge and minister," he seems aware that such an office is a punishing one which also punishes its representative with the fate of guilt for accidental slayings. Yet he continues to glory in such madness. Rightly to be great, we find him saying a scene later, is to "find quarrel in a straw" when honor is at stake; hence let "My thoughts be bloody or be nothing worth!" And when we see him again in Act V, he fights Laertes in the spirit of those impious giants who piled Peleon on Ossa in their war against the gods. Then, in a scene with Hora-

tio, he boasts of his statecraft in sending Rosencrantz and Guildenstern to sudden death, "Not shriving time allowed." Here, as in
his killing of Polonius, he is afterwards evading his own need for
shrift. Yet, superstitiously, he can believe in shrift enough to let
the thought of its being denied to his fellows enhance his sense of
triumph, his implicit boast of dooming these men eternally. By his
own hand he has done the sentencing—a vaunt worthy of a biblical
"scourge."

Some interpreters of the play would like to regard Hamlet as a
converted soul after his sea voyage—a man who is no longer a
scourge but now a "saved" minister.[71] But the facts of the play, it
seems to me, allow us no such conclusion. It is true that Hamlet
acknowledges, fatalistically, a "divinity that shapes our ends"; but
in doing so, he is praising not God ("in whose service is perfect freedom": Prayer Book), but rather "rashness" (in whose service Hamlet has found himself free to revenge). The "perfect conscience"
he is longing to attain is one which will sanction a slaying of Claudius by viewing him as "this canker of our nature"—not as a *man*
with a canker *in* him, but a mere evil substance. At the play's beginning, Hamlet had shown enough vestigial Christianity to cry
out "Angels and ministers of grace defend us." But in subsequent
moments of elation, including that at the play's ending, he forgets
any such considerations. He becomes himself the minister, rather,
of a poisoned chalice, and in that sense a fellow celebrant with
Claudius in a Black Mass. Here the ritualizing of revenge has
served to make it acceptable to the maimed consciences of Claudius
and Hamlet alike as a kind of impersonal duty. It is the play's final
instance of maimed rites.

For the gaming role of Black Priest, Hamlet has become ready
by a progressive callousness—figuratively like the crab going backward, to which he had alluded in II. ii. The "readiness" proclaimed by him in his "augury" speech of V. ii. 230 has nothing
in common with that enjoined in Scripture (Mt. 24:44): "Be ye
therefore ready, for in such hour as ye think not the Son of Man
cometh." The Scripture means being ready, through responsible
behavior, for the coming of Christ as judge. Hamlet means being
ready for rashness and the opportunity it can bring to play judge.
A biblical echo, the sparrow reference, when found in this upside-
down context, alerts us to the tragic parody in Hamlet's version of
readiness.

When calm returns to him on his deathbed, Hamlet regains enough residual humanity to answer Laertes' request for exchange of forgiveness with the reply: "Heaven make thee free of it" (that is, of my death). Yet it is noteworthy that he does not confess to any guilt of his own, as Laertes has done in his cry: "I am justly killed with my own treachery." Hamlet admits to no treachery, only to his wounded "name," which he would like Horatio to salve with a "tale." He is not contrite, as Laertes here is, or indeed as Claudius at least tried to be in the prayer scene of Act III. It is paradoxical that both these adversaries can be said to be intellectually more Christian than Hamlet, in that they know they have given "both worlds" to negligence, both "conscience and grace to the profoundest pit," in order to be revenged. To state the matter somewhat overbluntly: Claudius has knowingly defied Christian norms out of a love for Mammon, a mistaken worldliness, whereas Hamlet has confusedly evaded these norms out of a perverse idealism, a mistaken otherworldliness—a contrast in which Shakespeare is mirroring two polar kinds of moral evil, foils to each other. By evading, Hamlet has substituted a make-believe conscience, now so graceless that the deaths of his friends (and of his "brother" Laertes too) come "not near my conscience."

Such an attitude, we may say, has in it something of the language of "Cain's jawbone, that did the first murder." Medieval legend supposed that Cain used an ass's jawbone in murdering Abel,[72] very likely for a figurative reason—because Cain, when questioned by God, foolishly jawed back in retort, "Am I my brother's keeper?" Such disclaiming of responsibility for brother is analogous to Hamlet's behavior. There is emblematic irony therefore when Hamlet, in the graveyard, fondles the skullbone of an "ass . . . that would circumvent God." He himself is there jawing back, foolishly, at the Christian wit of the singing Gravedigger. This jolly delver, by implication, is obeying the sentence on Adam of Genesis 3:23, to "till the ground from which he was taken." At the same time, he is speaking (as metaphysical "delver") by truth's compass or "card," in an effort to correct the equivocation in Hamlet's world view. To this Gravedigger, man is but the "guest" of the pit of clay, and death can be a "quick lie" which will "away again." But Hamlet, with his eyes on the dust, not the charting stars, continues to steer his life's ship by equivocal reckonings which "undo" him both literally and spiritually. The rest is silence.

6 Divination, role-playing, and providence

From the vocation accepted by Hamlet on Elsinore's battlements
(to him a mountaintop revelation to be written on tables, yet actually a parody of Moses' experience)[73] has stemmed a career which
abuses noble and gracious values. Hamlet's "prophetic soul" has
accepted a vocation as seer, but a seer dedicated only to exposing
the crimes of his neighbors, through the use of what amounts to
demonic arts. This motif had been part of the story as told by Saxo
and Belleforest, who record that Hamlet astounded the King of
England by feats of clairvoyance uncovering ugly facts of the past.
Belleforest remarks, at this point, that demons do not have the
power to see into the future, but only to discover the past. Then
he adds: "Amleth . . . in the lifetime of his father had been indoc-
trinated in that science with which the wicked spirit abuses man."[74]
This passage could have provided Shakespeare the idea of associating Hamlet's "prophetic soul" with the arts of the *malin esprit*
known to Hamlet's father—known, that is, by implication in Shakespeare's reconstruction of the story, not overtly acknowledged.
Many lines in the play imply Hamlet's love of dark divination: for
instance, I. ii. 257; II. ii. 262 and 293; III. ii. 103; IV. vii. 45; and V.
ii. 4. In the "decoy" scene (II. ii), for which Dover Wilson supposed
that Hamlet has overheard Polonius, G. R. Elliott has offered the
more likely explanation that Hamlet senses a trap by his "almost
spectral power of divination."

When visiting Ophelia's closet Hamlet poses as a martyr and
judge of love, as no true lover should behave. The details of his
disarray parallel closely those Rosalind lists in *As You Like It* III.
ii. 392–402 when reporting the marks an old uncle taught her for
recognizing a "man in love." But we know from Rosalind's jesting
tone that she herself thinks such marks ridiculous as evidence of
true love. To Ophelia, Hamlet seems as if "loosed out of Hell / To
speak of horrors." As one recent critic has remarked, Ophelia "uses
this image as a metaphor, but for Hamlet it is a reality"—she has
"picked up the essence of his condition, not realizing how true it
is."[75] Hamlet's very posture, I would add, gives us an emblem of
this fact. His head turned back over his shoulder, as he walks from
Ophelia's room, seems designed by Shakespeare to remind us of
the evil Soothsayers in Dante's *Inferno* (Canto XX), whose form of
fraud is figured by their backward-facing heads. Let us call it dumb-

show; it imports the "argument" of Hamlet's dream drama.

We can detect in other scenes too something fraudulent in his preachments. When he cries out to Ophelia, "I say we will have no more marriages," these words have just enough similarity to one of St. Paul's counsels on marriage (in I Cor. 7:8 and 11) to alert us to the perverse gospel Hamlet is substituting. Likewise, when Hamlet berates his mother for making "sweet religion . . . a rhapsody of words," his own rhapsodizing of his father is our clue for recognizing that, in fact, he is but preaching idolatry in the name of religion. In today's language, we would say that he is here attempting to brainwash Gertrude—that is, convict her of guilt by his own propagandistic version of duty. Critics who have supposed that Hamlet in this scene is talking like a confessor equipped with Thomistic ethics[76] can hardly have read St. Thomas carefully. There is no sanction in Aquinas for a priest's being cruel and uncompassionate; nor for any teaching such as Hamlet's view of marriage. The theme Hamlet has harped on in his playlet before the court, that "A second time I kill my husband dead / When second husband kisses me in bed," has never been taught by the Christian church. Although St. Paul discouraged remarriage by widows, he nowhere condemned it (except in the Corinthian case of a mother's marrying *her son*).

The learned Catholic humanist J. L. Vives, in his *The Instruction of a Christen Woman* (1541, translated by R. Hyrde from the Latin edition of 1524, which Vives had dedicated to Catherine of Aragon, wife to England's king) wrote: "For to condemne and reprove utterly second marriages, it were a poynt of heresye." And his contemporary, Cornelius Agrippa, wrote that whoever says the grace of God is "void in such marriages" is "mocking that sacrament." J. W. Wadsworth, from whose recent article I am citing these passages, reports that in the sixteenth century when we find objections to a second marriage they are on practical grounds, rather than on moral—for instance, as one treatise puts it, the danger that the remarried woman will be always "either praising or praying for her first husband."[77] But Gertrude, surely, does not fall into *that* fault. It is her son, rather, who thinks she should be always praising her first husband. Through his Player Queen, Hamlet is trying to tutor Gertrude in his own doctrine:

> Both here and hence pursue me lasting strife
> If, once a widow, ever I be wife!

"Madam, how like you this play?" he queries.

It is to the credit of Gertrude's good sense that she replies: "The lady doth protest too much, methinks." That is, the Player Queen's view of marriage is scarcely credible, even in a fiction. It corresponds not at all to Gertrude's view. Gertrude sees no wrong in a second marriage, but seeks rather in the subsequent bedroom scene to counsel Hamlet on his duty to Claudius, "Thy father." Like the council of Denmark, she has no knowledge of an antecedent murder. Hamlet's whole effort is to make her feel guilty for remarrying —not by telling her of any legal impediment or citing any Christian norms, but by invoking those of his own ideal.

By the intensity of his castigations, Hamlet does succeed, momentarily, in making Gertrude confess guilt, although for precisely what she seems unable to say. The only guilt she heretofore has felt is for the "haste" of her remarriage. Hamlet's interpreting it as an act of sheer sensuality, however, is now driving her to feel shame, perhaps because she recalls a secret affection she had for Claudius (although without literal adultery) during the lifetime of the elder Hamlet. Also, she may feel that Hamlet's antic behavior reflects a shortcoming in her rearing of him. Self-criticism on these two counts, when exacerbated by Hamlet's harangue, provides probably the sole basis for her confessing to "black and grained spots." At the end of this scene, her promise not to tell on Hamlet reflects her emotional exhaustion, and also a desperate hope to prove herself a loving mother. That she nevertheless intends to continue a wifely duty to Claudius we can infer from the support she gives him in a subsequent moment of crisis, when Laertes threatens. Later, however, when the evident madness of Ophelia seems to corroborate Gertrude's sense of failure as a mother, she once again mentions an unspecified "guilt"—by now heightened, no doubt, because of her husband's command at the end of the graveyard scene, "Good Gertrude, set some watch over your [not *our*] son." Thus pressured, she becomes overeager to be a devoted mother, and in this way drinks the poison in the duel scene. This, ironically, is what Hamlet's preaching has caused.

Hamlet's delight in neoclassical theatre fare, meanwhile, has been his way of courting make-believe duty in another guise. The horror stories of this imaginary world help reinforce the morbid drama he has welcomed from the Ghost. Through calling for the Player's speech, and then following it up with an Italianate *Murder of Gonzago,* Hamlet can live vicariously in a world of sensational melodrama, can "make believe" this antique stuff as a wholly valid mirror of real life, and thus can suppress his residual Christian conscience. Only when he has thus drugged his natural reason (which by suggesting the Ghost may be a devil has offered obstacle to Hamlet's role-playing as Revenger) can a reckless mood be recaptured to

> drink hot blood
> And do such bitter business as the day
> Would quake to look on.

Yet when he faces the kneeling Claudius a moment later we can infer a remaining human reason which, although inarticulate, is not entirely drowned but is holding back his hand, while his passionate imagination compensates by devising a melodramatic reason for not striking. That is, I read his malice here as belonging to his make-believe Revenger's conscience, which he is now invoking by force of habit, while a subconscious moral sensibility in his deeper self is forestalling a Pyrrhus-like automatism. Hamlet's verbal malice, as belonging to his hypothesized role, is in a sense accidental to his drunken imagination of his duty, and thus not a directly willed malice. There is still enough humanity in him to balk at an act of open murder. It shunts his will into choosing, instead, a reaffirmation of his demonic dream of dignity, by which "act" he can escape from the real world into one of transcendent heroics.

The subsequent situation in the bedroom, however, offers a different kind of opportunity. Here the victim is veiled, hidden behind an arras, so that there is present no visible evidence to check the imagination in its naming of the object a rat. The killing of a rat can arouse no opposition on the part of natural human conscience, whereas to kill a man seen at prayer goes against the grain of any such conscience. This is not to say that Hamlet suspects nothing but a rat as the real creature behind the arras; it is to say, rather, that by encouraging an imagining of rat he can evade thinking on the real human being who may be there, and thus he can strike unhampered by native conscience. He can strike in ignorance of the true circumstances merely by neglecting to investigate. That neglect is due to impulsive passion, given rein from the scene's beginning and now allowed to distract his reason to a still further degree. Indeed, it is being encouraged by marginal memories of Italianate revenge situations, in which stabbings were done heroically without natural conscience ("dead for a ducat"). In the proper sense, Hamlet is here not really reasoning at all[78] but is welcoming the fictions he hopes will let him act.

And the situation in Hamlet's killing of Rosencrantz and Guildenstern is similar. When veiled behind a game of letters, these friends of Hamlet's can be imagined as nonhuman creatures, to be dealt with by their "mighty opposite," as in a play world of melodrama. By wilfully preferring such imagination, Hamlet can remain in an ignorance which will let him act. He can suppose himself in a play which the others have begun, and thus he can respond as an actor, rather than as a responsible agent in a life situation. Each of Hamlet's "successes" depends, in various ways, on his obliterating his residual human conscience by inviting a rash inspiration which will allow him to substitute the canons of a play-world conscience.

> They are not near my conscience; their defeat
> Doth by their own insinuation grow.
> 'Tis dangerous when the baser nature comes
> Between the pass and fell incensed points
> Of mighty opposites.

Hamlet can here fail to judge his act as murder, because his reason is distracted from common sense by his will's attachment to the code heroism of Senecan drama. In this sense, Hamlet's moments of melodrama are the "play within the play" of Shakespeare's larger drama. That is, they constitute the falsely simplified drama which Hamlet, as revealed by Shakespeare's overarching and more complex drama, is shown as longing to make believe (reductively) as the true measure of human tragedy.

No wonder, then, that henceforth Hamlet awaits the coming of another play-world situation. "Rashness," he hopes, may again empower him to some stunning and final victory. Praised be rashness! That's the roughhewing through which "divinity" can shape our ends! So, as fate would have it, an opportunity comes, the more easily because Hamlet refuses to heed his own mind's gaingiving. Claudius sets up a "play" of swords, and the added background of a Black Mass complete with chalice of poison—an ultra-Italianate situation in which Hamlet can "conscientiously" both kill and help administer a devilish communion, thus sealing his priesthood as a Scourge of God as the play ends. He has finally succeeded in doing accidentally what any human being would have difficulty in doing deliberately. He has succeeded, in fact, through courting accidents and awaiting their arrival with hopeful resignation.[79] After all, what he has desired all along is that his "solid flesh"[80] (his humanity) might melt, freeing his spirit for an imaginary self-hood. In a basic sense, a player is one who for his craft's sake accepts a kind of moral abnegation, substituting for his native conscience that of the fictive person he portrays. Hamlet as role-player thus transcends himself—but only for a demonic self which he makes believe as heroic, after casting himself at the Ghost's urging in the character of Revenger.

In Hamlet's total course of action there has been a constant inter-play between his natural self and the put-on character to which he works himself up. The revenger-character is, so to speak, his dream self, through which he finds release from his normal self. But the normal is not easy to banish or remold. Hamlet may suppose, in his first flush of elation, that he can divest himself at once of "all forms, all pressures past," yet in later acts it is almost as if his commitment had to be made all over again. Implicit is Shakespeare's meta-physical understanding of Hamlet's delay: a gifted and "sweet prince" can act revenge only after first dehumanizing himself through acts of imagination directed toward memorizing and memorializing stories of crime (crime not seen from within with psychological realism, but described from the outside like a sport-ing event, as in the Aeneas tale to Dido). Hamlet must stage a player's speech, or playlets, or the glassing of "pictures" which stereotype people, in order to induce the acting of his would-be role. Only as his melodramatic imaginings become frequent does he become bound by the habit of them. And only by accustoming himself to the practice of recklessness can his native humanity be-come effectively hardened. We may recall Macbeth's analogous tragedy, or the comment Augustine makes on the cumulative effect of vice: "Of a froward will was a lust made, and a lust served be-came custom, and custom not resisted became necessity" (*Confessions* VIII. 10). Never can habit utterly destroy a native goodness in the self, which is the original gift of the Creator (and which made possible Augustine's own ultimate breakthrough into freedom—for vice cannot, as he said, "tear up nature by the roots"); but the habit of sin can overlay nature and superinduce a fatalism.

By Act V, Hamlet's inward self has finally become so used to abandoning itself through yielding his nature as mere "instru-ment" to play-imagined revenges, that now he can fatalistically await one more denaturing of the self into the actor. The self—except for its flickering confession of an illness "here about my heart" (see likewise *Macbeth* V. iii. 19)—is now virtually lost in the character which the self has assumed. And this loss of inward self to outward role, whether in Macbeth or in Hamlet, makes the Hollow Man,[81] the walking shadow, the poor player—the ontological "nothing" toward which sin can progressively reduce life. It is all too true that "Use *almost* can change the stamp of nature." The fact that this maxim has earlier been preached by Hamlet himself, but in ignorance of its application to his own case, illustrates how deftly Shakespeare can place his dramatic ironies.

In his apology to Laertes, Hamlet declares that his madness, and not he himself, has wronged Laertes:

> Hamlet is of the faction that is wronged;
> His madness is poor Hamlet's enemy.
> Sir, in this audience
> Let my disclaiming from a purposed evil
> Free me so far in your most generous thoughts
> That I have shot mine arrow o'er the house
> And hurt my brother.

He is aware, in other words, that he has been "passion's slave," that his blood and judgment have *not* been well-commingled, that a "vicious mole" of nature has broken down the pales and forts of his reason, taking Hamlet away "from himself," so that only when "not himself" has he wronged Laertes. But this apology carries a deceptive half-truth. It overlooks Hamlet's own earlier thesis that "madness would not err, / Nor sense to ecstasy was ne'er so thralled / But it reserved *some quantity of choice* / To serve in such a difference" (III. iv. 73–76). Instead, it parallels strikingly, let me suggest, the Manichean version of responsibility which St. Augustine tells us he erroneously held during his days of pagan vainglory:

> I still thought, "that it was not we that sin, but that I know not what other nature sinned in us"; and it delighted my pride to be free from blame; and when I had done any evil not to confess I had done any . . . ; but I loved to excuse it, and to accuse I know not what other thing, which was with me, but which I was not.

Then Augustine adds: "But in truth it was wholly I, and mine impiety had divided me against myself: and that sin was the more incurable, whereby I did not judge myself a sinner."[82]

A sinner's acts are those of a divided and hence lamed will. But insofar as a vainglory is causing the lameness, is not such a man culpable for the willy-nilly acts which ensue? (We consider Claudius culpable for *his* acts, even though his very name means "the lamed one.") For Hamlet, the shrewd Gravedigger has a word of warning: "If the man go to this water and drown himself, it is will he, nill he he goes, mark you that."

What Hamlet's apology to Laertes has evaded asking is: How came upon Hamlet the madness which is wronging him? By whose willy-nilly will has this vicious mole been given a welcome within Hamlet's brain and allowed there to caper? Even Horatio, in his summation of the play's events, lacks the insight to speak precisely to that question. Yet Horatio's explanation is far truer than Hamlet's:

> And let me speak to the yet unknowing world
> How these things came about. So shall you hear
> Of carnal, bloody, and unnatural acts,
> Of accidental judgments, casual slaughters,
> Of deaths put on by cunning and forced cause;
> And, *in this upshot, purposes mistook*
> *Fall'n on the inventors' heads.*

Hamlet, reciprocally with others in the play, has been the inventor of a mistaken purpose. His (and their) unnatural acts have been the consequence of accidental judgments—that is, of decisions made on impulse and spur of the moment. From these have resulted Hamlet's "casual slaughters" of Polonius, Rosencrantz, Guildenstern, and Claudius, besides indirectly the deaths of Ophelia, Gertrude, Laertes, and finally of Hamlet himself. He, no less than Claudius and Laertes, has shot an arrow of revenge, now fallen, alas, on his own head. The put-on cause of the shooting of this arrow has been justice, but a justice forced or distorted by rash indignation and a blind desire for retaliation. Further, a voluntary cunning (in a series of earlier episodes no less than in this final manifestation) has attended this action. This much Horatio's generalized statement implies, or may be taken to imply.

We may note, incidentally, that Horatio's own actions in the play have had an element of moral negligence—although in a minor way, since he is a minor character and Shakespeare is proportioning each manifestation of Denmark's common tragedy. We can see Horatio's negligence in the fact that although it was he who

brought the distracted Ophelia to the Queen's attention (IV. v.),
he does not keep guard over Ophelia afterwards. "Follow her close,
give her good watch, I pray you," the King had requested. Yet
Horatio hastens off, instead, for a rendezvous with Hamlet, because
Hamlet has sent him a letter beckoning his attention: "I have words
to speak in thine ear will make thee dumb." Is this not analogous
to the Ghost's tempting of his son in Act I? Now, however, Hamlet
himself is the revenant who is luring attention by promising some
morbid delectation and appealing to a personal allegiance. Horatio
is thus distracted from his more immediate daylight duties to society at large. In his eagerness to hear what Hamlet may pour in his
ear, he forgets Ophelia and she drowns. A much earlier hint of neg-
ligent weakness in Horatio may be seen in Act I, scene 1. There
Horatio, although provided with lore by which to judge the Ghost
an "extravagant and erring spirit," stops short of making this judgment; he decides to "acquaint" Hamlet with the visitant, and without apprizing Hamlet as to its suspicious behavior. Later he does
try to stop Hamlet from following the Ghost, in I. iv, but gives up
under Hamlet's persistence, adopting the fatalistic attitude that
"Heaven will direct" the outcome. It is Marcellus who shows a
more Christian attitude at this point: "Nay," he says, "let's follow
him." (Compare Helena in *All's Well* I. i. 231: "Our remedies oft
in ourselves do lie, / Which we ascribe to Heaven.") But Marcellus
drops from the play after Act I—perhaps because Shakespeare could
not retain so charitable a person within the action without counteracting the play's tragic outcome.

In Horatio's summary speech on the tragedy, there are mysteries
of cause which even he does not penetrate, though they are latent
in the play's design as shaped by Shakespeare. One of these mysteries is that the cause of the "unnatural acts" lies in a self-love caused
by negligence of Divine Law. Involved in Hamlet's case is the moral
flaw of an evasion of those norms which are Denmark's and Hamlet's own baptismal heritage, and an idolizing, instead, of the man-
centered canons of an "antique" world of pagan chivalry, through
which man is betrayed into "antic" behavior. Through mistaking
revenge for a religious duty, Hamlet (and, in a different way,
Claudius and Laertes too) have allowed more than a little of the
spirit of Nero to enter the human bosom—even though there is not,
as in Nero's case, the extreme of a literal slaying of mother and a
literal suicide.[83] There has been, however, a figurative suicide in the
drowning of the natural conscience, and a figurative slaying of

mother in the disaster indirectly brought upon family and country, which are everyman's mother. Eight lives are sacrificed by Hamlet in a "purge" which parodies the purging action of Christian re- generation (for which, incidentally, the number eight is a tradi- tional symbol).[84] "Whosoever slayeth Cain," says Genesis 4:15, "vengeance shall be taken on him seven fold." If Claudius is sym- bolically Cain (III. iii. 37), then his slayer Hamlet (in legend, Lamech) suffers as God's vengeance on his revenge action the guilt for, and loss of, seven further family lives.

This tragic denouement manifests the mystery of divine judg- ment. True it is that in the corrupted currents of "this world," offense's gilded hand may shove by justice and preempt law, as Claudius has said.

> But 'tis not so above.
> There is no shuffling, there the action lies
> In his true nature, and we ourselves compelled
> Even to the teeth and forehead of our faults
> To give in evidence.

Hamlet has given us testimony that the true nature of his own action has been that of Heaven's minister as scourge. Further, the evidence of the play is that Hamlet, in using his father's signet to seal a sentence on his "friends," has usurped an authority to which he has not been publicly elected; and that in his whole role as scourge his justice has been of a tyrannical kind. Yet even a tyrant's deeds can subserve the justice of Heaven's wrath on the "something rotten" in Denmark, namely, all Denmark's neglect of brotherly love. According to Aquinas,[85] God permits scourges as his ministers because of the sins of the people. This fact does not excuse the wickedness of the scourge, but testifies rather to God's use even of the wicked to serve His providential purposes. The scourge in turn, Aquinas adds, suffers a divine vengeance, even in this world, in the fate of his self-made isolation from his fellow men and in the likelihood of his death by human retaliation. Is this not, indeed, Hamlet's fate? Meanwhile, however, a scourge's wild and cruel justice provides sinners an occasion to pray for Heaven's mercy—as Ophelia does before her death. And although we must say that Hamlet's final slaying of Claudius is an act of treason—as the bystanders rightly call it—yet it is also justice in a bleak mode, such as scourges are permitted to minister.

God's providence, although mysterious, is not as inscrutable as it seems to Hamlet. Boethius and Augustine understood it as an harmonious ordering of the disorder in nature introduced by man's cupidity. "A man's heart deviseth his way: but the Lord directeth his steps" (Proverbs 16:9). For Aquinas likewise, "all human affairs are subject to eternal law"—the affairs of good persons, by their acting in accord with it; but the affairs of wicked persons by their being imperfectly subject as to their actions, yet this imperfection on the part of action being "supplied on the part of passion, insofar as they suffer what the eternal law decrees concerning them, according as they fail to act in harmony with that law" (*S. T.* I–II. 93.6). And Nicholas Trivet could say of the sinner: "Although he recedes, with reference to the end, from the order of the divine will in one way, he nevertheless falls into the order of the divine will in another; for in leaving the order of mercy, he falls into the order of justice."[86]

Shakespeare himself offers for our pondering, in this connection, a comment by the witty First Clown in the graveyard scene:

> The gallows does well, but how does it well? It does well to
> those that do ill. Now thou dost ill to say that the gallows
> is built stronger than the church; argal, the gallows may
> do well to thee.

In other words, the man who prefers the justice of the gallows to the justice of the church may find the gallows doing well to him by punishing him for this ill judgment. But furthermore, as this Clown elsewhere remarks: 'Tis a pity that, in this world, "great folks" should have more countenance than their Christian fellows to drown or hang themselves. The whole world of the court, including the great Hamlet, is here being assessed through apt metaphor.

7 Atonement's tragic parody

If we are willing, finally, to entertain a theological perspective, there is one other and even more comprehensive way of viewing the tragedy of Hamlet. I find it suggested by St. Augustine's tracing of his boyish theft of forbidden pears to a "rottenness" in his own moral life. It involved, he says, his mimicking of a "maimed liberty," in perverse imitation of God:

> Wherein did I even corruptly and pervertedly imitate my
> Lord? Did I wish even by stealth to do contrary to Thy

> Law, because by power I could not, so that being a prisoner
> I might mimic a maimed liberty . . . a darkened likeness of
> Thy Omnipotency? Behold, Thy servant, fleeing from his
> Lord and obtaining a shadow. O rottenness . . .[87]

Here, perhaps, is an ultimate key to the logic of Hamlet's personal
tragedy. For Hamlet, without realizing it, does pervertedly imitate
his Lord. That is, he apes by his welcoming of rashness man's true
liberty of obedience to charity. Hamlet as scourge pervertedly
imitates Christ's role as suffering servant; his flight from reality
pervertedly imitates Christian pilgrimage; his being visited by a
ghost is darkly analogous to a baptism or a Pentecost; his longing
for "the witching time of night" reverses the Christian hope; his
gnostic wish that his flesh may melt and free him parodies Christian
desire for transcendence; his Manichean melodrama of "mighty
opposites" counterfeits the Christian concept of a warfare between
God and Satan. And, to sum it all up, Hamlet's stealthy strategy
for setting the world right is a perverse imitation of the method
of Atonement in Christian story.

Consider, in this last connection, St. Augustine's metaphorical
description of Christian atonement:

> The Redeemer came and the seducer was overcome. And
> what did our Redeemer to him who held us captive? For
> our ransom he held out *His cross as a trap*; he placed in it
> as a bait His blood.[88]

Or, again, this passage from Peter Lombard:

> Our Redeemer held up *His Cross like a mouse-trap* to our
> captor, and baited it with his Blood . . . God therefore be-
> came a man and died to overcome the devil.[89]

Yes, in a shadow-way, Hamlet does the same. With his celebrated
"mousetrap" (the staging of a murder play) he plays God, as it
were. He imitates Christ's work in a fascinatingly upside-down way.
Whereas God in Christ put on flesh, that is humanity, in order that
through this Man the world might be saved, Hamlet (substituting
a reverse kind of incarnation) relinquishes his humanity to put
on a mask of madness and thus visit a wicked world with his con-
demnation. Biblical echoes are here, but all of them in a trans-
valued version, a counterfeit version, an unwitting parody of
atonement.

"The decision to return to Elsinore," so Roy Walker has written, "is to Hamlet in his degree what the decision to go to Jerusalem was to Jesus."[90] Perhaps so, but what a difference in degree! In lauding the mysticism of Hamlet's "obedience to divinity within," Walker fails to see that this obedience is but a tragic perversion of Christian mysticism. Or, again, there is G. Wilson Knight's comment: "In his own Renaissance terms, he [Hamlet] has attained to his Kingdom of Heaven."[91] This may be true; but we must not be misled, as Knight seems to be, into a confusing of the true biblical kingdom with its demonic analogue. Nietzsche's gospel is not Christ's, nor as Knight seems to think, an approximation to Christ's. It is in fact its rival version. Hamlet's delight in playing the antic is a reverse parallel to St. Paul's willingness to be a fool for Christ; just as Hamlet's acceptance of fits of melancholy as a mode of mission is the tragic counterfeit of Paul's "When I am weak, then I am powerful" (II Cor. 12:10).

"Souls in their very sins," says St. Augustine, "seek but a sort of likeness to God, in a proud and perverted, and so to say, slavish freedom."[92] A playwright who knows this fact, it seems to me, has a basic clue for the structuring of Christian tragedy. He will recognize that tragedy can be a dark analogue of Christian redemption, a blind version of Atonement. Recall, for example, besides Hamlet's priestlike behavior, Macbeth's taking of a cup at the striking of a bell and celebrating pale Hecate's rites; or the elaborate language of sacrificial offering with which both Brutus and Othello envelop their crimes; or Romeo's drinking the cup at "Saint" Juliet's tomb-altar; or Richard II's imagined humiliation as a Christ betrayed by Judases. In each case, the tragic hero has taken as his god some imagination of his own heart, to which he then offers his life in an unintended mimicking of divine action.

The Shakespearean hero's defective action shadows Christian paradigm, in the same sense that falsehood inevitably depends upon truth, or the corruption of anything depends upon the good it corrupts. By ineradicable implication, a perverse nobility implies nobility, a defiled humanity implies something great that can be defiled. Waywardness is nothing but an ironic righteousness; just as evil is nothing but a deficient good. Thus tragedy, paradoxically, points us to the high calling man might have achieved, by showing us the empty shadow of it which he has chosen as his fate. In this respect, tragedy may be likened to an experience in Plato's cave, through which we are invited to discover that our backs are to the light. Or, it may be likened (as by Eliot) to a "wasteland" quest, whose apocalypse comes in a "decayed hole in the mountains," where there are no windows, but instead, magnificent towers "upside down in air . . . Tolling reminiscent bells." Reminiscent bells, deep-down inklings of the higher order betrayed, haunt the career of tragic man.

Understanding this, the Christian artist can perfect the logic of tragedy. He can give to any tragic downfall its proper shape as a "mistaken" version of religious self-abandonment, a topsy-turvy salvationism. Then, when the total action is rehearsed before an audience, some spectators will afterwards say, "How sad it had to be thus"; whereas others, who see the deeper meaning, will say: "How sad it had to be thus when it might have been otherwise." These two responses are the ones W. H. Auden has phrased in attempting to distinguish between the effect of Greek tragedy as compared with Christian. But I think this distinction can apply equally as well to two levels of our response to Shakespearean tragedy. For the levels are not necessarily mutually exclusive: the second can be added to the first as the fuller dimension of a progressive experience on the part of a spectator. The first is but an initial surface level of response to which all of us incline in our moods of half-enlightened paganism, whereas the second is a deeper level of response to which we may subsequently attain by drawing on the insight any man can have as a soul *naturaliter christiana*. Shakespeare himself dramatizes these two moods in a significant passage in *Richard III*. Commenting on the death of the two young princes, Richard remarks fatalistically: "All unavoided is the doom of destiny"—to which Elizabeth then replies, "True, when *avoided grace* makes destiny" (IV. iv. 218).

In wayside support of this perspective, we may wish to recall a recent remark by Hardin Craig:

> Theology tells us that the main functions of God are creation and redemption, and redemption may be said to be a universal human need. Therefore failure to achieve redemption is tragic.[93]

Or we may put beside it a recent generalization by Dolora Cunningham at the end of her essay on *Macbeth:*

> Macbeth makes his spirit inaccessible to the light of grace, as do practically all of Shakespeare's tragic heroes, in their various ways. If they had not done so, they would not finally be tragic, and the plays would not be tragedies,

but would belong rather with the group often called
romances—*Winter's Tale, Cymbeline, The Tempest*—in
which the threatened catastrophe is forestalled by the
working of grace in potentially tragic circumstances and
by the consequent ordering of otherwise destructive events
to a peaceful resolution. Such a comparison suggests that a
helpful distinction might be drawn between Shakespearian comedy and tragedy in terms of the effective operation
of grace as one method of organizing the happy ending and
its rejection or delay as a formative principle of the tragic
ending.[94]

We need not suppose that Craig or Cunningham would regard
their theological way of formulating tragedy as the only possible
one. Rather, it is a potentially final way, one which can include
other formulations of lesser dimension. That tragedy does in fact
include subordinate dimensions of explanation, even in Christian
tragedy, the kind Shakespeare wrote, has been one of the claims of
my present chapter.

I have tried to indicate how Shakespearean tragedy involves an
enlargement, by extension and transformation, of Aristotle's philosophical concepts. Greek tragedy has a less profound articulation
of the grain of tragic experience. But it nevertheless embodies
tragic form, in essence, with the basic elements of hamartia and
catharsis present in embryo. And we should recognize, further, that
Aristotle would not deny the name "tragedy" even to particular
tragedies which fall short of measuring up to his own requirements
for the best kind. Inferior kinds (of the sort Aristotle advises
against) can still function as tragedy. Tragedy, we may say, is any
serious story of magnitude which exercises our pity and fear—even
in versions, such as some twentieth-century ones, where pity sinks
to sentimental pathos or the fear to a contrived and sensationalized
dread. These are "tragedy" but in a diminished sense. Tragedy is
a form which each playwright fills with as much actuality as he can
envision. The full perfection of its potential, however, is achiev-
able only through a mimesis whose dimensions, as in Shakespeare's
practice, are even more comprehensive of the human situation than
in any drama know to Aristotle. What makes this possible is a vision
grounded in Christian wisdom. By this "gift" a playwright can perfect tragic form in art—just as, in the different but related realm of
life itself, nature is perfected by grace.

Drama as Parable

V

Moral Experience
and Its
Typology in
King Lear

Since tragedy is concerned with human downfall, any playwright working in this genre must bring to it his insight into the nature of evil. If he is a great artist we expect of him a governing perspective that is well integrated, not muddled or haphazard. We expect him to imply, through the way he shapes his play's evolving action, his distinctive understanding of the factors which lead to misery, and of the discoveries which can emerge out of anguish. For it belongs to the art of tragedy both to imitate human suffering and to do so significantly—that is, with signs by which its mystery can be illumined with intelligible meaning.

With what perspective, then, did Shakespeare come to the writing of *King Lear,* the tragedy which so many readers have considered his greatest? What view of human nature and destiny provided him his models and norms for delineating tragic mistake and its consequences? Increasingly of late, interpreters have characterized it as a Christian view—comparable to Dante's in *The Divine Comedy,* in the opinion of R. W. Chambers and John Danby, for instance.[1] And Miss Carolyn French, in concluding a recent brief essay on *King Lear,* gives as her judgment that behind the dramatic structure there is "a rationale derived primarily from Christian theology which orders the action on an intellectual level."[2] This contention seems to me justified. I should like to amplify its pertinence, however, by giving a closer and fuller attention to the structure and moral texture of the play's action. Only thus can we be quite sure that *King Lear* was not written in the spirit of, say, Beckett's *Endgame* and ought not to be read as if it were.

One obstacle, of course, to our grasping the Christian meaning in the play is the unmistakably pagan setting of the story, and more importantly, the force of the despair which is voiced time and again by Lear and Gloucester. If we rely on our momentary impressions only, it is easy to infer a stark and unrelieved pessimism in Shakespeare's outlook. And many a reader has drawn this inference. G. B. Harrison, to cite a recent example, feels that the "lesson, motive and motto" of the whole play is contained in Gloucester's words:

> As flies to wanton boys are we to the gods,
> They kill us for their sport.

This cry expresses the bitterness, Harrison believes, of a Shakespeare who had seen absolute evil—"a world in which good, however pure and refined, is futile and overwhelmed by evil."[3] But is such an inference valid?

1 Echoes of a biblical realism

Let us look at Gloucester's predicament in its full context. Can we say that the good of his recent act in aiding Lear has been futile? Actually, it has enabled Lear to escape to Dover. Further, it has inspired Cornwall's servant to risk his own life in defense of Gloucester, dying for him and slaying the torturer too. In this servant's act of sacrifice it is possible to see a major turning point in the play, one that signals and foreshadows an ultimate defeat for the forces of evil. Gloucester fails to see this implication when entrapped by his misery. Naturally so, for he has long been prone to judging superficially. His past life has been no simple case of "pure and refined" goodness. He has lived sportively, both in begetting and favoring Edmund, and later in blindly issuing orders for the death of Edgar. In this respect, Gloucester has behaved as recklessly as the gods whom he now accuses of sportive tyranny. There is a dramatic irony, then, in his imputing to the gods a wantonness so similar to his own.[4] And an element of this wantonness is still present in his despondent longing for suicide, in his request to be led to a cliff's edge. He is here forgetting the "kind gods" to whom he himself had cried out for forgiveness at the moment of his discovering that "Edgar was abused." He has relapsed into self-contradictory impulses. Yet this cannot mean that Shakespeare, as dramatist, is preaching a pessimism. Instead, he is revealing the residual ignorance of a desperate Gloucester.

Our inference becomes the more certain when we note, as a further dimension in Gloucester's real situation, the disguised presence of a providential rescuer. By Shakespeare's plotting, the banished Edgar is on hand to overhear his father's despair, and is about to contrive a medicine for it. Ignorant of this fact, Gloucester has just lamented his loss of Edgar, saying of him: "Might I but live to see thee in my touch, / I'd say I had eyes again!" This seeming impossibility will in fact be granted the blind man. He will be allowed a final leap into self-abandonment, but only that he may discover, at the bottom of his fall, the strange reality of a good earth under him and a cheerful neighbor ready to befriend him. When this discovery dawns, it has the wonder of a miracle. With amazement Gloucester then begins to view his life as preserved by "the clearest gods," and henceforth he is a changed man. Later we will hear him offer prayer to "the ever-gentle gods." And still later, he can die smilingly, on discovering that his unrecognized guide has all along been Edgar, whom he is now being asked to bless on the eve of Edgar's further mission, the deliverance of all England from Edmund's villainy.

One other episode, earlier, has contributed importantly to Gloucester's reeducation. He has encountered the mad Lear, and through grief over the King's misery has been cured of all self-pity. Moreover, he has listened to the hopeful words of a search party seeking to rescue Lear. A Gentleman leading this party speaks of a daughter who "redeems nature from the general curse / Which twain have brought."

The "twain" here referred to are Goneril and Regan. Yet the whole phrase has an abstractness which echoes at another level too. It was Danby, I believe, who first suggested that Shakespeare at this point intended his audience to be reminded of Adam and Eve, those "twain" ingrates of biblical story who brought on nature its first general curse. This archetypal level of suggestiveness may extend, I think, to other aspects of Lear's story as well. Let us recall that in Genesis, after the twainness of Adam and Eve in their joint cupidity, there follows an envy by Cain toward his brother, then later a general depravity of human nature which evokes a punishing flood from heaven, and still later an ambition for self-glory which ends in a Babel of tongues—four stages, all told, in the saga of evil's spreading curse. Does not each of these echo as a motif in Shakespeare's drama? For example, in Act III we find introduced a rainstorm which Lear interprets as a punishing flood, and afterwards there are scenes in which Lear's language breaks down into a babble of madtalk. There had been no such episodes in any earlier version of the Lear legend. One reason for Shakespeare's inventing them may have been to provide significant climax to the curse which is befalling Lear. Under this curse we see Lear flounder, an exile and a wanderer, until a rejected child of his takes on a role analogous to that of a Suffering Servant—and thus intervenes for the healing of the spiritual illness of a father who has come to epitomize, figuratively, St. Paul's concept of the "old man."

The total story, that is, has a kind of echoing parallel to biblical history. It is a family story dilated, as Maynard Mack has observed, into "a parable of society of all times and places," a "deeply metaphysical metaphor" of the human condition. And Lear's confession in IV. vi, during a moment of reason in madness, that all of us "came crying hither" to our world's great stage of fools, has been aptly compared by Mack to a traditional sentiment as voiced by the Elizabethan poet George Gascoigne: "We are all borne crying that we may thereby express our misery; for a male childe lately borne pronounceth A [for Adam] and a woman childe pronounceth E [for Eve]: So that they say eyther E or A: as many as discend from Eva."[5]

Lear at the climax of his alienation poses a haunting question (III. vi. 81): "Is there any cause in nature that makes these hard hearts?" He is asking this in reference to Goneril and Regan; and at the moment it seems an unanswerable question. But in the play as a whole we can find an answer simply by juxtaposing a second question, one raised implicitly by the spectacle of Lear's own plight. What is causing the "great breach in his abusèd nature," or the "cut to the brains" of which he complains? Is not his predicament that of a self-divided man—somewhat like, for example, the demoniac of Mark 5 who cried out from among the tombs, wishing death and cutting himself with stones?[6] Lear is being tortured by a hardheartedness, not solely in his daughters but principally in himself.

And its cause, basically, arises not from nature but from a fiendishness of spirit, which Lear's will has permitted to enslave his nature and abuse it. This truth is one which Gloucester (in IV. vi) seems to grasp while listening to Lear; for shortly afterwards Gloucester remarks: "Let not my worser spirit tempt me again." He is here associating Lear's plight with a similarly mad inclination to self-destruction which he himself suffered when influenced by a "fiend." But knowing himself now delivered from this fiend, Gloucester is praying to remain so. In Shakespeare's story a similar deliverance for Lear will come too.

The developing drama is thus thoroughly realistic in its accounting for evil, while at the same time not pessimistic as regards man's potentialities for regaining moral health. Gloucester comes to recognize in his unknown guide, the disguised Edgar, a sign of the "bounty and the benison of Heaven." Beside this, the justice of the gods can also be acknowledged. Edgar, after he has overcome Edmund, utters a generalization which critics have sometimes cited as Shakespeare's message to the audience:

> The gods are just, and of our pleasant vices
> Make instruments to plague us.

The context of these lines needs to be closely studied, however, if we are to grasp Shakespeare's full vision. Note that Edgar is not excluding himself from his generalized statement, and note further the significant words with which he began his speech: "Let's exchange charity." Is this reference to charity out of place in the pagan Britain of the play? Dr. Johnson thought so, accusing Shakespeare of a dramatic impropriety. But surely Shakespeare knew what he was doing.[7] Edmund on his deathbed has just confessed himself guilty as charged. Further, he has offered to forgive his unknown vanquisher "If noble." Edgar's response is to offer charity, while also identifying himself as Edgar, thus supplying as it were a two-level evidence of "noble" birth.

Only as subordinate to this reply do we hear Edgar's reference to the justice of the gods, no doubt in order to remind both himself and Edmund of the more-than-human laws to which man must answer. But then, immediately, Edgar goes on to reveal his own commitment to something higher than retributive justice. He turns to a telling of his "pilgrimage." That pilgrimage has involved more, even, than a verbal forgiving. It has included a caring for his wronger—for the father whose adultery has cost him his eyes. It has involved aiding this wounded man. Here, then, is a truth of deeper consolation than the truth that the gods justly make instruments of our pleasant vices to plague us. Edgar, in the name of the "clearest gods," has been working the cure of a father justly plagued for his pleasant vices. One recent critic, Harry Levin, has referred to Edgar as "that Good Samaritan" who "seems to be *anima naturaliter christiana*."[8] Another, Russell Peck, sees both Edgar and Cordelia as associated, by analogue, with "Christian configurations."[9] In the play itself, Edgar is significantly identified as Lear's "godson" (II. i. 93).

Juxtaposed to Edgar's tale of pilgrimage, Shakespeare has introduced the news of Goneril's suicide. This episode provides for Edmund a contrasting story—of how his own vicious life has become an instrument of plague both on Goneril and on himself. There is then a grim irony in his comment: "Yet Edmund was beloved." For is he not now aware that the love with which he has been beloved by Goneril is of a far different kind from the love Edgar bestowed on Gloucester? A love which inspires poisoning and suicide as its sacrificial offering contrasts *toto caelo* with that which inspires rescuing deeds. Edmund, a moment earlier, had confessed to being much moved by Edgar's story: it "shall perchance do good," he had said. And now, faced by new evidence of how deadly his own evil has been, he finds himself panting for "life" instead of for lust. He thereupon resolves to do "some good" despite his own nature. What has influenced this surprising conversion is quite evidently the charity embodied in Edgar, even more than Edmund's own experience of the justice of the gods in plaguing, although this latter truth has provided the negative ground for accepting a new positive hope.

Shakespeare critics who claim to see in *King Lear* only an exhibit of helpless virtue, passive and powerless, have a notion that the play's plot in Acts IV and V is ill adjusted to character. D. G. James, for instance, finds "a major flaw" in the plot and takes refuge in Granville-Barker's comment that these last two acts are "by comparison pedestrian," except for a few marvellous moments which are dramatically "incidental and not germane to the actual story." James complains in particular of the combat between Edgar and Edmund, which he thinks near to being "a piece of hollow stage trumpery." Edgar is here wrenched out of character, he believes, merely to serve as a plot device for getting on with the play.[10]

It seems to me, on the contrary, that this combat signals the emergence into public view of a redemptive power from the underworld of the *Lear* universe. On the stage trumpets are sounded to herald it. But because it comes out of the subplot it must as spectacle be abbreviated, so as not to overshadow Cordelia's martyrdom, the climactic event needed for the main plot. Both of these actions, moreover, have overtones of biblical Judgment Day (the signalling trumpets and the reference in line 263 to "the promised end"). Appropriately they have a quality of paradox and enigma, lest by consoling unambiguously they dissolve the tragic frame. To sustain effective tragedy, Shakespeare must keep uppermost our interest in Lear's anguish and our fearful pity over the decay of the secular upperworld which he has fathered. When considered in this context, the trial by combat is as germane to the total story as is, in another tragedy, the combat of Macduff against Macbeth. It is the subplot's counteraction mitigating the tragedy by revealing a token or earnest of future betterment.

If in *King Lear* the combat seems somewhat more huddled than in *Macbeth* we must take into account also a difference of theme in the two plays. Whereas the quest of Macbeth was for an earthly crown, the scope of Lear's initial quest is larger, nothing less than aged man's search for an infinite love. The ultimate outcome of a quest for infinite love can hardly be dramatized except as in a glass darkly; hence the final events in *Lear* have the quality of apocalyptic signs. They adumbrate, rather than fully declare, nature's secrets and unpublished virtues. Huddled flashes of episode, in such a context, need not be accounted as incidental makeshift; they are, rather, a valid reflection of Shakespeare's sense of history's shape. With due proportion they figure the possibilities the poet posits for man's development under divine providence. Belonging to this development, yet serving as a quasi-choral observer of it within the play, is the Duke of Albany. His reference to "This judgment of the Heavens" acknowledges, at the least, a divine governance over Goneril's fate. Yet obviously her downfall is related to earlier strokes of justice—notably, Edgar's intercepting of Goneril's letter and his overthrow of Edmund. Albany may therefore be aware (or we can be) that Heaven's "judgment" includes this whole sequence of episodes.

To Shakespeare's audience the ceremony of a trial by combat for the vindicating of truth and right would have suggested a medieval convention for establishing divine justice.[11] It may have reminded some auditors, further, of certain Old Testament roots for this convention. In Isaiah 41 and 45, the Persian King Cyrus is hailed as a "righteous man from the east," mysteriously raised up for the overthrow of Babylon and the release of its captives. In Isaiah's view, Cyrus is an anointed shepherd (45:1), through whom God has "made bare his holy arm in the eyes of all nations" (52:10). This deliverer's coming, moreover, is described in imagery pertinent to *King Lear*: it brings (see chapters 47–48) a day of doom on astrologers and "monthly prognosticators," and on trusters in wickedness who have said "I am, and none else besides me"; while at the same time it means a day of release for persons refined "in the furnace of affliction." If Isaiah could thus interpret the pagan Cyrus as a token (and a foreshadowing type) of divine Kingship, may not Shakespeare have patterned his pre-Christian Edgar in the light of such a paradigm? Edgar is Shakespeare's most distinctive addition to the Lear legend; and significantly it is Edgar who comes to rule in Britain as the play ends. This version is Shakespeare's way of suggesting, perhaps, how the meek can come to inherit the earth and the mighty be cast down from their seats.[12]

Moreover, the coast of Dover seems to have significance as moral geography. The Edgar who there emerges to vindicate justice comes, quite literally, out of the East, since Dover is Britain's easternmost port. Toward this same East, earlier, Edgar's blind father had groped, after discovering his own follies and "the times' plague." Thitherward, too, Lear is carried on a litter. In fact, once the play's action has revealed at England's geographical center of wild midlands an apocalypse of tyranny in the savage blinding of Gloucester in his own castle, all the characters in the play find themselves moving eastward, as if toward a place and moment of more final judgment and accounting. Dover's white cliffs figure, as does Lear's own white hair, a nature "on the very verge / Of her confine." They mark the brink of a known order, beyond which lies sea change and an encounter with mystery. At or near Dover's precipice, therefore, we witness the transformations which end an old order of life and open up a new—for instance, the "farewell" leap of Gloucester into miracle, and Lear's sleep which awakens into "daylight" under the ministrations of a Cordelia with "holy water" in her eyes. The promise of the new is further suggested by the acres of "sustaining corn" which flank Dover, whereas inland we had heard only of mildewed wheat and a bare heath.

2 Lear's basic flaw

But let us return our attention to Edgar's insight that "of our pleasant vices" the gods make instruments of plague. Does not this have a pertinence, not merely to Edmund's fate in Act V, but also to the fate of various other persons earlier in the play? Gloucester's pleasant vice of adultery, of which we hear him jesting as the play opens, costs him the gouging out of his eyes by the end of Act III. And in the main plot, Lear's pleasant vice of vanity reaps its plague too. For in his vanity he begets a bastard kind of justice, which becomes an instrument for cutting his own brains with madness.

When Lear prefers the flattering words of fair-faced Goneril and Regan to Cordelia's plain honesty, is he not committing, unwittingly, a kind of spiritual adultery? According to some modern psychoanalysts, he is seeking to tie his daughters to him as sweethearts, not merely daughters, and is thus demonstrating a "latent incestuous orientation."[13] If so, there is a lust in Lear's behavior not altogether unlike, although at a different level from, Gloucester's love of fleshly comfort. Lear's Fool will later comment, through riddling asides, that a preferring of one's "codpiece" before one's "head" brings lousiness and beggary as its plague, and that nights of wind and rain are provided for cooling a "courtesan." Metaphorically, these asides refer to Lear's vice (his preferring of rude will to wisdom, and his prostituting of true courtliness), whereby he has brought on himself a houseless misery and nights of mental storm. Out of Lear's own abuse of his role of king and father are made the disorders which plague him.

Granville-Barker has called the two protagonists of the play "wilful man" and "sensual man."[14] But the distinction between them can be stated also in other ways.[15] From the beginning Lear's tone and manner hint at a pride in outward ceremony, where Gloucester is jauntily evasive of ceremony's claims. Short-sighted "eyes" characterize Gloucester (who in scene ii talks about spectacles), while a narrow love of "I" characterizes Lear (who abandons his plural pronouns for singular ones the moment Cordelia displeases him). Further, if we measure these two against a Christian hierarchy of virtues, Lear's lack of charity makes him the appropriate protagonist of the main plot, while Gloucester's lack of faith fits him for the subplot, although perversions of charity and of faith inevitably interlock and hence are given an interdependent working out in the play's structure. Physical eyesight without faith, or an egoistic "I" without charity, are twin factors in tragedy. John Donne, I think, puns on both "I" and "eye" in his memorable adage, "No man is an Island."

We may say further, however, that what the play's two protagonists have in common is covetousness—the characteristic vice of old age, if one recalls for example *The Castle of Perseverance,* in which Sir Covetous has a scaffold of his own from which he commands the other sins, and to which he wins the hero when old age has made him immune to other forms of sin. From covetousness, Shakespeare is able to show, springs the irresponsibility and self-undoing of Gloucester and Lear. The dramatist's amplifications of this theme are of course the artistic product of his own insight, but its moral base is as ancient as Scripture, which names covetousness the root of all evil.

If we fail to see this root cause of tragedy in Lear (as well as in Gloucester), it is probably because our attention has been captured by secondary factors. Such is the case, it seems to me, with various critics who have attributed Lear's downfall to simple senility, or to his blindness to the hypocrisy of Goneril and Regan; or with other critics who blame centrally Lear's passion of wrath or its counterpart, an obstinacy in Cordelia; or with still others who would trace the tragedy to Lear's "absolutizing" of his office, or to the reverse of that, his decision to abdicate office and divide up England. But all these factors at most are no more than symptoms of a deeper ill. Behind them we can discern in Lear, although he cannot, a coveting of honor and glory, which is parallel to Gloucester's coveting of sensible and sensory goods. Neither hero, let us note, covets anything mean or base, such as money, lands, or political profiteering. This fact insures our sympathy, since the greed in question is seemingly noble, and hence tragic rather than villainous. Moreover, it masks itself with its moral opposite: generosity (in Lear's case) and conviviality (in Gloucester's).

Irving Ribner tends to locate the tragedy chiefly in a political sin—in Lear's decision to divide his lands in three parts under the rule of three dukes.[16] A Jacobean audience, he argues, would have seen in this plan a horrible "violation of the king's responsibility to God," from which only chaos could follow. But I doubt Shakespeare intended this emphasis. How could an audience know what would have happened in England had Cordelia received her intended share, the central and "more opulent" third of territory? Her power and her husband's might well have sustained order. Granted that we hear rumors, several times in the play, of a falling-out between the other two dukes; yet that the cause of this was rival ambition for power is by no means clear, since there seems to be a deeper ground simply in the differing moral values held by Albany and Cornwall. In any case, this rumored antipathy between them does not prevent their armies from fighting side by side in the defense of England as a whole. Moreover, Lear's original plan is presented as having the prior consent of his counsellors. And recent critics such as G. R. Elliott and H. V. Jaffa[17] have defended this plan as being sane and politically shrewd. At least some of Shakespeare's auditors, I would add, might have viewed it in the light of Joshua 11:23. Joshua in his old age "took the whole land . . . and gave it for an inheritance unto Israel according to their divisions by their tribes." The Bible reports no chaos from this act. May we not conclude therefore that not Lear's plan itself but his mismanagement of it, with a "darker purpose" than its surface aim, is for Shakespeare the basic cause of the tragedy?[18]

Lear's opening words about a "darker purpose" carry a Shakespearean irony, since the purpose is here indeed darker than its speaker knows. He identifies his purpose as a publishing now of the dowries of his daughters in order that future strife may be prevented. The way in which he goes about this purpose, however, actually elicits strife—not only between the daughters as they are invited to compete in giving Lear adulation, but between himself and the favored daughter who fails to honor him to his liking. The incitements to strife lurk both in his imperiousness of manner (his commands to "Attend. . . . Tell me. . . . Speak") and in the lush description he gives of the lands to be awarded. The very map of them so absorbs Lear's imagination that nothing is said of their magistracy, of the responsibility of ruling them. And then when his preferred child attempts a reply of impartial judgment, we see how superficial is his own imagined impartiality. Lear's actions thus publish to us his deeper purpose, an unacknowledged love of esteem which is at odds with his professed purpose of self-abnegation in resigning the throne.

Moreover, the self-abnegation itself is voiced in ominous phrasings. Lear says his "fast intent" is to "shake all cares." May this not mean a shaking off of all caring for human welfare? He speaks of desiring to be unburdened that he may "crawl toward death." Does not this suggest an unburdening of concern for life—and of his duty simply as a man to do something other than crawl? The Leir of Shakespeare's source play (dated about 1594) declared an intention to resort to "prayers and beades," whereby he might "thinke upon the welfare of my soule." Shakespeare's Lear uses no such language. He seems to be interested, rather, in his present opportunity for some *show* of self-abnegation by which to appear praiseworthy in the public eye. In dramatizing himself as one who will "crawl toward death," he is unaware that ironically he will be reduced to just such a crawl as the consequence of deluding himself regarding his real inner intentions.

Lear's purpose is dark enough to involve him in unwitting hypocrisy. He evades mentioning, until late in the scene, his intent to retain "the name and all the additions to a king." Furthermore, when he confesses that he had "thought to set my rest" on Cordelia's "kind nursery," he omits referring to the hundred knights he intended bringing into that nursery to serve him; mention of them is deferred until he can tuck in this detail subordinately to his granting of new largess to Goneril and Regan. What he gives must seem everything, and what he retains inconsequential. Yet Goneril will later describe Lear's retainers as making her castle "more like a tavern or a brothel / Than a graced palace." And allow as we may for exaggeration on Goneril's part, it nevertheless is clear that Lear's hidden purpose has been to buy by his "giving" a private preserve for self-indulgent living. Dramatically we have been shown a contradictory "divesting." Lear has resigned the crown, but not with a desire to resign worldliness for humility. Instead his longing is for a superworldly status—essentially for the freedom of a demigod, accountable to no one outside himself.

This subconscious and ignorant motive precipitates Lear's tragedy. Rightly, Granville-Barker has noted in the opening scene "something not far from godhead" in Lear's Olympian tone and isolation.[19] And W. H. Clemen has characterized Lear's initial speeches as "monologic dialogue," the speech of a person talking chiefly to himself, unconcerned to communicate with others.[20] This peculiarity continues through the play, in fact, until Lear's awakening in Cordelia's tent. On the heath he attempts both to defy the storm as if he were a superman, and at the same time to command it as if he were himself a god. That is the high point of his pretensions. But later he acknowledges that when the storm would not cease at his bidding he began to smell out the false religion which his daughters had encouraged in him. "They told me I was everything," he says, but that was "no good divinity."

Why, then, did Lear yield to this no good religion of self-idolatry? For one reason, surely, because he had always "but slenderly known himself," as Regan tells us in Act I. And Goneril mentions, further, his long-ingrafted rashness. Ignorance and rashness thus antedate the play's opening. As habits they are conditioning causes of his downfall. But the precipitating cause in Act I is Lear's covetousness of glory, which takes the form of his improvised "love test." In conducting this test he implicitly equates love with a publication of his merit above all else. He proceeds as if the proof of love were to be found in an estimate-giving, rather than in a caring for the welfare of the beloved one. With this perspective Lear blindly ignores his own duty to love human welfare, and ends by banishing the persons most concerned for his welfare. In seeking to justify himself, he undoes himself.

Two further points may be noted in this situation. One is that Shakespeare highlights the illogic of Lear's reasoning. Lear swears "by the power that made me," but avoids seeing the implications of the fact that he did not make himself. Is it not contradictory to swear by "all the operation of the orbs / From whom we do exist" and in the same breath to disclaim "all my paternal care" of the child Lear's own operations have generated? Or again, is it not illogical to invoke "the sacred radiance of the sun" and yet act like a dragon? Lear is taking his gods' names in vain, as Kent plainly tells him. Hence if this be a case of a tragic hero's acting in ignorance, such ignorance is wilful ignorance; it is not due to Lear's lacking all basis for knowing better. He is neglecting truths which at least fugitively he is aware of. This point accords with St. Paul's explanation, in Romans 1, of how the Gentiles are culpable for their own tragedy: they have ignored a knowledge they partly had and could have had more fully. It accords also with the explanation in Aristotle and Aquinas of how an incontinent man reasons negligently.

Secondly, the exact phrasing of Lear's question in his posing of the love test warrants attention. "Which of you shall we say doth love us most?" he asks. A question very much like this one can be found in the Bible: "Which of them therefore will love him most?" Jesus asks Peter (Luke 7:42). But in the Bible this question is preceded by a story of a creditor who forgave two debtors. Peter is able therefore to answer rightly: "He, I suppose, *to whom he forgave the most.*" This insight, that love shows itself most in forgiveness, which in turn draws love from those we forgive, is a point quite beyond Lear's understanding in Act I. We shall see him discovering it experientially, however, in Act IV, scene vii. It belongs potentially to everyman's knowledge. Hence Lear can come to learn it when his own unnatural behavior in the name of nature has reduced him to a ragged nature.

"The verdict of the play," as Miss Parker has well said, "is the paradox of Christian doctrine, that nature without grace *is* unnatural."[21] Grace is, so to speak, the "blest secret" at the creative ground of nature. Natural love if understood reductively as egoistic impulse degenerates into animalistic appetite (like that of the "barbarous Scythian, / Or he that makes his generation messes" for his gorging); and if understood, on the other hand, as a merely legal bond it becomes rationalistic and sterile; only when subdued by experience to charity, which is the "bond of perfection" (Colossians 3:14), does it become truly natural and humane. The play, among other things, is a testing of various myths of nature which emerge during the process of primeval man's search for the truth of nature.

3 Cordelia's development and Kent's

Even Cordelia, we must recognize, does not initially understand love as forgiveness. Her behavior in the opening scene's crisis, while less gravely faulty than Lear's, is nevertheless allied to his and helps precipitate his "hideous rashness." For she too seeks self-justification and acts from a sense of rightness tinged with self-regard.[22] How else explain the fact that she, who later (by Act IV, scene iii) "heaved the name of Father / Pantingly forth,"[23] can not in this opening scene "heave / My heart into my mouth"? She is of course here under constraint from Lear's subconscious coveting of esteem, which encourages the like in her; and she is as flustered by her sisters' apparent dishonesty as Lear is by her ungraciousness. But the sad result is that she becomes so absorbed in proving her own honesty that she ends by parading it as a rebuke to her sisters. She falls victim thus to an irony of self-contradiction. For how honest is it to declare that one can say "Nothing," but then to allow oneself to sermonize at length? Moreover, her sermon views love as a commodity to be measured and apportioned, and thus overlooks merciful love, an unmeasured sharing of fellowship. In this sense, her answer ironically is a "nothing," because it is defective as a response; and Lear's glib adage that "Nothing will come of nothing" proves to be, in one sense, immediately true of both her efforts and his, in that only defect comes from defect. (In another sense, however, this adage is a defectively Lucretian one, blind to the Christian truth of creation *ex nihilo*.) As any reader of Scholastic philosophy knows, evil is by definition a defect in being, a privation or lack, a no-thing. It is what life sinks back into when deprived of love's creative Word.

Cordelia's reply falls back on a merely legalistic reasoning: she will love her father according to her bond, the bond of her conventional obligation, which calls for a returning of duties for debts, no more and no less. She cannot pretend to love her father "all," she argues, because when she marries she will owe half her love to her husband.[24] This mathematical formula for a dividing of love in halves according to merit is strangely like Lear's proposal to divide his land in thirds according to merit. Both cases imply a substitution of calculation for the spirit of free giving. Moreover, to pride oneself on the rightness of dividing one's love hardly agrees with the biblical adage, "Be fruitful and multiply." Divided love virtually epitomizes tragedy.

Thus the love test has miscarried in polar ways. By eliciting a boastful self-righteousness in both Lear and Cordelia, it has made a great breach in the abused nature of love instead of fostering love. Quite absent, in both tester and tested, is any awareness that the proper proof of love is (as in the Bible), "Feed my sheep." Later in Shakespeare's play, however, Cordelia will learn a shepherding love —when she harbors the homeless Lear, clothes the naked Lear, and visits him when sick and imprisoned. In meeting thus the criteria for Last Judgment (see Matthew 25), she will modify her first judgment. But in her initial test she fails, principally because she is interpreting filial love without brotherly love. She is viewing her father only as a demanding creditor, not as a fellow man who, having fallen among thieves, needs compassion.

But how does Shakespeare bridge the change to the new Cordelia? Dramatically he cannot present on stage each of the phases in her transformation; for he is developing his tragic focus around Lear, whose savagery must lead him to an abyss of disintegration, preparatory to the miracle of his moral reintegration by a Cordelia of charity in full blossom. To whet our anticipation, her advent as rescuer can be rumored in interim scenes, and thereby a modification of her earlier outlook can be inferred by us. But first, as a basis, we need to be shown some seed of change in her—as the aftermath of her banishment, and before the close of Act I. Here is where Shakespeare's introduction of the King of France (a wooer of far different mold from the Petrarchan prototype of the old *Leir* play) is of crucial importance. The realism of France's courtship lights up the wreckage of Lear's love test with a glimmering of high romance, alien to the England we have seen. His love begins, in fact, the renovation of Cordelia.

The very plight of Cordelia enkindles in France a rescuing love. Her unprized state as a penniless outcast makes her newly "precious" in his eyes. "Be it lawful I take up what's cast away." Here is love according to a new kind of law, which does not measure by merit, or by favors received, or by any customary bond of obligation:

> Love's not love
> When it is mingled with regards that stand
> Aloof from the entire point.

Out of compassion, which gives him an insight into the hidden worth of what Lear has dismissed as "that little seeming substance," Cordelia's soul, France takes Cordelia and makes her his queen. France does not argue that Cordelia's answer was faultless. Instead, he urges Lear to realize that her offense cannot be believed to be "of such unnatural degree" as to make her a monster. Is it not, rather, a "tardiness in nature" which has but left "unspoke / That it intends to do?" With this faith France espouses her.

The attitude of France signalizes a transcending both of Lear's

morality tied to impulse and of Cordelia's morality tied to deserving, while at the same time it accords with what is for him both
lawful and naturally spontaneous. He has acted from a morality
open to the possibility of miracle, open to that supernatural ground
of community which is implicit in natural community. He has
taken to himself a bride, that he may perfect her—a concept that is
basic to the New Testament idea of marriage. In this sense his act
is figurally Christian, although he lives in pre-Christian times. We
may contrast his outlook with the despairing naturalism of Gloucester who, when seeing the King fall "from bias of nature," idly accepts this bias. Whereas Gloucester regards "eclipses in the sun
and moon" as nature's fortune-telling, France's response to eclipses
of human judgment and love is in accord with the New Testament
concept that such signs (see Luke 21:25) are occasions for men to
"lift up your heads," since redemption draws nigh when there is
"distress of nations with perplexity." Elizabethan auditors of
Shakespeare's play could have recalled that this apocalyptic hope is
the Prayerbook's "Gospel" for the second Sunday in Advent, and
they therefore could have sensed in the figure of France an Advent
truth.

France's faith begins soon to be justified. For by the end of the
scene we find Cordelia saying to her sisters:

> Use well our father.
> To your professed bosoms I commit him.
> But yet, alas, stood I within his grace,
> I would prefer him to a better place.

A shift in Cordelia's attitude is here I think discernible, although
Shakespeare is too careful of psychology to permit its emerging as
an abrupt change. Cordelia has not modified her suspicion of her
sisters, but she is acquiring the patience not to name their faults.
And she is no longer justifying herself to her father, and in their
hearing, as being rich by not having a "glib and oily art" and a
"still-soliciting eye." Instead, her eye is now solicitous for "our"
father's future welfare, and full of regret for having lost his grace.
Considering the fact that this speech follows directly after Lear's
own ungracious command to her to "be gone" without his love and
favor, her compassion for his situation is noteworthy. We can antic-
ipate that such a spirit will grow and deepen in her as Lear's plight
worsens. Thus a possibility has been established for that eventual

great scene of reconciliation, in which father and daughter will kneel each to the other, forgiving and giving benediction.

The Earl of Kent had defended Cordelia's blunt reply to the love test, declaring on her behalf that she had thought "justly" and had "most rightly said." But Shakespeare, as I have suggested, can scarcely have thought that Cordelia spoke "most rightly." Rather, he has been highlighting an initial flaw in her perspective. Equally he highlights, as the play proceeds, the similar flaw in Kent's perspective. Kent continues to champion a blunt and ungracious kind of justice during his disguise role as Lear's servant. But by this attitude he merely gets both himself and Lear deeper into trouble. We all delight, of course, in seeing Kent criticize the sycophant Oswald (using toward him a bold masculine raillery); such action parallels Cordelia's indignant criticism of her sisters (using toward them a feminine innuendo). Yet there is truth in Cornwall's comment that Kent's so-called "honest mind and plain" constrains nature from its proper manner.[25] We may also recall how, at the play's very beginning, Kent had condoned a constraining of nature from its proper manner. "I cannot wish the fault undone," he had said of Gloucester's marital infidelity, "the issue of it being so proper." Kent can be loyal (the play is ironically saying): loyal to a fault!

But as with other characters in this play, a combination of suffering and strange new discoveries gradually enlarges Kent's understanding. We notice the change particularly in Act V, when there is reported to us Kent's surprise on discovering that Edgar has been secretly championing a justice of another kind than Kent's. Earlier, in Act III, Kent had shunned the society of the disguised Edgar. But now on learning this beggar's true identity and real story, he has thrown his arms around Edgar's neck. The next we hear of Kent is when, after Edgar's victory, he enters on stage undisguised to offer, as he says, a bidding of "good night" to Lear, his master. A few minutes later Lear enters, carrying the body of Cordelia, and Kent kneels before him with the cry, "Oh, my good master!" But getting no welcome, Kent must probe for it. "Where is your servant Caius?" he asks Lear. This way of bidding for recognition implies still, I think, a residual element of self-centeredness; there is something self-dramatizing about it. Perhaps A. C. Bradley's perplexity as to Kent's purpose in preserving his incognito until this final scene can be answered by saying that Kent has wanted to stage a surprise at some public moment, when Lear might be properly impressed by his servant's devotion and bestow on Kent a noble reward. If so, Kent has now a newly ironic surprise in store. For the response he receives is deflating. To the question about Caius, Lear replies with a comment which is (by Shakespeare's subtle art) profoundly true:

> He's a good fellow, I can tell you that.
> *He'll strike, and quickly too. He's dead and rotten.*
> (Italics mine)

That is, Caius is now dead to a Lear who has progressed beyond him. When Kent then cries "No, my good lord, I am the very man," this admission scarcely helps his case. Even after further explanation, he is rewarded merely with Lear's curt "You are welcome hither"—after which Lear turns to his more cherished servant, the dead but *not rotten* Cordelia, on whose lips there may yet be life. Kent, after watching Lear in these last moments, realizes that he himself has a "journey" still to go.

The total role and significance of Kent has been much changed from that of his prototype Perillus in the old play *Leir*. Perillus was never banished. From motives of loyalty and pity he sought out the abused Leir at Goneril's house, and from then on functioned as a spiritual guardian. He reinforced Leir's quickly repentant mind, joined him in expostulations of Christian meekness, and protected him from a hired murderer by converting this villain through sermonizing. Then he persuaded Leir to go with him to France to seek forgiveness and aid from Cordelia. His "true love" was lauded by Leir in the very last speech of the play, when Leir (happily restored to his throne, in contrast to Shakespeare's ending) vowed to reward Perillus "the best I can." Shakespeare's version has introduced several important modifications of story: Lear's repentance is depicted as a slow and agonizing one, attained only by stages and after a breakdown into madness; its human agents are principally the Fool, Edgar, and Cordelia, rather than Kent; and at the end Lear expresses no indebtedness to Kent. Kent's past contribution is thus placed as one of equivocal and intermediate value. Yet his stoic virtue has, as its ultimate potential, a sense of call to a new kind of service—spoken of as a "journey" once Kent has witnessed, besides Edgar's pilgrimage, the sacrifice of Cordelia and Lear's parting summons to "Look there!" Insight rather than an accolade is Kent's true reward. That fact is thematic for Shakespeare's play as a whole.

4 Stages in Lear's development

The final scene of Lear's bending over the limp body of the hanged Cordelia, cherishing her as "my poor fool," is revelatory in mysterious ways. It might, I think, have reminded an Elizabethan audience of many a medieval painting of the Deposition from the Cross. I mean, of course, by analogy to the biblical scene.[26] For Lear's anguish is much like that of a disciple assisting at the burial of all his earthly hopes. Lear's feelings (like those of an onlooker at Calvary) are caught up within a frame of grief-stricken tragedy. As was true on Good Friday, no Easter vision has yet become available to the sufferers of this moment's desolation. Nevertheless, amid the deep despair there can be (if pictured by an artist of psychology like Shakespeare) occasional flickerings of a transcendent hope to punctuate the moment of darkness. For are not the darkest hours just before dawn, and is not the Dark Night of the Soul the traditional preface to mystic vision?

A. C. Bradley offered the opinion that the agony in which Lear dies is actually "one not of pain but of ecstasy." Noting that Lear's very last words are

> Do you see this? Look on her, look, her lips,
> Look there, look there!

Bradley remarked that an actor would be false to Shakespeare's text if he did not express with these lines "an unbearable *joy*."[27] This reading perhaps overstates just a little. Lear's situation, as I see it, is that of "a time of tension between dying and birth" (if I may borrow words from the end of T. S. Eliot's *Ash Wednesday*); he is therefore, like the speaker in Eliot's poem, still "between the rocks" of hopelessness and hope, yet able finally to cry out to the veiled "sister" of his garden, "Suffer me not to be separated." Bradley's view seems to me, however, much nearer the truth than that of his sceptical opponents, who see Lear as dying with a "cry of utter despair" (G. B. Harrison), or under "illusion" and "driven insane" (J. Stampfer), or retreating into "the happiness of delusion" (Nicholas Brooke).[28]

It is quite evident that Lear's emotion turns in cycles between despair and hope as he tries his various tests: with a mirror, then a feather, then with an ear or eye to Cordelia's lips in search of evidence that she lives. But must we hold, with Stampfer, that Lear is sane only when declaring her dead? Is his other talk merely a wild self-deception of temporary madness? Why not see Lear's reactions, instead, as those of a mind searching for truth through successive modes of evaluation? There is a kind of spiralling upward in the very grammar of Lear's grief. Note, for instance, the progressive mood of his verbs: how they start out in the imperative ("Howl, howl, howl, howl!"), then progress into a struggle between the indicative ("She's dead . . .") and the subjunctive (with the word "if" cropping up twice), and end at last in the interrogative ("Do you see this?"), followed by a hopeful and thus higher-level imperative ("Look there!"). The verbs as carriers of action have cycled upward. We need not claim that they signalize, at the end of this psychological climb, a Lear completely assured of a resurrected life in Cordelia, but rather that his love-impelled reason is converging toward (and verging on) such a faith beyond reason. A dream of new life is summoning him—as, indeed, had been his experience once before, when he awoke to an imagination of Cordelia as "a soul in bliss" yet qualified that judgment with the caution "I fear I am not in my perfect mind." Lear's bewilderment in both episodes (the one in Act IV, the other at the play's end) seems to me to picture a mind groping toward supernatural fact.[29] Nor should we overlook the thematic pertinence of a sentence spoken elsewhere in the play: "Nothing *almost sees miracles* / But misery."*

Kent had blurted out those words earlier in the play when, himself in stocks, he was finding comfort by perusing a letter from Cordelia. The miracle he could then almost see was her coming with an army to restore his own and Lear's earthly fortunes—in this sense to "give / Losses their remedies." But at the end of the play, when for the first time since her coming Kent actually sees Cordelia, the miracle she presents is no restitution at all in material terms, but instead her own dead body as a hanged fool. Yet now Kent beholds Lear reading in this dead body a sign (a spirit instead of a let-

---

* This line seems to me to gain added weight by its ambiguity. It can mean either "When brought to nothing but misery, man can almost see miracles"; or "When brought to nothing almost, man sees miracles but misery along with them."

ter), by which Lear can *almost see* the higher miracle of her coming
to him with life—to "redeem all sorrows / That ever I have felt." Is
not the drama presenting us a structural analogy between Kent in
stocks comforted by a letter, and Lear "upon the rack of this tough
world" seeking comfort in a sign, and at death's door glimpsing it?

Those critics who see Lear as dying deluded and insane are
arbitrarily truncating the logic of moral discovery which has characterized the play's whole structure. They seem to assume, moreover, that Lear in his final cry is pointing to a supposed return of
natural breath to Cordelia's lips. But Shakespeare's text does not
say this; it leaves appropriately mysterious what Lear saw. The
imagery of nature still lingers in the speech of any man who would
communicate his vision of supernatural reality, for it is only by
such language, used analogically however, that he can express what
he sees. We know that in Christian language, for instance, the basic
concept of resurrected life does not mean the resuscitation of a
corpse. "How are the dead raised up?" St. Paul asked in I Corinthians 15 (the well-known Burial Office passage), and he replied by
saying that the body being "sown a natural body" is raised "a
spiritual body"—something in a different order of reality. This
spiritual and supernatural life was what Paul had in mind when he
declared his own vision of a resurrected Christ. Some of his auditors,
it is true, considered him mad for talking in such terms (see the
comment of Festus in Acts 26); but would Shakespeare have
thought so? The playwright and most of his Elizabethan auditors,
I am suggesting, would have been able to distinguish between
madness and a valid faith. In the comparable case of Lear's final
cry, therefore, they would not have inferred, as the modernist
Nicholas Brooke does, that the play at its ending *invalidates* the
Christian hope of redemption. Only a blind or dogmatic skepticism
would so infer. The fact that Lear earlier has called Cordelia dead,
and has resorted to using his sword against her capturers, cannot
be said to preclude a more final hope, since we know from such
paradigms as Peter's use of a sword at Gethsemane or Paul's disbelief until his Damascus vision that such are the phenomena which
can preface man's break-through into new understanding. This is
the existential reality of the learning process, rightly imitated by
Shakespeare's art.

As various commentators have remarked, Lear's cry that "my
poor fool is hanged!" ambiguously associates Cordelia with the

court Fool of earlier scenes. A symbolic connection, through similarity of role, is here being implied. The innocent Cordelia's "folly" of companionate suffering, we may say, has become complementary to (and paradoxically the fulfilment of) the court Fool's worldly jests and shrewd folk wisdom. A. C. Bradley, who reasoned only in literal terms, was puzzled by the Fool's being dropped from the play in Act III without Shakespeare's informing us as to this character's ultimate fate; he supposed this due to the dramatist's carelessness or his impatience to reduce overloaded material. But symbolically, I think it is clear that the Fool's humble devotion to helping Lear (and Kent) "see" better is carried forward when rephrased in a new embodiment in Cordelia. That is, the Fool's verbal *riddles* are continued, at another level, in the *mysteries* of Cordelia's person. On the stage, moreover, the two roles could have been played by the same boy actor.[30]

The focus of any tragedy, however, must be on the defeat of all worldly hopes as the necessary preface to whatever higher intuition may be granted. Lear's "Never, never, never, never, never" is the drama's signal of his final resignation to a death of human wishes. His "Pray you, undo this button" suggests a readiness to be unclothed of life itself, which is empty of meaning apart from what Cordelia represents. By attention to the play's consecutive metaphors of unclothing, therefore, we can trace stages in Lear's learning of self-abnegation. At the start, he had divested himself of "cares of state," but basically out of a covetous desire for his own adulation. Later he had relinquished his hopes of courtly pomp, but in a spirit of savage bitterness: "Off, off, you lendings! Come, unbutton here." Only at the play's very end does the unbuttoning take on a genuine and gentle humility, contaminated no longer by self-will. This third stage of Lear's unclothing marks also his tragedy's denouement. Thelma Greenfield has aptly noted its likeness to the ending of Man in the morality play *Nature,* in which Man "prepared for his heavenly salvation by casting off his garments."[31]

The total story of Lear's purgation, if we study its windings for the essential pattern, can be seen as his gradual learning to put off, not so much his "lendings" as his initial self-centeredness. At Regan's house he would rather embrace the storm than ask his daughter's blessing, rather go mad than admit human weakness. A parallel in our own day might be cited from W. H. Auden's *Age of Anxiety,* which pictures man as preferring "rather to be ruined than changed," and willing to torture himself rather than let die the illusion he holds of himself as a god. In following such reasoning, however, Lear suffers a breakdown of judgment into wild ravings. And this releasing of his heart enables him both to expose his mad pretensions and to punish them with self-mockery.

A mock trial in Tom's hovel is followed later by Lear's mock crowning of himself with weeds. Here he is enacting the irony of his own lostness, in the light of which fact he can then proceed to repudiate the "no good divinity" that "I was everything." Thereafter we hear no more the self-justifying claim, "I am a man more sinned against than sinning." That illusion has been abandoned, as Lear probes deeper to mock his own self-righteousness. His own flesh, he realizes, has begotten the pelican daughters Goneril and Regan; and if there are simpering dames in this world, there are also hypocritical judges who plate their own sin with gold. Seeing then that the judge in office may be as guilty as the culprit he arraigns, Lear cries out: "None does offend . . . I'll able 'em." As Edgar remarks, here is "reason in madness." For when Lear can thus mock his earlier pretensions he is accepting the fact of his own moral bankruptcy. His image of a "rascal beadle," whipping a whore for the very vice which this man of authority hotly lusts to enjoy, is an epitome of Lear's predicament. His old edifice of moral claims is now in ruins, crumbled by its admitted contradictions.[32] He is thereby learning the truth of how *this* world goes, the world of "this great stage of fools." Yet in accepting such a this-worldly realism there is implicit a longing for something better. Once Lear knows himself utterly self-humiliated, he can call out for "a surgeon," and can half-conjecture some kind of "rescue." He is thus being made apt for a new "stage" in another world.

The higher world of Cordelia's love, when it dawns miraculously on an awakening Lear, seems to him like a resurrection from the dead. "You do me wrong to take me out of the grave," he demurs. But this reluctance of his, due chiefly to remorseful shame and bewilderment, is dissipated by the "Fair daylight" of a strange new realm of forgiveness. In the symbolism of the story, Cordelia's tent becomes a kind of holy place—which to a Christian audience might easily suggest the tent tabernacle of Old Testament times, wherein deliverance from an Egyptian bondage was celebrated. After this experience there then can be but one further step for Lear, at the very end of the play, when he accepts and welcomes a loosening of the garments of earthly existence itself, prompted to this typologically second Exodus by his gazing on a hanged Cordelia. The story of Lear's divesting is then complete. For at last he is fulfilling, in a way quite different from what he had anticipated at the play's beginning, a resigning of cares of "state." That purpose, proclaimed earlier in a pompous ceremony, is now in reality accomplished but in a transformed sense—just as likewise his earlier coveting of an infinite love is now transformed into a personal commitment to infinite love. Lear's quest has come full circle.

5 Edgar's sin and penance

Probably no Shakespearean play illustrates so well as *King Lear* the thesis of St. Augustine in the *City of God,* Book I, that calamities are profitable, both for refining away the selfishness in good men and exterminating the corruption of wicked men. Both kinds of men, says Augustine, are punished together,

> not because they have spent an equally corrupt life, but because the good as well as the wicked, though not equally with them, love this present life; while they ought to hold it cheap, that the wicked being admonished and reformed by their example, may lay hold of life eternal. (I. 10)

That there is a refining process through adversity in Lear's case has been acknowledged by most critics. They have given less attention, however, to the effect of adversity on the play's more relatively "good" characters, Cordelia and Edgar. In our present chapter we have already noted Cordelia's initial shortcomings, and how they are mended through her exile, marriage, and subsequent vocation of suffering service. But what about Edgar? Does not he too, as the subplot's counterpart to Cordelia, also have an initial flaw which is refined away by the uses of adversity? Let us return our attention to Edgar, with a focus now on the early part of his story.

For perspective on Edgar's minor flaw, however, we need to begin by assessing his father's more obvious weakness. Old Gloucester's sensuality, we may say, is an aspect of what Augustine calls love of "this present life." The immediate goods of everyday existence—ease, idle gossip, and saving one's skin—are Gloucester's chief concern. In Act I he watches from the sidelines his King's fall into folly without intervening. In this sense, Gloucester is a "tolerant" man, evading responsibility. He can accept fatalistically human eclipses of reason and judgment, whether in Lear or in himself. We are shown his eclipsed kind of reasoning in the play's opening lines. We hear him there admitting that he esteems his bastard son Edmund no less than his legitimate Edgar. He has "so often blushed to acknowledge" Edmund, he says, that now he is "brazed to it." With a flippant worldliness he jests about the whoreson's having come "something saucily into the world." Is it surprising, then, that in Act II he becomes, through sheer spiritual laziness, an easy victim of Edmund's deceit? Neglecting the duty of a father to himself examine the truth of the charges against Edgar, he prays Edmund to seek out Edgar and "wind me into him." "Frame the business after your own wisdom," he says; "I would unstate myself to be in a due resolution." And thus he does indeed *unstate* himself.

In a similar way the naive Edgar unstates himself. Like Cordelia, he too has a touch of his father's pleasant vices. Though to a lesser degree than his father, Edgar loves too much this present life, is too curious of its secrets, and too eager for the seductive kind of friendship offered by a bastard. Specifically, Edgar unstates himself by listening to Edmund's astrological lore, and then to Edmund's proposal that Edgar protect himself against danger, not by seeking reconciliation with the father, but by seeking safety in evasion and masquerade. Such a course of action soon leads to antics very much like those of black magic:

> Here he stood in the dark, his sharp sword out,
> Mumbling of wicked charms, conjuring the moon,
> To prove's auspicious mistress.

These lines give us Edmund's fabricated account to Gloucester of what Edgar was doing before he fled. Literally the report is false but figuratively it shadows a truth: Edgar has let himself become an assistant to a conjuring Edmund,[33] who has trapped him into dealing with his father not in a sensible way but in a spellbound, quasi-lunatic way. Edgar, although initially no devotee of astrology, has allowed himself a quizzical interest in such lore when Edmund tempted him with a report of what he "read this other day," namely, that eclipses portend "unnaturalness between the child and the parent" and "needless diffidences." Lured by this half-truth, Edgar is trapped into reading a horrible unnaturalness in his own father, and then into treating that father with a needless diffidence.

We have already seen, in Gloucester's case, the hypnotic attraction which fatalistic imaginings can have: they paralyze the will by offering a convenient excuse for the will to abnegate responsibility. Eclipses portend a falling-off of friendship, says a Gloucester who has already evaded the duties of true friendship, but who is enabled by his astrology to see friendlessness not in himself but in external forces in the universe. The observation "Love cools" becomes an anodyne to a person in whom love is already cool—cool enough to indulge the self-pity of imagining himself a helpless pawn in a loveless world. (St. Augustine in his *Confessions* comments on astrology as a religion of self-exculpation.) Edmund's success rests on his preaching for villainous purposes a melancholy view of life—in this case, "with a sigh like Tom o'Bedlam." For if he can induce Edgar to believe "the excellent foppery of the world," that our disasters have no relation to our wishes, but solely to compulsive circumstances, he can in effect hypnotize Edgar's will and thus figuratively make him a lunatic. That is, he can make of him one of those "great ones" (as Lear will later call them) who ebb and flow by the moon.

Although Edgar's fault shows up thus as a pliable weakness of will, in contrast to the show of stubborn will by Cordelia at her first testing, there is a kind of polar analogy in the way these two children respond to their fathers. For example, we first see Edgar indignant that "some villain hath done me wrong"—just as Cordelia reacted with indignation toward her sisters; then Edgar's tack is to "retire" from his difficulty into hiding—as Cordelia tried to hide from answering her father when challenged; but next Edgar consents to "go armed" and thereby gets drawn into masquerade— as Cordelia, similarly, offered show of self-justifying argument. What Shakespeare presents us, in sum, is a foolish self-defensiveness in both cases, a futile shadowboxing which misrepresents to the father the true nature of the child, and thereby provokes in the father a rage and retaliation. Both children, we may say, have allowed the light of their genuine love to be eclipsed by sublunary considerations. They dis-grace themselves in analogous ways. A reader of Shakespeare may be reminded here of the two cousins of whom Rosalind speaks in *As You Like It* (I. iii. 7): one "lamed with reasons, and the other mad without any."

Forms of folly thus interrelated lead to polar versions of exile and to polar modes of expiation. Cordelia's subsequent fate in the play is to become (as in Greek legend) a discarded child who is then (figuratively) adopted and raised by a king of another country, after which she becomes (as in Christian legend) an atoning child who goes about her father's business. "O dear Father, / It is thy business that I go about" (IV. iv. 24)—compare Luke 2:49. Edgar's fate, on the other hand, is to become (both literally and metaphorically) a hunted and haunted refugee, to whom all worldly ports are closed, and who by this fact is turned to seeking his better haven in a straw hovel, and a safer journeying under the garb of a beggar.

May we not say that such action is emblematic, within a pagan setting, of the biblical logic of purgation? St. Augustine, when commenting on the initial fault of Moses in slaying an Egyptian, had written:

> In minds where great virtue is to come, there is often an early crop of vices, in which we may still discern a disposition for some particular virtue, which will come when the mind is duly cultivated. (*Reply to Faustus* XXII. 70)

Even Peter, he adds, had to outgrow the crop of vice he showed when, in unwise defense of his Lord, he cut off the ear of an assailant.

Edgar decides to put off his old Edgarhood ("Edgar I nothing am," he confesses) and to accept instead the lot of a Tom of Bedlam. Whether or not Shakespeare had the fact in mind, this Elizabethan name for lunatics carries biblical associations. Bedlam derives from Bethlehem, the name used extrabiblically by the medieval monks for their hospital for the insane near London. To an Elizabethan playgoer, moreover, a recalling of the biblical Bethlehem might easily come, a moment later, when Shakespeare introduces the straw hovel to which a nobly born but now "poor" Edgar must turn, since for him there is no room in the ancestral castle-inn. To its adjacent mere cattle-shed shelter even Lear is content to be led, once his "wits begin to turn." Its vile straw can then seem "precious" to Lear; and before entering he stops to pray. Significantly, his first deed of real charity in the whole play comes when he invites his Fool to enter here ahead of him. And once inside this place of refuge, Lear finds himself learning "philosophy" from Tom, whose seeming madtalk has been described by a recent critic (Leo Kirschbaum) as expressing "the formal Christian viewpoint" but in an arcane way and "not ostensibly."[34]

We know from Edgar's sane statement, when first he put on the rags of Tom, that his intention was henceforth to employ lunacy along with "prayers" as a means to enforce "charity." He was then thinking of a charity on the part of others than himself; yet his own commitment to humiliation implies on his part a pilgrimage in search of charity. And in this quest his taking on of a disguise role enables him, in actual fact, to work out a kind of penance.[35] As a beggar he is associating himself with society's outcasts; he is suffering imaginatively their miseries as a way of eliciting fellowship from his neighbors. Thus he is undoing the alienations in which he, and others, have been caught. At the end of his experiences in the hovel and farmhouse, we will hear him soliloquize that his own pain has become "light and portable" through a partnership in the woes of others. Moreover, the lunatic role permits confession. Under its surface wildness, Edgar can rehearse (albeit in a heightened and surrealist form) the causes and consequences of his personal folly. Confession in this mode provides medicine for himself and also aids a fellow sufferer, Lear.[36] On Tom there thus devolves an opportunity to serve obscurely as his King's tutor.

The Lear who enters Tom's hovel is a king whose pride has already been punished by exile, and whose judgment has been mocked—pelted not only by the storm but by the gnomic proverbs of his loyal Fool. Under the impact of such lessonings Lear's mind is beginning to turn ambiguously toward madness and toward a deeper level of insight. There are now occasional flashes of self-criticism, and of pity for the poor, amid Lear's otherwise denunciatory thunderings. In this condition he is apt for the further education which Tom, assuming wildness, can offer covertly. Typologically, Lear may be said to resemble the Nebuchadnezzar of Daniel 4, who was driven from among men "to eat grass like an ox" until his reason returned and he learned to bless.

Tom's outward destitution and the nightmarish account he gives of himself serve to review for Lear, in parable form, the consequences of courtly debauchery. Once a servingman proudly arrayed, who "slept in the contriving of lust and waked to do it," Tom has been reduced to a scavenger vexed by a fiend. Such is the pitiful story he tells. Various of its details regarding the false servingman, as Kirschbaum has noted, duplicate facts in Shakespeare's portrait of Oswald, so that Tom's fantasy provides the play's audience a kind of mirror of the spiritual truth about Goneril's sycophant servant.[37] But more importantly, Poor Tom's whole predicament serves Lear as in some sense a mirror of his own story. And we can see why, since Lear in his own way has served a lust of heart and become vexed by a foul fiend. Indeed, if we but recall how Lear has been invoking blasts and fen-suck'd fogs and other "terrors of the earth," and has been abjuring roofs in order to be "comrade with the wolf and owl," we immediately realize that Tom's imaginary fiend has scarcely played on Tom tricks any worse than those of Lear's inner fiend. "Who gives anything to Poor Tom? Whom the foul fiend hath led through fire . . . and whirlpool . . . that hath laid knives under his pillow and . . . made him proud of heart . . . to course his own shadow . . ." Such description could well apply metaphorically to poor Lear.

Yet Tom's fictional confession carries also basically a genuine truth about Edgar himself, provided we allow for the exaggeration of its surrealism. Was not Edgar, figuratively, tempted by Edmund to play with knives and hunt his own shadow? And now his reference to "False of heart, light of ear, bloody of hand" deftly alludes to vices latent in an earlier Edgar, who was (we may recall) false enough of heart to put his own safety first, light enough of ear to listen to Edmund's reports, and bloody enough of hand to pretend a swordfight. Granted that these spiritual flaws in the early Edgar may be sensibly judged by us to have been minor ones, mere shadowy vices if compared to the blatant vice of wicked Edmund, nevertheless they warrant some mode of confession on the part of a probing and genuinely truth-seeking imagination. Further, we may note that among the fiends whom Tom names there is one called Flibbertigibbet, the fiend who "squints the eye" until cock-crow. May not this suggest Edgar's former malady? Edgar has been possessed—but only until cock-crow—by Flibbertigibbet, who caused him to see squint-eyed!

This temporary benightedness, once Edgar can recognize it in confessing it through Tom, becomes the experience out of which he can claim the right to offer Lear brotherly counsel. "Bless thy five wits!" Tom admonishes. "Bless thee from whirlwinds, star-blasting and taking!" Lear is far from ready to follow such good advice; he replies with a blast of curses (supposedly on Tom's behalf) calling on all the plagues of the air to light upon daughters. For he prefers to think Tom's penury the result of "unkind daughters," rather than of the "fiend" Tom has blamed. Tom thereupon reiterates his warning: "Take heed o' the foul fiend." He goes on to add, moreover, five further injunctions—a kind of catechism of universal moral principles. These paraphrase (at least to any Christian ear) five of the Ten Commandments of the Old Testament:

> Obey thy parents, keep thy word justly, swear not, commit
> not with man's sworn spouse, set not thy sweet heart on
> proud array. (III. iv. 82)

There is irony in beginning this list with an echo of the commandment which Lear had imagined he was enforcing in Act I: "Honor thy father . . ."! And the last counsel in the list, "Set not thy sweet heart on proud array," glances at the biblical "Thou shalt not covet," which we have earlier noted as the key to Lear's basic fault. Tom's five counsels (as well as the five blessed wits he has invoked) balance nicely over against Tom's list elsewhere of five fiends (IV. i. 58), a contrast perhaps deliberately structured thus by Shakespeare.

Lear, of course, continues to evade the duties enjoined in Tom's mumblings. What fascinates his attention instead is the image of naked man which the seemingly lunatic Tom presents. And further, Tom's revulsion against court life and its deceptions accords with Lear's own disillusionment with the court. Bitterly he hails Tom as a professional wise man—a "learned Theban" and "good Athenian," whom he will cling to as "my philosopher." And in this spirit Lear himself philosophizes that man, when unaccommodated and stripped of clothes, is no more than a "forked animal" such as Tom. This view grasps, obliquely, a half-truth only.[38] For in fact Tom is more than a forked animal; he is a penitent man who has accommodated himself to poverty. But this larger truth eludes Lear, not only because he is ignorant of the literal Edgar underneath the Tom, but also because he has not fully hearkened to what Tom has been saying.

A scene later, in the farmhouse, Lear sets up Tom as a pretended judge in a mock trial. Here again we can discern Tom's covert efforts to educate Lear. The snatches of madtalk which Tom intrudes into the proceedings are seemingly haphazard but in fact very shrewdly relevant. They provide comment, through analogy, on the nonsense of Lear's stance. Lear's clamor for justice, so Tom hints, is like the futile hornblowing of a silly shepherd.

> Sleepest or wakest thou, jolly shepherd?
>   Thy sheep be in the corn,
> And for one blast of thy minikin mouth,
>   Thy sheep shall take no harm.

Tom's point here, I think, is the ludicrousness of Lear's sounding off now with a call for justice, when the damage has already been done and furthermore is due to the plaintiff's own negligence. For making this point nursery rhyme serves well. Lear, like Little Boy Blue,[39] has been a delinquent shepherd. His belated horn-blowing is now (ironically) quite powerless to harm the feeding which his sheep are illicitly enjoying.

A similar irony is carried in Tom's reply, twenty lines later, to Lear's mad complaint that "the little dogs and all" are barking at him. Here Tom's absurd comment is: "Tom will throw his head at them. Avaunt, you curs!" As if a tossing of one's head (or as in Edwin Booth's acted version, a throwing away of a crown on one's head) were a sensible method of silencing dogs! Yet, metaphorically, is this not the method Lear has been using all too foolishly toward his doghearted daughters? By giving them his crown, or later by wagging his head at them in disapproval, he has not silenced them; he has merely lost his head. Tom's nonsense lines are thus a gentle parody for the focusing of Lear's predicament.

We therefore infer, both here and at other moments of the seemingly irrelevant talk, that Edgar under the mode of Tom is employing lunacy for surrealist commentary. The surface irrelevancies have a choric function for the play's audience. Moreover, they are Edgar's way of acknowledging his own kinship with irrational imaginings, and hence establishing fellowship with Lear, while also attempting the King's enlightenment through sympathetic chiding. When Tom's invention flags, Shakespeare moves the play's action onward to new episodes. But what Edgar has learned through his companionship with lunacy is summed up in two simple lines:

> The lamentable change is from the best;
> The worst returns to laughter.

In other words, human disorder at its worst elicits a comic sense, which by reminding us of our absurdity, points the mind toward a recovery of order.[40]

6   The play's patterned significance

Many of us are familiar with Kenneth Burke's and Francis Fergusson's schematization of the rhythm of tragic action in terms of the stages of Purpose, Passion, and Perception.[41] A focus on these can be helpful in any understanding of tragedy; hence much of my commentary has illustrated their presence in *King Lear*. But while thus studying the action's rhythm, we can be equally attentive to the literary devices by which the poet has endowed the action with amplitude of implication. Basic to this, it would seem, is another set of "p's"—paradox, parallelism, and prefiguration—along with a background sense of parable, which in *King Lear* turns about the possibilities for human progress under providence. When commenting on this aspect of the play, I have focused on paradoxes such as Heilman brought to our attention in his *This Great Stage: Image and Structure in "King Lear"* (1948), and on structures of parallelism such as Kernodle emphasized in his essay on "The Symphonic Form of *King Lear*" and traced to medieval art,[42] and on aspects of prefiguration to which critics such as Bethell and Levin have in part introduced us. These artistic features deserve our close study. The architectonics of *King Lear*—its balancings of character, its foreshadowings of theme, and its placed analogies of spiritual development—are much more intricate than many of us have supposed. And the total shaping of the tragedy is evidently guided by a perspective of the kind Auerbach discerned in medieval art: "everything tragic was but figure or reflection of a single complex of events, into which it necessarily flowed at last—the complex of the Fall, of Christ's birth and passion, and the Last Judgment."[43]

Readers will no doubt continue to differ in their views of the play as a whole. But debate over whether its message is nihilist, Stoic, or Christian is best resolved, it seems to me, along the lines of J. C. Maxwell's statement that "*King Lear* is a Christian play about a pagan world."[44] That is, the play is Christian in its implicit world view, while not so in its setting or explicit atmosphere. A Christian view of pagan history can discern in the panorama of that history a place for nihilistic, Stoic, and other attitudes such as the initial Epicureanism of Edmund. These can be seen by a Christian dramatist as variant responses to life's trials, through which pagans (and we too in our potentially pagan moments) typically stumble into disaster but then, more hopefully, can grope upward toward self-understanding. Modes of defective response, within Shakespeare's own times, were evident in the Renaissance currents of barbarism, cynicism, neoclassicism, and Machiavellianism. Their indirect benefit was a crisis in man's sense of identity, to which the shortcomings of these philosophies led, but out of which providentially could then arise, for some sufferers at least, a rediscovery of truths essentially Christian.

Although the achievement of self-understanding in any final sense waits upon Christian apocalypse, yet all men can have foreshadowings of it through natural revelation. It may be recalled that Aquinas considered the Gentile mind capable of attaining, through natural reason, a belief in immortality, in spirits, or in God; and that Calvin recognized in some pagans "the peculiar graces of God."[45] Within the world of *Lear* we can see emerging a native capacity for natural theology. The most notable instance of it is in Cordelia's invocation of "All blest secrets, / All you unpublished virtues of the earth." Here the earth itself (which Psalm 24 says is the Lord's and the fulness thereof) is looked to for healing. This insight has a universal base, while also being in accord with the Christian belief that nature itself has secret blessings, and virtues discoverable independently of a written Scripture or an institutional Church, once men are led by the crises of adversity to seek them. For this indeed was a way by which the ancient Hebrews found revelation, before ever setting down their discoveries in Holy Writ. According to medieval thought, there are two books of revelation, that of nature showing the way to that of Scripture, where then the historical crises of man in nature are more fully illumined.

Shakespeare, by placing his story in primeval times, perhaps wished to suggest to his Elizabethan audience the pit from which they were digged. That is, they could here review the agonizing quest that would be necessary to make progress once again toward Christian mystery, should England ever be deprived of its Christian heritage.[46] In 1606 Shakespeare may have prophetically seen this as a modern possibility, arising from the decay of England's Christian ethos.[47] Should that decay ever engulf the land, Englishmen would have to begin where Lear begins and relearn the meaning of life. Meanwhile, the play *King Lear* might serve as a medicine against such an eventuality, a homeopathic dose of it for the purging of the human soul. That continues to be the play's latent efficacy in our day as well.

VI

The Reshaped
Meaning
of
Coriolanus

Although Shakespeare mentions Coriolanus in 1594 in *Titus Andronicus,* not until about 1608 did he undertake to dramatize the story of this early Roman. By then his turning to it could have been prompted by its pertinence to his own times. An insurrection in the midlands in 1607 by peasants with economic grievances was a sign of the presence in England of class antagonisms not unlike those between the plebs and patricians of the Coriolanus legend.[1] And parallels to other aspects of ancient Rome were evident in English military attitudes and practices. Many an Elizabethan soldier-aristocrat had come to fame by exploits based more on a concern for personal glory than for the welfare of his troops. Moreover, in contemporary books on military matters a Roman austerity and rigor were being commended; and recruiting for war was being used by the government to drain off the social discontent arising from shortages of grain in England.[2] These aspects of the age Shakespeare had already somewhat analogized in his *Henry IV* and *Henry V,* there touching on them as comic ironies—for instance, in Falstaff's dragooning of peasant troops, and in Fluellen's bookish adulation of Roman military usages. The deeper implications of such attitudes, however, could be explored more seriously within the genre of tragedy, especially in a drama distanced appropriately to antique times.

Perhaps, as Kenneth Muir has suggested,[3] Shakespeare found his attention redirected to Coriolanus by some reading in the *Foure Paradoxes, or Politique Discourses* (1604) of Thomas and Dudley

Digges, since one aspect of the Coriolanus story is there treated. Dudley Digges (the stepson of Shakespeare's overseer, Thomas Russell) had devoted his fourth paradox to arguing "That the Antique Roman and Graecian discipline Martiall doth farre exceede in Excellency our Modern." Modern practice, he had urged, should learn from ancient example—particularly as regards the usefulness of foreign war for the curing of domestic broils. In developing this point, Digges had cited "that wise proceeding of the *Senate of Rome* in *Coriolanus* time." Peace had at that time occasioned a famine, he explained, which stirred up "lewd felowes" to exasperate the desperation and envious malice of the common people against the nobility, who in turn had grown so proud, through sloth and luxury, as to condemn and injure the poorer people. Thus a heat of contention had made *"Ex una civitate duas";* the body politic was suffering from a consumption which needed to be purged. The senate therefore, like a good physician, applied a "sovereigne medicine"—one which, in Digges' view, would have well prevented all the causes of trouble if only it had been applied earlier. They resolved on a war with the Volsces, to ease the city of its famine by diminishing the number of its people, and to "appease those tumultuous broyles, by drawing poore with rich, and the meane sort with the Nobilitie, into one campe, one service, and one selfesame daunger: sure meanes to procure sure love and quietnesse in a contentious Commonwealth." From this example Digges inferred a further paradox: "That warre sometimes [is] lesse hurtful and more to be wisht in a well governed State than peace."

Such reasoning, may we comment, has no doubt seemed attractively convincing to some theorists in all ages. It echoes, for instance, in the advice Shakespeare's Henry gave Prince Hal (2 *Henry IV* IV. v. 214) to keep "giddy minds" busy with "foreign quarrels." And even in our twentieth century occasional politicians have resorted to such bleeding of a state as a medicine, hopefully, for curing internal strife. But how good does Shakespeare think this remedy? Its equivocal and short-lived benefit in his *Henry V* suggests, I think, a fraudulent panacea. Does his *Coriolanus,* on the contrary, imply that a foreign war can be a "sure meanes to procure sure love" in a commonwealth? Scarcely so, if we consider the play's underlying irony, its attention to the tragedy of *procured* love.

Yet Digges had developed his thesis out of Plutarch, who had said that Rome's wise men and consuls hoped "by the meanes of forreine warre, to pacifie their sedition at home." They thought it mete—so we read in North's Plutarch—to clear Rome of its mutinous persons, who were its "superfluous ill humours"; and they hoped that putting "the meane sorte with the nobilitie . . . in one campe, and in one service, and in one like daunger" would make them together "more quiet and loving."[4] Shakespeare seems to have been prompted to ask: How truly was this hope fulfilled? By tracing the total Roman story through the lifetime of Coriolanus, Shakespeare's play reveals moral paradoxes not perceived by Plutarch or Digges.

At the outset, without attributing directly to Rome's senate or consuls the policy cited by Digges and Plutarch, Shakespeare lets the patrician-bred Marcius voice it:

> we shall ha' meanes to vent
> Our mustie superfluity.

As thus presented, the idea seems less a theory of the senate's calculating than an impulsive rationalization on the part of one young aristocrat who holds the plebs in contempt. The pride of this hero is such as Digges might have approved, since it has not grown out of any sloth or luxury on his part. It arises, rather, out of a devotion to valor, honor, and excellence. Shakespeare shows Marcius railing at the plebeian mutineers for their cowardice, and taunting them to acquire food by following him to the wars where, as rats, they may gnaw the garners of the Volsces! The plebs, when thus shamed by Marcius' tongue and roused to patriotism by his lure, duly follow him to a victory whose spoils provide a plentiful feasting. Rome's internal strife is thus seemingly cured. Yet Shakespeare lets us see how superficial the remedy is. The war's very success feeds an envy by Rome's tribunes toward Marcius, while at the same time it has fed this hero's paradoxical pride. As if magnanimously, he refuses to accept a greater share of the spoil than the other warriors; yet in doing so he refers to them as spectators, men who merely have "beheld the doing" of *his* sword. And instead of being grateful for their good will, he interprets it as flattery and a bribery "sauced with lies"—insinuating thereby the ineffable excellence of his own singular and sole modesty. Predictably, a Roman unity achieved around this version of love soon ruptures.

As Shakespeare's drama develops, the "sure love" which Digges had supposed procurable through "one camp" enlisted for war is shown to be, at bottom, a love of spoil and pageantry—Rome's legendary appetite for *panis et circenses*. And we see this love taking on whirlpool gyrations. We see the very hero who had justified war as a venting of the state's superfluity turning, under new circumstances, to a venting of his contempt for Rome, and then being himself vented from the city; after which he finds peace for himself in a revenge compact with his former enemy, Aufidius, now linked to him in true love—that is, in their mutual ambition to pour war into the bowels of Rome. Such politic unity, in turn, is shown by Shakespeare to be as unstable as the earlier union of Rome's rival classes. It, too, bursts apart over rivalry once the foreign campaign is halted. What the discipline of warfare has not purged is the *libido dominandi* of its participants. This is a theme Shakespeare had touched on when associating the motifs of rape and war in his early *Lucrece*, although there within a somewhat simpler circumstantial setting.

In *Coriolanus* the Plutarch-Digges thesis is nevertheless given its due, as a comic half-truth, when we overhear the servants of Aufidius voicing it in IV. vi. "Let me have war, say I," remarks one of these servants. "It exceeds peace as far as day does night, it's spritely . . . and *full of vent* [Italics mine]. Peace is a very apoplexy. . . . Aye, and it makes men hate one another." To which his fellow servant replies: "Reason, because they then less need one another." Shakespeare's implicit paradox here is that the need which war supplies in this instance is merely for companions in sport—for allies in the game of ravishing.

Shakespeare's perspective thereby not only remolds but transcends that of Digges or of Plutarch. And how could he have come by his fuller, more penetrating view? One available resource could have been the perspective on Rome which Christian tradition provided, especially in St. Augustine's well-known *City of God*. Although Augustine in his review of Rome's history does not specifically mention Coriolanus, he has a good deal to say regarding the civil dissensions of this early period. Repeatedly he refers to them in connection with his own analysis of Rome's tragic civilization. His comments therefore may provide us a base from which we can launch a further inquiry into Shakespeare's outlook and the import of his fable.

1 An Augustinian perspective

Augustine quotes Sallust's account of how the patricians treated
the people as their slaves, tyrannizing over them just as the kings
had done, until the people in their resentment seceded to Mount
Aventine and thereby obtained tribunes for their protection. He
cites this event in order to comment ironically on Sallust's overall
thesis that in this primitive period Rome was at its fairest and best,
with "equity and virtue" prevailing among its citizens "not more
by force of law than of nature." Can such a thesis be true when, by
Sallust's own admission, dissensions had existed from the beginning? In Augustine's view, the advocates of either party in this
clash, and in subsequent ones between the aristocracy and the plebs,
"were actuated rather by the love of victory than by any equitable
or virtuous consideration." Admirers of Rome, he goes on to say,
"have need to inquire whether, even in the days of primitive men
and morals, true justice flourished in it." Citing Sallust's statement
that after Tarquin's banishment the state "grew with amazing
rapidity" because a great "desire of glory had taken possession of
it," Augustine acknowledges that an eagerness for praise accom-
plishes "many wonderful things, laudable doubtless and glorious
according to human judgment." Yet in these things, he remarks,
liberty alone was not the goal but added to it domination and war
for the sake of display of valor. Rome's heroes suppressed desire of
wealth and many other vices—but for the sake of "this one vice,
namely, the love of praise," which the Romans accounted a virtue.
The Romans, indeed, have continued to think that it ought to be
excited and kindled up, supposing it beneficial to the republic; thus
even Cicero has recommended that the "education of a chief of
state" be nourished on love of glory, since through this desire
Rome's ancestors did illustrious things. But Augustine calls Cicero's
opinion a "poisonous" one because it has led the Romans to build
temples to Virtue and Honor (thus "worshipping as gods the gift
of God"), and has fed their desire for an "insane pomp of human
glory," in which "they have received their reward." They have
merited fame through war, and even have brought some good to
the unjust peoples whom they have subjugated. Yet the victories of
which they boast have been "not the substantial joys of the happy,

but the empty comforts of wretched men, and seductive incitements to turbulent men to concoct disasters upon disasters."[5]

The vigor of Augustine's critique must be understood, of course, in the light of his own contemporary purpose of apologetic. He is arguing for a Christian world view as the needed answer to Rome's ills. His definition of Rome's tragic flaw is therefore trenchant and thorough. But also it is balanced by Augustine's own pity for Rome's tragedy, and by his quasi-admiration for the zeal of the Romans in their devotion to a merely relative and shadow good. It is further qualified by his recognition of the "well nigh" to Christian virtue of occasional humble Romans, such as Regulus, Cincinnatus, and Fabricius—for whom Shakespeare's equivalents may be Cominius and Titus Lartius. Thus qualified and proportioned, Augustine's view has remained the traditional Christian one,[6] and Shakespeare can scarcely have been ignorant of it.

In fact, the play *Coriolanus* provides much evidence that Augustine's estimate of Rome's typical shortcomings was shared by Shakespeare. The drama's various additions to Plutarch's story—for instance, the role of Volumnia in training her son in a love of human glory, and later her tempter's role at the tragedy's very middle (with no warrant from Plutarch)—indicate on Shakespeare's part a perspective on Roman civilization not unlike Augustine's. Further, the victory of which the Romans boast in Act II of the play does indeed prove to be a seductive incitement to turbulent men (to the envious Tribunes, to the ambitious Volumnia, and to Coriolanus himself) to concoct, unwittingly, disaster upon disaster. It therefore seems to me wholly likely that Shakespeare brought to his reading of Plutarch an Augustinian clue for the reunderstanding of Coriolanus and his times. Too easily in the past have many scholars, although not all, been prone to agree with Tucker Brooke's judgment (made in 1909), that Shakespeare's figure of Coriolanus "is taken from North practically unchanged," and that Shakespeare's political views are "closely paralleled by those of Plutarch." Curiously, Brooke offered this judgment despite his awareness that "seven at least" of the scenes in *Coriolanus* "show only the very barest traces, if any, of Plutarchan influence."[7] More recent examination of these invented scenes, and of Shakespearean alterations elsewhere, has begun to modify this older view, but with no wholly satisfactory alternative emerging to replace it. An Augustinian perspective can perhaps therefore help us.

We do not know exactly when Shakespeare first became acquainted with North's translation of Plutarch's *Lives*. Perhaps, as T. J. B. Spencer surmises,[8] he dipped into the beginning pages of this huge folio volume for information on Theseus while at work on *A Midsummer Night's Dream*, but then postponed further explorings until about the time he was writing on *Henry V*, in which a comic parallel between the lives of England's Harry and Greece's Alexander appears in Fluellen's talk. Let us note, however, that Fluellen's "learned" dabbling in the Plutarchan method of parallel biography implies that Shakespeare found it (by 1599) voguish enough to parody. And the fact that Shakespeare here makes comic fun of Plutarch's method may imply that he had some reservations as to its adequacy, perhaps judging its philosophic premises to be somewhat shallow. I think we can say that his own *Julius Caesar*, begun in the same year, gives evidence that he had been reading Plutarch with an eye to getting below and around Plutarch's sandwich-style moralized portraits. Then about eight years later, in *Antony and Cleopatra*, followed immediately by *Coriolanus*, we see Shakespeare engaged in refashioning still more of Plutarch's Roman subject matter.

The increasing attention being given to Roman history by Shakespeare's contemporaries could have provided an incentive. Ben Jonson had published his *Sejanus* in 1605; Marston his *Sophonisba* in 1606; and Thomas Heywood's *Lucrece* (though probably staged much earlier) reached print in 1608. Perhaps, in particular, this published *Lucrece* served to remind Shakespeare of his own earlier probing into primitive Roman legend and thus nudged him into dramatizing the story which immediately follows Lucrece's in Roman historiography. In any case, his *Coriolanus* of 1608 contains tucked-in references to King Tarquin, along with other details of historical background. Moreover, Shakespeare's care for accuracy with regard to manners and customs in the early republic is scrupulous, as if to rival Ben Jonson's boast of historical learning. Yet Shakespeare's way of using such details is not antiquarian like Jonson's, nor does he didactically adopt, as Jonson did for his "truth of argument," the simplistic moral outlook of the Roman historians. A modern classicist such as Gilbert Highet can praise Shakespeare for having rendered better than anyone else, better even than the sources which he used, the essence of the Roman republic and its aristocracy.[9] Such an accomplishment must have required a superior point of view from which to understand the Roman story.

But if Shakespeare's superior point of view was, as I have suggested, basically an Augustinian one as regards the essence of Rome's civilization under the republic, his poetic art is nonetheless in accord with Aristotle's concern to discern essence within a concrete action, and to reveal it through a significant fiction. Turning therefore to Plutarch for some particular event of magnitude, whose potential form he could develop dramatically, Shakespeare found in the narrative of Coriolanus a convenient subject. He no doubt felt that by deftly altering or adding to Plutarch's details he could universalize more properly this story's ultimate meaning. Aristotle had said that drama should imitate the form of an action as it "ought to be"—that is, as it would be if the action (in tragedy, by convention, a historical action) could fully disclose its innate potential. He had assigned to plot the ordering of episodes "according to the law of probability," in order that the action's final outcome might arise naturally and inevitably by a sequence of causal interrelationships. Shakespeare's sense of what is probable in the action of Coriolanus and in this hero's Roman background is somewhat different from Plutarch's. His drama achieves a more unified and convincing story, sometimes by developing causal factors merely latent in Plutarch's account, other times by improvising wholly new episodes and interrelating these in a way which makes the progress of the action more naturally inevitable. By such poetic deepening, the Coriolanus story becomes under Shakespeare's revision the tragedy of an ethos.[10] It carries thus a quality of parable for the Elizabethan age, and for all time.

2 Three other perspectives transcended

Apart from Augustine's general perspective on Roman history, what sources of more immediate information on Coriolanus could have been available to an Elizabethan dramatist? And what interpretation did these accounts carry? Some brief survey of the variant readings of Coriolanus which had developed in the course of the centuries may be helpful to our understanding of the critical problem Shakespeare faced, and may help illuminate, as well, the debates among critics in our own day as to the meaning and success of Shakespeare's version.

We have remarked that Shakespeare fictionalizes history for the sake of a deeper truth. But a similar motive, it can be said, lies behind the earliest Roman versions of the legend. The Annalists of the second century B.C., who first worked Coriolanus into their chronicles of the Rome of about 500 B.C., drew heavily on their own latter-day customs and interests to embellish a contemporary meaning. Modern historians point out, for example, that in the developed legend the power of the tribunes and the practice of distributing grain are elements which belong not to primitive Rome, but more properly to the period of the Gracchan revolution in the second century B.C.; that the bestowing of surnames for valor cannot be attested earlier than the third century; and that the story of Coriolanus' taking refuge with Aufidius is probably an invention modelled on a similar story regarding Themistocles of Athens. About the only early fact the Annalists had to build on, most modern scholars think, was a general memory of an early period of famine and wars, to which popular storytelling added various accretions.[11]

Our earliest extant accounts of Coriolanus come from later Roman writers, from Cicero onwards, who drew as they wished from the now lost accounts of the early Annalists. And it is worth noting that these later writers offer various and differing evaluations of Coriolanus. We can discriminate, in fact, three major schools of interpretation.[12] Cicero's two references to Coriolanus (in a letter of 49 B.C. and in the *De Amicitia* of 44 B.C.) point to him as an example of treason and condemn him as "impious." This Ciceronian view can be found later in Aulus Gellius, in Lucius Ampelius, and in Eutropius. But in Livy's history (about 20 B.C.) we find an admiring view of Coriolanus, and the first extended account of him. Since Livy's purpose was to glorify the pristine virtue of Roman heroes of a golden past, his portrait stresses the greatness of Coriolanus as· a military leader and his later generosity in sparing Rome when petitioned by his mother and family. Rome's banishing of its hero is interpreted by Livy as a political misfortune, caused by a commons spitefully "set upon mischief" and by tribunes hostile to the patricians, whose cause Coriolanus had sought to advance. Close to Livy's patrician view is that of the Greek historian Dionysius of Halicarnassus in his *Roman Antiquities* (about 7 B.C.).[13] Here too Coriolanus is pictured as the noble victim of ambitious tribunes and a base rabble, and as a man who showed affectionate duty to his mother by relinquishing revenge on Rome. Livy had pictured Coriolanus as living on in exile till old age. Dionysius heightens the pathos by telling of a death by stoning by a Volscian faction—a sad fate for this magnificent Roman, who "is still praised and celebrated by all as a pious and just man." This evaluation, which is contrary to Cicero's as noted above, echoes in later accounts by Valerius Maximus (about 30 A.D.) and by Appian (about 150 A.D.). But a third view appears in Plutarch's *Parallel Lives*, in which each great man's virtues are weighed against his vices, as if to cast up a ledger and arrive at some moral score. Thus Plutarch applauds, on the one hand, the military exploits of Coriolanus, while on the other hand criticizing him for arrogance toward Rome's populace. Plutarch's balanced portrait is clearly the most adequate, as it is also the fullest in detail, of all the ancient accounts. Its deficiencies we shall be noting as our essay proceeds.

But first a word about interpretations of Coriolanus in Renaissance times. As might be expected, we can here again find samples of each of the three variant perspectives which antiquity had developed. The Ciceronian tradition lives on in William Painter, whose *Palace of Pleasure* (1566) cites Coriolanus as an instance of a man who abused the Roman state by his traitorous plot with the Volscians; and this is the view adopted likewise by La Primaudaye, whose *French Academie* (1586) discusses Coriolanus in a chapter entitled "Of Seditions." Livy's eulogizing view, on the other hand, has its Elizabethan advocate in Ludovic Lloyd, who in his *The Consent of Time* (1590) pictures Coriolanus as an honorable warrior banished for his virtues.[14] Earlier, Boccaccio had taken this view, and Lydgate had parroted it in *The Fall of Princes*, emphasizing also the great mercy of Coriolanus in later sparing the city.[15] The Plutarchan perspective can be found, however, in Golding's translation of the *Politicke, Moral, and Martial Discourses* (1595) of Jacques Hurault. This work moralizes more forcefully even than does Plutarch on the ruin Coriolanus brought on himself by his choler and pride. Shakespeare thus had available alternate interpretations to adjudicate between—or to transcend by his own higher synthesis.

This situation warrants mention, because among reactions by modern critics to Shakespeare's own version there have been positions taken which in a general way continue the three outlooks noted above. On the one hand, we have interpreters who much admire Coriolanus, attracted especially by his aristocratic bearing, and who therefore read Shakespeare as locating the cause of the tragedy in the hero's unworthy environment rather than in any initial flaw in him.[16] They reject the notion that Coriolanus displays any sin of egoism, and see in him instead a kind of goodness too noble to compromise with a base and ignoble world. Essentially this interpretation resembles Livy's. At the opposite pole, however, is a second group of readers to whom the behavior of Coriolanus seems so egregiously faulty as to make him, in O. J. Campbell's phrase, "partly an object of scorn."[17] He is a subject for satire, they believe, rather than for tragedy. He so alienates our sympathy, they insist, that an audience can only view him with detachment. Is not this view similar to Cicero's attitude of moral reprobation? It overlooks the testimony, noted above, of those other modern readers who feel no such aversion of sympathy. The Plutarchan perspective, which attempts a mediating stance, can be found in a third modern camp. Here we may instance Bullough's view that Coriolanus is a glorious patriot ruined by "his lack of Henry V's affability," with the result that he excites both our admiration and our disapproval, a "balanced judgment."[18] William Rosen's recent commentary likewise reflects this evaluation. In Rosen's view, Shakespeare's Coriolanus is a portrait built on balancing estimates of the hero, in this respect an expansion of Plutarch's method. Shakespeare used this approach, Rosen thinks, in order to show us with dispassionate analysis a hero who "achieves perfect virtue in war, [but] cannot live successfully in time of peace."[19]

Yet it is significant that Rosen, after reading Coriolanus in a Neo-Plutarchan light, finds the play as a whole unsatisfying: "we are continually put in a position," he complains, "of judging and evaluating" the protagonist, rather than being able to feel in rapport with him. Our sympathy and compassion are held in check, he believes; and in confirmation of this reaction he cites Granville-Barker's comment that Shakespeare has treated Coriolanus "as a judge might, without creative warmth," and A. C. Bradley's feeling that the hero's faults "chill our sympathy." Bradley's attempted explanation, shared in part by Rosen, was that North's Plutarch here so constricted Shakespeare's talents that "his whole power in tragedy could not be displayed." Is this explanation really credible? Is it likely that the vastly experienced Shakespeare of 1608 would

allow his own craft in tragedy to be spoiled by deferring to Plutarch's method or perspective? Perhaps, rather, a full appreciation
of Shakespeare's play must depend upon our being able to see
clearly how he bettered Plutarch—first of all as a moralist, by tracing alike the faults and the virtues of Coriolanus to an underlying
idealism, a grandly misguided idealism; and at the same time as
dramatist, by enlisting our pity and fear for the progressively
emergent self-destructiveness of that idealism.

The "only cause" of Coriolanus' misfortune, says Plutarch in a
final "Comparison of Alcibiades with Martius Coriolanus," was
"the austeritie of his nature, and his hawtie obstinate minde." By
"austeritie" Plutarch means a stern rudeness of manner. By
haughty obstinacy he means much the same thing: a lordly in-
solence. As he explains in the biography itself, when commenting
on the impatience of Coriolanus on being rejected for the consul-
ship, this showed a man too full of "passion and choller" and too
much given to "over selfe will and opinion." In short, Coriolanus
lacked the "affabilitie that is gotten with judgment of learning and
reason." Plutarch implies that the hero's faults were accidental evils
of excess, to which an inherently good nature is liable unless dis-
ciplined by education. He likens them to the weeds which can crop
up alongside the herbs in a rich but unmanured soil. The "naturall
wit and great harte" of Marcius he finds praiseworthy; it stirred up
a courage to do and attempt notable acts. The honor given those
acts, he says, quickened a manly appetite to show a daily increase of
valiantness. Men marvelled that Marcius was "never overcome with
pleasure, nor money," and endured easily all manner of pains and
travails. But on the other hand, Marcius had never been taught "by
compasse and rule of reason" to be civil and courteous, and to like
"the meane state" better than the higher. This defect was due, in
Plutarch's view, to his having been left an orphan by his father. On
balance, therefore, Plutarch offers as the story's moral that although orphanage brings many "discommodities" to a child, it does
not hinder him from excelling in "vertue above the common sorte."

How does Shakespeare's portrait differ? In many ways which we
shall be discerning as this chapter proceeds. But to begin with, let
us note a point well argued by Willard Farnham: that Shakespeare
has "changed radically" the nature of the combination of good and
bad qualities.[20] Instead of keeping the two sets separate, says Farnham, Shakespeare has bound them more closely together, making

them "seemingly inseparable and even seemingly interdependent." He has made them, in fact, paradoxical aspects of an underlying pride. This pride is something more deeply rooted than the haughty obstinacy of which Plutarch speaks, and it brings in its train a deep-seated wrath. For Plutarch, the "vehemencie of anger and desire of revenge" with which Coriolanus was carried away when sentenced to banishment is attributed simply to choler; it showed, he said, that the choleric man can be "so altered, and mad in his actions, as a man set afire by a burning agewe." But Shakespeare closely relates the hero's anger, both here and on earlier occasions, to a pride which is at the very basis of his self-respect and sense of worth. The hero's apparent virtues—his valor, honesty, and refusal to flatter—are likewise grounded in this pride. It inspires his righteous indignation at human baseness and the resistance he offers to the temptation to dissemble. But with all its apparent excellence, this pride nourishes defects too. "There is no sign," says Farnham, "that this man of proud virtue is *ever* led to be noble in spirit by a natural love for *all* that constitutes nobility of spirit. Thus is raised the delicate question *whether the virtue of Coriolanus is in truth worthy of admiration,* since it is dependent upon something so vicious as his pride" (Italics mine).

Plutarch had never raised any such question, and it is indeed a delicate one. It is possible for us to raise it, I think, because our own sense of "all that constitutes nobility of spirit" is a latently Christian one, as is likewise our sense of the dimensions of pride. At least many in Shakespeare's audience could have had this sense, and the poet himself could make use of it to give the Roman legend a more credible moral structure than Plutarch as pagan moralist could quite formulate. This is not to say that Shakespeare put any Christian doctrines into the heads of any of the Roman persons of his story. It is to say rather that the actual facts of the Roman story, as involving universal truths of human nature, are more fully conceivable when we come to them with a Christian perspective (as, for example, Augustine did), and that aided by such perspective a dramatist can present the moral grain of Roman experience with more subtlety (and a more coherent showing of the "probable" pattern of causation) than any Roman author could discern in his own civilization's story.[21]

But if we read the pride of Coriolanus as in the Christian sense a deadly sin, is there not also another sense in which this same pride is at the root of those noble deeds for which Coriolanus wins public acclamation from his fellow citizens at the end of Act I, and the approval of Plutarch as well? This is the problem that troubles Farnham, who finds in it a bewildering paradox: a Coriolanus who is "supremely guilty of pride the vice and at the same time supremely noble in pride the virtue." The proper resolution of this paradox, I believe, lies in understanding Augustine's concept of *splendid* vice—that is, of action that is quasi-admirable because nobly ignoble. Lacking this Augustinian clue, Farnham finds Coriolanus so puzzling that he concludes by calling the whole play "a magnificent failure." A noble hero so deeply flawed, he asserts, takes tragedy into an area "beyond the effective reach of merely human pity," thus destroying tragic validity.

In testimony against this charge of failure, we might cite T. S. Eliot's opinion that *Coriolanus,* along with *Antony and Cleopatra,* is Shakespeare's "most assured artistic success."[22] Or, as against the charge that this play's hero repels pity, there is M. W. MacCallum's testimony in his classic study of the Roman plays:

> Shakespeare glorifies Coriolanus in the same way that he glorifies Hamlet or Brutus or Antony. That is, he appreciates their greatness and explains their offenses so that we sympathize with them. . . .[23]

Farnham's negative reaction to Coriolanus can be traced partly at least to his prior assumption that Hamlet and Brutus are heroes in a quite different category—in his view not deeply flawed, not guilty of sins but of mistakes merely, and never led by their flaws "into the doing of evil." In contrast to these heroes of "incorruptible heart," he finds Coriolanus "monstrously deficient as a human being." But I regard this contrast as untenable. Do not all of Shakespeare's tragic heroes exhibit deep moral paradox? Hamlet from his own point of view has a strong sense of moral duty; yet a Hamlet who longs to "fatten all the region's kites" with the carcass of his country's king can scarcely be (I would think) any less sinful than a Coriolanus who would burn an unworthy Rome. Both are prideful justicers, championing revenge on the ground of personal honor. Each has deficiencies as a human being; and these stem, not principally from melancholy or choler or obstinacy, but from the kind of greatness desired as life's ideal. Each loves, in a self-centered way, his own virtue and honor. From this motive spring actions which can be admired as virtuous from one perspective but not from another. And if in *Hamlet* there is the hero's piety toward his father, which can attract our sympathy and make him seem like us (Aristotle's stipulation), there is similarly in *Coriolanus* the hero's piety toward his mother. Yet both these forms of piety, as we watch their emerging consequences, make us question the moral validity of such piety. Insofar as we recognize similar pieties in us, our own pieties come under judgment. They are instances of virtue misdirected and turned vice, but dignified by actions that yield some measure of earthly benefit even in their deficiency. Human virtue misapplied to self-honor is a proper matter for our pity and fear.

3 The paradox of a dragon god

I have been suggesting that a tragedy succeeds best when its audience can respond with a combination of sympathy and detachment. An auditor should feel (at least eventually, after reflection) that the hero is noble enough to be admired, yet mistaken enough not to be emulated. The hero's virtues should, by their splendor, elicit in us at least some degree of empathy arising from a potential likemindedness in us, while at the same time we withhold full identification because we sense, perhaps at first only dimly, ominous danger signals in the use the hero is making of his virtues. Thus we are held in tension between allure and caution, in an appreciative fearsomeness that grows toward awesome pity as the implications of the hero's flaw begin to loom as both monstrous and ruinous. Shakespeare's *Coriolanus*, it seems to me, is constructed to arouse and develop such a tension in our emotional experience.

By what dramatic considerations does Shakespeare elicit our sympathy for Coriolanus? Chiefly by his directing our attention at the outset to the hero's social context, in particular to the environing presence of less noble citizens. Their cruder forms of selfishness can make the hero's own prideful virtue seem admirable by comparison. Thus the play opens with a mutiny by the citizens, against which the hero's contemptuous words seem almost justified. We tend to discount, as being the cry of a demagogue, the First Citizen's charge (stronger than any in Plutarch) that "Caius Marcius is chief enemy to the people." For when this judgment is followed by "Let us kill him, and we'll have corn at our own price," the baseness of this proposal highlights, by contrast, the nobler motive which this same Citizen assigns to Coriolanus in seeking to derogate his services to country: he did them "to please his mother and to be partly proud, which he is, even to the altitude of his virtue." This estimate of the hero's motive—although actually a very accurate one, as the play will later show—seems to us in the present context scarcely damaging to the worth and nobility of Marcius. The seditious pleb, we note, is unable to gainsay a defense offered by the Second Citizen: "You must in no way say he is covetous." Moreover, when later the tribunes complain of the pride of Coriolanus, do not their own faults of jealousy and guile (added to a pride of power which Menenius mocks so trenchantly in II. i) undercut their right to criticize? Their tactics of baiting and of rigged trial in Act III exhibit a treachery which makes almost ludicrous their charging him with treason. Meanwhile, we have been shown pride aplenty among his supporters too. Menenius, although never choleric in his arrogance, is a foolishly vain man and one who, at least in private, views the plebs as rats. Volumnia similarly is proud—not merely of her son's valor and fame, but of her own status as mother, her own claims as counsellor, and her rank as a patrician. Hence, if we are to accuse Coriolanus of pride, we must realize that his cultural environment is riddled with this same vice, only in versions more petty or pretentious, less based on merit or concern for moral virtue than his. Shakespeare has in this respect improvised a good deal of detail not found in Plutarch, in order to establish a social background of moral obliquity, in relation to which the hero's tragic flaw can be more generously assessed and in part extenuated.

Moreover, the very citizens who in the play's opening scene had thought death-worthy the pride of Marcius are shown lauding him to the skies on his return from Corioli. They had called him "a very dog to the commonalty"; but when he returns with victory and spoils from his proud hunt they are enraptured. Crowds cast their garments in his path, as to some Roman messiah. The nobles bend to him "As to Jove's statue." Even the envious Brutus remarks that it is

> As if that whatsoever god who leads him
> Were slyly crept into his human powers,
> And gave him graceful posture.

Aside from the tribunes, all in the city dote on him—all except the First Officer, and Virgilia in her "gracious silence" and tender tears. (Obviously these two are introduced here by Shakespeare for their counterpointing attitude, and Virgilia's loving concern for the human Marcius underneath his mask of bloody honor is especially notable.) Soon, however, this moment of idolization passes. Its afterglow lasts just long enough for the citizens to promise Coriolanus their voices (more explicitly than in Plutarch's story) when he stands for consul; yet they retract these when the foxy tribunes arouse a selfish fear. Giving an uncritical ear to the tribunes, the citizens become a mindless mob, crying "To the rock, to the rock with him." Nevertheless, in Act IV, their attitude turns about once again, moved by renewed admiration: "I ever said we were in the wrong when we banished him . . . So did we all." Significantly, no one in Rome now berates Coriolanus for his pride, and no one criticizes him for having turned traitor to his city. "Who is't can blame him?" asks Cominius; "Your enemies and his find something in him." And Menenius adds:

> If he could burn us all into one coal,
> We have deserved it.

Thus the Coriolanus whom Menenius only one act earlier had conceded to be a diseased limb of the city is now regarded as a noble demigod. The patricians prepare guiltily to kneel to him for mercy, while predicting that the citizens who had hooted him out will soon roar him in again.

As is appropriate to tragedy, this situation carries a rich dramatic irony. For almost the whole city is made up of fearful admirers of the very kind of excellence which now threatens their destruction. Their awe implies that they too have a *libido dominandi,* in which Coriolanus has but outdone them. Cominius, Rome's best general and wisest statesman, comments that this Marcius now leads the Volscians

> like a thing
> Made by some other deity than nature
> That shapes man better.

In comparison to this god-man, Menenius views himself and other Romans as "us brats." Thus among the Romans, no less than among the Volsces, human worth is measured by an ideal of military might: the conqueror is reverenced, the man who can revel in slaughter and spoliation. In the Volscian camp, meanwhile, we are shown how readily a love for such revels can turn former enmity to sudden love, once Marcius offers his valor in their service. We hear a Volscian servant comment that the enmity was but a matter of fashion, and that now, "when they shall see, sir, his crest up again and the man in blood, they will out of their burrows, like conies after rain, and revel all with him." In anticipation of how Coriolanus will "mow all down before him," they are glorifying him "as if he were son and heir to Mars." The fact that he is a turncoat driven by a revenge motive does not trouble them (no more than it does Marcius himself, whom we see attributing his change to "chance, some trick not worth an egg"); what matters is his support for their own dreams of glory (and their support for his). It was on similar grounds that the Romans had idolized Marcius in Act II. And now, in Act V, when haplessly these Romans find him relentless against them, they nevertheless regard his dragon-like proceedings as those of a godlike emperor. "He sits in his state as a thing made for Alexander," says Menenius; "He wants nothing of a god but eternity and a Heaven to throne in."

This moral dilemma of the Romans, let me remark parenthetically, may have been calculated by Shakespeare to challenge the consciences of his own Elizabethan auditors. How many of them —like Fluellen in *Henry V*—were disposed to idolize an Alexander (despite his "rages, and his furies, and his wraths") or to take as their model of greatness "the pristine wars of the Romans"? How many, on the other hand, might recall Spenser's listing of Alexander (in *F. Q.* I. 5. 48) alongside such primitive heroes as Nimrod, Ninus, and Rome's Romulus and Tarquin, as self-doomed victims, all of them, of the ruinous vice of pride? Shakespeare is offering his contemporaries a trap for meditation when dramatizing the pristine awesomeness of Coriolanus, a hero so appealing in his very frightfulness to the Roman (and perhaps Elizabethan) imagination. He is revealing also, however, what Plutarch had not reported of Coriolanus—a humanity turned inhuman by its savage "divinity."

Shakespeare's paradox, that of a beast-man apotheosized, is distinctly one of his major additions to the Plutarchan narrative. Nowhere in Plutarch was Coriolanus likened either to a Mars or to a male tiger. Plutarch had pictured him as choleric but still tactically *human* in his revenge. Thus, for instance, when the Volscian plebs show (in Plutarch) no immediate readiness to follow Coriolanus into war, he and Aufidius together urge a grievance to arouse them; then, in approaching Rome, Coriolanus employs astutely politic considerations, sparing the lands of the patricians in order to foment dissensions in Rome as an aid to his conquest; and finally, when he receives ambassadors from Rome, they come bringing not naked pleas for pardon (as in Shakespeare) but an offer to restore his lands, and he replies with what he calls "honest and just" peace terms.[24] He demands that the Romans "let fall their pride," restore to the Volscians the lands seized from them in war, and agree further to accord the Volscians a freedom in Rome such as had been accorded the Latins. He even grants a thirty-day reprieve for the working out of a settlement. This portrait, that of a shrewd but basically reasonable hero, is far different from the picture which, in Shakespeare's version, Cominius gives when reporting on his fruitless appeal to Coriolanus:

> He was a kind of nothing, titleless,
> Till he had forged himself a name o' the fire
> Of burning Rome.

Fire, rather than peace terms, is this hero's concern. And there is no readiness to spare the patricians:

> His answer to me was
> He could not stay to pick them in a pile
> Of noisome musty chaff. He said 'twas folly,
> For one poor grain or two, to leave unburned,
> And still to nose the offense.

True, we hear later and indirectly of peace conditions contained in a letter, but since no one tells us what they were we infer their utter insignificance as a motive in the action. Shakespeare has deemphasized them, in order to portray a Coriolanus of single-minded revenge, an inhuman and superhuman engine of destruction.

We recognize in this portrait, moreover, a logical completion of the one given us in Act II after the exploits of Marcius at Corioli. There, too, Shakespeare has altered and enlarged on Plutarch's version. Plutarch had reported simply that after the battle Cominius, "in the presence of the whole armie, gave thankes to the goddes for so great, glorious, and prosperous a victorie: then he spake to

Martius, whose valliantnes he commended beyond the moone."
Shakespeare, instead, pictures Cominius giving some impromptu
praise before the army, devoid of thanks to the gods. But then, as a
supplement to the battlefield scene, Shakespeare invents a spectacular Triumphal Entry into Rome. Here we see honor given the
hero *as if himself a god*. And we hear him likened by Cominius to
a planet striking Corioli—thus (in a literal but non-Plutarchan
sense) commended beyond the moon.

In the oration of Cominius as invented by Shakespeare, the valor
for which Coriolanus is praised is detailed in lurid terms. A suprahuman butchery is suggested in the lines:

> From face to foot
> He was a thing of blood, whose every motion
> Was timed with dying cries.

> he did
> Run reeking o'er the lives of men as if
> 'Twere a perpetual spoil.

Yet Cominius in offering this tribute has prefaced it with a qualifying subjunctive:

> It is held
> That valor is the chiefest virtue and
> Most dignifies the haver. If it be,
> The man I speak of cannot in the world
> Be singly counterpoised.

The "If" is our clue to a doubt which Cominius may be repressing,
caught up as he is in the general admiration of the moment, and
brought up as he has been to accept the values conventional in his
society. He is here doing his public duty as the army's official
spokesman, and doing it generously—but we are allowed to see in
him a man of potentially higher ideals than the chief one he is here
lauding.

His description of the ravaging Coriolanus, let us note, is strikingly like the portrait given in *Hamlet* of Pyrrhus, an oversized
Senecan-type hero:

> Head to foot
> Now is he total gules, horridly tricked
> With blood of fathers, mothers, daughters, sons. . . .

And Shakespeare had used similar imagery when introducing, in
another play, the tragedy of the "bloody man" Macbeth:

> For brave Macbeth—well he deserves that name—
> Disdaining fortune, with his brandished steel,
> Which smoked with bloody execution,
> Like valor's minion carved out his passage. . . .

Macbeth had "unseamed" and canonaded all foes, as if with intent
to "bathe in reeking wounds, / Or memorize another Golgotha."
Shakespeare's mention of Golgotha implies his own estimate of
such valor: it is savage and blind. (Compare the connotations of
Golgotha in *Richard II* IV. i. 144.) Shakespeare was aware that
Macbeth's bravery was Roman in kind—if not that of the Roman
fool who commits suicide, yet that of those hardier Romans who
trusted to sword-wielding as if they were suprahuman. So Macbeth
appropriately, like Coriolanus, ultimately meets his death while
breathing out defiance. Of both these soldier-heroes we could say
what Lartius says (in I. iv) of Coriolanus—that he is "Even to
Cato's wish, not fierce and terrible / Only in strokes" but also in
"grim looks" and "thunderlike percussion." But it is evident that
Shakespeare is implying a different evaluation of "Cato's wish"
than does Plutarch in his stamping of Coriolanus with Cato's approval.

A successful soldier but an unsuccessful politician—this seems to
have been Plutarch's estimate of Coriolanus, and it is one often
repeated by modern readers of Shakespeare's play. But it involves
understanding "successful" in an equivocal sense. How successful,
we may ask, is a soldier who fights (in G. Wilson Knight's phrase)
like "a slaying-machine of mechanic excellence"?[25] And how successful a politician can we rate a man who boasts of having drawn
"tuns of blood" from an enemy to whom he then offers services
"Against my cankered country with the spleen / Of all the under-
fiends"? Here is a hero with the spirit of *aut Caesar aut nihil,* who
wills to dominate either by slashing other men or by offering them
his own throat to be cut (the very tactic which the Senecan revenger Richard III had used in winning Anne, and which is used
by three Romans—Caesar, Antony, and Cassius—in *Julius Caesar*).
Yet this is a hero whose name is used by other soldiers "as the grace
'fore meat" (IV. vii. 3). He elicits this reverence, we are told, by
"what witchcraft's in him." Witchcraft it indeed is, by any standard; but to pagan imagination it seems a valid kind of supernatural worth. What Shakespeare has done is to play up the paradox of
a quasi-divine, inhuman superhumanity, as the measure not only

of the hero's tragic ideal but of a whole civilization's confused and blind ethos. The art of tragedy requires that the dramatist make such heroism seem attractive to us. But he will also show, before his play ends, that the victories of which such a hero or such a civilization can boast turn out to be in reality Pyrrhic ones, all self-defeating.

4 The embassy scene

We have been speaking chiefly of the extra dimensions by which Shakespeare amplified the martial virtue of Plutarch's hero, giving it the glory of a metallic brilliance and ironic divinity. But there is also an important complementary aspect: the hero's virtue of filial piety. Here an apparent humanity is being counterpoised for our attention. It is dramatized early in the play when Marcius kneels to his mother on his return from Corioli, and later more climactically when he kneels to her in the embassy scene. These kneelings are Shakespearean additions to Plutarch's account, and they signalize the hero's acknowledgment of an obligation to kin, which the mother can then urge in her embassy pleading. After reminding him, "Thou art my warrior—I holp to frame thee," does she perhaps bring him to regain his more native humanity?

From this scene's very beginning it becomes evident that Coriolanus has repressed, without quite extinguishing, his ties to flesh and blood. Natural impulses of affection and instinct are awakened when he is confronted by a pleading mother, wife, and child. They erode his desperate determination to stand "As if a man were author of himself / And knew no other kin." He begins to feel like an embarrassed player:

> Like a dull actor now
> I have forgot my part and I am out,
> Even to a full disgrace.

In particular, he is aware of being challenged by his mother's kneeling, for his sense of duty to her rests on sanctions inbred from his youth. Can he be so unatural as to let Olympus bow to him? Can he restrain from her a debt of filial duty which her action and later her verbal reminder invoke? Eventually, after she has pled for eighty lines and twice knelt to him, he yields, even though intuiting as he does so that the "happy victory" she has won will prove "most mortal" to himself.

Does his capitulation mark a change into full and proper humanity? Does it involve a basic renovation of character? Distinguished critics have differed in their judging of this matter. In A. C. Bradley's view, Coriolanus has "saved his soul" in yielding to his mother.[26] G. Wilson Knight has written similarly: here love has proved stronger than swords and now "rules this metallic world." The hero "is now purified," says Knight, and both he and his mother for the first time in their lives love purely, achieving a nobility in the bankruptcy of their pride.[27] But D. J. Enright, on the other hand, asks: "Do we not rather feel that it is a victory less of love than of Volumnia's prestige and of her hardness . . . : that the mother has had what is really the last word . . . ?"[28] And Willard Farnham has declared, more forthrightly, that what good she does for her son comes far short of balancing the ill,

> because, though she brings him to the point of saving his native Rome, she cannot bring him to the point of saving his soul as a Roman. She cannot make him reaccept the old allegiance after she has made him turn false to the new, and she cannot even make him feel repentance—not the smallest—for having betrayed Rome in the first place.[29]

Even more recently, Eugene Waith has commented on the rhetorical strategy of Volumnia, which he finds more impressive than the validity of her arguments. Elizabethans, Waith remarks, were "acutely aware of the trickiness of oratory, and eloquence on stage could be a danger-signal as well as a badge of virtue." In the present instance, Waith comments, Volumnia "plays on her son's attachment to her, just as she had done previously when urging on him a course of moderate hypocrisy." Her persuasions reduce him now to a broken man, but has he been ennobled? Volumnia's appeals to nature have melted his valor but lead to his destruction. "Nature, instead of opening a new way to the hero, blocks an old one and teaches him his mortal finitude," nothing more.[30]

That there is something lacking in the hero's quality of mercy in this episode was evident to Plutarch. In his "Comparison of Alcibiades with Martius" he commented that the granting of the women's request by Coriolanus was, to say truly, a grace "very odious and cruell, and deserved no thankes of either partie, to him that did it." For, on the one hand, Coriolanus withdrew his army without the consent of the Volscians, at whose charge the war had been made, and whom he ought to have consulted because of the trust they had reposed in him; and on the other hand his sparing of Rome was done, not at the entreaty of its public ambassadors but solely to gratify the request of his mother. That was "no acte so much to honour his mother with, as to dishonour his contrie by," since it preserved the country "not for love of it selfe," but merely for "the pitie and intercession of a woman." In Plutarch's view, "he had no reason for the love of his mother to pardone his contrie, but rather he should in pardoning his contrie, have spared his mother, bicause his mother and wife were members of the bodie of his contrie and city, which he did besiege." Such comment suggests something less than the purified love which Wilson Knight finds in this scene, or the adult understanding which Dover Wilson sees in it. To Plutarch it suggests a deficient sense of social responsibility in the hero. I shall be commenting, later, on the limitations of Plutarch's ethic of civic sociability. That Shakespeare sees by a deeper standard we may infer from his drama's contrast between the fashionable sociability of Valeria, smart in her civic sophistication, and the retiring habits of Virgilia, stemming from a more gracious love. By either author's standards, however, the capitulation of Coriolanus to his mother falls short of an adequate concern for other people.

Shakespeare seems to invite us to ask: Has this hero taken thought for the plight of his wife and child, if left husbandless by the consequences of his decision? On the other hand, has he yielded out of a motive of love for Rome? When he turns to Aufidius with the comment, "Mine eyes sweat compassion," is there not something equivocal in this compassion? It is prefaced by "And, sir, it is no little thing"—as if the speaker were taking pride in being compassionate. This has the earmarks of a compassion for his own ideal, for his own image of his nobility. Shakespeare more than hints later that no love for Rome has been its motive. We hear Coriolanus justifying his action to Aufidius with a kind of boast:

> I am returned your soldier,
> No more infected with my country's love
> Than when I parted hence.

It is an evasive statement, yet paradoxically true. What he now prides himself for bringing back as a benefit is "no less honor to the Antiates / Than shame to the Romans."

The Antiates understandably have little appetite for an honor which is being imposed on them without their having been consulted in the matter. Enlarging on Plutarch's complaint of dishonor in the episode, Shakespeare shows Aufidius upbraiding Marcius for having never asked the advice of his council of war when yielding to his "nurse's tears." We hear Aufidius complain privately that those tears were cheap and deceitful:

> At a few drops of women's rheum, which are
> As cheap as lies, he sold the blood and labor
> Of our great action.

And more basically, Aufidius resents having been treated all along "as if / I had been mercenary"—no partner, but a servitor of the fame which Marcius has gathered up all to himself. Yet we know that Aufidius has no genuine wish (any more than Coriolanus does) to be a partner; his deeper wish, under a guise of patriotism and honor, is to be (as we would say) top dog. To renew his own fame, he resolves on the death of Marcius (even as Marcius, for a similar reason, had resolved on the destruction of Rome), going about it with tricky rationalizations and half-truths.

May Shakespeare be suggesting in Aufidius an analogy to Volumnia's motives? Was she perhaps, when contending with her son in the embassy scene, dissembling in order to renew her own fame? In her case, this motive could be working subconsciously, rather than (as is evident in Aufidius) from a deliberate envy. Her evading of the fact that she is in effect asking her son's death may indicate a wished-for ignorance on her part, an ignorance necessary to her own self-deception, through which she can triumph. In yielding to her, has not her son made himself a tragic victim of Volumnia's love of honor and of his own love of an imagined magnanimity? Such magnanimity, in turn, although it be nobler than a revenge in the name of honor, is not really charity. I cannot suppose, as Paul Siegel does, that Coriolanus has here exchanged a Hotspur-like concept of honor for the forgiveness of Christian humanism.[31] Actually he has forgiven no one. He has instead yielded to his mother's version of honor as the only natural way to be noble— as necessary, therefore, to his self-esteem. If this be charity, it is of a kind (as Aufidius remarks, V. vi. 11) that empoisons with its alms.

Self-esteem prevails in Coriolanus to the end. He can no better withstand Aufidius' taunt of "boy of tears" than he could Vol-

umnia's taunt of "This fellow had a Volscian to his mother" (which
is paradoxically true if we consider how cruelly she badgers him).
He is like his mother when he breaks out into scolding. Boasting
to Aufidius of his triumph at Corioli, he dares him to "Cut me to
pieces"—a taunt equivalent to Volumnia's dare, "If I cannot persuade thee . . . , thou shalt . . . tread . . . on thy mother's womb."[32]
Such is the fashion of high Roman heroism. Shakespeare has been
emphasizing in these personages of his tragedy a desperate love of
glory. In the hero this love is a cause of misfortune more basic than
the lack of affability which Plutarch had named as chief cause. And
it derives, as Plutarch had not suspected, from the education which
Volumnia has given her son.

The mother's pleading in the embassy scene warrants our close
scrutiny. Of her arguments as reported by Plutarch, several appeal
to Marcius' sense of honor. All of these Shakespeare uses and more
besides. According to Plutarch, she urged that a "gayle deliverie
of all evills" would benefit both countries but be "most honorable
for the Volsces"; and *if* it so come to pass, "thy selfe is thonly au-
thour, and so hast thou thonly honour." This emphasis is developed even more attractively by Shakespeare's Volumnia. The play
shows her proposing that Marcius reconcile both sides, so that each
may

> Give the all-hail to thee, and cry "Be blest
> For making up this peace."

Her confident *may* has here taken the place of *if* as to the outcome.
But at the same time Shakespeare allows a telltale *if* to preface her
proposal: if her suit, she says, might be thought poisonous to
honor, she would not be urging it. Why this defensive preamble?
Surely it is because Shakespeare knows that the whole proposal is a
make-believe argument, which for its success must be masked in
the making.

Do we wonder how Volumnia can possibly take her own proposal seriously in an Italy of dog-eat-dog rivalries? Only by evading
reality under the lure of imagined honor; only by thus dissembling
with herself and with her son. This is the import of the action
Shakespeare is dramatizing, and he has prepared us for it by the
character he gave Volumnia earlier in Act IV, scene ii. There (in
an episode having no source whatever in Plutarch) she had assured
her son:

> I would dissemble with my nature where
> My fortunes and my friends at stake required
> I should do so in honor.

Is not this, then, precisely the task to which she is devoting herself in Act V? Her friends now are at stake, and she has a chance to make her fortune by dissembling with her nature in the name of honor. In Act III she had sought to complete her son's education by urging:

> If it be honor in your wars to seem
> The same you are not, which, for your best ends,
> You adopt your policy, how is it less or worse
> That it shall hold companionship in peace
> With honor . . .

Now, in the embassy scene, she is urging him to seem (i.e., to see himself as) a reconciler (something he, indeed, is not), and to adopt that as his policy for his own postulated "best end" of fame and honor. And while urging this she is hiding as best she can, probably subconsciously, the fact that she herself is but seeming to be a suppliant—whereas in reality she is battling to establish her authority over him for her own best end of honor for herself.

Honor is the guise under which Volumnia argues; it is also the lure with which she argues. She warns her son that if he conquers Rome his chronicle will be thus writ:

> "The man was noble,
> But with his last attempt he wiped it out,
> Destroyed his country, and his name remains
> To the ensuing age abhorred."

Shakespeare is letting her elaborate on an argument reported by Plutarch, but he has her add a touch of flattery not in Plutarch's account:

> Thou hast affected the fine strains of honor,
> To imitate the graces of the gods . . .

And this provides her a preface for the question (reported in Plutarch): "Think'st thou it honorable for a noble man / Still to remember wrongs?" Here Volumnia is invoking the virtue of magnanimity, as a reason for her son's duty to show her a courtesy. In Plutarch's version, however, this duty is spoken of at first in general terms, as a noble man's duty of gratitude to "parent" and "countrie"; and then there is mentioned as its corollary the son's duty to grant "without compulsion" his mother's "reasonable request" (presumably for the country). By contrast, in Shakespeare's version Volumnia appeals directly to the duty which "To a mother's part belongs." Shakespeare is making explicit the thrust of her demand for honor to her. Moreover, he has her add upbraidings ("he lets me prate / Like one i' the stocks"), and a self-flattering reminder of her own labors for his honor ("she, poor hen, fond of no second brood, / Has clucked thee to the wars and safely home, / Loaden with honor"). Then Shakespeare has her say: "Down, ladies, let us shame him with our knees." It is the second time Volumnia has knelt in this scene, both times with the purpose of shaming her son into yielding. No such connotation is present when Plutarch says: "And with these wordes, her selfe, his wife and children, fell downe upon their knees before him." Shakespeare has designed for the total scene a meaning Plutarch had not understood.

There were perhaps among Shakespeare's auditors a few who, on hearing Volumnia's use of the hen image, would have recalled its wholly different use in Matthew 23:37: "Jerusalem, Jerusalem . . . How often would I have gathered thy children together, as the henne gathereth her chickens under her wings, and ye woulde not" (Geneva version). A true hen protects her children from the hawk. Since Volumnia, instead, has in fact reared her child to be a hawk (an osprey), who (in IV.v) has called his city one of "kites and crows," her terming herself a "poor" hen is Shakespearean irony. Christ's use of the hen image derives from Psalm 91:4, where it figures God's longing to protect His children. It may be pertinent to recall Thomas More's commentary:

> And how often like a loving hen He clucketh home even
> those chickens of His that wilfully walk abroad into the
> kite's danger, and will not come at His clucking. But ever
> the more He clucketh for them, the farther they go from
> him. (*A Dialogue of Comfort* II. 10)

Insofar as this biblical aura of associations might be evoked in a playgoer listening to Volumnia's diction, the irony of her posing as a pious hen would be the more evident.

Plutarch had pictured the ladies as frequenting the temples of the gods for prayer before undertaking their embassy as a "noble device" inspired "by some god as I thinke." When some "god above" inspired the modest Valeria, she with other ladies proposed the embassy to the passively grieving Volumnia and Virgilia; together they then acted "for the safetie of our countrie." But Shakespeare omits any mention of ladies at prayer, and along with it Plutarch's elaborate account of Valeria's being prompted by the gods. He allows us to infer that Volumnia rather than Valeria has proposed the embassy, and he keeps its inspiration problematic.[33] All we hear is the rumor reported by Cominius:

> all hope is vain
> Unless his noble mother, and his wife,
> Who, as I hear, mean to solicit him
> For mercy to his country.

May not this embassy's solicitation, at least in the mother's case, be motivated partly by a desire to outdo the men as ambassadors? Unlike the version in North's Plutarch, there has been no previous embassy of bishops and priests—unless we reckon Menenius as Shakespeare's ironic equivalent. Following up Menenius, Volumnia acts like a self-delegated Mother Priestess on the city's behalf, marshalling her acolytes in the name of household pieties.

One important aspect of the scene has been well commented on by H. C. Goddard.[34] He sees the largely silent Virgilia and her innocent child as more effective in the success of the embassy than the loquacious Volumnia. He points out that at the approach of the women it is Virgilia's "dove's eyes" and the boy's "aspect of intercession" which affect Coriolanus most powerfully. Also, whereas in Plutarch "first he kissed his mother and embraced her a pretie while" (although his wife came first in the procession), Shakespeare's Coriolanus kisses first his wife. Moreover, he turns to his mother only after referring to Virgilia as "Best of my flesh" and commenting on the sweetness of her kiss. Then a moment later he turns to another solicitor, "Dear Valeria," and hails her as "The moon of Rome," chaste as the icicle from purest snow that hangs on Diana's temple. His confession that instinct is melting his role of tyrant comes well in advance of his mother's oration and its reasons. And those reasons receive for a long while no visible response, thus forcing Volumnia to invoke repeatedly her son's attention to wife and child for support to her petition.

Goddard is probably right that Volumnia's attendants, rather than she, touch the hero's humanity most deeply. But the decision this hero then makes seems to me to owe its form and conscious motive to Volumnia. I discern two forces at work in the scene: Great Nature, and additionally man's second nature, custom—which is nature as fashioned by human art or artifice. Of this latter, the mother is spokesman and symbol. And it is to her that Coriolanus attributes his yielding, crying out "O Mother, Mother! What have you done?" Thus although his wife is associated in his mind with "dove's eyes," and Valeria with the moon, the mother looms higher than these two in his firmament of conscious values. He associates her with Olympus, and the stars, and the sun! Hence, significantly, he has turned from the wife to kneel to mother. And from then on, his mother's voice—as embodied in personage, speech, and action—subjects him to a two-pronged discipline: on the one hand, her rebuke for his filial impiety; on the other hand, her dangling the lure of a public worship that may be his if he grants her suit. Using this stick-and-carrot strategy, Volumnia dominates the scene. And her crowning device is to set before his eyes four kneelers jointly petitioning him.

Even Virgilia has been cajoled into participating in this final spectacle—a shaming one in a sense of which she is unaware. For by her yielding to Volumnia's "Down . . . Down," Virgilia has unwittingly compromised her dignity as wife, which earlier in the scene she was so graciously maintaining. The meeting had opened with her own simple-hearted greeting to Coriolanus: "My lord and husband." When to this he had replied solicitously, "These eyes are not the same I wore in Rome"—meaning, we infer, that they are now tearful—her gentle apology had been: "The sorrow that delivers us thus changed / Makes you think so." Then, during the remainder of the scene, she had been almost wholly silent. Letting Volumnia take over the managing of the embassy, Virgilia had stood weeping as if aloof from Volumnia's tactics,[35] never so much as flattering her husband with the adjective "noble." Virgilia's one interjection into the suit had come when Volumnia offered as a dare her mother's womb to be trodden on, if Rome were invaded. Virgilia then interjected:

> Aye, and mine,
> That brought you forth this boy, to keep your name
> Living to time.

Here her appeal to remember his child, through whom he can best preserve a living name, is on a tack different from Volumnia's. Yet coming where it does, as if in support of Volumnia's dare, it involves an inadvertent collaboration. And this prepares the way for Virgilia's yielding, a moment later, to the kneeling which Volumnia proposes. Perhaps Shakespeare's point is that eyes dimmed by tears can be shortsighted in a moment of crisis. We have known, from the beginning of the play, that Virgilia within her own household has been overshadowed by the mother-in-law. But now she has been brought, so to speak, under this mother's roof. For now the dove-like devotion of Virgilia, with its gracious power to revive a humanity in Coriolanus, has been diverted by Volumnia to support a framed mode of mercy.

A group kneeling is the only kneeling reported by Plutarch, who saw its motive as pure supplication. Livy had reported no kneeling at all; and neither he nor Plutarch gave the wife any speeches whatever in this scene. Shakespeare alone appreciates the tragedy of the kneeling and of Virgilia's participation in it. Yet most commentators have overlooked the sinister underside of Volumnia's success. Goddard by doing so can conclude that she becomes "genuinely maternal" in her embassy. Coriolanus, he writes, "never had a mother till this moment." Perhaps so—by Rome's or Plutarch's canons of motherhood. But would Shakespeare's Elizabethan auditors have approved without qualm such motherhood?

May not at least some of them have judged maternal love by a traditional Christian model, that of the biblical Mary? Mary's meekness—which Dante noted (*Purg.* XV) in her gentle questioning, "My son, why . . .?" and which at other times was evidenced by a silent suffering—defines a norm far different from Volumnia's. Early in the play, Shakespeare has shown Volumnia rejoicing to see "the only son of my womb" prove himself a man by coming home with "brows bound with oak." Now in the embassy scene she is shown invoking this son's duty to her womb—for a sacrifice which he senses will be most mortal. By persuading him to it, he says, she deserves to have a temple built to her. But may not Shakespeare intend us to see here a blind analogue to Christian story? Volumnia is an unwitting parody of Mary, who reverenced the fruit of her womb, her son, instead of asking for womb-worship. The womb-centeredness of Rome is correlative with its belly-centeredness, of

which I shall speak later in this chapter. The theory of G. Wilson
Knight, that drama is an "expanded metaphor," can apply in ways
which might surprise Knight himself.

5 A harlot-mother's triumph

Scarcely fifty lines after Volumnia's mission Shakespeare gives us
evidence, marginally at least, that he is reading her triumph by the
light of a bibilical symbolism. Plutarch had mentioned Rome's
opening of its temples to give sacrifice to the gods, then for the
honoring of the ladies a decree that a temple be built to Fortuna,
as the ladies requested. Shakespeare instead invents a triumphal
entry, accompanied by salutations which in effect parody those of
Palm Sunday gospel. A messenger reports:

> The trumpets, sackbuts, psalteries, and fifes,
> Tabors and symbols and the shouting Romans,
> Make the sun dance. Hark you!

These lines carry an allusion, as Richmond Noble has pointed
out,[36] to the list of musical instruments thrice named by Daniel in
his account of Nebuchadnezzar's ceremonies.

This Babylonian king, having set up a golden image, commanded everyone to fall down and worship it "when ye heare the
sounde of the cornet, trumpet, harpe, sackbut, psalterie, dulcimer,
and all instruments of music" (Daniel 3:5, Geneva version). The
story is one of the best known in the Bible, where it functions as a
paradigm of the false worship celebrated by heathen rulers. Shakespeare, by glancing at it, may be indicating to us the Babylonish
nature of Rome's ceremony invoked for the ladies.

And particularly for the lady Volumnia—for it is she who is
chiefly adored. Menenius hails her as worth a cityful of consuls. A
senator then adds:

> Behold our patroness, the life of Rome!
> Call all your tribes together, praise the gods,
> And make triumphant fires, strew flowers before them:

The pronoun "them" is appropriately ambiguous here, referring
equally to the ladies and to the gods whom they are regarded as
representing. Shakespeare does not record, as Plutarch had done,

the actual building of a Roman temple to Fortuna Muliebris. Instead he has dramatized the Roman worship of feminine Fortune as imaged in Volumnia.

Did Shakespeare perhaps remember Augustine's jibe at Fortuna Muliebris in *City of God* IV. 18? Comparing this goddess with an earlier one, Felicitas, whom the Romans had largely neglected, Augustine remarks: "Let the bad worship her [Fortuna Muliebris], who do not choose to have merit by which the goddess Felicitas might be invited"; and he adds (Ch. 23) that the Romans might better have found in Felicitas a goddess, who alone would have sufficed in place of their veneration of many gods. This evaluation, of course, could have been mediated to Shakespeare by Christian sources subsequent to Augustine.

Since in Christian lore Fortune is a strumpet, and since Shakespeare has associated Volumnia with "some harlot's spirit" in Act III when Coriolanus first yielded to her arguments, may we not regard this mother's final triumph, perhaps, in one other light—as the triumph of the great harlot? It is at least possible, I think, that Shakespeare understood it as such—although of course without breaking his dramatic illusion to allow any Roman to suspect this meaning. His Elizabethan audience, however, was made up of people who almost daily were bombarded by polemical references to the whore of Babylon. To Protestants she signified the Roman Catholic church; to more accurate students of Scripture, she signified a cultish paganism in ancient Rome. How many Elizabethans would have been able to recognize her, if her "genius" appeared in a Roman play in the Globe theatre? It is a tantalizing question.

Chapter 17 of the book of Revelation begins: "Come I will show you the great harlot who is seated upon many waters." For the Apocalyptist, as I assume Shakespeare knew, this harlot symbolized the diabolic within Roman civilization.[37] Verse 5 calls her "Babylon the great, mother of harlots and of earth's abominations." Further, we are told that she rides on a beast with many heads (verse 15). Thus supported, she "makes war on the Lamb" (verse 14). Is not this imagery relevant to Shakespeare's play? We have heard Coriolanus called a "bear" that simulates a "lamb"; and (in IV. i) he has characterized Rome as a "beast / With many heads [which] butts me away"; and a moment later he has likened himself to a "lonely dragon" going to a fen, his watery marsh. Figuratively, then, does not this whole civilization—of which Coriolanus is one of its would-be heads and finally its most threatening head—constitute a many-headed beast, a kind of sea monster with a multitude of "voices" as changeable as the watery Fortune it revels in?[38] When at the play's end this beast hails as its patroness the woman Volumnia, is she not the woman of Revelation, mistress of the beast? Theologians have often explained fornication in a metaphorical sense—a fornication of the human mind with its own fancies, to the neglect of living truth. Is such meaning inapplicable to Volumnia? In Revelation 18:4, a "voice from heaven" cries with reference to the harlot: "Come out of her my people, lest you take part in her sins." This sentiment, I think, could well have been Shakespeare's as he contemplated Volumnia.

With this interpretation in mind, let us review her total career as Shakespeare has sketched it, noting especially how it departs from Plutarch's account. Plutarch had given the mother no important role until the embassy. Earlier than that, he had reported of her no speeches. We are told merely that she was a widow whom her son delighted to honor, that he established his wife and family in her house, and that before going into banishment he came home to comfort the weeping and shrieking women. According to Plutarch, the son's desire to deserve honor through valiant deeds was "bred" in him by nature and by his seeing the joy his mother took in hearing everybody praise and commend him—"teares ronning down her cheekes for joye" when he returned from the wars crowned with a garland. Shakespeare has deftly retouched this portrait. He gives Volumnia no tears as characteristic of her joy. He gives her harsh, masculine characteristics: she has deliberately sent Marcius to "seek danger where he was like to find fame"; she cares more for his "good report" than for his life. She thinks his bloody forehead lovelier than the breasts of Hecuba, and she thanks the gods on hearing that he is returning wounded. Each of his battle scars she enthusiastically catalogs. She is at her proudest when he kneels to her at his homecoming. None of these details come from Plutarch.

Then Shakespeare adds further Volumnia's ambition to have her son made consul, and her emergent advocacy of dissimulation. He provides a basis for this in her disdain for the common people, an attitude she has taught Marcius. From her, the boy has learned to regard them as "things created to buy and sell with groats."

Hence he can be tempted in Act III by her urgings that he use toward these citizens "such words that are but roted in / Your tongue, though but bastards . . ." From her comes instruction how to mountebank their loves and cog their hearts. Let him go to them hat in hand and with "knee bussing the stones," thus "framing" himself as "hereafter theirs." These phrases carry a Shakespearean irony: it is indeed by framing himself the people's friend that Coriolanus will be brought to his knees.

Volumnia's policy is one we would speak of nowadays as Machiavellian. There is no suggestion of it in Plutarch's Volumnia, or in his Coriolanus. Yet elsewhere, in his account of Alcibiades, Plutarch claims to know well what tricky policy is. Alcibiades, he tells us, "ever studied by all devise he could, to currie favor with the common people," deceitfully. Then Plutarch goes on to say that he himself thinks this "lesse to be blamed" than the disdainful attitude which Coriolanus took toward the populace. An interesting remark! For may we infer from it that Plutarch would have half-approved the policy which Shakespeare shows Volumnia advocating? Probably so. Flattery at least has the merit of an outward courtesy; it demonstrates affability, which is the cure Plutarch repeatedly recommends for the faults he sees in Coriolanus. Yet the Plutarch who considered policy not so bad, on balance, could not imagine the disdainful Coriolanus being tempted to adopt this leaf from Alcibiades. Plutarch has overlooked the possibility of Alcibiadean advice being offered to the hero by his "civilized" mother— on the ground of its need in straitened circumstances—and approved on this same ground by the educated and "learned" Menenius. Such a reconstruction of the story is Shakespeare's.

Martial manliness and politic beggary are the successive parts Volumnia would teach her son to play. (They cohere in her own creed and foreshadow her later behavior.) The first of these Marcius has come to regard as natural to him: "I play / The man I am" (III. ii. 15). Yet here he does not realize that the man he has been playing masks a spirit in himself greedy for lionization; that in fact he took on his early role of warrior less through nature than through his pride's response to a habit custom-made by his mother's praisings.[39] Nor does he realize that hope of praise has induced him next, by Menenius' prodding, to submit to candidating for office. He has thought to reserve his own sense of honor in the candidating by half-candidly imitating those who "will practice the insinuating nod." But when his mother requests, further, that he "perform a part / Thou hast not done before," that of a dissimulating knee-bussing, he senses in such a role a dreadful "surcease to honor my own truth," a yielding to "Some harlot's spirit." Deliberate counterfeiting, we infer, offends his natural conscience. It involves acting not merely a role less noble than the one he had acted when masked in blood on the battlefield—a role he could play without awareness that it involved pretence and insincerity, without perceiving that his professed love of country disguised an ambitious love of self.[40] It involves, now, the humiliation of conscious disguise, which would be shaming, he feels, both to his "own truth" and to the dignity his merits deserve. Yet he agrees to it—under the pressures of his political dilemma and the urgings of his mentors —because of a fatalistic feeling that "What custom wills, in all things should we do't" (II. iii. 124). He agrees to counterfeit the lamb. At the trial, however, when his antagonists insult him, he breaks out of his sheepskin to roar like a lion, growl like a bear, and proclaim (in short) his own appetite for dominion, that universal wolf which has been bred into Rome's ethos since the days of Romulus. Has he not, like Romulus, been suckled by a wolfish mother?

In Act III we see Volumnia's policy, based on considerations of fortune, defeated by the superior craft of the tribunes. They have only to challenge Coriolanus' self-image by calling him "traitor," whereupon he abandons his promises to answer mildly:

> The fires i' the lowest Hell fold in the people!
> Call me their traitor!

He differs notably from the Coriolanus of Plutarch, who knew in advance of the charge of treason, yet consented to stand trial to it and indeed answered sucessfully until other charges were added. Even then, Plutarch reports no vituperative answer, merely Coriolanus' ill-considered praisings of those soldiers he had rewarded with spoils, thus exciting the rabble's envy and their vote for his banishment. Shakespeare's change emphasizes the wrath which any attack on the hero's self-image could elicit. A concern for merit overrides all considerations of political expediency and temporal vantage, the burden of Volumnia's recent coaching. In exposing contempt for the people, Coriolanus is nevertheless reflecting his

mother's true sentiment, that commoners can go hang, "Aye, and
burn too." This attitude, to Elizabethans, could suggest Nero, a
Roman prototype of fire-lovers and (as *King Lear* tells us) an angler
in the lake of darkness.

Menenius had accused the tribunes of being firebrands (III. i.
197). Volumnia, both by her premises and her advice, has prepared
her son to be one. Even the tactic of begging, which she and Menenius have urged, can be used by him later to serve revenge. To win
Volscian voices, Coriolanus does not hesitate to put on "mean ap-
parel"—since now his motive is no base desire "to save my life," but
a noble "spite / To be full quit of those my banishers." Such are the
moral confusions of self-love, its upside-down versions of nobility
and humility. Name saving is worthier than life saving. With this
outlook, Coriolanus turns to Aufidius, the enemy who has been
seeking to kill him, but whose concern equally is fame. It then becomes ironic that Aufidius must five times ask the visitor's name,
not at all recognizing him by face, but only at last through his proc-
lamation of the hurts he has given the Volscians. Through this
name—of injurer and mischief-maker—Coriolanus thinks to rehabilitate his honor by offering to devote it to the enemy's like-
minded appetite for pouring war into Rome's bowels. Aufidius, on
finding in Coriolanus this appetite (essentially for rape), embraces
him with more joy than a "wedded mistress." Aufidius' phrase here
implies, in Shakespeare's irony, that Coriolanus is being welcomed
as a kind of male harlot after his unmuffling of his manly charms
and advertising their availability for the sport of war. Forgotten
now is the hero's earlier claim (in I. vi. 72) to love Rome "dearer
than himself." For the sake of a quarrel not worth a "doit," he has
turned to Antium as a "goodly city." Thus his love, strumpet-like,
follows "chance" for the sole gain of vainglory. He is his mother's
son now, though in a mode she had not anticipated in Act III.

Meanwhile, Shakespeare has added to Plutarch further scenes
involving Volumnia, which show in her a revenge spirit parallel to
her son's as aftermath to the defeat of her strategy. "Now the red
pestilence strike all trades in Rome / And occupations perish!" is
her reaction to her son's banishment. Here, and in her scene with
the tribunes, she unpacks her heart with words and falls a-cursing
—like the "very drab" of which Hamlet speaks. She berates the
tribunes as "bastards" and as

> Cats, that can judge as fitly of his worth
> As I can of those mysteries which Heaven
> Will not have earth to know.

There is dramatic irony here: mysteries of Heaven are matters which indeed Volumnia will never know. And with equal truth she confesses: "Anger's my meat. I sup upon myself." Shakespeare is continuing to portray her as the matriarch of Rome's mad sense of what is noble.

We may recall, in this connection, the fear expressed by Menenius in III. i. 290, that Rome "like an unnatural dam" may "eat up herself." Menenius was there referring to a Rome dominated by the tribunes, but his words are equally applicable to Volumnia's blind appetite for vantage. We may note, also, one of the phrases with which Coriolanus praises his mother on his going into exile: "If you had been wife to Hercules . . ." The wife of Hercules, let us recall, gave him a tragic gift—a robe which ate up his flesh. The various roles which in the course of the play Volumnia successively gives Coriolanus to put on may be likened to such a robe. They eat up his humanity, and eventually his mortal life. Appropriately, Shakespeare elsewhere lets Volumnia liken herself to Juno, since the traditional trait of this goddess was that of female jealousy.

Volumnia's final appearance in the play, as we have noted, is her silent basking in Rome's plaudits. Is she sublime at this moment, as Bradley supposed?[41] Other readers have felt puzzled by her silence, since it seems to imply an unconcern for the tragic fate to which, in reality, she has consigned her son. Shakespeare has provided no later scene, as did Alexandre Hardy in his *Coriolan,* in which the mother suffers twinges of conscience on hearing of her son's death and cries out: "O Mère parricide! O Mère criminelle!" Such an ending would imply a degree, at least, of moral insight on her part. Shakespeare avoids this. Dramatically, it would too overtly call in question the illusion of righteous patriotism which Shakespeare, following Plutarch, is maintaining for this Roman matron—maintaining it, I have argued, as his ironic measure of a self-deception endemic in Rome's ethos. The basic bent of that ethos is pragmatic, not introspective. In such a context, Rome's ceremonies support a psychological need to avoid self-examination. They induce euphoria, like an opiate religion.

Shakespeare's understanding of the ultimate meaning of Volumnia's sacrifice, I think, was close to that which T. S. Eliot has voiced in his *Coriolan* poems:

> Now they go up to the temple. Then the sacrifice
> Now come the virgins bearing urns, urns containing
> Dust

Eliot is here ironically hailing Rome's (and imperial Britannia's) rites of sacrifice, characterizing them as the blindly pagan rituals of a worldly city, as profitless as urns of dust. Hidden from the eyes of this city is the mystery figured, as Eliot suggests, by the "dove's wing" and the "turtle's breast." Instead, here is a city dedicated to oak leaves, flags and trumpets, stone and steel, and dependent for its inspiration on "dingy busts, all looking remarkably Roman"— and on a matriarch who is helpless to aid her frustrated son.

Alongside this interpretation we may put some comments by another, more recent, reader of Shakespeare's story:

> We see nothing to make us hope for better things in either Rome or Corioli, as a result of his [Coriolanus'] loss. They [the opposing cities] are much alike, and it seems probable that they will continue in their habitual courses of envy, political scheming, and strife. . . . Both cities have used him for their own ends . . .[42]

We need add only that since the ends both cities serve are those of self-glorification, Volumnia's emergence as Rome's patroness is, at best, an equivocal achievement.

6 The blindness of a belly-polity

Any study of the play's deeper import must take into account the fable of the belly. Why did Shakespeare so richly enlarge upon this and assign it the focal position in his drama's opening scene? Theatrically, of course, it serves to make Menenius the more impressive, since with his first appearance we see dramatized his unusually jovial gifts as orator and crowd queller. We see him casting, like a practiced angler, his well-timed "pretty tale" as a lure to the mutineers, and then with it playing them into submission. (Meanwhile, off-stage, other mutineers—perhaps a more practical group, the hard core of the revolt—have to be appeased by the senate in a more substantial way, by a grant of five tribunes.) Yet in itself the fable carries a dramatic impact beyond its immediate value as entertainment and political tactic. It epitomizes a theory of society, an interpretation of the proper constitution of the state. It holds up, as an answer to Rome's conflicting appetites for power, the republic's need to accord respect and honor, centrally, to the belly of the body politic. It provides thus a major metaphor or emblem in relation to which the play's recurrent imagery of appetite, food, and feeding finds a contextual setting. Menenius' apologia for the beneficent belly effectually defines—surely with a dramatic irony on Shakespeare's part—Rome's belly-centered ethos.

Drawing on the ancient analogy of the body politic to a human body, Menenius pictures the belly as the smiling wiseman of the whole social organism. Indeed, he imagines this digestive member as able to speak—not as realism might suggest, through indecorous burping or farting, but with fabulous sagacity—as if the body's rightful teacher, or the city's resident Professor of Natural Philosophy:

> Your most grave belly was deliberate,
> Not rash like his accusers, and thus answered:
> "True it is, my incorporate friends," quoth he,
> "That I receive the general food at first,
> Which you do live upon, and fit it is,
> Because I am the storehouse and the shop
> Of the whole body. But, if you do remember,
> I send it through the rivers of your blood,
> Even to the Court, the heart, to the seat o' the brain.
> And through the cranks and offices of man,
> The strongest nerves and small-inferior veins
> From me receive that natural competency
> Whereby they live."

Note how this picture of the corporate life presupposes the primacy of the belly's office: the other members, even the heart and the brain, are viewed as dependents of the belly. From him, they are reminded, all receive "the general food" they live upon and "that natural competency" whereby they live. Do they live, then, by no other food than the belly's? If so, have they truly human life, or a merely animal existence? Shall the "storehouse" and "shop" govern the whole life of a commonwealth?

Surely Shakespeare, and at least some of his auditors, were marginally aware of a different view—for instance, the biblical view that man "does not live by bread alone" (Deut. 8:3 and Matt. 4:4),

supported further by St. Paul's warning that those "whose God is
their belly" will come to destruction by their minding of "earthly
things" (Philip. 3:19). The reference by Menenius to the "grave
belly" carries a Shakespearean pun: the belly is indeed a "grave"
member, since it turns to dust whatever it receives. No other organ
of the body is so wholly and grossly occupied with those goods of
life that are perishable. An Elizabethan auditor of the play, on
hearing the belly magnify its office through the speech given it by
Menenius, might well recall St. Paul's warning that those who
"serve their own belly" deceive the hearts of the simple by "fair
speeches" (Rom. 16:18).

Plutarch, and likewise Livy, report the fable with no hint as
to its critical shortcomings. Shakespeare, however, suggests these
through an interruption offered spontaneously by First Citizen:

>   What!
> The kingly crowned head, the vigilant eye
> The counsellor heart, the arm our soldier,
> Our steed the leg, the tongue our trumpeter,
> With other muniments and petty helps
> In this our fabric, if that they—

At this point Menenius in turn interrupts, to jibe with fine patrician snobbery at this pleb's assay into oratory:

> 'Fore me, this fellow speaks! What then? What then?

And the pleb, accepting this taunt, continues his thought as far as
he can. What if these nobler organs of the body, he asks,

> Should by the cormorant belly be restrained
> Who is the sink o' the body—

But having said this much, First Citizen gives way and is soon reduced to a pliant listener—both by Menenius' persistent "What
then?" and by his own curiosity to hear the rest of the fable. When
Menenius has finished with a flourish, the pleb is nonplussed and
replies: "It was an answer. How apply you this?" He senses something wrong with the fable, but because he lacks intellect enough
to specify reasons for his misgivings he yields to his opponent's line
of thought, and thereafter he is kept continually off balance by
Menenius' use of distracting jibes. For a perceptive theatre audience, nevertheless, what this Citizen has managed to half-articulate
serves to undercut the validity of the moral propounded by the

belly. How indeed do the belly's services to the rest of the body relate to those of the body's kingly "head" or counsellor "heart"? Is
Menenius about to bypass the claims of these higher organs and
identify "the sink o' the body" with Rome's ruling class?

Thoughtlessly, and buoyed up by self-assurance, Menenius does
just that. He applies his fable as follows:

> The Senators of Rome are this good belly,
> And you the mutinous members. For examine
> Their counsels and their cares, digest things rightly
> Touching the weal o' the common, you shall find
> No public benefit which you receive
> But it proceeds or comes from them to you
> And no way from yourselves.

Here we have a political pronouncement which essentially is absurd: no benefit, it asserts, can come to the members of a commonwealth except from its senators. One recent critic, John Palmer, has
described this as a "monstrous assertion." Palmer realizes, however,
that it represents an outlook not unusual in human history:
"Menenius is Shakespeare's portrait of an average member of the
privileged class in any community, the speaking likeness of an
English squire removed to a Roman setting."[43] H. C. Goddard
similarly sees Menenius as offering the "old sophistry" to which the
privileged in all ages tend to resort.[44]

Not only has Menenius assumed as dogma what would today be
called a "trickle down" theory of economics; he has also completely
ignored the public benefit that comes to a commonwealth from the
guidance appropriate to a kingly head, or from the protection given
by a soldier's arm, or from the legwork furnished by commoners.
Moreover, if the senate is to be identified, as Menenius asserts, with
the belly of the body politic, then this senate has in effect abnegated
its proper role of "counsellor heart." The traditional function of
"fathers" is thereby reduced to the lesser one of storekeeper and
manufacturer. We may recall, from more recent times, the jibe of
Napoleon that England was but a nation of shopkeepers. Did
Shakespeare perhaps discern, already in his own Jacobean England,
a tendency toward a mercantile-centered body politic? Was he
glancing at a tendency on the part of England's property-minded
new nobility, or equally on the part of the business-minded Puritan
class, to regard itself as the seat of government, thus ignoring the

commonwealth's need for a king from above to direct the flowering (as distinct from the flour-making) of the state, and its need likewise for a peasantry, from below, to till the earth and develop nature's fruitfulness? May not Shakespeare indeed have had in mind to analogize this two-sided blindness in terms of the Roman republic's tragic perspective? A commonwealth defined as Menenius has pictured it is essentially unprogressive: it is no ship of state with a harbor to reach, nor a band of pilgrims seeking a promised land. Instead, it is essentially a trade association catering to its entrepreneurs, and much like an octopus in its belly-centered unity.

In the history of political theory the body metaphor had not always been developed in the way Menenius fashions it. One of the notable treatises of the Christian Middle Ages was the *Policraticus* of John of Salisbury in the twelfth century. In that treatise what is mentioned as of first importance is the "soul" of the body (its pontiff or priestly power) and then the "head" (the prince) as the body's governor under the soul's guidance:

> The place of the head in the body of the commonwealth is filled by the prince, who is subject only to God and to those who exercise His office and represent Him on earth, even as in the human body the head is quickened and governed by the soul.[45]

Note how completely different this is from the view of Menenius, who has mentioned neither any prince nor any priestly authority—although, ironically, Shakespeare may be letting us see in Rome's belly senators a kind of comic surrogate for the prince which a commonwealth ought to have, and in Menenius himself a kind of comic pope.

Menenius, indeed, seems quite ready to speak, in the name of the gods, his own oracular judgment. Rome's recent famine, he sermonizes, is a punishment from heaven rather than something for which the senators are responsible. Accordingly, he would summon the plebs (but not the patricians) to penitence:

> For the dearth,
> The gods, not the patricians, make it, and
> Your knees to them, not arms, must help.

His pronoun "them" is nicely ambiguous: it refers to "gods" whom the plebs have offended in some obscure way; but also it could refer to the patricians, of whom it is implied the plebs ought to beg forgiveness for having slandered them. Pontifically, Menenius warns the plebs:

> you may as well
> Strike at Heaven with your staves as lift them
> Against the Roman state . . .

—implying by his rhetorical bridging of "heaven" and "state" a virtual identification. Then, as a final comfort, he refers the plebs to "The helms o' the state, who care for you like fathers." Again ambiguous: Does he mean the helms *over* the state, the steering gods? Or those *of* the state, its patricians?

First Citizen, acutely enough, takes the lower meaning and replies:

> Care for us! True, indeed! They ne'er cared for us yet. Suffer us to famish, and their storehouses crammed with grain; make edicts for usury to support usurers; repeal daily any wholesome act established against the rich, and provide more piercing statutes daily to chain up and restrain the poor. If the wars eat us not up, they will, and there's all the love they bear us.

His complaint, in essence, is that these "fathers" are cormorant, care-full in greed. Paradoxically, we will hear in Act III a similar complaint raised by Menenius himself when the tables are turned and the tribunes are in power. Rome, he then fears, is like an "unnatural dam" ready to "eat up her own." To a theatre audience observant of these and other turns in the story, Rome's domestic "feeding" habits take on a quality of cannibalism, although Shakespeare does not openly introduce the word "cannibal" until late in the play (IV. v. 201). Earlier, however, Act II opens with some dialogue as follows: "Pray you, who does the wolf love?"—"The lamb"—"Aye, to devour him . . ." And this is spoken when Rome is prosperous, not famine-stricken. The motif of savage dining, whichever party is in power, is effectively raised.[46]

According to John of Salisbury, the proper role of senators in a true body politic is to serve as the "heart":

> The place of the heart is filled by the Senate, from which proceeds the initiation of good works and ill. The duties of eyes, ears, and tongue are claimed by the judges and governors of provinces. Officials and soldiers correspond to the hands. Those who attend upon the prince are likened

to the sides. Financial officers and keepers (I speak now not of those who are in charge of the prisons, but of those who are keepers of the privy chest) may be compared with the stomach and intestines, which, if they become congested through excessive avidity, and retain too tenaciously their accumulations, generate innumerable and incurable diseases so that through their ailment the whole body is threatened with destruction.[47]

The "disease" which John has here described is precisely that which Shakespeare shows Rome's commoners attributing to the patricians as the play opens.

What authority surfeits on would relieve us. If they would yield us but the superfluity while it were wholesome, we might guess they relieved us humanely . . .

But then, as we have noted, the tale which Menenius offers in reply bypasses the charge of avidity. It merely pictures the belly as "good" because (so the sophistic argument runs) the belly is the dispenser of food to the body's other members. Quite evaded are at least two objections: 1) an economic objection, that this belly is not distributing as a good belly should; and 2) a political objection, that belly is attempting to substitute for heart. To the charge of patrician heartlessness, Menenius has but answered in effect: Your senators serve you heartily as the state's belly! First Citizen, therefore, is more right than he knows in suspecting that "our disgrace" is being fobbed off with a tale. What is being fobbed off as a big heart is in fact only a hearty stomach, while the name of "senators" is being sounded pompously to grace a function in Rome's body politic which John of Salisbury would have assigned to "financiers" merely, warning at the same time that this class in society is peculiarly liable to swollenness.[48]

The fulsomeness of Menenius' own rhetoric is an appropriate linguistic correlative of such swollenness. His speech is portly in its self-assurance, deceptively ample in its pragmatic illogic. And other instances of this proclivity can be found in speeches by other personages in the play: the gap between their sound and their sense, or between their "voices" and their "heart," is one of the play's recurrent motifs. Shakespeare is mirroring a flaw that is typical of Roman oratory yet representative of a tragic fact endemic to some extent in all ages.

It is important to grasp John of Salisbury's normative model of the body politic, which we have been citing from *Policraticus* V. 2, if later we wish to understand aright John's comic perversion of this model in *Policraticus* VI. 24. This later passage, interestingly, is the one which presents a fable identical with Livy's and close to Plutarch's. And John very impishly (although perhaps truthfully) puts it into the mouth of Pope Adrian IV. Since he thus gives it a setting almost as dramatic as Shakespeare's and equally parabolic, let us digress to notice how John handles it.

During a friendly conversation, Adrian asked John how men felt concerning himself and the Roman church. John "explained without reserve the abuses which I had heard of in the different provinces." He told Adrian what was "said by many," that the Roman church "shows herself to be not so much a mother as a very stepmother." And in developing this report he went on to say, among other things:

> Even the Roman pontiff himself is a grievous and almost intolerable burden to all; the complaint is everywhere made that while the churches which were built by the devotion of the fathers are falling into ruin and collapsing, he has built for himself palaces, and walks abroad not merely in purple but in gold. The palaces of priests dazzle the eye, and meanwhile in their hands the Church of Christ is defiled. They rend apart the spoils of the provinces as if they strove to refill the treasuries of Cresus. (Dickinson edition, p. 253.)

When asked by Adrian what he himself thought, John took refuge in quoting the opinion of a cardinal, Guido Dens, that "in the Roman church there inheres a certain root of duplicity and stimulant of avarice which is the source and root of evils." This comment prepares the reader for John's account of Adrian's reply —as does, likewise, John's frank admonition to Adrian: "Father, you are wandering in the trackless wilderness and have strayed from the true way." For John recounts that Adrian then laughed, congratulated John on having spoken frankly, and in apology put forth the fable of the belly. Significantly, John has entitled this whole chapter: "That the *vices* of rulers are to be endured because they embody the hope of the public well-being, and because they are charged with the disposal of the means of public health, even as the stomach in the body naturally dispenses nourishment; *and this on the authority of the Lord Adrian*" (italics mine).

I mention this because the Elizabethan historian Camden picked up John's story, recounting it his *Remaines* (1605); and because Geoffrey Bullough has recently reprinted the passage from Camden as a source for Shakespeare's *Coriolanus*. I fear that the sly humor of Camden (which in this respect follows John's) may be overlooked. Actually, Camden is using the fable as a jibe at the papacy—specifically, at Pope Adrian's foolish pretensions to confute and answer John of Salisbury. Observe how Camden begins:

> Pope Adrian the Fourth, . . . noted in his Papacy for using the Emperor Frederick the Second as his page in holding his stirrop, demanded of John of Salisbury, his countrey-man, what opinion the world had of the Church of Rome and of him, who answered: The Church of Rome which should be a mother is now a Stepmother, wherein sit both Scribes and Pharisees; and as for yourself, whereas you are a father, why do you expect pensions from your children? Adrian smiled, and after some excuses told him this tale which, albeit may seem long, and is not unlike that of Menenius Agrippa in the Roman History, yet give it the reading, and happily you may learne somewhat by it.

This is Camden's way of asking us to learn how Roman this pope is in his conception of his fatherhood.

The story which then follows tells how the body's members once mutinied against the stomach, until, themselves becoming faint as a result—

> they all with one accord desired the advise of the Heart. Then Reason layd open before them that hee against whome they had proclaimed warres, was the cause of all this their misery: For he as their common steward, when his allowances were withdrawne of necessitie withdrew theirs fro them, as not receiving what he might allow. Therefore it were a farre better course to supply him than that the limbs should faint with hunger. So by the persuasion of Reason, the stomacke was served, the limbs comforted, and peace re-established. Even so it fareth with the bodies of common-weale; for albeit the Princes gather much, yet not so much for themselves, as for others: So that if they want, they cannot supply the want of others; therefore do not repine at Princes herein, but respect the common good of the whole publicke estate.[49]

Here we see a pope who is justifying himself not as priest but as a prince—and one so devoid of piety that he unwittingly parodies the office of "Father" by identifying it with the belly's function, on which he regards the whole public good as dependent. (Recall, for comparison, Milton's more blunt way of making the same point in *Lycidas*, where he uses the phrase "blind mouths" to describe *episcopoi*—who ought to be "seers," i.e. see-ers instead of mouths, as Ruskin has so well explained in commenting on this passage.) Camden's Pope Adrian, instead of being a steward of the mysteries of God, regards himself as a steward of a very common good indeed —namely, of the food allowances he exacts from others (no mention being made of the heavenly food he should be receiving from God and offering gratis). And the only heart he has is one which uses reason to defend and advocate such a primacy! It is as Prince Belly, really, that he would comfort the commonwealth and reestablish its peace (ignoring Christ's "peace . . . not as the world giveth"— John 14:27). Hence Camden's unstated but implicit question to his readers is: Is not this Father, even as John of Salisbury had suggested, actually a blind Pharisee? And is not the Church he represents really a stepmother, rather than true mother?

Does not Shakespeare expect auditors or readers of his play to be nudged into asking a similar question regarding ancient Rome's parental figures, Menenius and Volumnia? That is: May we not see in Menenius the pharisaical pope of its pagan religion, and in Volumnia its stepmother church or temple; and in both together its popular oracles and vain peacemakers? I have already commented on the religious honors accorded Volumnia by Rome. And that Menenius functions in some sense as its surrogate priest is hinted by the fact, in Act V, that his embassy is substituted by Shakespeare for the embassy in North's Plutarch of "all the bishoppes, priestes, ministers of the goddes, and keepers of holy things." During his embassy, Menenius makes much of his status as foster father to Coriolanus; just as Volumnia, whose entrance immediately follows, appeals on the authority of her motherhood. Of Menenius, Coriolanus himself remarks that this old man "Loved me above the measure of a father— / Nay, godded me indeed"—a statement which to an Elizabethan ear would suggest a spiritual guardianship, the role of godfather in effect. All students of the play agree that Shakespeare has greatly enlarged the roles of both Menenius and Volumnia as found in Plutarch. What I am analyzing is the figurative significance of this enlargement.

In Act II we see these two guardians jointly delighting in a counting up of the wounds which their son has received. Then, in Act III, we see them urging him to stoop to pretense in order to save the status quo and their stake in it—this policy being rationalized, of course, as for his own and Rome's best ends. In reality they are asking Coriolanus to humiliate himself for the sake of their own prestige and for the patrician class interests on which they thrive. Thus the humility they teach, and the precious wounds they glorify (not Calvary's five, but the battlefield's twenty-seven), constitute a kind of secular parody of Christian piety.

I would suggest, therefore, that the situation here is analogous to the one touched on by Camden, that of the Pope's using of the Emperor Frederick as a stirrup-holding page to his own mounted authority. Republican Rome of course has no emperor, having recently exiled its Tarquin; but its near equivalent of emperor even before the play opens is its recently oak-crowned hero, Coriolanus. We are told of his early eminence by Shakespeare's Cominius in Act II:

> He bestrid
> An o'erpressed Roman, and in the Consul's view,
> Slew three opposers. Tarquin's self he met,
> And struck him on his knee. In that day's feats
> When he might act the woman in the scene,
> He proved the best man i' the field, and for his meed
> Was brow-bound with the oak.

Incidentally, the meaning of this episode is subtly changed by Shakespeare: whereas Plutarch had said that Marcius was awarded the garland for his *saving* of the life of a fallen fellow soldier, Shakespeare implies that it was given for a *slaying* of enemies while *bestriding* a fellow soldier, and for proving to be the best man by bringing even Tarquin to his knees. That is, Marcius has superseded in valiancy not merely his fellow soldiers but Rome's former king. He is thus potentially Rome's most natural monarch (if Rome were again to have a monarchy); and the play elsewhere makes clear that he is also Rome's most outspoken advocate of a centralized government—a point of view which gets him accused of wanting to be Rome's tyrant. In short, he looms, both by his convictions and his services, as Rome's most likely emperor—especially if we consider his ardent defense of the state in the name of the senate, alike against foreign invasion and domestic troublemakers. Yet we see him being used by Menenius and Volumnia as a page boy to their own ambitions.

In fact, we hear Coriolanus (in III. iii) likening his imposed role to that of a hostler:

> *Men.* Calmly, I do beseech you.
> *Cor.* Aye, as an ostler that for the poorest piece
>   Will bear the knave by the volume. The honored gods
>   Keep Rome in safety, and the chairs of justice
>   Supplied with worthy men! Plant love among's!
>   Throng our large temples with the shows of peace
>   And not our streets with war!

There is an undertone of bitterness in these words. He is agreeing to play a role in "shows of peace" for Rome's "temples"; but will those who chair the shows be "worthy men"? In using the word "chair," Shakespeare may have been aware of the ecclesiastical overtones this word can carry: every bishop's seat of authority is his chair, or *cathedra*. In effect, Menenius has been speaking *ex cathedra* by Shakespeare's implication, although this be quite beyond the awareness of Menenius himself. It is an instance of dramatic dialogue doing double duty—as imitation of natural speech and, at another level, as symbolic characterization. Menenius has been acting as a papa-moralist but with a questionable kind of peacemaking, so Coriolanus feels, in making him bend to the injustice of tolerating mobsters in office.

Throughout this scene, Menenius is revealed as a pathetic guardian to a regal but boyish Coriolanus. We see Menenius delivering up his ward to the hostile crowd with a sanctimonious plea. Let them consider, he begs, the soldierly wounds of Coriolanus, "which show / Like graves i' the holy churchyard." Then he does nothing at all to insure that the trial will proceed, as had been promised, by lawful form. His feeble efforts at justice consist solely of two interjections to Coriolanus: "Nay, temperately—your promise"; and "Is this the promise that you made your mother?" Much more appropriately, the consul Cominius tries to intervene by asking the people for a respectful hearing in the name of love of country:

>   Let me speak.
>   I have been Consul, and can show for Rome
>   Her enemies' marks upon me. I do love
>   My country's good with a respect more tender,

> More holy and profound, than mine own life,
> My dear wife's estimate, her womb's increase
> And treasure of my loins.

For Cominius, country is more important than womb. But this statesman's noble effort comes too late and is brushed aside, both by the demagogues and by an incensed Coriolanus.

The situation is thus similar to an earlier one, III. i., in which a bungling Menenius had thought to restore peace by crying out foolishly:

> Confusion's near. I cannot speak. You, Tribunes
> To the people! Coriolanus, patience!
> Speak, good Sicinius.

By such peacemaking he had but loosed the tribunes to ply their tactics for kindling, not quenching, disorder and violence. In that crisis, it was Cominius who momentarily saved the situation by helping protect Coriolanus with his sword and calling on friends to "stand fast." Menenius, instead of learning anything from this near-disaster of his policy of accommodation, confidently turned again

to trying his wit in a parley with the tribunes, relying on his ability to "patch" with "cloth of any color." The result was his foolish concession to a public trial of Marcius by the tribunes, thus blindly inviting the kangaroo court justice of scene iii. And when the swaggering tribunes have triumphed, we see Menenius pliably accepting the new order. He can speak them fair without a quaver of conscience or self-criticism:

> All's well, and might have been much better if
> He could have temporized.

Politic temporizing is indeed the chief virtue of Menenius, Rome's chameleon father-oracle.

In still other scenes, we see reflected his humorous trust in belly values. He jests with the tribunes about his reputation for loving hot wine and revels, and responds amiably to the taunt of Brutus that "you are well understood to be a perfecter giber for the table than a necessary bencher in the Capitol." In Act V, when Cominius returns defeated from his embassy to Coriolanus, Menenius has an explanation: the approach must have been made at an inopportune moment when Coriolanus "had not dined" and hence was unapt for giving or forgiving. Men have "suppler souls," he believes, when their blood is stuffed with "wine and feeding." He therefore plans to set upon Coriolanus at a better time, namely, after dinner. He relies also, as we see in the interview itself, on a plentiful use of sentiment. Not only does he refer to himself as "thy old father Menenius" and cry out "O my son, my son"; he points to his own tears and sighs when pleading that the "good gods" may assuage wrath. A piety thus garnished with self-dramatization has more than a little hypocrisy in it. We are not surprised, therefore, when he takes his rejection nimbly with a stoic grace. Such graciousness as he has, here and elsewhere, is the stock in trade of a humorous patrician angling for popularity.

As compared with the masculine Volumnia, Menenius is something of an old woman in his crotchety affectations, his susceptibility to flattery, and his busybody garrulousness. He pairs well with Volumnia as having hermaphrodite characteristics. And this fits in with Shakespeare's whole perspective on Rome as a city in which human beings have forfeited true humanity for "monstrous" simulations of humanity—monstrous in that a proper distinction between male and female is blurred, even as also a proper distinction between man and beast is blurred. It is a motif which Jonson had developed with satirical emphasis in characterizing the modern Italy of *Volpone*,[50] but which Shakespeare tucks in more subtly as an irony in ancient Rome's tragedy. Along with it, Shakespeare supplies other ironies. In Rome, belly and womb govern because neither the soul nor the total body of man is given its proper due. People live for appetite and the wearing of roles rather than for incorporating an integrity of purpose and action. Coriolanus has been allowed no true childhood and attains no true adulthood, but remains perpetually boyish. Rome has no king (being ruled instead by politic senators or guileful tribunes) and no priests (except for lay surrogates such as Menenius and Volumnia), and is thus a hybrid state-church, quasi-civil and quasi-religious. In Menenius and Volumnia, Shakespeare is highlighting the immediate "family" background of Coriolanus as set within a "city" background of factional rivalries and against an "outer-world" Antium which serves as foil. The causes of tragedy in the play's hero are thus proportionately distributed. And through such distribution, Coriolanus' own personal responsibility for his failure is realistically modified and extenuated.

Shakespeare also revises thereby the thesis with which Plutarch introduced his biography of Coriolanus. Plutarch had announced that "the life we intend now to write" teaches us by experience that "orphanage bringeth many discommodities to a childe, but doth not hinder him to become an honest man," and that it thus disproves a contention commonly offered by underprivileged youths, that their lack of caretakers to "see them well brought up" has been the occasion of "their casting awaye," that is, of their failures in life. Shakespeare shows, instead, that Plutarch's hero was hampered, both as child and as man, by a faulty education on the part of would-be "parents" of vainglorious virtue, who unwittingly treat their son like an orphan by abandoning him to the fickle loves of a wolfish society.[51] Into how honest a man is a child likely to grow in such a situation? Let Coriolanus' own confession, in Act V, suggest the answer:

> Aufidius, though I cannot make *true* wars,
> I'll *frame* convenient peace. (Italics mine)

Here is a paradoxical honesty: on the one hand, confessing to a dishonesty in war; on the other hand, offering a peace which confessedly is but framed for convenience. And behind this lies a double self-deception: both as to his own ability to make peace between rival camps (the same blindspot which made a fool of Menenius), and as to the cost of such peace as he does procure (the blindspot we noted in Volumnia).

Shakespeare's revised and total fable provides us a realistic parable of the true history of Rome. It does this by placing the small fable of Menenius within the encompassing fruits of that fable—an era that has "widowed and unchilded many a one" (V. vi. 153), not in Antium merely but in Rome as well. Plutarch had understood neither this larger parable of the times nor the true implications of the fable of Menenius. May we comment with a biblical reference to Christ's observation (Matt. 13), that some people cannot understand parables, because having eyes they see not, and with ears they hear not, since their hearts are hardened? This is the very complaint of unheeded First Citizen in the play: Rome's heartlessness.

7 Menenius as Plutarch

The way in which Shakespeare's perspective transcends Plutarch's can now be suggested in still another way—by noting how Shakespeare has assigned to Menenius various echoes of Plutarch's own outlook. Besides the belly fable, there is for instance the effort of Menenius to strike a balanced view of Coriolanus. When annoyed equally by the violence of the tribunes and by Coriolanus' failure to "speak 'em fair," Menenius cries out:

> Hear me speak.
> As I do know the Consul's worthiness,
> So I can name his faults—.

Here we have the very epitome of Plutarch's method. Elaborating it, Menenius proceeds, on the one hand, to defend Coriolanus as "a limb that has but a disease— / Mortal to cut it off, to cure it easy" —then concedes, on the other hand, that a limb deserves less respect when diseased. The rudeness of Coriolanus he traces, as Plutarch did, to a lack of formal schooling:

> Consider this. He has been bred i' the wars
> Since he could draw a sword, and is ill schooled
> In bolted language—meal and bran together
> He throws without distinction.

The corrective needed, so Menenius thinks, is for Coriolanus to learn to answer to the people in a calm way, thus mending the "something too rough" in his manner. Further, he should learn courtesy enough to "stoop to the herd" when the physic of the state so requires. But counterbalancing this assessment of flaw, Menenius is full of praise for the nobility of Coriolanus on the battlefield. We may almost imagine Plutarch speaking when Menenius says to the Volscian senators:

> I have been
> The book of his good acts, whence men have read
> His fame unparalleled haply amplified.

Furthermore, the role of Menenius as Rome's philosopher and quasi-priest has a parallel in Plutarch's own life. Plutarch is known to have been both a defender of Rome's political constitution and a priest of the Delphian Apollo.

It has often been suggested by literary critics that Shakespeare is using Menenius as a chorus to the drama. That may well be so, provided we do not take the further step of assuming, as some of these critics do,[52] that this choral character is Shakespeare's mouthpiece for his own views. Rather, Menenius functions much as the Chorus in *Henry V* does—as spokesmen for what may be called a "popular conscience" within the civilization being dramatized. Just as in *Henry V* the Chorus serves to voice the patriotic perspective of the Elizabethan historian Edward Hall, so likewise may Menenius be regarded as spokesman for the patriotic perspective of Plutarch. But at the same time Shakespeare hints, in various marginal ways, the inadequacies of this choral observer's perspective. Shakespeare brings Plutarch's outlook under judgment by putting Plutarch figuratively within the play in the person of Menenius.

Plutarch's central criticism of Coriolanus, as we have noted, was that he was prone to self-opinion and lacking in affability. This criticism is introduced, for instance, when Plutarch is commenting on the "passion and choller" Coriolanus showed after his rejection on election day. Shakespeare, at this same point in the action, shows us Menenius voicing this criticism. "Be calm, be calm," Menenius admonishes, as Coriolanus begins to react to the news. The advice proves ineffective, yet Menenius returns to it as the melee ends: "Put not your worthy rage into your tongue." And a scene later, he insists: "Repent that you have spoke." What he is asking is a change of tactics more than of heart. He reflects, in this respect, Plutarch's politically centered ethic, his concern for the civilities of civic life. We know Plutarch to have been (in Dr. Johnson's phrase) an eminently "clubbable man," a man often host or guest at banquets— as Menenius is reported to be in Shakespeare's play. To such a man, the amenities of urbane speech were a part of the gentleman's code.[53] It is understandable, therefore, that what Plutarch finds objectionable in Coriolanus is his seeming to have no "regard" for people, his inability to let them "be acquainted with him, as one citizen useth to another in a cittie." But nowhere does Plutarch charge Coriolanus with lack of *love* for people. Shakespeare, on the other hand, implies that Rome's need—for the sake indeed of its own political good—is brotherly love, a more radical requirement than simple "seeming regard" for acquaintances.

We can discover this if we but look closely at Shakespeare's handling of the candidating scene, which in the play precedes the election day reversal. Menenius is not here present, having departed just before the soliciting of votes begins. His later criticisms of Coriolanus, therefore, do not apply to this scene. But had he observed it, would he have discerned any fault in the candidate? Very likely not; for we here see a Coriolanus who keeps his temper and makes every effort to be accommodating. Shakespeare seems to explain this by the fact that Coriolanus has received from Menenius, just before the latter's going, some very timely advice. Coriolanus has been reluctant to act the candidate, protesting:

> Plague upon't! I can not bring
> My tongue to such a pace. "Look, sir, my wounds!
> I got them in my country's service when
> Some certain of your brethren roared, and ran
> From the noise of our own drums."

To us the candidate's pride in his own excellence is here conspicuous; and we may sense also, incidentally, a distortion of the truth, since we saw no soldiers at Corioli run away in fright of their own drums. Does not such a speech indicate a prejudiced polishing of one's self-image? But to Menenius what is alarming about it is solely its impolitic attacking of the people's faults. Coriolanus should not focus on those, says Menenius. "You must desire them / To think upon *you*" (italics mine). And with this he exits, begging his pupil to speak to the people in "a wholesome manner." In what follows, Coriolanus applies this counsel. He desires the citizens to think upon him—upon "Mine own desert," and on his worthiness in not wishing to trouble the poor by begging alms of them. He is willing to accommodate, nevertheless, to their stated price for office, a "kindly" asking of it. He replies courteously:

> Sir, I pray, let me ha't. I have wounds to show you, which
> shall be yours in private.—Your good voice, sir, what say
> you?

Here his kindness consists in his use of the respectful "Sir" and of a begging form of address, together with a proffer of intimate tokens "in private" and of esteem for the *good vote* the citizen can give him. And is not Coriolanus being kind, further, in wearing the customary gown to please his voters? To a residual complaint by Fourth Citizen, that "You have indeed not loved the common people," Coriolanus replies peaceably that he considers it "the more virtuous" not to have been "common" in his love, but that he is quite ready to oblige them, since they wish it, with such shows of love as popular politicians use—and he imitates a few for their entertainment.[54] Asked then about his wounds, he replies in effect: I'm sure I've no need to show them, since I know I can trust to your good voices without troubling you further. The citizens, apparently satisfied, respond: "The gods give you joy, sir, heartily."

In only a minor matter, it would seem, has Plutarch's account been altered: Coriolanus here has bypassed a showing of his wounds, although Plutarch had said "he shewed many woundes and cuttes apon his bodie." We may doubt that Plutarch would have raised an eyebrow over this omission, so modestly has it come about. Yet this change is basic to Shakespeare's conception of the hero's tragic flaw, and at the same time is integral with other small changes which revamp Plutarch's assumptions. For example, Plutarch had commented that in those days of Rome's pristine purity, offices were "not geven by favor or corruption"; there was no "buying and selling" of offices. But Shakespeare has introduced Third Citizen, who says: "You must think if we give you anything, we hope to gain by you"—to which Coriolanus replies: "Well then, I pray your price o' the counsulship?" Plainly, Coriolanus is willing to purchase favor. But on the other hand, whereas Plutarch had implied that favor and corruption alike are departures from justice, Fourth Citizen is presupposing that love for the common people, rather than mere justice in dealing with them, belongs to kindliness. To be kindly without love is to be noble yet not noble; it is something less than friendly.

If the citizens support Coriolanus despite his equivocal answers, it is (as Fifth Citizen says) because "We *hope* to find you our *friend*, and therefore give you our voices heartily" (italics mine). When later they reject him, it is (as Shakespeare's subsequent scene shows) because they have come to doubt the likelihood of his being their friend—particularly when they recall how he evaded showing them his wounds. True, he has named his wounds ("two dozen odd"), and his battles ("thrice six"), and thereby he has won the hearty voices of the people—but not really their hearts. Second Officer had argued (in II. i.) that it would be ungrateful of the people not to confess with their tongues the worthiness of a Coriolanus who has "planted his honors in their eyes and his actions in their hearts." But to plant spectacles of honor for admiring eyes is not the same as to feed hearts with a gift of love, love for the people as kinfolk. Deeper than the disposition of people to admire is the need of their natures for kindliness, in the sense of a kin-ly sharing of self.

First Officer had called attention to this latent need in saying of Coriolanus: "That's a brave fellow, but he . . . loves not the common people" (II. i. 5). A paradox here: a fellow who loves not fellowship; a fellow who takes the attitude that he is some superior fellow, not in their boat. In answer to Fourth Citizen's similar complaint (II. iii. 98), that "You have not indeed loved the common people," Coriolanus has replied, "I will, sir, flatter my sworn brother, the people, for to earn a dearer estimation of them." But of what worth is this swearing to brotherhood, if one's spirit implies that one regards the brother with condescension? This is the question Shakespeare raises, as Plutarch did not. Plutarch had thought it enough to be kindly of tongue. Shakespeare reveals the merely quasi-validity of such an ethic. The *dearer* esteem it earns one is merely *costlier,* ruinously so.

True, Plutarch's ethic suffices for his criticizing elsewhere a "too lordly" manner in Coriolanus. That is, he can recognize the cruder manifestations of the "hawtie obstinate minde" which he finds to be, in general, the "onley cause" of Coriolanus' misfortunes. But to focus on haughty obstinacy, we may say, is to see an adjacent flaw rather than the essential flaw; it is to mistake what is only a proximate cause for the root cause. That is why, we may infer, Plutarch finds nothing specifically objectionable in Coriolanus' behavior prior to his reaction to being rejected by the voters. Shakespeare, however, has been careful to show the hero's contempt for the plebs from the play's beginning, and during the candidating scene a conviviality which barely masks scorn. This conviviality, because not churlish, is not identifiable as scorn by the citizens until they are challenged afterwards, by the tribunes, on the question of "love." Then what they resent is the candidate's implicit scorn beneath his outward courtesy.

Plutarch had reported that Coriolanus, when candidating, faithfully followed Rome's customs. But let us note Plutarch's explanation of the customs. It overlooks what to Shakespeare, and to us, is their deeper potential of meaning. The "meane apparell" of a "poore gowne," Plutarch explains, was devised in order to move people the more; and the showing of wounds was devised to give testimony of the candidate's "valiantnes." Shakespeare implies more, by making the gown "wooluish" (Folio's spelling)—i.e., a woolen one—which Coriolanus tells us in soliloquy he finds humiliating to wear. The occasion thus becomes a test of the hero's willingness to beg and to be lamb-like—a test he passes in an equivocal way, accommodating his manners to this role, yet evading a deeper humility potential in the lamb symbolism. For Shakespeare, moreover, the custom of showing wounds implies a test not centrally of the candidate's valiantness but of his humanity—regarding which a few citizens at least have lurking doubts.

Plutarch reports the people as saying to one another, "We must needes choose him Consul," since to refuse so valiant a man would be shameful. To what, then, can Plutarch attribute the people's overnight reversal of good will into hatred? He traces it simply to their last-minute fear of putting into office a man "somewhat partial toward the nobilitie, and of great credit and authority amongest the Patricians"—to which North adds as marginal comment: "See the fickle mindes of common people." North and Plutarch alike seem unaware here of any moral fault in Coriolanus. Only the people's envy is noted, with the comment that the senate took it as a shame to themselves rather than to Marcius, and were "marvellously offended" with the people. Shakespeare, however, understands the hero's partiality to the nobility in a deeper sense: not centrally as a political partisanship, but rather as a moral partiality toward aristocratic deservings. Through this, Coriolanus is evading the citizens' hope of a free and reciprocal love. An ironic jibe by one of the tribunes, "We pray the gods he may deserve your loves," is then enough to put the fat in the fire. For now each citizen feels, with a rising indignation, that the candidate's begging has been more mock than real. This indignation the tribunes then exploit until it becomes in Act III the blind cry: "The people are the city!" Such perverting of the citizens, Shakespeare makes clear, has been possible only by reason of a hollowness in the hero's affability. His concern to earn their "dearer estimation" has been too exclusively politic. May we not say: too Plutarchan?

Why has Shakespeare invented, as the key clue to this hollowness, a reluctance to show Hob and Dick one's "unaching scars"? Why second-guess Plutarch at precisely this point? Let me suggest, besides the considerations I have mentioned, one other. I think Shakespeare may have had in mind here to figure a contrast to a well-known biblical paradigm, the episode in John 20 of Christ's showing his wounds to doubting Thomas, not merely to see but to touch and feel. To Christian imagination, that story provided an ultimate model of victorious candidacy—an honorable valiantness, which in charity seeks to draw into fellowship even the lowly straggler. By the light of this paradigm, it becomes appropriate for

Shakespeare to dramatize the Roman world's central defect in terms
of its ignorance of this norm. That is, Rome's hero, its quasi god-
man after Corioli, can be shown as loving "this painting / Wherein
you see me smeared," but not as loving to offer his wounds for his
neighbors' benefit. And this dramatized paradox, insofar as it may
awaken in a Christian audience some memory of the gospel paradigm it inverts, signalizes to that audience the basic flaw in
Coriolanus.

Perhaps I have dwelt overlong on this scene. But my purpose has
been to discriminate within it three kinds of morality: 1) the hero's
natural morality, as exhibited before he meets his voters; 2) his
politic morality, in obedience to the schooling by Menenius; and
3) the citizens' morality of gratitude for friendship—this third kind
so mixed, however, with a human weakness for idolizing, that it
falls victim, first to the superficial kindness offered by Coriolanus,
then to the false neighborliness offered by the tribunes. The drama's
indication that the people's gratitude is exploitable and unstable
is properly realistic. But what is significant is that the norm of
gratitude is present, in germ at least, in a pagan society. It marks
Shakespeare's understanding of the pagan world's point of contact
with Christian morality, its latent desire for grace in the common
man's fitful efforts at gratitude. We have seen a fuller blossoming
of common grace in the high-born Virgilia—whose very name perhaps suggested to Shakespeare that of the almost-Christian Virgil.
And we have noted also an unselfish love of country in Cominius.
But except for these rare instances of graciousness in high places,
and at lower levels a probing for it by the wise First Officer and the
Fourth Citizen, the Roman world was, as we know from our general
knowledge of history, not congenial to a morality of gratitude and
fellowship in love. Shakespeare, I am suggesting, knew these facts of
history and designed his drama appropriately and proportionately.

8 The ironies in a pagan magnanimity

But now that I have suggested three levels of perspective, I should
like to take advantage of them to clarify further the way in which
Shakespeare has structured his play. And here let me invoke aid
from a recent book, one not written about *Coriolanus* but never-

theless pertinent, a study by Maurice B. McNamee entitled *Honor and the Epic Hero* (1959). McNamee has described three versions of the concept of magnanimity—the Aristotelian-Greek version, the Ciceronian-Roman version, and the Christian version in Augustine and Aquinas. The first, as he points out, reflects a self-centered ethic; the second a state-centered ethic; the third a God-centered ethic, in which magnanimity is redefined to reflect charity and humility. Now I would not claim that Shakespeare's *Coriolanus* has in its cast of characters any unequivocal representatives of Christian magnanimity. Virgilia and Cominius, who approximate the Christian sense of this virtue, are yet caught within a Roman ethos which defeats their better instincts. Shakespeare's realism on this score is remarkably deft. His historical insight permits him, however, to suggest a foreshadowing of Christian magnanimity in these best of the Romans, and to place it in contrast to two other versions of magnanimity, both classically pagan: the Roman one in Menenius, and a predominantly Greek one in Coriolanus.[55] It will be worth our while to explore these latter two versions in their bearing on the tragedy. They seem to me to be, through a complex interplay, joint causes of the hero's disaster.

In commenting on the choleric behavior of Coriolanus when refused office on election day, Plutarch complains that Marcius behaved "as one thincking that to overcome alwayes, and to have the upper hand in all things, was a token of magnanimitie." What does Plutarch himself understand by magnanimity? Evidently something different from his hero's view of this virtue. Plutarch's view, I think, can be recognized as close to Cicero's—probably because his philosophy was chiefly Platonist, as was Cicero's, and because he had absorbed from his Roman acquaintances their sense of the primacy of man's societal obligations. John Oakesmith has described Plutarch as typically Roman in his stress on the dominant claims of the practical life and of the state. Confident of Rome's divine mission, says Oakesmith, Plutarch was critical of many aspects of Greek culture, which he regarded as childish compared with Rome's adult focus on civic welfare. The spirit of compromise, tolerance, and temperance was central to Plutarch's ethics. Reason, common sense, and good taste were the norms to which he submitted religion; and his philosophy was syncretistically ethical, rather than metaphysical.[56]

Cicero's concept of the magnanimous man is well indicated in the various passages which McNamee has cited from the *De Officiis,* notably this one:

> Neither must we listen to those who think that one should indulge in violent anger against one's political enemies and imagine that such is the attitude of a great-spirited, brave man. For nothing is more commendable, nothing more becoming in a pre-eminently great man than courtesy and forbearance. . . . If punishment or correction must be administered, it need not be insulting; it ought to have regard to the welfare of the state, not to the personal satisfaction of the man who administers the punishment or reproof. (I. xxv. 88)

Cicero urges the winning of "good will," principally through "kind services" and through "all those virtues that belong to gentleness of character and affability of manner" (II. ix. 32). And he wishes to correct the opinion of "most people," that the achievements of war are more important than those of peace. Rather, "there have been many instances of achievements in peace more important and no less renowned than in war" (I. xxii. 74). Plutarch and Shakespeare's Menenius, in the main, reflect these principles.

In his *Lives,* however, Plutarch gives ample evidence of the strong support Coriolanus had for a different outlook. He tells us that the "lustiest" young gentlemen of Rome, those that came "of nobler race," encouraged Coriolanus in his indignation when rejected for consul. They flocked about him as their captain because he stirred up in them "a noble emulation of honor and valliantnes." May we infer that these aristocrats admired Coriolanus, not merely as Plutarch does, for his "temperaunce and cleane handes from taking of bribes and money"—on which score Plutarch says Coriolanus may be compared "with the most perfect, virtuous, and honest men of Graece"—but also for something Grecian in this hero's proud love of honor? This group of young noblemen is not pictured in Shakespeare's play, but their spirit is caught rightly enough in Coriolanus himself.

The anger of Shakespeare's Coriolanus over public disrespect for his worth, we may notice, is grounded in a view of social order which differs from that of Menenius. We have heard Menenius describe the state in nautical terms (the patricians as "helms" to an armored ship), or in organic terms (the senators as belly to the body), or in family terms (the senators as father-caretakers). Coriolanus, on the other hand, uses language which stresses hierarchical order. The noble senate, he tells the plebs, "Under the gods keep you in awe, which else / Would feed on one another." The patricians, he argues in Act III, will debase the nature of their seats, if they let in "crows to peck the eagles." The senate, in his view, is "the fundamental part of state," where "gentry, title, wisdom" reside. It is "a graver bench / Than ever frowned in Greece" (III. i. 106). This comment seems to reflect a Spartan view of society, emphasizing the prerogatives of class and caste. Coriolanus would tie the worth of rulers to their valor in defending merit and rewarding it. Nobles who let the rabble's voices prevail, to the injury of a hero's deservings are "dastard" nobles, he later says. A city's chief duty, he implies, is to accord proper honor to natural excellence. It is on this point that his perspective is Hellenic and may be compared with that of Aristotle's magnanimous man.

The fact that a Coriolanus of 490 B.C. could not have read what Aristotle wrote around 325 B.C. would have been irrelevant to Shakespeare. In *Troilus and Cressida* he had shown Hector citing Aristotle, because it suited a figurative purpose in that play to have Hector represent an Aristotelian sensibility. In *Coriolanus,* likewise, when Volumnia thinks of her son in terms of a Hector, Shakespeare is indicating Rome's primitive tie with Hellenic values. The career he develops for Coriolanus is like Hector's, while also akin to that of Achilles. We can see this ambivalence in the subconscious love which Coriolanus has for his Volscian rival, Aufidius. At one point they join forces. But finally Aufidius, like Achilles, slays a Hector-like Coriolanus by underhanded means. Plainly these two exemplars of valor are but foils to each other, almost interchangeable. Of the two, however, Coriolanus is the more nearly a figure of Aristotelian magnanimity.

Let us recall some of the features of the virtue of *megalopsychia,* "greatness of soul," as pictured in the *Nicomachean Ethics* IV. 3–4. This virtue, the crown of all others, turns about a right attitude toward great honors. The magnanimous man, says Aristotle, claims these in accordance with his merits. He will not claim more than is his due, but he would be pusillanimous not to claim recognition for the superior excellence he in fact has. He despises honors given on trifling grounds, or when given by his social inferiors. But he will take moderate pleasure in great honors when conferred on him by good men, that is, by men as great or nearly as great as he. In accepting them, however, he will indicate a carelessness for praise, because praise is not something to be admired but rather a tribute to be accepted temperately; and more basically, because he realizes that nothing others can bestow on him is really great as compared with his own inner sense of worthiness. It is a mark of the magnanimous man to ask for "scarcely anything," but to give help readily to others. He is in fact somewhat ashamed of receiving benefits, since to receive suggests some inferiority to the giver. When he receives benefits, therefore, he is apt to confer greater benefits in return to manifest his superiority. To make clear this superiority, he is quick to remember what he has done for others, but apt to forget what has been done for him. He is a man of few deeds, but of great and notable ones. He avoids running into small dangers, but in great dangers is unsparing of his life. He desires to possess beautiful and profitless things, rather than profitable and useful ones, for this is more proper to a character that suffices to itself.

Before pursuing further the details of Aristotle's portrait, let us pause to observe how aptly those so far mentioned fit the behavior of Coriolanus. To almost everyone in the play Marcius seems careless of praise, and no more than temperately pleased with the great honors given him after Corioli by Cominius and by the senate. So temperate is he, indeed, that Cominius gently chides him for being "too modest." He seems ashamed to receive the benefit of praise for his "deserving" and says abashedly, "I have some wounds upon me, and they smart / To hear themselves remembered." Yet, paradoxically, by mentioning his wounds he is revealing the magnanimous man's tendency to be quick to remember what he has done for others, while apt to forget the favor they are doing him—forgetting, as Cominius chides, to be "grateful / To us that give you truly." Shakespeare is aware of this paradox. He is aware also that his hero's modesty does not involve any pusillanimity in claiming honors appropriate to high merit. Marcius accepts with thanks his General's gift of "My noble steed, known to the camp" and also the gift of the name Coriolanus. "I mean to stride your steed," he says, and to "undercrest" the awarded name. Understandably so; for these are indubitable symbols of preeminence—of superiority to Cominius, in fact. That they have been given in token, and in "sign of what you are" rather than to reward things done, adds to the magnanimous man's feeling that his worthiness transcends all honors men may bestow. At the same time, moreover, Marcius has disdained the reward of a tenth of the spoils of the war. He looks on those, Cominius comments admiringly, as the "common muck of the world" and seems content to reward his own deeds simply "with doing them." Here Shakespeare would have us see, I think, the Aristotelian claimer of beautiful things rather than profitable ones—the honors of a man sufficient to himself. But there is also, no doubt, an underside of Shakespearean irony as regards the "profitless" honors of the self-sufficient man.

Having received the benefit of honors, Marcius immediately manifests his superiority by bestowing a favor. He begs "my lord General" to give freedom to a prisoner, a poor man of Corioli who once "used me kindly." In this he shows the magnanimous man's inclination to ask "scarcely anything" but to give readily. Shakespeare has added, however, an ironic touch in the fact that Marcius cannot remember the name of the poor host he would honor, even in the very act by which he would "undercrest" his own name to make *it* memorable. The kindliness of hosting him becomes that of some nameless inferior.

And there are other "forgettings" in this Grecian magnanimity. We can observe them if we attend closely to how Corioli was captured. We see Marcius becoming the hero of the hour by dashing into the city all alone (exceeding thus Plutarch's report). But is it solely by Marcius' valor that the city is captured? Superficially, it would seem so. Let us notice, however, in I. iv, that he has been able to enter the city because its gates have been left open by its soldiers when fleeing a charge from Marcius' *men*. Titus Lartius, on arriving a moment later, barely has time to speak praises of the shut-in hero when the gates reopen, to reveal a Marcius being driven out. Lartius then shouts, "Let's fetch him off"—and he and his men do so, by charging into the city and taking it. A dozen lines later, we hear Marcius asking Lartius to take "Convenient numbers to make good the city," while he himself hastens off "to help Cominius," he says. The actual taking of the city, if we read closely, has depended (and still depends) on the work of Lartius and others.

Moreover, the help Coriolanus offers on arriving at Cominius' camp is not without some dramatic irony, too, if we are aware that he has left behind him a half-finished conquest. He says to Cominius:

> Where is the enemy? Are you lords o' the field?
> If not, why cease you till you are so?

To which Cominius replies:

> Marcius,
> We have at disadvantage fought, and did
> Retire to win our purpose.

Which of these two commanders, Shakespeare may be nudging us to ask, is behaving the more modestly? Has not Coriolanus himself retired from Corioli—and with a self-advertising purpose? Cominius, we know, has retired only to "breathe" his soldiers for the moment, while he commends them as "friends" who have fought well, and while he invokes help from the gods. Marcius has denounced as "rascals" the troups he has left behind, but now is recruiting new adulators from the army of Cominius.

After the battle, how much acknowledgment does Coriolanus give his helpers? Very little. When Lartius enters to praise Marcius, his speech gets cut off by the latter's reply:

> I have done
> As you have done, that's what I can—induced
> As you have been, that's for my country.

Is love for country really what has prompted Marcius? And is that the motive which is inducing him now to minimize the deeds of Lartius and others? Through forgetting their valor in rescuing him, Marcius can the more readily focus, a moment later, on his own magnanimity in standing "upon my common part with those / That have beheld the doing." Have these others been but beholders? Shakespeare's dramatic ironies tell us how to place and judge this Grecian magnanimity.

It is not surprising that modern translators of Aristotle have often found "pride" to be the nearest English equivalent for his *megalopsychia*. W. D. Ross, for example, so translates because of the note of "self-absorption" central to Aristotle's whole concept. It anticipates, Ross suggests, the Stoic sage but without the Stoic's self-abasement before the ideal of duty. It differs from the Ciceronian ideal, McNamee has observed, by its defense of the superior man's right to disdain people who are inferiors in honor, and by stressing his duty to disdain all worldly goods as inferior to the prize of honor, "which people of position most aim at." The magnanimous man of Aristotle's portrait "despises justly," since he thinks "truly" regarding superior and inferior merits. But in what way, we may ask, does this true thinker show a just despising? He is not given, says Aristotle, to blaming or speaking evil, even of his enemies— "except from haughtiness." (I am using Ross's translation.)

Does not this qualifying phrase provide a considerable loophole —one that would permit a haughty Coriolanus to do a good deal of blaming, especially under provocation? There are similar loopholes elsewhere. It might seem at first glance, for instance, that Coriolanus could not fit Aristotle's statement that the magnanimous man adopts an unassuming manner among humble people. But note Aristotle's explanation: one can be superior to the lower classes without difficulty, hence it would be vulgar to display against them one's full superiority. That is, one can condescend, while still remaining superior. And note this further description:

> He must be open in his hate and in his love (for to conceal one's feelings, i.e., to care less for truth than for what people will think, is a coward's part), and must speak and act openly; . . . [for] he is given to telling the truth, except when he speaks in irony to the vulgar. (Ross translation)

Everywhere in Shakespeare's play, surely, we see a Coriolanus who, because contemptuous, speaks freely the truth of his loves and hates, except when speaking in irony to the vulgar voters in the candidating scene. He evidently accords with the ideal of Aristotle, who does not expect, as does Plutarch, that a hero be always affable. Are Plutarch's strictures against haughty opinionatedness relevant to a hero great enough to disdain the concealing of his "true" opinions and "just" hatreds?

At only one point does Coriolanus fall short of Aristotelian magnanimity—in his harboring as long as he does his grudge against Rome. Aristotle says it is "not the part of a proud [great-souled] man to have a long memory, especially for wrongs, but rather to overlook them." But what is meant by a long memory? May one, against injuries done to his honor, retaliate for awhile—long enough to have one's merits reappreciated? As McNamee has pointed out, a revenging of dishonor is approved in Homer's *Odyssey;* and in the *Iliad* no one blames the great Achilles for his resentment over the taking away of his war prize. The pleaders criticize Achilles only for continuing his grudge after Agamemnon has admitted fault and declared a willingness to offer indemnity. This is his tragic error. Finally, when he does relent, he confesses he was "wrong in supposing that a man could nurse a grudge forever" (Rieu's translation). He then blames his stubbornness on Ate, a blind power that has possessed him, but he confesses to no mistake in his original resentment, or for having acted to vindicate his honor. We infer that his anger has been of excessive duration, but justifiable otherwise. His relenting, we further note, is effected by two kinds of persuasion: his detractors have been brought to their knees, and he finds alluring the prospect of new fame in the slaying of Hector. By returning to the doing of a publicly honored deed, Achilles fully reestablishes his superiority.

There are striking parallels in all this to the behavior of Coriolanus. Shakespeare's hero banishes Rome at the end of Act III with a speech much like that of Achilles when withdrawing his services from the Greek camp. Achilles says to Agamemnon:

> The day is coming when the Achaeans one and all will miss me sorely, and you in your despair will be powerless to help them as they fall in their hundreds to Hector killer of men. Then will you tear your heart out in remorse for having treated the best man in the expedition with contempt. (Book I, tr. E.V. Rieu)

Coriolanus departs with a similar taunt. Let your enemies, he says,

> Fan you into despair! Have the power still
> To banish your defenders, till at length
> Your ignorance, which finds not till it feels,
> Making not reservation of yourselves,
> Still your own foes, deliver you as most
> Abated captives to some nation
> That won you without blows.

There is great dignity in this rebuke, as if more in sorrow than in anger. The hero's self-sufficiency remains unruffled; and in that sense his reason is in control of his passion. Indeed, he can gently disdain in the next scene the efforts of his few friends to comfort him. He comforts *them* instead, by citing the adage that "extremity" is "the trier of spirits" and by giving assurance that he will "exceed the common." If in such circumstances he then invokes a "noble cunning," may we not justify this by the Greek ideal of resourcefulness?

On learning of his league with the enemy, do any of his country-men blame him? They do not, but fall back on pleading that he remember how royal it is to pardon "when less expected." By now, however, Coriolanus has become red of eye, and is in danger thus of losing honor by carrying indignation to excess. It is at this point, therefore, that Volumnia puts to him the question: "Think'st thou it honorable for a noble man / Still to remember wrongs?" For if he would imitate the graces of the gods, she argues, he needs to recall that the gods load their thunder with a bolt which only splits the oak, no more than that. If he exceeds this and wipes out the Romans, the benefit will be ill fame and an abhorred name; but if he relents, there is a new exploit he can undertake for enhancing his honor and bringing greater praises than ever. This argument, substantially, was the one used in the *Iliad* to persuade Achilles to desist from revenge. Both heroes yield, less out of a sense of public responsibility than to ennoble themselves.

There are two significant differences, however, from the Greek story. One is that the new honor-winning exploit which Volumnia is proposing involves peacemaking rather than war-making, and thus an exchanging of Coriolanus' excellence as conqueror for a civic kind of excellence in which, in fact, he has never been success-ful, that of reconciler of rival sides. How, conceivably, could he suc-ceed? By talking two greedy opponents into being generous to each other? As I have already indicated, that is a fool's errand which only a Menenius should undertake—a man content with patchwork de-vices, if only these can bring some fleeting moment of vain popu-larity. Volumnia evades looking at her proposal's requirements, focusing instead on the fame it may bring, in order thereby to ex-cite the aspiration of Coriolanus to magnanimity. And secondly, she ties her request to an appeal to filial duty—a sanction distinctively Roman. Through this appeal she socializes her son's Grecian virtue by insisting on a courtesy to mother as the duty which completes personal honor. Aristotle had spoken of honor as "that which we render to the gods" finally, but Volumnia is asking that it be rendered to her. No wonder then that Coriolanus says, when he consents: "You deserve / To have a temple built you." The "happy victory" she has won is, in essence, that of a Roman goddess to whom he is rendering honor. Volumnia has subdued his Grecian haughtiness. But the ironic result is that he is thereby made, in fact, the scapegoat for Rome's convenience.

On so complex a tragedy, several perspectives are concurrently possible. If we read with Plutarch's eyes, as some critics would, we can view Shakespeare's play as the tragedy of a "choleric man."[57] Yet such a summing up is limited and reductive. It ignores what Farnham and others have perceived as the root cause of the choler, the hero's pride in self-excellence. And historically-minded critics, I think, can recognize in this pride an aspiration to an Aristotelian magnanimity—man's crowning virtue for the Greeks, but in Christian eyes a source of vice. We know that Elizabethans, at least some of them, viewed pagan magnanimity critically. Thomas Watson's additions to *Antigone* (1581) present "Magnanimitas" as leading a pageant of tragic sin; and Fulke Greville contrasts Christian humility to Aristotle's magnanimity.[58] Shakespeare himself, in *Henry V*, associates the "magnanimous" Alexander with "Alexander the Pig." And in *Coriolanus* he has presented an Alexander-like greatness which manifests a tragic magnanimity.

But at the same time the tragedy of Coriolanus can be said to result, in part, from his being influenced by the kind of magnanimity Plutarch prefers—that of the non-obstinate man who is courteous to others out of a desire to have their favor. This was Plutarch's ideal. It is an ideal which Shakespeare's hero approximates in the candidating scene, and again when he relents in the embassy scene out of a desire for his mother's favor and his city's acclaim.[59] Yet this very obligingness ironically proves to be no less ruinous to Coriolanus than the haughty imperiousness which it ostensibly replaces. There is tragedy in this new magnanimity as much as in the old, because a concern for honor solely is still the hero's guiding motive. Coriolanus in Shakespeare's view is thus tragic on two counts: by aspiring originally to a Grecian excellence, and by accommodating to a Roman one, its philosophical cousin.

There is paradox in the fact that although Coriolanus does not fully measure up to Plutarch's ideal, he dooms himself by trying to. By his very bendings to show courtesy, this hero victimizes himself. Does not this fact imply a deceptive realism in Plutarch's ideal, its quasi-validity? Plutarch's ethic of social obligation can be said to be midway between the Greek ethic of individual honor and the Christian ethic of communal charity. Thus positioned, it has a kind of intermediary correctness in assessing the fault of Coriolanus. But at the same time it contributes to his disaster by providing no adequate substitute for the hero's sense of personal integrity, which it in fact compromises by absolutizing a duty to social convention. Plutarch's fable of the belly has precisely this inadequacy. My earlier comments have criticized it, not because it is altogether without merit in its stress on the mutual interdependence of the body's members, but because its ultimate import is defective. It is workable only at the cost of bastardizing human duty. Human interdependence on solely pragmatic grounds is but the rationale, as St. Augustine long ago remarked, of a pirate society, not a truly just society. Shakespeare's play, among its other achievements, places the merely relative validity of the Greek and of the Roman ideals as joint causes of the tragedy of Coriolanus.

Appropriately, Coriolanus does indeed ultimately attain fame, but by becoming its victim. "He shall have a noble memory," says Aufidius magnanimously, after having treacherously slaughtered him (in Achilles fashion) in order to refurbish Aufidius' own self-image of virtuous superiority. And meanwhile in Rome, Coriolanus gains the public acclaim he has desired—but, ironically, as an absentee hero:

> A merrier day did never yet greet Rome—
> No, not the expulsion of the Tarquins.

Now that he is unlikely to return, the senate can afford to propose gratefully:

> Unshout the noise that banished Marcius,
> Repeal him with the welcome of his mother.

This senate had done nothing earlier to negotiate with Marcius a rescinding of his banishment. But now to propose repeal can be tactically expedient for the senate's own popularity. Its power is now firmly reestablished, since the threat of a Coriolanus becoming Rome's king has been effectively removed. In an equivocal sense, then, the hope held out to Coriolanus by Volumnia in her suit has been fulfilled: he has reconciled the Volscians and the Romans— that is, has reconciled each, within its own camp, to a reestablishment of the internal power structure with which the play began. In this sense,

> each in either side
> Give the all-hail to thee, and cry "Be blest
> For making up this peace!"

Coriolanus has in nowise reconciled, however, the rival ambitions *between* the two camps. His death has merely resanctified an original status quo.

In my analysis of the play as a whole I have sought to bring out meanings which the text offers through its resonances of language and structure. But also I have attempted to show how our receptivity to what the text implies can be aided if we bring to it a sensibility sharpened by historical knowledge. Historical knowledge becomes most accurately pertinent to a grasp of Shakespeare's outlook, I have contended, when it includes a sense of the Christian perspective on history. This perspective Plutarch obviously did not have. His story of Coriolanus differs from Shakespeare's; and the difference is not explainable in terms simply of a shift in genre from biography to drama. Shakespeare has changed the figure-in-the-carpet in order to reveal in the tragedy a fuller dimension. His innumerable reconstructions of detail have configured the action with a deeper truth. And we can intuit that truth as we ponder the revised shape of Shakespeare's fiction.

The Christian dimension of this play about pagan times, let me say again, is not present in terms of Christian ideas voiced in the play—except insofar as Virgilia's voicing of love is that of a soul *naturaliter christiana,* and insofar as the fugitive concern of various citizens for love, gratitude, and friendship, and for a body politic ruled by head and heart, represent anticipatively the principles which nourish Christian order. These seeds of health are seen as germinally present in ancient Rome but thwarted. In a final sense, the Christian art of the play resides in its symbolic statement of pagan deficiencies, using for this a symbolism (of wolf, dragon, hostler, and harlot, for instance) which, while wholly natural in any pagan setting, at the same time evokes, for any reader knowledgeable in Christian lore, the larger aura of significance available in biblical texts and in Christian tradition. At the highest level of perspective, it is this Christian dictionary of implications which offers the key for understanding the vicissitudes of Roman history, so obscure to the Roman participants themselves and to their historiographer, Plutarch.

APPENDIXES

NOTES

INDEX

I

Two Augustinian
Echoes

1 The "limed soul" of Claudius

In *Hamlet* III. iii, at the climax of the action, Claudius attempts to pray. But on finding that he is unable genuinely to repent, he cries out:

> O wretched state, o bosom black as death,
> O limed soul, that struggling to be free,
> Art more engaged! (C. J. Sisson's edition)

Here "limed," meaning caught as with birdlime, sums up graphically his spiritual predicament. Yearning to wing his soul upward, Claudius finds it entangled in a kind of glue, while inwardly it is wasting into an "O" or cipher of itself. Earlier, Claudius has agonized over an entrapment of his hand in guilt—a "cursed hand" thick about with brother's blood. From that bondage he could hope to be freed, if only he could elicit heaven's mercy through prayer. But when then he finds his soul unable to form true prayer, the adjective *limed* gathers into focus his sense of desperate plight. A worldly snare is gumming his will.

Casually dropped into the drama's diction, the metaphor is an instance of Shakespeare's genius. But it may not be mere happy accident. The language is echoing a famous Christian story. Commentators have failed to note that the birdlime image occurs in several memorable passages in St. Augustine's *Confessions*. In X. [xxx.] 42, we read:

> Thou wilt increase, Lord, Thy gifts more and more in me, that
> my soul may follow me to Thee, disentangled from the birdlime
> of concupiscence; that it rebel not against itself . . . (Pusey's trans.,
> Everyman edition)

By "concupiscence," Augustine has just explained, he means "the lust of the flesh, the lust of the eyes, and the ambition of the world" mentioned in the Epistle of John. These, we therefore infer, are the birdlime *(viscum)* which entangles man's soul, causing it to turn rebel to itself.

Is not Claudius in just such a situation? His soul's strong "intent" to amend has been rendered impotent by a rebel desire to "retain the offense" which he would like to have pardoned and "past." The cause of this dilemma is his three-fold lust for "My crown, mine own ambition, and my queen." His situation thus parallels that of *Confessions* VI. [vi.] 9:

> I panted after honours, gains, marriage. . . . Behold my heart, O Lord, who wouldest I should remember all this, and confess to Thee. Let my soul cleave unto Thee, now that Thou hast freed it from that fast-holding birdlime of death. How wretched was it!

Note how the final words of this passage appear in *Hamlet* only slightly rearranged: "O wretched state, o bosom black as death, / O limed soul . . ." We could compare also a third passage in the *Confessions* (VI. [xii.] 22), in which the "birdlime" of pleasure's snares is associated with thraldom to a death-like misery. The metaphor is thematic.

In essence, Claudius' difficulty is what Augustine had described his own as having been—a gaping after honor, gains, and a wife. As these held Augustine back from the "conversion" he had begun to desire, so they detain Claudius. As long as his thoughts anchor on these and heaven too, Claudius is "like a man to double business bound." He cannot will anything singly. Though "inclination be as sharp as will," he stands "in pause" where to begin.

The doubleness of will here so accurately and fully presented by Shakespeare echoes Augustine's painstaking analysis, elsewhere in the *Confessions,* of this same psychological phenomenon. Describing his moral struggle, Augustine tells how he wanted to amend his life but could not by himself, because he had a mind "partly to will, partly to nill"—in short, "two wills, for that one of them is not entire: and what the one lacketh the other hath" (VIII. [ix.] 21). Or, again, he writes:

> When, above, eternity delights us, and the pleasure of temporal good holds us down below, it is the same soul which willeth not this or that with an entire will; and therefore is rent asunder with grievous perplexities, while out of truth it sets this first, but out of habit sets not that aside.
> Thus soul-sick was I, and tormented, accusing myself much more severely than my wont, rolling and turning me in my chain (VIII. [x–xi.] 24–25, tr. Pusey).

For Augustine, escape from this soul-sickness was possible only as he succeeded in achieving a complete humility, aided from the outside by the ministry of friends and the voice of a child. This is a direction in which we see Claudius looking: "Help, angels! Make assay! / Bow, stubborn knees, and heart . . . / Be soft as sinews of the newborn babe!"

Why does this noble effort not succeed? Unlike Augustine, Claudius lacks neighbors to lend him spiritual aid. Hamlet, at this moment, lurks in the background as a Black angel. Claudius, left unassisted, finds his thoughts unable to ascend with his words:

> My words fly up, my thoughts remain below.
> Words without thoughts never to Heaven go.

One further reason for the failure is that Claudius has not ordered quite aright his attempt to pray. He has omitted to bring into it petitions like those of the Lord's Prayer. Though his words glance at two of that Prayer's petitions when he declares that prayer's twofold force is "To be forestalled ere we come to fall / Or pardoned being down," he does not quite translate this into "Lead us not into temptation, But deliver us from evil." Nor has he begun his prayer by a hallowing of the name, kingdom, and will of "Our Father," or continued it with a plea to "forgive" as we forgive others. Caught between his guilt and an echo of King David's petition ("Wash me, and I shall be whiter than snow"—Psalm 51), Claudius is more anxious to wash his hand than his heart and is not thinking on mercy toward his own neighbor as a way to honor Heaven. His hope that "All may be well" therefore comes to naught. Perhaps, on a second attempt, he might have done better. Our pity is for a remorseful soul struggling toward a genuine penitence. When despair is reinforced, fortuitously, but ungraciously, by Hamlet's committing a crime which threatens Claudius, a fear for name and status prompts Claudius to shuffle with conscience and banish Hamlet under secret instruction for his death.

It is evident, however, that what may be called the universalizing features of Claudius' soliloquy at prayer, those elements which stiffen it with a more than personal import, depend either on the Bible (as in the allusions to Cain and to the Lord's Prayer) or on Western Europe's most famous book of Christian psychology, Augustine's *Confessions*. No wonder Abraham Lincoln declared this speech—rather than any of Hamlet's —his favorite passage in the play.

Whether Shakespeare ever read the *Confessions* in Latin (Sir Tobie Matthew did not publish his English translation until 1620), or whether he came by the substance of Augustine's outlook indirectly, we can only guess. But we do know that Augustine was the most popular, the most often invoked, of all Church Fathers in the age of the Renaissance-Reformation. And the Elizabethan public, in that era of lively theological interest, bought and read more religious books than all other kinds put together. Critics of later times too often forget this fact. Preoccupied with the more narrowly professional aspects of literature, they have sought clues to Shakespeare's diction far more often in the writings of his liter-

ary contemporaries than in the major classics of Christian tradition by
which (through direct or indirect permeation) the roots of Elizabethan
culture were being fed.

Considering *Hamlet* as a whole, we may remark further that one of
the dramatic functions served by Claudius' analysis of repentance is that
of providing a foil or counterpoise to Hamlet's statements on this same
theme. From the King's confession of murder we move, a scene later, to
Hamlet's meditation on another slaying, that of Polonius. And how
different the terms:

>   For this same lord,
> I do repent; but Heaven hath pleased it so,
> To punish me with this and this with me,
> That I must be their scourge and minister.

Absent here is the whole Christian framework of repentance. Instead of
seeing himself, as does Claudius, faced by the "bar" of heaven and compelled by it to "give in evidence" even to the "teeth and forehead of our
faults," Hamlet sees his fault as ordained by heaven. And later when he
asks pardon, not of God or heaven but only of Laertes, the ground he
proposes for pardon is that the evil he has done was not "purposed" by
him. He would excuse the human will and remove thereby the duty of
restitution. A case for the toleration of "distraction" is substituted. Hamlet's equivocal repentance is thus a self-forgiveness in the name of fatalism. The piety of it is morally bankrupt. Claudius' earlier speech has
provided us, the audience, a touchstone for intuiting this fact.

2 Iago's Pelagianism

In *Othello* I. iii. 321 ff., Iago sets forth his theory of the will. Roderigo
has just pleaded an inability to reform himself: "I confess it is my shame
to be so fond, but it is not in my virtue to amend it." Iago thereupon
lessons him:

> Virtue! A fig! 'Tis in ourselves that we are thus or thus. Our
> bodies are gardens, to the which our wills are gardeners. So that
> if we will plant nettles or sow lettuce, set hyssop and weed up
> thyme, supply it with one gender of herbs or distract it with many,
> either to have it sterile with idleness or manured with industry—
> why, the power and corrigible authority of this lies in our wills.
> If the balance of our lives had not one scale of reason to poise
> another of sensuality, the blood and baseness of our natures would
> conduct us to most preposterous conclusions. But we have reason
> to cool our raging motions, our carnal stings, our unbitted lusts,
> whereof I take this that you call love to be a sect or scion.

The lecture is neat, academically considered. The professor, loftily brushing aside his pupil's troubles, has reduced the problem to straightforward, easy-to-remember terms. One simple proposition, backed up by two picturesque illustrations, each developed with parallelism and balance and the whole controlled by a commonsense optimism—who could wish a happier explanation?

On closer scrutiny, however, the explanation has some obscurities. Just what the various herbs signify remains shadowy, and how the gardener comes by his supply of them is not stated. The assumption seems to be that the garden of the body has these herbs in root form. They connote various types of possible action which the human will can choose among and develop. The gardener-will, then, decides and regulates the character of the crop which his garden-body shall yield. Without logical transition, Iago's explanation then jumps from the garden metaphor to a scales metaphor. As the first was a picture of man's freedom of action, the second is a picture of his freedom in choosing. That is, the will is to be seen as free not only as to what it chooses but also in the very act of choice. Man's passions, Iago is saying, do not necessitate his choices, inasmuch as he has reason to balance against passion. Our lives need not be led to "preposterous conclusions," since a corrigible authority resides in our wills. Both illustrations would enforce the thesis that whatever we do is "in ourselves" and of our making.

Yet the explanation has a blind spot. As regards the act of deciding, it overlooks the power which habit has in disposing the will to favor passion. Roderigo has just said he "will incontinently drown" himself; he has just confessed he has no real will to check his passion, even though ashamed of it. Iago's explanation has omitted to consider what it is that disposes the will to prefer certain herb-possibilities and to cultivate them. Roderigo's state is that of having no incentive to amend: "It is silliness to live when to live is torment" he has said a moment earlier. Thus Iago's theory obscures the human will's need to be disposed toward the good and to be empowered by the order of such a disposition. (Virtue is "an ordered disposition of the soul," "a good quality of the mind" in Scholastic definition.[1]) Iago would have Roderigo amend his life according to his own will and merely by invoking that will, when it is already predisposed to self-destruction!

The theory must be suspect, also, because the teacher of it is himself headed for defeat. His own wife Emilia will ultimately act by a virtue for weighing love of truth as life's chief value, rather than by using reason to curb her passion. Such unexpected behavior will bewilder Iago. And earlier we see a frustration in Iago on his perceiving that Cassio's life has in it a "daily beauty" which makes his own ugly by comparison.

Iago cannot by his own will's power succeed in removing that ugliness in himself.

Readers of *Hamlet* may recall, moreover, that Claudius in that play found himself unable by reason alone to amend his life. Like Roderigo he confessed to a sense of shame, because of a lack of power actually to will a change. The cry by Claudius, "Help angels! Make assay!" acknowledged his sense of need for aid from outside to perfect his will. That outlook is in contrast to Iago's in *Othello*.

Iago's theory may be compared, however, with that of Pelagius, a fifth-century Christian heretic. Pelagius in his *Defense of the Freedom of the Will* was not, of course, so silent about God as Iago is. As a Christian theorist, Pelagius acknowledged that God had set the stage for man's choices by creating him and nature round about him. Yet Pelagius excluded God from qualifying in any way man's volitions and actions. Man was seen as the sole author of his own character. Pelagius pictured man as endowed at birth with a capacity for freedom, the bare possibility for acting either in the direction of evil or of good. How man used this inborn capacity determined his character, and the use was wholly in man's own power. Volition and action were entirely his own work.[2] "That we really do a good thing, or speak a good word, or think a good thought proceeds from ourselves."[3]

In support of this thesis, Pelagius used also a garden motif and a scales motif. Man's inborn possibility for actions, good or evil, said Pelagius, "resembles a root which is most abundant in its produce of fruit." This root "yields and produces diversely according to man's will." It is capable "either of shedding a beautiful bloom of virtues or of bristling with the thorny thickets of vice."[4] Man's choice decides the issue. Iago has amplified this garden metaphor, let us grant, in slightly different language from Augustine's; the flowering that emerges, Iago says, depends on which plantings man cultivates. Yet inasmuch as the herbs of Iago's parable represent the root possibilities man begins with and which he then cultivates as he wills, so that the character of the flowering is thereby of man's making, I think we may recognize an affinity of basic idea. As for the scales idea, it is reflected in Pelagius' thesis that man is not handicapped in his freedom by Adam's fall, not predisposed either toward virtue or vice. The possibilities are evenly balanced. "We are formed naturally without either virtue or vice; and previous to the action of our own proper will, the only thing in man is . . . a capacity for either conduct."[5] Handicapped by no bias, man does not need the enabling power of grace.

St. Augustine criticized this view as being contrary to experience and also to Scripture. Man's present freedom, he contended, is in a state like that of the wounded man in the parable of the Good Samaritan. It is half-dead, and needs a restoring grace to empower liberty of action.[6] In and of himself, man has a will that is sickly. His situation may be either that of a will without power, or that of a power without the will in immediate control.[7]

This view of Augustine's, it may be of further interest to note, seems to accord with the comment of some of Shakesepare's personages outside of *Othello.* "As we are ourselves, what things are we!" exclaims one of the French Lords in *All's Well* IV. iii. 24—to which his companion replies: "Merely our own traitors." The two men are commenting on Bertram's indulgence of his will in his clandestine affair with a young lady. And the second Lord goes on to remark: "he that in this action contrives against his own nobility, in his proper stream o'erflows himself." In other words, Bertram's will in this case is his own enemy. His will, left to itself, is plainly not exercising the "corrigible authority" Iago posits for the will. Elsewhere, in *Romeo and Juliet* II. iii. 28, Friar Laurence expresses a theory also different from Iago's. He sees two opposed foes

> In man as well as herbs, grace and rude will;
> And where the worser is predominant,
> Full soon the canker death eats up that plant.

Here man is regarded as himself an herb, growing in grace predominantly or else in rude will predominantly. Grace, by implication, is the authority whose operation is needed to subdue rude will, if death is to be avoided. In this view, the "preposterous conclusions" against which Iago warns would be due not to sensuality primarily but to "rude will."

In the light of these passages, and in the light of the issues raised by the Pelagian controversy, we can react to Iago's speech somewhat more cautiously than is usually done. A recent opinion that "These are the sentences of a moral philosopher to whose thought few would take exception"[8] is, I think, uncritically hasty. Certainly at other moments in the play—for instance, when Iago is theorizing cynically on woman's virtue—most of us do take exception to the thought of this moral philosopher. Why not, then, here? If his character is to be of a piece dramatically, his theory must have some blind spot persistently. His reasoning must be continuously plausible but deceptive.

Iago's deceptiveness on such an issue as that of the freedom of the will could certainly have been penetrated by the wiser Elizabethans. Article IX of the Thirty-Nine Articles mentions the Pelagians for specific disapproval, and many of the collects in the Book of Common Prayer stress man's dependence on grace. The Pelagian tenor of Iago's argument would therefore have been scented more easily by auditors in that age than in our own. Even a century ago, however, when Christian teaching on original sin was all too often ignored, Coleridge could still perceive that Iago's estimate of man forgets his handicapped state. Iago, says Coleridge of this speech, is here the partisan of "a truth converted into a falsehood by the absence of all the necessary modifications caused by the frail nature of man."[9]

More recently, Hardin Craig has referred to Iago's argument as "a grand perversion of the theory that good is the end and purpose of reason."[10] And as regards Iago's garden metaphor, may we not apply D. W. Robertson's summary of the medieval view of this literary image? The nature of any garden, Robertson tells us, was seen as determined by whether Christ, or *sapientia*, is the gardener. "When Christ is the gardener, the garden is ruled by wisdom and suffused with the warmth of Charity. Otherwise it is ruled by worldly wisdom or *scientia* and suffused with cupidity."[11]

Lucrece in Other
Versions

1 Chaucer's legend

Sidney Lee, in 1905, wrote more truly than he knew when he remarked: "Like Chaucer, Shakespeare holds up Lucrece to eternal admiration as a type of feminine excellence."[1] What Lee did not understand—nor have many others since—was the particular kind of feminine excellence being held up, and the particular kind of admiration in which Chaucer and Shakespeare were holding it. The two poets, I believe, were not admiring Lucrece's moral excellence but, instead, the esthetic excellence of her vanity and of her feminine virtuosity in self-deception. Not as an epitome of truly human virtue, but as a beautiful instance of its blind abuse, she fascinated their attention. In her they could see what Shakespeare elsewhere calls the "one touch of nature" which makes the whole world kin, namely, love of vainglory. This frailty both authors can accept with compassion—but Chaucer with a more mischievous eye for its farcical side, Shakespeare with a more philosophical eye for its tragic significance.

The general thesis that Chaucer was writing satire or travesty in his *Legend of Good Women* was advanced by H. C. Goddard in 1908, and in a modified form was applied to the Cleopatra of Chaucer's *Legend* by R. M. Garrett in 1923.[2] Unfortunately their contention, perhaps because they supported it so thinly with details, has fallen by the wayside. Yet Goddard made some penetrating jibes. "Chaucer's principal formula for making a woman good," he remarks ironically of the *Legend*, "is to make her the victim of a bad man. All women, whatever their own part in the affair may have been, who are betrayed by false loves are—presto!—fit subjects for canonization; such is the delightful logic with which Chaucer manufactures new martyrs and sings the praises of women. A more exact, if less ironical title for the poem would be *The Legende of Bad Men*." Of the Lucrece story, Goddard noted two things. One is that Chaucer has assigned contradictory reasons for Lucrece's failure to cry

out in alarm, and that Chaucer's comment, "she seyde al that she can,"
implies that "al" was very little. Goddard's second point is to note what
has puzzled other critics too, Chaucer's seemingly confused memory of
the Bible in the allusive lines which end his poem:

> For wel I wot that Crist himselve telleth
> That in Israel, as wyd as is the lond,
> That so gret feyth in al that he ne fond
> As in a woman; and this is no lye.
> (Robinson's text, second edition)

This allusion, if traced to its closest verbal source (Matthew 8:10 and
Luke 7:9), turns out to be a reference to no woman at all, but conversely,
to a Roman centurion (literally one *man* in a hundred, an emblem perhaps of our smiling Chaucer).

These are useful clues, though they are also elusive ones which need
for their interpretation a fuller attention to both text and context. For
example, might not Chaucer in his biblical allusion have had in mind,
instead of the Roman centurion, the Syro-Phoenician woman of Matthew 15:28? Granted, this latter passage lacks Christ's explicit statement, as in the other episode, that "I have not found so great faith, no,
not in Israel"; yet plainly the Syro-Phoenician woman did have great
faith and (see verse 24) was not of the house of Israel. Why not therefore
accept this latter identification, as F. N. Robinson does in his authori-
tative edition, and consider the matter closed? Yet even Robinson adds
the qualifying clause: "unless Chaucer confused her story with that of
the centurion." Is it a confusion, and if so why? Might it, contrariwise,
be a case of a deliberate ambiguity? Perhaps Chaucer, great poet that he
is, can be saying several things at once, opening up thus, rather than
closing, the significance of his allusion.

The Syro-Phoenician woman and the Roman centurion, as any
thoughtful reader of their stories can discover, have in common two important characteristics which give their faith a unique quality: first, a
great concern for healing; and second, a great humility. Let us note that
the centurion, although accustomed as a Roman official simply to command his wishes performed, has gone out of his way to humble himself
before a subject Jew for the sake of curing a servant "sick of the palsy,
grievously tormented." Moreover, he asks no parade to his house, no
spectacle to grace his own fame. "Lord, I am not worthy that thou
shouldest come under my roof; but speak the word only and my servant
shall be healed." This Roman's prayer, in fact, is such a perfect epitome
of true faith that the sentence just quoted has been incorporated into
the Catholic Mass (with the word "soul" substituted for "servant"), as
everyman's proper prayer in preparation for holy communion. By implication it is Chaucer's faith. But the faith of the Syro-Phoenician

woman can be conflated with it, as being substantially the same. Morally she is a feminine equivalent of the centurion. This Gentile woman has so little vanity that she refers to herself, not even as a "lost sheep," but as a "dog" pleading for "crumbs" from a good man's table. Her one concern is for the cure of a daughter "vexed by a demon." Hence, if Chaucer's feminine readers are looking for a woman rather than any man, as their model, let them think on this biblical heroine—if they can!

Should they do so seriously, however, the large irony of Chaucer's tale would become evident: in every respect Lucrece is not at all the kind of woman we have found the Syro-Phoenician woman to be. Lucrece resembles, rather, that woman's demon-possessed daughter, in need of cure. Likewise, she resembles not the biblical centurion, but rather that noble Roman's sick servant, tormented by a palsy. For, as Chaucer has been hinting, Lucrece's fear for reputation both palsies her moral life and enslaves it to a demonic vanity. We may suspect that admirers of Lucrece (and perhaps also of Lucretius) were among the court ladies to whom Chaucer was dedicating his poem. For them, Chaucer is winding it up by alluding to a biblical woman the reverse of Lucrece, and saying that the rarity of *her* faith "is no lye." By implication, the faith of (or Chaucer's pretended praise of) any other kind of woman may be a lie—that is, a mere poetic fiction.[3]

Thus the biblical allusion at the poem's ending is of crucial importance. As a gratuitous addition on Chaucer's part, how can it be accounted for except as a clue to his own interpretation? His seeming fumbling of it, as we have now shown, masks a rich ambiguity of reference. He is being as bold an ironist as he dare risk. Once we realize this fact, we can become alert to watch for irony elsewhere, in passages where the signaling of it is less overt. Consider, for example, Lucrece's final glory, that of having her dead body paraded through the streets. Such glory contrasts *toto caelo* with that accorded the centurion or the Syro-Phoenician woman. And here Chaucer, although leaning on Livy's mention of a funeral parade, has surrounded this fact with overtones of horror and oppression. Lucrece was carried on a bier, he says,

> Thurgh al the toun, that men may see and here
> The horryble dede of hir oppressyoun . . . .

The loose syntax and the ambiguous pronoun *hir* (which can be either singular or plural in reference) permit of a double entendre. Whose "oppressyoun," and precisely what "horryble dede" are being set forth? On the surface, the references may be to *their* (the Tarquins') oppression of her. But, conversely, the poet could mean Lucrece's oppression of men's eyes and ears by the horrible deed of her suicide.

And what precisely has Rome-town gained by canonizing her?

> Ne never was ther kyng in Rome toun
> Syn thilke day; and she was holden there
> A seynt, and ever hir day yhalwed dere
> As in hir lawe . . . .

What *hir* law has hallowed, Chaucer is emphasizing, is the abolition of kingship. He is making explicit what Ovid implied by telling this story under the date of February 24, Rome's holiday commemorating the "Fuga Tarquinii Superbi." But did the medieval Chaucer think the overthrow of monarchy a holy event? He may well have remembered what Augustine had written (*City of God* III. 16): "How calamitous a year was that in which consuls were first created, when the kingly power was abolished."[4] Besides, as a Christian poet Chaucer was surely aware that whereas paganism's calendar may celebrate the exiling of kings, the Christian calendar has always preferred to celebrate an Advent of true Kingship. What he thinks of Lucrece's sainthood he hints broadly enough at the very beginning of his poem:

> Now mot I seyn the exilynge of kynges
> Of Rome, for here horible doinges

The pronoun *here*, with its ambiguously singular or plural reference, can be taken as meaning either *their* (the kings') horrible doings or *hers*. Chaucer, I suggest, is challenging us to a double vision, by which both readings are true.

For the covert working of his irony, however, Chaucer must seem to slide away from this opening theme. "But for that cause telle I nat this storye," he hastens to add apologetically. He will draw the Lucresse who has been commended by the pagans "for hyre wifhod and hire stede-fastnesse," and who "in oure legende" has been held in "grete compassioun" by Augustine, because she "starf in Rome toun." Will Chaucer's readers now fall into the trap of supposing that *our* legend of Lucrece (the Augustinian one) is the same as the Roman legend? "Starf" is a verb Chaucer can use elsewhere (*Troilus,* 1844) of Christ's death—but in that case as an example of our need for *his* compassion, not of his need for ours. Christ's death was a ransoming one, to "beye" our souls from bondage to "feynede loves." Was Lucrece's death that kind of death? Precisely because it was morally the exact opposite, an instance of bondage to fained loves, it warranted Augustine's compassion along with his judicious censure. But this fact of Augustine's censure of Lucrece, and his grounds for it, our shrewd Chaucer in his assigned task of praising Lucresse must discreetly omit from mention. It is enough that he has established the paradoxical tone he needs for the praise he will in the rest of the poem bestow on her *steadfastness.* Exactly what kind of love she was steadfast in he has not stated, except by implication in saying that "these payens" (Ovid and Livy) commend it. But at the end of his poem he will return to ironic praise of her particular kind of steadfast-ness:

> I telle hyt, for she was of love so trewe,
> Ne in *hir wille she chaunged for no newe;*
> And for *the stable herte,* saddle and kynde,
> That in these wymmen men may alday fynde.
> Ther as they kaste hir herte, there it dwelleth.
>
> (Italics mine)

To never change one's will can imply impenitence—a continuing to dwell wherever the heart has been cast. Thus "stable," as a term of praise, is equivocal. A stable, incidentally, was the place where, midway in the poem, a "knave" was said to be. Might even that bit of background de-tail carry a Chaucerian wordplay and theme?

Chaucer in his *Legend* has been faithfully carrying out a Prologue instruction to "Spek wel of love." But just how can a Christian author speak well of Cupid's saints? Through a poet's enigmatic art of praise. While narrating in a tone of steadfast admiration and kindly sadness, Chaucer is using this mode of naive obedience both to represent well the unexamined love characteristic of Lucrece and other noble pagans and, at the same time, to tuck into his story marginalia which undercut their whole perspective by revealing, all too well to an alert reader, the moral blindness through which good women fall into mental muddle and tragic self-victimization. Chaucer's own stable but knavish art, we may say, is thus gracing with a lurking disgrace the sentimental liking of his noble social superiors for Cupidinous love.

From the start of his story, Chaucer pretends to be following Ovid, yet any close reader will soon be aware of subtle transformations. Ovid be-gins with mention of the tedium of the siege of Ardea, relieved by Tar-quin's inviting his men to drink and good cheer, which then inspires the men to eulogies of their wives. Chaucer, in retelling this sequence, man-ages to suggest a general idleness, with probably a pun on idol-ness (an association made in *The Second Nun's Tale,* lines 7–14, 269, 285, 298)—here by soldiers more interested in "japes" than in a serious prosecution of the war:

> Ful longe lay the sege, and lytel wroughten,
> So that they were half idel, as hem thoughten;
> And in his pley Tarquinius the yonge
> Gan for to jape, for he was lyght of tonge,
> And seyde that it was an ydel lyf;
> No man dide there no more than his wif.

It is perhaps this "ydel lyf" (equally true of man and wife) that is about to be put to the test. To "ease oure hearte," suggests Tarquin, "Preyse every man his owene." Thus stated, Tarquin's words carry an invitation to idolize (i.e., to idolatry, by any Christian standard). And Chaucer shows Collatine immediately responding. His wife, Collatine boasts, "Is holden good of alle that evere hire knowe." (We may wonder: In what sense do men get to know her and hold her?) A hunt now begins.

And what do the men find when they arrive at Lucrece's house? They find, so Chaucer notes, no porter at the gate. This missing guardsman is a detail Ovid had used, but not of Lucrece's house. He had used it, instead, to describe the house in which the other Roman wives were revelling wantonly, the house which the noblemen first visited. Chaucer, by omitting this first stop, has contrived two things: 1) a seeming deference toward his feminine readers by avoiding any mention of Rome's loose women; and 2) an impression that he is dutifully remembering the "no porter" from Ovid, whereas actually he is inverting Ovid's import by placing this compromising fact at Lucrece's door. Then what are we told the visitors see when they peek into Lucrece's chamber? According to Chaucer, they see her sitting "by hir beddes side / Dischevele, for no malyce she ne thoughte." But is lack of malice an adequate explanation for the "Dischevele"? May not a reader suspect in Lucrece a subconscious love-longing, not unrelated to the open state of her house?

Ovid had not introduced Lucrece as disheveled, although he did include, among Tarquin's memories of her after the visit, the loveliness of her hair falling about her neck. Idyllically, Ovid had introduced her as engaged in spinning, with baskets of wool standing here and there about her couch. But Chaucer mentions the spinning only after first carefully locating her "by her beddes side / Dischevele."

> And softe wolle oure bok seyth that she wroughte
> To kepen hire from slouthe and idelnesse;
> And bad hire servaunts don hire besynesse,
> And axeth hem, What tydyngs heren ye?
> How seyth men of the sege, how shall it be?

Despite the deferential reference to "oure bok," Chaucer is not here following Ovid with genuine fidelity. According to Ovid, Lucrece's first words to her maids were an urging them on to the spinning of a votive war cloak, to be sent as soon as possible to their lord. Chaucer entirely omits this reason for working the wool. We are not told what, precisely, Lucrece is working at. Moreover, the "besyness" of her servants is "bad" in so ambiguous a way as to suggest that it may consist, perhaps, in providing Lucrece with whatever rumors they have picked up through associations with men! Evidently there are more ways than one of keeping oneself from sloth and idleness. Even Lucrece seems to be busy, less in spinning wool than (may we say) in mental woolgathering. Her very next words,

God wolde the walles were falle adoun!
Myn husbonde is to longe out of this toun,

hint at a concern for her sexual need—this, rather than her husband's
need for a war cloak. Whereas Ovid, at this point, had pictured Lucrece
as boastfully taunting the defenders of Ardea, and as imagining her husband rushing about with drawn sword, the very image of pugnacity,
Chaucer's Lucrece has no such militant spirit, nor does any ideal of a
fighting husband come to her mind. Ovid's account is being refocused.

Tarquin, after listening in on Lucrece's thoughts and then seeing her
rush to embrace her husband, comes away burning with a lustful desire.
As in Ovid's account, he presently girds on a sword and rides to Lucrece's
house. But the circumstances of his arrival differ. For Ovid, the time is
about sunset; in Chaucer's account it is after sunset, in the dark. Ovid
has Tarquin come as a kinsman and friend, who as such is entertained
at supper. Chaucer has him come as a thief. He pictures him entering
first "into a prive halke," then stalking "ful thefly" about in the night
until finding entrance "by wyndow or by other gyn." This change of
circumstances permits a suspicious reader to ask: Why not simply by
the door, which the earlier visit had shown to be unguarded? Could it be,
perhaps, that the thief-like behavior is as much a masquerade as was the
guise of friend assumed by Ovid's Tarquin? That is, has Chaucer's
Tarquin perhaps surmised that Lucrece subconsciously would prefer to
have a stranger intrude under pretense of villainy, since thereby she
would be provided an opportunity to attribute her yielding to force and
mischance?

Awakened by a sudden pressure on her bed, what can Lucrece say?
"What beste is that," she asks, "that weyeth thus"? Then on learning
that this *beste* is a king's son, with a sword in hand for silencing her, "No
word she spak, she had no myght therto." No might, we infer, for ma-
neuvering an escape. She "axeth grace, and seyth al that she can." Chaucer explains her scant speaking by saying that "hire wit is al ago." Yet it
seems this wit is not "ago" in any way that hinders its going about considering all the reasons for *not* resisting which Chaucer hypothesizes for
her. "Ryght as a wolf that fynt a lomb alone, / To whom shal she com-
pleyne?" (Can we be quite sure, in Chaucer's phrasing of this question,
that Lucrece finds being alone with this wolf anything to "complain"
of?) This consideration leads to a second: "Wel wot men that a woman
hath no myght." To a sophisticated reader, this can be one of the poem's
most amusing lines. It leads to Lucrece's third thought: "What! Shal she
crye, or how shall she asterte / That hath hire by the throte, with swerd
at herte?" (But how real is the danger that Tarquin might kill her, when
to do so would *ipso facto* deprive him of her sexual cooperation? Perhaps
the vague "That" which has her by the throat is not so much Tarquin's

hand as it is her own grasping for excuses.) When she "axeth grace," Tarquin replies with his second threat: to defame her. (Is not this a bit curious? What need is there for a second threat, if Tarquin really means his first threat and if Lucrece already believes herself helpless? Could it be, rather, that both threats are intended gallantly to provide Lucrece the "grace" of a face-saving excuse for her yielding?) Chaucer does not have Tarquin offer, as in Ovid's account, ardent pleas to Lucrece and promises of gifts to influence her along with his threatening sword. For Ovid, such begging and bribing highlights a Lucrece unmoved by love or money; hence Tarquin can overcome her only by a second tactic, his threat to defame her. Chaucer is more subtle in his insight. On the one hand, Tarquin must *look* like a robber; hence no pleading with pecuniary gifts, which might make him seem a seducer. On the other hand, as this rapist proceeds directly to his second threat, let him seal it with a grand oath: "As wisly Jupiter my soule save!" For this oath (added by Chaucer) not merely emphasizes Tarquin's awesome determination; it also suggests a secret inducement, by recalling (to an understanding ear, such as Lucrece's?) the wisdom of Jupiter, king of the gods, who disguised himself for adulterous purposes—and whose rapture no mortal woman should wish to resist!

Chaucer as ironist keeps these hints subdued. Ostensibly he is merely describing Tarquin's dreadfulness in order the more fully to exculpate Lucrece and sing her praises. He therefore credits Lucrece's yielding, as Ovid had done, to the overwhelming force of Tarquin's second threat. But, in fact, he outdoes Ovid—and thereby keeps alive his own irony. "Succubuit famae victa puella metu" had been Ovid's terse comment. Chaucer embellishes; he has Lucrece fall into a complete swoon:

> She loste bothe at ones wit and breth,
> And in a swogh she lay, and wex so ded,
> Men myghte smyten of hire arm or hed.
> She feleth no thyng, neyther foul ne fayr.

In such a lifeless condition, what pleasure could she have given Tarquin? Chaucer's exonerating details have reduced the situation to absurdity, perhaps in order to awake in the canny reader a few questions: Is this swoon a faint or a feint—or compounded of both? Is Lucrece dead, maybe, only in arm and head, those parts of her body not needed for a sexual response? Or are the lines telling us figuratively that Lucrece has lapsed now into a moral deadness, in which ability to discriminate between good and evil is gone? Any of these readings is possible. Meanwhile, Chaucer has covered his tracks by piously stressing the love of good name and the dread of public shame which characterized "Romeyn wives." (Even here, possibly, there is a hidden pun on "roaming"—cf. *Man of Law's Tale,* 558: "To pleyen and to romen to and fro.") Chaucer's comment derives from Augustine's. But it substitutes for Augustine's open criticism of name worship (which Chaucer dare not voice) a praise of it which becomes double-edged, chiefly through the poet's deft picturing of the pathetic-idiotic consequences of such a love.

A thoughtful reader of the rape account Chaucer has given might be prompted to recall, further, Augustine's question: "What if she was betrayed by the pleasure of the act, and gave some consent to Sextus . . . ?" She alone knows, had been Augustine's reply. For since he was speaking, as he says, to "those who are unable to comprehend what true sanctity is," he was content to focus on Lucrece's subsequent sin of suicide. Yet note his explanation of what caused this later act: not a genuine love of purity, but her "burning" with a "proud dread" at the thought of human suspicion—a distress which the "Roman love of glory in her veins" could not endure. Does not this permit any reader who does understand true sanctity to continue to surmise that Lucrece's earlier yielding to Tarquin was influenced, likewise, by this Roman love? And if thus influenced, could she have been, actually, as chaste as her admirers believe? Is not an idolizing of human glory likely to adulterate with equivocations one's responses in a rape situation? Would not a subconscious shame promote, in those circumstances, a masking of the will's role under idle modes of self-excuse? Such an interpretation of the subtle interrelation between the psychic and sexual areas of human behavior seems implicit in Chaucer's story.

The poem's overt comment on the rape concludes with a stanza of rebuke for Tarquin, after which Chaucer returns to "the story I rede." But again he reads with a difference. Whereas Ovid's Lucrece, the next morning, sends only for her old father and her husband, Chaucer says she sends for "hir frendes alle." As in Ovid, she sits now with disheveled hair, but the accompanying simile is altered: Ovid's "Ut solet ad nati mater itura rogum" is turned into—

> In habit switch as *women* used tho
> Unto the *buryinge* of hire frendes *go*
> (Italics mine)

—a phrasing which hints that Lucrece is now about to bury her friends in her own grief, using a "habit" for this which women have. Her countenance and her story, Chaucer goes on to say, arouse in the whole assemblage a woe impossible to tell. Impossible to tell, we may suspect, because involved in it are so much mental confusion and moral irony.

Lucrece's contradictions are latent in Ovid's account, but Chaucer is making capital of them. He has Lucrece say that

> for hir gylt ne for hir blame,
> Hir husbonde shulde nat have the foule name,
> That wolde she nat suffre, by no wey.

The four piled-up negatives are both pathetic and humorous. They conspicuously invert the wise adage: Accentuate the positive, eliminate the negative. Moreover, what precisely does her statement mean? If she is saying that she will in no wise allow her husband to receive a foul name for what is *her* guilt and *her* blame, she is admitting her own guilt. But if, on the contrary, she is saying that she refuses to accept, as any guilt or blame of hers, her husband's receiving of a foul name, she is shuffling off on her audience the blame for giving him such a name and the guilt of misjudging her. Or she may be quite muddled as to what she means. Chaucer, I think, means to show her as floundering in contradictions and exploiting ambiguities. These, inevitably, are the consequences of her pagan fear of losing fame for self and husband—and of her evading of the truth that a violated body signifies the guilt, properly, only of the will which connives in its violation.

But Lucrece's audience is floundering similiarly. They now answer, "upon hir fey" (which to Chaucer may be the very thing most suspect),

> That they forgave yt hyr, for yt was ryght,
> It was no gilt, it lay not in hir myght.

Appropriately the pronoun "it," four times repeated, here roams loosely in four different directions. And the final noun, "might," is likewise ambiguous. "Might" could mean physical strength; or it could mean willpower. If we entertain the second sense, that Lucrece lacked strength of will to resist sin, it makes nonsense of the judgment "no guilt." (In Livy's account the citizens specify that they exonerate her on the premise that her will gave no consent. Chaucer presumably could have been as specific, had he not preferred an ambiguity.) Even more significant is the contradiction imbedded in the first line. Is it logical to forgive an action that is *right?* A right action can sometimes need exoneration; but to forgive it is nonsense. Lucrece's reply to their offer therefore carries, ironically, a more consistent logic:

> "Be as be may," quod she, "of forgyvyng,
> I wol not have noo forgyft for nothing."

That is: she will not have them forgive where there is nothing to forgive. Such, at least, is one possible reading of her piled-up negatives.

Yet if there is nothing to be forgiven, there is nevertheless in Lucrece's view a "foule name" to be removed, and this she undertakes to do by removing herself from life to fame! She will have nothing to do with forgiveness (which Chaucer's readers ought to know is the *sine qua non* of Christian virtue); yet she will give everything else for the sake of a picture of "clennesse," which she can create as she falls dead! What she supremely cares about is *how she falls:*

> And as she fel adoun, she kaste hir lok,
> And of hir clothes yet she hede tok.
> For in hir fallynge yet she had a care,
> Lest that hir fet or suche thyng lay bare.

In *that* she is steadfast—in a concern for her *covering*, and in glancing *downward*. Such is Chaucer's measure of "Hir herte . . . so wyfly and so trewe."

The meaning I have been drawing out for attention is not the only possible one but rather the covertly ultimate one. At the surface level, of course, readers may see merely the simplistic meaning which Lucrece sees in events, a meaning larded with lurking contradictions which Lucrece overlooks in her emotional self-righteousness, and which Roman legend has glorified through its uncritical admiration. But Christians, at least potentially, can read with a subtler sensibility—as indeed any man can, if he is genuinely sophisticated in matters of human experience and intellectual enough not to let emotion blur insight as he reflects on the total story. Such a man was Chaucer, aided by the illuminating realism and compassion of Augustine.

The poem has therefore been offering us a traditional enigma—a story with two levels of meaning—while tantalizing our reflective capacities by various casual, and seemingly naive, variations from the details in pagan legend. Besides parenthetical references to Augustine and the Bible, Chaucer has supplied for our aid sly clues of many sorts, notably the following: 1) a repeated use of the pronoun *hir* or *here* in an ambiguous sense; 2) a transfer of the "no porter" to Lucrece's house; 3) a characterizing of Collatine and company as "half idel," thus inviting us to discern a similar idleness in Lucrece when later her words betray less concern for responsible work than for idle fancy; 4) an assigning to Tarquin of tactics which imply a complex plan for encouraging Lucrece to fancy herself as helpless; 5) a "defense" of Lucrece's yielding which challenges us to see, rather, her concern for self-justification, and her swooning as half self-induced—somewhat like Lady Macbeth's faint after the murder of Duncan; 6) an associating of her steadfastness with impenitence and with a keeping up of appearances at all costs; and 7) a sympathetic account of the nevertheless confused reasoning in her martyrdom, which covertly reveals it as truly absurd.

This reading of Lucrece, let me remark in conclusion, need in no way diminish our esthetic appreciation—either of the poem, or of its heroine's feminine excellence, or of the splendor of that civilization (both ancient and perennial) to which she belongs. Rather, our sense of an art in all things, whatever their kind, is I think immeasurably enhanced. For if the biblical author of Proverbs could declare himself awed by "the way of a serpent upon a rock" and "the way of a man with a maid," he could in the same passage confess as *wonderful* "the way of an adulterous woman": "She eateth and wipeth her mouth, And saith, I have done no wickedness" (30:20). To a Christian eye, indeed, there is no thing in which the beauty of order may not be found. As Augustine so wisely puts the matter:

> Many have spoken fully and *truly in praise* of ashes and dung. What wonder is it then if I say that a human soul . . . wherever it is and whatever its quality . . . is beautifully ordered, and that *other beauties arise even from the penalties* it undergoes.[5]

Or again, as he says elsewhere: just as "the beauty of a picture is increased by well-managed shadows, so, to the eye that has the skill to discern it, *the universe is beautified even by sinners . . .*"[6] Chaucer, like Shakespeare, was aware of this fact. It was for both writers the keystone of their art.

And can any art be more relevant to the human condition than this? Are not most of us, much of the time, sinners—especially in the evasions by which we mask this fact from ourselves for the protecting of our ignorance? A poetic which mirrors such a truth can be our best introduction to reality.

2 Heywood's play

Within a few months after Shakespeare's *Lucrece* appeared, another Elizabethan poet was providing the public a stage version. So we can infer from a passage in Drayton's *Legend of Matilda* (December, 1594), where mention is made of:

> *Lucrece,* of whom proude Rome hath boasted long,
> Lately reviv'd to live another age,
> And here ariv'd to tell of *Tarquins* wrong,
> Her chast deniall, and the Tyrants rage,
> Acting her passions on our stately stage . . .

This acted *Lucrece* cannot be identified, unless (as seems credible) we accept Allan Holaday's argument that Thomas Heywood's *The Rape of Lucrece* (first published in 1608) has behind it an earlier version, on stage by the late summer of 1594.[7] A revival of this version around 1600 would account then for Jonson's reference, in *Cynthia's Revels* (1601), to making "a face like a stabb'd Lucrece." Regardless of this hypothesis, however, Heywood's play as a published text warrants a comparison with Shakespeare's poem. Evidently it was an equally popular work. It reached a fifth edition by 1638, besides its performances at the Red Bull theatre and elsewhere.

Yet here is an instance in which the comparable commercial success of two contemporary versions of a story seems to testify a response, not precisely from the same public, but rather from different segments of the Elizabethan populace. Audiences of that day, we may need to be reminded, were no more monolithic in their tastes than today's audiences. Both they and the authors who wrote for them brought variant perspectives and values stemming from the diverse heritage of the Renaissance. In Heywood's case, the perspective used in his telling of the Lucrece story is notably Livy's rather than St. Augustine's. Basically what we find in Heywood's play is a heightening of Livy's moral vision with an overlay of Tudor didacticism, while at the same time there is interspersed for comic relief some native clowning and a dozen or more catches of popular song (increasing to twenty-two by the fifth edition).[8] In the play's central episode, the rape story, various echoes from Shakespeare's *Lucrece* indicate that Heywood has absorbed what he could of that poem. But plainly his reading has been superficial, and predetermined by Livy's interpretation. For he gives us a Lucrece designed to be in every respect a model for our moral admiration. Thus his version has nothing of Shakespeare's or Chaucer's sense of the irony of Lucrece's virtue, or of the tragic limitations of Rome's sense of values.

For Heywood, Lucrece's tragedy has its cause (as in Livy) in the tyranny begun by Tarquin's parents when they usurped the throne. Further, the tragedy's whole meaning turns about a simple contrast between the lust of the Tarquin family and the virtue of a chaste Lucrece and of a pious Brutus, who suffer from tyranny's ravages and die to free Rome from them. Such tragedy, if compared with Shakespeare's, is simplistic and neoclassical. It rests, we may suppose, on Livy's idea that Tarquin Superbus initiated a tragedy like that of the Greek Atreus-Oedipus: "For the royal house of Rome produced an example of tragic guilt, *as others had done,* in order that the loathing of kings might hasten the coming of liberty, and that the end of reigning might come in that reign which was the fruit of crime."[9] Livy as historian was an apologist for republicanism; hence for him the era of the Tarquins is a tragic phase from which Rome was delivered by the republican spirit of Brutus. The passage I have quoted from Livy would account for the subtitle Heywood gives his play: "A true Roman Tragedy."

Yet in structuring the composition of his work, Heywood's own additions of balladry and clownage are surely something less than Roman. These mix English variety show devices with classical chronicle, and thus achieve a domestication of neoclassical tragedy. A. M. Clark regards this amalgam as "debasing some of the noblest legends of Livy."[10] But the typically middle-class patrons of the Red Bull theatre seem to have found congenial to their taste this play's Senecan rhetoric and spectacle, its in-

terludes of minstrelsy and racy dialogue, and its morality of platitudi-
nous patriotism. Heywood's play no doubt pleased most of his auditors.
Shakespeare's poem, on the other hand, if we may credit Gabriel Harvey's estimate, was best appreciated by a "wiser sort" of reader.

Among this wiser sort, if I may digress for a moment, can be included
the young poet Thomas Middleton. His *The Ghost of Lucrece* (1600; ed.
J. Q. Adams, 1937) is written in the same stanza form as Shakespeare's
poem. But it is cast in the literary form of a complaint, such as one finds
in Daniel's "Rosamond" or in *The Mirror for Magistrates*. It presents
the ghost of Lucrece coming from hell, where she has been "sucking at
Revenge's dugs," and where her companion "spirits of sin" include Tarquin, Tereus, and Philomela. She revisits earth to tell the sad story of a
"hell-eyed Lust" figured in herself. The candle of her shames, she confesses, "stinks before the throne of Chastity," because her lack of chastity
has "painted the mouth of lust" on her heart and "made my ghost reel to
hell." Her twofold sin is plainly stated:

> . . . lust and blood are mingled in one lamp
> To seal my soul with Rape and Murder's stamp. (27–28)

Middleton's perspective, clearly, is an orthodox Christian one.[11] We
may suppose he saw this implied in Shakespeare's *Lucrece,* but saw also
an opportunity for himself to bring the story's moral into open statement
by continuing Lucrece's life into an afterworld, where she could appropriately discover the truth about herself and confess it.[12]

We should note, however, that a very different estimate of Lucrece
continued to be available to Elizabethans. The Roman perspective of
Ovid and Livy was kept alive not only in their writings but by Boccaccio,
Chaucer's·Italian contemporary. Boccaccio's *De claris mulieribus* (1360–
74; printed in 1473 and later editions) had treated Lucrece as a supreme
model of chastity and conjugal fidelity. His estimate of her (I quote from
the English translation by Lord Morley in the 1540s) was that she "can
neuer be to muche commendyde and praysede."[13] From Boccaccio this
view was copied by Lydgate in *The Fall of Princes* (written in the 1430s;
printed 1494 and later). Lucrece, says Lydgate, was clean and innocent
in heart and thought, and her chaste will "dede non offence." He excuses himself from telling her story, by saying Chaucer has already
written of her "a legende souerayne." Yet Lydgate devotes nineteen
seven-line stanzas to versifying, from Boccaccio, a complaint made by
Lucrece regarding the injury done her by Tarquin; and elsewhere he
versifies an account from Collucius, which is devoted largely to Collatine's reassuring his wife that her soul is free from corruption and a
lantern of good example, but to which she replies with a counterargu-
ment concluded by her suicide.[14] It seems evident that Lydgate must have

read Chaucer superficially, with eyes blinded by Boccaccio. The simplistic Roman interpretation is the one adopted also by Gower in his brief tale of Lucrece in the *Confessio Amantis.*

Whether Heywood had ever read Chaucer's story of Lucrece, or Boccaccio's in Latin, or Lydgate's echoing of Boccaccio, or Gower's versifying, we do not know. He seems merely to be following Livy, while absorbing a few touches from Shakespeare's popular poem and dressing up the whole with his own inventions of spectacle and naive moralizing. Heywood is obviously more interested in melodrama than in any subtleties of human psychology.

His play opens with a reluctant husband, Tarquin Superbus, being urged by his wife Tullia to seize the crown. This situation is obviously comparable to that in Shakespeare's *Macbeth,* and critics have often claimed that Heywood's text of 1608 strongly reflects *Macbeth.* Perhaps so. Yet the basis for Heywood's characterization of Tullia and Tarquin is in Livy's history, and the style he has chosen for developing the story is obviously Senecan rather than Shakespearean. Heywood's Tarquin pleads feebly, "Heare me wife." Whereupon (I am using Holaday's edition) Tullia thunders:

> I am no wife of Tarquins if not king:
> Oh had *Jove* made me man, I would have mounted
> Above the base tribunals of the earth,
> Up to the Clouds, for pompous soveraignty.

A moment later she is proposing to "lave our brows then in that crimson flood" of the blood of Servius, her own father. Then, after the assassination, she not only rides her chariot over the body of this father, as Livy mentions, but in doing so declares her delight to "wash my Coach-naves in my father's blood." Such rant I think we may call pseudo-Tamburlainean. It bears no relation to Lady Macbeth's boast: "Had he not resembled / My father as he slept, I had done't." Shakespeare's lines carry a pathos which Heywood's lack. Moreover, Lady Macbeth eventually cannot repress fears and guilt feelings for the blood on her hands, whereas when we see Tullia again, toward the end of Heywood's play, her bravado is undiminished. "Mercy I scorne . . . / Come on ye slaves and make this earth divine" is her taunt as she dies fighting.

It accords with Heywood's sense of drama to show Tullia's son Sextus Tarquin arriving a moment later (from his fighting elsewhere "Knee deep in blood") to shout now his boast: "I ravisht the chaste *Lucrece; Sextus* I, / . . . 'twas for my Rape, / Her constant hand ript up her innocent brest, / 'Twas Sextus did all this." By such language Heywood thinks he is epitomizing the "black sin" that has descended from mother to son with all the fatalism of an organic disease. Yet (unlike Oedipus under hereditary curse), Sextus has developed no remorse.

Shakespeare had given us, as his final vignette of Sextus Tarquin, a man slinking away in shame after the rape. Livy, with a concern rather for the political consequences, had reported of him that after Rome's decree of banishment he departed to the Gabines and was there slain by old enemies. But Heywood at the end shows Sextus returning from banishment with an army to besiege Rome, very likely because Heywood can thus stage him meeting Brutus in a spectacular duel.[15] The last words of Sextus are here boldly impenitent (and with none of the undertone of remorse of Shakespeare's Macbeth):

> I repent nothing, may I live or die,
> Though my blood fall, my spirit shall mount on hie.

Then, as ravisher and punisher clash, each falls slain by the other, and Heywood can round off his play with the funeral honors bestowed on Brutus, including the award of a laurel crown. Meanwhile, two other episodes of heroism which Livy had reported as happening somewhat later—Horatius at the bridge, and Mutius Scevola's self-mutilation by fire—have not been overlooked by Heywood. He has worked these into an earlier battle scene for their value as stage spectacle.

Within this large framework of chronicle (the epic story of Tullia's irreligious monarchizing until the purging of her dynasty by a devout patriotism embodied in Brutus), Heywood sets the personal tragedy of Lucrece in a central section of about a thousand lines. Slightly earlier, Lucrece makes a brief first appearance on stage, significantly, to upbraid one of her maids for casting "wanton looks" at the Clowne. She warns:

> Know hence-forth there shall no lascivious phrase,
> Suspitious looke, or shadow of incontinence,
> Be entertain'd by any that attend on Roman Lucrece.

This establishes the tone of Heywood's portrait. In a later scene showing Lucrece with her maids, just before the testing lords burst in, we hear her lecturing these maids against revelling, and expounding to them her sense of duty:

> Since all his businesse he commits to me,
> Ile be his faithful steward till the Camp
> Dissolve, and he return, thus wives should do . . .

And she refuses a supper invitation from Lord Turnus. As Allan Holaday has remarked, "She moves about, robot fashion, speaking the cherished moral platitudes of Heywood's day."[16]

When Sextus Tarquin comes later, alone, to visit this Lucrece, he is able to gain entrance only because, pretending a goodwill visit, he has beforehand lured Collatine into furnishing him a ring as a token to ensure welcome. Only because of this ring does Lucrece open the house gates to Tarquin. "Without that key you had not entered heere," she assures him. Then, at supper, she is so modest in remaining standing to serve him the meal, and so virtuous in her speaking (not of Collatine's fame, as in Shakespeare's version, but of Collatine's prizing of Sextus), that he is reduced to muttering exclamations to himself against the "impious lust" that has brought him here, and can eat little. When he has been ushered to his room, she retires to her bed, but not without a prayer to Jove, in which she commits her chastity to heaven's keeping. By innumerable touches of invention, Heywood is making sure that we view Lucrece as a perfect and saintly woman. His details show almost no dependence on Shakespeare's.

Next we hear Tarquin soliloquize on the "blacke mischiefe," and the bad madness, that is driving him to destroy himself in betraying "divinest" Lucrece. He knows the rape will bring down on him men's contempt and curses, but fate is propelling him to "make my dayes harsh" for the sake of one sweet night. (The utter fatalism of his psychology here goes beyond Shakespeare's.) Then he awakens her to make his proposal. She replies, "Heaven such sinnes defend!" and she begs him for Rome's sake not to havoc his own worth and not to wrack her chastity. When he threatens, "By *Jove* ile force thee," she replies:

> By a God you sweare to do a devils deed, sweet Lord forbear.
> By the same *Jove* I sweare that made this soule,
> Never to yeild unto an act so fowle.

And she cries "Helpe, helpe." Notice here Lucrece's gracious plea, her forthright rejection of Tarquin's proposal, her sensible cry for help, and her conspicuously Christian theology, even though as a Roman her name for God is Jove. Heywood has almost no historical sense of the difference between Roman and Christian civilizations.

When Tarquin now immediately threatens to pillow any shrieks, Heywood's Lucrece quietly assures him she prefers death to dishonor. She begs him not to exile pity from his heart, and to look on her tears as orators pleading on Collatine's behalf. To Tarquin's second threat, to defame her by placing her murdered beside one of "thy basest Groomes," she replies: "Then make my name foule, keepe my body pure." This answer would have quite surprised Ovid or Livy. It implies a contempt for fame as compared to chastity. Further, Tarquin can overcome her only by physical strength, by seizing and dragging her off-stage, while she cries out, "Jove guard my innocence," and Tarquin boasts:

> Lucrece th'art mine
> In spite of *Jove* and all the powers divine.

Rape under such circumstances, I think we may say, would have been regarded even by St. Augustine as no loss of true chastity by Lucrece.

Quite inconsistent, however, with the largely Christian behavior of Heywood's heroine prior to the rape is her insistence afterwards on revenge and suicide. Here we can only suppose that Heywood's admiration for Roman valor, and his feeble understanding of Christian ethics, made it easy for him to take at face value a legend so stunning in its theatrical possibilities. His inaptitude for psychological insight may have led him to suppose, further, that he was following Shakespeare in the kind of nobility he now pictures in Lucrece. He may even have thought he was bettering Shakespeare by not assigning to Lucrece any withdrawal into dallyings with grief. She sends at once for the lords.

Before they arrive, Heywood invents for her a single speech of complaint, in which she questions why the gods have allowed her victimization:

> ... oh you powerfull Gods,
> That should have Angels guardents on your throne
> To protect innocence and chastite! oh why
> Suffer you such inhumane massacre
> Of harmlesse vertue?

If it is her fate, she reasons, to bear the shame of being "a staine to women," she will be "no more woman" but "Devote to death and an inhabitant / Of th' other world." Dressed therefore in "funerall blacke" and in the ornaments of widowhood, she greets Brutus and Collatine courteously. Asked to tell who has wronged her, she replies: "Ere I speak my woe, / Sweare youle revenge poor Lucrece on her foe." They so promise immediately. Then, asking them to sit, she straightforwardly announces her mangled reputation, speaks of her "innocent" thoughts but "body soild," and names Tarquin and how he gained admission by the ring.

> This Ring, oh *Collatine!* this Ring you sent
> Is cause of all my woe, your discontent.

Up to this detail (which is Heywood's way of emphasizing the element of fatal mischance in her tragedy), the scene has been in general accord with Livy's version.

So also is Lucrece's summary, next, of Tarquin's threats and of how his threat to "make me hated" by all the world "Ravisht and kild me at once." At this point (as in Lydgate's version) Collatine personally commends what she did:

> Yet comfort Lady, I quit thy guilt, for what could
> Lucrece doe more than a woman? hadst thou dide polluted
> By this base scandall, thou hast wrong'd thy fame:
> And hindred us of a most just revenge.

Evidently Heywood intends us to approve both fame and revenge as
human motives. Immediately they are given religious sanction, as Brutus
invites the lords:

> Lay your resolute hands upon the sword of Brutus,
> Vow and sweare, as you hope meed for merit from the Gods,
> . . .
> And joyne with *Brutus* in the just revenge
> Of this chaste ravisht Lady, sweare.

When they at once do so, Lucrece says this hope removes her grief.

> Yet Lords, that you may crowne my innocence
> . . .
> Ile not debare my body punishment:
> Let all the world learne of a Roman dame,
> To prise her life lesse than her honor'd fame.

Then she stabs herself. By thus phrasing her dying words, Heywood implies that she is deliberately setting an example of true virtue in order
to revive it for Rome.

Brutus orders a display of the body in the marketplace, to kindle
Roman wrath to "a most just revenge"; and the remainder of the play
(about 500 lines) turns about the successful expulsion from Rome of the
Tarquinian "viperous brood" and the defeat of all counterattacks. In
the end Brutus gives his life to chastise the Tarquin "Lust" and "Pride."

From the play's beginning this has been Brutus' sense of the destiny
he was "borne to"—to purge the state's "infected blood, bred by the pride
/ Of these infested bloods" (220–223). The Tarquins, like giants of old,
have warred against the gods. The success of their sacrilege has caused
Brutus to ask: "*Jove* art thou just; hast thou reward for pietie?" And,
again: "What's the reason then, / Heaven spares his rod so long?" But
he himself has answered: "*Jove* oft delayes his vengenance" until the
fruit of pride is ripe for a fall into rot. Heywood, following Livy, has
shown Brutus visiting the oracle at Delphi and there gaining a confirmation of his mission. "He that first shall kiss his mother / Shall be power-
full, and no other" says the oracle. Brutus reads the hidden meaning by
falling to kiss the earth, man's mother. Thereupon the oracle adds a
comment invented by Heywood:

> Then *Rome* her ancient honours wins,
> When she is purg'd from *Tullia's* sins.

It is this message which Brutus treasures, while he bides his time under
cover of madness until Lucrece's victimization provides him the opportunity to bid for popular support. In the name of the gods, he then accepts the leadership of an army of purgers. Critics such as Irving Ribner

have seen in this story a similarity to Malcolm's action in Shakespeare's *Macbeth*. But surely Malcolm's retirement to the court of pious Edward is significantly different from Brutus' escape into pretended madness, satiric wit, and the comfort of a secret oracle. This aspect of Brutus makes him similar, rather, to Shakespeare's Hamlet.

Heywood would have us thoroughly approve not only Lucrece and Brutus but also Collatine. From the start Collatine is portrayed as simply an affectionate and merrily confident husband, an adaptable and generous courtier. Newly married, he's at home during the *coup d'etat,* and when summoned to court he accepts the "new humours" of his friends as a way of living "safe." On hearing that Tarquin Superbus has rewarded his son Sextus for betraying the Gabines, Collatine's attitude is: "Leave all to heaven." By this, Heywood intends to stress Collatine's piety.[17] To insure further that we view him as a good husband, he is shown making frequent visits home to his wife—once when his clown comes to say that Lucrece intreats his return, again when he brings friends for a dinner in his home, and a third time in connection with the wager. Heywood alters also the circumstances of this wager. What prompts it is Collatine's being teased for not drinking at a camp feast. Horatius jests that Collatine will "pledge no health unless it be to his Lucrece." Sextus then jibes: "What's Lucrece but a woman, and what are women / But tortures and disturbance unto men?" At this point, several of the men rise to a defense of their wives, thus impelling Collatine to say: "I should wrong my Lucrece not to stand for her." Heywood is implying that Collatine is no boaster but a modest man put on the defensive. Sextus is shown baiting him by questioning cynically whether any wives can be trusted in their husbands' absence. Here again, Collatine does not speak first. Rather, Brutus answers that some wives, no doubt, are vicious and "apt to sinne," yet others are "angels and sweet featur'd saints." Collatine then says: "Such is my virtuous Lucrece"—whereupon the other men boast that their own wives are superior. Only when thus challenged does Collatine say:

> Ile hazard all my fortunes on the vertues
> Of divine Lucrece, shall we try them thus?

And he proposes an immediate visit, with the stakes being a "horse and armour" for the man adjudged to be the winner. Such a bet implies, simply, a confidence in Lucrece's merits.

Elsewhere in the play, as well, Heywood maintains our favorable view of Collatine—no falls into trance or into blubbering, as in Shakespeare's version. To Collatine, at the end, is given the curtain speech which sums up the play's message:

> March on to Rome, Jove be our guard and guide,
> That hath in us veng'd Rape, and punished Pride.

Such faith in Jove, Heywood makes us feel, is equivalent to good and true religion. It supports a pious heroism which Heywood evidently regards as thoroughly admirable, a moral model for Elizabethan approval.

Heywood's *Lucrece* has been praised as an "attempt to give dramatic form to a vision of man's relation to the forces of evil in the world which is distinctly Shakespearean."[18] I would doubt that it is such an attempt, but would say that if it is, it quite fails in that attempt. The distinctively Shakespearean vision is, as I have tried to show, something quite different—less sentimental, less jumbled, less subject on the one hand to the values of the source materials it works with and on the other to the vague religiosity of bourgeois Renaissance humanism. To point out what such a distinction can mean for the precise appreciation of literary texts has been the purpose of our present survey. If we have succeeded, our long excursion into comparative literature will have placed Shakespeare's achievement in better perspective.

Our study has focused on the significant difference between the Roman perspective on Lucrece and the medieval-Christian perspective. We have shown how, among Elizabethan versions of her story, Shakespeare's rests fundamentally on the view taken by Augustine and Chaucer, whereas Heywood's merely amplifies Livy's view with Tudor embellishments. We have noted also how this divergence of perspective is evident, likewise, in a contrast between the Renaissance view of Boccaccio and Lydgate, on the one hand, and the ultra-Augustinian view of Middleton on the other. Thus we have illustrated the intellectual cross-currents of the times. But we have demonstrated further that not all intellectuals are equally intellectual. The shrewder can deploy the vision of the shallower by making it the rind, not the core, of truth.

Notes

I Shakespeare's Re-Vision of Lucrece

1. F. T. Prince, *The Poems* (1960), Introduction, pp. xxxiii-xxxviii.

2. Harold R. Walley, "*The Rape of Lucrece* and Shakespearean Tragedy," *PMLA*, LXXVI (1961), 480–87.

3. Thus Sidney Lee, in a 1905 edition of *Lucrece,* laments that Shakespeare fell victim to the very faults of which he accused his contemporaries, a wasting of his ingenuity in devising grandiose language and "bombastic periphrases." From Furnivall, in 1885, to Douglas Bush's *Mythology* of 1932, and C. S. Lewis' *English Literature* of 1944, there runs a reiterated complaint that Lucrece's agonies have been made too rhetorical. Swinburne, in 1879, described the poem as a whole as having "fits of power and freaks of poetry," but not a good poem. Bush finds it "soulless," "wearisome," and "quite bookish."

4. Geoffrey Bullough, *Narrative and Dramatic Sources of Shakespeare,* I (London, 1957), 182–83.

5. T. W. Baldwin, *On the Literary Genetics of Shakespeare's Poems and Sonnets* (University of Illinois Press, 1950), p. 153.

6. Baldwin decides in favor of these, while also showing that most of Livy's variant details were included in the notes of a Renaissance edition of Ovid by Marsus (1508 and later editions). He considers Chaucer's version to be of "negligible influence," and follows Wilhelm Ewig [*Anglia,* XXII (1899)] in concluding that Shakespeare made no use of Augustine. Bullough in his *Sources* has included Chaucer's version, remarking that Shakespeare "certainly knew" it; but he offers no discussion of points at which Chaucer could have influenced Shakespeare. He omits Augustine entirely as a source.

7. The prose style of the Argument, and its moral perspective as well, seem to me closely imitative of Livy. James M. Tolbert, in "The Argument of Shakespeare's *Lucrece,*" *Texas Studies in English,* XXIX (1950), 77–90, after noting the Argument's Latin-like connectives and absolute constructions, has speculated that it was written not by Shakespeare but was supplied at the last moment by a publisher's assistant who in rote manner consulted some Latin epitome of Livy. I think this an ingenious but mistaken hypothesis.

8. Charlotte Porter, Introduction to her edition (1912), p. ix.

9. See Hyder Rollins, New Variorum edition of *Shakespeare: The Poems* (Philadelphia, 1938), p. 423.

10. A recent essay by D. C. Allen independently lends support to the view I am developing. In "Some Observations on *The Rape of Lucrece*," *Shakespeare Survey*, 15 (1962), 89–98, Allen writes (p. 91): "We must, I think, face the fact that Shakespeare read the story of Lucrece in its Christian context. There was no question in his mind about its tragic import, but he felt that it must be glossed in terms of Christian options. Lucrece should have defended herself to the death, or, having been forced, lived free of blame with a guiltless conscience." Allen, however, does not review Shakespeare's poem systematically in the light of this view; he merely reports the existence of a Renaissance controversy between those humanists who quoted Ovid and Vergil in defense of Lucrece's chastity and other humanists who, following Augustine, saw in her an "imperfect" chastity; and then he refers to a few of Shakespeare's passages in which the latter view is suggested, or would have been recognized by readers familiar with Landino's and Petrarch's moralization of Troy's fall (to which Shakespeare has Lucrece liken her own). Troy, for Petrarch, is "the voluptuous city, victim of its own passions"; for Landino, it is "the youthful life of man when reason slumbers."

11. Baldwin, *Literary Genetics,* p. 135, has noted this allusion.

12. In *Richard III* (written in 1592 or 1593) Shakespeare had already dramatized this point of psychology in the scene of the slaying of Clarence by the two murderers (I. iv.). In *King John* (about 1595), on the other hand, he dramatizes in the scene between Hubert and Arthur (IV. i.) the only psychology by which a tyrant's psychology can be quelled —by innocent Arthur's nonresistant charity. The fact that Arthur does not make use of negative sermonizing to combat Hubert's aggression is noteworthy, particularly since Shakespeare's source play, *The Troublesome Raigne,* had pictured Arthur as converting Hubert by preaching negative warnings. Evidently Shakespeare knew (as Jesus did in contrast to the Pharisees of his day) that negative moralizing, however pious, has no efficacy against radical evil. In Lucrece, therefore, he has shown us the futile Pharisaic response.

13. The vanity of worldly fame is the basic theme of Chaucer's *House of Fame.* That poem, and its rootage in the medieval Christian view of fame, is expounded by B. G. Koonce, *Chaucer and the Tradition of Fame* (Princeton University Press, 1966).

14. Whereas Ovid and Livy do not locate this "slave" in any particular household, Shakespeare follows Chaucer in naming him Lucrece's; and, on a second mention of him, Shakespeare's Tarquin calls him "some rascal groom," a variation of Chaucer's "thy knave . . . in the stable."

15. Thus I concur with Walley's generalization (p. 480), that while the

I *Shakespeare's Re-Vision of Lucrece,* CONTINUED

poet's "preoccupations are basically those of a dramatist," our attention
in the poem is concentrated "rather on the deliberation which precedes
and lies back of drama."

16. Sidney Lee, as cited in the Rollins Variorum, p. 225. John Bailey's
similar comment in 1929 (Rollins, p. 514) is noteworthy as an example
of antimedieval prejudice: "Prolixities of this sort," says Bailey of the
digression on Troy, "whatever beauties they include, are survivals of the
incoherent irrelevancies of a Middle Age which had always too much
time on its hands. They remind us of those very long lanes for which
Chaucer sometimes allows himself to desert his main road of action."

17. Compare, in Marlowe's *Dido,* the irony of Dido's saying, after
hearing from Aeneas the tale of Troy: "O, had that ticing strumpet
ne'er been born!" (II. i. 300). Much later she admits that "all the world
calls me a second Helen" (V. i. 144).

18. The number 42 seems to connote evil in *Romeo and Juliet* and in
Antony and Cleopatra, as I shall be noting in later chapters. Since number symbolism is currently out of fashion, I recognize the riskiness of
even mentioning it. Yet it may have had for Shakespeare, in a minor
way, a figurative import.

19. According to the *OED,* a repeated *he,* as in *he he,* represents
laughter. Aelfric is cited as an initial authority on this meaning; and its
punning use in connection with confession of adultery is illustrated from
Wycherley's *Country Wife* (1675), II: "He! he! he! he's my wife's gal-
lant." This furnishes us ground for reading Lucrece's *he he* as a kind of
blind glee, through which Shakespeare is inviting us to see the farcical
side of her supposed ecstasy of chastity.

20. Shakespeare's own estimate of Nestor (and also of Ulysses and
Sinon, whom we shall presently mention) is indicated clearly in *Henry
VI, Part III,* a play which antedates *Lucrece.* He shows us the monstrous
Richard boasting that

> I'll drown more sailors than the mermaid shall;
> I'll slay more gazers than the basilisk;
> I'll play the orator as well as Nestor,
> Deceive more slyly than Ulysses could,
> And, like a Sinon, take another Troy. (III. iii. 186–190)

II In Search of an Adequate Perspective

1. Robert Heilman, *Magic in the Web* (University of Kentucky Press,
1950), p. 240.

2. For my citations, see *Johnson on Shakespeare,* ed. Walter Raleigh (Oxford University Press, 1908) and *Shakespeare Criticism,* ed. D. Nichol Smith (Oxford University Press, 1934).

3. See Arthur R. McGee, "Macbeth and the Furies," *Shakespeare Survey,* 19 (1966), 55–67.

4. *Johnson,* ed. Raleigh, p. 161. It is noteworthy, however, that Johnson's view was not shared by Addison. To the contention of Dennis, that every tragedy ought to show a "particular Providence . . . plainly protecting the good and chastizing the bad," Addison replied that Tate had subjected *King Lear* to a "chimerical Notion of Poetical Justice." See Clarence Green, *The Neo-Classic Theory of Tragedy in England During the Eighteenth Century* (1934; repr. New York, 1966), pp. 139–46.

5. F. R. Leavis, *The Common Pursuit* (London, 1952), pp. 107–111. Jean Hagstrum, in *Samuel Johnson's Literary Criticism* (rev. ed., University of Chicago Press, 1967), p. 68, admits that Johnson's universe "had neither angels nor devils, neither a heroic Christ nor a magnificently rebellious Satan." The consequence of this, I would say, was that both radical good and radical evil were excluded from Johnson's sense of probability.

6. H. C. Heffner, *The Nature of Drama* (Boston, 1959), p. 343.

7. H. C. Goddard, *The Meaning of Shakespeare* (University of Chicago Press, 1951), p. 557.

8. W. J. Bate, *Prefaces to Criticism* (Garden City, 1959), p. 135.

9. *Coleridge's Writings on Shakespeare,* ed. Terence Hawkes (New York, 1959), p. 65. My further citations are from other pages in this text.

10. W. K. Wimsatt and Cleanth Brooks, *Literary Criticism: A Short History* (New York, 1957), pp. 406–407.

11. George Santayana, *Interpretations of Poetry and Religion* (New York, 1900). Later in life, he gradually changed his opinion of Shakespeare. John M. Major, in "Santayana on Shakespeare," *SQ,* X (1959), 469–79, quotes him as writing before his death to Corliss Lamont: "perhaps he [Shakespeare] might be set down for a Humanist or Naturalist of our sect . . ." (p. 477). Richard Butler, *The Mind of Santayana* (Chicago, 1955), has described his overall philosophy as "a curious combination of Platonic idealism, Kantian transcendentalism, and the crude materialism of Democritus" (p. viii).

12. On Shaw's views, see E. B. Adams, "Bernard Shaw's Pre-Raphaelite Drama," *PMLA,* LXXXI (1966), 428–38; also Sylvan Barnet, "Bernard Shaw on Tragedy," *PMLA,* LXXI (1956), 888–99; and the criticism collected in *Shaw on Shakespeare,* ed. Edwin Wilson (New York, 1961).

13. For instance, Theodore Spencer, *Shakespeare and the Nature of Man* (New York, 1942), p. 148; and G. B. Harrison, *Shakespeare: The Complete Works* (New York, 1948), p. 1137.

II *In Search of an Adequate Perspective,* CONTINUED

14. A. C. Bradley, *Oxford Lectures on Poetry* (London, 1909), pp. 69–92.

15. A. C. Bradley, *Shakespearean Tragedy* (Second edition reprint, London, 1950), pp. 37–38.

16. Bradley, *Shakespearean Tragedy,* ed. cit., pp. 21, 78.

17. Jacques Maritain, *On the Philosophy of History* (New York, 1959), p. 24.

18. George Thomas, *Religious Philosophies of the West* (New York, 1965), p. 256.

19. See Appendices A and B in Lily B. Campbell, *Shakespeare's Tragic Heroes: Slaves of Passion* (New York, 1959 edition), esp. pp. 281–86.

20. Bradley, *Shakespearean Tragedy,* ed. cit., pp. 83–84, 198, 364; cf. also 324.

21. Bradley fails to reconcile this statement (p. 100 and p. 174) with his statement elsewhere (p. 343) that in *Macbeth* the witches "are dramatically on the same level as the story of the Ghost in *Hamlet,* or the falsehoods told by Iago to Othello."

22. Bradley, *Shakespearean Tragedy,* ed. cit., p. 25.

23. Roland Frye, *Shakespeare and Christian Doctrine* (Princeton University Press, 1963), pp. 43, 57–58.

24. Bradley, *Oxford Lectures on Poetry,* pp. 352–53.

25. A recent instance of this contrary direction is Norman Holland's view in his *Psychoanalysis and Shakespeare* (New York, 1966), pp. 305–306. Holland thinks fictional characters have no implied freedom of choice. "A psychological vocabulary," he says, "describes men choosing actions in the real world, but dramatic characters do not exist in the real world nor do they choose." I would say, rather, that the *dramatis personae* imitate human life and action, including the action of choice-making by the self being represented. That assumed self's *liberum arbitrium,* it seems to me, is an aspect of the action being enacted. We see developing in the action the kind of character the self is choosing to affirm.

26. Bradley, *Shakespearean Tragedy,* ed. cit., p. 37.

27. L. C. Knights, *Explorations* (London, 1946), pp. 18–36.

28. See D. A. Traversi, *An Approach to Shakespeare* (Garden City, 1956), pp. 150–81; M. M. Mahood, *Shakespeare's Wordplay* (London, 1957), pp. 129–42; and Dolora Cunningham, "Macbeth: The Tragedy of the Hardened Heart," *SQ,* XIV (1963), 39–47.

29. Francis Fergusson, *The Human Image in Dramatic Literature* (New York, 1957), pp. 115–25.

30. E. E. Stoll, *Othello* (Minneapolis, 1915), p. 33; Campbell, *Shakespeare's Tragic Heroes,* Ch. XIII; Bernard Spivack, *Shakespeare and the Allegory of Evil* (New York, 1958), pp. 421–22.

31. E. E. Stoll, *Art and Artifice in Shakespeare* (Cambridge University Press, 1933), p. 163.

32. E. E. Stoll, *Shakespeare's Young Lovers* (Oxford University Press, 1937); my citations are from pp. 4–8, 34, and 42.

33. Stoll, *Young Lovers*, p. 3.

34. Heilman, *Magic in the Web*, p. 270.

35. Campbell, *Shakespeare's Tragic Heroes*, p. 248.

36. Augustine, *City of God* XII. 8; XIV. 6–9; XIX. 21.

37. Aquinas, *Summa Theologica* I–II. 73. 2; 74 entire. In my "Hamlet's Apostrophe on Man," *PMLA*, LXVI (1951), 1073–1113, I showed how the moral philosophy of Aquinas fits the action of the play *Hamlet*, whereas a Platonic and Stoic philosophizing dominates the reasoning of Prince Hamlet, who thereby fails to understand rightly the realities of his own action.

38. W. C. Curry, *Shakespeare's Philosophical Patterns* (Baton Rouge, 1937), pp. 97–137.

39. Frye, *Shakespeare and Christian Doctrine*, p. 36.

40. Alice Walker, "The Reading of an Elizabethan," *RES*, III (1932), 264–81, describes Lodge's borrowings from Scholastic authors.

41. See my article, "The Grounds of Religious Toleration in the Thought of John Donne," *Church History*, XI (September, 1942), 241.

42. Frye, *Shakespeare and Christian Doctrine*, p. 14. He believes (p. 100) that Luther's teachings are the closest in conformity with Shakespeare's dramatic practice. But this is sheer guess, unsupported by any systematic comparison of Luther's position with others, and unattended by close study of any one of Shakespeare's plays. Frye seems not to know of C. J. Reimer's *Der Begriff der Gnade in Shakespeares "Measure for Measure"* (Marburg, 1937), which surveys the meaning of grace in Luther, in Calvin, and in Catholic theology, and concludes that the Catholic meaning is the closest in accord with the play's passages. Peter Milward, S.J., has criticized Frye's rejection of allegory; see "Shakespeare and Christian Doctrine," The Shakespeare Society of Japan *Shakespeare Studies*, IV (1965–66), 36–56.

43. L. L. Schücking, *The Meaning of "Hamlet"* (New York, 1937), pp. 1–30.

44. Eliot's "Introduction" to G. W. Knight's *Wheel of Fire* (1930). In what follows I summarize from his essays "Shakespeare and the Stoicism of Seneca" (1927) and "Hamlet" (1919). For a critique of Eliot's stance, see René Wellek, "The Criticism of T. S. Eliot," *Sewanee Review*, LXIV (1956), 398–443.

45. Leavis, *The Common Pursuit*, pp. 128, 131–33, and 152. The limitations of Leavis' criticism have been well commented on by Vincent Buckley, *Poetry and Morality* (London, 1961), pp. 198–205 and 227–33.

II *In Search of an Adequate Perspective,* CONTINUED

46. L. C. Knights, *Further Explorations* (Stanford University Press, 1965), esp. pp. 24–32 and 66–72. See also his lecture, "Shakespeare's Politics," in *Proceedings of the British Academy,* XLIII (1957), 115–32.

47. For this view of *Lear,* see, e.g., R. Y. Hathorn, *Tragedy, Myth, and Mystery* (Indiana University Press, 1962), p. 176; Kenneth Myrick, "Christian Pessimism in *King Lear,*" in *Shakespeare 1564–1964* (Brown University Press, 1964), ed. Edward A. Bloom, pp. 56–70; Virgil K. Whitaker, *The Mirror up to Nature* (San Marino, 1965), pp. 211–40; James Kirsch, *Shakespeare's Royal Self* (New York, 1966), p. 316; James H. Jones, *Shakespeare's Transformation of His Sources in "King Lear"* (University Microfilms, Ann Arbor, 1965); and others to be noted hereafter in my chapter on *Lear.* A particularly fine case for the play's medieval "homiletic structure" has been developed by Maynard Mack, *"King Lear" in Our Time* (University of California Press, 1965), esp. pp. 45–80. For a contrary view, however, see William R. Elton, *King Lear and the Gods* (San Marino, 1966). Elton sees a "pagan universe" of metaphysical absurdity as the play's ultimate meaning.

48. L. A. Cormican, in *Scrutiny,* XVII (1950–51), 186–202 and 298–317; M. D. H. Parker, *The Slave of Life* (London, 1955). Further, Miss Honor Matthews has focused on Christian imagery in her *Character and Symbol in Shakespeare's Plays* (Cambridge University Press, 1962); and Patrick Cruttwell's *The Shakespearean Moment* (London, 1954) is devoted to characterizing in a general way the medieval quality of poetic style in Shakespeare and in Donne.

49. Nevill Coghill, "The Basis of Shakespearian Comedy," in English Association *Essays and Studies,* n.s. III (1950), 1–28. This view is held also by Glynne Wickham, "Shakespeare's 'Small Latine and less Greeke'," in *Talking of Shakespeare* (London, 1954), ed. John Garrett, pp. 209–30. Further, William B. Toole in his *Shakespeare's Problem Plays* (The Hague, 1966), pp. 39–97, endorses and supplements Coghill by offering an excellent review of Dante's allegory, of Christian typology, and of the structure of English mystery and morality plays.

50. Especially by G. W. Knight, *The Wheel of Fire,* Ch. IV; R. W. Battenhouse, *"Measure for Measure* and Christian Doctrine of the Atonement," *PMLA,* LXI (1946), 1029–59; Nevill Coghill, "Comic Form in *Measure for Measure,*" *Shakespeare Survey,* 8 (1955), 14–27; Toole, *Shakespeare's Problem Plays,* Ch. V; and E. T. Sehrt, *Vergebung und Gnade bei Shakespeare* (Stuttgart, 1952), pp. 121–97.

51. S. L. Bethell, *The Winter's Tale: A Study* (London, 1947); and J. A. Bryant, "Shakespeare's Allegory: *The Winter's Tale,*" *Sewanee Review,* LXIII (1955), 202–22.

52. Robert G. Hunter, *Shakespeare and the Comedy of Forgiveness* (Columbia University Press, 1965).

53. *The Tempest,* ed. Frank Kermode (London, 1954), pp. xxx and lxxxiii; my "Shakespeare and the Bible," *Gordon Review,* VIII (1964), 20.

54. *Pericles,* ed. F. D. Hoeniger (London, 1963), pp. lxxxviii–xc. Concurrently, the scriptural motifs in Shakespeare's earliest comedy, his *Comedy of Errors,* are being given increased attention as clues to the drama's meaning; see Arden edition by R. A. Foakes (London, 1962), pp. xlvi–li and 113–15.

55. Barbara Lewalski, "Biblical Allusion and Allegory in *The Merchant of Venice,*" *SQ,* XIII (1962), 327–43; and her "Thematic Patterns in *Twelfth Night,*" *Shakespeare Studies,* I (1965), 168–81. George W. Slover has attempted a full-fledged exercise in medieval four-fold interpretation in his "A Comparative Study of the Symbolism in the Sources of the *Merchant of Venice*" (Indiana University M. A. dissertation, 1960).

56. J. A. Bryant, *Hippolyta's View: Some Christian Aspects of Shakespeare's Plays* (University of Kentucky Press, 1961). The chapters on comedies seem to me more successful than the others.

57. J. V. Cunningham, " 'Essence' and the *Phoenix and Turtle,*" *ELH,* XIX (1952), 265–76; repeated in his *Tradition and Poetic Structure* (Denver, 1960), pp. 76 ff. Let me mention also an excellently learned and convincing explication of Sonnet 146 by Charles Huttar, "The Christian Basis of Shakespeare's Sonnet 146," *SQ,* XIX (1968), 355–65.

58. For example, Whitaker, *Mirror,* p. 152; Robert Speaight, *Christian Theatre* (New York, 1960), pp. 65–88; Paul Siegel, *Shakespearean Tragedy and the Elizabethan Compromise* (New York University Press, 1957), p. 82; Eleanor Prosser, *Hamlet and Revenge* (Stanford University Press, 1967), pp. 249–50. For earlier commentators, see "Shakespeare and Religion: A Bibliography," *The Shakespeare Newsletter* (December, 1960).

59. S. L. Bethell, *Shakespeare and the Popular Dramatic Tradition* (Westminster, 1944), p. 82.

60. Curtis B. Watson, *Shakespeare and the Renaissance Concept of Honor* (Princeton University Press, 1960), p. 449.

61. For a survey of this recent trend, see D. R. Howard, *The Three Temptations: Medieval Man in Search of the World* (Princeton University Press, 1966), pp. 3–31.

62. R. E. Kaske, "The *Canticum Canticorum* in the Miller's Tale," *SP,* LIX (1962), 479–500.

63. R. E. Kaske, "The Summoner's Garleek, Oynons, and eek Lekes," *MLN,* LXXIV (1959), 481–84.

II *In Search of an Adequate Perspective,* CONTINUED

64. For further interpretation of the symbolism of *Henry V,* see my "Henry V as Heroic Comedy," in *Essays on Shakespeare and Elizabethan Drama in Honor of Hardin Craig,* ed. R. Hosley (University of Missouri Press, 1962), pp. 163–82.

65. G. Wilson Knight, *Wheel of Fire* (New York, 1957 edition), pp. 235–36; see also 250–51.

66. Frye, *Shakespeare and Christian Doctrine,* p. 34.

67. See G. Wilson Knight, "Shakespeare and Theology: A Private Protest," *Essays in Criticism,* XV (1965), 95–104.

68. G. Wilson Knight, *Principles of Shakespearean Production,* 2nd edition (Pelican Books, 1949), pp. 166–67.

69. Northrop Frye, *Anatomy of Criticism* (Princeton University Press, 1957), p. 214.

70. Frye, *Anatomy,* pp. 207–10. Incidentally, Frye is incorrect in saying (p. 213) that Augustine teaches that "time begins with the fall."

71. E. J. Tinsley, *Christian Theology and the Frontiers of Tragedy* (Leeds University Press, 1963), pp. 11–13. Italics mine.

72. Jarold Ramsey, "Timon's Imitation of Christ," *Shakespeare Studies,* II (1966), 162–73.

73. Perhaps this is why even a Freudian critic such as Norman Holland, in a wayside remark in *The Shakespearean Imagination* (New York, 1964), p. 132, can say (although without amplifying) that the events of *Julius Caesar* are "ordered in a Christian way" and prove both Cassius and Brutus wrong.

74. Goddard, *Meaning,* pp. 514–15.

75. Jane H. Jack, "*Macbeth,* King James, and the Bible," *ELH,* XXII (1955), 173–93; Siegel, *Shakespearean Tragedy,* p. 144; Bryant, *Hippolyta's View,* p. 161; Matthews, *Character and Symbol,* p. 37.

76. Siegel, *Shakespearean Tragedy,* p. 126; on Judas, p. 131.

77. Whitaker, *Mirror,* pp. 245–53, traces Othello's tragedy to his making Desdemona a kind of god (in II. i. 186–209). It should be added, however, that Othello's idolatry of Desdemona is also paradoxically a neglect of the true child of God in her, i.e., of the self which can be and later is a witness to heaven. John Seaman, "Othello's Pearl," *SQ,* XIX (1968), 81–85, notes that in Rev. 21:21 the gate for each of the entrances to the heavenly city is a pearl. In losing Desdemona, Othello loses a gateway to heaven.

78. See Margaret Ranald, "The Indiscretions of Desdemona," *SQ,* XIV (1963), 127–39.

79. See, e.g., his essay in *Myth and Symbol,* ed. Bernice Slote (University of Nebraska Press, 1963), pp. 3–20. Frye's interest in myth, however, seems to be more Nietzschean than Christian. In his recent *Fools*

of Time: Studies in Shakespearian Tragedy (University of Toronto Press, 1967) he praises Nietzsche as "illuminating for Shakespeare" (p. 10), then proceeds to misread and caricature Dante's concepts and those of Christianity in general as being melodramatic and brutalizing (pp. 79–81). It is a pity that so eminent a critic has fallen into such confusion in matters of theology.

80. Susan Snyder, "Marlowe's *Doctor Faustus* as an Inverted Saint's Life," *SP*, LXIII (1966), 565–77.

81. E.g., Robert West, "The Christianness of Othello," *SQ*, XV (1964), 333–43.

82. John Arthos comments well on this point, in *The Art of Shakespeare* (New York, 1964), pp. 26–28.

83. G. I. Duthie, ed., *Romeo and Juliet* (Cambridge University Press, 1955), pp. xix–xxi. Other instances are G. A. Bonnard, *"Romeo and Juliet:* A Possible Significance?," *RES*, II (1951), 319–27; and Geoffrey Bullough, in *Narrative and Dramatic Sources of Shakespeare,* I (London, 1957), 276–77. In answering this view, I am elaborating remarks of mine in *The Tragic Vision and the Christian Faith,* ed. Nathan Scott (New York, 1957), pp. 89–93.

84. Ulrici suggested this about a century ago. The lovers, he said, "mar their rare excellence by making idols of each other, and fanatically sacrificing all things to their idolatry" (quoted in Variorum *Romeo and Juliet,* ed. Furness, p. 452). Da Porto implies idolatry when he has Romeo cry out at Juliet's tomb: "O beautiful body, ultimate goal of my desire . . ." I use the translation of Da Porto's story by M. Valency and H. Levtow, in *The Place of Pleasure* (New York, 1960), 128–53.

85. The real sin behind courtly love was the "idolatrous deification of another human being," Rosemond Tuve remarks in her *Allegorical Imagery* (Princeton University Press, 1966), p. 262n. She supports this conclusion with an extended review of Jean de Meun's *Roman de la Rose,* showing how the author constantly implies his own standard of *caritas* by presenting ironically the many forms of love which lack it and which are figured at the end by the Pygmalion lover who finds his "rose" in a stone lady fashioned as his idol.

86. Granville-Barker, *Prefaces,* II (Princeton University Press, 1930), p. 8.

87. Stoll, *Shakespeare's Young Lovers,* p. 22.

88. John Vyvyan, *Shakespeare and the Rose of Love* (London, 1960), pp. 149–50.

89. An association of Juliet with Helen can be found in Brooke's poem. Just before the day set for her wedding with Paris, Juliet says that even if her beauty excelled that of "the famous Grecian rape" (2237, Bullough text) she would dress it up for Paris' sake. Note also that

II *In Search of an Adequate Perspective,* CONTINUED

Thisbe, in Shakespeare's *Midsummer-Night's Dream,* V. i. 200, likens herself to Helen.

90. Douglas L. Peterson nicely establishes this point in his *"Romeo and Juliet* and The Art of Moral Navigation," *Pacific Coast Studies in Shakespeare* (University of Oregon Books, 1966), ed. Waldo McNeir and Thelma Greenfield, pp. 33–46. In this same volume, Stanley Stewart's essay (pp. 47–67) on "Romeo and Necessity" argues similarly that Romeo becomes a prisoner of Venus, not by any astrological determinism but by wilfully electing the dark garden of Capulet's orchard. However, when both Peterson and Stewart further argue that Friar Laurence is the play's spokesman for moral responsibility, I think this contention only half valid, and in fact as misleading as Franklin Dickey's view on which I comment hereafter.

91. Erwin Panofsky, *Studies in Iconology* (Oxford University Press, 1939), p. 112, points out that blind Cupid was in medieval times associated especially with "blindfold death" and with the classical *caeca Fortuna,* because these three were blind both in an intransitive and a transitive sense—i.e., not only as personifications of "an unenlightened state of mind" but also as personifications of "an active force behaving like an eyeless person." All were associated with night and with infidelity. The concept of Cupid as purblind is elaborately stated in *Love's Labor's Lost* III. i. 181–98.

92. Shakespeare omits, e.g., the physical tremblings which Brooke records of the lovers' first meeting (lines 264–73 and 418), his coarse pausing over the sensuous delights of their wedding night (903–24), and his reference to Juliet as a lusty jennet (723).

93. Francis Fergusson, *Romeo and Juliet,* Laurel edition (New York, 1958), p. 16.

94. Denis de Rougemont, *Passion and Society,* tr. Montgomery Belgion (London, 1940), esp. pp. 55–102.

95. Mahood, *Shakespeare's Wordplay,* pp. 56–57. But Miss Mahood, by failing to follow through on De Rougemont's lead, becomes inconsistent in her interpretation. After acknowledging the plausibility of the view that Romeo and Juliet exemplify a "tragic passion that seeks its own destruction," she shifts (p. 65) to the contrary view that their love is "not . . . in its nature tragic" but instead a victory. She then speaks of the "Pyrrhic victory" of society over them.

96. Aquinas, *Summa Contra Gentiles* III. 85. Peterson, in *Pacific Coast Studies,* pp. 35–36, quotes this along with similar statements by Elizabethan authors.

97. Actually, the feud between the houses is more supposed than real. Da Porto had indicated this by having Juliet's mother on one occasion

comfort her by saying: "cry no more; we will give you a husband to your liking, even if you wanted one of the Montecchi" (Montagues). In Shakespeare, old Capulet thinks highly of Romeo, would do him "no disparagement," and even intervenes as host to forbid Tybalt to frown at him. Noting Capulet's attitude, H. B. Charlton, in *Shakespearian Tragedy* (Cambridge University Press, 1948), p. 61, thinks the play a failure, because the feud is too weak a cause for the tragedy. Artistic failure is the complaint also of Whitaker, *Mirror*, p. 110; and of D. A. Stauffer, *Shakespeare's World of Images* (New York, 1949), p. 56. These critics fail to see that Shakespeare, by emphasizing the fact that there is no longer any remembered grievance to support the feud, is calling our attention to the motive of human vanity which uses the feud as an excuse. The servants of the play's opening scene, and Tybalt on a later occasion, relish the feud as an opportunity for showing off, while on the other hand the lovers use it as an excuse for clandestine doings.

98. So does the Juliet of Brooke's account, who is specifically aware of Dido's ill fame (line 391) and hopes to avoid this by nominal marriage. In further justification she tells herself this alliance may produce a peace between the houses (the argument Shakespeare gives to Friar Laurence). Brooke comments: "O how we can persuade ourselves to what we like!" I think Shakespeare is implying this same comment.

99. "Old Ninny" is a comic name for Ninus, who in Christian historiography is remembered as the founder of the Earthly City, Babylon. Let us recall, also, that when St. Augustine's pupil, Licentius, was writing a poem on Pyramus and Thisbe, Augustine advised him to condemn libidinous love *by the way in which he arranged* his poem; see D. W. Robertson, *Preface to Chaucer*, p. 60, citing Augustine's *De Ordine* I. 8. 24.

100. These critics and others have been surveyed by Herbert McArthur, in "Romeo's Loquacious Friend," *SQ*, X (1959), 35–44. McArthur argues for the modern romantic view, that the purity of Romeo and Juliet needs an opposite, the sordid and trivial world of Mercutio, out of which to rise to a love beyond the ken of their friends.

101. Significantly, Shakespeare has removed all traces of the Christian piety which Brooke's account attributes to Romeo at this point. Brooke has Romeo kneel repentantly in prayer to "Lord Christ." This kind of deathbed repentance was a stock feature of much Protestant drama (e.g., in Bale's *King Johan*), but Shakespeare avoids it, maintaining firmly his portrait of Romeo's substitute love religion.

102. On Chaucer, see for instance Chauncey Wood, "The April Date as a Structural Device in *The Canterbury Tales*," *MLQ*, 25 (1964), 259–71.

103. Thus Bonnard, *"Romeo and Juliet,"* *RES*, II (1951), 321, says

II *In Search of an Adequate Perspective,* CONTINUED

Shakespeare devised his time scheme "to render his lovers innocent of any suspicion of double-dealing and so worthy of the whole-hearted sympathy of the audience." I would say to render them seemingly innocent and seemingly worthy; for in tragic art the author must strive to contrive a sympathetic surface level while hiding the real truth underneath.

104. T. S. Eliot uses "nine" for similar irony in *The Waste Land.* In a secularized London, the "stroke of nine," as Robert A. Day comments (*PMLA,* LXXX, 287–90), marks "the beginning of another day among drafts and invoices" for the bank clerk, but also it is a masked religious symbol which cues us to "a parody of the Mass" and of the sacred event which the Mass symbolizes, Christ's death at the ninth hour.

105. Augustine, *City of God* XIX. 17.

106. Brooke quite overlooks this possibility, assuming throughout his poem that Escalus is a "prudent" prince of sage decrees. Brooke's attempt to contrast Prince and Friar, the one wise and the other foolish, reflects a popular Protestant attitude of Elizabethan times. Shakespeare does not adopt it.

107. See W. H. Auden's comment in the Laurel *Romeo and Juliet,* p. 23. Da Porto had said the Friar hoped his project might "redound to his great honor with the prince and everyone else."

108. The Friar in Masuccio's version (1474) is induced by a bribe to perform the secret wedding; in Da Porto's (c. 1530) he has built up a friendship with Romeo by telling him about magic arts, and he uses wiliness in proposing the potion to Juliet; in Bandello's (1560) he is called a "great distiller" in chemistry. See Olin Moore, *The Legend of Romeo and Juliet* (Ohio State University Press, 1950).

109. An auspicious indication of this defect is the negative note on which his first soliloquy ends. While recognizing theologically that both "grace" and "rude will" are factors in human life, Friar Laurence chooses to extrapolate the second of these solely: "And when the worser is predominant, / Full soon the canker death eats up the plant." Why is he not emphasizing, rather, the good life which is nourished through grace? Because to do so would not suit tragedy, the kind of story Shakespeare is writing. Laurence is shown as reasoning somewhat like Marlowe's Faustus, who reduced the meaning of Scripture to a half text ("The wages of sin is death"), ignoring the other half of his text and thereby being led to prefer magic to Scripture. Laurence, however, is not a toweringly bold rebel, as Faustus is, since Shakespeare wishes to picture a more common flaw, more pathetic in kind—a nominal piety, which unwittingly has become decadent by leaving undeveloped the "gracious" or upward side of its inherited Christianity.

110. Franklin Dickey, *Not Wisely But Too Well* (San Marino, 1957), pp. 106–15.

111. A warning against being swept away by passion, as were Romeo and Juliet, is traditional with the story. Brooke, Bandello, and Painter all voice this moral. Paul Siegel has traced its frequency in various comparable love tragedies of Elizabethan fiction; see his "Christianity and the Religion of Love in *Romeo and Juliet*," *SQ*, XII (1961), 371–92. But I think Siegel errs at the end by confusing Christian sainthood with the Cupid sainthood of Shakespeare's lovers. For a medieval view of Cupid's devotees, see for instance John Gower's moralizing on Pyramus and Thisbe, in *Confessio Amantis*, ed. G. C. Macaulay (Oxford, 1901), Bk. III. These lovers, with hearts set afire by Cupid, says Gower, became guilty of a "will to deie" (line 1512); their suicides were due to "folhaste" and waste of wit (lines 1497–98).

112. M. A. Shaaber, "Shakespeare 1963–1964," *Renaissance News*, XVIII (1965), 179.

III Toward Clarifying the Term "Christian Tragedy"

1. John Masefield, pp. 9 and 29; A. C. Bradley, *Shakespearean Tragedy* (London, 1904; 2nd ed. repr., 1950), p. 25; Churton Collins, *Studies in Shakespeare* (Westminster, 1904), p. 296; J. M. Robertson, *The Religion of Shakespeare* (London, 1887), pp. 9–10. Robertson went on to attack Christianity and its morality in *The Dynamics of Religion* (London, 1897; second edition, 1926). I shall be occasionally borrowing, in the first half of this chapter, from my "Shakespearean Tragedy as Christian," *The Centennial Review*, VIII (1964), 77–98.

2. O. C. Quick, *Doctrines of the Creed* (New York, 1938), p. 45.

3. John Arthos, *The Art of Shakespeare* (New York, 1964), p. 33.

4. Irving Ribner, "Shakespeare, Christianity, and the Problem of Belief," *The Centennial Review*, VIII (1964), 105. Note also Ribner's contention (p. 103) that "all great literature must have its allegorical dimension, in that it must mean far more than it literally states."

5. Frye's procedure has been criticized, on various counts, by Ribner in *Tulane Drama Review*, X (1966), 265–74.

6. László Kéry, "Shakespeare in Washington," *The New Hungarian Quarterly*, VII (Autumn, 1966), 62.

7. If one wishes to be more precise, one can distinguish further between puritan and medieval strands within Christian tradition. Thus, for instance, one could say that the principles of discrimination operative in the anonymous *King Leir* are predominantly puritan, whereas those guiding Shakespeare's *King Lear* are more medieval. Old Testament allusions in *King Leir* are frequent and explicit, while at the same time the play's principles of justice are influenced by neoclassical concepts.

III *Toward Clarifying the Term "Christian Tragedy"*, CONTINUED

8. See Clifford Leech, *Shakespeare's Tragedies and Other Studies in Seventeenth-Century Drama* (London, 1950), pp. 3–20. These pages have been anthologized in *Tragedy: Modern Essays in Criticism,* ed. Laurence Michel and Richard Sewall (Englewood Cliffs, 1963), pp. 161–74, and in *Shakespeare's Tragedies: An Anthology of Modern Criticism,* ed. Laurence Lerner (Penguin Books, 1963), pp. 285–98. Michel and Sewall also reprint an exchange between J. C. Maxwell and Leech, from *Essays in Criticism,* V (1955), 175–81, over the question of the incompatibility of tragic drama and Christianity. Maxwell briefly questions Leech's thesis, chiefly by pointing to the fact that many tragedies have been written for Christian audiences, and by authors who nowhere overtly reject a Christian outlook. Leech replies that Christians might write or enjoy tragedies on days of the year when their religious opinions were not powerful, their vision then being "a-Christian." This answer, it seems to me, presupposes that tragedy is a mood picture rather than, as Aristotle said, an imitation of an action. Do playwrights write tragedy simply to express a sub-Christian mood which has overtaken them, and without relation to their usual creedal basis for understanding life?

9. See D. W. Robertson, "Chaucerian Tragedy," *ELH,* XIX (1952), 1–37, revised in his *A Preface to Chaucer* (Princeton University Press, 1962), pp. 463–503.

10. William Elton, *King Lear and the Gods* (San Marino, 1966), pp. 333–38.

11. See further, M. D. H. Parker, *The Slave of Life: A Study of Shakespeare and the Idea of Justice* (London, 1955), pp. 217–21.

12. Richard Sewall, *The Vision of Tragedy* (Yale University Press, 1959), pp. 68–79; and see also pp. 4–5; 150; and 159.

13. Una Ellis-Fermor, *The Frontiers of Drama* (London, 1945), pp. 17–18 and p. 146. Miss Ellis-Fermor uses the term "Manichaeistic" loosely rather than with philosophical accuracy. For her, it means (pp. 127–33) the poet's balancing of "two impressions made by his experience"—one of a malevolent world order, the other of a beneficent one; hence of "manifest evil and immanent good"; or of evil in outward action but implicit good in the inner action of the "thought-life" of characters. She speaks of Shakespeare as counterpoising in *King Lear* the "thought-world" of Cordelia and Kent against the events which shape and are shaped by other characters. Such analysis seems to me fuzzy, half-Hegelian and half-mystical.

14. I. A. Richards, *Principles of Literary Criticism* (London, 1925), p. 246. For a similar view, see Murray Krieger, *The Tragic Vision* (New York, 1960), pp. 243–48.

15. See A. P. Rossiter, *Angel with Horns* (London, 1961), pp. 180, 186, 261–65.

16. D. D. Raphael, *Paradox of Tragedy* (Indiana University Press, 1960), p. 53; for my other references, see pp. 31, 41, and 51–52.

17. Laurence Michel, "Hamlet: Superman, SubChristian," *Centennial Review,* VI (1962), 230–44.

18. Sylvan Barnet, "Some Limitations of a Christian Approach to Shakespeare," *ELH,* XXII (1955), 81–92.

19. Denis de Rougemont, "Religion and the Mission of the Artist," reprinted in *The New Orpheus* (New York, 1964), ed. Nathan Scott, pp. 59–73.

20. Laurel edition of *Romeo and Juliet* (New York, 1958), p. 38.

21. See, for instances, Miguel A. Bernard, "The Five Tragedies in *Macbeth,*" *SQ,* XIII (1962), 49–61. Bernard distinguishes five dimensions of Macbeth's tragedy: 1) physical fall; 2) psychological impoverishment; 3) moral downfall into total callousness; 4) social disruption and sickness; and 5) the theological dimension of damnation, Macbeth's "greatest tragedy." See also Harry Morris, "*Macbeth,* Dante, and the Greatest Evil," *Tennessee Studies in Literature,* XII (1967), 23–38; and Herbert Coursen, "In Deepest Consequence: *Macbeth,*" *SQ,* XVIII (1967), 385–87; also Glynne Wickham, "Hell-Castle and Its Door Keeper," *Shakespeare Survey* 19 (1966), 68–74. The whole of *Shakespeare* 19 is devoted to *Macbeth.*

22. S. L. Bethell, "Shakespeare's Imagery: The Diabolic Images in *Othello,*" *Shakespeare Survey,* 5 (1952), 62–80; Paul Siegel, *Shakespearean Tragedy and the Elizabethan Compromise* (New York, 1957), pp. 131 and 140; see also Honor Matthews, *Character and Symbol in Shakespeare's Plays* (Cambridge, 1962), pp. 135–38, and Virgil Whitaker, *The Mirror up to Nature* (San Marino, 1965), p. 253.

23. H. S. Wilson, *On the Design of Shakespearian Tragedy* (University of Toronto Press, 1957), pp. 26–31; Irving Ribner, *Patterns in Shakespearian Tragedy* (London, 1960), pp. 26–34; Siegel, *Shakespearean Tragedy,* pp. 84–85. For a fuller statement of Siegel's view, see his *Shakespeare in His Time and Ours* (University of Notre Dame Press, 1968), esp. pp. 88–107.

24. W. H. Auden, Laurel edition, pp. 33 and 38–39.

25. For instance, G. R. Elliott, *Flaming Minister* (Duke University Press, 1953), pp. 230–42; M. D. H. Parker, *The Slave of Life,* pp. 126–30; Ribner, *Patterns,* pp. 113–15.

26. Whitaker, *Mirror,* pp. 191–99.

27. Ribner, *Patterns,* p. 80, lists ten of them in support of his own advocacy of a "saved" Hamlet. To that list can be added Miriam Joseph, Bryant, and Prosser.

28. Eleanor Prosser, *Hamlet and Revenge,* (Stanford University Press, 1967), pp. 229–37.

29. Wilson, *On the Design,* pp. 46–48.

III *Toward Clarifying the Term "Christian Tragedy"*, CONTINUED

30. For a discussion of Plutarch's *De sera numinis vindicta,* and of his doctrine of providence in general, see R. H. Barrow, *Plutarch and His Times* (Indiana University Press, 1967), pp. 95–102. On providence in Plotinus, see my *Marlowe's "Tamburlaine"* (Vanderbilt University Press, 1941), p. 125.

31. Roland Frye, *Shakespeare and Christian Doctrine* (Princeton University Press, 1963), pp. 138–39.

32. H. B. Charlton, *Shakespearian Tragedy* (Cambridge, 1948), p. 103.

33. Moody Prior, "Hamlet and the Modern Temper," *ELH,* XV (1948), 274–284.

34. E. M. Tillyard, *Shakespeare's Problem Plays* (London, 1951), pp. 25–30.

35. See, for instance, Jacques Maritain, *On the Philosophy of History* (London, 1959), esp. pp. 41–50; and C. A. Patrides, *The Phoenix and the Ladder* (University of California Press, 1964), pp. 1–48.

36. These are the three section headings in the translation by F. L. Battles, in *The Library of Christian Classics,* Vol. XX (Philadelphia, 1960), from which I have been quoting.

37. Maynard Mack, "The World of Hamlet," in *Yale Review* (1952) and reprinted in *Shakespeare: Modern Essays in Criticism* (New York, rev. ed., 1967), ed. Leonard Dean, p. 260.

38. For further comment, see my "Hamlet's Apostrophe on Man," *PMLA,* LXVI (1951), esp. pp. 1097–1102.

39. John Vyvyan, *The Shakespearean Ethic* (London, 1959), p. 155. Vyvyan's handicap is that he takes his perspective from the mysticism of Aldous Huxley, under which he would subsume truths drawn from the New Testament, Buddhism, Taoism and Jung; see pp. 158 and 185. Roland Frye, in a more recent book, stops short of attributing salvation to Richard, yet seems to imply this in saying that Richard in prison "prepares himself for heaven by the disciplines of humility and affliction"; see *Shakespeare and Christian Doctrine,* p. 180.

40. G. Wilson Knight, *The Imperial Theme* (London, 1931), p. 289. Knight's two long chapters, pp. 199–326, orchestrate a mystical reading of Wagnerian kind. For a less mystical but otherwise thoroughly romantic interpretation, a recent sample is Sheila M. Smith's " 'This Great Solemnity': A Study of the Presentation of Death in *Antony and Cleopatra,"* *English Studies,* XLV (1964), 163–176.

41. Dover Wilson, the New Cambridge *Antony and Cleopatra* (1950), p. xxxvi.

42. M. R. Ridley, the New Arden *Antony and Cleopatra* (1954), p. liii; William Rosen, *Shakespeare and the Craft of Tragedy* (Harvard University Press, 1960), pp. 150–53.

43. Regarding the shortcomings of Antony's self-understanding, Robert Heilman provides some excellent comment in his essay, "From Mine Own Knowledge: A Theme in the Late Tragedies," *The Centennial Review*, VIII (1964), 19–28.

44. Sylvan Barnet, in "Recognition and Reversal in *Antony and Cleopatra*," *SQ*, VIII (1957), 331–34, identifies Antony's anagnorisis with his perceiving, at this moment, that "without Cleopatra—whom he cannot now have—he has nothing"; and he identifies Cleopatra's anagnorisis with the moment when she realizes that her plot has brought death to the man she loves. I regard these two moments as having a larger context and as being the climax of what I would call an incremental and *distributed* recognition.

45. North's Plutarch had reported: "Then she dried up his blood that had berayed his face, and called him her Lord, her husband, and Emperour, forgetting her own miserie and calamity, for the pitie and compassion she tooke of him." Geoffrey Bullough, *Narrative and Dramatic Sources of Shakespeare*, V (London, 1964), 310.

46. On the comic undertones of Antony's death, see Matthew N. Proser, *The Heroic Image in Five Shakespearean Tragedies* (Princeton University Press, 1965), pp. 206–13.

47. L. J. Mills, in "Cleopatra's Tragedy," *SQ*, XI (1960), 154, sees here "no admitting, apparently no perception, of the fact that she is responsible for [Antony's] defeat and death." That this is the apparent situation, I would agree, but it seems to me the truth is haunting her subconscious mind and being repressed. Mills rightly says that she is "never penitent" but "does change somewhat" (p. 161).

48. In Plutarch's account and in Daniel's, Dolabella furnishes this information only after Caesar's visit; and there is no separate scene with Dolabella. Plutarch construes her scene with Caesar simply as her attempt to deceive Caesar as to her desire to die; he reports that she appealed for life and pardon by falling at Caesar's feet, disfigured and blubbering, using her martyred appearance to elicit pity and color her excuses. Daniel follows Plutarch's account of her actions, but additionally gives her speeches which more than imply, under her wailing face and rent hair, an artful grace attempting to seduce Caesar, a mischief which Caesar detects and rejects, moralizing on it to Dolabella. Shakespeare agrees with Daniel in positing seduction as Cleopatra's purpose, but he invents a more magnificent way for her going about it, and he lets her hint this motive so craftily that no explicit comment on it emerges.

49. We can find this same pun in Daniel's *The Tragedie of Cleopatra* (1599). His Chorus speaks of Egypt as "the most unholy of all Lands, that *Nylus* border"; a Nuntius reports how Cleopatra admired the aspic as "The fairest creature that faire *Nylus* feedes"; and Nylus is hailed for

III *Toward Clarifying the Term "Christian Tragedy"*, CONTINUED

its "free bankes uncontrould." Lines 1195, 1494, and 1693, Bullough's edition.

50. Barnabe Barnes, however, in *The Divil's Charter* (1607) points up this irony. He refers to Cleopatra's asps as "birds" fed on *Nylus* slime, which when substituted for her two lovely boys, give "princely" magnificence to *Ptolemy's* wife! The passage is quoted in the new Arden *Antony and Cleopatra* (1954), p. xxxi. We know, moreover, as Martha Golden has pointed out in *Shakespeare Research Opportunities*, ed. W. R. Elton, I (1965), 13–14, that a woman with serpents at her breasts was a common medieval emblem for Luxuria.

51. The marvel of Shakespeare's irony is that he keeps it implicit rather than letting it become explicit as in the Garnier-Pembroke *Tragedie of Antonie* (1595). In this earlier work, Cleopatra is allowed to cry out, "Antony . . . take me with thee to the *hellish* plaine," and to express a hope of being a "wandering shade . . . where brookes of *hell* do falling seeme to mone." She is offering "due rites" of tears, she says, because "me the heaven's wrath / *Into a stone not yet transformed* hath." (Bullough, *Sources*, V, 404–405, esp. lines 1896, 1950, 1974; italics mine.)

52. In Daniel's version, a similiar point is made by having Cleopatra praise the "mysteries" of "strange divinitie" which Egypt's priests found in the âspic. They rightly assign it offerings and worship, she says, because it can open the door of life to a death of "pleasing sleepe" which enlarges our soul by stealing our selves from ourselves in a gentle and cunning theft. See lines 1500–1527, Bullough's edition.

53. See Leeds Barroll, "Enobarbus' Description of Cleopatra," University of Texas *Studies in English*, XXXVII (1958), esp. pp. 63–66. Barroll also points out the many ways in which Cleopatra becomes a type of Voluptas, so that Shakespeare's tableau of her on her barge at Cydnus may be described as "*Voluptas* gone a-sailing," a nautical Bower of Bliss (p. 76).

54. Cited by Franklin Dickey, *Not Wisely But Too Well* (San Marino, 1957), p. 156.

55. See Dickey, *Not Wisely*, pp. 148–52 and 163–64.

56. Willard Farnham, *Shakespeare's Tragic Frontier* (University of California Press, 1950; repr. 1963), pp. 200–203.

57. See Ribner, *Patterns*, pp. 182–84; H. C. Goddard, *The Meaning of Shakespeare*, (University of Chicago Press, 1951), pp. 586–87.

58. S. L. Bethell, *Shakespeare and the Popular Dramatic Tradition* (Westminster, 1944), pp. 129–31; J. A. Bryant, *Hippolyta's View: Some Christian Aspects of Shakespeare's Plays* (University of Kentucky Press, 1961), pp. 183–91.

59. See Wilson, *On the Design*, pp. 211–13.

60. Michael Lloyd, "Cleopatra as Isis," *Shakespeare Survey*, 12 (1959), 94.

61. In Antony, moreover, there is a trio of vices, Gluttony-Lechery-Sloth, as Leeds Barroll points out in "Antony and Pleasure," *JEGP*, LVII (1958), 708–20.

62. Bullough, *Sources*, V, 274.

63. Bullough, *Sources*, V, 346.

64. See Robin Moffet, "*Cymbeline* and the Nativity," *SQ*, XIII (1962), 207–18.

65. See Bryant, *Hippolyta's View*, p. 182.

66. Interestingly, Scarrus does not appear under this name in the text until after the sea battle, of which he had disapproved. Earlier than that, he appears under the name of "Souldier," one whose visible wounds offer a sign of his devotion to Antony. When Antony later remarks to Scarrus, "Would thou and those thy scars had once prevailed" (IV. v. 2), it is as if Shakespeare were suggesting Antony's recognition of having neglected a martyr's testimony. Note that Scarrus, in his days as anony-mous soldier, opposed the influence of Cleopatra; only after his becom-ing "Scarrus" does he fight maliciously and thus merit the "armor all of gold" awarded him by Cleopatra. Gold, in such a context, is a worldly reward which implies his moral ruin. The textual problems have been discussed by Leeds Barroll, in "Scarrus and the Scarred Soldier," *HLQ*, XXII (1958), 31–39; but Barroll does not sense, as I do, a figurative sig-nificance in the name change.

67. Peter Seng, "Shakespearean Hymn Parody?" *Renaissance News*, XVIII (1965), 4–6. Seng acknowledges Richmond Noble's earlier obser-vation, in *Shakespeare's Use of Song* (Oxford, 1923), that the well-known pentecostal hymn *Veni creator spiritus* has here its Bacchanalian equiva-lent. The *Veni sancte spiritus*, however, is a more exact model.

68. Barroll, "Enobarbus' Description of Cleopatra," Texas *Studies in English*, XXXVII (1958), 77.

69. Ethel Seaton, "*Antony and Cleopatra* and the Book of Revela-tion," *RES*, XXII (1946), 219–24.

70. When Antony describes it as the embracing of "such a twain" (I. i. 38), we may recall the doomed "lovers twain" of Bottom's play in *Midsummer-Night's Dream* (V. i. 51), or the phrase in *King Lear* (V. vi. 211) regarding "the general curse / Which twain have brought." Twain-ness implies divisive rivalry; and Cleopatra's comment, "Excellent false-hood!," describes its peerlessness more aptly than she knows.

71. See *The Dramatic Works of Thomas Dekker*, ed. Fredson Bowers, II (Cambridge, 1955), 561–63.

72. Thomas S. Kepler, *The Book of Revelation* (New York, 1957), p. 140, gives a table of the ten Roman emperors from Tiberius to Domi-

III *Toward Clarifying the Term "Christian Tragedy"*, CONTINUED

tian, whom St. John intends as the immediate reference of his apocalyptic image. According to St. Irenaeus, Revelation was written during the reign of Domitian. This emperor was outstandingly pretentious in claiming an Hellenic divinity for himself, and his era was one of much persecution of Christians in Asia Minor.

73. Leeds Barroll, "Shakespeare and Roman History," *MLR*, LIII (1958), 330–32.

74. Jean Daniélou, *From Shadows to Reality*, tr. Dom Hibberd (Westminster, 1960), pp. 72–73, notes the equivalence of Leviathan, sea serpent, and Egypt in biblical typology.

75. See Kepler, *The Book of Revelation*, pp. 119 and 143.

76. Bradley, *Shakespearean Tragedy* (edition of 1950), p. 260.

77. Dover Wilson, New Cambridge *Antony and Cleopatra*, p. xiv.

78. See W. K. Wimsatt, "Poetry and Morals: A Relation Reargued," *Thought*, XXIII (1948), 294–95.

79. Wilson, *On the Design*, p. 4. Wilson selects four plays (*Romeo and Juliet, Hamlet, Othello*, and *Macbeth*) as reflecting a Christian "order of faith"; but he then argues—erroneously, I think—that these plays are not strictly tragic, because their events culminate in "a resolution of tragedy into comedy."

80. See Marvin Herrick, *The Poetics of Aristotle in England* (New Haven, 1930), pp. 15–34; and John Hazel Smith, *A Humanist's "Trew Imitation": Thomas Watson's Absalom* (University of Illinois Press, 1964), esp. pp. 43–47. Actually, Watson mixed Senecan with Aristotelian principles.

81. For example, H. S. Wilson, in *On the Design*, pp. 221–27; John Vyvyan, in *The Shakespearean Ethic*, p. 13; and Northrop Frye, in *Fools of Time* (University of Toronto Press, 1967), p. 34.

82. See Whitaker, *Mirror*, pp. 50, 55, 91. Note also that Lane Cooper, in his *Aristotle on the Art of Poetry: An Amplified Version with Supplementary Illustrations* (Cornell University Press, revised edition, 1947), often applies Aristotle's principles to Shakespeare.

83. A review of these samplings of Elizabethan theory, and of others like them, can be found in Lily B. Campbell, *Shakespeare's Tragic Heroes* (New York, 1959 reprint), pp. 25–38; in Whitaker, *Mirror*, pp. 56–81; and in my *Marlowe's Tamburlaine* (Vanderbilt University Press, 1941), pp. 114–20.

84. See Norman Pratt, "The Stoic Base of Senecan Drama," *TAPA*, LXXIX (1948), 1–11.

85. S. H. Butcher, *Aristotle's Theory of Poetry and Fine Art*, fourth edition (New York, 1951), p. 316.

86. Note how Aquinas, in *S. T.* II–II, 1–3, sets Aristotle's understanding of pity in the context of the virtue of mercy.

87. See Baxter Hathaway, *The Age of Criticism: The Late Renaissance in Italy* (Cornell University Press, 1962), pp. 224–37.

88. Herrick, *The Poetics of Aristotle in England,* p. 19.

89. See Butcher, *Aristotle's Theory,* p. 255n; D. M. Hill, "Catharsis," *Essays in Criticism,* VIII (1958), 113–19. Yet note that Scripture uses the phrase "bowels of comparison" to signify a desirable kind of pity. The error of modern interpretation is to identify pity with what is expelled, rather than with that activity of the soul (analogous to the bowel activity of the body) which is completed when it discards the impurities in the mixed good it has fed on.

90. Gerald Else, *Aristotle's Poetics: The Argument* (Harvard University Press, 1957), pp. 230–32; 436–46.

91. Roy Morrell, "The Psychology of Tragic Pleasure," reprinted from *Essays in Criticism,* VI (1956), by Michel and Sewall in *Tragedy: Modern Essays,* pp. 276–89.

92. Ronald S. Crane, *The Languages of Criticism and the Structure of Poetry* (University of Toronto Press, 1953), p. 172.

93. Crane, *Languages,* p. 171–73.

94. See Wayne Booth, "Shakespeare's Tragic Villains," reprinted in *Shakespeare's Tragedies* (Penguin Books, 1963), ed. Laurence Lerner, pp. 188–89.

95. Helen Gardner, *The Business of Criticism* (Oxford, 1959), p. 59.

96. Jan Kott, *Shakespeare Our Contemporary* (New York, 1964), p. 86.

97. R. A. Foakes thinks this Prayer Book litany a pertinent response to the defects we see in Shakesepare's tragic heroes, Hamlet alone excepted; but I think Hamlet no exception. See Foakes's comment in *Stratford-Upon-Avon Studies 5: Hamlet* (London, 1963), ed. J. R. Brown and B. Harris, p. 148, and my rejoinder in *Shakespeare Studies,* I (1965), 356, ed. J. Leeds Barroll.

IV Hamartia in Aristotle,
Christian Doctrine, and *Hamlet*

1. R. S. Crane, in *The Languages of Criticism and the Structure of Poetry* (University of Toronto Press, 1953), pp. 42–43, comments on how the science of poetry becomes truly comprehensive only by dependence on "many other sciences or arts" for its subsidiary principles.

2. For example, that of Petrus Victorius, with accompanying Greek text (pub. 1560, often reprinted; second ed., 1573) and that of Antonio Riccobini (pub. 1579, reprinted 1584). There were also, of course, translations into Italian—notably Castelvetro's (1570) and Piccolomini's (1572).

IV *Hamartia in Aristotle, Christian Doctrine, and* Hamlet, CONTINUED

3. For a full marshalling of the evidence, see Peter Munz, *The Place of Hooker in the History of Thought* (London, 1952).

4. E. M. Simpson and G. R. Potter in their edition of *The Sermons of John Donne,* X (University of California Press, 1962), p. 364, rate his indebtedness to St. Thomas as "very considerable." Their index lists over fifty references to Aquinas and a hundred more to the Schoolmen.

5. Of the extent of Shakespeare's relations with Roman Catholics or their sympathizers we have only fragmentary knowledge. His father's name appears on a list of suspected Papists in 1592, and his daughter Susanna's name on a listing in 1607. One of his early schoolmasters, Simon Hunt, departed for Douay in 1575 and joined the Jesuits. We know that in the College of Douay the theological instruction was chiefly from the *Summa* of St. Thomas; on this specific point, see Philip Hughes, *The Reformation in England,* III (London, 1954), 291. Was Shakespeare familiar, we may wonder, with any of the English or Latin treatises of Thomas Stapleton, the recusant whom Anthony Wood later praised as "the most learned Roman Catholic of all his time"? Marvin R. O'Connell, *Thomas Stapleton and the Counter Reformation* (Yale University Press, 1964) gives an excellent account of the Thomistic orientation and patristic learning of Stapleton.

6. In taking over Aristotle's philosophy, St. Thomas also profoundly modified it. On this point, see F. C. Copleston, *Medieval Philosophy* (New York, 1961), p. 87; and H. V. Jaffa, *Thomism and Aristotelianism* (University of Chicago Press, 1952), esp. pp. 187–92.

7. Note Milton B. Kennedy's conviction, in *The Oration in Shakespeare* (University of North Carolina Press, 1942), p. 223, that Shakespeare's dramatic theory is "consciously or unconsciously Aristotelian." Virgil Whitaker, in *The Mirror up to Nature* (San Marino, 1965), p. 143, believes that Shakespeare wrote "quasi-Aristotelian tragedy," but he associates this with Sidney's Neo-Aristotelianism (p. 85) more closely than I would.

8. Ingram Bywater, *Aristotle on the Art of Poetry* (Oxford, 1909), p. 215. This view, that hamartia is solely an intellectual failing, is held also by Humphry House, *Aristotle's Poetics* (London, 1961), pp. 93–96.

9. S. H. Butcher, *Aristotle's Theory of Poetry and Fine Art,* 4th edition of 1911, reprinted (New York, 1951), p. 318. Others who have argued for a moral aspect in hamartia include P. W. Harsh, in *Trans. Am. Philol. Assn.* 76 (1945), 47–58; Lane Cooper, in *Classical Journal,* 43 (1947–48), 39–40; and R. Y. Hathorn, in *Tragedy, Myth, and Mystery* (Indiana University Press, 1962), pp. 85–87. Cedric Whitman, *Sophocles* (Harvard University Press, 1951), pp. 28–35, agrees that the moral interpretation of hamartia is "the only one that is consistent with Aristotle's thinking." But then, curiously, he argues that Aristotle's concept does

not fit Greek drama, contradicts its facts, and is superimposed distort-
ingly on the values of the older poets. To sustain this contention, Whitman would insist that criticism of tragic heroes by the Chorus is in no
way identifiable with the playwright's view. Whitman's reading of Sophocles, and a similar one by Bernard Knox (mentioned hereafter in footnote 15), seem to me mistaken. But let me say that, even if my own quite
different reading of Sophocles, which relies on the support of other
notable critics, should be a wrong one, this would not invalidate the
thrust of my main argument. My concern is with how Aristotle could
have understood Sophocles, whether rightly or wrongly. Aristotle's sense
of hamartia, whether or not it was shared by Sophocles, was later taken
up and modified by Christian writers, and in this form became Shakespeare's heritage.

10. W. K. Wimsatt, *Literary Criticism: A Short History* (New York,
1957), p. 41. Lane Cooper, in *Aristotle on the Art of Poetry: An Amplified Version with Supplementary Illustrations* (Cornell University Press,
revised edition, 1947), pp. 40–41, carries this emphasis further by defining hamartia as a "blindness of heart." It involves a flaw, he says, both
in the heart and in the head of the agent. He cites Creon's reference to
"the wretched blindness of my counsels" and relates this imperfection to
man's "first disobedience" as described by Milton.

11. Hathorn, *Tragedy,* p. 86. Hathorn is arguing that ignorance is
not ethically neutral. Later, in discussing *Hippolytus* (pp. 100–105), he
finds this play a study in "intentional blindness." Theseus, he notes,
rejects investigation; Hippolytus rejects adult experience; and Phaedra
forswears her own better knowledge. Particularly noteworthy is Phaedra's statement: "though insanity is bad, it at least has the advantage
that one is destroyed without knowing it." Here may be a parallel, I
think, to Hamlet's attitude.

12. Robert B. Heilman, " 'Twere Best Not Know Myself': Othello,
Lear, Macbeth," in *Shakespeare 400* (1964), ed. James G. McManaway,
pp. 89–90. An interpretation much like Heilman's, stressing the hero's
rejecting of opportunities for self-knowledge, has been developed by
Lillian Feder, in " 'The Unwary Egotist': A Study of the *Oedipus Tyrannus,"* *Centennial Review,* V (1961), 260–80.

13. Butcher, *Aristotle's Theory,* pp. 320–24.

14. Citing widely from Aristotle's works, Martin Oswald has distinguished between *hamartia,* as denoting a shortcoming inherent in the
disposition of the agent, a quality of his temperament which gives him
the possibility of making mistakes, and *hamartema,* which denotes an
actual blunder and resides in the act rather than the agent. See his "Aristotle on AMARTIA and Sophocles' Oedipus Tyrannus," in a *Fest-
schrift Ernst Kapp* (Hamburg, 1958), pp. 93–108.

15. Butcher, *Aristotle's Theory,* pp. 309–10; Bernard Knox, *The He-*

IV *Hamartia in Aristotle, Christian Doctrine, and* Hamlet, CONTINUED

roic Temper (University of California Press, 1964), p. 116; Maritain, *The Responsibility of the Artist* (New York, 1960), p. 31. Butcher here jeopardizes his own theory that an unselfish goodness is inappropriate to tragic heroes. Knox, on the other hand, is radically modern. He assumes (see p. 55) that Sophocles' personal religion involved a worship of the grave itself, and of those heroes who by their passionate anger seemed to exceed ordinary humanity. After giving an excellent summary of the heroic temper of Antigone—audacious, uncompromising, and stubbornly self-sufficient—Knox would have us suppose all this justified by her "love." He downgrades Creon for ultimately lacking in nerve. In *Oedipus at Thebes* (New Haven, 1957), Knox insists that Oedipus "is not a man guilty of a moral fault" (p. 49). The play, he thinks, does not fit Aristotle's description of tragedy but instead exemplifies the very thing Aristotle thought a tragedy should avoid—the spectacle of a virtuous man brought to misery (p. 31). In short, Knox dismisses Aristotle's theory as inapplicable for understanding Sophoclean tragedy. Knox's view is today popular, but I regard it as the consequence of a modernist incompetence in the discipline of philosophy alongside a myopia in literary criticism.

16. Gilbert Norwood, *Greek Tragedy* (New York, 1960), pp. 137–41; A. C. Schlesinger, *Boundaries of Dionysus* (Harvard University Press, 1963), pp. 27–28, and for my other citations, pp. 69 and 37. Lane Cooper's view is cited approvingly by Wimsatt, *Literary Criticism,* p. 39. On Watson's view, see Whitaker, *Mirror,* pp. 82–84.

17. Knox, *The Heroic Temper,* p. 115.

18. On this point, see Vernon Bourke, *Will in Western Thought* (New York, 1964), pp. 30–33 and 55–71.

19. Aquinas, *Summa Theologica* I–II, 85, 2–3. All my citations of this work will be from the translation by the English Dominicans, First Complete American Edition in Three Volumes (New York, Benziger Brothers, 1947).

20. Quoted by E. Przywara, *An Augustine Synthesis* (New York, 1936), p. 124. Compare Donald Howard, *The Three Temptations* (Princeton University Press, 1966), esp. p. 53.

21. Anders Nygren, *Eros and Agape* (London, 1953), p. 284.

22. "Sin," *Kittel's Bible Key Words,* tr. Coates (1951), pp. 33–38.

23. *Kittel,* p. 49.

24. Augustine, *City of God* XIV, 11, relying on I Tim. 2:4, where Adam's and Eve's modes of culpability are distinguished. Augustine says Adam's mode can be seen in Aaron's and Solomon's consentings to idol worship, and Eve's mode in the blandishments of the women who persuaded Aaron and Solomon. I use the translation by Marcus Dods, in *Nicene and Post-Nicene Fathers,* First Series, Vol. II (Buffalo, 1887).

25. Augustine, *On Free Will* III. 53. tr. J. H. S. Burleigh, in *The Library of Christian Classics,* VI (Philadelphia, 1953), 202.

26. Aquinas, similarly, believes liberation possible by consulting conscience. He supposes that human beings have *synderesis,* a natural habit for understanding certain true and unchangeable rules and seeds of virtue, by which the reason can judge in particular acts which apply these principles (*S. T.* I. 79. 12–13). Jaffa, *Thomism and Aristotelianism,* pp. 114 and 143, comments that in Aristotle, however, it would seem that men learn of virtue and vice simply from public opinion. Aristotle has no concept of conscience.

27. Aquinas, *S. T.* I–II. 77. 4.

28. Aquinas, *S. T.* I–II. 2. 7–8; II–II. 25. 7; 26. 3.

29. Aquinas, *S. T.* I–II. 19. 4; I–II. 74. 7.

30. Dover Wilson, *What Happens in Hamlet,* 3rd. ed. (Cambridge, 1951), pp. 220–29; 307.

31. J. H. Brock, *The Dramatic Purpose of Hamlet* (Cambridge, 1935), esp. pp. 10, 26.

32. See, e.g., the kinds of slander warned against by Francis de Sales, in *Introduction to the Devout Life* (1609), ed. J. K. Ryan (1950), Pt. III, ch. 29.

33. Aquinas, *S. T.* I–II. 77. 4–7; 82. 3; 84. 2.

34. A. H. Fairchild, *Shakespeare and the Tragic Theme* (University of Missouri, 1944), pp. 105–17. This seems to me more convincing than Paul Siegel's attempt, in *Shakespearean Tragedy and the Elizabethan Compromise* (1957), p. 97, to distinguish between Shakespeare's "comparatively innocent" heroes and guilty ones.

35. John Vyvyan, *The Shakespearean Ethic* (London, 1959), p. 103. This apparent allusion to Judas, interestingly, is by Leontes in *The Winter's Tale,* where the cultural setting is not specifically Christian but rather the fictional world of antique Romance. Thus, I would say, the phrase has a universal meaning for all auditors, while at the same time auditors familiar with Christian story can understand the phrase's meaning in a full and ultimate sense by recalling the paradigm of Judas. Truth is one and the same for all men; but a knowledge of the Bible can assist and amplify our understanding of it.

36. See, e.g., the comment on *Hamlet* in Francis Fergusson, *The Idea of a Theatre* (Princeton University Press, 1949), pp. 145–46; Rebecca West, *The Court and the Castle* (Yale University Press, 1957), pp. 27–28; and G. K. Hunter, "Hamlet Criticism," *The Critical Quarterly,* I (1959), 31.

37. Peter Alexander, *Shakespeare's Life and Art* (London, 1939), p. 161. Similarly, W. H. Clemen, in *The Development of Shakespeare's Imagery* (Harvard University Press, 1951), p. 110, speaks of Hamlet's "ability to penetrate to the real nature of men and things," and praises

IV *Hamartia in Aristotle, Christian Doctrine, and* Hamlet, CONTINUED

him for calling "things by their right names." Even G. Wilson Knight, who in *The Wheel of Fire* emphasizes the "inhuman cynicism" of Hamlet's vision, shifts inconsistently to a romantic view in saying that this vision "is right" and sees "the truth." My own view is that Hamlet by reason of his tragic psychology, gives us a distorted, reductionist, and split version of the truth.

38. W. F. Trench, *Shakespeare's "Hamlet": A New Commentary* (London, 1913), p. 115; H. B. Charlton, *Shakespearian Tragedy* (Cambridge, 1948) pp. 90–96; Robert Speaight, *Nature in Shakespearian Tragedy* (London, 1955), pp. 11 and 26; Ernest Jones, *Hamlet and Oedipus* (London, 1949). C. S. Lewis, "Hamlet: The Prince or the Poem?," *Proceedings of the British Academy*, XXVIII (1942), 152, speaks of Hamlet's "inability to understand either himself or his fellows or the real quality of the universe..."

39. L. C. Knights, *An Approach to "Hamlet"* (London, 1960), pp. 80–81. This book develops and refines the view Knights set forth in *Explorations* (London, 1946), pp. 66–77. The earlier essay, however, was spoiled somewhat by a conjecture that, at least in part, Hamlet's "immaturity" was reflecting Shakespeare's immaturity at the time of writing.

40. Vyvyan, *Shakespearean Ethic,* pp. 55–56. See also B. R. Pollin, "Hamlet, a Successful Suicide," *Shakespeare Studies,* I (1965), 240–60.

41. Aspects of my interpretation have appeared in "Hamlet's Apostrophe on Man," *PMLA,* LXVI (1951), 1073–1113, and in "The Ghost in *Hamlet*," *SP*, XLVIII (1951), 161–92.

42. A *locus classicus* on this point is *City of God* V. 24. Princes are happy, says Augustine, "if they be slack to avenge, quick to forgive: if they use correction for the public good and not for private hate ... and if they do all things not for glory but for charity, and with and before all, give God the due sacrifice of prayer and contrition for their imperfections."

43. Compare R. A. Foakes, "An Approach to *Julius Caesar,*" *SQ,* V (1954), 259–70. Foakes traces the way in which various themes of that play are used "to suggest a full circle of events." Let me point out, further, that this circle involves, in Acts I–IV of *Julius Caesar,* a motif sequence which is telescoped within Act I of *Hamlet*. That is, the three motifs—of Caesar's triumph celebrated, his reign supplanted, but his spirit then returning to haunt—are all paralleled in the opening situation of *Hamlet*. The Ghost in Hamlet may therefore be equivalent to Caesar's spirit—which Antony foresees (III. i. 270) as "ranging for revenge, / With Ate by his side come hot from hell," to cry havoc. Note that in the anonymous play *Caesar's Revenge,* the ghost of Caesar comes specifically from hell (III. i).

44. *City of God* XII. 13. Augustine's insight into the cyclical nature of wrong-doing has a parallel in Gilbert Murray's theory of Greek tragedy in his *Five Stages of Greek Religion* (New York, 1925). Murray sees ancient tragedy as reflecting the pride and punishment of the Year-Daemon. Each Year, as it arrives and waxes great, commits the sin of hubris, for which it is then slain. The death is deserved, but the slaying itself is a sin; hence the new year comes as an avenger, or resurrection of the Wronged one, and repeats the cycle.

45. Salvador de Madariaga, *On Hamlet* (London, 1948), pp. 22–23.

46. The hint for thus characterizing Hamlet comes from Belleforest: "je ne sçay lequel des Grecs et Romains eussent eu l'honneur de l'avantager en vertu" (quoted by Stabler, *PMLA*, LXXXI, 213). But Shakespeare makes Hamlet's pagan virtue emblematic of a lapsing from Christian virtue.

47. And especially by its reading of Hamlet's sex disgust as Shakespeare's own, as Jones does, seeing in the act of playwriting an essentially neurotic activity and a technique for evading infantile guilt. Marshall Stearns in "Hamlet and Freud," *College English*, 10 (1949), 272, has rightly objected that this reductive view neglects the point that the artist may be in conscious command of his illusions, making them serve "a more concrete relation to reality." For a full survey of Freudian criticism, see Norman N. Holland's recent *Psychoanalysis and Shakespeare* (New York, 1966). But note that James Kirsch, who invokes Adler and Jung in his *Shakespeare's Royal Self* (New York, 1966), doubts (p. 182) that Hamlet has an Oedipus complex in the Freudian sense.

48. Critics such as Bradley, Dover Wilson, and Granville-Barker have supposed that Gertrude was guilty of adultery with Claudius during the lifetime of Hamlet's father. I accept, rather, the arguments against this view by John Draper in *The Hamlet of Shakespeare's Audience* (Duke University Press, 1938) and by Carolyn Heilbrun in "The Character of Hamlet's Mother," *SQ*, VIII (1957), 201–206. The Ghost's word "adulterous" does not actually charge Gertrude with unfaithfulness *before* his death; and his complaint that Claudius dispatched him of his life, his crown, his queen, may indicate the sequence in time of the takings. Moreover, the Gonzago playlet does not accuse its Queen of infidelity while her husband lived, nor does the Dumbshow show the poisoner wooing the Queen until afterwards. I interpret this evidence to mean that Hamlet (and his father) interpret as "adulterous" the mere fact of a second marriage.

49. Vyvyan, *Shakespearean Ethic*, p. 30.

50. See Josephine Bennett, "Characterization in Polonius' Advice to Laertes," *SQ*, IV (1953), 3–9; and "These Few Precepts," *SQ*, VII (1956), 275–76.

IV *Hamartia in Aristotle, Christian Doctrine, and* Hamlet, CONTINUED

51. Augustine, *City of God* XIV. 4. Two passages in Shakespeare's *All's Well* seem to reflect this same doctrine: 1) the comment by two lords, in IV. iii. 23, that "as we are ourselves" we are "merely our own traitors" unless "God delay our rebellion"; and 2) Parolles' reference, in I. 1. 158, to "self-love" as "the most inhibited sin in the canon."

52. Augustine, *On the Morals of the Catholic Church,* chapter xxvi. Compare the comment of H. N. Hudson in his edition of *Hamlet* (New York, 1909), p. 38: "a man who fixes on no higher principle than that of being true to himself will never be really true to himself. This is one of those cases wherein a man must aim at the greater, or he will attain the less."

53. G. R. Elliott sees here a "wild vow," and comments further that in capping it with "the far wilder vow" to absolute secrecy Hamlet in effect dedicates himself to "a proud, inhuman, and irreligious solitude." See *Scourge and Minister* (Duke University Press, 1951), pp. 38–40. With other aspects of Elliott's study, however, I cannot agree—for example, with his view that the Ghost's speech contains "contrary motives" of revenge and "heavenly charity"; or with his view that later in the play Hamlet discards revengefulness for "eventual charity and magnanimity." I find Elliott's canons for judging charity far too loose, reflecting perhaps his background in the humanism of Norman Foerster.

54. In our 1960s, "honesty" has become the banner of radical student movements on U. S. A. college campuses, where (as at Berkeley) an ideal of "free" speech comes to mean freedom for "filthy" speech. The basic thrust of such honesty is not charity but rather a contempt for what is obsessively described as the "phony" in the social order. Such "honesty," usually justified as an instinctive or "gut" morality, and imagined as "realism," easily drifts toward nihilism and irresponsibilty—a modern analogue to Hamlet's psychology.

55. Aquinas, *Compendium of Theology,* tr. Cyril Vollert (St. Louis, 1948), ch. 174.

56. See Wilson, *What Happens in "Hamlet,"* pp. 146 and 150; and the contrary arguments of Lawrence, in "Hamlet and the Mouse-trap," *PMLA,* LIV (1939), 709–35; of Speaight, in *Nature in Shakespearean Tragedy,* pp. 32–34; and of W. W. Greg, in "The Mousetrap—A Postscript," *MLR,* XXXV (1940), 8–10.

57. Trench, *Shakespeare's "Hamlet,"* pp. 85–90 especially, has much to say about Hamlet's persistent tendency to "let himself go." Trench rightly associates this with a kind of suicide, since suicide is an act in which the will renounces responsibility to everything but its own desires.

58. Its most recent exponent is Sister Miriam Joseph, in her "Discerning the Ghost in Hamlet," *PMLA,* LXXVI (1961), 493–502. Paul Siegel

in *PMLA*, LXXVIII (1963), 148–49, rebuts much of her argument. Critics who judge the Ghost to be a spirit of darkness tempting Hamlet to evil are now many. A listing would include, besides myself, the following: Knight, *Wheel of Fire*, p. 42; Goddard, *The Meaning of Shakespeare*, pp. 354 and 382; Vyvyan, *Shakespearean Ethic*, p. 31; Speaight, *Christian Theatre* (New York, 1960), p. 66; Knights, *Approach*, pp. 46–48; Whitaker, *Mirror*, p. 191; William Hamilton, "Hamlet and Providence," *Christian Scholar*, XLVII (1964), 203; James Kirsch, *Shakespeare's Royal Self*, pp. 37–54; and Eleanor Prosser, *Hamlet and Revenge* (Stanford University Press, 1967), pp. 97–142. This emerging consensus is too important to be ignored.

59. To the evidence offered in my article, let me add mention of John Gerson's *De Probatione Spiritum*, ed. Paschal Boland (Washington, D.C., 1959). Gerson stresses the importance of testing spirits by norms taken from Holy Scripture, and cites as one such norm (sec. 27) the following text from James 3: 17: "The wisdom that is from above is first of all chaste, then peaceable, moderate, docile, in harmony with all good things, full of mercy and good fruits, without judging, without dissimulation."

60. More relevant to the Ghost is Plato's saying (*Phaedo*, 80–81) that souls tainted and impure at the time of death will through fear of Hades be dragged back into the visible world and hover about tombs. "Of course these are not the souls of the good, but of the wicked, and they are compelled to wander about these places as a punishment for their bad conduct in the past."

61. More specifically, in medieval symbolism, the willow represented sterility in good works. Since the willow is a tree bearing no fruit, it was associated with the waters of *cupiditas*. See D. W. Robertson, "The Doctrine of Charity in Mediaeval Literary Gardens," *Speculum*, XXVI (1951).

62. His attitude has nothing of the spirit required in the Catholic office of Extreme Unction. That office (I quote a modern text) requires the penitent (or his representatives) to confess that he has "sinned exceedingly . . . through *my* most grievous fault" and to invoke the prayers of the saints on his behalf. Also, the office begins with a prayer which includes these words: "Let no demons have access here; let the angels of peace be present and all hateful dissension leave this house."

63. Fredson Bowers, *Elizabethan Revenge Tragedy* (Princeton University Press, 1940), esp. p. 37; and C. B. Watson, *Shakespeare and the Renaissance Concept of Honor* (Princeton University Press, 1960), esp. pp. 127–35.

64. Robert H. West, "King Hamlet's Ambiguous Ghost," *PMLA*, LXX (1955), 1107–14.

IV *Hamartia in Aristotle, Christian Doctrine, and* Hamlet, CONTINUED

65. See A. P. Stabler, "King Hamlet's Ghost in Belleforest?," *PMLA,* LXXVII (1962), 18–20.

66. The dispositive cause of idolatry, Aquinas explains (*S. T.* II–II. 94), is a defect of nature on the part of man, either through ignorance in his intellect or disorder in his affections, both of which involve guilt. Further, idolatry (which is a species of superstition) is the gravest of sins, since it lessens the divine sovereignty by setting up another God in the world, and "there is no kind of sin that idolatry does not produce at some time, either through leading expressly to that sin by causing it, or through being an occasion thereof."

67. Nevill Coghill, *Shakespeare's Professional Skills* (Cambridge University Press, 1964), p. 11, citing from the Malone Society Reprint (1937).

68. Lines 1260–64 (Arcite's lament), Coghill's Penguin edition, p. 59. The basic metaphor, likening a soul ignorant of its true good to a drunkard who can not find his way home, derives from Boethius, *Consolation,* III, pr. 2.

69. See Heilman, " 'Twere Best Not Know Myself': Othello, Lear, Macbeth," in *Shakespeare 400* (1964), ed. McManaway, pp. 88–98; and Heilman's "To Know Himself: An Aspect of Tragic Structure," *REL,* V (1964), esp. pp. 48–49.

70. For Elizabethan commentary on this concept in Isaiah, see my *Marlowe's "Tamburlaine": A Study in Renaissance Moral Philosophy* (Vanderbilt University Press, 1941), pp. 13 and 108–13; and see additionally, Anthony Munday, *A View of Sundry Examples* (1580), p. 80.

71. For example, Fredson Bowers, "Hamlet as Minister and Scourge," *PMLA,* LXX (1955), 740–49.

72. In medieval allegory, *jawbone* signified "the devil's malice"; see *Art Bulletin,* XXIV (1942), 212.

73. I have elaborated this point in my article in *SP* (1951), pages 176–77. Note also Augustine's generalization (*Confessions* III. 16) that "in acts of violence where there is a wish to hurt, whether by reproach or injury"—whether for revenge, or to avoid some evil, or through envy—such iniquity is that of men who "live ill" against the Ten Commandments.

74. See Israel Gollancz, *The Sources of Hamlet* (London, 1926), p. 237, a passage which A. P. Stabler has called to my attention.

75. Kirsch, *Shakespeare's Royal Self,* p. 62.

76. For example, M. D. H. Parker, *The Slave of Life* (London, 1955), p. 95. Irving Ribner, similarly, speaks of Hamlet's "Christian concern for his mother's salvation" in this scene (*Patterns in Shakespearian Tragedy* [London, 1960], p. 78). But I see an analogy to Othello, the demonic priestly confessor of V. ii, whose behavior is remarkably like Hamlet's.

77. J. W. Wadsworth, "Webster's *Duchess of Malfi* in the Light of Some Contemporary Ideas on Marriages and Remarriages," *PQ,* 35 (1956), 394–407.

78. Cf. Granville-Barker, *Prefaces to Shakespeare: Hamlet* (London 1946), 113 n.

79. I would agree with Heilman's comment (*REL,* V, 55), that Hamlet has an "instinct" for "provoking the adversary into hostile steps that will make [his own] action mandatory, automatic, and pure"—but pure only because Hamlet hides from recognizing his actually impure motives in provoking the threats which will permit him the legalistic justification of self-defense.

80. Although Fredson Bowers and others have suggested "sullied flesh" as an emendation, the Folio's reading of "solid flesh" has been strongly defended in recent articles by Richard Flatter in *SQ,* XI (1960) and Sidney Warhaft in *ELH,* XXVIII (1961).

81. For further comment on Hamlet as Hollow Man, see my *PMLA* article "Hamlet's Apostrophe on Man," (1951), p. 1113.

82. *Confessions,* V. [x.] 18 (tr. Pusey, Everyman edition).

83. See William Montgomerie, "More an Antique Roman than a Dane," *The Hibbert Journal,* LIX (1960), 67–77, regarding parallels between Nero and Hamlet. Montgomerie lists the following: both had a flair for playacting and poetry; Nero is said to have sung the "Sack of Ilium" while Rome burned (compare Hamlet's fascination with the Aeneas tale to Dido); and Nero died by suicide at age 30, as Hamlet dies at 30 after having long *desired* suicide. Nero occasionally identified himself with Orestes and with Oedipus.

84. Regarding traditional number symbolism, see Russell Peck, "Number Symbolism and the Idea of Order in the Works of Geoffrey Chaucer" (Indiana University Dissertation, 1962). The number eight can signify either renewal (as in the eight souls saved in Noah's ark), or conversely it can signify a false renewal (as in the eight bushels of florins in Chaucer's *Pardoner's Tale*). Shakespeare specifically uses the ark reference for the four couples whose marriage concludes *As You Like It;* and his *Measure for Measure* ends likewise with a marriage feast for eight persons. But *Hamlet,* as a tragedy, appropriately provides an upside-down version of comedy's pattern.

85. Aquinas, *On Kingship,* tr. Phelan and Eschmann (Toronto, 1949), Ch. VI–VIII.

86. Trivet, as cited by D. W. Robertson, *Preface to Chaucer* (Princeton University Press, 1962), p. 26. See also Augustine, *City of God* XXII. 2.

87. Augustine, *Confessions* II. [vi.] 14 (Everyman ed., p. 29). Compare Marcellus: "Something is rotten in the state of Denmark."

IV *Hamartia in Aristotle, Christian Doctrine, and* Hamlet, CONTINUED

88. Augustine, Sermon LXXX, *Post-Nicene Fathers,* First Series, VI, 499.

89. Peter Lombard, *Sentences* III. 19, as quoted by C. Lattey, *The Atonement* (Cambridge, 1928), p. 164.

90. Roy Walker, *The Time is Out of Joint* (London, 1948), pp. 143–44. More recently, Richard Foster has interpreted Hamlet as a messianic figure; see "Hamlet and the Word," *UTQ,* XXX (1961), 229–45.

91. G. Wilson Knight, *Wheel of Fire,* 5th ed. (New York, 1957), p. 323.

92. Augustine, *On the Trinity* I. 11. 5.

93. Hardin Craig, *New Lamps for Old* (Oxford, 1960), p. 101.

94. Dolora Cunningham, "*Macbeth:* The Tragedy of the Hardened Heart," *SQ,* XIV (1963), 46.

V Moral Experience and Its Typology
in *King Lear*

1. R. W. Chambers, "King Lear," *Glasgow University Publications,* LIV (1940), 20–52, reprinted in part by Paul Siegel, *His Infinite Variety: Major Shakespearean Criticism* (New York, 1963), pp. 353–75; John Danby, *Shakespeare's Doctrine of Nature* (London, 1949), pp. 122–25, and 204–205.

2. Carolyn French, "Shakespeare's 'Folly': *King Lear,*" *SQ,* X (1959), 524. See also Peter Mortenson, "The Role of Albany," *SQ,* XVI (1965), 224: "*King Lear* . . . explores the Christian rationale and affirms it without retreating to clichés or easy rewards."

3. G. B. Harrison, *Shakespeare's Tragedies* (New York, 1953), p. 159.

4. The *Malleus Maleficarum,* a Renaissance compendium by Catholic divines, explains the name Beelzebub as meaning "Lord of the Flies, that is of the souls of sinners who have left the true faith of Christ"; see section I. 4, as cited by Robert West, *The Invisible World* (University of Georgia Press, 1939), p. 69. This meaning has been revived for our attention in William Golding's *Lord of the Flies* (1953), in which this god is worshipped by wanton boys who exhibit, in Golding's allegory, the power of original sin. Let us recall, also, that St. Francis used the epithet "brother fly" to refer to slothful men (see Bonaventura's *Life of Francis,* ch. V, sec. 6). Shakespeare's Gloucester is obviously a slothful man. At this point in the play he is superstitiously honoring demonic gods—of the kind St. Paul describes in Ephesians 6 when exhorting Christians to fight against such powers by putting on "the whole armor of God."

5. Maynard Mack, "*King Lear*" *in Our Time* (University of Cali-

fornia Press, 1965), pp. 111–12. My other references to Mack are from pp. 101 and 115; see also his comment (p. 71) that the play has a "homiletic structure" for setting forth a vision of the nature and destiny of man.

6. Russell Peck draws this analogy in his essay on "Edgar's Pilgrimage: High Comedy in *King Lear*," *SEL*, VII (1967), 229, noting also that this passage in Mark 5 is alluded to in four other plays of Shakespeare.

7. Shakespeare has "by negligence," said Johnson, given to a heathen "the sentiments and practices of Christianity." But Johnson was himself neglecting the fact that the Old Testament tells us of some pagans who were saints, and that (as Jean Danielou has recently emphasized) the domain of Christ extends beyond the limits of the explicit revelation of Christ. In every age and every land, says Danielou, there have been men who have "believed in Christ without knowing Him" and thus have belonged "invisibly to the visible Church." See Danielou, *Holy Pagans of the Old Testament* (London, 1957), esp. p. 10.

8. See Harry Levin's essay, "The Heights and the Depths: a Scene from *King Lear*," in *More Talking of Shakespeare* (London, 1959), ed. John Garrett, p. 95.

9. Russell Peck, "Edgar's Pilgrimage," p. 235.

10. D. G. James, *The Dream of Learning* (Oxford, 1951), pp. 111–15. Leo Kirschbaum, who contrary to James regards *King Lear* as "Christian in content," nevertheless also fails to see any psychological unity in Edgar. Surveying Edgar's succession of roles—dispossessed son; Poor Tom; a *deus ex machina* at Dover cliff; a dialect-speaking peasant; a letter-bearer; a knightly challenger—Kirschbaum regards these as the actions of a multifunctional "puppet," necessitated by plot alone "rather than being motivated into action by psychology." See his *Character and Characterization in Shakespeare* (Wayne State University Press, 1962), 59–75.

11. Frederick Pollock and F. W. Maitland, *History of English Law* (Cambridge University Press, 1962), II, 600, point out that trial by combat was considered in the Middle Ages a "sacral process." "What triumphed was not brute force but truth. The combatant who was worsted was a convicted perjurer."

12. K. Muir, Arden *Lear*, p. xlviii, cites Luke 1:52 as in his view the "perfectly clear" meaning of an earlier scene, the trial in the hovel in Act III. If so, then I would add that Act V repeats the theme in a larger way—in this respect like the incremental parallelism of biblical poetic structure.

13. See the essays by Arpad Pauncz (in *American Imago*, IX) and by John Donnelly (in *Psychoanalytic Review*, XL), reprinted in excerpt in *The King Lear Perplex* (San Francisco, 1960), ed. Helmut Bonheim.

V *Moral Experience and Its Typology in* King Lear, CONTINUED

Note also the Fool's comment (I. iv. 187) that "thou madest thy daughters thy mother." It implies that Lear has perverted fatherly love into a childish love of being mothered.

14. H. Granville-Barker, *Prefaces to Shakespeare: First Series* (London, 1933), p. 179.

15. Josephine Bennett, for example, compares the two as "blind of heart" and "blind of eye," and specifically terms "blindness of heart" Lear's "tragic flaw." See "The Storm Within: The Madness of Lear," *SQ*, XIII (1962), 149–50. Had Mrs. Bennett consulted Ephesians 4:17 ff. (Epistle for 19 Trinity in the Prayer Book), she would have discovered that "blindness of heart" is a hardening of the heart which causes Gentiles to walk in the vanity of their mind, having the understanding darkened; and that this plight is characteristic of what St. Paul calls "the old man," corrupt in deceitful lusts. The same passage goes on to contrast the "new man": one who is angry but sins not; who lets himself speak only what may minister grace to hearers; who is tenderhearted and forgiving. These norms, and with them the motif of conversion from "old man" to "new man," seem to me very pertinent to the developing logic of Shakespeare's play.

16. Irving Ribner, *Patterns in Shakespearian Tragedy* (London, 1960), pp. 118–20.

17. Excerpted in *The King Lear Perplex,* ed. Bonheim, pp. 159–63 and 169–72. For an enlargement of this argument, see H. V. Jaffa and Allan Bloom, *Shakespeare's Politics* (New York, 1964), pp. 118–28. Lear's plan, Jaffa infers, was to balance in England three ducal powers, while retaining for himself the name of king with intent to exercise the dominant influence from a base at Cordelia's court. But this shrewd plan for a unified England was ruined when, by dividing the land instead into two parts, Lear in effect tempted the one power to overthrow the other, while leaving himself no mediating base.

18. Francis G. Schoff has recently argued that the play contains no evidence that Lear is to be regarded as a horrible example of either senility, or wrathfulness, or sin against the responsibilities of kingship. In Schoff's view, however, the story can be given no satisfactory motivation whatever and Shakespeare is doing all he can to prevent us from accounting for its opening incidents in any logical way. See his "King Lear: Moral Example or Tragic Protagonist?" *SQ*, XIII (1962), 157–72. I regard this argument as a distortion of a half-truth. That is, I would agree that Shakespeare is not making his tragedy into a didactic *exemplum* of the moral consequences of senility, wrath, or sin against Tudor political philosophy; yet these factors seem to me not inconsequential, as Schoff would suppose, but consequential in a secondary way,

as aspects or reflections of a deeper moral motivation working in and through them. The deeper moral motivation is Lear's subconscious desire for godlike authority—an attitude indicated clearly enough by his comment to Cordelia: "Better thou / Hadst not been born than not to have pleased me better." Lear's greed to please himself at all costs, his self-centered glorification, is in my view the basic moral flaw Shakespeare is implying in Lear. Because Schoff overlooks this more subtle causation, he champions Stoll's notion of an incredible opening scene which an audience must simply accept uncritically.

19. Granville-Barker, *Prefaces,* p. 164.

20. W. H. Clemen, *The Development of Shakespeare's Imagery* (Harvard University Press, 1951), p. 135.

21. M. D. H. Parker, *The Slave of Life* (London, 1955), p. 132.

22. Arthur Sewell makes this point in his *Character and Society in Shakespeare* (Oxford, 1951), p. 115. The first Act, he says, shows all the characters, except the King of France, determining their conduct by "self-regarding" reason.

23. Could Shakespeare here be echoing St. Paul's idea, in Romans 8:14–16, that "as many as . . . have received the Spirit of adoption" cry out "Abba, Father," since they "have not received the spirit of bondage again to fear"? Cordelia's experience, in any case, seems analogous at a secular level to what St. Paul is describing.

24. This answer is both rational and absurd: in short, the rationalistic reasoning of self-justification. A recent critic, Ivor Morris, stresses the absurdity of Cordelia's answer, but tries to explain it by supposing (mistakenly, I think) that she is deliberately reproducing Lear's error in order intentionally to parody it. See "Cordelia and Lear," *SQ,* VIII (1957), 141–58. Morris might have pointed out, but does not, that his solution would be at least halfway in line with early versions of the legend, such as Geoffrey of Monmouth's, in which Cordelia gives as the second part of her answer the mocking reply: "So much as thou hast, so much art thou worth, and so much do I love thee." But Shakespeare's Cordelia, by comparison, is no "wise child" of folktale concerned to teach her father through verbal riddle. Rather, she is betraying her own tragic weakness, an attitude *riddled by* inner contradictions and hence unwittingly foolish in reply.

25. O. J. Campbell, convincingly, has identified Kent's role as that of the Stoic "plain man," a frank speaker who (like Epictetus) understands duty in terms of rebuking evil in other people. Noting that Kent's plain speaking is ineffectual, Campbell comments: "Here, as elsewhere in the play, Shakespeare insists that the stoic way to salvation from turbulent and unworthy emotion is psychologically unsound." See "The Salvation of Lear," *ELH,* XV (1948), 103. Coleridge, on the other hand,

V *Moral Experience and Its Typology in* King Lear, CONTINUED

declared Kent to be "perhaps the nearest to perfect goodness in all Shakespeare's characters."

26. On points of analogy between Cordelia and Christ, see for instance S. L. Bethell, *Shakespeare and the Popular Dramatic Tradition* (Westminster, 1944), p. 60, and Paul Siegel, *Shakespearean Tragedy* (New York, 1957), p. 186. Critics hostile to all such readings should be reminded perhaps that analogy does not mean identity.

27. A. C. Bradley, *Shakespearean Tragedy* (London, 1950 reprint) p. 291. Bradley's interpretation here has been seconded by critics such as Siegel, Granville-Barker, and R. W. Chambers.

28. Harrison, *Shakespeare's Tragedies*, p. 183; Stampfer, "The Catharsis of *King Lear*," *Shakespeare Survey*, 13 (1960), 2–3; Brooke, *Shakespeare: King Lear* (London, 1963), pp. 55–60. For a rebuttal of these critics, see Paul Siegel's "Shakespeare's Kneeling-Resurrection Pattern in King Lear," in his *Shakespeare in His Time and Ours* (University of Notre Dame Press, 1968), pp. 108–121. Siegel assembles evidence from *Lear,* and also from many of Shakespeare's comedies, of a conjunction of kneeling with resurrection and new birth. I have listed other Christian interpretations of *Lear* in Chapter II, footnote 47.

29. Thus my own view is close to that of Mrs. Bennett in "The Storm Within: The Madness of Lear," *SQ*, XIII (1962), 154, who reads all of Lear's actions in this scene as "evidences not of insanity, but of hope and love"; and to that of C. J. Sisson, in *Shakespeare's Tragic Justice* (London, 1962), p. 76, who rejects the notion of illusion and interprets Lear as having a glimpse "round the corner of this known world of time" into the otherworld of eternity, where he sees his beloved Cordelia awaiting him, her lips smiling again for him. Yet, as befits tragedy, the play must stop short, I believe, of resolving Lear's agony into simple bliss. His situation, rather, is somewhat like that of Simeon in Eliot's *A Song for Simeon:* "Not for me the ultimate vision . . . I am dying in my own death and the deaths of those after me." Simeon's paradoxical experience of undergoing a "birth season of decease" seems to me aptly analogous to Lear's at the end of Shakespeare's play.

30. On this point, see Thomas S. Stroup, "Cordelia and the Fool," *SQ,* XII (1961), 127–32.

31. Thelma Greenfield, "The Clothing Motif in *King Lear,*" *SQ,* V (1954), 285.

32. John Holloway, in *The Story of the Night* (University of Nebraska Press, 1961), p. 87, sees in Lear's discovery at this point—rightly, I think —a parallel to the truth more analytically stated by St. Paul in Romans 2:21–23.

33. That Edmund's whole plot is a work of black magic is signalized

for the audience by the tune he hums ("Fa, sol, la, mi") immediately before he first accosts Edgar. Harry Levin (*More Talking,* ed. Garrett, p. 91) has identified these notes as the *mi contra fa,* "the forbidden interval known as *diabolus in musica.*"

34. Kirschbaum, *Character and Characterization,* p. 65.

35. J. A. Barish and M. Waingrow come close to this interpretation in saying that Edgar returns "to enact a kind of purgatorial masquerade." See "Service in *King Lear,*" *SQ,* IX (1958), 351.

36. In some respects Tom's role seems to suggest, by analogy, the hide-and-go-seek tactics of the Jesuit missioners in Elizabethan England. Their methods of exorcising devils, perhaps only half-understood by critics, were pilloried in Harsnett's *The Declaration of Egregious Popish Impostures* (1606). What was the relation in Shakespeare's mind, we may wonder, between Jesuit practices of exorcism and the tricky exorcism he lets Edgar practice on Gloucester? We know that in writing *King Lear* Shakespeare borrowed from Harsnett a host of details and overtones, most recently catalogued by K. Muir in *Shakespeare's Sources,* I (London, 1957), 147–61. Perhaps Shakespeare is suggesting, for Jesuits and non-Jesuits alike, an imaginative mode of exorcism by which any man can work for community redemption, and in the process expiate his own past mistakes.

37. Kirschbaum, *Character,* pp. 66–69.

38. As Muir rightly remarks (Arden edition, p. liv), Lear's judgment here "is only an interim report on the human condition; it is not the answer provided by the play as a whole."

39. Regarding a possible source for today's Little Boy Blue ballad in Elizabethan verses about Cardinal Wolsey, see K. E. Thomas *Real Personages of Mother Goose* (Boston 1930), pp. 87–91.

40. G. Wilson Knight, in his general essay on "King Lear and the Comedy of the Grotesque," argues a somewhat similar point: "A shifting flash of comedy across the pain of the purely tragic," he declares, "both increases the tension and suggests, vaguely, a resolution and a purification." See his *Wheel of Fire,* 4th rev. ed. (London, 1949), p. 160.

41. See Fergusson, *The Idea of a Theatre* (Garden City reprint, 1953), p. 31.

42. George R. Kernodle's essay is in *Elizabethan Studies and Other Essays in Honor of George F. Reynolds* (Boulder, 1945), pp. 185–91.

43. Erich Auerbach, *Mimesis* (Garden City reprint, 1957), p. 279.

44. Maxwell, in *MLR,* XLV (1950), as quoted approvingly by Muir in the Arden *Lear,* p. lvi. Compare Alfred Harbage's view (Pelican *Lear,* Introduction) that the play is "rather inclusively than exclusively Christian."

45. Aquinas, *Contra Gentiles,* I and II; Calvin, *Institutes,* II. iii. 4.

V *Moral Experience and Its Typology in* King Lear, CONTINUED

46. S. L. Bethell comes close to making this suggestion in his *Shakespeare,* p. 54.

47. Harrison, *Shakespeare's Tragedies,* pp. 160–62, cites various evidences of the degeneracy of English morals and manners in the years 1605 and 1606. We may note also that Thomas Dekker, assuming a prophet's role in his *The Seven Deadly Sinnes of London* (1606), warned of "seven Divels" needing to be cast out; see H. F. B. Brett-Smith's edition (Oxford, 1922), p. 11.

VI The Reshaped Meaning of *Coriolanus*

1. See E. C. Pettet, "*Coriolanus* and the Midlands Insurrection of 1607," *Shakespeare Survey,* 3 (1950), 34–40. A briefer uprising had occurred in 1597 in Oxfordshire. Geoffrey Bullough reprints accounts of both in his *Narrative and Dramatic Sources of Shakespeare,* V (London, 1964), 553–58.

2. See Paul Jorgensen, "Shakespeare's Coriolanus: Elizabethan Soldier," *PMLA,* LXIV (1949), 221–35.

3. Kenneth Muir, "The Background of *Coriolanus,*" *SQ,* X (1959), 137–40.

4. Bullough, *Sources,* V, 516. Livy, more briefly, refers to "fear of forraine dangers" as being "the greatest bond of civile concord," since it knits together hearts "hatefull afore one to the other" (*Sources,* p. 503). I shall be using throughout the chapter Bullough's reprint of sections from North's Plutarch (1579) and Holland's Livy (1600).

5. My quotations have come from *City of God* I. 17–18; III. 17; and V. 12–17 (tr. Marcus Dods), in each of which sections Augustine cites the early days of the Republic as a kind of paradigm for Rome's later history.

6. We can find a different view, however, in a less traditional writer such as Martin Luther. Roland Frye, in his *Shakespeare and Christian Doctrine* (Princeton University Press, 1963), p. 98, has cited Luther's eulogizing of ancient Rome. Its boys, by age twenty, says Luther, had been reared into "wise and excellent men, skilled in every art and rich in experience, so that all the bishops, priests, and monks in Germany put together would not equal a Roman soldier. Consequently their country prospered . . ." We know that Luther held what has been called a "two kingdom" doctrine, which posited a disjunction between the realm of politics (in which he accepted "heathen virtue" as the norm) and the realm of saving faith (for which gospel grace was requisite). Applying to the realm of politics a heathen ethic, Luther during the Peasants War

could exhort rulers to "smite, slay, stab, and kill" as their duty. Scholars such as Ernst Troeltsch, Karl Barth, and Dietrich Bonhoeffer have criticized Luther's ethical dualism as being conducive to the Prussian militarism of recent centuries.

7. Tucker Brooke, *Shakespeare's Plutarch* (London, 1909), II, xiv–xv.

8. T. J. B. Spencer, *Shakespeare: The Roman Plays* (London, 1963), pp. 14–15.

9. Gilbert Highet, *The Classical Tradition* (New York, 1957), p. 198.

10. That *Coriolanus* reveals the tragedy of a whole society has been recognized by Matthew Proser, *The Heroic Image in Five Shakespearean Tragedies* (Princeton University Press, 1965), esp. p. 138; and by W. I. Carr, " 'Gracious Silence'—A Selective Reading of *Coriolanus*," *English Studies*, XLVI (1965), 221–34. Carr calls Coriolanus "the scapegoat for the terrible deficiencies of his training" and a victim of his city's "self-sufficient politics" of mere adroitness and intelligence—adding that "A judgment upon Coriolanus is a judgment upon the world which made and admired him."

11. See Carl A. Roebuck, "Coriolanus: the Story," *Northwestern University Quarterly*, II (Spring, 1960), p. 35.

12. See Alan D. Lehman, "The Coriolanus Story in Antiquity," *Classical Journal*, 47 (1952), 329–35.

13. Bullough, *Sources*, V, 462–72, summarizes from the Loeb translation the story of Coriolanus by Dionysius, but acknowledges that it was unavailable to Shakespeare in any English version.

14. Willard Farnham, *Shakespeare's Tragic Frontier* (University of California Press, 1950), pp. 212–17, surveys Lloyd's view, along with the similar view found in the French drama *Coriolan* (c. 1600) by Alexandre Hardy. He then contrasts these two with the Plutarchan view found in Golding's translation of Hurault.

15. Lydgate, *Fall of Princes*, Book III, 1891–2072, ed. Henry Bergen (Oxford University Press, 1924), II, 381–86. Note, however, that in Lydgate's version the mother pleads by offering herself as a hostage and by reminding her son how fondly she cared for him in his infancy—two motifs not found in any of the Roman accounts. Lydgate shows the city receiving its hero back with great "solempnite," although later, unaccountably, it banishes him again. If Shakespeare knew Lydgate's account, he must have rejected its characterization of mother and son as being unhistorically chivalric.

16. A recent defender of this view is H. J. Oliver, in "Coriolanus as Tragic Hero," *SQ*, X (1959), 53–60; but earlier variations of this same outlook have been expressed by Barrett Wendell (1894), George Brandes (1900), and W. H. Clemen (1951).

17. Oscar J. Campbell, *Shakespeare's Satire* (New York, 1943), 198–

VI *The Reshaped Meaning of* Coriolanus, CONTINUED

217. Somewhat similarly, Norman A. Brittin argues in "Coriolanus, Alceste, and Dramatic Genres," *PMLA,* LXXI (1956), 799–807, that Coriolanus is a "humour" character and the play itself an "odd dramatic type." G. B. Shaw in his introduction to *Man and Superman* wittily labels *Coriolanus* "the greatest of Shakespeare's comedies."

18. Bullough, *Sources,* V, 494–95.

19. William Rosen, *Shakespeare and the Craft of Tragedy* (Harvard University Press, 1960), p. 209; see also p. 186. Yet some of Rosen's remarks elsewhere are not exactly consistent with this formulation. On p. 191 he notes the "foolhardiness" of Coriolanus in war, and on p. 207 speaks of his "egocentric" emotions. Can Coriolanus, in that case, be said to have "perfect virtue" even in war?

20. Farnham, *Shakespeare's Tragic Frontier,* esp. pp. 207–17; 240; 244.

21. William F. Lynch, in a recent defense of "Christian imagination," argues a thesis with which I would in general agree, that such imagination in no way cancels out the facts of history nor imposes on them an external reading, but rather probes these facts more deeply in order to illumine a theological "dimension" which the human situation latently has. See his *Christ and Apollo* (New York, 1960).

22. T. S. Eliot, *Selected Essays* (New York, edition of 1950), p. 124.

23. M. W. MacCallum, *Shakespeare's Roman Plays* (London, 1910), p. 471.

24. Similarly, in Livy's account, Coriolanus replies to the first embassy: "If so be the Volscians had their lands restored to them againe, then there might be some parle and treatie of peace"; but that if the Romans insist on retaining their booty, then he will continue to hold in remembrance the "private wrongs" done him by his countrymen and the "courtesie" shown him by strangers, the Volscians. See Bullough, *Sources,* V, 503.

25. G. Wilson Knight, *The Imperial Theme* (London, third edition, 1951), p. 168.

26. A. C. Bradley, *Shakespearean Tragedy* (London, second edition, repr. 1950), p. 84.

27. Knight, *The Imperial Theme,* pp. 196–98. Compare Dover Wilson's view, *Coriolanus* (Cambridge, 1960), p. xxxiv, that the hero here "grows up, comes to know himself and to understand the meaning of life for the first time."

28. D. J. Enright, "*Coriolanus:* Tragedy or Debate?" *Essays in Criticism,* IV (1954), 19.

29. Farnham, *Shakespeare's Tragic Frontier,* pp. 258–59.

30. Eugene Waith, *The Herculean Hero* (New York, 1962), pp. 139–41.

31. Paul Siegel, "Shakespeare and the Neo-Chivalric Cult of Honor," *Centennial Review*, VIII (1964), 63–64.

32. In the account by Dionysius of Halicarnassus, the mother more bluntly threatens simply to kill herself, should Coriolanus refuse to spare his country. See Bullough, *Sources*, V, 471.

33. In Holland's Livy, as in Shakespeare's play, there is no mention of heavenly inspiration. It is reported simply that Rome's dames came flocking to the mother and the wife, and Livy comments: "Whether this proceeded from any publike counsell and was done in pollicie, or came onely of womens feare, I find but little in any records" (Bullough, *Sources*, V, 503). Perhaps Shakespeare is implying Livy's clue, but understanding the motives of "pollicie" and "feare" in a different and less favorable sense.

34. H. C. Goddard, *The Meaning of Shakespeare* (University of Chicago Press, 1951), pp. 605–10.

35. Although Aufidius upbraids Coriolanus for yielding to his "nurse's tears," we have no evidence in the embassy scene that Volumnia weeps, except in line 100, where she may be momentarily simulating what she describes. Shakespeare's account seems in part influenced by Livy's, which characterized the mother as "falling in steede of praiers into a fit of choler." Plutarch had softened this; his Volumnia speaks of "our prayers" and questions the choler of her son.

36. Richmond Noble, *Shakespeare's Biblical Knowledge* (London, 1935), p. 243.

37. The Apocalyptist had in mind, in particular, the Rome of his day—that of Domitian, a consul who insisted on being called *dominus et deus*, who wore Greek dress and a golden crown in the senate, and who persecuted Christians for "irreligion." Plutarch was a visiting philosopher-lecturer in the Rome of this period.

38. The play's persistent imagery of voices has been reviewed by Leonard Dean, "Voice and Deed in *Coriolanus, UKCR*, XXI (1955), 177–84. Its animal imagery has often been noted—for example, by J. C. Maxwell, "Animal Imagery in *Coriolanus*," *MLR*, XLII (1947), 417–21, and by Maurice Charney, *Shakespeare's Roman Plays* (Harvard University Press, 1961), pp. 163–69, although not by them in the context I am suggesting.

39. The influence of worldly praise in the forming of human character, and its deforming effect on a child's natural innocence, is one of Augustine's major themes in his *Confessions*, esp. I, 27–30.

40. Regarding his self-love, false modesty, and "subtle imaginative effort at evasion" and self-deception, even during his role as patriot, see the excellent discussion by Charles Mitchell, "Coriolanus: Power as Honor," *Shakespeare Studies*, I (1965), 199–226.

41. See Bradley's British Academy Lecture on *Coriolanus* (1912).

VI *The Reshaped Meaning of* Coriolanus, CONTINUED

42. H. S. Wilson, *On the Design of Shakespearian Tragedy* (University of Toronto Press, 1957), pp. 110–11.

43. John Palmer, *Political and Comic Characters of Shakespeare* (London, 1962 reprint), pp. 254–55.

44. Goddard, *Meaning of Shakespeare,* p. 617.

45. *The Statesman's Book of John of Salisbury,* V. 2., ed. John Dickinson (New York, 1927), p. 65. It is of interest that John of Salisbury claims here to be borrowing from "The Instruction to Trajan" in a letter by Plutarch, although modern scholars are sure the purported letter cannot be from the pen of the historical Plutarch but is the invention, rather, of some medieval Christianizer of Plutarch.

46. Mitchell, "Coriolanus," *S. St.,* I, 213, has noted how the play's imagery associates war with feasting. I would add that the metaphor of slaying as a *supping* had been used by Shakespeare in *Troilus and Cressida* V. viii. 19, there associated with Achilles.

47. *Statesman's Book,* V. 2, ed. Dickinson, p. 65. Compare E. E. Kellett's remark (cited in the New Variorum *Coriolanus* [Philadelphia, 1928], p. 646) that the First Citizen's reference to the "counsellor heart" makes us "begin to suspect Shakespeare of Medievalism. . . . For in the medieval writings on law and politics, it is almost always *cor* or *pectus* that is *senatus*."

48. Aquinas had issued a similar warning against "tradesmen" in *On Kingship,* tr. G. B. Phelan and I. T. Eschmann (Toronto, 1949), p. 76; and it is a frequent theme in medieval treatises.

49. Bullough, *Sources,* V, 552.

50. See Jonas A. Barish, "The Double Plot in *Volpone,*" *MP,* 51 (1953), 83–92.

51. Norman Rabkin has theorized that in *Coriolanus* Shakespeare was embarking on "a new kind of tragedy," in which the hero and his chief associates are "determined by social and psychological forces over which they have no control." He would attribute to Shakespeare the pessimistic view that a "rational and humane order cannot be restored because it cannot exist in society." See his article, "*Coriolanus:* The Tragedy of Politics," *SQ,* XVII (1966), 211. I would say, rather, that Shakespeare is showing how Roman society has become disordered by its psychology of vainglory. This endemic vice is thwarting native capacities for virtue in Coriolanus and in the plebs, and even in Cominius and in Virgilia.

52. See, for instance, Millar MacLure, "Shakespeare and the Lonely Dragon," *UTQ,* XXIV (1955), 115, and Dover Wilson's edition of *Coriolanus* (Cambridge, 1960), p. xx. Menenius, says MacLure, "is the criterion by which all political action in the play is to be judged." The

Fable of the Belly, says Wilson, has been placed by Shakespeare at the very forefront of his play, because it expresses "the point of view of all right-minded persons in his audience."

53. With his gentlemanly manners, however, Plutarch could be unmerciful. An interesting story has come down to us of some dialogue of his with a slave he was having whipped. The slave cried out that Plutarch was not the philosopher he pretended to be; that he had written on clemency and against anger but was now contradicting his precepts by abandoning himself to choler. "How is this, Mr. Varlet?" answered Plutarch. "By what signs and tokens can you prove that I am in passion? . . . I am not of opinion that my eyes sparkle, that I foam at the mouth . . . or that my voice is more vehement, or . . . that I either shake or stamp with madness; that I say or do anything unbecoming a philosopher." Then, turning to the officer doing the scourging, he added: "While he and I dispute this matter, mind your business on his back." (M. W. MacCallum, *Shakespeare's Roman Plays,* p. 102) We may compare this situation with the scene in *Coriolanus* in which Menenius dresses down the tribunes, jovially but with patrician hauteur.

54. In my view, the lines "I will not seal . . ." should be pronounced cavalierly, submerging the wilfulness of the verb *will* under a modesty that is more surface than genuine.

55. Rodney Poisson has written on "Coriolanus as Aristotle's Magnanimous Man," in *Pacific Coast Studies in Shakespeare* (University of Oregon Books, 1966), ed. McNeir and Greenfield, pp. 210–24. The present chapter was composed before this article appeared and therefore duplicates some of Poisson's evidence. However, my conclusion is different. Whereas Poisson uses Aristotle's concept to justify the attitudes of Coriolanus, even to the point of suggesting that his dragon-like anger "need not outrage Christian principles" (p. 224), I see the hero's Aristotelian magnanimity as un-Christian and also a root cause of his tragedy; and further I see in the hero's attempt to modify his Greek attitudes to fit Roman standards another and concurrent cause of his tragedy. H. V. Jaffa, *Thomism and Aristotelianism* (University of Chicago Press, 1952), p. 130, has commented on the fact that Aristotle's magnanimous man is imperfect in relation to friendship. Michael McCandles, "The Dialectic of Transcendence in Shakespeare's Coriolanus," *PMLA,* LXXII (1967), 44–53, has emphasized the fact that Coriolanus, in his drive for transcendence, paradoxically finds his selfhood defined "only insofar as it is made the object of someone else's attention" and that the result is both "the apogee of his egoism and a total void." With these observations I agree.

56. John Oakesmith, *The Religion of Plutarch* (London, 1902), esp. pp. 5–10 and 79–86.

VI *The Reshaped Meaning of* Coriolanus, CONTINUED

57. This view is taken by Dover Wilson, *Coriolanus,* p. xxvii; and by
S. K. Sen, "What Happens in *Coriolanus,*" *SQ,* IX (1958), 343.

58. See Virgil Whitaker, *Mirror Up To Nature* (San Marino, 1965),
p. 83; and C. B. Watson, *Shakespeare and the Renaissance Concept of
Honor* (Princeton University Press, 1960), p. 308. Aquinas, as McNamee
shows (*Honor,* pp. 123–28), retains magnanimity as a virtue, but only by
changing Aristotle's dimensions of the concept, giving it a new orientation and spirit.

59. The fact that Plutarch criticizes, as I noted earlier, the hero's manner of yielding does not mean he would wish him unyielding. Plutarch
approves both the embassy's purpose and Volumnia's argument. He
criticizes solely the element of rudeness in the hero's seeming to care for
his mother's favor only, neglecting that of Rome's other citizens and that
of his Volscian allies. Plutarch would wish a diplomatic bidding for
everyone's favor—although precisely how Coriolanus could have done
this he omits to say. Does he suppose Coriolanus might have won the
Volscians to accept Rome's peace terms by using a tale like that of
Menenius?

Appendix I
Two Augustinian Echoes

1. Aquinas, *Summa Theologica* I–II. 55. 2–4.
2. See Augustine, *On the Grace of Christ* I. 4–5.
3. Cited in *On the Grace of Christ* I. 17.
4. Cited in *On the Grace of Christ* I. 19.
5. Cited by Augustine, *On Original Sin,* ch. 14.
6. Augustine, *On Nature and Grace,* ch. 50.
7. Augustine, *On the Spirit and the Letter,* ch. 53.
8. Donald Stauffer, *Shakespeare's World of Images* (New York, 1949),
p. 174. Similarly, G. L. Kittredge, *Shakspere* (Harvard University
Press, 1926), p. 45, thinks Shakespeare is using Iago "for the utterance
of great truths," the most remarkable of which is Iago's "sublime assertion [to Roderigo] on the supremacy of will and reason"; and J. V. Cunningham, *Woe or Wonder* (University of Denver Press, 1951), p. 27, calls
Iago's argument "orthodox and true."
9. Coleridge, as reprinted in *Shakespeare Criticism,* ed. D. Nichol
Smith, (London, 1916), p. 302.
10. Hardin Craig, *The Enchanted Glass* (New York, 1936), p. 27.
11. D. W. Robertson, "The Doctrine of Charity in Mediaeval Literary
Gardens: A Topical Approach Through Symbolism and Allegory," *Speculum,* XXVI (1951), 31–32.

Appendix II
Lucrece in Other Versions

1. Quoted by Hyder Rollins, in *Shakespeare: The Poems* (New Variorum edition, Philadelphia, 1938), p. 420.

2. Goddard's two-part essay is in *JEGP,* 7 (1908) and 8 (1909). Garrett's, on " 'Cleopatra the Martyr' and her Sisters," is in *JEGP,* XXII (1923), 64–74.

3. It is further just possible (so rich is Chaucer's ambiguity) that even a third biblical passage may be shadowed under Chaucer's allusion; namely, Christ's encounter with the Samaritan woman in John 4. The Samaritan woman lacked the "living water" of the spirit of truth; also she was dwelling with a man who was no true husband to her. In these respects she resembles, figuratively, Lucrece. Note, however, that Christ did not commend this Samaritan woman's faith. Instead, he amazed her with his knowledge of "all things that ever [she] did" (verse 39), and by telling her that she was ignorantly worshipping "that which ye know not" (verse 22). Perhaps Chaucer is intending a similar surprise for his feminine auditors.

4. In *City of God* III. 15, Augustine points with strong disapproval to the murder by which the elder Tarquin originally succeeded to the office of kingship; but at the same time he notes the ironic fact that "when he was afterwards banished by the Romans, and forbidden the city, it was *not for his own* but for his son's wickedness in the affair of Lucretia—a crime perpetrated not only without his cognizance, but in his absence" (italics mine). I am using Marcus Dods' translation, in *Nicene and Post-Nicene Fathers,* II (Buffalo, 1887), ed. Philip Schaff.

5. Augustine, *Of True Religion,* 77, in *Augustine: Earlier Writings,* tr. J. H. S. Burleigh (Philadelphia, 1953), p. 265. Italics mine.

6. Augustine, *City of God* XI. 23, tr. Dods. Italics mine.

7. See Introduction, in Allan Holaday's edition of Heywood's *The Rape of Lucrece* (University of Illinois Press, 1950). Among other points, Holaday reminds us that Heywood had already attempted to imitate Shakespeare's *Venus and Adonis* in his own *Oenone and Paris* (1594), and that his extraordinary fluency made him quite capable of composing a play in a month's time if need be. Revisions of its text could have followed later, with probably a major revision in 1607 before sale to the booksellers.

8. Irving Ribner, *Jacobean Tragedy* (London, 1962), pp. 59–60, suggests in justification of the comic songs that they are "concentrated in those central scenes where the dramatist wishes to stress the escape of the Roman lords into wanton amusement and self-indulgence in the

face of Tarquin's tyranny." This explanation has plausibility. Yet why did Heywood continue to stuff in more and more of such "escape" songs? From at least one passage in the play, it could be inferred that he considered them harmless. Collatine proposes (lines 987–88):

> By my consent lets all weare out our houres
> In harmeles sports: hauke, hunt, game, sing, drink, dance.

And later (2475), Brutus refers to the songs as "humorous toyes."

9. Livy, *History* I. 46. 3, tr. Foster, Loeb edition. Foster interprets Livy's words here as a reference to the Atreus-Oedipus story.

10. A. M. Clark, *Thomas Heywood, Playwright and Miscellanist* (Oxford, 1931), p. 219. He explains (p. 220): "It grafts on a plot of classical tragedy the rude, incongruous and unashamed stock of the native interlude."

11. Only a few years earlier the young Middleton had published a verse paraphrase of a portion of Scripture, his *The Wisdom of Solomon* (1597).

12. J. Q. Adams, the modern editor of *The Ghost of Lucrece* (New York, 1937), is in error, I think, in supposing that Middleton saw in Shakespeare's *Lucrece* "a beautiful celebration of chastity" (p. xix).

13. See *Forty-Six Lives from Boccaccio,* ed. Herbert G. Wright (Oxford University Press, 1943), p. 159. Henry Parker, Lord Morley, had read so widely in Roman history that he himself seems to have adopted, uncritically, the Roman view. His translation remained in manuscript until Wright's edition for The Early English Text Society.

14. For Lydgate's passages, see *The Fall of Princes,* ed. Henry Bergen for the E. E. T. S. (Oxford University Press, 1924), I, 226–37 (Bk. II) and II, 354–60 (Bk. III).

15. Livy, however, could have provided the hint, when he tells how Arruns Tarquin met Brutus in a combat that cost both their lives. Heywood needed only to replace Arruns with Sextus.

16. Holaday, ed., *The Rape of Lucrece,* by Thomas Heywood, p. 41.

17. As Ribner remarks, *Jacobean Tragedy,* p. 68, Collatine here voices the traditional Tudor doctrine of passive obedience, which Heywood espouses in his other plays. But was this doctrine also Shakespeare's? *Richard II* shows John of Gaunt espousing it; but the consequences which then ensue seem to imply its inadequacy. I think Shakespeare assessed mere passive obedience with a critical eye.

18. Ribner, *Jacobean Tragedy,* p. 71.

Index

Aaron, 430
Abel, 93, 138, 216, 251
Abraham, the patriarch, 107
Abraham, servant to Montague, 122
Absalom, tragedy by Watson, 183, 426
Achilles, 25, 32, 212, 269–70, 365, 371, 373, 448
Achitophel, 101
Adam, 90, 94, 95, 202, 216, 218, 219, 237, 251, 271, 272, 382, 430; Old Adam and New Adam, 91
Adams, J. Q., 398, 452
Addison, Joseph, 409
Adrian, IV, Pope, 348–50
Advent, 285, 388
advice-giving, in tragedy, 19, 83, 122, 125, 236, 304, 329, 358
Aeneas and Dido, 112, 163, 257
agape, 74, 88, 109, 115, 170, 176
Agrippa, Cornelius, 253
Ahab, 94
alabaster image, 96
Albany, 49, 275, 279
Alcibiades, 314, 337
Alexander, Peter, 227, 431
Alexander the Great, 87, 157, 178, 320, 372
allegory, 75, 78, 84, 85, 86, 95, 105. *See also* typology
Allen, D. C., 407
Allen, William, Cardinal, 239
All's Well, 85, 383, 434
ambiguity, in action, 15, 297; in phrasing, 26, 30, 33, 34, 110, 166, 289, 394; of pronouns, 334, 345, 387, 388. *See also* wordplay
Ambrose, St., 78, 79
anagnorisis, or tragic discovery, 120, 156–67, 423
analogy, 18, 24, 87–100, 112, 157, 170, 171, 257, 263–64, 274, 350–51, 365, 442; to Christian ritual, 26, 33, 100, 115; to Holy Week, 117, 288; to sexual climax, 27; within the drama, 72, 119, 120, 122, 125, 290, 295; polar analogy between characters, 29, 28–39, 251, 354. *See also* figura, metaphor, and parable
animal imagery, in *Hamlet*, 249, 255–56; in *Coriolanus*, 335, 338, 340, 346

anima naturaliter christiana, 274, 374
Antigone, 210–12, 214
Antiochus Epiphanes, 180
Antony, 21, 64, 67, 161–83 passim, 323
Antony and Cleopatra, 22, 151, 161–83, 309, 316, 408; the developing anagnorisis of the lovers, 162–66; ironies in Cleopatra's suicide, 166–68; Cupid's saints and their parody of Christ story, 169–73; Scarrus, 173–74, 425; Eros, 175–76; echoes of biblical apocalypse, 176–81; Egypt understood typologically, 181
apocalyptic signs, 275, 285, 426
Apocalypse, *see* Bible, Revelation
Appian, 312
Aquinas, St. Thomas, 76, 79, 83, 84, 90, 135, 214, 244, 253, 302, 411, 416, 428, 430, 437; on moral psychology, 77, 78; on the influence of the stars, 110; on evils as medicinal or satisfactory, 138–39; on remorse, 151; on original sin, 139, 215–16, 224; on reason as man's "proximate" rule only, 220; on self-love, 220; on negligence and the sin of omission, 221, 246; on ignorance, 221–22, 223, 225–26; on eternal law, 220, 225, 262; on incontinence, 223, 247, 282; on conscience, 225–26, 431; on purgatory, 239; on idolatry, 246, 436; on kings as scourges, 261; on pity, 426; on tradesmen, 448; on magnanimity, 450; his modifications of Aristotle's concepts, 207, 214, 215, 217–18, 220–23, 225–26, 428; editions of the *Summa Theologica* in Elizabethan times, 206
archetype, 23, 74, 91, 93, 106, 271. *See also* paradigm and typology
Aristotle, 137, 149, 154, 186, 199, 227, 243, 266, 317; use of his thought in Elizabethan times, 183–84, 206–07; his *Poetics* in relation to his *Ethics*, 205; modern rejectors of his poetic concepts, 143, 183, 426, 428, 430; modern defenders, 183, 194, 426–30; his concept of character, 66; of anagnorisis, 156–160, 161; of villainy, 188; of catharsis, 192–95; of hamartia, 207–208, 428; of ignorance, 209–210; of incontinence, 213–14, 217, 282; of self-love, 220; of probability, 310; of magnanimity, 365–69; Christian

Malcolm, 60, 71, 72, 153, 195, 197
Machiavelli, 80, 82
Mack, Maynard, on Hamlet, 157; on *King Lear*, 272, 412, 422, 438–39
MacCallum, M. W., 316, 446, 449
MacLure, Millar, 448
McArthur, Herbert, 417
McCandles, Michael, 449
McGee, A. R., 409
McManaway, James, 429
McNamee, Maurice B., 363, 364, 368, 369, 450
McNeir, Waldo, 416, 449
Madariaga, Salvadore de, 231, 433
magnanimity, 327, 329, 362–72; its pagan version in Christian estimate, 372
Mahood, M. M., 110, 410, 416
maimed liberty, 12, 262
maimed rites, 55, 250, 340
Maitland, F. W., 439
Major, J. M., 409
make-believe, a characteristic of tragic action, 22, 161–62, 165, 183, 251, 254–55, 257, 328
Malone, Edmund, 6
Manichaean world view, its relation to tragedy, 141–42; Augustine's criticism of, 217; Hamlet's apology in the light of Augustine's remarks, 258
Marcellus, 260
Maritain, Jacques, 65, 154, 210, 410, 422, 430
Marlowe, Christopher, 135; *Dido*, 408; *Dr. Faustus*, 100, 106, 418
Marston, John, *Sophonisba*, 309
Marsus, edition of Ovid, 406
martyrdom, its false mode in Lucrece, 18, 25, 28; and in Cleopatra, 168; truly figured in Cordelia, 274, 288
Mary Magdalene, 96, 97
Mary Magdalene, the Digby play, 85
Mary, mother of Christ, 333
Masefield, John, 131, 419
Masuccio, Salernitano, 418
Matthews, Honor, 412, 414, 421
Matthew, Tobie, 379
Maxwell, J. C., 301, 420, 447
Mercutio, 57, 113–14, 160
Measure for Measure, 4, 39, 58, 81, 84, 89, 175, 178, 246, 412, 437; Coleridge's view, 58; Bradley's, 65
Menenius, 318–20, 337, 340, 363; his fable of the belly analyzed, 341–50; his stepfatherly care of Coriolanus, 350–55; embodies Plutarch's attitudes, 355–58; dramatized by Shakespeare to reveal their tragic blindness, 358–62
Merchant of Venice, 85, 117, 124, 235, 413
Meres, Francis, *The Sinner's Guide*, 77, 78; *Palladis Tamia*, 78, 222
metaphor, 47, 50; drama as "expanded metaphor," 89, 125, 236, 334; three metaphors of tragedy's dimensions, 204–205; *King Lear* as "metaphysical metaphor," 272; the metaphor of rape

as rapture in *Lucrece*, 30, 33; courtly love's thematic metaphors in *Romeo and Juliet*, 105–109; disregarded pearl and deadly kiss as twin metaphors in *Othello*, 96; in *Hamlet* the allied metaphors of misaimed arrow, 228, maimed rites, 250, and poison pouring, 236, 260; in *Coriolanus* the major metaphors of belly and womb worship, 334, 342, and of savage dining, 346; in *Lear* the metaphors of divesting and unstating, 280, 291, 294
Michel, Laurence, 144–45, 420, 421, 427
Middleton, Thomas, 452; *The Ghost of Lucrece*, 398
Midsummer Night's Dream, 112–13, 309, 416, 425
Mills, L. J., 423
Milton, John, 108, 429; *Samson*, 134; *Lycidas*, 350
Milward, Peter, 411
mimesis, 38; includes imitating the moral quality of an action, 103; not to be confused with the fact of human tragedy, 143–45; the eschatological dimension of action included, 145–49; three dimensions of its subject matter, 204
miracle, 285; in Gloucester's experience, 271; France's mention of, 276, Kent's, 289
Mirror for Magistrates, 398
Mitchell, Charles, 447, 448
Moffet, Robin, 425
Moore, Olin, 418
Montague, 117, 118
Montaigne, 80, 82
Montgomerie, William, 437
moral doubletalk, instances of, 25, 32, 160, 240, 249, 360
moral geography, 276
morbid imagination, attributed to Shakespeare, 4; "morbid excess" as understood by Coleridge, 53; psychoanalytic explanation of Hamlet's morbidity, 233; associated with demonic arts, 252
More, Thomas, *Dialogue of Comfort*, 330
Morley, Henry Parker, Lord, 398, 452
Morrell, Roy, 195, 427
Morris, Ivor, 441
Morris, Harry, 421
Mortenson, Peter, 438
Moses, 252, 296
Much Ado About Nothing, 85
Muir, Kenneth, 303, 439, 443, 444
Munday, Anthony, 436
Munz, Peter, 428
Murray, Gilbert, 433
Myrick, Kenneth, 412

Napoleon, 344
Narcissus, 170, 172; narcissistic love, 98, 231
Nashe, Thomas, 186
Nebuchadnezzar, 179, 297, 334